THE INSTITUTE FOR POLISH–JEWISH STUDIES

The Institute for Polish–Jewish Studies in Oxford and its sister organization, the American Association for Polish–Jewish Studies, who are responsible for the publication of *Polin*, are learned societies, established following the International Conference on Polish–Jewish Studies held in Oxford in 1984. The Institute is an associate institute of the Oxford Centre for Hebrew and Jewish Studies, and the American Association is linked with the Department of Near Eastern and Judaic Studies at Brandeis University.

Both the Institute and the American Association aim to promote understanding of the Polish Jewish past. They have no building or library of their own and no paid staff; they achieve their aims by encouraging scholarly research and facilitating its publication, and by creating forums for people with a scholarly interest in Polish Jewish topics, both past and present.

Each year since 1986 the Institute has published a volume of scholarly papers in the series *Polin: Studies in Polish Jewry* under the general editorship of Professor Antony Polonsky joined, in 2015, by Professor François Guesnet of University College London. Since 1994 the series has been published on the Institute's behalf by the Littman Library of Jewish Civilization. In March 2000 the entire series was honoured with a National Jewish Book Award from the Jewish Book Council in the United States. More than twenty other works on Polish Jewish topics have also been published with the Institute's assistance.

The editors welcome submission of articles for inclusion in future volumes. In particular, we are always grateful for assistance in extending the geographical range of our journal to Ukraine, Belarus, and Lithuania, both in the period in which these countries were part of the Polish–Lithuanian Commonwealth and subsequently. We also welcome submission of reviews, which are published on the website of the American Association. We are happy to translate articles or reviews submitted in Polish, Russian, Ukrainian, Lithuanian, Hebrew, or German into English. Submissions should be sent to one of the following: Dr Władysław T. Bartoszewski (email: wt@wtbartoszewski.pl); Professor Antony Polonsky (email: polonsky@brandeis.edu); Professor François Guesnet (f.guesnet @ucl.ac.uk); Professor Joshua Zimmerman (email: zimmerm@yu.edu).

Further information on the Institute for Polish–Jewish Studies can be found on its website, <www.polishjewishstudies.co.uk>. For the website of the American Association for Polish–Jewish Studies, see <www.aapjstudies.org>.

THE LITTMAN LIBRARY OF
JEWISH CIVILIZATION

Life Patron
Colette Littman

Dedicated to the memory of
Louis Thomas Sidney Littman
*who founded the Littman Library for the love of God
and as an act of charity in memory of his father*
Joseph Aaron Littman
and to the memory of
Robert Joseph Littman
who continued what his father Louis had begun

יהא זכרם ברוך

'Get wisdom, get understanding:
Forsake her not and she shall preserve thee'

prov. 4: 5

*The Littman Library of Jewish Civilization is a registered UK charity
Registered charity no. 1000784*

POLIN
STUDIES IN POLISH JEWRY

VOLUME THIRTY-SIX

Jewish Childhood in Eastern Europe

Edited by
NATALIA ALEKSIUN, FRANÇOIS GUESNET
and
ANTONY POLONSKY

Published for
The Institute for Polish–Jewish Studies
and
The American Association for Polish–Jewish Studies

London
The Littman Library of Jewish Civilization
in association with Liverpool University Press
2024

The Littman Library of Jewish Civilization
Registered office: 14th floor, 33 Cavendish Square, London W1G 0PW

in association with Liverpool University Press
4 Cambridge Street, Liverpool L69 7ZU, UK
www.liverpooluniversitypress.co.uk/littman

Managing Editor: Connie Webber

Distributed in North America by
Oxford University Press Inc., 198 Madison Avenue
New York, NY 10016, USA

© Institute for Polish–Jewish Studies 2024

All rights reserved.
No part of this publication may be reproduced,
stored in a retrieval system, or transmitted, in any form or by
any means, without the prior permission in writing of
the Littman Library of Jewish Civilization

The paperback edition of this book is sold subject to the condition
that it shall not, by way of trade or otherwise, be lent, re-sold, hired out
or otherwise circulated without the publisher's prior consent in any
form of binding or cover other than that in which it is published
and without a similar condition including this condition
being imposed on the subsequent purchaser

Catalogue records for this book are available from the
British Library and the Library of Congress

ISSN 0268 1056
ISBN 978–1–802070–34–7 (cloth)
ISBN 978–1–802070–35–4 (pbk)

Publishing co-ordinator: Janet Moth
Copy-editing: Mark Newby
Proof-reading: Andrew Kirk and Joyce Rappaport
Index: Bonnie Blackburn
Production, design, and typesetting by
Pete Russell, Faringdon, Oxon.

Printed and bound in Great Britain by
CMP Books.

Articles appearing in this publication are abstracted and indexed in
Historical Abstracts and America: History and Life

This volume is dedicated to the memory of
Sir Ben Helfgott
Pabianice, 22 November 1929 – Harrow-on-the-Hill, 16 June 2023

*Holocaust survivor, Olympic weightlifter, and
long-standing supporter of Holocaust remembrance*

*Former chairman and life patron of the
Institute for Polish-Jewish Studies*

∎

This volume benefited from grants from
THE MIRISCH AND LEBENHEIM CHARITABLE FOUNDATION
TAUBE PHILANTHROPIES

Editors and Advisers

Editors

Monika Adamczyk-Garbowska, Lublin
Israel Bartal, Jerusalem
François Guesnet (co-chair), London
Antony Polonsky (co-chair), London
Michael Steinlauf, Philadelphia
Jonathan Webber, Kraków

Editorial Board

Eliyana Adler, University Park, Pa.
David Assaf, Tel Aviv
Władysław T. Bartoszewski, Warsaw
Glenn Dynner, Bronxville, NY
David Engel, New York
David Fishman, New York
Laura Jockusch, Waltham, Mass.
Ronald Liebowitz, Waltham, Mass.
Joanna Michlic, London
Elchanan Reiner, Tel Aviv

Jehuda Reinharz, Waltham, Mass.
Moshe Rosman, Ramat Gan
Szymon Rudnicki, Warsaw
Robert Shapiro, New York
Adam Teller, Providence, RI
Magdalena Teter, New York
Daniel Tollet, Paris
Joshua Zimmerman, New York
Steven Zipperstein, Stanford, Calif.

Advisory Board

Elissa Bemporad, New York
Andrzej Chojnowski, Warsaw
Norman Davies, Oxford
Havi Dreifuss, Tel Aviv
Michał Galas, Kraków
Frank Golczewski, Hamburg
Olga Goldberg, Jerusalem
Andrzej Kamiński, Washington DC
Hillel Levine, Boston, Mass.

Heinz-Dietrich Löwe, Heidelberg
Joanna Degler (Lisek), Wrocław
Anna Michałowska-Mycielska, Warsaw
Joanna Nalewajko-Kulikov, Warsaw
David Sorkin, New Haven, Conn.
Scott Ury, Tel Aviv
Marcin Wodziński, Wrocław
Piotr Wróbel, Toronto

Preface

VOLUME 36 of *Polin: Studies in Polish Jewry* is an examination of children, childhood, and childrearing in eastern Europe. The understanding of childhood and children's roles has undergone a significant transformation in recent years, and there has been considerable new research on the ways in which children participate in determining their own lives. This turn to children's experiences, in historical scholarship as well as in literary and cultural studies, has extended from examination of the lives and self-representation of young individuals and the family to a focus on how such research can shed light on larger historical questions.

The history of childhood has been a somewhat neglected topic in research on the history and culture of east European Jewry in general, and Polish Jewry in particular. Rather, children have featured in broader studies of education and childbirth, viewed through the lens of educational projects and women's history, and seen as objects of communal assistance. In this volume, we have endeavoured throughout to let children and teenagers speak for themselves and, while aware of the limits of their freedom of action, to assess their degree of agency. At the same time, we have paid close attention to ideas and ideals regarding Jewish children and Jewish childhood expressed by those with a degree of power over these children's lives—not only their parents, but religious and communal leaders, educators, medical professionals, and political activists engaged in mobilizing young people. We have sought to examine how these individuals developed specific agendas on the raising and education of children, and on what values should be instilled into them according to their age, class, and gender.

■

Polin is sponsored by the Institute of Polish–Jewish Studies, which is an associated institute of the Oxford Centre for Hebrew and Jewish Studies and of the Department of Hebrew and Jewish Studies, University College London, and by the American Association for Polish–Jewish Studies, which is linked with the Department of Near Eastern and Judaic Studies, Brandeis University. As with earlier issues, this volume could not have appeared without the untiring assistance of many individuals. In particular, we should like to express our gratitude to Professor Ron Liebowitz, president of Brandeis University, to the late Mrs Irene Pipes, president of the American Association for Polish–Jewish Studies, and to David Dahlborn, treasurer of the Institute for Polish-Jewish Studies. These four institutions all made substantial contributions to the cost of producing the volume. A particularly important contribution was that made by the Mirisch and Lebenheim Foundation, and the volume also benefited from a grant from the Taube Foundation for Jewish Life and Culture. As was the case with earlier volumes, this one could not have been published without the constant assistance and supervision of Connie Webber, managing editor of the Littman Library, Janet Moth, publishing coordinator, Pete Russell, designer, and the tireless copy-editing of Mark Newby, the proofreading of Andrew Kirk, Julja Levin, and Joyce Rappaport, and the staff at Liverpool University Press.

Plans for future volumes of *Polin* are well advanced. These will focus on encounters of the Jews of Poland with Germans and German Jews and their respective cultural traditions, on gender and the body in eastern European Jewish history, and on how the concept of 'the other'—whether Jewish or Polish—has been represented in works of art in the cultural sphere in the Polish lands. We should welcome articles for these issues. We should also welcome any suggestions or criticisms. In particular, we are always grateful for assistance in extending the geographical range of our journal to Ukraine, Belarus, and Lithuania, both in the period in which these countries were part of the Polish–Lithuanian Commonwealth and subsequently.

We note with great sadness the death of Sir Ben Helfgott, Holocaust survivor, Olympic weightlifter, and former chairman and life patron of the Institute for Polish–Jewish Studies. He was among the pioneers in Britain to raise awareness of the Holocaust. A native of Piotrków Trybunalski, he worked tirelessly to improve Polish–Jewish relations, and was awarded the Commander's Cross of the Order of Merit of the Republic of Poland. Another very sad loss was that of Irene Pipes, long-standing president of the American Association for Polish–Jewish Studies. Irene came from a family that was well integrated in Polish society but retained strong Jewish ties. As president of the American Association for Polish–Jewish Studies from the early 1990s, she employed her considerable diplomatic talents to foster dialogue and discussion in an open manner on difficult and divisive issues. Her enormous contribution to Polish–Jewish understanding was recognized in the award to her by the Polish government of the Commander's Cross of the Order of Merit of the Republic of Poland. We are also much saddened by the passing of Shevach Weiss, Speaker of the Knesset from 2000 to 2004 and a committed worker for Polish–Jewish understanding, and of Peter Pulzer, a great scholar and unfailing supporter of this yearbook and of the Institute for Polish-Jewish Studies. Marian Fuks, who died in October 2022 at the venerable age of 108, was the author of a large number of studies of Polish Jewish history, including the history of the Jewish press and the role of Jews in music in Poland. They will all be sadly missed.

Contents

List of Contributors   xii

Note on Editorial Conventions   xiv

Introduction   1
NATALIA ALEKSIUN, FRANÇOIS GUESNET, AND ANTONY POLONSKY

1   CHILDHOOD AND FAMILY

Children and Childhood in Hasidic Courts before 1939   19
GADI SAGIV

Representations of Boyhood in Nineteenth-Century Hebrew Literature   42
ROTEM PREGER-WAGNER

The Beautiful Manor House: Glimpses of Jewish Childhood in the Galician Countryside   65
YEHOSHUA ECKER

Advocacy and Practice in CENTOS Journals   89
SEAN MARTIN

2   THE MEDICAL TREATMENT OF CHILDREN

The Child in Traditional Jewish Medicine around 1900   104
MAREK TUSZEWICKI

Newborn Care and Survival among Jews in Early Modern Poland   122
ZVI ECKSTEIN AND ANAT VATURI

Who Nursed the Jewish Babies? Wet-Nursing among Jews in the Late Russian Empire   140
EKATERINA OLESHKEVICH

TOZ Summer Camps: Modern Welfare for Weak and Exhausted Jewish Children in Poland, 1924–1939   162
RAKEFET ZALASHIK

3   THE EDUCATIONAL EXPERIENCE

What Kind of Self Can a Pupil's Letter Reveal? The Tarbut School in Nowy Dwór, 1934–1935   181
DAVID ASSAF AND YAEL DARR

State Schools as Polish–Jewish Contact Zones: The Case of Tarnów 199
AGNIESZKA WIERZCHOLSKA

Working Children and Young People as Seen by Contributors to
Mały Przegląd 220
ANNA LANDAU-CZAJKA

Through Their Own Eyes: Jewish Youngsters Describe Their Holidays in
Interwar Poland 241
ULA MADEJ-KRUPITSKI

Autograph Books of Polish Jewish Schoolgirls as Historical Documents 267
NATALIA ALEKSIUN

From Relief to Emancipation: Cecylia Klaftenowa's Vision for Jewish Girls in
Interwar Lwów 291
SARAH ELLEN ZARROW

4 CHILDREN AND TRAUMA, 1914–1947

Zionist Care and Education for Galician Refugee Children in Austria
during the First World War 309
JAN RYBAK

Jewish Children Seeking Help from Catholic Institutions in Kraków
during the Holocaust 327
JOANNA SLIWA

'It was easier with a child than without': Creating and Caring for Polish
Jewish Families in the Wartime Soviet Union, 1939–1946 342
SARAH A. CRAMSEY

Voices of Soviet Jewish Children Documenting the Second World War 365
ANNA SHTERNSHIS

Jewish Child Survivors in the Aftermath of the Holocaust 390
JOANNA MICHLIC

The Rehabilitation of Jewish Child Holocaust Survivors, Poland, 1944–1947 399
BOAZ COHEN

5 CHILDHOOD IN POST-1945 POLAND

Beyond Post-Holocaust Trauma: Polish Jewish Childhood in Dzierżoniów,
Lower Silesia, 1945–1950 418
KAMIL KIJEK

Blurred Spots of Revolution: Polish Communists of Jewish Origin and
 Their Early Political Socialization 448
ŁUKASZ BERTRAM

Index 471

Contributors

NATALIA ALEKSIUN is Harry Rich Professor of Holocaust Studies at the University of Florida.

DAVID ASSAF holds the Sir Isaac Wolfson Chair of Jewish Studies in the Department of Jewish History at Tel Aviv University.

ŁUKASZ BERTRAM works at the Institute of Political Studies, Polish Academy of Sciences, Warsaw.

BOAZ COHEN is Head of the Holocaust Studies Program at the Western Galilee College, Akko.

SARAH A. CRAMSEY is an assistant professor of Judaism and diaspora studies and professor by special appointment of central European studies at Leiden University.

YAEL DARR is Chair of the MA Program in Culture Research at Tel Aviv University.

YEHOSHUA ECKER teaches early modern and modern Jewish history at the Center for Jewish Studies, University of Florida, Gainesville, and at the Graduate School of Jewish Studies, Touro University, New York.

ZVI ECKSTEIN is currently serving as Dean of the Tiomkin School of Economics and the Head of the Aaron Economic Policy Institute at Reichman University, and is a visiting professor at the Wharton School of the University of Pennsylvania.

FRANÇOIS GUESNET is Professor of Modern Jewish History at University College London.

KAMIL KIJEK is an assistant professor at Taube Department of Jewish Studies, University of Wrocław.

ANNA LANDAU-CZAJKA is a professor at the Institute of History at the Polish Academy of Sciences.

ULA MADEJ-KRUPITSKI is an assistant professor in modern Jewish history in the Department of Jewish History at McGill University.

SEAN MARTIN is associate curator for Jewish history at Western Reserve Historical Society, Cleveland, Ohio.

JOANNA MICHLIC is Hedda Andersson Visiting Professor of Contemporary History and the Holocaust at Lund University.

EKATERINA OLESHKEVICH is a doctoral candidate in the Department of Jewish History and Contemporary Jewry at Bar-Ilan University.

ANTONY POLONSKY is Professor Emeritus of Holocaust Studies, Brandeis University, and Chief Historian of the Global Education Outreach Program at the Polin Museum of the History of Polish Jews, Warsaw.

ROTEM PREGER-WAGNER received her doctorate from Ben Gurion University. She has taught in the Child and Youth Culture Research programme at Tel Aviv University.

JAN RYBAK is Early Career Research Fellow at the Birkbeck Institute for the Study of Antisemitism, London.

GADI SAGIV is an associate professor at the Open University of Israel.

ANNA SHTERNSHIS is Al and Malka Green Professor of Yiddish Studies at the University of Toronto.

JOANNA SLIWA is a historian at the Conference on Jewish Material Claims Against Germany (Claims Conference), where she also administers the Saul Kagan Fellowship in Advanced Shoah Studies and the University Partnership in Holocaust Studies.

MAREK TUSZEWICKI is a deputy director of the Institute of Jewish Studies, Jagiellonian University, Kraków.

ANAT VATURI is a faculty member at the Department of Jewish History and the Interdisciplinary Unit for Polish Studies at the University of Haifa.

AGNIESZKA WIERZCHOLSKA is a fellow at the Moses Mendelssohn Center for European Jewish Studies, Potsdam.

RAKEFET ZALASHIK is a professor of medical humanities at the Azrieli Faculty of Medicine, Bar-Ilan University.

SARAH ELLEN ZARROW is Associate Professor, Endowed Chair of Jewish History at Western Washington University, Bellingham.

Note on Editorial Conventions

Place Names

Political connotations accrue to words, names, and spellings with an alacrity unfortunate for those who would like to maintain neutrality. It seems reasonable to honour the choices of a population on the name of its city or town, but what is one to do when the people have no consensus on their name, or when the town changes its name, and the name its spelling, again and again over time? The politician may always opt for the latest version, but the hapless historian must reckon with them all. This note, then, will be our brief reckoning.

There is no problem with places that have accepted English names, such as Warsaw. But every other place name in east-central Europe raises serious problems. A good example is Wilno, Vilna, Vilnius. There are clear objections to all of these. Until 1944 the majority of the population was Polish. The city is today in Lithuania. 'Vilna', though raising the fewest problems, is an artificial construct. In this volume we have adopted the following guidelines, although we are aware that they are not wholly consistent.

1. Towns that have a form which is acceptable in English are given in that form. Some examples are Warsaw, Kiev, Moscow, St Petersburg, Munich.

2. Towns that until 1939 were clearly part of a particular state and shared the majority nationality of that state are given in a form which reflects that situation. Some examples are Breslau, Danzig, Rzeszów, Przemyśl. In Polish, Kraków has always been spelled as such. In English it has more often appeared as Cracow, but the current trend of English follows the local language as much as possible. In keeping with this trend to local determination, then, we shall maintain the Polish spelling.

3. Towns that are in mixed areas take the form in which they are known today and which reflects their present situation. Examples are Poznań, Toruń, and Kaunas. This applies also to bibliographical references. We have made one major exception to this rule, using the common English form for Vilna until its first incorporation into Lithuania in October 1939 and using Vilnius thereafter. Galicia's most diversely named city, and one of its most important, boasts four variants: the Polish Lwów, the German Lemberg, the Russian Lvov, and the Ukrainian Lviv. As this city currently lives under Ukrainian rule, and most of its current residents speak Ukrainian, we use the Ukrainian spelling unless another form is required by the context.

4. Some place names have different forms in Yiddish. Occasionally the subject matter dictates that the Yiddish place name should be the prime form, in which case the corresponding Polish (Ukrainian, Belarusian, Lithuanian) name is given in parentheses at first mention.

Transliteration

Hebrew

An attempt has been made to achieve consistency in the transliteration of Hebrew words. The following are the key distinguishing features of the system that has been adopted:

1. No distinction is made between the *alef* and *ayin*; both are represented by an apostrophe, and only when they appear in an intervocalic position.
2. *Veit* is written *v*; *ḥet* is written *ḥ*; *yod* is written *y* when it functions as a consonant and *i* when it occurs as a vowel; *khaf* is written *kh*; *tsadi* is written *ts*; *kof* is written *k*.
3. The *dagesh hazak*, represented in some transliteration systems by doubling the letter, is not represented, except in words that have more or less acquired normative English spellings that include doublings, such as Hallel, kabbalah, Kaddish, rabbi, Sukkot, and Yom Kippur.
4. The *sheva na* is represented by an *e*.
5. Hebrew prefixes, prepositions, and conjunctions are not followed by a hyphen when they are transliterated; thus *betoledot ha'am hayehudi*.
6. In the transliteration of the titles of works published in Hebrew, only the first word is capitalized; other than in the titles of works, names of people, places, and institutions are capitalized following the conventions of the English language.
7. The names of individuals are transliterated following the above rules unless the individual concerned followed a different usage.

Yiddish

Transliteration follows the YIVO system except for the names of people, where the spellings they themselves used have been retained.

Russian and Ukrainian

The system used is that of British Standard 2979:1958, without diacritics. Except in bibliographical and other strictly rendered matter, soft and hard signs are indicated by *y* before a vowel (e.g. Ilyich) but are otherwise omitted, and word-final -й, -ий, -ый, -ій in names are simplified to -*y*.

Introduction

NATALIA ALEKSIUN, FRANÇOIS GUESNET
AND ANTONY POLONSKY

Behold, children are a heritage from the LORD; the fruit of the womb, a reward. Like arrows in the hand of a warrior are the children of one's youth. Blessed is the man who fills his quiver with them! He shall not be put to shame when he speaks with his enemies in the gate.

Psalm 127: 3–5

Poland has brought me up as a Pole, but brands me a Jew who has to be driven out. I want to be a Pole, you have not let me; I want to be a Jew, but I don't know how, I have become alienated from Jewishness. (I do not like myself as a Jew.) I am already lost.

Abraham Rotfarb, autobiography submitted to YIVO competition, 1939

Reconstructing the experiences of the past can only be done by asking questions which directly address the child's most intimate feelings, which still often fester with unhealed wounds. The goal of educators should be to raise a healthy Jewish generation, unburdened by psychological traumas. Regardless of these, we must confront the child with the past and acquire a faithful picture of children's reactions and the psychological changes that have occurred as a result of the difficult experience.

Genia Silkes, 'Kwestionariusz dla zbierania zeznań
i materiałów o dzieciach żydowskich w czasie okupacji niemieckiej' (1945)

IN THIS VOLUME of *Polin: Studies in Polish Jewry*, we have attempted to examine the history of children, childhood, and child-rearing in Jewish eastern Europe. Historians have long delved into how the understanding of childhood and children's roles changed over time and studied the ways in which children participated in determining their own lives. In recent years, however, in historical scholarship and literary and cultural studies there has occurred 'a turn to children's experiences', which have been investigated not only as a means of examining the lives and self-representations of young individuals and the family but also because of the light such research can shed on larger historical questions.[1] This approach has its critics. In the October 2020 issue of the *American Historical Review*, Sarah Maza argued that 'writing the history of children is difficult . . . because of the nature of a group of people incommensurable with any other in the field's canon'. Children, she claimed, produce few sources in their own voices, have very limited agency, and as individuals and a group soon grow out of their subaltern status. Accordingly, she advocated an approach that focuses rather on issues beyond children themselves and examines the cleavages within adult societies over the nature of childhood, the way it is thought of, imagined, and deployed. What we need, she claimed, is a history written *through* children rather than *of* them.[2] In this volume, we take issue with this view and seek to write a history which, in the words of Steven Mintz, author of a major work on American children, *Huck's Raft*, is imbued with 'children's agency, experience, consciousness, and autonomous action'.[3]

In the research on the history and culture of east European Jewry in general, and Polish Jewry in particular, the history of childhood has not been studied in depth. Rather, children feature in sections of broader studies of education or childbirth or are discussed through the lens of educational projects or women's history or as they feature on the receiving end of community assistance.[4] While scholars have increasingly integrated age, alongside gender, ethnicity, and class as an important category of analysis, rarely do they focus on children's own agency.[5] The subject is also still largely absent from studies of the social and cultural history of pre-modern Poland, while the literature on the Holocaust and its immediate aftermath seems to be growing at a much greater pace.[6]

We have endeavoured throughout to let children and teenagers speak for themselves and, while aware of the limits of their freedom of action, to assess their degree of agency. At the same time, we pay close attention to ideas and ideals about Jewish children and Jewish childhood expressed by those with a degree of power over their lives: not only parents but also religious and community leaders, educators, and political activists seeking to mobilize young people. We therefore pay close attention to the views expressed by such individuals on how children ought to be raised and educated and what values should be instilled into them, according to their age, class, and gender.

The chapters in this volume build on recent scholarly interest in children and childhood. They also rely on diverse earlier projects that stemmed from a concern for proper child-rearing, the desire to raise productive members of the Jewish community and society, and a sense that children are worth studying in their own right. In the twentieth century ethnographers, sociologists, pedagogues, public health specialists, and historians took a keen interest in customs related to childhood and the lives of Jewish children. In 1904 Regina Lilientalowa published a pioneering study, 'Dziecko żydowskie', which investigated the ethnography of Jewish childhood, analysing proverbs and customs about offspring from the moment of conception, dealing with the difficulties of conceiving, ways to increase the chances of having a son, and how to facilitate childbirth. An expanded edition was published posthumously in 1927.[7] Her study also familiarized her audience with the customs surrounding ritual circumcision.[8] The autobiography competitions for young Jews organized by YIVO in 1932, 1934, and 1939 encouraged the contributors to reflect on their childhood and adolescence.[9] Driven by their understanding of childhood as the period which shapes a person's personality, habits, and approach to life, Jewish reformers in the twentieth century sought to mobilize community resources to help children in need and to transform adolescence from a period of deprivation and suffering into one imbued with promise for the future.

Soviet policy-makers also grappled with issues related to children and childhood. From the inception of the Soviet Union, they were confronted with the huge number of orphans created by civil war and famine. The Soviets saw these children as an important element in building socialism and sought, above all in the orphanages which were then established, to transform them, with mixed success, into committed citizens of the socialist state. A second wave of orphans emerged after 1930 as a result of Stalin's policies of collectivization, forced industrialization, and terror. By now the regime lacked the resources to carry out the policy which it had implemented in the 1920s, and these orphans ultimately became victims of the worsening political climate.[10]

In dealing with this group of traumatized children, Soviet policy-makers drew on research which had developed in the late tsarist era on what was described as 'subnormality' and 'pathology' in the Russian child population. This evolved in the late 1930s into a concept of the clinically established pathological 'impairment' of such orphans and led to a much more repressive approach to childcare.[11] At the same time the Soviet regime published a large range of books for children and set up professional theatres for them, seeking in this way to foster their aesthetic and cultural education. However, from the late 1920s these were transformed into ideological instruments of the totalitarian state.[12]

Throughout the twentieth century the plight of underprivileged children was hauntingly portrayed by photo-journalists such as Jacob Riis and Lewis Hine, who explored child poverty and deprivation. In this new world, children had a unique ability to appeal to sentiments of sorrow and hope and the humanistic instincts to pity and protect. Roman Vishniac and Alter Kacyzne appealed to this sense of loss and pity in their photographs of east European Jewish children just before the Second World War was to wipe them out. Widespread poverty, coupled with anti-Jewish violence and the Holocaust, which wreaked havoc in the lives of Jewish children, resulted in the breaking up of Jewish families, produced thousands of Jewish orphans in need of urgent assistance, and heightened a sense of communal responsibility. After the Holocaust Jewish organizations and community leaders were involved in locating, assisting, and rehabilitating Jewish child survivors and facilitating parenting, child-rearing, and childcare in new political and familial settings, often in transit from eastern Europe.

This volume is divided into five parts, each focused on different research questions, methodological approaches, and sources. They showcase the wealth of material that can be utilized to examine children's experiences, representations of childhood, and approaches to adolescence. They also provide an important corrective to key questions of Polish and east European Jewish history by complicating neat chronological divisions and assumptions about what it meant to grow up Jewish in eastern Europe and how communal ideas and organizations moulded Jewish childhoods. This is particularly evident in the chapters devoted to the interwar, wartime, and post-war periods. However, rather than organize these chapters chronologically, we have decided to focus first on conceptions of childhood and the family in Jewish eastern Europe in a number of milieus and contexts. The first part discusses a variety of familial settings in connection with communal ideals. The second part examines medical discourses and the treatment of children from the early modern period to

1939. The third part analyses the educational experience of Jewish children in interwar Poland and after the Holocaust, and delves into the issue of children's agency in a number of educational frameworks. The fourth part investigates children's experience of trauma between 1914 and 1947, and focuses on how Jewish institutions and children themselves sought remedies for such experiences. The fifth and final part discusses childhood and its problems in a Jewish milieu rebuilt after the Holocaust.

The discussion of conceptions of childhood highlights both those features which were common to all the inhabitants of eastern Europe and those specific to Jews. Some of these common features are reflected in the similarity between Yiddish and Polish proverbs. Thus the Yiddish 'Kleyne kinder lozn nit shlofn; groise kinder lozn nit ruen' is paralleled by the Polish 'Małe dzieci nie pozwolą ci spać; duże dzieci nie pozwolą ci żyć' (Little children won't let you sleep; big children won't let you live); 'Kleyne kinder, kleyne frydn; groyse kinder, groyse leydn' by 'Małe dzieci, małe kłopoty; duże dzieci, duże kłopoty' (Little children, little trouble; big children, big trouble); 'Kinder un gelt; a sheyne velt' by 'Dobre dziecko jest skarbem matki' (A good child is a mother's treasure); and 'A kindersher seykhl iz oykhet a seykhl' by 'Dziecko prawdę ci powie' (A child will tell you the truth).[13] Different kinds of Jewish childhood were also shaped by the familial context of relationships and obligations. 'Obligations of parents to children and of children to parents are specified in the legal literature, but they are not contractual or reciprocal in the same way as are the obligations of husbands and wives.'[14] At the same time, the Talmud and rabbinic literature stress that a child is one of the three major blessings that God can confer on a person.[15]

The nineteenth century saw the enormous expansion of hasidism in eastern Europe, a Jewish religious revival with strong traditional characteristics. As Gadi Sagiv shows, children were venerated in this movement in a manner common to many cultures and religions. Children of hasidic leaders were groomed for leadership and sometimes even became *tsadikim* while they were still young. This was strongly criticized by the maskilim, the supporters of Jewish Enlightenment, who saw it as one of the many primitive aspects of the hasidic movement. Obviously, this was not a view shared by the hasidim. They accepted the inversion inherent in the veneration of *yenuka*s (child leaders). This meant that, in contrast to the common practice in the movement when the *tsadik* was an older person whom they could trust, consult, and rely on, the child leader was perceived as the dominant figure in the relationship, and older hasidim were dependent on him. For them, a child who would grow up to be a *tsadik* became living proof of the stability and continuity of the dynasty.

In her chapter, Rotem Preger-Wagner describes the changing conceptions of childhood in Hebrew literature. As she shows, the nineteenth century saw a major change in the way childhood was perceived, with the child now being understood as distinct from the adult and worthy of note. As Philippe Ariès has documented for European societies more generally, this had not been the case before.[16] Child characters in Hebrew literature were increasingly depicted in a manner derived from ideas articulated by Enlightenment philosophers and the Romantics. This view was succeeded by what Preger-Wagner describes as the emergence of the figure of 'the child protagonist, who speaks "from within himself", giving the child the position of narrator', a process which resonates with trends in European literature more generally.

In 'The Beautiful Manor House', Yehoshua Ecker explores a very different milieu by focusing on coming of age in the families of the increasingly acculturated Jewish landowners of Galicia, where Jews were given the right to own land in the nineteenth century. While noting that such a Jewish setting was unique, he examines the social and spatial interactions embedded in the networks of the Jewish landowning families in Galicia and Jewish manor houses in the Galician countryside.

One feature of the modern period is the way governments and political movements began to use the concept of childhood as a vehicle for developing and promoting social values. Thus, confronted with the humanitarian crisis caused by the flight to Vienna and Prague of Galician Jews when the province was occupied by Russian forces, local Zionist activists sought to advocate for Jewish national solidarity and self-reliance through the institutions they created. In 1917 the Jewish National Fund (founded in 1901 by the Zionist Organization with the purpose of purchasing land in Palestine) justified its call for donations as follows: 'The rescue of Jewish children is a great national mission. Jewish children are the most valuable national asset our Jewish nation has and we cannot shy away from any difficulty or obstacle in order to fulfil this holy duty.'[17]

As Sean Martin shows in his chapter, CENTOS, the Central Society for the Care of Orphans, founded in Warsaw in 1924, avoided explicit Zionist propaganda but had as its goal raising Jewish children as Jews and promoting Jewish self-help and cooperation. These ideals were clearly set out in the movement's journals, *Unzer kind*, *Dos kind*, and *Przegląd Społeczny*.

Part 2 discusses the medical treatment provided to Jewish children as the early modern period in Poland gave way to modernity in the nineteenth century. The earlier concern of the Jewish community for its children is reflected in the large body of literature dedicated to their care. Many of the remedies it advocated were derived from customs and rabbinic teachings which saw illness as a punishment for sin. They also integrated the traditional practices of the surrounding societies, as Marek Tuszewicki discusses in his chapter. These treatments were particularly concerned to facilitate conception and healthy birth and prevent unwanted pregnancies. Recourse was often had to spells and amulets and to religious intercession, such as the recitation of psalms. In this traditional form of medicine, children not only were patients but sometimes functioned as caregivers and even healers. As in the surrounding societies, they were seen as having access to the interface between this world and the next. Medical treatments also drew on classical medicine as it had developed in Greece and Rome and had been taken up by Arab and Jewish physicians. Such treatments, based on both ancient medicine and folk medicine, were dominant until the end of the eighteenth century. They then came up against the growing prestige of modern medicine, which demonstrated its effectiveness in combating smallpox, cholera, and infant mortality. Confidence in doctors grew steadily, particularly among the Jewish elite, in spite of the high cost of their services and the fact that their definitions of illness and the role of the patient were clearly at odds with traditional understandings. The triumph of modern medical practice, however, was never more than partial.

The Jewish population of Poland–Lithuania increased rapidly in the early modern period. From between 150,000 and 200,000 in the mid-seventeenth century (out of a total population of 11 million) it grew to around 750,000 (out of a total population of between 12 and 14 million) by 1764, when the first, not very adequate, census was taken. Jews then made up about 6 per cent of the population. Half a century later their number on the lands of the now non-existent Polish–Lithuanian Commonwealth had risen to perhaps a million. The rapid rise of the Jewish population continued throughout the nineteenth century until the arrival of modern methods of contraception and an increase in the age of marriage among Jews. By the late nineteenth century, for which much more accurate statistics are available, the Jewish birth rate began to fall below that of the general population.[18]

How far is the increase in the size of the Jewish population to be explained by differences in medical practice in childcare?[19] Celibacy was rare, and Jews suffered fewer deaths on the battlefield. They may have been more resistant to diseases because of the hygienic requirements of their religion. *Kehilot*, the Jewish community organizations, provided basic support for the poor, which may have limited the impact of outbreaks of disease. Jews may also have found it easier to get hold of food in times of famine because of their access to Jewish traders and agents in agricultural goods.[20] Even more important was the Jewish ideal of early marriage, which was justified on both moral and religious grounds, and the facilitation of this practice through the *kest* system, whereby the parents, usually those of the bride, supported the young couple until they were ready for economic independence.[21] *Kest* was probably limited to the wealthier stratum of Jewish society, and the proportion of families able to follow the practice diminished as the size of the Jewish community grew. At the same time the fact that the elite married early may have led to attempts by the rest of Jewish society to follow suit.[22]

This issue is discussed in the chapter by Zvi Eckstein and Anat Vaturi. Examining Jewish care of newborns in the seventeenth and eighteenth centuries, they argue that, while there were discrepancies between Jewish law and custom and actual practice, 'the customs, beliefs, and norms governing post-partum breastfeeding and wet-nursing that were standardized as "good" among Jews in early modern Poland, favoured infant survival'. They thus constituted one of the factors that lowered infant and child death rates, which do seem to have been lower than the corresponding rates among Christians, particularly those living in the countryside.

The Talmud enjoined maternal breastfeeding and the early first feeding of the newborn, which was to take place 'immediately after birth, but in any event before twenty-four hours have elapsed, even if the navel has not yet been cut'.[23] This gave the newborn the benefit of the first milk, known as colostrum, which contains a range of antimicrobial elements and substances that strengthen the immune system, of which the medical profession only became aware in the nineteenth century. At the same time it does seem that the employment of wet nurses, both Jewish and Christian, including both those who lived in the house of the parents of the child and those who cared for such infants in their own home, was widespread, particularly among wealthier families. It was stressed in the Jewish literature that changing wet nurses should be avoided. Wet nurses were primarily employed when a mother had died, when she could not breastfeed herself, or when she was unwilling to do so. This was common among rich families, who did not want to wait the twenty-four months between pregnancies that the rabbis decreed was necessary if the mother was breastfeeding. This was in spite of the fact that using Christian wet nurses was criticized in the ethical literature.

More detail of Jewish infant-feeding practices is to be found in the chapter by Ekaterina Oleshkevich. She demonstrates that wet-nursing in its two variants—live-in and live-out—was widespread among the Jewish community of the tsarist empire. This should have occasioned little surprise, as wet-nursing was a normal practice in Europe until the nineteenth century, as it was also in better-off circles in Russia. Affluent mothers believed that to breastfeed was inappropriate to their social status, so that wet-nursing was 'a low-prestige and poorly paid job'.[24] Oleshkevich argues, in contrast to Eckstein and Vaturi, that 'alongside normative texts, the rabbinic responsa also affirmed that affluent women were not expected to breastfeed and mentioned women who explicitly linked their unwillingness to breastfeed with their social status'. As a result, affluent mothers who wished to breastfeed were seen as unconventional and going beyond what was necessary.

Of the two types of wet nurse, the live-in variety, although more expensive, was generally preferred, particularly by the Jewish elite, since it afforded parents greater control. Usually the baby was nursed for one to two years, and live-in wet nurses were often single mothers (widows, divorcees, and unmarried women), both Jewish and non-Jewish. Married women who wanted to be employed as live-in wet nurses had to agree to give up their own infants, since it was believed that a woman could only breastfeed one baby at a time. These babies, like the children of poorer Jewish families, were often looked after in baby farms, sometimes described as *fabriki angelov* (angel factories), which had appallingly high death rates.

Less expensive and therefore resorted to by less affluent families was the practice of hiring a wet nurse who took the baby with her to her own home and brought the child back to the parents when it was weaned, between the ages of 1 and 2. It is not known how widespread this practice was, but Oleshkevich points out that it is frequently referred to in newspapers, fiction, and rabbinic responsa and seems never to have been regarded as unusual. There were even cases where affluent families resorted to it.

Employment of non-Jewish wet nurses, both live-in and live-out, for Jewish babies was widespread in the Russian empire in the nineteenth century. It was difficult to find a Jewish wet nurse outside the Pale, and many parents preferred to avoid the bureaucratic hassle this required. The ethno-religious origin of a wet nurse was usually not a decisive factor. More important were the wages, her physical condition, and the quality of her milk.[25]

As the century progressed the perception of 'good motherhood' changed and increasing pressure was put on Jewish women to nurse their own babies. Maternal breastfeeding was now increasingly favoured, something that was linked with the gradual medicalization of child-rearing, which accepted wet-nursing only if the mother had a severe medical condition that prevented her from breastfeeding. This argument was Europe-wide. In the rapidly growing towns of western Europe, the emerging medical profession attacked the practice of feeding infants with cow's milk, which was seen as both dirty and indigestible by infants. It was often given to babies in the baby farms. When babies fed in this way developed colic, they were frequently given 'mother's kindness', a draft of gin or an opiate. This practice was responsible, at least in part, for the high infantile mortality in the region, which, it was believed could be reduced by breastfeeding.

Rakefet Zalashik's chapter on the camps run by the Society for the Protection of the Health of the Jewish People focuses on a scientific attempt to improve the physical state of poor Jewish children in the interwar period. The camps came to play an important role in the lives of the children and their parents and emerged as an important institution for the Jews of interwar Poland, who sought to safeguard the health of their young generation without government funds.

While the first two parts rely on the voices of Jewish children filtered through the lens of memory and memory politics, the voices of children and adolescents are most clearly to be heard in the third part, which examines their educational experience in interwar Poland. On the basis of the autobiographies submitted to YIVO, Kamil Kijek constructed a compelling portrait of what he described as the 'generation of independence'.[26] The radical political and social transformations which occurred in the early twentieth century alienated the members of this group from their parents and their view of the world, whether embodied in Jewish religious Orthodoxy or in maskilic and integrationist approaches to Jewish issues. The introduction of compulsory education led to the rapid adoption of the Polish language and to an admiration for Polish culture and literature at a time when the intensification of antisemitism, particularly in the 1930s, made integrating into Polish society much more difficult. As a consequence the members of this group felt compelled to adopt a 'radical modernism' which took the form of active participation in new political parties and movements, above all Zionism, Bundism, and communism.

These issues are reflected in the chapters in this part which use ego-documents to illuminate how young people experienced the crisis. That by David Assaf and Yael Darr makes use of a rare collection of some ninety letters written between 1934 and 1935 by boys and girls up to the age of 11 who studied at the Tarbut primary school in the town of Nowy Dwór Mazowiecki, approximately 35 kilometres north-west of Warsaw, to examine their social and emotional life. This is seen as a paradigm for the experience of those children who attended Hebrew elementary schools in Poland between the two world wars. The letters were part of a classroom project for pupils to write to pen pals in Palestine, which was an established practice in the Tarbut institutions in Poland, intended both to train pupils in writing Hebrew and to create a living connection with the Jewish community there. Most were addressed to the school's director, Zvi Plesser, on the eve of his departure for Palestine. As the authors argue, these letters reveal not only loyalty to the school and to Plesser personally but also the 'deep and complex relations between pupils and teachers and a torn or divided self rather than a decisive Zionist ego'. This is reflected, above all, in the constantly repeated contrast between the idyllic image of the Land of Israel and the gloomy reality of their lives in Poland.

School education played a key role in the nationalization project of the Second Polish Republic, which had as its goal the raising of young citizens of the resurrected Polish state, both ethnic Poles and members of ethnic minorities. Most Jewish children in interwar Poland—about 80 per cent—attended Polish state schools.[27] Using the minutes of the teachers' meetings of two schools in Tarnów in the former Galicia, Agnieszka Wierzcholska discusses the difficulties Jewish children faced in Polish primary schools. The Czacki and the Staszic schools were located in an overwhelmingly Jewish, working-class part of the town, which had a population of 40,000, of whom 50 per cent were Jewish, and were tasked with fostering Polish acculturation. Wierzcholska's chapter offers unique insights into the views of teachers who interacted with a large number of Jewish students and suggests a great degree of individual agency among teachers and—in particular—headmasters. While the Czacki school ostensibly offered the opportunity for inclusiveness and democratization, it was the Jewish students that the teachers identified as problematic because of their poor level of Polish, failure to attend school on Saturday, and what was seen as unruly behaviour, such as playing soccer on Saturdays (which clearly transgressed the precepts of Judaism) instead of attending school or synagogue service. Their presence was seen as diminishing the educational opportunities of their Catholic classmates. In the Staszic school the teachers were aware of these difficulties but sought solutions that addressed the needs of the Jewish students.

Two chapters in this part, by Anna Landau-Czajka and Sarah Ellen Zarrow, explore the issue of children and adolescents and their labour or professional training from very different angles. Landau-Czajka examines child labour through the lens of letters sent by children and young Jews to *Mały Przegląd*, the popular Polish-language supplement to the Jewish daily *Nasz Przegląd* intended for young people and published in Warsaw from the second half of the 1920s. The contributors provided a largely negative picture of the effect of work on their lives. They complained of the impact of their work in the house and outside it on their ability to pursue long-term education. Landau-Czajka describes children assuming parental duties. Perceiving their situation as unfair, the children decried their lack of opportunities. Expectations of education changed in the 1930s, as more young children finished primary school; however, adolescents began to express anger at not being able to attend secondary school. Landau-Czajka highlights how many of these reports express regret for what their authors saw as a lost childhood. An exception was, however, made for work in Palestine or in preparation for moving there.

Sarah Ellen Zarrow focuses on Cecylia Klaftenowa's vision for Jewish orphans and other children in interwar Lwów (Lviv). She examines Klaftenowa's educational project, the Women's Vocational School of the Association of Handicraft Workshops for Jewish Girls, which focused on Jewish girls and sought to produce a cohort of independent women with practical skills in addition to their general education. Zarrow argues that this vision was closely connected to the broader project of the productivization of Polish Jewry, understood as an emancipatory project which would not only include girls from impoverished homes. Embedded in the material culture of the region, the school offered a successful model for Jewish life in interwar Poland.

Another analysis of Jewish children's experiences outside school is provided by Ula Madej-Krupitski, who also has recourse to the voices of children themselves. Her chapter, 'Through Their Own Eyes', analyses the holiday culture of young Jews in a number of settings: spontaneous or organized, with family members and among other children. Holidays offered Jewish children unique opportunities to experience Poland and Polish culture, to reflect on social and gender norms, and to be socialized into political ideologies.

Natalia Aleksiun's chapter offers a different perspective on the experience of Jewish children who attended Polish schools in the Second Polish Republic. By looking at autograph books and the inscriptions collected by teenage Jewish girls during the Second World War, she sheds light on the enduring culture in which Polish poetry continued to be cited in the midst of the Soviet and German occupations. While examining the rituals connected with attending Polish schools, which offered an inclusive space for friendships, she also delves into the emotional lives of the children during the Holocaust.

According to the Yiddish proverb, 'a child's tears reach heaven'. The twentieth century certainly saw Jewish children and young people undergoing appalling suffering. In the fourth part, 'Children and Trauma, 1914–1947', Jan Rybak's chapter shows how Zionist organizations in Vienna and Prague attempted to care for child refugees from Galicia during the First World War. In 1914 the Russian advance had led to between 340,000 and 600,000 refugees either fleeing or being expelled from Galicia. About half of them were Jewish,[28] many of whom were children. The need to care for them was a major preoccupation of the Jewish leadership in Vienna and Prague. The Zionists, who saw helping suffering Jews not only as a necessary task but also as a way to broaden their influence within the Jewish community, took a major role in these relief activities. Throughout the war Zionist activists invested considerable resources in providing rescue and assistance for Jewish refugee children from Galicia, whom they saw as potential future pillars of the nation, and in creating institutions in which these children would be educated in a new and progressive manner. This was eloquently expressed at a 1918 youth conference in Vienna: 'Do not allow the *ḥeder* to revive; create in its stead true educational institutions, modern Jewish kindergartens into which sun, air, and light stream in and from which emerge our children strengthened in body and spirit.'[29]

Far more tragic was the plight of Jewish children during the Holocaust. Their mortality rate was extremely high and very few survived in Poland, Lithuania, Belarus, or Ukraine. In recent years, much attention has been paid to the testimonies of these young survivors, which can certainly provide new insights into such topics as the rescue and betrayal of Jewish fugitives, local anti-Jewish violence, family dynamics, Jewish self-help, and relations with non-Jewish neighbours. These topics are examined in the chapters dealing with the Holocaust.

Joanna Sliwa turns her attention to Jewish children's efforts to survive by seeking help from Catholic institutions in Kraków. She explores different groups of Jewish children who found their way to convents, suggesting that age and status—such as being accompanied by a parent—determined their experience and, in particular, their attitudes to baptism and conversion. Drawing both on the children's own accounts and on institutional documentation, she sheds new light on the delicate balance between Jewish children, their relatives, and members of the clergy. The continued family bonds and the reconstruction of Jewish families after the war are at the centre of Sarah Cramsey's contribution. Her chapter, '"It was easier with a child than without"', follows Jewish families who escaped Poland to the east and survived the Holocaust in the Soviet Union, and the complex challenges they faced as they made fateful decisions about their future.

A poignant account of the sufferings of children in Romanian-occupied Transnistria during the Second World War is provided by the material collected in 1945 by the ethnomusicologist Moisey Beregovsky (1892–1961) and his team from the Folklore Section of the Department for the Study of Jewish Culture at the Ukrainian Academy of Science in Kyiv. Their goal was not specifically to document survivors' stories but rather to collect and publish Yiddish-language songs, stories, jokes, and folklore that had circulated during the war. In all, they interviewed hundreds of survivors and collected 263 original songs. At least one-third of those they interviewed were under 18 in 1945. Believed to have been lost, the project was rediscovered in 1990 in the basement of the Ukrainian National Library. Anna Shternshis's chapter focuses mainly on children and adolescents who survived in the Bershad ghetto in the Vinnitsa region, which was one of the largest in the area, some of whom could still be interviewed in the 1990s. In all, twenty-six songs from the ghetto have been preserved, shedding unique light on these children's experiences.

Jewish children, especially the youngest, had the slimmest chance of survival of any age group during the Holocaust except the very elderly. Those who did so often owed their lives to the assistance of non-Jewish helpers. After the war surrogate parents and Jewish organizations, both legal and semi-legal, faced a dilemma about child survivors and their future. Relatives and Jewish organizations tried to locate the children, hoping to place them with Jewish institutions. Some of those who had sheltered Jewish children relinquished them out of a sense of moral obligation. For about two years, beginning in April 1942, Michalina Pawel sheltered a 12-year-old boy,

Wolf Katz, the son of Mojżesz Katz from Mościska near Lwów. The child lived with her in the village of Lacka Wola (Volytsya), and she continued to care for him after the war. She explained in a letter to the Central Committee of Jews in Poland:

After liberation, I kept the defenceless and destitute child with my family, knowing that nobody in his family had survived. I felt therefore obligated to take care of the underage boy and I treated him in the same way as my children, until I received information about the existence of children's homes organized especially by the Jewish committees. Not wanting to cut him off from his normal mode of living, I have given him the possibility of returning to the Jewish community.[30]

She asked for assistance for her own family to compensate her for hiding a Jewish child. Other helpers demanded to be paid before they would hand over the children.[31] It was for children like this that a myriad institutions were created that were to improve their health, help their emotional rehabilitation, and prepare them for the future in Europe or beyond.

There is a vast literature on the experiences of Jewish child survivors in Europe and their difficult path to a new life in Palestine/Israel, the United States, and elsewhere. A growing number of memoirs offer insights into childhood in the aftermath of the war and in transit.[32] In particular, it has been argued that, although the camp system separated families, the creation of new bonds there helped inmates by providing them with a network of mutual support. Arguably, many women imprisoned in camps bonded in this way, caring for one another and increasing their chances of survival. Some of those who survived did so by being harboured by non-Jewish families.[33] For some of the children, these non-Jews acted as their surrogate families, and emotional bonds persisted after the war, even when children returned to their biological families and adults began rebuilding their lives.[34] For most, however, these bonds were severed when the children were removed from the families and as Jews emigrated from Poland. Some wartime caretakers became the legal parents of rescued children and raised them after the war as their own, at times without revealing their Jewish origins. Some young Jews who formed relations with non-Jews remained committed to their wartime bonds.

The aftermath of the Holocaust has become a major topic in recent years. Examining questions of institutional and political continuities, scholars have described survivors' experiences, communal efforts to rehabilitate them, and the activities of Jewish organizations.[35] In these studies, the efforts to recover Jewish children are particularly important,[36] and scholars have increasingly examined the experiences of such children. In her study of child survivors, Rebecca Clifford noted that, after the war, they found themselves in a 'strange world' in which 'apparent truths could be instantly, shockingly upended ... The truth was often unknown, but equally often it was hidden from the children.'[37] The plight of Jewish child survivors is discussed in three chapters here. Seeking to uncover the post-war lives of such children, Joanna Michlic's chapter, 'Jewish Child Survivors in the Aftermath of the Holocaust', describes the reconstitution of Jewish families and the adoption of Jewish children by previously unknown Jewish relatives or even complete strangers. Highlighting the children's vulnerability, her chapter underscores the emotional difficulties they continued to face. Her contribution encourages further research into the lives of child survivors, including their relationships with their rescuers and their difficulties in overcoming the bitter experiences of the war.

Boaz Cohen's 'The Rehabilitation of Jewish Child Holocaust Survivors' offers a compelling picture of the efforts undertaken by educators and pedagogues in preparing children scarred by their wartime experiences to be reintegrated into institutional and familial settings and to overcome their mistrust, self-hatred, and anger. This chapter explores the rehabilitative work with Jewish child and teenage survivors in the aftermath of the Holocaust in Poland. It looks at the perception of these children by adults, and the educational challenges they presented to their educators and to the Jewish community in general. In the children's homes, educators and caregivers developed new educational practices. Cohen describes how they attempted to re-establish the children's trust and identity through such practices as self-government and children's courts.

Part 5 deals with Jewish childhood in Poland after the war. Kamil Kijek's chapter, 'Beyond Post-Holocaust Trauma', a microhistorical examination of one town, delves into the Jewish experience of childhood in post-war Poland. He describes the often competing visions of how children should be brought up in the new political conditions, and children's own trajectories into adulthood in a town with a uniquely dense post-Holocaust Jewish population. As he demonstrates, Jewish childhood in Dzierżoniów in the immediate post-war years, like that in other towns of the newly incorporated areas of Poland, was fundamentally different from that elsewhere in the country. The size of the Jewish community and the wartime experiences of parents undermined state-sponsored political indoctrination and the associated pressure to assimilate and created a strong Jewish identity. In addition, Jewish children in Dzierżoniów benefited from educational opportunities not available to their parents' generation, as is clear from the biographies of some of those described in the chapter. This phenomenon can be observed both among those who remained in Poland and those who emigrated.

Finally, engaging with the notion of Polish Jews' political activism, and, in particular, building on the scholarship underscoring the centrality of politics for Jewish youth, Łukasz Bertram examines the accounts of childhood and adolescence of Polish Jewish communists who came of age and became radicalized in the Second Polish Republic. His chapter analyses private and public accounts of childhood constructed after the war and maps out how adults narrated their coming of age. Filtered through their later experiences and their ideological entanglements, these accounts help explain how this cohort perceived itself and its path to communist ideology and activism. Comparing an array of personal accounts—including memoirs, autobiographies, questionnaires and CVs produced for the Communist Party, and oral history interviews—of adults who narrated their childhood as defined by left-wing politics allows him to delve into what they perceived as an ideal communist childhood and youth. Paying close attention to narrative strategies, Bertram makes it clear how in their autobiographies members of this group tend to minimize the importance of Jewishness and the role of antisemitism in family socialization and socialization to communism.

Conclusion

Gershon Hundert argued that studying the experience of children and the attitudes towards coming of age offers an important corrective to how the Jewish past is perceived.[38] This volume proves the potential of this lens for such topics as local history; the history of education and charitable institutions; the histories of medicine, emotions, and gender; and Polish–Jewish relations, to name just a few. The chapters concentrate on diverse cohorts of children, in different time periods, geographical settings, and contexts in eastern Europe. At the same time, they also offer insights into prescriptive projects for Jewish childhood and approaches to child-rearing. Although the majority of the contributors focus on the twentieth century, the volume's wide chronological range makes it possible to investigate children's experiences and individual and community approaches to child-rearing over the *longue durée* in the Polish lands. Its individual chapters also show that, in studying Jewish childhood in eastern Europe, the generational lens turns out to be closely tied to other key categories, such as gender and class.

The contributors to this volume underscore the ongoing centrality of these issues, as well as shifting approaches to children and ideas about the desired outcome of a Jewish childhood. Whether focusing on children's own self-understanding or on how they were moulded by adults, the volume emphasizes how the lens of children's history can offer a nuanced and dynamic understanding of Jewish studies in eastern Europe. Likewise, the different chapters raise methodological questions. They use a variety of sources and disciplinary approaches, from personal accounts, to community reports, to journalism and literature. All the contributors reflect critically on their sources: what are their limitations and how can they best be interpreted to understand the experience of Jewish childhood? They are constantly mindful of the inherent gaps and silences in them. There are questions about Jewish children and their experiences we would wish to raise, for the answers to which we often lack a record or the ability to probe their voices fully. However, the volume does what it can to reproduce the voices of many Jewish children and adolescents. In particular, we know what those born before the war could not have been aware of—that their world would be almost totally destroyed within a few years. The dreams which they so eloquently expressed were never to be realized. This volume is a modest memorial to their lost hopes.

Notes

1 Among many recent examples, see C. Heywood, *A History of Childhood: Children and Childhood in the West from Medieval to Modern Times* (Cambridge, 2001); J. Humphries,

Childhood and Child Labour in the British Industrial Revolution (Cambridge, 2011); J. Helgren and C. A. Vasconcellos (eds.), *Girlhood: A Global History* (New Brunswick, NJ, 2010); S. E. Chinn, *Inventing Modern Adolescence: The Children of Immigrants in Turn-of-the-Century America* (New Brunswick, NJ, 2009); *The Routledge History of Childhood in the Western World*, ed. P. S. Fass (London, 2013); on children and childhood in the Polish lands, see K. Jakubiak and A. Winiarz (eds.), *Nauczanie domowe dzieci polskich od XVIII do XX wieku* (Bydgoszcz, 2004); M. Dąbrowska and A. Klonder (eds.), *Od narodzin do wieku dojrzałego: Dzieci i młodzież w Polsce*, i: *Od średniowiecza do wieku XVIII* (Warsaw, 2002); E. Mazur (ed.), *Od narodzin do wieku dojrzałego: Dzieci i młodzież w Polsce*, ii: *Stulecie XIX i XX* (Warsaw, 2003); D. Żołądź-Strzelczyk, *Dziecko w dawnej Polsce* (Poznań, 2002); M. Delimata, *Dziecko w Polsce średniowiecznej* (Poznań, 2004); M. B. Koval, *Childhood in Medieval Poland (1050–1300): Constructions and Realities in a European Context* (Leiden, 2021).

2 S. Maza, 'The Kids Aren't All Right: Historians and the Problem of Childhood', *American Historical Review*, 125 (2020), 1261–85: 1262–3.

3 S. Mintz, 'Children's History Matters', *American Historical Review*, 125 (2020), 1286–92: 1286; see also id., *Huck's Raft: A History of American Childhood* (Cambridge, Mass., 2006).

4 See H. Pass Freidenreich, *Jewish Politics in Vienna, 1918–1938* (Bloomington, Ind., 1991), 156–7; C. Weissler, '*Mizvot* Built into the Body: *Tkhines* for *Niddah*, Pregnancy, and Childbirth', in H. Eilberg-Schwartz (ed.), *People of the Body: Jews and Judaism from an Embodied Perspective* (Albany, NY, 1992), 101–16; A. Sommer Schneider, 'The Survival of Yidishkeyt: The Impact of the American Jewish Joint Distribution Committee on Jewish Education in Poland, 1945–1989', in Eilberg-Schwartz (ed.), *People of the Body*, 353–77.

5 See I. Bassok, *Teḥiyat hane'urim: mishpaḥah veḥinukh beyahadut polin bein milḥamot ha-'olam* (Jerusalem, 2015); id., 'Darkhei ḥinukh bamishpaḥah hayehudit bepolin bein milḥamot ha'olam: nisayon behistoryah antropologit', *Gal-ed*, 24 (2015), 75–106; K. Kijek, *Dzieci modernizmu: Świadomość, kultura i socjalizacja polityczna młodzieży żydowskiej w II Rzeczypospolitej* (Wrocław, 2017); A. Bar-El, 'Jewish Children's Periodicals in Poland between the Two World Wars—in Three Languages', *Rocznik Historii Prasy Polskiej*, 16/1 (2013), 5–48; A. Szyba, '"Czy można zniszczyć kopiec mrówek?" Nauka przyrody w szkołach Centralnej Żydowskiej Organizacji Szkolnej (1921–1939): Teoria i praktyka', *Kwartalnik Historii Żydów*, 268 (2018), 743–61; K. Person, '"The children ceased to be children": Day-Care Centres at Refugee Shelters in the Warsaw Ghetto', *Polin*, 30 (2018), 341–52; S. Martin, 'Jewish Youth Between Tradition and Assimilation: Exploring Polish Jewish Identity in Interwar Krakow', *Polish Review*, 46 (2001), 461–77; id., 'How to House a Child: Providing Homes for Jewish Children in Interwar Poland', *East European Jewish Affairs*, 45 (2005), 26–41.

6 M. Botticini, Z. Eckstein, and A. Vaturi, 'Child Care and Human Development: Insights from Jewish History in Central and Eastern Europe, 1500–1930', *Economic Journal*, 129 (2019), 2637–90. On child survivors of the Holocaust, see e.g. K. Nili, 'Children', in *The Holocaust Encyclopedia*, ed. W. Laqueur (New Haven, Conn., 2001), 115–19; P. Heberer, *Children during the Holocaust* (Lanham, Md., 2011). The issue is also dealt with in the testimonies collected in I. Ehrenburg and V. Grossman, *The Complete Black Book of Russian Jewry*, trans. and ed. D. Patterson (New York, 2017); R. Braham, *The Politics of Genocide: The Holocaust in Hungary*, 2 vols., rev. edn. (New York, 2016); J. Ancel, *The History of the Holocaust in Romania* (Lincoln, Neb., 2012); D. Deletant, 'Transnistria', in G. D. Hundert (ed.), *YIVO Encyclopedia of Jews in Eastern Europe* (New Haven, Conn., 2008).

7 R. Lilientalowa, 'Dziecko żydowskie', *Materyały Antropologiczno-Archeologiczne i Etnograficzne Akademii Umiejętności w Krakowie*, 7 (1904), 141–73; Ger. trans.: R. Lilienthal, 'Das Kind bei den Juden', *Mitteilungen zur jüdischen Volkskunde*, 25 (1908), 1–24; expanded edn.: R. Lilientalowa, *Dziecko żydowskie* (Kraków, 1927).

8 Lilientalowa, *Dziecko żydowskie*, 15–17.

9 See YIVO Archives, New York, RG 4, 'Autobiographies of Jewish Youth in Poland (1932–1939)'; *Awakening Lives: Autobiographies of Jewish Youth in Poland before the Holocaust*, ed. J. Shandler (New Haven, Conn., 2002); *Ostatnie pokolenie: Autobiografie polskiej młodzieży żydowskiej okresu międzywojennego*, ed. A. Cała (Warsaw, 2003); *Alilot ne'urim: otobiyografiyot shel benei no'ar yehudim mipolin bein shetei milḥamot ha'olam*, ed. I. Bassok (Jerusalem, 2011).

10 A. M. Ball, *And Now My Soul is Hardened: Abandoned Children in Soviet Russia, 1918–1930* (Berkeley, Calif., 1996); id., 'Survival in the Street World of Soviet Russia's "besprizornye"', *Jahrbücher Für Geschichte Osteuropas*, 39 (1991), 33–52.

11 See A. Byford, 'The Imperfect Child in Early Twentieth-Century Russia', *History of Education*, 46 (2017), 595–617.

12 M. Van de Water, *Moscow Theatres for Young People: A Cultural History of Artistic Innovation and Ideological Coercion, 1917–2000* (New York, 2006); L. Shpet, *Sovetskii teatr dlya detei: Stranitsy istorii 1918–1945* (Moscow, 1971); A. Burgess, 'The Artful Propaganda of Soviet Children's Literature' (15 June 2017): Atlas Obscura website, 'Stories', visited 10 Dec. 2022.

13 See F. Kogos, The Book of Yiddish Proverbs and Slang (Secaucus, NJ, 1970); Emily, '28 Yiddish Phrases about Children' (30 Apr. 2018): Jewish Food Hero website, visited 23 June 2022.

14 M. Walzer, M. Lorberbaum, N. J. Zohar, and M. Kochen, 'Parents and Children', in eid. (eds.), *The Jewish Political Tradition*, iii: *Community* (New Haven, Conn., 2018), 155–222: 157.

15 Ibid.

16 See esp. P. Ariès, *L'Enfant et la vie familiale sous l'Ancien Régime* (Paris, 1960); Eng. trans.: *Centuries of Childhood: A Social History of Family Life*, trans. R. Baldick (New York, 1962). Heywood, however, notes that Ariès's thesis played an important role in opening up the discussion of childhood. It has since been put into question by historians who expanded his research (Heywood, *A History of Childhood*, 11–15).

17 Central Zionist Archives, Jerusalem, L6 103: Jewish National Fund, memorandum on Jewish children's relief (1917(?)).

18 This is a matter which has been extensively discussed (see esp. G. Hundert, 'Population and Society in Eighteenth-Century Poland', in J. Michalski (ed.), *Lud żydowski w narodzie polskim / The Status of Jews in the Polish Nation* (Warsaw, 1994), 12–19).

19 Ibid. 12–13.

20 Ibid. 13.

21 Ibid. 14–15.

22 S. Stampfer, 'Hamashma'ut haḥevratit shelnisu'ei boser bemizraḥ eiropah bame'ah ha 19', in E. Mendelsohn and C. Shmeruk (eds.), *Studies on Polish Jewry: Paul Glikson Memorial Volume* (Jerusalem, 1987), 65–77; G. Hundert, 'Jewish Children and Childhood in Early Modern East Central Europe', in D. Kraemer (ed.), *The Jewish Family: Metaphor and Memory* (New York, 1989), 81–94: 89.

23 J. Preuss, *Biblical and Talmudic Medicine*, trans. and ed. F. Rosner (Lanham, Md., 2004), 405.

24 S. Grieco and C. Corsini, *Historical Perspectives on Breastfeeding: Two Essays* (Florence, 1991), 34.
25 From antiquity, there were many criteria on how to choose a proper wet nurse and how to check the quality of the breastmilk (see V. A. Fildes, *Wet Nursing: A History from Antiquity to the Present* (Oxford, 1988), 18–23; N. A. Mitsyuk, 'Materinstvo u dvoryanok tsentral'noi Rossii vo vtoroi polovine XIX – nachale XX v.: Istoriko-antropologicheskii i etnokul'turnyi aspekty', habilitation thesis (Institute of Anthropology and Ethnography, Russian Academy of Sciences, 2016), 571–76).
26 K. Kijek, *Dzieci modernizmu*, 26.
27 The figures varied greatly by region: in Lwów, Kraków, and Tarnopol, the proportion was 90 per cent or more (G. Bacon, 'National Revival, Ongoing Acculturation: Jewish Education in Interwar Poland', *Jahrbuch des Simon-Dubnow-Instituts*, 1 (2002), 71–92: 76).
28 B. Hoffmann-Holter, *'Abreisendmachung': Jüdische Kriegsflüchtlinge in Wien, 1914–1923* (Vienna, 1995), 29–30.
29 'In den Kindergarten oder zurück in den Cheder?', *Jüdische Zeitung*, 17 May 1918, p. 3.
30 Archiwum Żydowskiego Instytutu Historycznego, Warsaw, 303/VIII, 'Centralny Komitet Żydów w Polsce: Wydział Opieki Społecznej, 1944–1950', 235, fo. 1: Pawel Michalina, letter to Central Committee of Jews in Poland, Warsaw (received 16 May 1947).
31 For a recent study of negotiating the return of the children to the Jewish community in Poland, see A. Bikont, *Cena: W poszukiwaniu żydowskich dzieci po wojnie* (Wołowiec, 2022).
32 Several volumes of children's testimonies have been published by the Children of the Holocaust Association in Poland (see *Dzieci Holocaustu mówią...*, i, ed. W. Śliwowska (Warsaw, 1993); ii, ed. J. Gutenbaum and A. Latała (Warsaw, 2001); iii, ed. K. Meloch and H. Szostkiewicz (Warsaw, 2008); iv, ed. K. Meloch and H. Szostkiewicz (Warsaw, 2012); v, ed. A. Kołacińska-Gałązka (Warsaw, 2013); Eng. trans.: *The Last Eyewitnesses: Children of the Holocaust Speak*, i, trans. J. Bussgang and F. Bussgang (Evanston, Ill., 1998); ii, trans. J. Bussgang, F. Bussgang, and Simon Cygielski (Evanston, Ill., 2005)).
33 For children's perspectives during the Holocaust, see N. Belsky, '"Am I a Jew?": Soviet Jewish Youth and Antisemitism on the Home Front during the Second World War', *Holocaust and Genocide Studies*, 34 (2020), 274–94; J. Sliwa, *Jewish Childhood in Kraków: A Microhistory of the Holocaust* (New Brunswick, NJ, 2021). For child survivors' experiences, see N. Bogner, *At the Mercy of Strangers: The Rescue of Jewish Children with Assumed Identities in Poland* (Jerusalem, 2009); E. Nachmany Gafny, *Dividing Hearts: The Removal of Jewish Children from Gentile Families in Poland in the Immediate Post-Holocaust Years* (Jerusalem, 2006); M. Marrus, 'The Vatican and the Custody of Jewish Child Survivors after the Holocaust', *Holocaust and Genocide Studies*, 21 (2007), 378–403; J. B. Michlic, 'What Does a Child Remember? Recollections of the War and the Early Postwar Period among Child Survivors from Poland', in ead. (ed.), *Jewish Families in Europe, 1939–Present: History, Representation, and Memory* (Waltham, Mass., 2017), 153–72.
34 On surrogate bonds in the context of hiding, see N. Aleksiun, 'Uneasy Bonds: On Jews in Hiding and the Making of Surrogate Families', in E. R. Adler and K. Čapková (eds.), *Jewish and Romani Families in the Holocaust and Its Aftermath* (Rutgers, NJ, 2020), 85–99.
35 D. Engel, *Bein shiḥrur liveriḥah: nitsolei hasho'ah bepolin vehama'avak al hanhagatam, 1944–1946* (Tel Aviv, 1996); N. Aleksiun, *Dokąd dalej? Ruch syjonistyczny w Polsce (1944–1950)* (Warsaw, 2002); A. Grabski, *Centralny Komitet Żydów w Polsce (1944–1950): Historia polityczna* (Warsaw, 2015).

36 H. Datner-Śpiewak, 'Instytucje opieki nad dzieckiem i szkoły powszechne Centralnego Komitetu Żydowskiego w Polsce w latach 1945–1946', *Biuletyn Żydowskiego Instytutu Historycznego*, 119 (1981), 37–51; Bogner, *At the Mercy of Strangers*; Nachmany Gafny, *Dividing Hearts*; Sliwa, *Jewish Childhood in Kraków*; Michlic (ed.), *Jewish Families in Europe*; A. Helman (ed.), *No Small Matter: Features of Jewish Childhood* (Oxford, 2021); Bikont, *Cena*.

37 R. Clifford, *Survivors: Children's Lives after the Holocaust* (New Haven, Conn., 2020).

38 Hundert, 'Jewish Children and Childhood in Early Modern East Central Europe', 90.

1. CHILDHOOD AND FAMILY

Children and Childhood in Hasidic Courts before 1939

GADI SAGIV

> The nineteenth century saw the dynamic expansion of hasidism in east and central Europe, a Jewish religious revival with strongly traditional characteristics. Children were venerated in this movement in a manner common to many cultures and religions. However, there was something specific about the way the children of hasidic leaders were groomed for leadership and sometimes even became *tsadikim* (spiritual leaders) while they were still children. This involved an inversion of roles, since most hasidim viewed *tsadikim* as spiritual fathers, older men whom they could trust, consult, and rely on in all domains of life. However, a child hasidic leader was invested with spiritual authority, and when he grew up to be a *tsadik* he came to be seen as a living example of the stability and continuity of the movement.

ACCORDING TO A HASIDIC TRADITION, Rebbe Israel of Ruzhin (1796–1850) once confessed plaintively 'I was never a boy.'[1] He intended in this way to explain why he had not, like most children, learned to read or write properly. However, his words can be understood as a more general articulation of the fact that the childhood of a future hasidic leader was hardly an ordinary one. How did these boys experience their childhood? To what extent were the children of hasidic leaders expected to behave like adult hasidic leaders themselves? How far does the perception of a lost childhood among the children of hasidic leaders correspond with the well-known contention of Philippe Ariès that 'in medieval society the idea of childhood did not exist'?[2]

The underlying premise of this chapter is that childhood as an important stage in human life has not thus far received adequate attention in the otherwise vast scholarship on hasidism. This lacuna is glaring, given the fact that, from its early history, kinship and dynasties played such a prominent role in hasidism. From hasidism's early stages, its social structure consisted of groups of hasidim, each led by a *tsadik*, or rebbe, with leadership being bequeathed to one of his descendants. Early scholarship on hasidism focused on *tsadikim*, whereas later scholarship began to focus on the ordinary hasidim themselves. However, those who belonged to the hasidic elite but who were not leaders, such as members of the *tsadik*'s family and his entourage, remained beyond the focus of scholars. This chapter is thus not only part of a growing interest in childhood in Jewish history but also an attempt to fill in gaps in the study of hasidism.

In this chapter, I focus on the experiences of children, both boys and girls, who were descended from hasidic leaders, from the emergence of the movement in the last decades of the eighteenth century to the eve of the Second World War. I do not examine the childhood experiences of the ordinary members of the hasidic movement, although the childhood of those who did not belong to the elite does merit its own study. There are various possible contexts for such a discussion: a cultural one, of images of childhood in world religions;[3] a literary one, of hagiography and depictions of child saints or the childhood of saints;[4] a Jewish social one, of Jewish children and childhood in eastern Europe;[5] and a non-Jewish one, of non-Jewish elites, such as children and childhood among the eighteenth-century Polish nobility or in Russia at the beginning of the twentieth century.[6] I will treat childhood as encompassing the period from birth to marriage, which, among hasidim, customarily took place in the teenage years.[7]

The sources I have employed reflect primarily the point of view of those who belonged to the hasidic movement and thus offer an internal view of the topic. They include the perspectives of *tsadikim*, descendants of *tsadikim* who did not serve as *tsadikim* themselves, and ordinary hasidim. They also take account of the evaluations of those who left the movement (some of whom became secular) and criticized hasidism or Orthodox Judaism, and those who remained faithful to Orthodox Judaism and to the hasidic movement. The sources encompass the rich hasidic biographical traditions (that are often hagiographical) and ego-documents which involve such diverse genres as autobiographies, memoirs, diaries, and letters. Obviously these internal sources do not necessarily reflect childhood as it was; rather, they usually convey the idea of childhood from an idealized point of view, as it should have been.[8] In addition to the body of internal hasidic sources, some external, maskilic, sources will be used, usually embodying a critical view of the topic.

The diversity of the hasidic movement—which consisted of a wide variety of dynasties dispersed across many regions of eastern Europe with different social characteristics and over many years—makes it difficult to construct a uniform history of hasidic children and childhood. However, the movement did share some common characteristics across virtually all regions, periods, and groups. Among these were, first and foremost, the figure of the *tsadik*; secondly, the development of dynasties; and, finally, the hasidic court both as a place and as an institution. While not ignoring the specificity of each hasidic group, I believe that these three features allow for a discussion of the common characteristics of childhood among the hasidic leadership.

In addition to the disparity between the images of childhood and the social reality noted above, the images themselves also change. In her study of childhood in Russia between 1890 and 1991, Catriona Kelly noted the permanent tension, discernible in European culture since the mid-eighteenth century, between a rationalist, Enlightenment-oriented view that children are 'budding adults' and a sentimentalist, romanticist view that the child is 'a unique form of human individual'.[9] Kelly argued that in Russia, 'by the late nineteenth century, a huge increase in the influence of the "sentimentalist" view had taken place'.[10] However, the rationalistic view continued to dominate outside the Russian cultural elite. In the discussion that follows, I will occasionally refer to this distinction, but, in the hasidic case, it was not directly influenced by modernizing cultural trends but rather by earlier Jewish traditions.

An exploration of the characteristics of childhood in hasidic courts can shed new light on the general characteristics of the hasidic movement, including the role of the *tsadik*, the movement's dynastic structures, and the relationship between its leaders and their followers, not to mention the light it sheds on gender relations. Moreover, such an exploration is not only important for the history of hasidism; it also reveals the expectations of children of leaders of mass movements in traditional societies and the challenges these children encountered in attempting to meet or evade these expectations. This enquiry also shows how the followers of such leaders shaped images of those leaders' children and how the relationship between the leaders and their followers influenced, and were influenced by, those images.

The Child and Hasidic Hagiography

A hagiographical legend about the hasidic leader Kalonymos Kalman Epstein of Kraków (1754–1823), whose teachings were published in the book *Ma'or vashemesh*, includes the following story:

> I heard that when the author of *Ma'or vashemesh* was a child he studied in a yeshiva with old Torah scholars because he was very sharp and pious. One day, after he had finished studying, he went outside and saw a young goat standing there and rode on it. His old disciples told him: Rabbi, you are embarrassing us as your students. He responded that every human being must have childhood which is called *vildigkeyt* [wildness]. This is an act of youthfulness, and I thought to myself that it is good to do acts of youthfulness, now [rather] than when I am 20 years old.[11]

This story presents Epstein in two seemingly opposing ways. On the one hand, he is described as leading an intellectual circle of older people, which presents him as a wunderkind or *puer senex* (a child with the wisdom of an old person);[12] on the other hand, he is seen engaging in childish acts, unfitting for a senior spiritual leader. These acts are later imbued with an explanation that frames them not as childish but, rather, as having the intentions of a grown-up. The legend presents a positive perspective on childhood as a necessary part of human life and seems to exhibit the rationalist view that a child is an adult in the making.

The legend about Epstein is representative of hasidic literature, as most of the sources on the early childhood of *tsadikim*—prior to barmitzvah at the age of 13—are hagiographical traditions recorded by hasidim. These appeared primarily in the form of collections of stories, beginning in 1814 with *Shivḥei habesht*, followed by three major waves: in the 1860s, prior to the First World War, and between the wars. They presented childhood as but one aspect of the unique status of *tsadikim*. In addition, in the second half of the twentieth century new collections of legends dedicated to the childhood of *tsadikim* appeared, sometimes as part of a broader literature of childhood legends about those regarded as Jewish saints.[13] Those later collections, which include solely tales of the childhood of *tsadikim*, are tailored for all Orthodox (not just hasidic) children, and seek to inculcate those values which will ensure they become pious Jews.[14] In the eyes of educators, it was important to present the *tsadik* as a role model, and thus the portrayal of their childhood plays a pivotal role in such accounts. Notably, all hagiographical collections deal with male children who later became *tsadikim*. Voices of female children can be heard only in autobiographical accounts, which will be discussed in the following section. In addition to hagiographical legends recorded by their followers, there are a few personal accounts by the *tsadikim* themselves: most are self-praising, and in this respect akin to the hagiographical traditions.

Legends about the childhood of *tsadikim* are characterized by a diversity of motifs, many of which can be found in the earlier hagiographical traditions of Jewish as well as non-Jewish religious figures.[15] In the legend about Epstein, the wunderkind motif was highlighted, as was the motif of childish acts that are later explained as representing hidden wisdom. Both motifs can be found in legends about non-Jewish saints[16] and in other hasidic hagiography. An example of the wunderkind comes from a legend according to which Uri of Strelisk (1757–1826) explained that he wept in his childhood because he lamented for the Shekhinah (the divine presence, held in some rabbinic sources to be in exile with the Jewish people), a weeping and an explanation that befitted an older person.[17] An example of the projection of a future characteristic into the childhood of a *tsadik* comes from a story about Shraga Feivel Danziger (1792–1848), who as a child imitated the prayer movements of Levi Yitzhak of Berdichev when Levi Yitzhak visited his family home. Confronted by the embarrassment of the child's parents, Levi Yitzhak promised them that these childish acts indicated that Shraga Feivel would grow up to be a great spiritual figure.[18]

The wunderkind motif is common in several Jewish cultural contexts,[19] including east European Jewry of the early modern period.[20] However, there is another image which sheds important light on hasidic childhood: the *yenuka*, the wunderkind of the Zohar.[21] The stories about the *yenuka* in the Zohar are not hagiographical but rather mystical narratives that underscore the wunderkind's status. Yet as I shall show, this literary trope was attributed to more than one hasidic leader.

An example of the retrospective explanation of childish acts surfaces in a tradition about the Besht himself. According to the *Shivḥei habesht*:

After the death of his father the child grew up. Because the people of the town revered the memory of his father, they favoured the child and sent him to study with a melamed. And he succeeded in his studies. But it was his way to study for a few days and then to run away from school. They would search for him and find him sitting alone in the forest. They would attribute this to his being an orphan. There was no one to look after him and he was a footloose child. Though they brought him again and again to the melamed, he would run away to the forest to be in solitude. In the course of time they gave up in despair and no longer returned him to the melamed. He did not grow up in the accustomed way.[22]

This legend does not describe the Besht as a wunderkind. Although his behaviour seems reckless, the people around him and later readers of this legend realized that he did not really need a teacher. Having no need for a teacher is certainly appropriate for a person who would evolve into a spiritual master without outside assistance. In addition, the story of a child who did not conform to social conventions is appropriate for the future founder of a new social movement. The story might also give a place to the romanticist view that childhood is a unique phase of life that does not necessarily anticipate adulthood.

The stories about the special qualities of *tsadikim* did not always originate with the hasidim. At times *tsadikim* themselves spoke about their childhood. Thus, some childhood memories of the prominent hasidic leader Simha Bunem of Przysucha (1765–1827) are reported to have been written down by his scribe. In these accounts it is possible to find testimonies of intellectual brilliance in his early childhood.[23] According to Sandz hasidim, their founding father, Hayim Halberstam (1793–1876), recalled that from his early childhood he had an extraordinary memory and intellectual capabilities.[24] The mystical autobiography by the Galician *tsadik* Itzhak Yehudah Yehiel Sofrin (1806–74), the rebbe of Komarno, also extols his own virtues. He praises himself not only as a child but also as a soul before birth. Here is an example of what he wrote about his early childhood:

Between the ages of two and five years I attained wondrous visions and divine inspiration. I spoke prophetic words when a person would ask about divine matters, and literally gazed from one end of the world to the other. My teacher and uncle, the awesome holy person, our teacher, Rabbi Zevi of Zhidachov, gave me two Rhenish coins every week so that I would tell him what I had seen and respond to everything that he would ask of me. I clearly and precisely answered all the questions that he asked me and donated the money to charity.[25]

Sometimes, the description of childhood in these ego-documents is laconic. This is the case in the autobiography of Rabbi Yehoshua Heschel Rabinowicz (1860–1930), the rebbe of Monastyryshche. In general, it seems that Rabinowicz tried to portray himself favourably. Writing at the age of 70, Rabinowicz noted that he did not remember his early childhood, but added that he heard that his grandfather had forecast a glorious future for him. He also praised his own barmitzvah sermon, which delighted the audience and anticipated his future leadership.[26] Thus, with regard to his childhood, Rabinowicz's autobiography is in fact hagiography based on what others said about him.

The fact that most of the sources about early childhood contain hagiographical motifs such as that of the wunderkind does not imply that all of them were about the exceptional intellectual prowess or the high spiritual level of the child. In the rather exceptional case of Nahman of Bratslav (1772–1810), his childhood is characterized by depression because of his feeling of not being heard by God:

He would often speak to God in heartfelt supplications and pleas . . . but nevertheless he felt he wasn't being noticed or heard at all. On the contrary, it seemed to him that he was being pushed away from the service of God in all kinds of ways, as though he were utterly unwanted. Days and years passed by, and still he was far from Him; he had not attained any sense of nearness at all . . . Despite all this, he would fortify himself and refuse to leave his place. At times he would become depressed, when he saw that despite all his begging and pleading to draw near to God's service, no attention was being paid to him at all. At such times he would cease his private prayers for a number of days. Then he would catch himself and be overcome with shame for having called the goodness of God into question . . . and he would begin again to plead before the Lord as before. All this happened to him any number of times.[27]

Although at first glance this text does not seem to be hagiographical, it does conform with Rabbi Nahman's unique image among hasidic leaders as one whose inner life was characterized by constant attempts to overcome the feeling of an existential distance from God. Attributing this characteristic to their master's early childhood can be thus understood as yet another projection of the features of the mature *tsadik* into his earlier years. However, in contrast to common descriptions of outstanding intellectual capabilities attributed to other *tsadikim* in their childhood, this description of alienation seems less conventional: perhaps it alludes to the young *tsadik*'s real emotional difficulties. In any event, this feature of Rabbi Nahman's life became an ethos for all Bratslaver hasidim.

There is one hagiographical motif that is rare in hasidic hagiography: the motif of the ignoramus who became a late bloomer. Such was, for example, the ancient rabbinic legend of Rabbi Akiva.[28] This motif is rare in hasidic hagiography, because the vast majority of its heroes were born to hasidic leaders and were expected to succeed them. The descendant of a *tsadik* cannot be an ignoramus. The motif of the late bloomer could have been applied to the Besht, but, although the Besht is described in *Shivḥei habesht* as having received his wisdom at the relatively old age of 14, the legend about his earlier childhood quoted above does imply that he already possessed spiritual capabilities.

The hagiography of the childhood of *tsadikim* needs to be understood against the broader cultural backdrop of the discourse on children and sainthood in various cultures and religions, which rests upon more general perceptions of children and childhood.[29] Carl Jung's observations on the 'child' archetype and its foundational presence in numerous myths are relevant here.[30] In certain religious traditions, particularly Judaism and Christianity, children can be attributed messianic roles, in particular when a child belongs to a dynasty of which there are messianic expectations. The verse from Isaiah 9: 6, 'For unto us a child is born, unto us a son is given: and the government shall be upon his shoulders', was interpreted by both Jews and Christians as heralding the birth of the future redeemer. There are also traditions from later periods about children who deliver messianic prophecies. In the context of east European hasidism, most notable is the description of the messiah as a child in the *Megilat setarim* of Bratslaver hasidism.[31] In contrast to most hasidic sources about the early childhood of *tsadikim*, this text describes a vision or prophecy with a messianic content. Zvi Mark has demonstrated that the anonymous child-messiah in this vision corresponds with the image of a particular hasidic leader, Nahman of Bratslav. Moreover, scholars argue that Nahman hoped that his only son, Shlomo Efraim, would become the messiah when he grew up, but Shlomo Efraim died at the age of 4.

The legends about hasidic leaders, whether by their followers or their own first-person accounts, are usually full of hagiographical conventions. While these accounts could contain aspects of the real lives of the leaders, it would be safer to assume that they represent the image of childhood as perceived by hasidim in later periods or as the *tsadikim* would have preferred to be remembered. The descendants of *tsadikim* who did not become *tsadikim* themselves have fewer hagiographical conventions and more revealing autobiographical accounts, as I shall show in the following section.

Childhood Memories

There are a few autobiographical accounts by descendants of *tsadikim*, male and female, who did not become leaders or spouses of such leaders. As they did not hold any particular position, they were perhaps at greater liberty to speak. From their descriptions, much can be learned about the economic situation in which they were reared, their relationships with their family members, and their education. The writers of these accounts were more or less the same age: they were born around the beginning of the twentieth century and their memories cover the period from then until the First World War. This is not a coincidence: the majority of these accounts were written after the Holocaust, often after family members had been murdered or emigrated from Europe, to preserve something of the destroyed world of east European Jewry. There are also autobiographical accounts of the followers of *tsadikim* who visited their courts, which provide an external view of hasidic childhood.

Malka Shapiro (1894–1971) was the daughter of the hasidic leader Yerahmiel Moshe Hapstein, the rebbe of Kozienice. After her arranged marriage to her first cousin, the hasidic leader Avraham Elimelekh Shapiro of Grodzisk, she became a religious Zionist and a modern Hebrew author. Together with her husband and children she emigrated to Palestine in 1925 and settled first in Haifa, then in Kefar Hasidim (a settlement near Haifa co-founded by one of her brothers), and finally in Jerusalem. As the wife of a hasidic leader, she maintained her hasidic lifestyle as a pious Orthodox Jewish woman. She wrote short stories about the hasidic court in Kozienice, where she grew up. These stories are her childhood memories told with a great degree of nostalgia. They can also be understood as a post-Holocaust attempt to shape the image of hasidism in general and the Kozienice court in particular.[32]

Golda Finkler (1903–91) was a descendant of two hasidic dynasties. Her father was the rebbe of the Modzitzer hasidim, and her mother was the daughter of Avraham Eiger, the rebbe of Lublin. Since her parents divorced when she was 3 years old, she lived with her mother at the residence of her grandfather in Lublin. A memoir of her life there between 1903 and 1914 (and to a large extent also after that year), was published by her daughter in 2012.[33] Although less nostalgic than Shapiro, Finkler describes her life at the court favourably, with particular admiration for her grandfather, the rebbe of Lublin.

Malka Shapiro and Golda Finkler remained faithful to Orthodox Judaism and to hasidism. Hence, in their accounts, they express sympathy with how children were reared in hasidic courts. However, in the memoirs of descendants of *tsadikim* who left hasidism, the nostalgia for life in the court is interrupted by the discovery of the world around it in the years of adolescence. Accordingly, it is often possible to hear a critical voice in their accounts. Three examples are Ita Kalish, Shmuel Abba Horodezky, and Yohanan Twersky. Ita Kalish (1897–1994), a few years younger than Malka Shapiro, was the daughter of the Polish *tsadik* Menachem Mendel Kalish (d. 1919), the rebbe of Otwock, who was the great-grandson of a leading *tsadik*, Itzhak Kalish (1779–1848), the founder of Warka hasidism. In her autobiography, Ita Kalish wrote about her childhood and adolescence in her father's court at Otwock, where she lived between 1906 and 1914.[34] Like Malka Shapiro, Ita Kalish described her early childhood favourably. Although her mother died when she was about 9 years old, she described the period when her family lived in Otwock as full of love,[35] in which her father and his mother played notably positive roles.[36] However, in contrast to Shapiro, her descriptions are gradually coloured by a sense of disillusionment with traditional Jewish life. Kalish did not remain in the hasidic world, to the disappointment of her father. Her private tutor exposed her to non-religious Jewish and Polish culture, and she grew increasingly critical of the lifestyle of traditional and Orthodox Judaism: eventually, she became secular. After her arranged marriage at the age of 15 to a descendant of a wealthy family of Gerer hasidim, she ran away from home, but was later persuaded by her father to return to her husband. However, she did not abandon her modern and non-Orthodox tendencies. In 1919 she left her husband's family home, leaving behind her husband and 2-year-old daughter.[37] Eventually she moved to Berlin, divorced her husband, reunited with her daughter, and they emigrated together to Palestine in 1933.

Shmuel Abba Horodezky (1871–1957), a historian of Judaism, was a grandson of Rabbi Gedaliah Twersky, the rebbe of Malin, an offshoot of the Chernobyl dynasty. Shortly before his death in Tel Aviv, where he had settled in 1938, Horodezky published his memoirs, in which an entire chapter is dedicated to his childhood in Malin and Chernobyl.[38] Until the age of 10 Horodezky grew up in the court of Malin and then moved to Chernobyl. His grandfather the rebbe treated him harshly, once punishing him by not allowing him to go home after *ḥeder* and forcing him to stay there all night. However, in general, the hasidim paid Horodezky respect as the rebbe's grandson.[39] At the age of 10 he moved to Chernobyl, where he lived not in the local court but rather with his other grandfather, Rabbi Baruch Horodezky, who had refused to be appointed rebbe. Horodezky wrote that although he did not live in the Chernobyl court, his grandfather's house was like a house of a *tsadik*, with all its visitors and rituals.[40] He also wrote that until the age of 15 he was immersed in hasidism, having simple faith in the 'holy fathers' of hasidism: 'My inner world was complete, full of naivety and faith.'[41] However, an Orthodox Jew who was familiar with the Haskalah settled in Chernobyl, met Horodezky in the *beit midrash*, and introduced him to books written by maskilim.[42] His writings on hasidism from later periods are characterized by admiration for the founding fathers together with harsh critiques of the later generations.[43]

Yohanan Twersky (1900–67) was the son of Menahem Nahum Twersky of Warsaw, but he grew up in his grandfather's court in Turiysk, another branch of the Chernobyl dynasty. His book, *Heḥatser hapenimit*, is a description of three hasidic courts of the Chernobyl group and is explicitly based not only on his own memories but also on memories of other family members, primarily those of his mother, Haya, the daughter of Mordechai Twersky, the rebbe of Shpikov.[44] Twersky's account emphasizes the role of the daughters of *tsadikim*, the secular education they received alongside their traditional education, and the somewhat subversive influence they had on their children due to that secular education. Twerksy, who was reared under the significant influence of his mother, received a secular education and was implicitly critical of the masculine hasidic establishment.

The writings of these descendants of *tsadikim* show that they grew up like children of the east European elite, enjoying material wealth. In addition to grand residences, lavish food, and fine clothing, they had private nannies and went on daily trips to the areas surrounding the courts, escorted by the rebbe's servants.[45] In addition, they took part in the hasidic custom of travelling to famous spas.[46]

Their material wealth was also manifested in the importance afforded by *tsadikim* to the private education they provided for their children, especially girls, inside the court. Haya Twersky related that her brother Yitzhak Nahum studied in the Shpikover *beit midrash* while she and her sisters were educated by two Jewish tutors. One taught them reading and the other writing, especially the writing of letters of various genres and styles. This teacher also taught several other Jewish children in Shpikov. However, while children outside the court used to go to the tutor's residence to study, for the daughters of the *tsadik*, he used to come to the court and teach them there. A few other girls joined the lessons given to the Twersky sisters. They were all daughters of important Jewish functionaries in Shpikov, such as the local rabbi and the rebbe's *gabbai* (personal secretary). It is likely that, if the Twersky sisters had not been provided with a private tutor, the other girls would not have had this opportunity to learn.[47] To give another example, Golda Finkler studied for some time at private schools for girls in Lublin, but later her mother hired private tutors, who taught her French and Polish, in addition to Yiddish and Russian, which she already knew.[48]

In contrast to the boys, the girls' education at the hasidic court was less restricted—they were more exposed to secular education, including foreign languages and literature. Haya Twersky was even secretly exposed to Enlightenment literature and read Russian literature and German literature translated into Russian.[49] Moreover, sometimes secular education was an overt requirement. Ita Kalish wrote that, before her wedding, she was informally tested by her future in-laws to confirm that she had read the contemporary Polish author Gabriela Zapolska, known for her satirical comedies: such reading was held to be almost mandatory for young girls in bourgeois Jewish families.[50] Golda Finkler also noted that in her early years she used to read stories in Yiddish about rebbes but later began reading Russian and Polish literature.[51] This was not unique to daughters of hasidic leaders. In nineteenth-century eastern Europe, many daughters of non-hasidic rabbis and daughters of hasidim who were not *tsadikim* also enjoyed a secular education, unlike their brothers.[52] Yet it seems that daughters of hasidic leaders were still educated in their homes at the courts. Hence, under these circumstances, their reading of secular non-Jewish literature seems notable.

Another expression of the privileged position of such children can be seen in the relationships they were permitted to have, which reflected a high degree of social stratification. The girls of the Kalish family were allowed to spend time only with the elite families that lived near the court in Otwock, whereas the boys' social ties were restricted to their peers in the *beit midrash*.[53]

Notwithstanding the preference for private education with a tutor, there were courts in which this was not customary, perhaps due to financial constraints. Unlike the well-to-do courts of Kozienice and Otwock, the court in Malin suffered from a relatively low income, despite its familial connection to the rich courts of the Chernobyl dynasty. Horodezky relates that during his childhood in Malin he was sent to a *ḥeder* together with nine other boys and that his studies took place at the teacher's house rather than his grandfather's court. In contrast to the excellent tutor hired for Haya Twersky and her sisters, Horodezky's tutor was neither well known nor particularly successful. Hence, he took on a second job—preparing snuff—which he did during *ḥeder* hours, assisted by his students.[54] Another example is that of the Hebrew author Yehudah Leib Levine (1844–1925), grandson of the hasidic leader Moshe of Kobrin. The rebbe wanted his grandson to live in the court, so he could personally take care of his education, but the rebbe's wife, his grandmother, objected due to financial constraints.[55]

There were also accounts by hasidim who visited the courts and reported on what they saw or heard. One such visitor was Yitzhak Even (1861–1925), whose book includes memoirs from the court of Avraham Yaakov Friedman (1819–83) in Sadegura, including a few pages on how children from the Ruzhin-Sadegura dynasty were reared.[56] Even wrote that, in general, those children in the Sadegura court who were descended from rebbes were reared and educated like the children of monarchs (as Even imagined such an education). When they (Even most likely referred to boys) reached the age of 3, they were taken out of their nanny's hands and transferred to the charge of two servants and a *melamed*, who was responsible for teaching them to read Hebrew, the Bible with Rashi's commentary, and rabbinic literature. The *melamed* also educated and groomed them for the role of a *tsadik*: he shared legends about hasidic masters and showed them how to behave among hasidim and other visitors. When the child was a bit older, another teacher joined the team, and taught writing Hebrew, Yiddish, and some German. Child-rearing by servants was customary among families of the eighteenth-century Polish nobility and nineteenth-century bourgeoisie.

Even also described the dress code of the children in the Sadegura court. Until the age of 13 boys were dressed like princes or clad in the uniform of military generals with swords on their belts. However, at the age of 13 their clothing changed and became the silk attire of grown-up hasidic leaders.

The fact that children of hasidic leaders were reared by servants might have led to exploitation. Yitzhak Even recalled that sometimes, when hasidim were waiting to see the *tsadik*, a servant would bring the child to ask for money in return for the honour of being touched by the child's fingertips, as grown-up leaders of the Sadegura court did.[57] Even implies that the servant was the one who enjoyed the money, exploiting the tremendous respect the hasidim had for their leaders' family.

Living in economic prosperity, enjoying a private education, and maintaining high-class social ties were not characteristics only of the hasidic leadership. They were a feature of the lifestyle of the relatively restricted group of Jewish bourgeois families in the region. This raises the question of what was distinctively hasidic about the affluent childhoods of the descendants of *tsadikim*. One such feature was who such children encountered. They would frequently come into contact with active hasidic leaders who were their parents' friends and colleagues, in addition to other *tsadikim* who were part of the family. Hasidic leaders always maintained close social ties among themselves, either because they were disciples of the same *tsadik* or because of the inter-dynastic marriages that were customary for them. Of course, these social practices were not unique to hasidism; however, in the context of hasidism, they were not based solely on social and economic status; they also had a significant spiritual aspect of allowing for intimate connections between holy men, who pursued the spiritual way of the Besht, thereby inspiring the children and serving as role models. The aforementioned Nahman of Bratslav, who was the great-grandson of the Besht, told his followers that when he was a child, many *tsadikim* visited his parents' house in Mezhibozh during their pilgrimage to the Besht's gravesite.[58] Such immediate access to holy men was not often available to children who were not descendants of *tsadikim*.

A second specific characteristic of the experience of children at hasidic courts was the constant presence of hasidic stories and storytelling. Recounting the acts of their leaders was a well-established hasidic custom,[59] a practice that resulted in numerous volumes of hagiography (some of which have already been referred to). While this practice was customary in families of *tsadikim* and hasidim, among *tsadikim* it had a unique significance: for *tsadikim*, many of these stories were not just stories about remote legendary rebbes but rather memories of their own ancestors. When Nahman of Bratslav mentioned the *tsadikim* who visited his parents' house, he also claimed that they told him many stories about other *tsadikim*. Some of the stories might have referred to his great-grandfather. Rabbi Nahman postulated that these stories contributed to his religious awakening.[60] In her memoir, Ita Kalish wrote that during her childhood in the court of Otwock, her grandmother used to tell her offspring—not only Ita and her brothers but also her father, the rebbe—stories about the ancestors of the dynasty.[61] Thus, in families of hasidic leaders, at least some of the stories relayed about the *tsadikim* were actually family memories transmitted orally from generation to generation.

A third feature, common for at least some children of *tsadikim*, is the significant role that preparation for their future office as *tsadik* played in their upbringing. Tutoring a child to perform the role of *tsadik* was customary among many families of *tsadikim*. For example, there is quite a long hasidic teaching attributed to Mordechai Twersky (1770–1837) with the following note: 'a teaching our master delivered in his childhood when he engaged with the hasidim'.[62] While there is no mention of Twersky's age at the time, for the hasid or hasidim who wrote it down he was still a child.

A fourth characteristic is the influence of hasidic marriages. Hasidic leaders tended to establish relationships with each other through marriages arranged between their descendants. These inter-dynastic marriages acquired symbolical status since they were seen as connecting sacred families. The marriage of descendants of *tsadikim* did not necessarily change the status of the couple from children to adults. After marriage, which sometimes took place as early as the age of 13, the couple often continued their previous lifestyle, with the sole difference that they moved in to live together in the house of one of their in-laws, usually the bride's parents. However, these weddings sometimes led to estrangement, on occasion more intensely than in families of non-*tsadikim*. While the son of a *tsadik* knew that he would be expected to continue his father's dynasty, he often had to adapt to the customs of a different dynasty—and under the watchful eye of his in-laws and the hasidim of that dynasty. For example, Yissachar Dov Rokeah (1854–1926), who was to become the third Belzer rebbe, encountered such problems when, at the age of 14, he married the daughter of Rabbi Aharon Twersky of Chernobyl. The Chernobyl hasidim harassed him in an unsuccessful attempt to make him abandon some of his Belz customs.[63] Sometimes a young groom felt uncomfortable with his newly married status in his in-laws' home. Hayim Halberstam of Sandz confessed that even at the age of 17, some four years after he had married Rochel Feyga, daughter of Rabbi Boruch Frenkl Thumim, the rabbi of Lipník nad Bečvou in Moravia, while he lived with his in-laws he still behaved like a child, asking his father-in-law to let him return to his parents' house for a while.[64]

While some descendants of *tsadikim* experienced delayed maturity and seem to have continued to feel that they were still children even after they had married, the 'ascension to the throne' appears to have had a sudden sobering effect, requiring the immediate adoption of an adult role. This was the case with Mordechai Twersky of Shpikov, who grew up in his father's court free of all responsibility. However, his life changed dramatically and abruptly when his father died suddenly in 1887 and he had to succeed him as *tsadik*. Although he was already 25 years old, one of his hasidim quoted Mordechai as saying that until that moment he was still in his adolescence.[65]

The Death of the *Tsadik* Father: Adoption and Child Leaders

Up to this point I have concentrated on the more or less uninterrupted childhood of the children of *tsadikim*. However, their lives were sometimes disrupted when their father died while they were still young. In such cases, there existed several strategies for coping with the ensuing crisis that affected not only the direct descendants of the *tsadik* but also his entire court and circle of followers.

One strategy was for other *tsadikim* to adopt the children, even when their mother was still alive. The practice of relatives adopting orphans was not limited to the descendants of *tsadikim*;[66] however, adoption among the hasidic elite had unique features, as sometimes the adopting *tsadikim* were not relatives of the orphans. This was the result of solidarity among the hasidic elite and the orphans' high prestige, which made adopting them an honour. Notably, the sources only mention the adoption of male orphans who later became *tsadikim*; there is no information about female orphans. Thus, there are stories about the children of Rabbi Abraham 'the Angel', son of the Magid of Mezerich, who died in 1776 at the age of 36, while his wife was still alive. According to hasidic hagiography, *tsadikim* competed for the right to adopt the children. Eventually, Shlomo of Karlin triumphed and adopted the elder, Yisrael Hayim, while Nahum of Chernobyl adopted the younger, Shalom Shekhna.[67]

Adoption benefited both sides: the adopting *tsadik* acquired the prestige of the deceased *tsadik*, while the orphan received an elite education and hasidic training for leadership that included not only the study of rabbinic literature, kabbalah, and the teachings of previous *tsadikim*, but also training in practices unique to the *tsadikim*, such as performing miracle-working rituals. A hasidic tradition recounts that Nahum of Chernobyl sent some of his hasidim who had asked for his help to Shalom Shekhna.[68] This constitutes a further confirmation of the view, mentioned above, that the descendants of *tsadikim* began practising as rebbes in their childhood.

There were, however, instances when a widow opposed the adoption of her children. One example involved the children of Shalom Shekhna. When he died in 1812, his widow continued to raise their children. One of them became the famous *tsadik* Israel Friedman of Ruzhin. According to hasidic hagiography the mother took her children to prominent *tsadikim*, who were astonished by their intellectual achievements. At the same time, the mother's decision had far-reaching implications —as mentioned earlier, Rabbi Israel lacked a fundamental rabbinic education. Assuming that he did not suffer from a learning disability,[69] had he been adopted and educated by a hasidic leader he possibly would not have had such striking gaps in his education.

Alongside the adoption of descendants of deceased *tsadikim*, there were cases of young orphans who received the formal office of the *tsadik* while still a child, usually upon becoming a barmitzvah. A child leader of this sort was known as a *yenuka*, an allusion to the wunderkind of the Zohar. While the *yenuka* phenomenon was not widespread, it gained considerable public attention when it occurred, among hasidim and non-hasidim alike. The sources reveal conflicting opinions about child leaders.

While the followers of a *yenuka* tended to describe him as a full *tsadik*, followers of opposing groups and opponents of hasidism perceived the *yenuka* as undermining the office of the *tsadik* and as disrespectful towards his hasidim.

The figure of the *yenuka* brings together two topics mentioned above: the hagiographical motifs used to describe early childhood and the more realistic descriptions of the growing involvement of future *tsadikim* in leadership during adolescence. The *yenuka* is also an example of the tension between the rationalist view that children are small adults and the romanticist view that they are unique individuals superior to older human beings. This can be illustrated with four cases: Yisrael Perlov (1868–1921), who became the *tsadik* of Stolin in 1873 when he was not yet 5 years old; Shlomo Bentsion Twersky (1870–1939), who ascended to leadership in Chernobyl in 1881 at the age of 11; Menahem Nahum Twersky (1869–1915), who was accepted as a *tsadik* in Talne in 1882, at the age of 13; and Yaakov Yitzhak Perlov (1901–18), who was nominated *tsadik* in Koydanow in 1915, when he was 14 years old.[70]

Although elevating a child to the position of *tsadik* can be understood within the rationale of the dynastic process, it raised questions regarding his ability to lead a court and a congregation of followers. These concerns are clearly set out in a letter sent to the Karliner hasidim soon after the crowning of the *yenuka* of Stolin, Yisrael Perlov, which attempted to justify the decision. The author of this letter, one of several sent to the Karliner hasidim in different localities, was Baruch Mendelbaum, a rabbi from Turów, one of the central figures of the Karlin court. In his letter, Mendelbaum urged the hasidim to go to the court on the Jewish festivals. He praised Perlov's spiritual stature, arguing that believing in the *tsadik* was worth more than listening to his discourses, if a child of that age was even capable of giving such discourses. In his view, merely touching the *yenuka*'s hand was like touching an amulet.[71]

Mandelbaum's letter, which adduced numerous arguments setting out Perlov's qualifications to hold the office along with calls to support him, clearly suggests that he was not universally accepted by his hasidim. Possibly some of them avoided the court because they feared that a child would not be able to fulfil the various roles of a hasidic leader—mystic, miracle-worker, spiritual guide, personal counsellor, and public face of the community. The emphasis on the importance of believing in the *yenuka* and the significance of touching him was intended to encourage travel to the court. It reveals some of the fears of the court's personnel that so young a child could not respond properly to serious petitions made by his hasidim. Yehudah Leib Levine, the maskilic author who included this letter in a satirical account of the affair, was explicit about this, writing sarcastically:

The rabbi of Turów [Mandelbaum] knows that . . . some of the Stolin hasidim have little faith and that in spite of all the energy he invests in promising them [the benefits of travelling to the court], it is possible that when they travel and arrive [in Stolin] and see [the *yenuka*], their hearts will hesitate because they will not hear and not see anything. Neither Torah, nor piety, but only a small child walking around in a fox-fur hat, wearing a sash over a long silk coat. And if they ask him anything, he might not respond properly because he is a 5-year-old child and might even do something obscene, which is understandable given that he is a child. Then, all of the rabbi's efforts [to bring the hasidim to the court] will be in vain. That is why he repeats two or three times that the most important thing is faith [in the *tsadik*].[72]

Levine clearly believed that expecting a child to behave like an adult was absurd. Hence, describing this child as having the capabilities and powers of a fully fledged *tsadik* was patently dishonest.

How did a child function as a hasidic leader? Usually, he was aided by older members of the court, who had served as his father's or grandfather's hasidim. These key figures functioned as regents. They reared the child and made sure that he got the appropriate education and training for future success as a hasidic leader, while taking upon themselves some of the roles of leadership. In the case of the *yenuka* of Stolin, Mendelbaum wrote that the *yenuka*'s mother had appointed a few older figures in the court as regents. He also referred to the biblical precedent of Joash, king of Judah, who was crowned at the age of 7 by Jehoiada the priest, who functioned as a regent (2 Kgs 11–12; 2 Chr. 22–4). It seems that Mandelbaum did not choose this example randomly. By associating the Karlin dynasty with that of King David, he not only legitimized the crowning of the child but also endowed it with the messianic promise inherent in the dynasty of the kings of Judah.

An account of the daily life of the *yenuka* of Stolin under the supervision of his advisers can be found in the memoirs of one of his hasidim:

My grandfather, Rabbi Pinhas Yosef Shapira, may his soul rest in Heaven, used to travel to Stolin on the festival of Shavuot or on Hanukah or on other days because of some frequently recurring events—when he had to pay his rent to the landlord but there was no money or when one of his sons was threatened with being drafted into the army and so on . . . When had to return home from Stolin, he would approach Rabbi Yisrael Binyamin [Glauberman, the *gabbai* of the *yenuka*], to deliver a *kvitl* [petition] and a *pidyon* [monetary gift] and they went through the long corridors to find the rebbe and obtain from him a farewell blessing. When they found him immersed in play, the *gabbai* would address him politely: 'Rebbe, Pinhas would like to return to Gritsev, and he has come to get a farewell blessing.' 'Let him travel, no one is stopping him, farewell Pinhas!' Rabbi Pinhas would then approach the *yenuka* saying: 'Rebbe, my son David Aharon has been summoned for induction into the army and asks for your blessing so that he will be released.' 'Let it be, as you say, Pinhas, let him be released.' 'Rebbe, I wish my income would improve.' 'Fine, fine, let it improve! Farewell Pinhas!' And while they were still standing there, the *yenuka* would return to his play. The *gabbai* would calmly repeat the *yenuka*'s phrases: 'Farewell Rabbi Pinhas. God will help you and with the assistance of the *tsadikim* your son will be released from the army and your livelihood will improve, God willing.' The *yenuka* remained occupied in play, and the hasid [Pinhas] would shake hands with Rabbi Yisrael Binyamin and return to his home and family, encouraged and full of hope.[73]

This story was not told by a hostile maskil but by the grandson of a hasid of the *yenuka* of Stolin, who nostalgically recalled the *yenuka*'s early years. Even assuming that many people resented child leadership, it is clear that there were also at least some who accepted it. Karliner hasidim later argued that the rebbe's manner of undertaking children's play actually hid his deep spirituality and that his childish acts revealed to his hasidim his elevated spiritual stature. Moreover, they remembered that when he was seated at the table, he used to hide under it, claiming that he could not sit at it as long as Almighty God was in front of him.[74]

A child leader, even one that was older than the *yenuka* of Stolin, prompted discomfort. A good example is the *yenuka* of Chernobyl, Shlomo Bentsion Twersky, whose opponents were followers of his uncle, Baruch Asher Twersky, who also lived in Chernobyl and wanted to be recognized as *tsadik*. They wrote a letter to the oldest *tsadik* of the family, Avraham Twersky, asking him to support their master:

Empty and simple people have gathered, workmen and craftsmen, coarse and crude, who do not know how to distinguish right from left. And they have congregated to desecrate the Holy Name in public and have built themselves a shrine, placing this little child [Shlomo Bentsion] on the throne of the rabbinate. And he is an immature and suckling child who has never read and studied [the Torah] and his precious soul that descended from the source of the holy is assimilated into those ignorant people who disturb his spirit and body, giving him *pidyonot* leading him to the gravesite of his father where they call him 'rebbe'. Here they ask his advice and he does not understand what they are saying, as if 'they said to wood: you are my father' [Jer. 2: 27]. And in addition they do not give the child time to study the Torah of the Lord, which should show him the way of the Lord ... They [also] disturb him and do not leave him in peace until he will have grown up and his beard become full and in so doing they destroy a precious soul, God forbid.[75]

For the writers of the letter, the supporters of the *yenuka* were too uneducated to crown a hasidic leader, and the child, who did not have enough rabbinic educational background, was not yet capable of leading a congregation, as his inability to respond to his followers' queries made abundantly clear. However, the writers distinguish between the *yenuka* and his supporters. While the simplicity of the followers is described negatively, the child is characterized as a precious soul which has descended from its elevated spiritual origin into the midst of these worldly hasidim, wasting his time attempting to fulfil their requests and forfeiting the opportunity to complete his education. Their argument thus claims to focus on the child's true interests. In a subsequent passage, the writers also expressed concern that the child would not succeed in preserving his followers' faith, as was expected of a hasidic leader. Yet beyond these concerns, they seem more concerned about the failure to recognize their own master, whom they saw as the natural candidate for leadership.[76]

Considering the large number of objections which the practice aroused, what was it that spurred hasidim to insist upon crowning a child? Usually, they feared that the position of *tsadik* would be given to a family member from a different court, that the hasidim would become his followers, and the court would cease to exist. In the case of the *yenuka* of Stolin, his hasidim feared that his mother would succeed in crowning her eldest son from her first marriage, whose father was from the Kozienice dynasty.

If that happened, the Karlin dynasty might perish. Similar concerns are discernible in the cases of other *yenuka*s.

The fear that another family member would be crowned explains the central role played by the mothers of *yenuka*s.[77] Crowning the *yenuka* not only preserved the mother's prestige, it also secured an income for her son, herself, and usually other family members as well. From this vantage point, the *yenuka* was responsible from a young age for his family's livelihood. However, the mother's central role also generated discontent on the part of the hasidim. In a letter sent from Talne to the newspaper *Hamelits* in the summer of 1883, the writer claimed bitterly that since the crowning of the *yenuka* of Talne, a woman, his mother, had become the court's ruler.[78]

The reasons for supporting the *yenuka* were not only practical, economic, and political, going beyond the hope that the young *tsadik* could ensure the survival of the court after his father's death; they also had a spiritual basis. Decades after Horodezky left Orthodox Judaism, he wrote in his autobiography a nostalgic description of the crowning of Shlomo Bentsion Twersky on the day of his barmitzvah:

> Hundreds of hasidim gathered, arriving from near and far to see the splendid spectacle. For on that very day, [Shlomo Bentsion] became a mature *tsadik*,[79] and from thenceforth would himself receive *kvitlekh*, deliver blessings, give out amulets and protective charms. He would preside at the table and conduct the singing on the sabbath.[80]

The new *tsadik* entered the room, performed Kiddush (the ceremony of blessing), sat down at the table, and began the ritual meal. These acts made a strong impression on the hasidim or at least on the young Horodezky:

> It was quiet in the hall. The hasidim, most of whom had had the honour to sit at the table of the deceased *tsadik*, saw and felt now the same vision and feeling they felt then. There was no difference between the old deceased *tsadik* and the young living *tsadik*. And all the audience that had assembled looked at him alone, no one removed his eyes from his gestures. And he sat as if he were an old and self-confident *tsadik*.[81]

Then the *yenuka* began singing the sabbath songs, surprising his audience with a new melody and delivered the *shirayim* (the symbolic distribution of the leftovers). After he left the room,

> great joy burst out and took hold of all the hasidim. Love and fraternity flared up in all of them, rich and poor, scholar and ignoramus. All of them as one began dancing and singing: 'For unto us a child is born, unto us a son is given: and the government shall be upon his shoulders' [Isa. 9: 6]. Finally, he showed up again and joined the dancing. They said that at that time everyone saw the face of the Shekhinah.[82]

The child leader thus fulfilled the expectation that he could behave like a mature man. In addition, his ascension to the throne was described using a verse with messianic overtones. From the perspective of the hasidim the *yenuka*'s coronation was a redemptive act that saved the dynasty from extinction.

Another expression of admiration for the actual acts of the *yenuka* can be seen in the case of the *yenuka* of Koydanow in Belarus. In a recently published manuscript that includes some of his sermons recorded by a disciple, Yaakov Yitzhak Perlov, who served as a *tsadik* in Koydanow between the ages of 14 and 17, from 1915 until his death in 1918, is depicted conducting regular ritual meals like an adult *tsadik*. At these meals he delivered sermons, conversed with the hasidim, and answered their questions. To the best of my knowledge, this is the only true record of a *yenuka* undertaking actual teaching in his early years rather than a hagiographical fiction.[83]

Conclusion

Research into the childhood of Jews in eastern Europe has shown a significant gap between the Orthodox image of Jewish childhood in the shtetl and its reality. Orthodox literature portrays a normative image of pious Jewish childhood that identifies childhood with learning Torah, either in the *ḥeder* or the *beit midrash*. However, autobiographies of numerous east European Jews show that children were not always bound to that pious lifestyle but rather lived like children in other societies, spending a significant part of their time outside educational institutions.[84]

The gap between image and reality is more complicated in the case of descendants of hasidic leaders. While there were families of *tsadikim* who wanted their children to grow up like children of the families of the rabbinate or the economic elite, and while this was often the case for female descendants, male descendants of hasidic leaders were much more bound by the hasidim's expectations. The hasidim for the most part considered such male children as extraordinary figures and attributed great importance to the symbolic and mythical aspects of their childhood. Male children of hasidic masters were raised in an environment that destined them for leadership from a very early age, and they were expected to mature earlier than their contemporaries. Accordingly, they are often reported to have skipped, and perhaps missed out on, some of their contemporaries' childhood experiences, such as play or meeting other children. Childhood was considered by hasidim a privilege their masters could not afford.

Consequently, the transition from childhood or adolescence to adulthood did not depend on the children themselves, and sometimes not even on their parents, but rather on the hasidim. The moment of crowning was a critical moment in the childhood of hasidic leaders. Until they were crowned, they could continue acting like some kind of eternal child, a sort of Peter Pan; from the moment they were crowned they were forced to become adults. Yet in some cases, such as when a *tsadik* died prematurely, such a transition could occur when the individual was still a child. In these cases, the formal ascension to leadership did not necessarily occur at an age that might be considered developmentally appropriate.

The veneration of children in the hasidic movement can be seen both in the retrospective praise of the childhood of grown-up *tsadikim* and in the actual veneration of *yenukas*. This reflects perceptions of childhood common to various cultures and religions. The child carries the past and embodies hope for the future. The child symbolizes simplicity, innocence, and purity; primordial unity, preceding any split and fragmentation; and it maintains a safe distance from the constraints of the normative social system. The unity attributed to the child constitutes him as connecting the earthly and the divine.[85] This final quality, often attributed to hasidic leaders, explains to some extent why it was not unheard of to ascribe the completeness of a *tsadik* to a child.

One of the general motifs that found expression in hasidic discourse about childhood, of both *tsadikim* and *yenukas*, is the association between children and old people. Children and old people are located at the two limits of human life: the child at the beginning, the old person at the end. This affinity seems to have imbued the image of the child with the wisdom of the elderly, which might be lacking in the middle-aged.[86] In fact, hasidic claims that descendants of *tsadikim* skipped their childhood may also be understood as reinforcing this perspective. Hence, the *yenuka* exemplifies both the rational and the romanticist views of childhood: on the one hand, the *yenuka* was expected to behave as a grown-up; on the other, there were unique features of his childhood that legitimated his ascension to the throne.

Many hasidim viewed the *tsadik* as a spiritual father, an older person whom they could trust, consult, and rely on in all domains of their life. In the case of the *yenukas* there was an inversion of these roles: the child leader was perceived as the older person, the father, whereas older hasidim were like children. Still, a child developing into a grown-up *tsadik* was for the hasidim a living example of the stability and continuity of the dynasty which symbolized the continuity of Jewish life, especially during times of turmoil.

Notes

1 D. Assaf, *Derekh hamalkhut: r. yisra'el miruzin umekomo betoledot haḥasidut* (Jerusalem, 1997), 88; Eng. trans.: *The Regal Way: The Life and Times of Rabbi Israel of Ruzhin*, trans. D. Louvish (Stanford, Calif., 2002), 38.

2 P. Ariès, *Centuries of Childhood: A Social History of Family Life*, trans. R. Baldick (New York, 1962), 128.

3 e.g. W. B. Clift, 'Child', in *Encyclopedia of Religion*, 2nd edn., 15 vols. (Detroit, 2005), iii. 1566–9.

4 e.g. M. Koval, *Children and Childhood in Medieval Poland (1050–1300): Constructions and Realities in a European Context* (Leiden, 2021), ch. 5.

5 G. D. Hundert, 'Jewish Children and Childhood in Early Modern East Central Europe', in D. Kraemer (ed.), *The Jewish Family: Metaphor and Memory* (New York, 1989), 81–94.

6 B. Lorence-Kot, *Child-Rearing and Reform: A Study of the Nobility in Eighteenth-Century Poland* (Westport, Conn., 1985); C. Kelly, *Children's World: Growing Up in Russia, 1890–1991* (New Haven, Conn., 2007).

7 The Hebrew term *yaldut*, referring to childhood, appears in the Hebrew Bible (Eccles. 11: 10), suggesting an early awareness of childhood as a distinct period. This term occasionally appears in hasidic hagiography. Gershon Hundert noted that 'eighteenth-century sources usually use the term *na'ar* to apply to people up to eighteen years of age', suggesting that

'the age of majority decreased slightly between the sixteenth and the eighteenth centuries' (Hundert, 'Jewish Children and Childhood in Early Modern East Central Europe', 89).

8 For a similar premise, see T. Berner, 'Constructions of Childhood in Early Modern Jewish Ego-Documents', *Journal of Family History*, 39 (2014), 101–13: 102–3.

9 Kelly, *Children's World*, 54–7.

10 Ibid. 55.

11 Y. M. Gruenwald, *Likutim ḥadashim* (Warsaw, 1899), 51a.

12 T. C. Carp, '"Puer Senex" in Roman and Medieval Thought', *Latomus*, 39 (1980), 736–9.

13 e.g. Y. Klapholz, *Gedolei yisra'el beyaldutam*, 3 vols. (Tel Aviv, 1967); Y. Arigur, *Gedolei yisra'el beshaḥarutam* (Tel Aviv, 1975).

14 e.g. A. Fader, *Mitzvah Girls: Bringing Up the Next Generation of Hasidic Jews in Brooklyn* (Princeton, NJ, 2009).

15 S. Galley, 'Holy Men in Their Infancy: The Childhood of *Tsadikim* in Hasidic Legends', *Polin*, 15 (2002), 169–86; P. Gaffney, *Constructions of Childhood and Youth in Old French Narrative* (Farnham, Surr., 2011), 20–1.

16 e.g. Koval, *Children and Childhood in Medieval Poland*, 104. Koval distinguished between saintliness shown *despite* childishness (the *puer senex* motif), and demonstrating saintliness *through* childishness.

17 Galley, 'Holy Men in Their Infancy', 181.

18 *Tiferet raboteinu me'aleksander*, ed. Y. L. Makover (Benei Berak, 1966), no. 6 (p. 10).

19 On wunderkinds in Jewish literature, see e.g. S. A. Horodezky, 'Yanuka', *Moznaim*, 10/10 (1929), 7–9; 10/12 (1929), 8–10; G. Scholem, 'Mekorotav shel "ma'aseh rabi gadi'el hatinok" besifrut hakabalah', in *Devarim bego*, ed. A. Shapira (Tel Aviv, 1976), 270–83.

20 D. Ruderman, 'Three Contemporary Perceptions of a Polish Wunderkind of the Seventeenth Century', *AJS Review*, 4 (1979), 143–63.

21 M. Oron, 'Motiv hayenuka umashma'uto besefer hazohar', *Te'udah*, 21–2 (2007), 129–64; J. Benarroch, *Sava veyanuka: ha'el, haben, vehamashiaḥ besipurei hazohar* (Jerusalem, 2018).

22 *In Praise of the Baal Shem Tov: The Earliest Collection of Legends about the Founder of Hasidism*, trans. and ed. D. Ben-Amos and J. R. Mintz (Lanham, Md., 1970), 11–12. For a brief discussion of the text, see Galley, 'The Childhood of *Tsadikim* in Hasidic Legends', 180–1.

23 e.g. Shmuel of Sieniawa, *Ramatayim tsofim* (Warsaw, 1881), 167. On these accounts, see G. Dynner, *Men of Silk: The Hasidic Conquest of Polish Jewish Society* (New York, 2006), 184.

24 Klapholz, *Gedolei yisra'el beyaldutam*, iii. 8–9.

25 *Jewish Mystical Autobiographies: Book of Visions and Book of Secrets*, trans. M. Faierstein (New York, 1999), 276.

26 Y. H. Rabinowicz, 'Ḥayei yehoshua', in *Sefer hayovel*, ed. S. L. Horowitz (New York, 1930), 49–75: 50.

27 N. Sternharz, *Shivḥei haran* (Jerusalem, 1961), 11–12; trans. in A. Green, *Tormented Master: A Life of Rabbi Nahman of Bratslav* (Tuscaloosa, Ala., 1979), 27.

28 Galley, 'Holy Men in Their Infancy', 178.

29 Clift, 'Child'.

30 C. G. Jung, 'The Psychology of the Child Archetype', in id., *Aion: Researches into the Phenomenology of the Self*, Collected Works of C. G. Jung, 9/1 (London, 1959), 151–81.

31 *The Scroll of Secrets: The Hidden Messianic Vision of R. Nachman of Breslav*, ed. Z. Mark, trans. N. Moses (Brighton, Mass., 2010), 121–57.

32 M. Shapiro, *Medin leraḥamim* (Jerusalem, 1969); Eng. trans.: *The Rebbe's Daughter: Memoir of a Hasidic Childhood*, trans. N. Polen (Philadelphia, Pa., 2002); S. E. Jelen, 'Ethnopoetics in the Works of Malkah Shapiro and Ita Kalish: Gender, Popular Ethnography, and the Literary Face of Jewish Eastern Europe', in S. E. Jelen, M. P. Kramer, and L. S. Lerner (eds.), *Modern Jewish Literatures: Intersections and Boundaries* (Philadelphia, Pa., 2011), 213–36; D. Perets, 'Malka shapira (1894–1971): soferet ivrit umanhiga hasidit', MA thesis (Open University of Israel, 2022). Thanks to Polen's translation, English readers have access to one of Shapiro's books. However, she published several others with her childhood memories in them.

33 K. Finkler and G. Finkler, *Lives Lived and Lost: East European History Before, During, and After World War II as Experienced by an Anthropologist and Her Mother* (Boston, Mass., 2012).

34 I. Kalish, *A rebishe heym in amolikn poyln* (Tel Aviv, 1963); Eng. trans.: 'Life in a Hassidic Court in Russian Poland toward the End of the 19th and the Early 20th Centuries', *YIVO Annual of Jewish Social Science*, 13 (1965), 264–78; expanded Heb. edn.: *Etmoli* (Tel Aviv, 1970); see Jelen, 'Ethnopoetics in the Works of Malkah Shapiro and Ita Kalish'; A. Bar-Levav, R. Margolin, and S. Feiner, 'Mavo', in eid. (eds.), *Tahalikhei ḥilun batarbut hayehudit*, 2 vols. (Ra'ananah, 2013), i. 36–61.

35 Kalish, *Etmoli*, 61.

36 Ibid. 48–60.

37 Years later she revealed that she was actually banished by her mother-in-law, who discovered that she was in correspondence with Zionists.

38 S. A. Horodezky, *Zikhronot* (Tel Aviv, 1957), 11–25.

39 Ibid. 11–12.

40 Ibid. 21–2.

41 Ibid. 23.

42 Ibid. 23–4.

43 S. A. Horodezky, *Haḥasidut vehaḥasidim*, 2nd edn., 4 vols. (Tel Aviv, 1927–43).

44 Y. Twersky, *Heḥatser hapenimit: korot mishpaḥah* (Tel Aviv, 1954). On Haya and her sisters, see D. Assaf, *Untold Tales of the Hasidim: Crisis and Discontent in the History of Hasidism*, trans. D. Ordan (Waltham, Mass., 2010), 210–13.

45 e.g. Shapiro, *The Rebbe's Daughter*, 20; ead., *Medin leraḥamim*, 24; Twersky, *Heḥatser hapenimit*, 191; Finkler, *Lives Lived and Lost*, 46.

46 For example, Golda Finkler wrote about the summer vacations of her grandfather's family in Otwock and the travels of his descendants to spas (Finkler and Finkler, *Lives Lived and Lost*, 47–9); Yohanan Twersky noted a visit to a spa resort in Otwock that ended abruptly due to the outbreak of the 1905 revolution (Twersky, *Heḥatser hapenimit*, 204–9). On the travels of hasidic rebbes to spas, see M. Zadoff, *Next Year in Marienbad: The Lost Worlds of Jewish Spa Culture* (Philadelphia, Pa., 2012), 87–90.

47 Twersky, *Heḥatser hapenimit*, 170–1.

48 Finkler, *Lives Lived and Lost*, 56–7.

49 Twersky, *Heḥatser hapenimit*, 163, 180.

50 Kalish, *Etmoli*, 77; ead., *A rebishe heym in amolikn poyln*, 63–4.

51 Finkler, *Lives Lived and Lost*, 57.

52 I. Parush, *Reading Jewish Women: Marginality and Modernization in Nineteenth-Century Eastern European Jewish Society* (Waltham, Mass., 2004), 172–206; E. Adler, *In Her Hands: The Education of Jewish Girls in Tsarist Russia* (Detroit, 2011), 94; see also R. Manekin, *The*

Rebellion of the Daughters: Jewish Women Runaways in Habsburg Galicia (Princeton, NJ, 2020), 13; ead., '"Mashehu ḥadash legamrei": hitpatḥuto shel ra'ayon haḥinukh hadati levanot ba'et haḥadashah', *Masekhet*, 2 (2004), 63–85.
53   Kalish, *Etmoli*, 45–6.
54   Horodezky, *Zikhronot*, 12.
55   Y. L. Levine, *Zikhronot vehegyonot* (Jerusalem, 1968), 39.
56   Y. Even, *Funm rebin's hoyf: zikhroynes un mayses* (New York, 1922), 118–20.
57   Ibid. 119.
58   Galley, 'Holy Men in Their Infancy', 170–1.
59   D. Biale, D. Assaf, B. Brown, U. Gellman, S. C. Heilman, M. Rosman, G. Sagiv, and M. Wodziński, *Hasidism: A New History* (Princeton, NJ, 2017), 220–1.
60   See J. Weiss (ed.), *Magelei siaḥ: leket siḥot vehanhagot shel r. naḥman mibraslav* (Jerusalem, 1947), 54–5; cited in Galley, 'The Childhood of *Tsadikim* in Hasidic Legends', 170–1.
61   Kalish, *Etmoli*, 55.
62   M. Twersky, *Likutei torah hashalem*, ed. M. Wieder (Monsey, NY, 2002), 213.
63   Y. Klapholz, *Admorei belz*, 4 vols. (Benei Berak, 1972–8), iii. 20–1.
64   D. Assaf, *Hetsits venifga: anatomyah shel maḥloket ḥasidit* (Tel Aviv, 2012), 429 n. 31.
65   M. Glubman, *Ketavim* ([Jerusalem], 2005), 130–2.
66   On such adoptions among early modern Ashkenazi Jews, see T. M. Berner, *Al pi darkam: yeladim veyaldut be'ashkenaz* (Jerusalem, 2018), 78–80.
67   Assaf, *Derekh hamalkhut*, 60–2.
68   Ibid. 68–9.
69   Ibid. 88–90; see Assaf, *The Regal Way*, 37–9.
70   Three of these four cases were discussed in greater detail in G. Sagiv, '"Yenuka": al tsadikim-yeladim baḥasidut', *Zion*, 76 (2011), 139–78. I was informed about the *yenuka* of Koydanow only recently.
71   See Y. L. Levine, 'Hitgalut hayenuka bestolin', *Hashaḥar*, 6 (1875), 25–44; for Mandelbaum's letter, see ibid. 36–42; on the composition of this text by Levine and other sources about the *yenuka* of Stolin, see Sagiv, '"Yenuka"', 146–8.
72   Levine, 'Hitgalut hayenuka bestolin', 41 n. 23.
73   Y. Shapira, 'Hayenuka vehagabai', in *Stolin: sefer zikaron likehilat stolin vehasevivah*, ed. A. Avatihi and Y. Ben-Zakai (Tel Aviv, 1952), 153–5: 154.
74   A. A. Schore, 'Al shoshilta dedahava venishmato hakedoshah shel maran or yisra'el mistolin zyaa: 3', *Kovets beit aharon veyisra'el*, 34 (1991), 147–63: 161–2.
75   The National Library of Israel, ARC 4°1699, 10/b: Jews of Chernobyl, letter to Avraham Twersky, 14 Aug. 1882(?).
76   Notably, the opponents of the child wrote that he took the *kvitlekh* to his father's grave to consult with the dead. They presented this as an example of his incapability to lead. However, reliance on the authority of the former leader is discernible also among older *tsadikim*. The last Habad leader, Menachem Mendel Schneerson, was known to have connected with his father-in-law in this way. See e.g. A. M. Ehrlich, *Leadership in the HaBaD Movement: A Critical Evaluation of HaBaD Leadership, History, and Succession* (Lanham, Md., 2000), 108–9.
77   N. Polen, 'Rebbetzins, Wonder-Children, and the Emergence of the Dynastic Principle in Hasidism', in S. T. Katz (ed.), *The Shtetl: New Evaluations* (New York, 2007), 53–84.
78   Hadover Emet (pseud.), letter to the editor, *Hamelits*, 22 June 1883, p. 698.

79 Horodezky wrote 'gadol', which can be also translated as 'great'.
80 Horodezky, *Zikhronot*, 19.
81 Ibid. 20.
82 Ibid.
83 Yaakov Yitzhak Perlov, *Sefer imrei ya'akov*, ed. S. Erlich (Benei Berak, 2021).
84 M. Zalkin, '"Et hadar hateva lo yadu ve'et tekhelet hashamayim lo ra'u"? yaldut baḥevrah hayehudit hamasortit bemizraḥ eiropah', *Zmanim*, 102 (2008), 58–65.
85 Clift, 'Child'.
86 In this context, it is interesting to note the post-Jungian discussion of the *peur senex* (see J. M. Benarroch, '"Hasaba-yenuka" veḥanokh-metatron ke'arkhitip seneks-puer ("zaken-na'ar"): kriah post-yungianit basifrut hazoharit (al pi yames hilman)', in R. Hacohen-Pinczower, I. Pardes, R. I. Cohen, and G. Hasan-Rokem (eds.), *Hadimyon haparshani: dat ve'omanut batarbut hayehudit behekshereiha* (Jerusalem, 2016), 46–71). However, this approach seems to be less suited to the current discussion.

Representations of Boyhood in Nineteenth-Century Hebrew Literature

ROTEM PREGER-WAGNER

The discourse of childhood in Hebrew literature emerged through a gradual and cumulative process, which was intertwined with the profound concerns raised by the modernization processes occurring in Jewish society. The basic argument of this chapter is that children served as a conduit for the reformulation of discussions about Jewish identity. This contention emerges in the many dimensions that reveal how childhood was transformed from a marginal and neglected life chapter to a central component of self-understanding. The impact of nationalism on Hebrew literature led to the emergence of the child protagonist with an individual point of view who is assigned the role of narrator, a process which was similar to general developments in European literature.

Introduction

When and where do representations of children and childhood first appear in Hebrew literature? What are the thematic, aesthetic, ideological, and gendered features of these representations, and what role did they play? What were the social, cultural, and literary contexts of their emergence, and what were the reasons for it? In this chapter, I examine these questions in respect of the formative period of modern Hebrew literature in nineteenth-century Europe. From a methodological viewpoint, the attempt to trace the emergence of representations of childhood is grounded in re-readings of nineteenth-century Hebrew narrative works and in the field of childhood studies. Combining literary enquiry with conceptual tools borrowed from childhood studies allows, on the one hand, narratives of childhood to be located within Hebrew prose, and, on the other, the assumptions and attitudes at work in the shaping of these narratives to be investigated.[1]

Pre-modern literature, both Jewish and non-Jewish, contains very few representations of children and childhood. This does not mean that pre-modern Jewish or European society did not relate to children or did not recognize their particular needs, but neither regarded them as a topic of cultural interest. An increasing interest in the representation of children in European literature began to develop in the eighteenth century and gained momentum in the nineteenth. The discourse on childhood in Hebrew prose begins, as I shall show, in the nineteenth century, following its appearance in European literature, albeit with a certain delay. It developed slowly, vacillating between the adoption of a modern outlook, which emphasized the crucial role of childhood in the formation of individual identity, and pre-modern approaches, which did not regard the period of childhood as having any value for literature.

The narrative genres that emerged in the early modern period—the autobiography, the memoir, and the novel—placed at their centre a new subject, 'I', an individual, usually male, whose formation occurs in relation to the society in which he is active. This subject was constructed, primarily, through providing a historical-biographical dimension: that is, by establishing a narrative that traces growth from childhood to adulthood. This narrative relied on the centrality of memory in the constitution of self-identity and on the increasing recognition of the crucial place of childhood in the formation of the adult personality. It is in the autobiography, the memoir, and the novel that, for the first time in the history of Western literature, reconstructions of childhood episodes appear as an indispensable link in the formation of the personality of the protagonist. Representations of children and childhood in literature thus emerged within the context of the modern idea of the self, and are intimately linked with the rise of the novel, which is the genre most characteristic of modern prose.

Modern Hebrew prose was created in nineteenth-century eastern Europe under unusual circumstances. The narrative genres that were introduced into European literature at this time were characterized chiefly by realistic representation, which drew its power and credibility from the layered nature of its language, including speech. The writers of the Haskalah (Jewish Enlightenment) were influenced by these genres and created their equivalents in Hebrew prose, although they worked in an environment in which Hebrew was not a spoken language but rather a holy tongue, employed chiefly for prayer and study. Lacking an actual spoken form of Hebrew, writers of Hebrew prose were required to artificially create the verisimilitude of a spoken Hebrew. This linguistic challenge is important because of its implications for the possibility of writing children's lives in Hebrew. The spoken language of Jewish children in eastern Europe was not Hebrew but Yiddish, and literary renderings of their experiences entailed a double challenge: the inherent artistic difficulties that the representation of children pose for an adult author because of the chronological and experiential gaps separating them, and the linguistic limitation that necessitated the invention of a spoken Hebrew which could be credibly used by children.

The turn to childhood and its inclusion in the concept of the self can be attributed to two revolutions on the political, symbolic, and conceptual planes derived from the Enlightenment. The first is the perception of human equality as innate and the dismantling of the status and symbolic hierarchies that had prevailed in pre-modern Europe, according to which the child was seen as weak and subordinate and therefore not as an autonomous subject. The second revolution is the recognition of the role of memory in the construction of identity that laid the foundation for the modern concept of the individual and for an entire range of literary forms that are grounded in the experience of the authorial 'I'. A turning point in the understanding of childhood is associated with Jean-Jacques Rousseau, a representative of the Enlightenment whose writing, paradoxically, anticipated the Romantic view of childhood. Under the influence of his works *Emile* and *The Confessions*, Romanticism became the first movement in cultural history to contemplate childhood as the edenic epoch of human life and to regard the child as the quintessential human being. Rousseau introduced two key elements in the emergence of the concept of childhood: the first is the development of a narrative of the self, in the novel and other genres, which depicted the subject as a psychologically complex individual who possessed an 'inner' history. The second is the child as a symbolic conduit in national-political narratives. Rousseau perceived the child as a creature unencumbered by society's ills and therefore as one who could cure them. This idea resulted in tethering the child to nationalist discourses and became a commonplace of modern literature.

As has been noted, the discourse of childhood in Hebrew prose was influenced in its formative stages by European literary models. The impact of these models is apparent in several of its basic features: in the turn towards diverse literary genres of the 'self', including 'coming-of-age' narratives whose starting point is in childhood; in a shift from indifference to glorification of childhood and its identification with the values of naturalness, innocence, originality, imagination, interiority, and emotion, which stimulated an interest in child protagonists and the period of childhood; in the development of the child figure from object to subject and from passive victim to active agent; in gender bias (the figure of the child is almost exclusively a boy[2]); and, finally, in the dialectical interaction between the description of the child's individuation and the exploitation of the child's symbolic importance for collective-national goals.

The discourse of childhood in Hebrew prose during its formative period developed gradually and shifted from the margins of narrative creativity to the centre. In this chapter I describe this process, focusing on the three main phases which developed over the course of the nineteenth century. The first phase, which provides the point of departure for the representation of childhood in Hebrew prose, is marked by *Avi'ezer*, the autobiography of Mordekhai Aharon Gintsburg (1795–1846), a member of the Vilna Haskalah, written over many years and published in 1864. Gintsburg began the story of his life with his childhood, thus establishing a basic template for describing Jewish childhood. For the first time in Hebrew prose, he created a narrative that wove a dense web of connections between an individual's childhood and their adult personality. By the 1860s these techniques had found their way into works of fiction.

The second phase is to be found in the work of Sholem Yankev Abramovitsh (1835–1917), known by his pseudonym, Mendele Moykher Sforim. Abramovitsh, the greatest Hebrew prose writer of the Haskalah, who was clearly influenced by Gintsburg, is the creator of the Jewish child in Hebrew fiction. Throughout his long literary career from the 1860s to the second decade of the twentieth century, he was engaged in the creation of child characters and accounts of childhood. The Jewish child figure that he created is derived in part from ideas about childhood articulated by Enlightenment philosophers, and in part from the Romantic perception of the child. His work is thus an important link between the two main sources that shaped the modern concept of childhood.

The third phase is embodied in the work of Mordekhai Ze'ev Feierberg (1874–99), a member of the generation of the Hebrew Revival. Feierberg's narrative works made a special contribution to shaping the world of the child and narratives of childhood at the end of the nineteenth century. He was responsible for creating the child protagonist, who speaks 'from within himself', giving the child the position of narrator. He thus for the first time gave shape to a realistic narrative world described from the perspective of the child, through his own experience and in his own language. The child in his stories is caught in the tension between the self-contained and self-referential world of childhood and the imposition on him of the national-collective mission which, in effect, takes over his childhood. His work provides a kind of artistic synopsis of the discourse about childhood which began with Gintsburg, as well as giving a literary illustration of the faltering and tortuous process by which the subjectivity of the child emerges in Hebrew prose in the course of the nineteenth century.

First Phase: *Avi'ezer* by Mordekhai Aharon Gintsburg

The starting point for the emergence of the discourse of childhood in Hebrew prose is the first Hebrew autobiography, *Avi'ezer* by Mordekhai Aharon Gintsburg,[3] which greatly influenced the Hebrew writers of the latter half of the nineteenth century. Gintsburg wrote his life history well aware of the novelty of his approach to Hebrew autobiographical writing. In the introduction to his book he remarked that whereas biographies of extraordinary persons had been written in the holy tongue, until his own book, the story of an ordinary person who wished to narrate his inner life had never been written down. These two observations—that the subject of an autobiography could be Everyman and that the chief concern of such a book was the life of the psyche—are among the features of modern autobiography as moulded by Rousseau, both in terms of the interest in the human being as an individual and in terms of the focus on his interiority and not necessarily on heroic adventures and 'great' deeds.[4]

When Gintsburg approached the narration of his inner life he started with his childhood. The mere fact that he was the first to compose a continuous narrative of Jewish childhood in Hebrew prose as part of his understanding of his adult personality is the overt and explicit reason for establishing him as the starting point for the discourse of childhood in Hebrew prose. However, this in itself is an insufficient reason. Gintsburg's own account of his life story is situated at the very centre of the period of the Haskalah and to a large extent embodies its values. Nevertheless, it is the first original Hebrew work that relates to the literary tradition that harks back to Rousseau's *Confessions* and which came, through various channels, to permeate Hebrew literature and whose influence became explicit in the autobiography of Solomon Maimon.[5] The foundational status of *Avi'ezer* in the Hebrew discourse of childhood is therefore inextricably linked to Rousseau. In the cases of both Rousseau and Gintsburg, autobiographical writing stemmed from a novel sense of selfhood and from the notion of a subject whose obscure opening chapter—childhood—was regarded as the source of everything which followed.

Claiming *Avi'ezer* is the seminal example of the Hebrew discourse of childhood means that the genesis of that discourse is to be found in the genre of autobiography from which it evolved and found its way into literary fiction.[6] The pioneering aspect of *Avi'ezer*, therefore, cannot be ascribed merely to the fact of its engagement with childhood as its subject matter or from the values and outlooks it drew from Rousseau. Rather, it also derives from its after-history: the fact that in the wake of its publication in the 1860s it became a point of reference and source of influence for the evolving discourse of childhood in Hebrew literature, a discourse that did not exist before its publication.

The canonical Hebrew literature of the Haskalah, at least that portion of it which was written before the 1870s, did not evince any explicit interest in the narrative of the self in general or of childhood in particular. According to Alan Mintz, the Hebrew autobiography emerged as an alternative to the maskilic novel. The 'autobiographical impulse', as he called it, was given expression in Gintsburg's pioneering work and in the autobiography of Moshe Leib Lilienblum (1843–1910), *Ḥatot ne'urim*, which appeared in 1876 and was reincarnated in fictional literary form towards the end of the century, with the rise of the new literary poetics.[7] In its initial stages, the story of Hebrew childhood is closely tied to the shift in genre described by Mintz from autobiographical to fictional literature. It begins to germinate in the first Hebrew autobiography, which was written in the context of modern European *Bildung* literature, and in some autobiographies that were written in the second third of the nineteenth century and which devoted some chapters to childhood, such as *Ḥatot ne'urim*, 'Al nehar kevar' by Yehuda Leib Gordon (1830–92),[8] and *Zikhronot miyemei ne'urai* by Avraham Ber Gottlober (1811–99).[9] However, its reception into the literary canon occurred in the last third of the century.[10]

Gintsburg's basic understanding of the child and childhood was, above all, maskilic. It was founded on the rationalist assumptions of the Enlightenment regarding the nature and role of the period of childhood in the formation of the adult. Children had been liberated from the moral and symbolic values that were attributed to them in pre-modern thought but had not yet been granted the ability to be understood as subjects. They were perceived as 'adults in waiting', in other words, as rational creatures in potential.[11] In the childhood chapters of *Avi'ezer*, these assumptions are manifested in the near-absolute dominance of the intellectual component of the self-narrative and in its moral and didactic bias. In his description of his childhood Gintsburg harshly criticizes traditional Jewish education, and to a large degree links this critique with his campaign to transform Jewish society and expose it to the values of the Haskalah.

The Key Elements of a Jewish Boyhood

Gintsburg's description of his childhood can be seen as an account of the key elements of the childhood of an east European Jewish boy, marked by the following milestones: until the age of 3 he was under the charge of his mother, was transferred at the age of 4 to that of his father and began to study, entered *ḥeder* between the ages of 5 and 6, advanced along various stages of learning while passing from the hands of one *melamed* to the next, encountered prospective brides for his arranged marriage at the age of 11, was engaged at around the age of 12, barmitzvah at 13, followed by marriage and residence with his in-laws at the age of 14. This narrative progression established the boundaries of his childhood: it is a brief childhood from the modern perspective, and also from that of Gintsburg himself.

Gintsburg describes his childhood almost exclusively in relation to his father, while almost entirely ignoring his mother. This stems from his understanding of his inner history as the constitution of the self in relation to the social order as embodied in traditional Jewish education. The father is identified with the beginning of the process of social formation, and to a significant degree with the entire process of education—the education of the son in Jewish society was the father's duty both within the home and outside it. The mother and anything related to aspects of life that were not mediated by the visible, explicit, and navigable social order were not perceived as contributing to the constitution of the self.

Accordingly, between the commencement of boyhood and its early conclusion, its key elements are outlined by describing the different stages of study, from the father's lap to the *ḥeder* and the various *melamedim* under whose tutelage the child finds himself. The identification of the progress of boyhood with Jewish learning in the *ḥeder* is founded on the realities of life for east European Jewish boys. This was also documented in Solomon Maimon's autobiography, which clearly influenced Gintsburg's work. However, it is not simply a representation of reality; on the contrary, its purpose is to actively construct a polemical discourse of Jewish boyhood. I do not mean to suggest that Jewish boys did not spend endless hours of their childhood in the *ḥeder*, but I also assume that their family members—however present or absent they may have been—occupied a place of no small significance in their lives. My argument is, rather, that the dominance of *ḥeder* life and education served as a kind of displacement or symbolic veil for the implicit narrative, whose essential element is the confrontation with the father.

Positioning the *ḥeder* at the centre of his childhood experience reveals the duality underlying the way the Jewish boy was formed—analogous to two sides of a page inscribed on the front as an individual subject and on the back as a national subject. As Ala Alryyes has shown, the appearance of the child figure in European literature is associated with the appearance of two types of discourse: of the novel and of the nation. In both, he argued, the child served as a representation of an original subject, who is simultaneously out of place and situated in a crucial place. The main argument in Alryyes's book is that both the emergent novel and the early modern national narrative placed the story of the child at their centre. The child functions as a symbolic conduit for the resistance to fictional and political representation identified with paternal authority. The early English novel is based, according to his argument, on the story of an unhappy child who runs away from its father's house. The national narratives of the seventeenth and eighteenth centuries—Alryyes discussed Locke's and Rousseau's understanding of the social contract as national narratives—

struggled against the absolutist myths of the state. The authority of the father-king was depicted as an authority whose time had passed, to be superseded by the community and the nation. As a result, childhood, both in the individual and in society, became a site where a confrontation took place over the introduction of a new kind of representation. In place of the metaphors of father-king and child-subject, alternative explanations of the relationship between political authority and subjectivity were provided.[12]

By criticizing ḥeder education, the maskilim in general, and Gintsburg in particular, identified the childhood of Jewish boys as a site of public and national significance. The ḥeder embodied the perception of the Jewish boy as a carrier of the Jewish heritage—trained from early childhood to accept the yoke of Torah study and observance of the commandments.[13] This heritage, which is unquestionably a patriarchal one, made the child into a national subject, a link in a chain that guarantees Jewish continuity. Identifying Jewish boyhood with ḥeder education is, in effect, an attempt to make a breach in the prevailing symbolic order of the traditional Jewish concept of childhood, while suspending the biographical father outside the boundaries of explicit criticism and engendering a new national subject. The critique of the ḥeder is an allegorization of a broader and more essential national conflict between sons and fathers, which characterizes the fault line marking the transition to modernity. Out of this confrontation the child figure would emerge.

Gintsburg's account of ḥeder education became a profoundly internalized model for the narrating of childhood in the nineteenth century, and was perceived by most as the archetypal representation of Jewish boyhood. This is apparent in Lilienblum's explicit statement that he did not need to describe his own education because Gintsburg had already done so.[14] Gintsburg thus sketched the contours of the childhood narrative, determined its course and its boundaries, and presented the key figures in the life of the Jewish boy: the father and the *melamedim*. No less important were the materials that were almost entirely omitted from this narrative: the mother, the parental home, the siblings, and anything unrelated to his formal education. This narrative, as I understand it, is a kind of code for deciphering the discourse of childhood and subjectivity that Gintsburg established in Hebrew narrative prose.

'Children's Talk'

Gintsburg used the phrase 'children's talk' (*siḥat yeladim*), when attempting to explain to his readers why he wrote about childhood. The phrase derives from *Pirkei avot*, and the original context is negative: 'Midday wine, children's talk, and sitting in the assemblies of the ignorant put a man out of the world.'[15] This need to justify himself illustrates in miniature the beliefs about childhood that prevailed in the traditional Jewish society in which Gintsburg was located and in relation to which he wrote.[16] Nonetheless, and given the fact that Gintsburg allocated space to 'children's talk', it is meaningful to ask what turned *Avi'ezer* into a work that set out for subsequent writers the essence of the Hebrew childhood narrative.

Beyond the construction of the Jewish childhood narrative, Gintsburg introduced a cluster of topics and features that became an inseparable part of the story of Jewish boyhood throughout the 'long' nineteenth century. The brutal corporal punishment employed by *melamedim* appears as a recurrent feature in most of the childhood narratives; the tensions between the Torah stories and the *pilpul* (casuistry) of the Talmud, between halakhah (law) and aggadah (narrative/legend), and between excessive intellectualization and imagination would emerge as the central frictions characterizing the child's state of being torn between contradictory tendencies and which inform the very quality of being a child. The too-brief childhood or the childhood utterly denied to the Jewish boy because he is perceived as a miniature adult—this too is an issue that would become a kind of trope; the wise, quick-witted boy with the phenomenal memory, destined to be a Torah genius, would become the archetypal child hero. 'Rebelliousness', that wild province of childhood in which the child violates the social conventions or rebels against them openly—this too would reappear as a childlike characteristic. As noted earlier, father–son relations would become the focal point for the representation of interpersonal relations within the family and, analogously as well as evocatively, they would act as the site of conflict between the child and Jewish society. When mothers and mother–son relations eventually do appear, their appearance reflects a kind of re-reading of the convention that Gintsburg innovated. Girls, it should be noted, scarcely appear in the childhood narratives of Haskalah literature or Hebrew Revival literature before the prose narratives of Devorah Baron (1887–1956). The *ḥeder*, as the quintessential space of Jewish boyhood, and the *melamed* as the central adult figure explicitly confronting the child, are perhaps the most recognizable features that can be traced back to *Avi'ezer*, and they would reappear in every boyhood narrative in subsequent decades. Attitudes towards these themes did indeed change and were sometimes even inverted, but they are nevertheless present as essential ingredients of the Jewish boyhood narrative.[17]

Gintsburg, who appears to have operated in a world of Jewish literary discourse that opposed 'children's talk', planted a seed, however immature, of a different discourse. This discourse broached the very question of Jewish subjectivity, including the relationships between childhood and selfhood and between childhood and nationalism. The fact that he included his own child-self in this enquiry provides the starting point for the rise of the discourse of Jewish childhood in Hebrew. The childhood story that he wrote introduced cracks into 'the self'—fissures that were inherent to a grappling with the establishment of a discourse of childhood: for example, the fact that the narrative of the self includes chapters that are unruly and inaccessible to memory, lapses of awareness which cast doubt on all of the remembered elements that ostensibly control the constitution of self-identity; and, conversely, that the narrative of the self, from its starting point in childhood, is an arena of struggle between various forces that determine and shape the discourse. These cracks, which Gintsburg exposed mostly unwittingly, stimulated and activated the literary imagination of Feierberg and of other contemporary authors.

Second Phase: Sholem Yankev Abramovitsh (Mendele Moykher Sforim)

Sholem Yankev Abramovitsh is considered the founding father of modern Jewish prose in Hebrew and Yiddish. He was a man of the Haskalah, active from the 1860s until the 1920s in the tsarist empire and revolutionary Russia, and was, in Hayim Nahman Bialik's words, the 'crafter of the style' of modern Hebrew prose.[18]

It is Bialik, rather than Abramovitsh, who is considered the creator of Jewish childhood in Hebrew literature. I would argue, however, that Abramovitsh is the pre-eminent writer dealing with children and childhood and the inventor of the child figure in Hebrew fiction. He regarded the child as an essential element in the artistic interrogation of Jewish issues and, more than any other modern Jewish writer, included childhood in his understanding of the self. His views about children and childhood were influenced by ideas that had developed in European literature and philosophy from the eighteenth century, and through his literary activity in this field he was an agent of change within the Haskalah movement.[19]

Abramovitsh dealt with the Jewish child and Jewish childhood in all his literary works, both his journalism and his stories. The deep and continuous interest he took in childhood has no parallel among his contemporary writers; however, parallels can be found among nineteenth-century writers in other languages. The scale and intensity of Abramovitsh's focus on childhood are manifested in the fact that almost every single work of his contains some treatment—whether extensive and explicit or incidental and marginal—of it. This is evident from the very first article he published while still a young man, 'Letter on Education',[20] down to the chapters of *Of Bygone Days* which he wrote in his old age.[21]

Abramovitsh's creative grappling with the childhood narrative extended over many years of writing and produced a complex and dynamic set of ideas which embodied his understanding of childhood. Its beginnings are rooted in the maskilic critique of Jewish education, and its later manifestation is in satirical-realist writings that also contain a few flashes of Romanticism. Despite this chronological development, the understanding of childhood in Abramovitsh's work does not follow a straight path. Expressions of a maskilic view of childhood can be found in later works, while glimmerings of a Romantic or pre-Romantic view appear in the early and intermediate ones. In fact, the maskilic–Romantic opposition does not adequately capture the matter.

Abramovitsh's writing evinces an affinity with perceptions of childhood that were prevalent in European literature from the eighteenth century onwards, and it integrates original reflections on the child and childhood in Jewish society with an artistic reworking of experiences from his own childhood. His work does not contain a consistent and coherent view of childhood but rather a range of forms, often incompatible with one another, including expressive representations of children and musings about childhood. What these share is a decades-long literary investigation of the child and childhood and of their place in the life of the adult human being.

The special place that Abramovitsh accorded to childhood in his literary creation derives from what Carolyn Steedman called 'a form of subjectivity' that emerged in European society during the nineteenth century.[22] The child became an object of literary and scientific enquiry, such that both Romantic poets and rationalist philosophers—from Wordsworth to John Stuart Mill—took an interest in children and their sensory perceptions. Children fascinated the rationalists because they were a convenient 'object' of observation and reflection; observation of the feelings and impressions of children was central to the period's scholarly outlook, and such observations were the foundation stones of modern psychology. For the Romantics, childhood also functioned, in Judith Plotz's words, as 'an adult imaginary kingdom and as an adult research institute'.[23] Abramovitsh's writings reveal the influence of these trends and the complex way that he implemented them in the Jewish context.

Abramovitsh began his engagement with childhood from a critical standpoint. Beginning with his early writings in the 1850s, he addressed himself to the problem of the education of Jewish children and responded on the immediate social plane to the treatment of children in Jewish society. Nevertheless, his critical treatment of Jewish education was not limited to the social sphere. It drove him, as mentioned earlier, towards an artistic interrogation of the nature of the Jewish child and Jewish childhood. The childhood chapters of his novel *The Wishing Ring* contain fragments of childhood life within the context of a biting maskilic critique, sometimes adduced merely as an element of a critical argument but nonetheless providing an opening for the emergence of a new artistic language with which to represent children's lives, and laying the groundwork for describing a Jewish subject who is also a child.[24]

At this point I would like to present the two poles of the child figure and of childhood in Abramovitsh's writing. One is the child portrayed in *The Wishing Ring*, a novel whose writing extended from the 1850s until the end of the century. At the other end lies *Of Bygone Days*, a semi-fictional autobiography written between 1894 and Abramovitsh's death in 1917, which remained incomplete. Between the early and later work the development of a self-conscious, artistic grappling with the representation of children's lives can be discerned.

The attitude to childhood in these two works is fundamentally different—*The Wishing Ring* is a critical maskilic novel, and its tone is mainly satirical—its narrator is Mendele Moykher Sforim. *Of Bygone Days* is primarily an epic and nostalgic novel, narrated mostly by Rebbe Shlomo, who reflects on his childhood from a distance. Despite the palpable difference in tone, atmosphere, and narrative technique, these two works share similar features in how they describe childhood. *The Wishing Ring* begins with a coming-of-age story rooted in childhood, which is later truncated, dispersed, and abandoned among other plot elements. *Of Bygone Days* is a consistent and self-contained coming-of-age story, despite remaining unfinished. The core of the plot in both novels is the story of a Jewish boy in a shtetl who is orphaned at the age of 13 by the death of his father.

Childhood in *The Wishing Ring*

The Wishing Ring begins with episodes from the childhood of its protagonist—the child Hershele. This part of the novel is the first prose attempt in Hebrew to provide elaborate description of the reality and experience of an east European boyhood, centring on the child protagonist from his birth to his barmitzvah. It includes a large mass of material on childhood, both in its plot design and in its exposition of the author's views. This section of the novel should be regarded as both pioneering and definitive in the genesis of the descriptions of childhood in contemporary Hebrew writing. With these chapters Abramovitsh shattered the framework of the maskilic childhood narrative by virtue of the diminished place he accorded to Hershele's formal education. The account of Jewish boyhood, as developed in *Avi'ezer* and in the maskilic genre of autobiography more generally, had centred, as noted above, on study in the ḥeder. Yet here, with the exception of a small passage that mocks the figure of the *melamed*, there is no meaningful portrayal of Hershele's time in the ḥeder. According to *The Wishing Ring*, the arena of Hershele's childhood is Kabtsieli Street, and not in the family or educational spheres.

The portrayal of the children's daily life on Kabtsieli Street is a succinct and intense summary of childhood experiences: a band of children with their games, conflicts, and play-acting, sloshing through the mud or trading in kids' treasures, be it a rusty nail, a pierced nutshell, or odd pieces of fabric. Children, according to this description, are sensual, curious, and vibrant creatures.

The abiding narrative focus on the daily life of Hershele and his companions is indeed pioneering; however, it is interrupted by a series of interpolations setting out the argument that childhood is stolen from Jewish children:

> Hershele's childhood was short-lived, and while still of tender years, old age overtook him, giving him the appearance of a child-Jew. The Jew is destined to suffer so many troubles during his short life, that he has no time to be a child. The childhood of a Jew is like sunshine on a rainy day, momentary rays that are instantly swallowed by clouds, darkness and mist. No more has the child's swaddling been removed—he is launched into Torah and good deeds, and lo, he is like an adult Jew in his gait, speech, and garb, in his misery and temper, and in every outer appearance.[25]

The world of Kabtsieli Street into which Hershele is socialized is a society of paupers and idlers, unable to control their fate and given to false dreams. It is a childish society in the negative sense of the word. Paradoxically, Hershele's childhood is very brief because there is nothing for him to mature into. Abramovitsh described how a Jewish child was born and grew up into a society that was thoroughly infantile. The theft of childhood was in essence its appropriation, an appropriation resulting from the adults' own childishness. What Abramovitsh was saying is that a society into which it is impossible to mature has no place for either the child or childhood. In order to extricate Jewish society from a condition that he perceived as perpetual infantilism, he gave birth to Hershele. And by engendering Hershele, in other words by assigning Jewish childhood to an actual child and demarcating it as a defined life stage, he sought to constitute a dual Jewish subject: first—the child, second—the adult.

The Wishing Ring is a kind of literary laboratory explaining the genesis of the Jewish child and the nature of Jewish childhood. Because it is a multilayered novel, with various genres and plots, it offers a glimpse into various artistic attempts to describe the Jewish child figure. These attempts combine sharp realistic observations and quasi-allegorical expansions, descriptions of a sensual and actual child and philosophical generalizations, a turn towards the child and childhood and a turning away from them. This multifaceted structure exposes the difficulties Abramovitsh had to deal with in his effort to establish a Jewish child-subject: how to critique Jewish education and assert the theft of Jewish childhood while simultaneously narrating a child's life; how to recount a child's life in the near-total absence of earlier Jewish childhood stories; how to relate a story of Jewish childhood reliably in Hebrew—a language not spoken by children. Was it possible to hold together a story of childhood, including all the trivial, prosaic detail expected of it, without harnessing it to some ideology? What lay between telling the story of a child's life and setting out one's view of what constitutes a worthy and desirable childhood? What lay between an adult author and his own childhood?

In *The Wishing Ring*, Abramovitsh provided radical answers to some of these questions. He disrupted the childhood narrative that he had inherited from Gintsburg and took Hershele out of the *ḥeder* into the street. The creation of a Jewish street child was radical in the sense that it extricated him from the social order and dominion of the father. This strategy implicitly argued for the need to dismantle the patriarchal structure in order to create a child-subject. This argument was derived from European literature, and it played a crucial role in the formation of the child in modern literature. The novel's deep-reaching analysis of Jewish society demonstrated that Jewish children lacked a childhood because Jewish society is childlike. The story of Hershele's childhood suggested that the creation of a genuine Jewish childhood required it to be separated from Jewish adulthood so that children could be children and grown-ups could attain adulthood. In so doing, Abramovitsh dispensed with the circularity of the maskilic argument about the non-childhood of Jewish children.

The novel thus lays the foundations, or rather the conditions, for the constitution of Jewish childhood. Although the child protagonist Hershele is transformed in the course of the novel from a particular child into a sort of allegory, the novel taken as a whole can be understood as an extended description of the child that is yet to emerge.

Of Bygone Days and the I-Child

Of Bygone Days is a fictional autobiography in which childhood occupies a large and extended space. It can be viewed as the consolidation of the modern conception of autobiography in the sense of an 'I' that engages in an ongoing dialogue with its own childhood. The story is narrated by the protagonist, Rebbe Shlomo, within a framing story which describes the event that led Shlomo to write the story of his childhood: a revelatory vision in which Shlomo became aware of himself as a child of tender years. The starting point for Shlomo's story is not in the parental home on the day of his birth, surrounded by family and embedded in his social background, but is rather an isolated, personal event of a childhood experience associated with revelation and the transformation of awareness. This enabled the child to form an awareness of a continuous self that was not dependent on others. How did this situation come about? Shlomo, the adult writer, linked the idea of writing about his childhood with a remote event in his childhood that he called 'self-realization'. The connection is metonymic: the writing vision appeared during a storm, just as the self-realization event of his early childhood had occurred during a storm:

My life is a turbulent ocean, my days and years are raging waves and my soul is the storm-battered ship; even my first conscious realization of myself began with a storm. It was springtime. Suddenly it got dark, and in the garden path, amid the fresh foliage, a young boy ran barefoot and half-naked, with nothing but a linen shirt on his body and a cap on his head. Now he hurried and now he stood still. His eyes took in everything, and his ears were cocked like a rabbit's. That boy was myself. That was the day when my eyes were opened and I was revealed to myself as I really am.

I was alone there; no living creature was with me, only the sky above and the earth below, and a fence on either side. All of a sudden there was thunder, a crashing sound from the sky, a noise rolling to the ends of the earth and exploding into many mighty sounds, while fiery serpents and angels of fire flitted about in the sky. I imagined this to be the thundering of God's chariot, the Lord of Hosts who rides the clouds, who cracks the whip and splits the tongues of fire.[26]

The entire passage is based on a combination of the Romantic view of childhood with verses and images from biblical and midrashic literature. The Romantic outlook is apparent in the epiphany acknowledging nature and creation. The child running barefoot and naked in a spring storm is like Adam in the Garden of Eden: he is alone, with only the heavens above and the earth below. The language is replete with verse fragments evoking the Creation story, the revelation on Mount Sinai, the prophets, and prophetic initiation scenes in both biblical and rabbinic literature. The innovative power of this epiphany cannot be overestimated. Abramovitsh presents here, for the first time, a fictional autobiography of childhood that does not begin within the parental, familial context but rather in an isolated and autonomous experience of self-realization of a child outdoors in nature, in the vein established by the European Romantic poets. The Romantic perception of the child as endowed with the ability to experience transcendence here receives a pioneering expression in Hebrew literature.

The framing story thus presents a sublime scene of self-revelation, which leads to the writing of the story and the return to the province of childhood. It is narrated by Rebbe Shlomo in the first person, although the major portion of his childhood narrative is told from the point of view of an omniscient narrator. This dual narrative offers two simultaneous perspectives on childhood: the first underscores the experiential, subjective, and memory-bound (and hence elusive) dimension of a return to the childhood narrative; the second accords the childhood story the character of a chronicle, like a recital of actual events, while upholding the distance and gap between the event of narration and the time of the narrative. The former produces a narrator who re-establishes the awareness of continuity between his adulthood and childhood. The second establishes the childhood episodes as a reality independent of the observer's viewpoint and detaches the individual narrator from the narrative. This duality renders childhood, on the one hand, as a separate, distant province, a kind of 'place in time' to which one can return by means of the story, and on the other as an active, interior component of an adult person's awareness, who recognizes it as a part of selfhood. The construction of childhood as a 'place in time' highlights the narrating subject as situated outside it and therefore as a subject who is split between his childhood and adulthood. The construction of childhood as a component of the adult self, as a part of the narrating I, produces a complex subject who holds different and contradictory life situations simultaneously. The former 'controls' his childhood as an object of description; the second experiences it.

What links these two novels is a complex evolution of how the Jewish child and Jewish childhood should be understood, both ideologically and aesthetically. If in *The Wishing Ring* Abramovitsh had to belabour the very distinction between children and adults so that the Jewish child might be a child, in *Of Bygone Days* he takes a diametrically opposed position—now that the child is a child, one can present an adult Jewish subject who is also a child. Being a child, therefore, is not merely a life stage but also has within it a certain ability to experience, reflect, feel, and create, which is not lost in adulthood. On the contrary, being a child is the foundation for an individual's complex and multifaceted character, especially in the case of the writer. In the change he experienced in the period between the writing of these two novels, Abramovitsh managed to realize two aspects of the modern understanding of childhood: the first is the separation of childhood from adulthood for the sake of establishing the child-subject; the second is the inclusion of the child in the perception of the adult self, for the sake of its reconstitution.

The grand movement of self-constitution rooted in childhood, which unfolds over the totality of Abramovitsh's literary oeuvre, also has an aesthetic aspect. The child in his early work continually skirted the border of allegorical representation. It represented an attempt to carve the character of a particular child out of neoclassical poetics, a poetics in which the child and childhood are an essence, an idea, a concept. In his later work, the allegorical elements were discarded in favour of childhood episodes steeped in realism which successfully render a concrete child character. This movement is of great importance. It reveals the twisting path that Abramovitsh had to walk in order to achieve a representation of children and childhood in Hebrew prose while facing an almost complete lack of earlier models, dealing with the difficulty of 'translating' a non-Hebrew childhood into Hebrew, and contending with prevailing images of early childhood as an 'empty' chapter, unworthy of literary or cultural engagement. In other words, Abramovitsh had to free himself from notions of childhood as an opaque essence—unimportant and generalized for the sake of limited symbolic purposes—in order to evolve his perception of childhood as a free-standing, formative chapter of human life. For this evolution to occur—as in Pinocchio's transformation from a puppet into a real boy—required the impact of the Romantic understanding of childhood as a formative chapter of a person's life and as a model of the artistic soul. Romanticism did indeed glorify childhood and enclose it within a certain image that suited its needs; however, at the same time it remade childhood as a constitutive phase in the formation of subjectivity. Hence its bridging role in viewing childhood as a central topic of literary and cultural interest and as an object of realistic representation, a point of view whose influence is clearly marked in Abramovitsh's narrative prose. Within the Jewish context, he elaborated an outlook on childhood that contained streaks of Romanticism or pre-Romanticism, but which was situated within an unquestionably non-Romantic narrative whole. To the maskilic, realistic, and biographical elements, he added the 'natural' Jewish child—wild, emotive, and imaginative—who embodies more than a fraction of the figure of the creative artist.

Third Phase: Mordekhai Ze'ev Feierberg

Mordekhai Ze'ev Feierberg was a writer of the Hebrew Revival, which was marked by psychological realism, neo-Romanticism, and symbolism. He died of tuberculosis at the age of 24, and left behind seven stories, a single essay, and several letters. Children are a major theme of his work: the three short stories 'In the Evening', 'The Amulet', and 'The Calf', all subtitled 'From the Memoirs of Hofni, Master of Imagination', form a narrative cycle centred on the child protagonist Hofni.[27] His well-known longer story 'Whither?' also includes the childhood experiences of its hero, Nahman the Madman. His first story, 'Yaakov the Guard', which is not a childhood story, also integrates childhood memory. The few stories he managed to write during his short life present a new approach to the representation of children and childhood in Hebrew literature.

In a letter that Feierberg sent to Ahad Ha'am, editor of *Hashiloaḥ*, in 1898, and which was appended to 'In the Evening', he wrote: 'In these memoirs I wish to present the entire world of a Jewish person; I began therefore with the period of childhood.'[28] The requirement of 'the entire world of a Jewish person' highlights the inclusion of childhood in the concept of personhood, an idea that even in the 1890s was not self-evident. However, Feierberg required even more: in the same letter, he revealed his desire that his stories should describe 'the shape of our most interior world'. His aspiration to depict the Jewish person from the inside out is premised on the concept of the child as a basic element of this interiority. This notion, which Feierberg formulated clearly and illustrated concretely in his stories, reflects the long journey that the writing of Jewish childhood had undergone during the nineteenth century since its rudimentary beginnings in Gintsburg's autobiographical writings. Unlike Gintsburg, Feierberg explicitly acknowledged that reflecting on childhood and adopting the child's point of view as part of a person's 'interiority' is a means for exploring subjectivity. His stories were an attempt to expand and deepen writing in Hebrew about the Jewish self 'from within its interior', while childhood is perceived as the site where this interiority is inscribed.

The Jewish Child in the Tales of Hofni

The Tales of Hofni correspond to three scenes from childhood that are unrelated in terms of chronology or causality. All three are recounted in the first person by Hofni, and all three grapple with the point of view, inner experience, consciousness, and language of a child. Each of them is a kind of initiation story: in 'In the Evening', the child's mother recounts a legend that is interpreted by Hofni as a demand to fight on behalf of his people and faith. In 'The Amulet', following an encounter with a kabbalistic master, Hofni decides to overcome his night-time fears and become a 'man of war'. In 'The Calf', the slaughter of a calf by his mother provokes Hofni to ask hard questions about the ways of the world and to recognize its cruelty.[29]

In these stories Feierberg presents a new kind of fragmentary description of Jewish childhood, as opposed to the structure derived from the *Bildungsroman* that had previously dominated it. This new structure contains vignettes from the life of a Jewish child that are not linked to a framing narrative. In other words, it is constructed of fragments of experience that have welled up in memory, without an elaborate social background and with hardly any exposition, thus drawing the reader closer to a child's perspective. What stands out is the child's present experience, without the explanatory or disciplinary interventions of an adult narrator. One cannot know whether Feierberg would have ultimately created a general framework for the Tales of Hofni, beyond the works' shared title and the stories' shared protagonist and childhood scenarios. In their present form, the stories offer a singular poetics of the life of a child and of childhood experience. Moreover, Feierberg did not shy away from engaging with the concrete realities of childhood: everyday items of no apparent importance, children's talk, and other realistic material effects.

The childhood narrative in the Tales of Hofni is unique on several levels, the first being the arena in which it takes place: it is located mainly in the parental home and focuses on the relations between the child and his parents, and especially on his relationship with his mother. The description of Jewish boyhood that Gintsburg developed, following Solomon Maimon, traced the different stages of ḥeder studies. Mendele's *The Wishing Ring* relocated this narrative from the ḥeder to the street. Feierberg transferred it from the ḥeder to the home. For the first time space was given to the parental home and to relations with parents as a quintessential arena of childhood. The 'big' questions regarding the child Hofni's destiny as a member of his people, which loom large in these stories, are an issue between him and his parents and are not mediated by the ḥeder.

Furthermore, the Jewish description of childhood as it had taken shape in Haskalah literature confronted the son with the father's symbolic heritage as embodied in the ḥeder. As far as any parental presence was concerned, it was limited to the father figure. In Feierberg's Tales of Hofni, he positioned the child mainly against his mother and involved her in various matters, some of which concerned her family role, such as food, sleep, a bedtime story, and some of which were linked to her by symbolic association. In 'In the Evening' the narrative is divided between the ḥeder and the home, while the story's emotional centre of gravity is the home. In 'The Amulet', the story plays out between the parental home and that of the kabbalistic master and focuses on the relationship between Hofni and his parents. Thus, for example, the legend told by his mother in 'In the Evening' aroused Hofni's imaginative world and affected him far more than his ḥeder studies. Not only was it delivered by his mother, it carried a symbolic weight that was set against the heritage of Jewish learning, which was the father's domain. The transposition of the childhood narrative into the home in the Tales of Hofni therefore entailed their transposition from the father and Torah study to the mother and her aggadic stories.[30] These trends of transferring the story of Jewish boyhood from the ḥeder to the home, from the sphere of the father and Talmud study to the sphere of the mother and the world of aggadah, were already manifested in the writings of David Frishman (1859–1922), Yitskhok Leibush Peretz (1852–1915), and Mikhah Yosef Berdichevsky (1865–1921) in the 1880s, but Feierberg made them central in his work.

In 'In the Evening', the arena in which the childhood narrative takes place is one of the story's major themes and is also concretized in its structure. The story is divided between the ḥeder and the home, and portrays Hofni in each of these arenas, while confronting them. The parental home is depicted as an arena of boyhood of no less value than the traditional one of the ḥeder. What is more, the effectiveness of the home in Hofni's world is immeasurably greater. As I have pointed out, the aggadic tale recounted by his mother as a bedtime story was an initiation event which spurred Hofni to crucial decisions. The evening ḥeder, on the other hand, left him mostly with a sense of boredom. Another level on which Feierberg transformed the narrative of childhood concerns the nature of this narrative: the Tales of Hofni are not typical plot-driven stories—the external development of the plot is of minor significance, while by contrast the internal drama taking place in the mind of Hofni the child hero is central. For example, 'In the Evening' describes a day in Hofni's life, which is divided between his evening ḥeder study and his mother's bedtime aggadic tale. On the story's realistic material plane there are 'small' everyday occurrences which add up to a narrative that could be characterized as 'a day of small things'. But the impression that these events left on Hofni receives expansive and elaborate treatment. 'The Amulet' also revolves around a daily occurrence in the life of a child and a family—Hofni suffered from nightmares and could not sleep and his father took him to be cured by a rabbi adept in kabbalah. Here too, the chief events are Hofni's feelings and experiences. In 'The Calf', the narrative revolves around a domestic incident: Hofni learned that his parents' cow had borne a calf. The calf filled his heart with joy, a joy which was then shattered when he learned that it was to be slaughtered. The majority of the story is a description of 9-year-old Hofni's thoughts and feelings in the face of the harshness of a world in which such things can occur.

These stories describe realistic and seemingly trivial events as they are experienced by a young child who is more impressed by the rebbetzin's act of illuminating the *ḥeder* with a candle than by the rabbi's stern demeanour or his blows. The way daily events are experienced in the child's consciousness constitutes their essential narrative. The Tales of Hofni thus constitute a new kind of narrative: firstly, because the action resolves around events in the life of a child which in earlier fiction of this type had not been seen as central; secondly, because the main action takes place in the child's interior world. Feierberg also used this shift as an artistic device: he created a poetics which rested on subjective experiences and the refraction of 'objective' reality. The child was the conduit of this extreme form of subjectivization:

I, Hofni, loved to stand at such times on a bench by the window of the heder and look out; I loved to watch the spray and the pockmarks that formed on the surface of the puddles when the rain spattered down on them; I loved to look at the doleful faces of the people as they fought their best with the flagstones and planks of wood that had been strewn about to make footpaths... I stood still and stared straight ahead. There was nothing that I wanted, nothing that I felt, nothing else that mattered in the whole world.[31]

Another unique aspect of the Tales of Hofni is their mode of delivery. The stories are narrated by Hofni, the child protagonist, in the first person. This has implications for the plot, which is subject to the point of view and the vacillations of the observing and reporting child. The very act of entrusting the story to the child protagonist is a decision of tremendous importance. First of all, this is an act of constituting the subject—for the narrator is the one who controls the point of view, artistic materials, and language. In other words, being made the narrator endows the child with power. Secondly, it reflects a recognition of the child's powers of reflection along with a willingness to contend with its limitations. In Hofni's case, the stories yield to the impassioned, sometimes fragmented, indecisive, non-perspectival character of his gaze, without 'filling out' the picture with broader background knowledge. On the contrary, they use the narrating child's gaze as a device that validates his extremely personal observation of an apparently familiar reality.

Boyhood in the Tales of Hofni is thus transformed on three levels: it moves the arena in which the action takes place from the *ḥeder* to the home and from the father to the mother, it diverts the focus from the 'outside' to the 'inside', and finally it makes the child's point of view central. This transformation, along with the fragmented structure of the stories, established a poetics of childhood whose essence is a turn towards the child as an observer and towards the way in which he experiences his surrounding reality.

In this respect, as Hamutal Bar-Yosef has pointed out, this is a realistic description of childhood.[32] Nevertheless, it is clear that Feierberg's achievements in rendering childhood in a realistic way are not devoid of a bias that favours specific characteristics of childhood: they emphasize imagination and feeling, fear and wonderment, an intense subjection of the self to impressions, with simultaneous powers of observation and reflection. In other words, the outlook is Romantic, centred on internal experience which nonetheless contains an element of sober realism and rationality.

The turn towards the child's consciousness is also an artistic device: by adopting the Romantic notion of the child as a being endowed with sensitivity, imagination, subjective perception, and interiority, Feierberg used the child figure as a means for revealing and understanding the life of the psyche. His is a crucial contribution to constituting the narrative of the self, in the sense of 'interiority', as forged by the child. It was this self-conscious attitude which privileged the experiences of childhood that Feierberg saw as central to his literary goals, as he described them in his letter to Ahad Ha'am.

Feierberg's attempt to allow the Jewish child to speak 'from within himself' was pioneering—he sought to explore Jewish identity through the figure of a child and expanded Hebrew prose into new regions of consciousness and psychology. He thus deepened and enriched the representation of the child and childhood as well as the narrative possibilities of writing from alternative and marginal points of view. The child-subject that he created was a national subject in every aspect. There was an attempt to break through into some kind of independent 'interiority', but this essence was composed of Jewish materials and was constantly caught up in the power relations of current and historical Jewish realities, with Jewish aspirations and struggles.

Conclusion

What connects these three artists—Gintsburg, Abramovitsh, and Feierberg—is a process of transition from a distant to a more immediate point of view, from the depiction of a child as an object to a subjectivization involving progressively greater detail. During the first half of the nineteenth century Jewish children were represented chiefly as social products, as unformed, and as victims. From mid-century onwards they were increasingly perceived as a topic for reflection and enquiry, around which accumulated a form of knowledge and sentiment that became a discourse of childhood. Towards the end of the century children were represented 'from within themselves' for the first time: they and their voices were entrusted with the role of narrator, their points of view and consciousnesses shaped the narrative world and the type of knowledge and experience constituted within it. This focus is also related to shifts in aesthetic attitudes, which were not necessarily indebted to perceptions of childhood but which had implications for the poetics of writing childhood. The literature of the Haskalah was for the most part neoclassicist, and to the extent that it dealt with children it tended to identify them with a specific trait and to distance the gaze. Childhood served this literature as an allegorical representation of a general but limited essence. Abramovitsh's probing and satirical realism was interested in the child and observed him at a distance. Feierberg, influenced by Romanticism and realism, shifted the gaze to the child himself and gave him a voice. Throughout the entire century the subjectivization of the child figure and the interest in childhood years carried the double burden of the new European developments in this area: the child slowly became constituted as a subject with rights, as an individual of psychological complexity capable of personal expression, and at the same time as a signifier in the symbolic national discourse.

In conclusion, the appearance of representations of children and childhood in Hebrew literature stemmed from an elaborate and complex web of themes. No single explanation can be given for the marginal presence of childhood in pre-modern Hebrew literature, and no single motive explains the awakening interest in this topic in nineteenth-century Jewish and Hebrew literature. The discourse of childhood in Hebrew literature emerged through a gradual and cumulative process, which was intertwined with the profound concerns raised by the modernization processes taking place in Jewish society. The basic argument set out in this chapter is that children served as a conduit for the reformation of discussions about Jewish identity. This argument is spelled out in the many dimensions that reveal how childhood was transformed from a marginal and neglected life chapter to a central component of self-understanding. The very appearance of childhood in Hebrew literature was related to the impact of the Enlightenment on Jewish society, to the social status it accorded to children, and to the links it nurtured between memory and identity. Childhood also served as an instrument for the critique of the Enlightenment's rationalism, following the influence of Rousseau, Romanticism, and the privileging of the singular, original, emotional subject, modelled on the 'child'. The Romantic perception of childhood, and especially the discovery that childhood was the formative period of life and simultaneously life's edenic epoch, had a crucial impact on the repositioning of children and childhood at the centre of culture. These ideas received expression in Hebrew narrative prose as early as the first third of the nineteenth century and went on to occupy a central place towards the end of the century.

Under the influence of Romanticism, childhood emerged as a topic for the development of autobiographical writing in Hebrew and for the new conception of the act of writing as a constitutive tool of selfhood. It played a role in the processes of individuation and secularization and at the same time served as a symbolic representation of the collective national subject. An additional axis that is connected to these developments is the role that children and childhood fulfilled in the development of aesthetic, literary, generic, and linguistic attitudes; making childhood central in autobiography and fiction stimulated and honed questions about language and representation—questions intensified by the condition of Hebrew as a non-spoken language. In addition, writing about children and childhood raised acute questions about the role of gender in how reality is represented in literature. Certainly, a critical feminist look at the nexus of gender and childhood exposes the real and symbolic connection between the marginality of women and the marginality of children, and demonstrated the limits in contemporary representations of their position. Above all, a critical reading of literary representations of children constitutes a powerful tool for exposing the ideological structures that shaped the processes of modernization in Jewish society and is thus an unexpected means of illuminating foundational concerns that motivated the emergence of modern Hebrew literature.

Translated from the Hebrew by Ilana Goldberg

Notes

1 R. Preger-Wagner, *Hayeled halaz ani hu velo aḥer: yeladim viyeladot basiporet ha'ivrit bame'ah hatesha-esreh* (Tel Aviv, 2018).
2 Philippe Ariés pointed out that the concept of childhood was applied first of all to boys. He referred to historical reality, but gender bias was also a feature of literary representations of children (see P. Ariés, *Centuries of Childhood: A Social History of Family Life*, trans. R. Baldick (New York, 1962), 61). 'The child' in nineteenth-century Hebrew fiction is also clearly a boy. Very few girls appear in the margins, but as secondary characters, who remain underdeveloped, partial, and blurry. The gender bias illustrates the construction of the child figure and the limitations of literary representation: The literary child figure, with all its innovation, replicated the prevailing perceptions of gender in Jewish and general society in the nineteenth century.
3 M. A. Gintsburg, *Avi'ezer: viduyo shel maskil*, ed. S. Werses (Jerusalem, 2009). Gintsburg began to write it in 1828. The first seven chapters were published in 1844, while he was still alive, but the entire work was only published in 1864, eighteen years after his premature death in 1846 (see S. Werses, 'Darkhei ha'otobiyografyah bitekufat hahaskalah', in id. (ed.), *Megamot vetsurot besifrut hahaskalah* (Jerusalem, 1990), 249–60).
4 See Rousseau's reflexive description of the act of writing: 'I did not promise the public a great personage: I promised to describe myself as I am, and to know me in my advanced age it was necessary to have known me in my youth' (J. J. Rousseau, *The Confessions*, bk 4). On the modern concept of interiority and its relationship to the narrative of childhood, see C. Steedman, *Strange Dislocations: Childhood and the Idea of Human Interiority, 1780–1930* (Cambridge, Mass., 1995), 4–5.
5 Werses, 'Darkhei ha'otobiyografyah bitekufat hahaskalah', 251. Maimon wrote his autobiography in German (*Salomon Maimons Lebensgeschichte* (Berlin, 1792/3); Eng. trans.: *The Autobiography of Solomon Maimon: The Complete Translation*, ed. Y. Y. Melamed and A. P. Socher, trans. P. Reitter (Princeton, NJ, 2018)). Fishel Lahover noted the influence of Rousseau's *Confessions* on Maimon in his introduction to the Hebrew translation (see F. Lahover, 'Shelomoh maimon vesefer toledotav', in S. Maimon, *Sefer ḥayei shelomoh maimon*, trans. Y. L. Baruch (Tel Aviv, 1953), 9–50: 24–5).
6 For an extended discussion of *Avi'ezer* as the starting point for the discourse of childhood in Hebrew literature, see Preger-Wagner, *Hayeled halaz ani hu velo aḥer*, 62–93; for a discussion of *Avi'ezer* in the context of the emergence of Jewish autobiography, see M. Moseley, *Being for My Self Alone: Origins of Jewish Autobiography* (Stanford, Calif., 2006), 336–44.
7 A. Mintz, *'Banished from Their Father's Table': Loss of Faith and Hebrew Autobiography* (Bloomington, Ind., 1989), 6; see M. L. Lilienblum, *Ḥatot ne'urim*, Ketavim otobiyografiyim, 1 (Jerusalem, 1970). Of *Ḥatot ne'urim*, Avraham Shaanan wrote: 'In several respects it is a link in the same chain of autobiographies of which Mordekhai Aharon Gintsburg is one of the most important. In truth Gintsburg exhibits much greater narrative and descriptive talent than Lilienblum. With the perspective of time the famous chapters of *Avi'ezer* appear to be the foundation stones for the development of Hebrew fictional realism, which cannot be said about Lilienblum's work' (A. Shaanan, *Hasifrut ha'ivrit haḥadashah lizerameiha*, 2 vols. (Tel Aviv, 1962), ii. 30).
8 Y. L. Gordon, 'Al nehar kevar', in *Kitvei yehudah leib gordon*, vol. ii: *Prozah* (Tel Aviv, 1960), 267–90.
9 A. B. Gottlober,' Zikhronot miyemei ne'urai', *Zikhronot umasaot*, 1 (Jerusalem, 1976).

10 Samuel David Luzzatto also wrote an autobiography, *Toledot shadal*, which was published in *Hamagid* between 1857 and 1862. However, as Werses noted, the documentary element overwhelmed the life story, and for the most part this work enumerates Luzzatto's spiritual achievements and offers an interpretation of his works. This trend is also apparent in the description of his childhood, even though in his letter he articulated a recognition of the importance of childhood for understanding the adult person. See Werses, 'Darkhei ha'otobiyografyah bitekufat hahaskalah', 254–5.

11 Nimrod Aloni concisely described the Enlightenment's educational philosophy according to the features of education put forward by Kant: development of the child's bodily, mental, and moral faculties and training them to adhere to the path of rationality (N. Aloni, 'Aliyato unefilato shel haḥinukh hahumanisti: mehaklasi lapostmoderni', in I. Gur Ze'ev (ed.), *Ḥinukh ba'idan hapostmoderniti* (Jerusalem, 1956), 13–42: 24–5).

12 A. A. Alryyes, *Original Subjects: The Child, the Novel, and the Nation* (Cambridge, Mass., 2001), 15–16, 117–27.

13 M. Zalkin, '"Et hadar hateva lo yade'u ve'et tekhelet hashamayim lo ra'u?" yaldut baḥevrah hayehudit hamasortit bemizraḥ eiropah', *Zmanim*, 102 (2008), 58–65.

14 Lilienblum, *Ḥatot ne'urim*, 84. On the way in which Lilienblum turned Gintsburg's story into a representative one, see Mintz, 'Banished from Their Father's Table', 29–30.

15 Mishnah *Avot* 3: 10.

16 Ephraim Kanarfogel discussed the interpretations of this *mishnah* and its influence until the Middle Ages. Its influence can be assumed to have persisted until Gintsburg's own time, otherwise he would not have needed to make any apologies (see E. Kanarfogel, *Haḥinukh vehaḥevrah hayehudit be'eiropah hatsefonit biyemei habeinayim*, trans. R. Bar Ilan (Tel Aviv, 2003), 48–50).

17 Thus, for example, in his story 'In the Evening', Feierberg upset the convention of the story of boyhood in the *ḥeder* and created a confrontation between the *ḥeder* and the home and, in effect, shifted the centre of gravity of childhood experience to the home and the mother (M. Z. Feierberg, 'Ba'erev', *Hashiloaḥ*, 4/24 (1897/8), 501–10; repr. in *Kitvei m. z. fai'erberg* (Tel Aviv, 1951/2), 39–55; Eng. trans.: 'In the Evening', in *Whither? and Other Stories*, trans. H. Halkin (Philadelphia, Pa., 1973), 81–105).

18 H. N. Bialik, 'Yotser hanosaḥ', in *Kol kitvei* (Tel Aviv, 1953), 245–6.

19 For an extensive discussion of Abramovitsh as the creator of the Jewish child in Hebrew narrative, see Preger-Wagner, *Hayeled halaz ani hu velo aḥer*, 98–178.

20 S. Y. Abramovitsh, 'Mikhtav al devar haḥinukh', *Hamagid*, 15 July 1857, pp. 121–2.

21 S. Y. Abramovitsh, *Bayamim hahem*, in *Kol kitvei mendele mokher sefarim* (Tel Aviv, 1966), 251–80; Yid. edn.: Mendele Moykher Sforim, *Shloyme reb khayims* (Warsaw, 1936); Eng. trans.: Mendele Moykher Sforim, *Of Bygone Days*, in *A Shtetl and Other Yiddish Novellas*, trans. R. R. Wisse (New York, 1973), 254–358.

22 Steedman, *Strange Dislocations*, 3.

23 J. Plotz, *Romanticism and the Vocation of Childhood* (New York, 2001), 3–4.

24 S. Y. Abramovitsh, *Be'emek habakha*, in *Kol kitvei mendele mokher sefarim*, 143–250; Yid. edn.: *Dos vintshfingerl* (Warsaw, 1865); Eng. trans.: *The Wishing Ring*, trans. M. Wex (New York, 2003).

25 Abramovitsh, *Be'emek habakha*, 153; see id., *The Wishing Ring*, 20–1.

26 Abramovitsh, *Bayamim hahem*, 257; Mendele Moykher Sforim, *Of Bygone Days*, 268–9.

27 Feierberg, 'Ba'erev'; id., 'Hakame'a', *Hashiloaḥ*, 4/22 (1897/8), 336–41; repr. in *Kitvei m. z. fai'erberg*, 56–64; Eng. trans.: 'The Amulet', in *Whither? and Other Stories*, 106–18; id.,

'Ha'egel', *Hashiloaḥ*, 2/11 (1896/7), 433–6; repr. in *Kitvei m. z. fai'erberg*, 128–32; Eng. trans.: 'The Calf', in *Whither? and Other Stories*, 73–80. For an extensive discussion of Jewish childhood in Feierberg's work, see Preger-Wagner, *Hayeled halaz ani hu velo aḥer*, 227–52.

28 M. Z. Feierberg, letter to Ahad Ha'am, 5 Jan. 1898, in *Kitvei m. z. fai'erberg*, 184.

29 Hamutal Bar Yosef identified the bildungsromanesque character of the Tales of Hofni (H. Bar Yosef, 'Eizeh min romantikan hayah fai'erberg?', *Bikoret ufarshanut*, 23 (1988), 87–116, esp. 103).

30 In 'Whither?', the last story written by Feierberg, he returned to the biographical structure and father–son relations (Feierberg, M. Z. 'Le'an', in *Kitvei m. z. fai'erberg*, 65–125; Eng. trans.: 'Whither?', in *Whither? and Other Stories*, 121–215).

31 Feierberg, 'In the Evening', 83; see id., 'Ba'erev', in *Kitvei m. z. fai'erberg*, 40.

32 Bar-Yosef, 'Eizeh min romantikan hayah fai'erberg?', 88.

The Beautiful Manor House
Glimpses of Jewish Childhood in the Galician Countryside

YEHOSHUA ECKER

The legal reforms of 1848 in the Habsburg monarchy led to the emergence of the phenomenon of Jewish landownership. By 1902 there were 532 Jewish-owned estates in Galicia as against 2,372 owned by Christians. The diary of Renia (Aurelia) Spiegel provides a unique picture of coming of age in one of the families of the increasingly acculturated Jewish landowners in Galicia, examining the social and spatial interactions in its social network. It raises larger issues. The challenges of raising children in a place with no Jewish communal infrastructure forced parents to decide what their priorities were and to take active steps if they wanted to provide a Jewish way of life and a Jewish education for their children. At the same time, childhood in a manor provided new opportunities away from communal pressures, making it possible for parents to choose other cultural and educational options. For children, growing up on a rural estate became the dominant experience of their childhood and framed their lives in a unique manner.

FOURTEEN-YEAR-OLD Renia (Aurelia) Spiegel began to write a diary on 31 January 1939 soon after she went to live with her grandparents in the city of Przemyśl. She had previously lived with her parents and younger sister on a secluded rural estate. Renia now experienced an abrupt change in her family setting: not only did she leave behind the home she had known for most of her life, but her mother and younger sister moved to Warsaw, while her father stayed behind in their old dwelling place. Renia decided to record her recent memories of happier times:

I used to live in a beautiful manor house on the Dniester River. I loved it there. I think these were so far the happiest days of my life. There were storks on old linden trees, apples glistened in the orchard, and I had a garden with neat, charming rows of flowers . . . All that remain are memories, sweet and lovely . . . I miss the house where we all lived together . . . the white manor house on the Dniester River.[1]

Thousands of Jewish children experienced manorial life and the realities of the country estates which Renia described as her childhood paradise. By 1939 there were hundreds of rural estates in Poland which were owned by Jews, hundreds more held on lease, and many thousands of Jews who made their living as administrators or managers of such estates. The largest group of Jewish landowners, leaseholders, and rural workers was found in the former Habsburg Galicia, where Renia and her family lived. Here, a growing number of leaseholders, managers, administrators, and owners had established themselves, particularly after the legal reforms of 1848.

The estate environment presented unique challenges and possibilities for Jewish parents and children. It constituted a social and physical space very different from the more common Jewish community settings in towns, cities, and villages. On the one hand, the challenges of raising children in a place with no Jewish community infrastructure forced parents to decide what their priorities were and to take active steps if they wanted to provide a Jewish way of life and a Jewish education for their children. On the other, living on an estate provided new opportunities away from community pressures and made it possible for parents to choose other cultural and educational options. From the point of view of the children, growing up on rural estates and in manor houses would be a formative experience that framed their lives in different ways from how their parents might have wished. Subject to the decisions of their parents, with limited agency of their own, their responses and experiences in the formative years of life are not well known and difficult to discover. This chapter seeks to examine these responses and experiences as reflected in Renia Spiegel's diary.

While thousands of Jewish children spent part of their lives on rural estates, written accounts of this way of life are few. In particular, there are only a handful of published memoirs and autobiographies. Among the better known are those by Oskar Kofler (1897–1979), born and raised on his family's estate of Petlikowce, and Karl Maramorosch (1915–2016), born on his family's estate of Soroki but raised and educated in Kołomyja (after finding refuge in Vienna during the First World War).[2] These offer clear descriptions of family life on rural estates: when children were raised on the estate and when the parents chose to raise their children in a nearby town in order to alleviate the challenges of remote rural life while still making regular trips to the countryside. Both Kofler and Maramorosch wrote their memoirs long after the events they describe, and their recollections are invariably coloured by their later experiences. Whereas some other memoirs do exist, diaries are even rarer: most diaries written by children on rural estates probably did not survive. Indeed, a full diary, written over an extended period of time from the point of view of a child who grew up on an estate, is a rarity. For the most part, children's points of view are absent and their immediate, unmitigated voices unheard. In this respect, Renia Spiegel's diary is unique and valuable, worthy of analysis in its own right.

Renia's Diary

Renia's diary was written close to the events she described and was initiated by a change in her personal situation brought about by the complexities of life in the countryside. While the diary continues into the war period and ends when Renia was killed in Przemyśl on 30 July 1942, it was not a direct product of the war. It deals with many matters in Renia's adolescent life. While the estate quickly fades into the background as more urgent and immediate matters emerge, it is always present, even if unmentioned. Renia recognized that life in the manor house had a great impact on her, and returned again and again to examine her memories and feelings about it and her life there before her move to Przemyśl. Leaving the manor house did not remove it from Renia's life. On the contrary, she remained connected with the world of the rural estates through family ties, as well as through her inner world and thoughts. Renia recorded in the diary her continued interactions with the estate, her changing attitudes and shifting viewpoints. These developed over time as she continued to reflect on her life on the estate, longing for it and analysing it.

Renia's published diary has the rare benefit of having an additional, second, voice, that of her younger sister Elizabeth (Ariana) Bellak, that can be heard in the 'Preface', 'Afterword', and notes.[3] Elizabeth shared many of Renia's experiences and knew most of the people Renia mentions. The combination of Renia's diary and Elizabeth's memoir creates a text about a shared childhood in two voices, one immediate, active, recorded in real time, addressing an audience of one; the other mature, retrospective, written in response to the first, with many decades' hindsight, addressing a much wider audience. A growing mass of additional material, including a documentary film[4] and other filmed and printed interviews with Elizabeth, multiplies Elizabeth's accounts and refracts her voice.[5] As the lives of Renia and Elizabeth unfold in the diary and the memoir, the nature of the idyllic childhood Renia described gradually emerges.

Elizabeth clarified many details which appear in the diary, giving names and dates and identifying places. She provided the name and location of the estate where she was born and lived as well as the estate her parents previously lived on, where Renia was born:

My name was Ariana . . . I lived with my father Bernard, my mother Róża and my sister Aurelia—Renia . . . My sister, Renia Spiegel, was born on 18 June 1924, in Uhryńkowce, in the Tarnopol province in south-eastern Poland . . . I came along on 18 November 1930 . . . By then, my family had moved to an estate . . . called Stawki . . . which was near the Dniester River and close to the Romanian border.[6]

We'd lived in a manor house, not a mansion. But we'd been comfortable. We'd had nannies and employees . . . For example, Renia had a nanny named Klara when she and my parents lived on the estate where she'd been born.[7]

The two estates of Uhryńkowce and Stawki played a central role in the lives of the Spiegels, combining the professional, social, and cultural aspects of their family life. These estates were the primary source of their livelihood. Even after the mother and daughters moved from Stawki, Bernard Spiegel continued to run the estate and support his family financially, and later also with food.[8] The estates played a pivotal role also in the upbringing of the two Spiegel girls. The manor house was a comfortable place to grow up in and the estate environment was supportive and nourishing, providing a rich world to explore and to cherish. Renia left Stawki at the age of 14, Elizabeth at 8, and their memories capture their experiences at these ages. They also left out important parts of the story, which also reflects their youth. Still, as Renia's diary shows, the small world of the Spiegel sisters encompassed quite a wide variety of experiences and locations and was connected with much wider circles.

Renia and Elizabeth's family belonged to the large group of Jewish medium-sized landowners, estate managers, administrators, and leaseholders. Although their parents were not large landowners, the sisters still experienced the benefits of rural life, its remoteness and at the same time various connections to urban and cultural centres, the privileges of life in the manor house, and the realities of life on an estate. The glimpses of the sisters' childhoods in the diary and the texts published with it show how these estates were incorporated into the wider worlds of villages, towns, and cities. They will serve here as a prism for exploring the development of local estates, local and regional interactions, and wider family networks.

Jews on Estates

Rural estates were one of the main engines of the Galician economy and the location of many industrial enterprises.[9] They formed a relatively independent space, not subject to the authority of the villages or towns in their vicinity. These estates dated back to not-so-distant feudal times. Historically they were the property of the local nobility, and they functioned as revered and privileged units of production, inherited, bought, and sold mostly by the nobility. Each estate had its own name, including those newly created by chipping off parts of older and larger estates, and an administrative registration number recorded by the Austrian authorities. The prestige associated with them lingered even after the nobility lost much of its political and economic power.[10]

While most Galician estates were not owned by Jews, the number of Jewish landowners grew significantly from the middle of the nineteenth century. The numbers presented in different studies do not always coincide, since they list either the number of Jewish landowners or the number of estates owned by Jews, but both lists show a continuous growth of Jewish landownership. There were at least nineteen individual Jewish owners in 1855, and thirty-eight in 1861, in all of Galicia. A detailed study found twenty-nine Jewish owners in forty locations, including twenty partnerships, in 1851, in Western Galicia alone, which suggests the numbers in Eastern Galicia were even higher. Later numbers indicate a faster rate of estate acquisition in the next two decades, slowing down towards the turn of the century: 324 Jewish owners in 1874; 289 Galician estates with Jewish owners in 1876; 418 Jewish owners in 1889; 532 Jewish owners as against 2,372 Christian owners in 1902; at least 561 Jewish owners in 1912. The 1931 census revealed 464 Jewish-owned estates in Galicia, whereas the number of Jewish-owned estates in the other parts of the newly created Polish state was much smaller: 145 in central Poland and 161 in eastern Poland. The fall in the number of Jewish landowners in Galicia also reflects shifts in ownership and the destruction of estates during the First World War.[11]

Prosperous Jewish families could legally become estate owners as a result of a long process that had culminated in the Fundamental Laws on the general rights of citizens that became part of the Austrian December Constitution of 1867. Promising equal rights to all citizens, including Jews, left no legal way to discriminate against Jews wishing to purchase landed estates. Earlier stages of this process had seen individual licences granted to specific Jews, a short period after 1848 when Jews were allowed to buy landed estates in Galicia before this was put on hold in 1852, and the period after 1860 in which permission was given to individuals based on education and profession. The 1867 legal reforms opened the gates to a large number of new Jewish landowners in Galicia.[12] While Jews were involved with the Galician countryside and the running of rural estates long before the reforms of 1848 and 1867, these legal changes brought increased opportunities. New respectability could be found in owning rural estates and in performing the social functions of the old nobility. The common expectation was for a long-term association between family and estate, securing the foundations of economic stability and social prestige.

Many estates that did not have Jewish owners were run by Jewish managers or leaseholders. Generally, about half of all estates were regularly leased out, and about half or more of those were leased by Jews. This added hundreds of Jewish leaseholders whose legal position was different from that of landowners but who generally lived on and operated the estates in the same manner. A study of 1,620 leaseholders of entire estates in 1893 found 783, or about half, to be Jewish. Of these, 718 were leased from Christian owners, while only 65 leased from Jewish owners (the geographical division was 165 and 13 in Western Galicia, 553 and 52 in Eastern Galicia). Of 4,000 estate administrators on large estates, approximately 30 per cent (about 1,300) were Jewish. The 1931 census data indicated that some 1,658 Jews were hired employees on Galician estates in agricultural professions, compared to about 1,220 in other parts of Poland (not including other employees, such as accountants or teachers).[13]

The actual number of Jewish landowners was small compared to the entire Jewish population of Galicia, and many of them were part of an increasingly cohesive social group, with intricate webs of kinship, marriage, and partnership. In addition, they introduced a growing number of other Jews into the estates and the Galician countryside. Jewish owners, managers, and leaseholders, and the large number of Jewish workers and employees they brought to the estates, formed a visible and influential social group that lived on, worked on, or frequented the rural estates. They would entertain guests and relatives, business associates and investors, contractors and developers, friends and holiday-makers, who could in this way regularly experience at first hand the various aspects of life on these estates. Family members, relatives, in-laws, partners, investors, managers, leaseholders, and various other workers, employees, and their families would follow, numbering thousands of households and linking the estates to the wider Jewish population in Galicia. Over decades several generations of owners and employees fostered a sense of belonging and attachment to rural estates and held on to memories of childhoods, careers, and entire lifetimes spent in the Galician countryside.

Estates as Sites of Jewish Childhood

Estates were unique sites of Jewish family life in general and Jewish childhood in particular. They constituted a separate space with particular social and physical features. Several aspects differentiated them from other spaces inhabited by Jews: estates were not subordinate to nearby towns and villages but were independent units. They were large agricultural facilities and usually included gardens, fields, pastures, forests, and other natural features such as ponds. Their population was usually much smaller than the village's, and the social hierarchy was very clear.

The combination of social and environmental factors that set childhood experiences on country estates apart is delineated in the Spiegel sisters' narratives and echoes many other voices. The most visible features in their descriptions include the manor house, the agricultural cycle, the farm animals, the wider surrounding nature, the social realities of workers and employees, and the particular trajectories of individual children within these worlds. These combined to create a world clearly distinct from Jewish childhood in large cities, small towns, and even villages.

Generally, most Jewish-owned estates in Galicia were smaller than those owned by the nobility. Some families and individuals held several estates which might be concentrated in one area, making up a very large tract of land; others leased or managed large estates owned by noblemen. From a child's point of view, the size of the properties made an unforgettable impression, especially the sense that this large area was available for gardening, playing, and exploring. Comparing the estate to other places made these differences abundantly clear. Both Renia and Elizabeth echo this sentiment in different ways: Renia in invoking the trees and flower beds and the view of the Dniester river; Elizabeth in stressing the many hectares of land the estate occupied.[14]

There was a wide range of manorial residences, from modest structures to veritable palaces. Even on smaller estates, the manor house, where the owner lived, was a substantial edifice in comparison with the regular village cottages and many town houses and apartments. On larger estates, the residences of their owners, leaseholders, or managers were even more imposing. The Spiegels' residence was somewhat modest, hence Renia's use of the Polish term *dworek* (little manor house). Modest as it may have been, the *dworek* which Renia longed for formed the centre of the sisters' life as well as that of the Stawki estate.

As the residence of the owners, leaseholders, or managers, the manor house was the central feature of the estate. It was larger, more elaborate, and more conspicuous than most other structures in the small world of the estate. It would often have modern amenities such as a radio, a record player, a telephone, and a library. A car might be parked outside, and a carriage and horses would be available to serve the needs of the residents. When the residents were Jewish, it constituted a privileged Jewish space, contrasting strikingly with the many non-Jewish households of the estate and neighbouring villages. It situated the residents in the upper echelons of local society and thus set the rural estate apart from most of the other spaces in cities, towns, and villages, where the Jewish presence, even if numerous or outnumbering other groups, did not enjoy a central social or symbolic position.

While Renia mostly recalled the manor house with fond emotions, Elizabeth added a more general description of the estate, pointing out those elements that were most vivid in her memory. Apart from the house and the size of the estate, she briefly noted the livestock, the farm products, and the natural world within which the estate was located:

We had these ponds, and because of the ponds it was called Stawki (*stawek* is Polish for pond). There was nothing around except our house... We had beautiful flowers in front of the house and they bloomed and gave nice smell... We had horses, we had chickens, and geese, and cows... We had pigs.

We'd had a chicken coop and a place to store bushels and bushels of wheat. We'd grown sugar beets that we sold to the factories for sugar. But most important, we'd lived on acres of fertile land.[15]

This natural world was also what Renia missed when she was forced to live in the town: 'To think it's May already, May, and I still haven't seen a tree in bloom, haven't smelled fields waking up, my fields.'[16]

Stawki, like numerous other rural estates, was a private property in which the occupants of the manor house stood at the top of the social ladder. In Stawki this was the Spiegel family. Unsurprisingly, Elizabeth's accounts reflect her father's central role in running all aspects of life in Stawki. As Elizabeth also recalled, the interaction with the workers and assertion of authority was a daily routine, and the children witnessed these relationships regularly and from an early age:

My dad... was busy doing what he'd always done—growing and harvesting wheat, tending to his sugar beets and overseeing the peasants who worked for him, many of whom were Ukrainian and lived in the little town of Tłuste [Tovste], which was a few miles from our house... My father... used to wake up early, put on his riding pants and leather boots, and walk out to check on the animals and workers.

I used to go sometimes with my dad to the fields... he used to look at things, how things were going.[17]

Life Outside the Estate

Estate life often had a mobile character, as the residents had limited access to some commodities and to the more developed life in towns in which they wished to participate, and they felt the need to leave the estate regularly for these purposes. Manorial life was therefore associated with travel to visit friends and relations, to go on holiday or to shop, to see to the needs of the estate, to sign contracts, to deliver livestock. This frequent travel distinguished life on an estate from that in villages, towns, or cities. Family visits usually involved travel, as most families did not reside in a single location in the countryside and many were originally from towns and cities, like Róża Spiegel (née Finkel), Renia, and Elizabeth's mother, who came from Przemyśl. As the move from Uhryńkowce to Stawki also shows, there could be professional reasons for moving from one estate to another. In the case of leaseholders and administrators, the end of the lease or the termination of employment would usually mean a move to another estate.

The family photographs that accompany the published diary and are presented in the documentary film and online come from Elizabeth Bellak's own collection. They indicate the availability of a camera and tell a vivid story of mobility. One photograph shows Renia on horseback in Zaleszczyki, a popular resort town. Another shows the sisters participating in a harvest celebration there. The image of the sisters dressed in special costumes greeting the mayor of Zaleszczyki captures their visibility in local social life. Also recorded are other visits to the town and to vineyards and farms in the area. Elizabeth recalled regular visits to nearby Tłuste and to Zaleszczyki.[18] The photographs also record more distant destinations, such as the town of Skole and family visits to Przemyśl.[19] Most of the trips recorded are for pleasure or to visit family.

Another important reason for travel by Jewish children from rural estates was education. Access to good education or professional training meant leaving the estate regularly or for an extended period of time. In this respect the links between rural estates and the most central cultural hubs were well established. The Spiegel sisters' lives illustrate this well. As Elizabeth related, the sisters exhibited a talent for reading poems in public, a talent that was clearly nurtured and encouraged as they were growing up. Their mother had ambitious plans for her daughters and pursued the opportunities this presented in the most prestigious venues. Elizabeth remembered a trip to Lwów to audition for a radio show which earned the sisters a spot reciting poetry. She noted that Renia decided to devote herself entirely to writing, but Elizabeth was taken by her mother to other auditions in Warsaw, which very soon established her as a child star. Elizabeth and her mother moved from Stawki to Warsaw, where she worked as an actress in the theatre and acted in films on location throughout Poland, relying on private tutors for her education. Renia was sent to the school her mother had attended under the care of her mother's parents and was in contact with many of her mother's childhood and school friends.[20]

Elizabeth's move from Stawki to Lwów and to Warsaw was easily accomplished, as was Renia's to a middle school in Przemyśl. When she began writing her diary, she attended a selective school in the city and was ranked at the top of her year, while Elizabeth was a fledgling child star in radio, theatre, and film, the 'Polish Shirley Temple'. Nothing suggests that their upbringing in the countryside in any way hindered their education or limited their opportunities. On the contrary, it seems to have been of great advantage. Remote as they were on the map of pre-war Poland, Uhryńkowce and Stawki served as an important stage in life trajectories that could lead to Lwów, Przemyśl, or Warsaw and to prospects of a successful career.

However, these opportunities had to be sought outside the small world of the estate. Parents who were raising children in the countryside had to make conscious decisions about their children's education and future career, because they needed to bring suitable tutors to the estate or send their children away to elementary schools, boarding schools, gymnasia, universities, or other institutions for vocational or professional training. Special talents had to be pursued in cultural hubs, usually in the big metropolitan centres of Lwów or Warsaw or, in earlier decades, Czernowitz, Vienna, Berlin, and other European cities.

Leaving Stawki coincided with the need to make a decision about the sisters' formal education. Their mother probably decided that in order to obtain a better education, her daughters would need to leave the estate. This also coincided with her decision to separate from her husband (she would later plan to dissolve the marriage). The move from Stawki was made more abrupt and traumatic for Renia because of Elizabeth's budding career and the better opportunities for her in Warsaw, which led to her separation from her mother and sister.[21] The clash between the expectations and limited possibilities of life on the estate and the desire to seize in full the opportunities which presented themselves in the big city may also have played a part. This tension clearly also existed in other countryside settings. Róża Spiegel had grown up in a city, studied in leading universities outside Poland (Berlin and Vienna), experienced a sophisticated and modern lifestyle, and was a newcomer to estate life.[22] Her hopes and expectations may not have coincided with what she found there. Bernard Spiegel's views on his daughters' education remain more difficult to characterize. Understanding his own background and his involvement in farming and estate management in the countryside will probably give a better sense of his views on this topic.

Leaving her home in Stawki was one of the factors behind Renia's diary. According to her sister, memories of Stawki seem to have inspired her creative writing—the diary and the poems she incorporated in it.[23] They also provoked Renia's inner discussions about the place of Stawki in her life. These might not have become so evident had she remained on the estate and had her life continued unchanged. At the age of 16, a year and a half after she began her diary and ten months into the war, writing in Soviet-occupied Przemyśl and about to go and see her father in his new home, Renia reviewed and re-evaluated her relationship with the glowing memory of the manor house of Stawki. Reflecting on her current feelings about her life in Stawki and after Stawki, she posed the question: 'I've lived in Stawki. Was I happy there? No, there were worries, Mama was seriously ill, there were money issues, family quarrels and rows, first Daddy, then Mama. My home's fallen apart. Worse still. Arianka went to Warsaw, she struggled there, lost her childhood, it vanished and that was wrong.'[24] In this way, the older and more aware Renia reduces her childhood paradise to a less idealized coming of age, removing the trappings of a beautiful manor house, fields, plants, and nature and focusing on the family relationships within the house, on pressing economic problems, and on the high hopes and aspirations of parents and children.

When she wrote these reflections, the manor house in Stawki had already been confiscated by the new Soviet regime, and the estate was a dream to which she could not return. Accordingly Renia focused her hopes more on having a family home than on resuming her carefree life on the rural estate. These concerns only intensified as she realized her mother was planning a future without her father. She also called into question her mother's decision to remove her sister from her family setting to pursue her career. Later musings even reveal Renia contemplating life as a farmer, which would have subjected her to physical labour and allowed her to avoid thinking at all, reflecting, perhaps, the option her father might have chosen over an urban lifestyle.[25]

Social Interactions: Family, Friends, and Playmates

Bernard Spiegel's past and family background can be partially reconstructed using the post-war testimonies of his few surviving family members, in particular the testimonies of his siblings, Maria (Mania, Manie) Königsberg (née Spiegel) and Mojżesz Szpigiel, recorded between January and March 1948.[26] Although they focus on the period between June 1941 and April 1944, these accounts reveal a wide family network of relatives and in-laws that would have been part of Renia's world. Like Renia's diary, they also leave out many details, particularly about the period before 1939 and the Soviet occupation between September 1939 and June 1941, which is common in accounts collected immediately after the war in communist Poland. They also do not mention all the members of the family by name, which could have a number of causes, including the political atmosphere at the time. They do, however, provide enough information to fill in some of the gaps in Renia's diary and its accompanying commentary. Renia occasionally mentioned the names of a few relatives (and Elizabeth mentions an extended family, most of whom died in the war and as victims of the Holocaust[27]), but the actual family network scattered near and far still requires reconstruction, as does its part in making Stawki what it was. The siblings' testimonies provide a rudimentary account that also points to the family's long involvement in farming and managing rural estates.

In one of her testimonies, Maria Königsberg provides the names of her parents: Henryk Spiegel and Salomea (née Solewiec). It is also possible to extract from the testimonies the names of some of their siblings and some details about their lives and families, though these are not described in any organized way. None of them mentions Bernard by name, which is strange, but he may be mentioned anonymously. Bernard's relatives, as reconstructed from the testimonies, included his eldest brother Markus Spiegel, his wife (Hinda), and their sons Józek and Witek (who all perished); his eldest sister Ewa Wachs (Waks) with her daughter Lila; a brother who was sent to Bełzec (Bernard?); a brother, Mojżesz Szpigiel, and his son Czesław (killed in January 1944, aged 14); and a sister Maria Königsberg, her husband (Hilary Hilel Königsberg, born in Czortków in 1895 to Dawid Königsberg and Paja Steckel) and their son (Edward (Edzio), born March 1937). After the outbreak of war in 1939, most of them found refuge in Horodenka, a town near Tłuste on the other side of the Dniester river. From there they eventually fled to the area of Tłuste, as the pressure of Nazi round-ups intensified between December 1941 and September 1942.[28]

According to his daughter Maria, Henryk Spiegel was 72 years old in 1943. This would place his birth around 1871. He was killed with his two grandchildren in July 1943. The birth dates and places of Henryk Spiegel's children pinpoint his movements. His eldest daughter, Ewa Wachs, was born in or near Lwów in 1895, Mojżesz (Moniek) was born in 1899 in Koszyce in the Rzeszów area, and Maria was born in 1907 in Święte near Radymno. In address directories of the 1920s Henryk Spiegel is registered as the owner of a small estate in Święte (183 hectares). His absence from the record before the First World War implies that he initially worked as a manager or leaseholder. In her testimony, Maria noted that her father was a farmer and recalled that his farm was among the first to provide training to ḥalutsim (prospective emigrants to Palestine) in 1918. This was evidently the farm in Święte. Maria was 11 years old at the time, and this was the one childhood experience she chose to mention in that context. Her siblings were born in different places and evidently spent parts of their childhood in different rural locations.[29]

The Spiegel relatives and in-laws were in the business of running rural estates, as farm managers, leaseholders, and owners. Their life histories demonstrate the kind of mobility experienced in these professions, revealing changes in location and position. Mojżesz Szpigiel gave his profession as farmer. Before the war he had lived in Tłuste and run one of the estates in the area, probably as the manager. Maria and Hilary Königsberg lived in a villa outside Tłuste. Königsberg was also identified as a farmer and had a knowledge of the local estates—before the war he had been a leaseholder and estate owner. Hilel's grandparents (Hersz and Roza Steckel) were leaseholders on the Stary Czortków estate, and his relatives were leaseholders of several estates near Tłuste, some of which were held in the family for several decades. Kos (Kohos) Königsberg (his brother) was the leaseholder in Hołowczyńce, Osias Stöckel in Śniatynka, Jakob Steckel (or Stöckel) in Różanówka. More distant relatives and in-laws, for example the Albin and Weisglas families, owned their own estates.[30]

Renia Spiegel thus had a wide circle of relatives and in-laws on other estates and farms between Tłuste and Zaleszczyki and beyond. Most are not mentioned in her diary. In the Przemyśl context they were not relevant. Those she does mention are not mentioned in the testimonies of her relatives from Tłuste, with the exception of her cousin Lila.[31] Lila Wachs, whom Renia called 'cousin and friend . . . the companion of my childhood', survived the war with her mother, Ewa, near Tłuste. Their post-war documents indicate that Lila and her mother were living with the Spiegels in Stawki. Ewa declared she was a house-owner in Stawki and that she left in September 1939. She then moved to Horodenka with Lila. They joined the rest of the family near Tłuste in July 1942.[32]

Lila, who was less than two years younger than Renia, evidently moved to Stawki at a young age and shared Renia and Elizabeth's childhood. When Renia travelled to visit her father in his temporary new home in Zabłotów in August 1940, she was joined by Lila at Horodenka, and the two were then picked up by Bernard in a horse-drawn cart for a four-hour journey. Both of them hoped they were returning to some version of their lost childhood paradise. Both, Renia wrote, were disappointed and disillusioned. Noting the difference between their previous lives and the present further dissipated any image of a childhood paradise that may have lingered in

Renia's memory. Renia observed Lila's reactions and the sense of not belonging anymore. This ended her hopes of any return to her former life, and they both decided to leave right away.[33]

Lila is the only childhood friend mentioned in the diary. Given Renia's detailed analysis of the social scene at her new school in Przemyśl and her daily reporting of shifts and changes in her social life, the absence of earlier references is striking. Nor is there any mention of school life before the sisters left Stawki. There is also no mention of tutors. Likewise, no other Jewish children or playmates are mentioned. Judging by what Renia and then Elizabeth wrote, there were not many children around to play with, Polish, Ukrainian, or Jewish. The impression is of the sisters mostly interacting within the family and living in the social world of the parents. This might have been a choice by the parents, but it is not made explicit. Lila may have been brought to the estate specifically to provide an acceptable playmate. In the light of this silence, Renia's time in Przemyśl was a period when she was thrust into a much more Jewish environment, with many Jewish friends and classmates living close by and meeting daily.

Renia's Jewish education also seems to have been limited. Clearly Renia's first and main language and cultural world was Polish. The diary is written in Polish and its cultural references are almost entirely from Polish and German literature. Hebrew and Yiddish play no role in her diary, and there is no mention of using them in any context. There is, however, a reference to learning French and English from scratch in Przemyśl. Whereas her mother was fluent in German, the younger daughter did not understand it. Elizabeth also clarifies that the family was not really observant, and in Stawki they only celebrated the High Holidays.[34] The move away from Stawki seems to have significantly expanded the sisters' educational and social horizons.

The sisters did, however, have a good level of Polish education. As noted above, Renia fitted well into her new school, and Elizabeth could perform very well in Polish. The language at home seems to have been only Polish. If the parents relied in some way on the local Polish elementary school, or employed special tutors, neither sister mentions it.

Other accounts from the interwar period suggest that, in the social circles of leaseholding families to which the Spiegels belonged, Polish was the main language spoken at home and the vehicle of schooling, cultural consumption, and creativity. Two autobiographical essays stemming from this social circle further elucidate the background and context of Renia's countryside childhood.

The Diary in Light of Related Childhood Accounts

Hundreds of autobiographical essays were submitted to the competitions organized by the YIVO Youth Research Division between 1932 and 1939, which were open to those between the ages of 16 and 22. Two of the essays submitted to the second competition in 1934 are very close to Renia's diary, not only in the time of writing and the age of the writers but also in their social milieu and place of origin. They highlight the similarities of their social contexts, although their different ages mean they experienced different historical events.

Marcel Königsberg, a 21-year-old third-year law student at Jan Kazimierz University in Lwów, sent an autobiographical essay of eleven pages, which was received on 1 July 1934.[35] His father was Kos Königsberg, the leaseholder of Hołowczyńce. Marcel's uncle and aunt, Hilary and Maria Königsberg, were therefore also the uncle and aunt of Renia and Elizabeth. Marcel and Renia belonged to the same family and social circles in the same region, but the experiences they recalled were different. This was not only because of the different medium of writing: a diary written for personal reasons and an autobiographical essay that followed instructions set out by YIVO. The decade that separated their births and the political events that shaped the reality of their early lives made the worlds of their childhoods drastically different.

Marcel described his life chronologically, quickly reaching his earliest memories from his fourth year, when his parents had fled to Prague with him and his elder sister in the wake of the Russian advance into Galicia. At the age of 6 he remembered riding a fine horse from the stables on his parents' leased estate. He recalled the movement of troops, the officers who played with him, and how he once rode away with the troops, and his parents had to dispatch a farmhand to retrieve him. His early childhood was shaped by war, exile, and the experience of foreign places; his view of home could never be the same as Renia's. His life story does not portray an idyllic childhood but rather the difficult circumstances of post-war rural reality.

Early on Marcel experienced the sometimes harsh reality of estate management, which depended on successful crops and demanded daily diligence. Their initial lease was in partnership with his more prosperous uncle; his father managed the estate by himself but received no salary. While the estate might be profitable, this did not translate immediately into money, and whereas there is no hint of them going hungry, cashflow was a constant problem. Though Marcel admitted he did not understand all aspects of their financial situation, he clearly sensed the difficult atmosphere at home.

Much of Marcel's essay recounts his unhappy educational experiences and his mistreatment by his teachers in different schools. Shortly after their return from Prague (where he attended a Jewish school), he was sent to the Polish primary school in Tłuste. He ascribed his good grades there to his parents' high local status and their ability to provide the teachers with supplies from their farm. He then attended a government gymnasium, but had to move to a private gymnasium, in a neighbouring town, in which he completed four years. He ascribed his bad grades to his father's failure to bribe the director and individual teachers, as was the case with other parents.[36]

When he was in the third year of the gymnasium his mother's health deteriorated further, and she died after an operation in Lwów. The loss of his mother, Luna, is the focal point of the essay, the lowest point in a progression of suffering. Marcel was then sent to live with one aunt, and his sister to another. After a clash with his teachers and being hit by one of them, he moved for the fifth year of study to the Jewish Gymnasium in Lwów, where he later graduated. He was not accepted at medical school, so he chose law, as it offered wide options of employment. Throughout his educational journey, he made friends in his early years in Tłuste among the children of the peasants and only in Lwów among the Jewish students.

Ludwik Stöckel (1914–2005), also a law student at Lwów, was Marcel Königsberg's second cousin and close friend. His parents, Osias Stöckel and Pesia (née Krasucka), were the leaseholders of Śniatynka. Ludwik submitted to YIVO a much more elaborate essay, comprising sixty-five pages of autobiography, written in Tłuste in 1934, and forty-four pages of poems, ballads, and letter excerpts, from the years 1928 to 1934. He was 20 years old when he sent the entry to YIVO, and it arrived in Vilna on 22 June 1934.[37] Ludwik was planning to emigrate to Palestine, much to the displeasure of his father. He carried out his plan in November 1935. His autobiographical essay summed up his life at a crossroads, when it was about to take a dramatic turn, and it traced his path from indifference to political activism in the name of the Jewish national idea.

Ludwik was born on the Zofiówka estate in Biała, near Czortków, on 14 February 1914. His elder brother Józek (Józef Salomon) had also been born there on 13 May 1906.[38] His parents leased the property, part of the Biała estate, until shortly after Ludwik's birth, when they moved to Śniatynka near Tłuste. Ludwik relied on his mother's accounts of the arrival of the Russian army, their taking all the good horses from their stables and leaving all the bad ones, and the subsequent escape of the entire family from the estate on a wagon together with two farm workers. They arrived in Debrecen, and there boarded a train to Vienna. When they returned from Vienna they found the estate in ruins, and had to live in the nearby village of Capowce and then relocate to Tłuste, until the manor house was rebuilt. Ludwik associated with Jewish children in town and picked up some Yiddish; he then also learned Ukrainian in the countryside, where he played with the children of the estate workers. He moved regularly between the town and the estate and wanted to learn to ride horses like his cousin Marcel, who was an excellent rider.

After attending four years of primary school in Tłuste, he followed his brother to Czortków high school[39] and then to Lwów University, spending every holiday back home at the estate, where he rode horses, swam in the pond, played with the dogs, and entertained friends and relatives who came from Kołomyja, Lwów, and Vienna, mostly engaging in sports, hiking in the forests in the area, or visiting harvest celebrations on different estates. He reports the movement of cousins and relatives in and out of the estate, the events of each summer holiday, and the new sports they were playing: ping-pong, introduced by the Viennese cousins, and then tennis, improvising a tennis court at Różanówka, his uncle's leased estate.

In the fourth year of gymnasium, in 1928, at around the age of 14, Ludwik started writing poetry and reading many more books and newspapers. Examples of his poems are reproduced in the material he submitted. At that time he also began travelling extensively with his father on business, visiting agricultural sales and fairs in the region. Marcel and his sister Julia were part of Ludwik's immediate social circle and took part in the holiday activities he described. He mentioned them often in his essay by their nicknames Celek and Jula. Marcel's essay also mentioned Ludwik, but only as 'my cousin'. Eventually Ludwik and Marcel studied law together in Lwów, until Ludwik emigrated.[40]

Both Ludwik and Marcel experienced the First World War, spent time as refugees in Vienna and Prague, returned to ruined properties, and had to resume their lives in the town of Tłuste. This fundamentally influenced their education and their choice of playmates and set their childhood apart from previous and later cohorts. Their experiences also indicate the particular post-war circumstances of rebuilding the estates. The post-war environment was marked by a significant drop in the numbers of Jewish households and the Jewish presence in the countryside. Renia and Elizabeth were born into this reality, and, from a child's point of view, this would have been taken for granted. Renia's coming of age in the 1930s was after that period, when farms had already been rebuilt and work relationships re-established. Evidently Renia and Elizabeth were also not fully immersed in family lore in the way Ludwik and Marcel were, with their mothers, aunts, and grandmothers recalling the events of the past. The specific timing of the sisters' births and of their leaving the estate, and possibly their relative isolation, limited this kind of knowledge.

School life, friends, teachers, and conflicts at school take up much of the descriptions of their childhood by Ludwik and Marcel. This accentuates the lack of stories about primary school in Renia's diary. Also prominent in the YIVO autobiographies are the holidays, spent mostly on estates and their surroundings, when cousins and friends would meet and exchange stories and the local environment would be explored. Ludwik's and Marcel's trajectories led both to education in a gymnasium and then on to Lwów University. Most of the direct descriptions of the estates in their essays come from when they returned to them during school holidays. Given that the common age of attending gymnasium was then 10 or 11 (as opposed to 14 in Renia's time), this meant much of their childhood was spent away. In comparison, Renia's account reflects the circumstances of her abrupt removal from the estate and generally lacks extensive descriptions of holidays.

The primacy of Polish language and culture is common to the accounts of Ludwik and Marcel, as it is to Renia's and Elizabeth's. Only Ludwik's particular experiences with his peers in town speaking Yiddish, and then his political choices that led him to learn Hebrew, set him on a different path. Marcel, with a similar path, could follow Yiddish only with difficulty. Both cousins chose to write their autobiographical essays in Polish, which was also the language of Ludwik's poems and letters. Ludwik goes on to analyse this cultural preference, explaining that his social circle was completely assimilated. He had no systematic Jewish education and no continuous study of Hebrew or Jewish texts. Furthermore, he and his peers were raised in an environment that was indifferent to many aspects of Jewish life, and immersed in Polish society.

Family Estates

Święte, Henryk Spiegel's estate, where his son Bernard probably grew up, is the family estate that Renia does not mention. Understanding where Bernard came from can illuminate his actions in Stawki and his choices in raising his family there. Święte was a very small place, and the Austrian and Polish censuses reveal how small its Jewish population was (see Table 1).

The estate and its neighbouring village differed in their religious constitutions. That of the estate changed significantly from decade to decade, reflecting changes in the composition of the workers and residents. Before the First World War the number of Jews and then the number of Roman Catholic Poles grew, while the number of Greek Catholic Ukrainians dropped significantly. The village, however, had a stable ratio, with Greek Catholic Ukrainians forming a very large majority, followed by small numbers of Jews and Poles, reflecting a much smaller turnover of residents.

The language of the estate's residents was predominantly Polish, while Ukrainian dominated in the village. This suggests a three-tier linguistic and cultural structure for Jews who lived on estates: some level of Jewish culture with either Yiddish or Polish or both spoken at home; Polish spoken regularly among permanent residents and workers in the estate environment; and Ukrainian spoken occasionally within the estate and regularly in the immediate rural world outside it. The tension between the home culture and the immediate Polish culture is reflected in the 1921 choice of six Jewish residents—very likely the Spiegel family—to declare their nationality as Jewish, while two Jewish residents (perhaps hired employees or some members of the family) chose to declare theirs as Polish.

Whereas in the village the Jewish population was culturally negligible, it made up a significant component within the estate. This created room for cultural and ideological differences. In 1921 the estate environment could tolerate 'Poles of the Mosaic faith', while the village environment fostered very clear divisions marked by religion and nationality.

The population numbers are so small that it is possible that all the Jews recorded were members of one household. This certainly encompassed a very limited Jewish environment, though in Radymno, not far away, there were more than 1,000 Jews, and there were other towns in the area with significant Jewish populations. Growing up in such a limited Jewish environment would certainly have prepared Bernard for life in Stawki and would explain his cultural habits and preferences. It also points to the links between one estate and another, often across great distances.

The particular history of the two estates that were central to the lives of the Spiegel sisters and the way they came to be associated with the family is another theme that is completely missing from their narratives. This may be another feature of the point of view of the young. Their existence in their home was evidently perceived as requiring no explanation. Comparison with other accounts reveals the gaps in the children's versions, which autobiographies written later in life usually cover.

Table 1 Populations of Święte estate and village 1880–1921

	Year	Houses	Residents	Religion			Nationality			Language	
				Jewish	Roman Catholic	Greek Catholic	Jewish	Polish	Ruthenian	Polish	Ukrainian
Estate	1880	1	29	7	5	17	–	–	–	29	–
	1890	2	40	16	2	22	–	–	–	17	23
	1900	3	48	20	22	6	–	–	–	48	–
	1910	–	61	–	–	–	–	–	–	–	–
	1921	1	34	8	10	16	6	12	16	–	–
Village	1880	145	757	24	11	722	–	–	–	757	–
	1890	137	820	35	16	769	–	–	–	16	804
	1900	149	845	22	18	805	–	–	–	39	806
	1910	–	1100	–	–	–	–	–	–	–	–
	1921	193	1082	30	16	1036	30	15	1036	–	–

Source: K. K. Statistische Zentralkommission, Special-Orts-Repertorien der im Österreichischen Reichsrathe vertretenen Königreiche und Länder, xii: Galizien (Vienna, 1886), 150–1; K. K. Statistische Zentralkommission, Special-Orts-Repertorien der im Österreichischen Reichsrathe vertretenen Königreiche und Länder: Neubearbeitung auf Grund der Ergebnisse der Volkszählung vom 31. December 1890, xii: Galizien (Vienna, 1893), 201–2; K. K. Statistische Zentralkommission, Gemeindelexikon der im Reichsrate vertretenen Königreiche und Länder: Bearbeitet auf Grund der Ergebnisse der Volkszählung vom 31. Dezember 1900, xii: Galizien (Vienna, 1907), 230, 232; K. K. Statistische Zentralkommission, Allgemeines Verzeichnis der Ortsgemeinden und Ortschaften Österreichs nach den Ergebnissen der Volkszählung vom 31. Dezember 1910 (Vienna, 1915), 339; Główny Urząd Statystyczny Rzeczypospolitej Polskiej, Skorowidz miejscowości Rzeczypospolitej Polskiej opracowany na podstawie wyników pierwszego powszechnego spisu ludności z dn. 30 września 1921 r. i innych źródeł urzędowych. xiii: Województwo lwowskie (Warsaw, 1924), 15–16.

Uhryńkowce and Stawki could be considered twin estates, very close to each other, similar in size, jointly owned and run for decades. Although registered as two separate entities, they were routinely described in administrative documents and handbooks as if they were one unit. The Spiegels' movement between the two demonstrates this connection. The estates had been among several that had been the property of the Kimelman family for several generations. Most of the land had been acquired between 1870 and 1880 by Moses and Isak Kimelman, and passed down to their children and grandchildren. By 1939, different branches of the Kimelman family had owned landed properties for sixty or seventy years, and some may have been held in lease even longer.[41] Stawki (576 hectares in 1929) was considered a subsidiary of the nearby estate of Uhryńkowce (460 hectares in 1929). Stawki and Uhryńkowce officially became the property of Moses and Isak Kimelman sometime between 1876 and 1882.[42] They were probably associated with the family even earlier.[43] The last owners were Oswald Kimelman,[44] Jadwiga Kimelman, and Luiza Lotta Liebentritt (née Kimelman).

The transformation of estates into Jewish spaces is revealed in the demographic information for Uhryńkowce and Stawki. The 1900 Austrian census, the last to provide substantial details, recorded nineteen houses on the Uhryńkowce and Stawki estates and 163 residents, of which 74 were Jews (about 45 per cent). Separate information for each estate only included the number of houses and the population: fourteen houses and 97 residents in Uhryńkowce, five houses and 66 residents in Stawki. In the nearby village of Uhryńkowce the census recorded 289 houses and 1,692 residents, of which 99 (less than 6 per cent) were Jews. While the village population was considerably larger than that of the two estates, the land belonging to the village and to the estate was almost the same, with a small advantage to the estate: 1,009 hectares registered for Uhryńkowce estate compared to 926 hectares for Uhryńkowce village.[45] This discrepancy captures part of the inherently privileged position of estates in relation to villages in Galician society of the time. In 1910 the number of residents of the Uhryńkowce estate was 141 and of the village 1,629.[46]

Earlier the number of Jewish residents was also significant, indicating a long involvement with the estates. In 1890 the Stawki estate had 34 Jewish residents and 90 non-Jewish residents, with fourteen buildings, and the Uhryńkowce estate had 41 Jews and 11 non-Jews, with eight buildings. The village had 102 Jews.[47] In 1880 the two estates had twenty-three buildings, 74 Jewish residents, and 105 non-Jews between them. The village had 57 Jews.[48] In 1869 the estates had 180 residents and twenty-four buildings.[49] As far back as 1869 the numbers indicate a continuation of a significant number of Jews. These numbers suggest that the Jewish leaseholder and subsequent owner developed the estate into a small-scale community, which partially solved the problem of a lack of any Jewish community infrastructure.

The upheavals of the First World War took a toll on these estates. The first Polish census of 1921 recorded only 1,500 residents in Uhryńkowce village, of which forty-three were Jews. The two estates fared much worse, with only twenty-one residents, two of them Jews. The number of buildings in the village was given as 346, whereas on the estates only two buildings were still recorded.[50] Like many other estates under Russian occupation and in areas on the front line that experienced heavy fighting, Uhryńkowce and Stawki suffered massive destruction in the war years. Hundreds of thousands of buildings were in ruins, livestock lost, and many estates were completely destroyed, never to regain their former condition.[51] The damage suffered by Uhryńkowce and Stawki is evident in the dramatic fall in the number of houses and residents. New people needed to be brought in to make good the losses. In addition, the 1920s and 1930s policy of parcelling up estates to be sold to individual farmers—which included the Kimelman holdings[52]—possibly prompted the changes that brought the Spiegels to Stawki as managers and ultimately owners.

The involvement of the Spiegels in Stawki may have been more of a family investment, with Bernard managing the family's interests. Not only was Bernard's sister Ewa a resident of the estate, his father Henryk was also associated with Stawki. An echo of this association is found in a long account of the war experiences of Herman Steinkohl Zenner in the area of Tłuste.[53] Zenner, who was in the work camp in Hołowczyńce between 7 June and 23 June 1943, mentions a 75- or 76-year-old estate owner from Stawki by the name of Spiegel, his daughter, his son, and his 15-year-old granddaughter who worked with him there. He relates how the older Spiegel described his plans to hide under the protection of his former gardener on the Stawki estate, choosing as his hiding place an old, half-ruined, single-storey building on his farm in Stawki.[54] The familiarity with Stawki and its workers suggests a much more frequent and closer link to the place and possibly a more formal attachment than might be construed from the Spiegel sisters' account.

Conclusion

Renia's diary offers a different—more engaged—insight into childhood on rural estates and the impact of the estate environment on Jewish children. It highlights the problems and challenges they found pressing, rather than those their parents dealt with. It also reveals their silence on matters where older writers might have written much more. Children's texts appear to require additional contextualization and more excavation of hidden layers and unspoken knowledge.

Children's perceptions of time matter. What appears to adults as a short period may seem much longer to a child. The time some families spent on particular estates might have been quite short, but to children these experiences were formative and memorable, as is revealed by the descriptions by Renia and Elizabeth, who both spent only eight years at Stawki and yet were fundamentally affected by it.

Likewise, children's experiences cannot be measured in generations but rather in cohorts, as the difference of a few years can mean very different experiences and realities. The gap between Renia's and Elizabeth's accounts and the YIVO autobiographies reveals different stages in the process of rebuilding local estates, with critical stages that the Spiegel sisters did not witness taking place just a few years before and after their births.

With source material scarce or scattered, children's texts and diaries have additional value as they may be the only sources available. Notably, the Spiegels of Uhryńkowce and Stawki are difficult to find in the official records. It is still unclear when exactly they came to be associated with the Kimelman estates and in what way. It is only Renia's diary and Elizabeth's recollections that link them to their estate lives. Renia's diary reveals a lacuna in knowledge of Jewish life in the Galician countryside and the need to use a wider array of sources to illuminate life on rural estates owned and run by Jews.

Renia's changing attitude to the estate in Stawki underscores the significant changes in children's understanding of their experiences and how they perceive them and respond to them throughout their growing up. Accounts written later in life tend to flatten this arc and present a more even approach to childhood realities. In Renia's case she had undergone a transformation, shifting from considering her estate childhood in terms of its external realities—buildings, nature, and daily routines—into a deeper analysis of human interaction and family dynamics as they were affected by financial difficulties and familial disagreement. She presents the potential for such shifts in similar settings.

Finally, Renia's and Elizabeth's unique and special paths show the potential of estate upbringing, with its less structured education, especially in the first decade of life, to send the children raised on estates on creative or reflective paths.

Notes

1 R. Spiegel, *Renia's Diary: A Young Girl's Life in the Shadow of the Holocaust*, trans. A. Blasiak and M. Dziurosz (New York, 2019), 1–2 (31 Jan. 1939); Pol. orig.: R. Spiegel, *Dziennik 1939–1942* (Rzeszów, 2016).

2 O. Kofler, *Żydowskie dwory: Wspomnienia z Galicji Wschodniej od początku XIX wieku do wybuchu I wojny światowej*, ed. E. Koźmińska-Frejlak (Warsaw, 1999); K. Maramorosch, *The Thorny Road to Success: A Memoir* (Bloomington, Ind., 2015).

3 E. Bellak, 'Preface', in Spiegel, *Renia's Diary*, 9–12; ead., 'Afterword', ibid. 277–89; ead., 'Notes', ibid. 293–318. Renia's mother and sister survived. The diary was preserved by Renia's boyfriend, Zymunt, who brought it to New York in the early 1950s and gave it to Renia's mother.

4 T. Magierski (dir.), *Przemyśl – złamane marzenia*, documentary (Smoking Mirrors Productions, 2019).

5 See e.g. United States Holocaust Memorial Museum, Washington DC, '80 Years after Kristallnacht: Diarists of the Holocaust' (6 Nov. 2018): YouTube website, visited 8 Mar. 2022; M. Teler, 'Ariana Spiegel: Niezwykłe losy "polskiej Shirley Temple"' (31 Oct. 2019): Histmag.org website, visited 8 Mar. 2022.

6 Bellak, 'Preface', p. xiii.

7 Bellak, 'Notes', 302 n. 7.

8 Ibid.

9 On agriculture remaining the primary economic occupation and field of production with wood and grain as the major products of the estates and a growing field for Jewish economic enterprise, see W. O. McCagg, *A History of Habsburg Jews, 1670–1918* (Bloomington,

Ind., 1992), 115; F. Friedmann, *Die galizischen Juden im Kampfe um ihre Gleichberechtigung (1848–1868)* (Frankfurt am Main, 1929), 14–16.

10 T. Gąsowski, 'From *Austeria* to the Manor: Jewish Landowners in Autonomous Galicia', *Polin*, 12 (1999), 120–36; Friedmann, *Die galizischen Juden im Kampfe um ihre Gleichberechtigung*, 21–2; M. Semczyszyn, 'Kryzys ziemiaństwa w Galicji Wschodniej na przełomie XIX i XX wieku (do 1914 roku)', *Prace Historyczne*, 146 (2019), 787–808.

11 Gąsowski, 'From *Austeria* to the Manor'; K. Ślusarek, *W przededniu autonomii: Własność ziemska i ziemiaństwo zachodniej Galicji w połowie XIX wieku* (Warsaw, 2013), 34, 57–9, 97; Friedmann, *Die galizischen Juden im Kampfe um ihre Gleichberechtigung*, 22; F. Bujak, *Galicya*, i: *Kraj, ludność, społeczeństwo, rolnictwo* (Lwów, 1908), 154, 272; J. Lestchinsky, 'The Industrial and Social Structure of the Jewish Population of Interbellum Poland', *YIVO Annual of Jewish Social Science*, 11 (1956/7), 243–69: 256.

12 See e.g. Gąsowski, 'From *Austeria* to the Manor'; A. Eisenbach, *Emancypacja Żydów na ziemiach polskich 1785–1870 na tle europejskim* (Warsaw, 1988), 371–8, 411–13, 436–43, 541–3; N. M. Gelber, 'Toledot yehudei levov', in id. (ed.), *Entsiklopedyah shel galuyot: levov* (Jerusalem, 1956), 21–390, esp. 269–72, 278–84, 305–6; Eng. trans.: 'History of the Jews of Lwow', trans. M. Y. Ecker (n.d.): JewishGen website, visited 8 Mar. 2022; Friedmann, *Die galizischen Juden im Kampfe um ihre Gleichberechtigung*, 21–3, 79–88; M. Śliż, *Galicyjscy Żydzi na drodze do równouprawnienia 1848–1914: Aspekt prawny procesu emancypacji Żydów w Galicji* (Kraków, 2006), 23, 57–62.

13 Gąsowski, 'From *Austeria* to the Manor', 124; Friedmann, *Die galizischen Juden im Kampfe um ihre Gleichberechtigung*, 22; Bujak, *Galicya*, i. 154, 418–19, 421; F. Morawski, 'Dzierżawy w obrębie własności tabularnej w Galicyi: Na podstawie sprawozdań wydziałów powiatowych', *Wiadomości Statystyczne o Stosunkach Krajowych*, 15/2 (1895), 1–22, esp. 12, 17–22; Lestchinsky, 'The Industrial and Social Structure of the Jewish Population of Interbellum Poland', 254–6.

14 Spiegel, *Renia's Diary*, 1 (31 Jan. 1939), 229–30 (16 Apr. 1942), 238 (2 May 1942); Bellak, 'Notes', 293 n. 1, 302 n. 6.

15 Bellak, 'Notes', 302 n. 6.

16 Spiegel, *Renia's Diary*, 15 (7 May 1939).

17 Bellak, 'Notes', 296 n. 2.

18 E. Bellak, opening monologue, in Magierski (dir.), *Przemyśl – złamane marzenia*, 03:45–05:30 min.

19 'Picture Section', in Spiegel, *Renia's Diary*, between pp. 144 and 145; Magierski (dir.), *Przemyśl – złamane marzenia*, 03:45–07:00 min.; 'Elizabeth Bellak' (n.d.): Zalishchyky website, 'Collections', visited 8 Mar. 2022.

20 Bellak, 'Notes', 293–5 n. 1.

21 Spiegel, *Renia's Diary*, 163–5 (22 Sept. 1941), 216–17 (12 Mar. 1941), 244–6 (12 May 1942); Bellak, 'Notes', 302 n. 7, 316–17 n. 23.

22 Bellak, 'Afterword', 283, 285; 'Notes', 293–5 n. 1, 304–5 n. 9.

23 Bellak, 'Preface', 46–7.

24 Spiegel, *Renia's Diary*, 46–7 (1 July 1940).

25 Ibid. 243 (9 May 1942).

26 Archiwum Żydowskiego Instytutu Historycznego, Warsaw (hereafter AŻIH), 301/3281: Maria Konigsberg, testimony, 17 Jan. 1948; 301/3491; Maria Kenigsberg, testimony, 15 Mar. 1948; 301/3492: Mojsesz Szpigiel, testimony, 10 Mar. 1948. For partial translations of these

testimonies into Hebrew, see *Sefer tluste*, ed. G. Lindenberg (Tel Aviv, 1965), 161–7, 178; see also *Memorial Book of Tluste (Tovste, Ukraine): Translation of* Sefer Tluste, ed. G. Lindenberg, trans. S. Mages (New York, 2020).
27 Bellak, 'Notes', 316–17; 'Acknowledgements', 319–20: 320.
28 Horodenka was where Renia's father is known to have found shelter as well and where he obtained work as a farmer, and evidently where he was later in the ghetto (Spiegel, *Renia's Diary*, 24 (16 Nov. 1939); 27 (26 Dec. 1939); Bellak, 'Notes', 302 n. 7, 314 n. 20)).
29 Maria Kenigsberg, testimony, 15 Mar. 1948, pp. 1, 8, 9; Maria Konigsberg, testimony, 17 Jan. 1948, p. 1; Mojzesz Szpigiel, testimony, 10 Mar. 1948, pp. 1, 4, 6, 7; AŻIH, 301/3889: Berł Glik, testimony, 2 Mar. 1948; Arolsen Archives, Bad Arolsen, 3.2.1 IRO [International Refugee Organization] 'Care and Maintenance' Program, CM/1 files from Germany, 79894919: Ewa Wachs, née Spiegel, care and maintenance form (n.d.). Various files state that Ewa Wachs was born in 1885, 1895, or 1905, but her brother stated that she was about 47 years old in 1943, and her father was then 72, hence the year given in her main file, 1895, is taken to be the correct one. The birth place Lwów might actually mean some smaller location nearby (*Księga Adresowa Polski (wraz z w.m. Gdańskiem) dla Handlu, Przemysłu, Rzemiosł i Rolnictwa, 1926/27* (Warsaw, 1927), 1370; *Księga Adresowa Polski (wraz z w.m. Gdańskiem) dla Handlu, Przemysłu, Rzemiosł i Rolnictwa, 1929* (Warsaw, 1929), 794).
30 Mojzesz Szpigiel, testimony, 10 Mar. 1948, pp. 1, 4; Maria Kenigsberg, testimony, 15 Mar. 1948, pp. 1, 3–5, 11–12, 17, 26, 36; AŻIH, 301/3337: Hilary Koenigsberg, testimony, 28 Mar. 1948, pp. 1, 3–4; *Sefer tluste*, pp. 29, 41, 49, 56, 243; Archiwum Główne Akt Dawnych, Warsaw (hereafter AGAD), 1/300/0/-/1970: p. 88, 1895 birth records; 'Karola Albin', 'Kos Koenigsberg', 'Marcel Koenigsberg', 'Julia Steckel', 'Josef Stoekel', 'Pesia Stoekel', 'Aneta Weisglas', 'Isidor Weisglas': Yad Vashem website, 'Central Database of Shoah Victims' Names', visited 11 July 2022.
31 Spiegel, *Renia's Diary*, 49 (8 Aug. 1940) (Lila). Renia casually mentions aunts Hela (ibid. 68 (20 Dec. 1940)) and Lusia in Przemyśl (ibid. 32 (19 Jan. 1940), 50 (21 Aug. 1940)) and a visit to an aunt in the countryside in the summer she visited Warsaw (ibid. 26–7 (15 Aug. 1939)). They do not seem to be among the relatives who converged on the Tłuste area during the war.
32 Ewa Wachs, née Spiegel, care and maintenance form; Arolsen Archives, 3.2.1 IRO, CM/1 files from Germany, 79395662: Leichter Jakob, care and maintenance form (27 Sept. 1948). Jakob was accompanied by Leichter Lila, born 27 May 1926, Lwów.
33 Spiegel, *Renia's Diary*, 50–1 (21–2 Aug. 1940).
34 Spiegel, *Renia's Diary*, 169 (17 Oct. 1941); Bellak, 'Afterword', 283; 'Notes', 297 n. 3.
35 YIVO Archives, New York, RG 4 (Autobiographies of Jewish Youth in Poland), Autobiography 3676: 'M. Konigsberg' (Pol., 1934).
36 See I. Bassok, 'Ma'amadot utefisah ma'amadit etsel yeladim uvenei no'ar yehudim bepolin bein hamilḥamot', *Gal-ed*, 18 (2002), 225–44: 236; id., 'Darkhei ḥinukh bamishpaḥah hayehudit bepolin bein milḥamot ha'olam: nisayon behistoryah antropologit', *Gal-ed*, 24 (2005), 75–106: 90, 101.
37 YIVO, RG 4, Autobiography 3675: 'Lud' (Pol., 1934); 'Ludwik Stöckel: Adventure Along the Way to My Goal', in *Awakening Lives: Autobiographies of Jewish Youth in Poland before the Holocaust*, ed. J. Shandler (New Haven, Conn., 2002), 141–96; '"Lud" (Ludwik Stöckel)', in *Ostatnie pokolenie: Autobiografie polskiej młodzieży żydowskiej okresu międzywojennego*, ed. A. Cała (Warsaw, 2003), 333–76; A. Cała, 'Obraz prowincjonalnej Polski w

autobiografiach młodzieży żydowskiej z kolekcji YIVO', in W. Mielewczyk and U. Siekacz (eds.), *Żydzi na wsi polskiej* (Szreniawa, 2006), 129–39: 133–5.
38 AGAD 1/300/0/-/2828: p. 3, birth record of Józef Salomon Stöckel (1906).
39 On the Juliusz Słowacki Gymnasium, see *Sprawozdanie Dyrekcji Państwowego Gimnazjum imienia Juljusza Słowackiego w Czortkowie za rok szkolny 1927/28* (Czortków, 1928), 21, 39.
40 On Marcel and his sister Julia, see N. Aleksiun, 'Story of Rescue: Klymko Jan' (Dec. 2014): Polin: Polish Righteous website, 'Stories of Rescue', visited 8 Mar. 2022; ead., 'Historia pomocy: Klymko Jan' (Dec. 2014): Polin: Polscy Sprawiedliwi website, 'Historie pomocy', visited 8 Mar. 2022, ; AŻIH, 349/24, 6532: accounts of rescue (1972, 1993–7).
41 K. Oksza Orzechowski, *Przewodnik statystyczno-topograficzny i skorowidz obejmujący wszystkie miejscowości z przysiółkami w Królestwie Galicyi W.X. Krakowskiem i X. Bukowinie, według najświeższych skazówek urzędowych* (Kraków, 1872), 44, 85, 92.
42 J. Michalewicz (ed.), *Informator statystyczny do dziejów społeczno-gospodarczych Galicji: Słownik historyczny zakładów przemysłu gorzelniczego Galicji doby autonomicznej*, 4 vols. (Kraków, 1988–93), iv. 119; *Rocznik Statystyki Przemysłu i Handlu Krajowego*, 1/3 (1885), 13–14.
43 A daughter of Moses Kimelman was born in Uhryńkowce, probably around 1874 (AGAD 1/300/0/-/591: birth record (1894)).
44 *Księga Adresowa Polski (wraz z w.m. Gdańskiem) dla Handlu, Przemysłu, Rzemiosł i Rolnictwa*, 1929, 1713; *Dziennik Urzędowy Województwa Tarnopolskiego*, 2/6 (1 June 1922), 21.
45 *Gemeindelexikon der im Reichsrate vertretenen Königreiche und Länder. Bearb. auf Grund der Ergebnisse der Volkszählung vom 31 Dezember 1900* (Vienna, 1900), 762, 764–5.
46 *Allgemeines Verzeichnis der Ortsgemeinden und Ortschaften Österreichs nach den Ergebnissen der Volkszählung vom 31. Dezember 1910* (Vienna, 1910), 392.
47 K. K. Statistische Zentralkommission, *Special-Orts-Repertorien der im Österreichischen Reichsrathe vertretenen Königreiche und Länder: Neubearbeitung auf Grund der Ergebnisse der Volkszählung vom 31. Dezember 1890*, xii: *Galizien* (Vienna, 1893), 659, 661.
48 K. K. Statistische Zentralkommission, *Special-Orts-Repertorien der im Österreichischen Reichsrathe vertretenen Königreiche und Länder*, xii: *Galizien* (Vienna, 1886), 476, 477.
49 K. K. Statistische Zentralkommission, *Orts-Repertorium des Königreiches Galizien und Lodomerien mit dem Grossherzogthume Krakau: Auf Grundlage der Volkszählung vom Jahre 1869 bearbeitet von der k. k. statistischen Central-Commission* (Vienna, 1874), 252.
50 Główny Urząd Statystyczny Rzeczypospolitej Polskiej, *Skorowidz miejscowości Rzeczypospolitej Polskiej opracowany na podstawie wyników pierwszego powszechnego spisu ludności z dn. 30 września 1921 r. i innych źródeł urzędowych*, xv: *Województwo tarnopolskie* (Warsaw, 1923), 23.
51 See e.g. M. Paździora, *Atlas historyczny Galicji* (Chrzanów, 2021), 100. On the deliberate and systematic destruction of Jewish-owned estates, see P. Zavadivker, 'Pogroms in World War I Russia', in E. M. Avrutin and E. Bemporad (eds.), *Pogroms: A Documentary History* (New York, 2021), doc. 5.1 (p. 115). The 1921 census data for Zaleszczyki-Tłuste area reveals extensive depopulation of Jews in the countryside, compared to the pre-war period.
52 It was included in lists of obligatory sales, in 1936 and 1939 ('Rozporządzenie Rady Ministrów z dnia 7 lutego 1936 r. o ustalenie na rok 1936 wykazu imiennego nieruchomości, podlegających wykupowi przymusowemu', *Dziennik Ustaw*, 1936, no. 11, item 108 (#55; 580 hectares); 'Rozporządzenie Rady Ministrów z dnia 11 lutego 1939 r. o ustalenie na rok 1939 wykazu imiennego nieruchomości podlegających przymusowemu wykupowi', *Dziennik Ustaw*, 1939, no. 12, item 65 (#28; 400 hectares)).

53 T. Friedman (ed.), *Wie Hermann Zenner aus Kolomea den Nazi-Krieg in 1941–44 ueberlebte: Hundert mal dem Tod entgangen* (Haifa, 1999); compare the testimony of Hermann Steinkohl Zenner, born in Kołomyja in 1906, regarding his experiences in the Kołomyja ghetto, Tłuste, Rohatyn, Horodenka, and in hiding (Yad Vashem Archives, Jerusalem, Testimonies, O3/3389: Hermann Steinkohl Zenner, testimony, 1946–7).

54 Hermann Steinkohl Zenner, testimony, 138–41.

Advocacy and Practice in CENTOS Journals

SEAN MARTIN

From the end of the nineteenth century, governments and political movements began to see childhood as a period conducive to developing and embodying social values. CENTOS, the Central Society for the Care of Orphans, founded in Warsaw in 1924, aimed to raise Jewish children as Jews and promote Jewish self-help and co-operation. These ideals were clearly set out in the movement's journals, *Unzer kind*, *Dos kind*, and *Przegląd Społeczny*. To achieve their goals, the leaders of CENTOS paid close attention to legal developments that offered protections for children, and to relationships with local officials who often provided funds, however small, for their work. CENTOS was not a political movement and avoided open identification with Zionism. Instead it devoted itself to organized social work, with its goal of the improvement of the health of the Jewish community in Poland.

WHAT IF YOU WROTE SOMETHING and no one ever read it? This was the question faced by the editors of the journals published by CENTOS (Centralne Towarzystwo Opieki nad Sierotami / Farband fun Tsentrales far Yesoymim Farzorgung in Poyln; Central Society for the Care of Orphans), founded in Warsaw in 1924. The editors of *Unzer kind* ('Our Child') estimated that the title never crossed the desks of 90 per cent of the presidents, vice presidents, and secretaries of the local Jewish associations that were themselves CENTOS members.[1] Michał (Meir) Peker, editor of *Dos kind* ('The Child'), wrote that most of the Jewish community's social and spiritual leaders did not even know the monthly existed, even after nine years of publication.[2] Lest this appear to be simply the dire situation among publications in Yiddish, an editorial in the Polish-language *Przegląd Społeczny* ('Social Review') confessed to the same problem. An unnamed author (presumably Józef Kohn, the journal's editor at the time) wrote in a 1930 article commemorating another year of the journal's publication that the same article from 1929 could simply be reprinted, outlining the same difficulties faced by the journal the previous year.[3]

These three journals, along with a few other titles published occasionally by CENTOS and some of the associations' annual reports, are the most important source for the history of Jewish orphan care in Poland before 1939. They appeared as monthly publications for much of the period between 1918 and 1939, and they are a record of the work of the social workers, teachers, physicians, and others who did so much to aid Jewish children. The indifference the editors described suggests it would be unwise to make any grand claims about their influence, whether among the general Jewish or non-Jewish public. The historian is then left with an intriguing phenomenon—journals that offer unusually thick descriptions not to be found elsewhere but that no one seems to have read or taken seriously. Still, the CENTOS associations were a remarkable part of Poland's vibrant Jewish civil society, and they deserve more study, both for what they can reveal about the development of that society and for what they can reveal about the lives of children.[4] This chapter is an effort to learn more about these topics by examining these publications, especially *Dos kind*, *Unzer kind*, and *Przegląd Społeczny*. The history of Jewish child welfare as reflected in these publications suggests the engagement of the Jewish community in both advocacy and practice that tied their nation to Poland, even as the editors and writers of them proclaimed the Jews' separateness. A discussion of the journals' rhetoric, with special attention to the development of Jewish child welfare, reveals how community leaders moved from orphan care to general child welfare and how they hoped to develop their work.

CENTOS brought hundreds of associations and committees from all three former partitions of Poland together under one organizational structure.[5] These associations were formed during and after the First World War in response to the need to care for war and pogrom orphans. Their work complemented the efforts of the pre-war community institutions serving Jewish children. Funded initially by private funds and later in large part by the American Jewish Joint Distribution Committee (JDC), the associations eventually joined to form CENTOS, with Senator Rafał Szereszowski as chair.[6] The efforts of CENTOS, led and developed by Polish Jews, saved orphaned and impoverished children, reinforced Jewish identity among the children, and represented Jewish interests to the larger Jewish and Polish communities. Nina Bar-Yishay and Marek Web have described how the development of CENTOS was a recognition of the fact that the community's basic needs could not be met through simple charity.[7]

In the absence of CENTOS's own records, the history of Jewish child welfare in interwar Poland must be told using the records of other Jewish organizations, notably those of the JDC; municipal and national government records that detail the activities of Jewish groups; the press; and the fragmentary memoir literature. Records from the Ringelblum Archive at the Jewish Historical Institute in Warsaw even tell the history of CENTOS during the war, to the extent it can be reconstructed from such fragmentary sources.[8] None of these sources, however, can replace the detailed observations found in the CENTOS publications. The journals no one read reveal the scope of the organization's interests and detail the results of the group's work.

CENTOS paired advocacy with practice, a combination evident from the beginning. By 1925, the year after CENTOS's founding, the group managed 423 sites and ninety-three children's homes, in which lived 4,057 children; 11,700 children were in foster care (with relatives or foster families); 14,000 received some kind of support to attend school; and 3,187 participated in vocational training programmes; 3,725 children went to summer camps; and 998 were in sanatoria.[9] The writer and editor Avrum Levinson described the Jewish orphan problem as 'a silent epilogue of our national tragedy', a result of the recent history of war and pogroms. Levinson lamented that care for orphans did not stem from a rational, nationalistic, religious, or even philanthropic impulse, but simply from the work of sensitive individuals who took up the task. Calling for significantly more support for orphan care as a part of Jewish national self-help, Levinson also offered a warning typical of the tone of many CENTOS editorials: those who did not want to or could not perform this duty would in the end 'look on our graves'.[10]

CENTOS drew on the work of many leaders who had been active in Jewish communities for decades. The group nonetheless occupied a specific niche within Poland's rapidly developing Jewish civil society. CENTOS was not a political organization, nor was it an educational or medical institution. CENTOS was about childcare, specifically orphan care, though it was not just a group of orphanages. CENTOS's publications included many promotional materials, such as booklets of brief articles or short overviews of the group's history, and other titles by the editors and writers of *Dos kind, Unzer kind,* and *Przegląd Społeczny*.[11] In an effort to tell others of their mission, one of the first CENTOS publications was *Dos elendste kind* ('The Loneliest Child'), published in 1925, which included articles by influential writers and community activists supporting the work of Jewish childcare. It seems that this was meant to be a regular periodical, but it only appeared once more, in 1927. These Yiddish publications were obviously intended for a Jewish audience; however, they included the voices of those connected to the community but more commonly encountered in Polish, such as Janusz Korczak and the linguist Jan Baudouin de Courtenay. Articles by Korczak, Baudouin de Courtenay, Moyshe Zilberfarb, Chaim Zhitlowsky, A. Levinson, Y. Rubin, and Moyshe Shalit appeared in the 1925 edition, while the 1927 edition featured the work of Yehoshua (Ozjasz) Thon, Aleksander Lednicki, Avrum Levinson, Aharon Zeitlin, Y. Rubin, Janusz Korczak, L. Noyshtot, Baudouin de Courtenay, M. Shneyorson, N. Gergel, and S. Tshernovitsh.

Given that CENTOS was a new group formed during trying historical circumstances, its publishing record appears rather impressive. While *Dos elendste kind* was published by the central office in Warsaw, two of the three most important CENTOS publications came from the work of local associations. The Centre for Orphan Care in the former Congress Poland published *Dos kind* starting in 1924, citing the Polish-language, non-Jewish journal *Opieka nad dzieckiem* as a model. *Przegląd Społeczny*, published by the Central Committee for the Care of Jewish Orphans in Lwów, appeared in 1927.[12] *Unzer kind*, the journal of the central office of CENTOS in Warsaw, first appeared under the title *Dos shutsloze kind* ('The Neglected Child') in 1928. These journals were only loosely affiliated: they were not published by the same association, but the associations were formally linked to each other through the organizational structure of CENTOS. The separate titles reflect the legacy of the partitions, but a reading of the contents shows that the journals shared not only common goals but also many of the same ideas and authors.

The CENTOS journals were quite similar. Published in a small format, they were all monthlies, with the occasional double issue throughout the year. Each issue was about forty pages long and followed a regular format: a brief editorial on the first pages followed by a selection of articles on a variety of topics, often written by well-known names such as Janusz Korczak or the parliamentary delegate Róża Pomeranc-Melcer. At about four or five pages long, these articles were quite accessible for the average reader. The final sections of the issue included book reviews, lists of the contents of journals in the field, and often lengthy reports from local committees. The publications reveal the range of CENTOS's activities, reflecting pressing needs and detailing local work. They also show a dedication to both accessibility and professional and scholarly ideals. Each of the journals sometimes included writings by the children receiving care in CENTOS institutions, but children's writings never appeared regularly. None of these journals were intended for an academic audience, nor were they simply newsletters of a professional association. The Yiddish titles were intended for anyone with a serious interest in the welfare of children, both professionals and parents. *Przegląd Społeczny* intentionally did not include parents in its audience and rejected the idea of popularization, yet it too was published in a format that was more accessible than academic.[13]

Broad, strongly worded statements of support for vulnerable Jewish children were published alongside descriptions of educational philosophy, reports of inspections of children's homes, and extensive reports from local committees. Reviews of relevant new laws and the latest in pedagogy abroad added to the mix, revealing the interest of CENTOS's leaders in practical work, professional development, and pedagogy. While much original work appeared in these journals, many issues included reprints of articles from the other journals (translated from Yiddish or Polish) or from non-Jewish Polish-language titles such as *Wiadomości Literackie* or *Opieka nad dzieckiem*. This shared content confirms my impression that the journals were quite similar in approach and content. The work of some authors appeared in several parts over the course of a year, and many authors published in two or three of the journals over their roughly fifteen years of publication. For example, Michał Friedländer, trained in the law but active as a teacher and pedagogue, published a series of articles on questions of gender in the raising of children over several issues in both *Przegląd Społeczny* and *Dos shutsloze kind*.[14] An article on the work of Friedländer as a popularizer of specialized knowledge by Iwona Michalska raised a question deserving of some consideration and, if possible, further research: that is, of the motivations of those who wrote for these journals. Michalska suggested that difficulties in employment offered Friedländer favourable conditions for freelance writing for professional journals;[15] this may very well have been true for many of his peers. The seeming co-operation among CENTOS editors may simply be the result of a small community in close contact, but it may also be a consequence of shared goals and a professional commitment to improving child welfare.

By the editors' own admission, the journals lacked readers. Notes of pessimism about the low circulation crept in as early as 1925, when Peker wrote that the journal did not enjoy the same support as other journals of its kind.[16] In 1926 the weak economic situation meant that subscribers were forced to let their subscriptions lapse and that institutions no longer had the money to subscribe.[17] In January 1927, the beginning of the journal's fourth year, Peker noted that 100 copies of the journal were sent to Białystok but only one or two to two other locations. Significantly, Peker wrote that Congress Poland was like Eastern and Western Galicia, where there was a singular lack of Yiddish and where Yiddish journals were not read.[18] Upon the journal's 100th issue in April 1932, Peker declared that this was not a cause for celebration because of the difficult economic times. He referred to what he did as 'silent work'.[19] Confident of the continued need for his efforts, he remained determined and optimistic in spite of indifference.

That *Przegląd Społeczny* was published in Polish must have helped it reach a broader audience among the intelligentsia to which its contributors belonged. Leon Weinstock, the chief editor in 1927, and Józef Kohn, who assumed the position in 1928, established a professional journal focusing on the theory and practice of social work. *Przegląd Społeczny* aimed to instruct Jewish social workers in the field, advocate for changes in Polish law that would benefit Jewish children, and establish standards of social work practice akin to those in western Europe.[20] The circulation, according to an article in *Przegląd Społeczny*, was approximately 1,500.[21] *Przegląd Społeczny* was also sent to state offices, orphanages, local political organizations, local Jewish community organizations, and members of the Sejm and Senate. In terms of publishing solid, provocative content, *Przegląd Społeczny*, like its Yiddish counterparts, was remarkably successful. In terms of reaching a wide audience, *Przegląd Społeczny* faced the same difficulties, with the exception that the choice to publish in Polish likely ensured it a greater readership (both among its contemporaries and among twenty-first-century scholars).

By 1928 there were already two journals devoted to Jewish child welfare, but that year a third appeared. Perhaps the central office wanted its own separate title. Peker, a medical doctor and author, seems to have dominated *Dos kind*, given his monthly editorials, so perhaps it arose from personal conflict or professional rivalry. A. Levinson, Leib Neustadt, and M. Shneyorson published the first issue of *Dos shutsloze kind* in January 1928. It attracted writers such as Pomeranc-Melzer and Tsemakh Shabad, a doctor and social worker from Vilna, and the first issue included an extended article on the history of the JDC in Poland, an article on the doctor's role in childcare, and another on the role of the teacher in an orphanage. Like *Dos kind*, the last pages included reports from the regions. It was not appreciably different in format or content from *Dos kind*. The name change to *Unzer kind* in 1930 reflected a more general approach and a determination to move away from 'the traditional, philanthropic concepts of the orphan and orphan care', which privileged work with orphans but neglected broader methods of caring for children.[22]

Two general trends can be identified in the editorials and articles of these journals. The first is a move away from orphan care towards care for all Jewish children, and the second is what the leaders of CENTOS described as the conscious effort to transform childcare from philanthropy into social work. As early as July 1924 there was a recognition that it was time to move away from emergency relief work and to acknowledge that the needs of all children, from the day of their birth to adulthood, must be considered.[23] The crisis of the war led to immediate needs among orphans, but it was time for the associations to establish broader goals. Peker was quite frank in declaring that the cardinal fault of the JDC was that it was temporary, that it had always planned to withdraw its commitment. He viewed orphan care as just one part of childcare, and he consistently advocated for all kinds of ongoing support for all children: medical, educational, spiritual, and social.[24] He stated that he did not want to divide children into those with parents and those without, and thought CENTOS would have a greater effect if it broadened its efforts beyond orphans. There was an integrity to Peker's approach that comes through clearly, if only out of sheer repetition over many issues. The care of orphans was also, in part, the care of adults. The CENTOS associations worked closely with the remaining parents of half-orphans and with family members, especially in the implementation of foster care. The call to improve the lives of children necessitated the teaching of adults—parents were among those in the intended audience of these journals, at least of *Dos kind* and *Unzer kind*.

Peker advocated for all forms of care to be included within CENTOS's work, including the establishment of children's homes, schools, schools for children with special needs, clubs, summer camps, evening courses, publishing projects, hospitals, sanatoria, pharmacies, baths, kitchens, trade workshops, laundries, and centres for school hygiene.[25] The needs of children led to the involvement of CENTOS associations in all of these activities, as far as they were able. Local leaders established orphanages; arranged for foster care; worked with children with special needs; arranged for orphaned children to attend appropriate schools; sent children to summer camps; and sponsored clubs, lectures, training courses, and libraries. They responded to children's needs as those needs became apparent and as their resources allowed.

The name CENTOS, which formally referred to orphans not children in general, remained in use until the group's dissolution during the war, but, in fact, CENTOS associations advocated for care for all children throughout nearly the entire interwar period. The renaming of *Dos shutsloze kind* indicates a formal shift, but the name of the organization stayed the same. A 1931 discussion of a possible similar name change for the western Małopolska association suggests the difficulty of a seemingly simple task, especially as the change does not appear to have been controversial. Objections were raised by both Leib Neustadt and Jan Landau, who argued that the name change could only be done in co-ordination with the other regional associations and the central office. A decision was made to accept the change, but only after further co-operation with the other groups and the main administration.[26] In 1932 Peker and Abram Perec launched another CENTOS journal, *Dziecko* ('Child'), with C. Indelman as editorial secretary. *Dziecko* only appeared for two years. Peker's insistence that conditions dictated the publication of a journal in Polish seems to have ignored the presence of *Przegląd Społeczny*, not to mention *Opieka nad dzieckiem*. Noteworthy, though, was the existence of the organization sponsoring the publication, the Central Organization for the Care of Jewish Children in Poland (Centralna Organizacja Opieki nad Dziećmi Żydowskimi w Polsce), established in 1927.[27] While the name of the new organization makes clear the change in the scope of work, the status of this group remains hazy, and I have yet to find other traces of its activities. Another indication of the turn to more general childcare work was the change in the subtitle of *Przegląd Społeczny* to indicate that the journal focused on both social issues and child welfare.[28] Still, CENTOS's leaders were broad-minded enough from the beginning to address the needs of all Jewish children.

CENTOS's leaders described the associations as the embodiment of the transformation of childcare from charity to professional social work, a successful effort by Jewish leaders to reform their community under difficult conditions.[29] CENTOS's editors described their work as fundamentally different from the efforts of those who had come before them, notably the community leaders and philanthropists who had established orphan homes from the mid-nineteenth century on. The work of these earlier leaders cannot be dismissed as mere charity: throughout the region, Jewish community leaders established orphanages, schools, and hospitals that were regarded as professional institutions, significant enterprises that arose out of the philanthropic work of the wealthiest of the Jewish community. In a fundamental way, the work of nineteenth- and early twentieth-century Jewish philanthropists in both eastern Europe and the United States made the work of CENTOS possible. The JDC, to which CENTOS owed its existence, was the most effective Jewish organizational response to the humanitarian crisis of the war. It seems clear, however, that the leaders of CENTOS distinguished themselves from their predecessors. This may have been simply a natural inclination to describe one's own work in the present as better than what came before or simply the growing pains of a child eager to strike out independently. It should be noted, however, that Peker and others described their work in explicitly national terms while operating in a vastly different context, both socially and politically. This self-perception persisted. A description of CENTOS in the 1938 *Almanach Szkolnictwa Żydowskiego w Polsce* makes this point clear: 'The system of CENTOS work corresponds to the ideology of the Union, which categorically rejects the older, philanthropic tradition of raising orphans and advances the principle of productivization through exemplary professional education.'[30] This description of CENTOS's work highlights vocational education, a fundamental part of the group's mission and an example of its work beyond simply housing children without homes.

Peker described care for children as rooted in religion, but he also rooted his group's work in the movement of national rebirth.[31] The future of the people was dependent on the physical and spiritual development of children as 'future citizens and fighters for the interests of the people'. Caring for children was very much a community activity. Significantly, the non-Jewish Baudouin de Courtenay, in his essay in the first volume of *Dos elendste kind*, also noted the distinction between religious and secular motivations.[32] In an article in the very first issue of *Dos kind*, Peker bristled at the notion that adults might use children for their own individual purposes (even as he drafted them into his own view of Jews as a nation), declaring that a child's misfortune should not just be used as 'a matter of charity for your sinful soul'.³³ The movement he was a part of was not just about clothing and shoes but about the duty to feed and educate and care for future generations.³⁴ Peker wrote that this duty should not treat care for the child as a private matter, placing the carer in the centre of the relationship, as an 'I'. Rather, he argued, care was a community responsibility. Writing in *Dos elendste kind*, Avrum Levinson echoed Peker's words, referring to care for children as a 'national obligation'.³⁵ Peker hoped to end the era of the lone guardian and philanthropist in favour of more centralized institutions that reflected the Jewish national goals of the CENTOS leaders.³⁶ While these plans were aimed squarely at improving the living conditions of the Jewish people in Poland, they were not explicitly political. Child welfare leaders avoided the period's ideological squabbles between Zionists, Bundists, and others, not least because funding from the JDC prohibited specifically ideological positions in working with children. While the role of ideology in the work of CENTOS associations deserves further investigation, the generally non-partisan stance of CENTOS stands out in a period marked by sharp internal Jewish divisions. Peker's call for a national Jewish response to what he saw as a generation in peril aimed to encourage his readers to take practical steps to aid Jewish children.

Beyond the rhetoric about the transformation from charity to social work, the new political context demanded co-operation among local Jewish leaders, Jewish community organizations, and municipal officials that was both challenging and complex. The question of who should care for the needs of minority populations in the new state of Poland—private organizations, municipal governments, or both— was far from settled. Maks Schaff asked this and related questions often in the pages of *Przegląd Społeczny*, not least because changes in Polish legislation affected the answers.³⁷ Schaff recognized the success of private initiatives in the field of childcare in the immediate aftermath of the war. How, then, should the state interact with these new organizations? How was the state going to benefit from what private groups, such as the CENTOS associations, had already done? Schaff's legitimate concerns were the result of the significantly increased involvement of the private (Jewish) sector in child welfare, apart from the official work of Jewish community organizations and the new role of the centralized Polish state. According to an article on this issue in Białystok's *Farn yidishn kind* ('For the Jewish Child'), local leaders recognized the need for government support to improve their work and lamented that government support was more coincidental than systematic.³⁸ The goal for CENTOS's leaders, in both the local associations and the central office, was to make the Jewish institutions as autonomous as the non-Jewish ones. The associations themselves acted as intermediaries between the Jewish community and international Jewish groups such as the JDC and between the Jewish community and Polish officials at the local and state level. With all of these groups, the CENTOS associations pressed the case for funding to develop broader services for children, especially funding from municipal governments, to which they were legally entitled. Whatever the merit of CENTOS's claim to have transformed child welfare, CENTOS differed from earlier individual and community responses to the needs of children in the coordination and scale of its efforts, efforts made possible at least in part by the traditional philanthropy that led to the formation of the JDC during the First World War.

The entangled relationships between Jews and Poles at the local level reveal that the separateness of the communities was clear and still taken for granted by both Jews and Poles. The transformation CENTOS's leaders envisioned was a realization of their goals of Jewish self-help, which, first and foremost, included raising Jewish children as Jews. The leaders of CENTOS recognized the assimilationist trend in schools and often discussed how to combat the idea that schools were suited only for Polish children and the Polish national ideal. The reprint in *Dos kind* of an article that originally appeared in the *Shedletser vokhnblat* in Siedlce evoked the fears of assimilation in the school system. The article was reprinted, according to an editorial note, precisely because the same issues in Siedlce were also present in other towns. The author wrote that the Polish elementary school simply did not give Jewish children a way to make a living and to stay tied to the Jewish people.[39] Nonetheless, Jewish fathers sent their children to Polish elementary schools, because they did not have to pay for tuition. As the author wrote, 'it is difficult to demand a non-Jewish teacher give a Jewish child his heart, his soul'.[40] In addition, antisemitism among Poles kept many Jewish teachers out of the public schools, as it was seen as a scandal for a Jewish teacher to teach a Polish child. In another minor example, CENTOS's leaders considered what their children read and were concerned by the statistics of a lending library at the CENTOS institution in Pińsk.[41] Jewish children borrowed Yiddish and Hebrew books, but they borrowed books in Polish at a much higher rate. The CENTOS journals reveal an organization that was not explicitly political: CENTOS was never associated with a specific political movement, for example, yet it did not shy away from efforts to fight what it saw as forced assimilation.[42] Transformation was not just about the provision of more services for children offered at an advanced professional level, it also involved the establishment and development of Jewish organizations that operated independently to achieve Jewish goals for the Jewish nation.

How much do these sources reveal about the children themselves? The men and women whose work appeared in the CENTOS journals were well educated, usually trained in western Europe, and active professionally and in the Jewish community. Largely due to the available sources, any history of CENTOS will primarily be a history of adults, of those engaged enough to have left traces of their work. The orphans themselves are for the most part nameless, and the CENTOS journals do not help much in naming them. Still, it is worth making the distinction between adults and children and considering what can be gleaned from these sources about who the children were, what they thought, and what they did. Just as the CENTOS journals combined advocacy and practice, an article on CENTOS should, as far as possible, include the voices of children as a corrective to the views of adults. Information about the children comes from the children themselves: from their writings and from the articles and reports from the local associations which often mention specific activities. These articles and reports tell of a variety of activities the children participated in, including the preparation of exhibitions of crafts and institutional newsletters.[43]

Children's writings did appear periodically in the journals, though never as a regular feature. This was quite unlike *Mały Przegląd*, the children's supplement to *Nasz Przegląd*, one of Poland's most important Jewish daily newspapers.[44] *Mały Przegląd* was the work of the children in Janusz Korczak's children's home, but, while Korczak was much admired in the pages of the CENTOS journals, the editors never truly picked up on his model of highlighting the children's work.[45] Still, it is clear that they recognized the importance of allowing children to speak for themselves, and furthermore, many authors provided descriptions of children and their living conditions. The selections of children's writing that did appear in the CENTOS journals offer intriguing insights into the lives of Jewish children.

Not surprisingly, the young people were very concerned about their futures. Given the persistent poor economic conditions, work, or the lack of it, is perhaps the foremost theme in these writings. In a special section of children's writings in the April–May 1934 issue of *Dos kind*, Yosef Vindman expressed concern about his future.[46] One evening in early spring, when he was standing on the balcony of the children's home in Brisk (Brześć), Vindman's thoughts turned to his work as an apprentice and his plans upon finishing school. He recalled his days of vacation in a small shtetl, where he noticed how many carpenters were without work, men with families and children, who went around miserable and depressed. 'From what did they make a living?' he asked. He went on:

And what about us, we who are still beginners, we who still need first to begin to learn a trade, from what will we make our existence? On what will we survive for even one day? Our parents, whom we don't have, will help us? Once, when students finished school, they became apprenticed to a master, but that was another time. That was a time when everybody could work and make money if they wanted, but today? Today you try to sell your hands and your brains, but no, nowhere's buying. When we go to and from school, we see thousands of people with haggard faces, sitting along the boulevards and waiting. Maybe? Maybe 'God' will send them something? On the other side walk others, satisfied, well-dressed, and not feeling hardship. And so I sit and think: No, something in our lives is not in order.[47]

Sitting on the balcony, he felt someone's hand upon him and turned to see his friend, who asked him what he was thinking about. Vindman asked him: 'What do you intend to do when you finish school?' The response: 'What kind of question are you asking me? I will work.' Vindman continued: 'You already have someone to work with? Thousands of workers go around without work and you have work? What does this mean?' His friend responded: 'I will go away to a kibbutz and then to Palestine.' Vindman replied: 'This means that those who think like Zionists, they can go to Palestine and get a chance to live, but those who think a little differently, they already can't live, can't exist.' Taken aback and momentarily struck silent, his friend then explained that Vindman could join an organization and then go to a kibbutz, too.

Vindman asked: 'What? Do you think I'm such a great idealist? To go to the Land of Israel I should already know what I will be doing there.' Thinking a bit more, Vindman continued, 'No! I will never do such a thing. I will not sell my soul to the devil just for a certificate [to go to Palestine]. For a certificate I won't do something which is against my conscience.' Vindman went to bed thinking: 'Is it worth it to dance the "Kelal yisra'el" just for a certificate? No, fifty times no! I will never do it.' And with such thoughts he fell asleep.

Vindman's discussion with his friend highlights both the necessity of work and the varying views young Jews held towards Palestine. While the developing Jewish community held out hope to many young Jews in Poland, not everyone was taken with the idea of emigrating, even when economic circumstances presented very few options, as Vindman himself had just lamented.[48]

Another story, a second submission from Brisk, was written as if to motivate young Jews to realize the importance of work, and verges on satire. In 'The File', Moyshe Dubrinski told of a fictionalized day's experiences at work.[49] This longer piece centres on an encounter with an instructor teaching a teenager to use a file, but the point of the story is one's attitude towards work. After the encounter with the instructor, young Khaim excitedly told his friend Hershele about a dream from the previous night. In the dream, he returned to a home where he met his brothers and sisters, who asked questions about his work and study and listened eagerly to tales of what he had already made as a worker. He thinks: 'It's good to be a guest!' In the dream he next went to the meeting of an organization, where he noticed a pretty girl. He thought to himself in his dream: 'I'm already not going back to Brisk.' Suddenly, another boy woke him up, calling out that the hour was already late. Startled awake, he realized that there was no home, no meeting, that first he had to go to school, that, simply, he did not know which world he was in. Telling his friend Hershele that he was ready to throw away the file to run after the pretty girl, Khaim is admonished. Hershele tells him:

No, my dear Khaim, you must not say such things. The file should be sacred for you! *The entire world exists by the file.*[50] The newest technology—this is all made by the file ... Take back your words! You should love the file because this is the basis of the world and the basis of life.[51]

The story concludes: 'Hearing Hershele's words, I felt more will to work and now I work more diligently.'[52]

Preoccupied with their fate during difficult economic times, these children longed for practical solutions. Vocational education was recognized as one of children's— and society's—most important needs. By 1938 CENTOS was serving over 30,000 children, providing services ranging from vocational training to housing to foster care.[53] The work of CENTOS was constructive, as evidenced by efforts to improve vocational education in the 1930s.[54] The leaders of the CENTOS associations made co-ordinated efforts to identify children's skills and to place them in appropriate educational programmes. As described in the CENTOS journals, CENTOS aimed to give children practical opportunities as a way of building up the Jewish nation.

The CENTOS publications can reveal much about both Jewish community leaders and the children they served, but there is still more of the group's history to uncover. Further biographical information about the editors would illuminate their place within the larger community of Jewish and Polish intellectuals and social workers. In addition, the bare facts outlined here suggest that there must be more to the story than a simple desire to increase awareness of the CENTOS mission. A second Yiddish publication was begun in 1928, when one title was already active. Peker established a second Polish title when the first was very much a going concern. Unfortunately, I can only speculate about professional rivalries or personal motivations, but it does seem likely that the personalities of CENTOS's leaders may have played a role in publishing decisions. In addition, my impression is that those most involved were not always the most prominent figures. The publications were run and written by professionals active in the field who chose this kind of journalistic work as a way to share their knowledge and as part of their professional development. There are also many outstanding questions about the relationships among the editors, writers, and other leaders of CENTOS and of Polish Jewry which the publications themselves cannot easily answer.

Though the CENTOS publications may not have had the audience they deserved, they document the group's work and ideals. The most pressing concern remained consistent throughout the period—how to raise Jewish children as Jews. To do their work, the leaders of CENTOS had to pay close attention to legal developments that offered protections for children and to relationships with municipal officials who often provided funds, however small, for their work. There was an emphasis on the Polish legal and political context at the same time as there was a lack of explicitly Zionist propaganda. The occasional publication of articles describing conditions for children in Palestine shows that the CENTOS journals did not ignore Zionism, but it should also be said that it did not feature prominently in their pages. CENTOS was Jewish national self-help in the broadest meaning of the phrase. It was not a political movement, but it was a pragmatic step towards improving the health of the Jews living in Poland. It was not simply emergency relief or charity but rather organized social work that established desperately needed institutions for Jews throughout newly independent Poland.

Notes

1 'Tsu unzere lezer', *Unzer kind*, Nov.–Dec. 1931, pp. 449–50.
2 M. Peker, 'Unzer yubiley (tsum dershaynen funem 100-tn numer *dos kind*)', *Dos kind*, Apr. 1932, pp. 2–3.
3 'Nasze drogi', *Przegląd Społeczny*, Jan. 1929, pp. 1–3; (untitled), *Przegląd Społeczny*, Jan. 1930, pp. 1–4.
4 See N. Bar-Yishay and M. Web, 'Yesoymim-farzorgung un kindershuts in poyln (1919–1939)', in J. Fishman (ed.), *Shtudyes vegn yidn in poyln, 1919–1939 / Studies in Polish Jewry, 1919–1939* (New York, 1974); S. Martin, 'A History of CENTOS', in *For the Good of the Nation: Institutions for Jewish Children in Interwar Poland. A Documentary History*, ed. and

trans. S. Martin (Boston, Mass., 2017), 1–59; see also Archiwum Żydowskiego Instytutu Historycznego, Warsaw, 117, 'Prace magisterskie napisane przed 1939 rokiem', 45: B. Lewin, 'Związek Towarzystw Opieki nad Żydowskimi Sierotami i Dziećmi Opuszczonymi Rzeczypospolitej Polskiej (CENTOS)', Master's thesis (University of Warsaw, 1938). The history of child welfare in Poland, including education and pedagogy, is well covered (see C. Kępski, *Dziecko sieroce i opieka nad nim w Polsce w okresie międzywojennym* (Lublin, 1991); S. Walasek (ed.), *Opieka nad dziećmi i młodzieżą: Studia z dziejów i oświaty w XX wieku* (Kraków, 2008), esp. Z. Cutter and E. Sadowska, 'Opieka nad ludnością II Rzeczypospolitej ze szczególnym uwzględnieniem mniejszości żydowskiej', 59–118); as is Jewish child welfare (see M. Łapot, *Z dziejów opieki nad żydowskim dzieckiem sierocym we Lwowie (1772–1939)* (Gliwice, 2011)).

5 Łapot, *Z dziejów opieki nad żydowskim dzieckiem sierocym we Lwowie*, 88–98; M. Balukiewicz, 'Działalność Towarzystwa dla Opieki nad Żydowskimi Sierotami we Lwowie (1916–1939)', in A. Bilewicz and S. Walasek (eds.), *Rola mniejszości narodowych w kulturze i oświacie polskiej w latach 1700–1939* (Wrocław, 1998), 291–9.

6 Y. Bauer, *My Brother's Keeper: A History of the American Jewish Joint Distribution Committee* (Philadelphia, Pa., 1974).

7 Bar-Yishay and Web, 'Yesoymim-farzorgung un kindershuts in poyln', 136.

8 Archiwum Żydowskiego Instytutu Historycznego, 200, 'Zbiór dokumentów Związku Towarzystw Opieki nad Dziećmi i Sierotami Centos w Getcie Warszawskim, 1941–1942'.

9 'Der farband fun di tsentrales far yesoymim-farzorgung', *Dos elendste kind*, 1925, pp. 3–7.

10 A. Levinson, 'Korbones fun a tsufal', *Dos elendste kind*, 1925, pp. 7–10.

11 These publications include *Dos elendste kind* (Warsaw, 1925); M. Shneyorson (ed.), *Dos elendste kind* (Warsaw, 1927); *Kinder far kinder: yesoymin-khoydesh 1927 yor* (Warsaw, 1927), which seems to have been intended as an illustrated supplement to *Dos elendste kind*; *Krótki zarys działalności Związku Towarzystw Opieki nad Sierotami Żydowskiemi Rzeczypospolitej Polskiej* (Warsaw, 1928), which also appeared in German and English; *Odbudowa i samopomoc* (Warsaw, 1930); M. Peker, *Vi azoy dertsien gezunte kinder?* (Warsaw, 1931); C. Hirsz Tarłowski and M. Peker, *Bay der arbet: zamlung fun pedagogishn notitsn un artiklen* (Warsaw, 1934); K. Lis, *Der hayl-pedagogisher anshtalt 'tsentos' un zayn dertsiung-sistem (sistem fun intimer dertsiung)* (Warsaw, 1937); M. M. Mejnster, *Fizjologia i higiena miesiączki* (Warsaw, 1937); and M. Unger (ed.), *Di produktivizirungs-tetikayt fun tsentos: farband fun gezelshaftn far kinder un yesoymim-farzorgung tsentos in poyln* (Warsaw, 1938). Local publications included *Farn yidishn kind* in Białystok and *Der yosem* from the Home for Jewish Children and Farm in Helenówek, Łódź, an institution not supervised by CENTOS but written about extensively in *Dos kind*. The publications edited by Moyshe Shalit should also be mentioned (*Fun yor tsu yor: ilustrirter gezelshaftlekher yorbukh* (Warsaw, 1929); *Oyf di khurves fun di milkhomes un mehumes: pinkes fun gegnt-komitet 'yekopo' in vilne: 1919–1931* (Vilna, 1931)). Many associations' annual reports can be found in *Dokumenty życia społecznego Żydów polskich 1918–1939 w zbiorach Biblioteki Narodowej*, ed. B. Łętocha, A. Cała, and Z. Głowicka (Warsaw, 1999).

12 For an introduction to *Przegląd Społeczny*, see M. Łapot, '"Nowe wychowanie" na łamach lwowskiego "Przeglądu Społecznego" (1927–1939)', *Pedagogika*, 12 (2003), 77–86; id., 'Lwowski *Przegląd Społeczny* jako trybuna walki o prawa dziecka', in T. Gumuła and S. Majewski (eds.), *Historia wychowania w kształceniu nauczycieli: Tradycja i współczesność, teoria i praktyka* (Kielce, 2005), 317–25; id., 'Zagadnienia teorii opiekuńczo-wychowawczej na łamach "Przeglądu Społecznego" (1927–1939)', *Pedagogika*, 18 (2009), 227–40.

13 See Łapot, *Z dziejów opieki nad żydowskim dzieckiem sierocym we Lwowie*, 176.

14 M. Friedländer, 'Zagadnienia płciowe w wychowaniu młodzieży', *Przegląd Społeczny*, June 1929, pp. 216–26; July 1929, pp. 244–53; Aug. 1929, pp. 293–302; Sept. 1929, pp. 329–31; Oct. 1929, pp. 373–85; *Dos shutsloze kind*, Aug. 1929, pp. 254–7; Sept. 1929, pp. 306–9; Oct.–Nov. 1929, pp. 346–56; Dec. 1929, pp. 413–16; *Unzer kind*, Jan. 1930, pp. 13–25; see also I. Michalska, 'Nauczyciel dla nauczycieli i wychowawców: Michał Friedländer jako popularyzator wiedzy o wychowaniu w latach międzywojennych', *Studia Edukacyjne*, 48 (2018), 133–49.
15 Michalska, 'Nauczyciel dla nauczycieli i wychowawców', 136.
16 M. Peker, 'Der tsveyter yorgang', *Dos kind*, Jan. 1925, pp. 1–2. CENTOS's publications did attract some attention from the press: *Haynt* published lists of the contents of many issues (see e.g. *Haynt*, 7 Mar. 1924, p. 10; *Haynt*, 10 Apr. 1924, p. 4).
17 M. Peker, 'Der driter yorgang', *Dos kind*, Jan.–Feb. 1926, pp. 1–2.
18 M. Peker, 'Der ferter yorgang', *Dos kind*, Jan. 1927, pp. 3–4.
19 Peker, 'Unzer yubiley', 3.
20 'Nasze drogi', *Przegląd Społeczny*, Nov. 1927, pp. 1–4; quoted in Łapot, *Z dziejów opieki nad żydowskim dzieckiem sierocym we Lwowie*, 176.
21 [Untitled], *Przegląd Społeczny*, Jan. 1930, pp. 1–4.
22 'Unzer kind', *Unzer kind*, Jan. 1930, pp. 1–2.
23 M. Peker, 'Fun yesoymim-farzorgung tsu kinder-hilf', *Dos kind*, July 1924, pp. 1–3.
24 M. Peker, 'Kindershuts oder yesoymim-farzorgung', *Dos kind*, Sept.–Oct. 1925, pp. 1–2.
25 M. Peker, 'Tsentrale yidishe kinder-shuts-organizatsye', *Dos kind*, Oct. 1926, pp. 2–3.
26 'Walne Zebranie Zachodnio-Małopolskiego Związku Towarzystw Opieki nad sierotami żyd. w Krakowie', *Przegląd Społeczny*, July 1931, pp. 270–5: 273–4.
27 'Centralna Organizacja Opieki nad Dziećmi Żyd. w Polsce – Sprawozdanie', *Dziecko*, 1932, no. 1, pp. 20–4: 20.
28 The subtitle changed from 'Organ Związku Towarzystw Opieki nad Sierotami Żydowskimi Rzeczpospolitej Polskiej "Centos"' ('The Organ of the Union of Societies for the Care of Jewish Orphans of the Republic of Poland "Centos"') to 'Czasopismo poświęcone zagadnieniom społecznym i opieki nad dzieckiem' ('A Journal Devoted to Social Issues and Childcare').
29 For a similar observation, see N. Meir, 'From Communal Charity to National Welfare: Jewish Orphanages in Eastern Europe before and after World War I', *East European Jewish Affairs*, 39 (2009), 19–34; see also id., *Stepchildren of the Shtetl: The Destitute, Disabled, and Mad of Jewish Eastern Europe, 1800–1939* (Stanford, Calif., 2020), 121; M. Zalkin, 'Charity', in G. D. Hundert (ed.), *YIVO Encyclopedia of Jews in Eastern Europe* (New Haven, Conn., 2008); M. Zalkin, 'Philanthropy', in Hundert (ed.), *YIVO Encyclopedia of Jews in Eastern Europe*.
30 'Centos', *Almanach Szkolnictwa Żydowskiego w Polsce*, 1 (1938), 462–73: 463.
31 M. Peker, 'Kinder-shuts oder yesoymim-farzorgung', *Dos kind*, Oct.–Dec. 1925, pp. 1–2.
32 J. Baudouin de Courtenay, 'Der yosem: als almenshlekher, iber-natsyonaler un iber-religyezer bagrif', *Dos elendste kind*, 1925, pp. 17–19.
33 M. Peker, 'Di kinder-farzorgung, als gezelshaftlekhe problem', *Dos kind*, Jan. 1924, pp. 3–5.
34 M. Peker, 'Nokh der konferents', *Dos kind*, Apr. 1924, p. 1.
35 Levinson, 'A natsyonaler khoyv', *Dos elendste kind*, 1927, pp. 8–13; quoted in Meir, 'From Communal Charity to National Welfare', 27.
36 Peker, 'Tsentrale yidishe kinder-shuts organizatsye'.

37 M. Schaff, 'Na pograniczu dwuch [sic] okresów', *Przegląd Społeczny*, Oct. 1928, pp. 1–7.
38 'Af naye vegn', *Farn yidishn kind*, June 1927, pp. 2–3.
39 'An alte tsore', *Dos kind*, Feb. 1929, pp. 32–4.
40 Ibid. 33.
41 Ben-Nakhman, 'Vos leyenen unzere kinder', *Dos kind*, Jan.–Feb. 1935, pp. 12–16.
42 For another example, see S. Z. Vulf, 'Vegn dertsiungs-shuln far yidishe kinder fun di 'povshekhne' shuln', *Dos kind*, July 1929, pp. 38–9. Vulf encouraged the establishment of schools like the supplementary Sholem Aleichem and Workmen's Circle schools in the United States.
43 See S. Martin, 'Future Generations: Associations for Jewish Children in Kraków, 1918–1945', *Polin*, 23 (2010), 291–319: 312; M.S., 'Jednodniówka', *Przegląd Społeczny*, Aug. 1929, pp. 321–4; Eng. trans.: M. Schaff, 'The Publication of the Home for Orphans in Lwów, Zborowska 8', in *For the Good of the Nation*, 64–71.
44 See A. Landau-Czajka, *Wielki 'Mały Przegląd': Społeczeństwo i życie codzienne w II Rzeczypospolitej w oczach korespondentów 'Małego Przeglądu'* (Warsaw, 2018); ead., 'Working Children and Young People as Seen by Contributors to *Mały Przegląd*', this volume.
45 See Łapot, *Z dziejów opieki nad żydowskim dzieckiem sierocym we Lwowie*, 212–17.
46 Y. Vindman, 'Unzer gedank', in 'Shafungen fun unzere kinder', *Dos kind*, Apr.–May 1934, pp. 15–17.
47 Ibid. 16.
48 Ibid. 16–17.
49 M. Dubrinski, 'Di fayl', in 'Shafungen fun unzere kinder', *Dos kind*, Apr.–May 1934, pp. 17–19.
50 Emphasis in original.
51 Dubrinski, 'Di fayl', 18–19.
52 Ibid. 19.
53 Martin, 'A History of CENTOS', 40–1; see also Bauer, *My Brother's Keeper*, 204.
54 'Centos', 464–5.

2. THE MEDICAL TREATMENT OF CHILDREN

The Child in Traditional Jewish Medicine around 1900

MAREK TUSZEWICKI

The traditional healing culture of Eastern Ashkenaz, as it had developed by the turn of the nineteenth century, made use of amulets and prescribed diets to ensure the birth of healthy and virtuous children. The traditional value system also helped to explain the death of a child when it occurred. At the same time, the development of modern medicine, which was very attractive to the Jewish elite and led to the emergence of many Jewish doctors, presented an increasingly successful challenge to the traditional Jewish medical world. In Jewish traditional medicine, children were not only patients, but sometimes functioned as caregivers and even healers. This was a role particularly assigned to adolescent girls, while medicines derived from children played an important role in traditional Jewish medical culture. Methods of protecting the community from evil forces were focused specifically on male children as well as on actions and rituals appropriate to the male domain of Judaism.

THE BEGINNING of the twentieth century was a time of rapid change for the Jewish population of eastern Europe, which participated in many aspects of the modernizing processes affecting the continent. This was a time when Yiddish and Hebrew literacy was growing dynamically, and the Jewish intelligentsia was also increasingly involved in the German, Russian, and (a little later) Polish press and publishing. The period is also marked by a wealth of testimony on changes in medical culture. This was produced by various groups and social circles with different objectives. Thus ethnographers, predicting the undoubted decline of the world of tradition, wished to preserve evidence of this cultural heritage for future generations. For their part, physicians sought to undermine 'folk medicine' or at least identify in its complex set of ideas and practices some glimmers of rational thought. The writers of growing numbers of autobiographies were eager to describe a medical world-view organically linked to a dying era which they remembered with nostalgia. Alongside these groups, which were critical of current medical practice, representatives of Jewish Orthodoxy also expressed their opinions. New books of customs[1] and handbooks of remedies[2] were produced, although they remained strongly rooted in a tradition of religious writing. Similarly, in the domain of halakhic and ethical literature, it is possible to perceive the impact of modernity, unavoidable given the fundamental challenges it posed for religious orthodoxy. Pious handbooks for newlyweds[3] and complex codices of Jewish law,[4] which also dealt with health issues, gained the approval of the Orthodox and became an important tool for resisting the challenge of modernity. In other words, a large and varied corpus of literature now emerged, devoted to how health issues were perceived, how illnesses were treated, and what preventative measures were taken in Jewish circles. This remained, to a great extent, connected to the traditional approach, although the individual works reflected very different attitudes to these issues.

A very large part of this literature was devoted to children: their conception, protection from illnesses, and treatment, and teaching them how to stay healthy. It thus reflects east European Jewish views on children and their well-being, and refutes Philippe Ariès's claim that the idea of childhood was only 'discovered' very recently; on the contrary, it testifies to the widely developed sense within Judaism of the uniqueness and specificity of childhood.[5] This literature shows direct inspiration from biblical history, although this is in accordance with talmudic tradition, midrash, and rabbinic literature, and is also linked to kabbalistic speculation. According to this literature, a child is one of the three major blessings that God can confer on a person —care for children thus results from a desire to ensure their success both in this world and in the next. At the same time the roots of many precepts concerning the health of children must be sought in classical medicine as it developed in ancient Greece and Rome and which, by way of Arab doctors and Jewish interpreters, triumphantly returned to Europe during the Renaissance. Until the final decades of the eighteenth century this represented the major strand of medical culture throughout eastern Europe, and its loss of influence, although never complete, occurred only as a result of developments in the nineteenth century, above all the successful battle of modern medicine against smallpox, cholera, and infant mortality. Alongside religious tradition and classical medicine, there was a full palette of beliefs and practices to which contemporaries gave such names as 'superstition' and 'anachronism', but which remained influential in the care of children at all stages in their development.

It is not surprising that, like other communities during the period of modernization, the Jews of eastern Europe had a large and varied collection of techniques to care for their young. This reflects a deep concern for motherhood and childhood and a clear definition of children as human beings different in many ways from adults. The literature nearly always focuses on children as the beneficiaries of folk medicine.[6] However, children also sometimes functioned as caregivers—administering medicines—and even as healers. This in turn created opportunities for them to take the initiative, to lay down conditions, or even oppose the rules imposed by tradition. The actual period of childhood also created a specific symbolism, which, integrated with mystical ideas, served society as a reference point in threatening situations. It thus affected communities even before a child was born.

In this chapter I want to examine the role of the child in Jewish medicine. I will consider what led to the enormous variety of treatments which can be found in the source material and investigate the circumstances surrounding the more active role taken by children in the treatment of illness. Did they thus gain a degree of independence or were they exploited instrumentally as performers of rituals, essential but involuntary participants in them? Did Jewish society differ in this respect from its environment or were its practices elements of a broader medical culture specific to eastern Europe? Finally, what were the reasons for the practice of seeking a reversion to childhood, even if only symbolically, to safeguard an adult's health and life?

I will start with an analysis of what is perhaps the most important stage in the development of a young life, that before birth. According to the Talmud, a child in its mother's womb is composed of three elements: white matter, which comes from the father and creates bones, muscles, fingernails and toenails, the brain, and the whites of the eyes; red matter coming from the mother, which forms skin, the body, hair, blood, and pupils; and the soul, which comes from God.[7] Sources from the beginning of the twentieth century do not limit themselves to this scheme, especially since it does not explain a great number of phenomena accompanying pregnancy and childbirth. The diagnostic methods proposed at first glance could suggest the use of spells, whose justification is based on a folk cosmology that can be difficult to decipher. They focus on the moment of a child's conception, which determines its sex and to a certain extent its health. To a great degree, however, they reflect the views of rabbis, both those expressed in the Talmud and those in later writings. They also draw indirectly on medical traditions that entered Jewish culture from outside. One of the most interesting traditionalist accounts of the prenatal period is the nineteenth-century handbook *Imrot shelomoh*, which claimed that at conception all the elements of a human being were present, while the mother's womb was like soil which was being sown.[8] It also speculated on the actual process of fertilization, which, linking the seed with moisture, was seen as comparable to the operation of yeast in the production of bread.[9] In this work there are speculations linked to traditions of classical medicine regarding the right (warm) and left (cold) sections of the uterus, which were derived from the belief that human health requires an equilibrium between the four main bodily fluids, or humours—blood, yellow bile, black bile, and phlegm. Each of the humours is built up from the four elements and displays two of the four primary qualities: hot, cold, wet, and dry. This theory, expounded by the Greek physician Galen and attributed to Hippocrates, took root in rabbinical teachings and was then modified in ethical texts.[10] It held that if the seed entered the warm section of the uterus then a boy would be born and if it entered the cold section then it would be a girl.[11] Based on this, attempts were made to establish the sex of a child by examining the future mother's body. If a pregnant woman's left breast was larger this was taken to mean that she was carrying a girl, and if the right one was then it was a boy.[12]

Attempts to discover a foetus's sex were included in the theory of humours, above all in the symbolism of blood, bile, and phlegm—fluids common to the parent and the child. These were also linked to popular beliefs about male characteristics (strength, aggression) and female characteristics (beauty, submissiveness) and sought analogies in the world of plants and animals. Thus, the author of *Imrot shelomoh* recommended throwing a piece of bread impregnated with menstrual blood to a dog. If the dog ate it, there would be a male child.[13] In turn, most of the advice drawn by the collection *Refa'el hamalakh* from the eighteenth-century guide *Mifalot elokim*[14] suggested examining the expectant mother's urine to determine the foetus's sex, and the couple's urine in the event of problems getting pregnant.[15] These practices, derived to a certain extent from the proximity of the urinary and sexual organs, were also connected to long-established diagnostic techniques of classical medicine which sought answers to medical issues in the consistency, colour, and smell of urine. In early modern Jewish society, midwives examined the mother's urine to establish the state of a pregnancy.[16]

The overwhelming majority of measures regarding pregnancy prescribed by Jewish handbooks were preventative, seeking to avoid the negative consequences of immoral behaviour. A relatively large number were also intended to protect against potential threats or to treat existing medical conditions. The handbooks rarely specify the appropriate moment for applying them, so it seems they were simply used at random. For example, two of the four plant species used ritually on the festival of Sukkot—the *lulav* (palm branch) and the *etrog* (citron)—could be used prophylactically during pregnancy and childbirth: untying the knots of the plaited holder used to bind the *lulav*, myrtle, and willow together on Hoshana Rabbah was held to reduce the risk of a miscarriage,[17] whereas biting off part of an *etrog*[18] was seen both as a prophylactic measure, when performed before the birth, and as a therapeutic one, if the delivery proved difficult. Many remedies were applied at moments of crisis when the pregnancy appeared to be at risk or before labour. Labour itself increased the danger to both mother and child, and ways were sought to ensure their safety, whether through intercession with God, warding off evil influences, or help from a traditional healer or a doctor.

The handbooks also espoused traditional values as a way to protect the unborn child. At almost every stage of a foetus's development the moral actions of the mother, the father, and sometimes other members of the family and even the community as a whole were held to be of fundamental importance. This was especially true before the child was conceived, reflecting the belief that children are a blessing and childlessness a punishment from God. Thus the Hebrew edition of *Refa'el hamalakh* advised a childless couple to follow punctiliously the order of daily prayers and the rules for ritual fringes, to ransom those in captivity, to pay for the copying of a Torah scroll and the publishing of religious books, and to eschew taking employment away from their neighbours, gossiping, and lying. This would supposedly gain them credit in the heavenly court and the blessing of children. The sin of pride, manifested in a woman's excessive attachment to beautiful clothes, was also seen as an obstacle to becoming pregnant.[19] This concern extended to the prenatal period. Here, the parents' behaviour was held to be influential in preventing the foetus from developing a deformity and ensuring it was endowed with the capacity for learning. *Imrot shelomoh* lists a series of talmudic prohibitions on sexual relations between a married couple, since every inappropriate action carried harmful consequences for the child.[20] Thus, great weight was given to ensuring that during intercourse the couple saw themselves as performing a commandment rather than satisfying their lust.[21] Fantasizing about other people or looking at other faces was regarded as especially perilous. The writer of *Imrot shelomoh* even forbade conversations 'in an alcove', so as not to arouse thoughts about other women.[22] However, a man devoted to good works and the commandments could expect wise, prosperous, and good offspring.[23]

Another significant group of practices was aimed at preventing unwanted pregnancies or ensuring that conception did not take place under circumstances which could endanger the foetus. The danger of malevolent forces was stressed. Most surviving sources provide advice on combating the evil eye, Lilith, demons, and other evil powers. These injunctions sometimes take the form of prohibitions: for instance, a man should not have intercourse with his wife within an hour of leaving the toilet since the demon associated with the place could cause infertility.[24] It was also forbidden to urinate under a new moon, since this activity was in general seen as harmful, and, if a woman was pregnant at the time, she could also be endangered.[25] At the same time there were also injunctions such as that a woman who was soon to give birth or had just given birth should have a knife to hand as protection against demons.[26] The greater part of such directives took the form of the use in specific circumstances of religious-cum-mystical traditions. *Shimush tehilim* recommended, for example, reciting Psalm 1 in order to avoid a miscarriage and Psalm 128 in the event of a difficult delivery.[27] In turn, *Refa'el hamalakh* recommended that the husband of a pregnant woman should, in the ninth month, perform the commandment of taking the Torah out of the Holy Ark or be called up to the final reading of the Torah.[28]

Amulets for the protection of pregnant women were also popular in east European Jewish society. Protection from the harmful influence of demons was provided, above all, by written amulets containing the holy names of God and the angels. Some examples are cited in *Refa'el hamalakh*, which took them from *Toledot adam*.[29] The preparation of amulets required the participation of a scribe, who was to use kosher parchment rather than paper if possible. These were hung on the forehead, around the neck, or on the thigh of the mother so that they lay on bare skin. Arranged with the letters upwards, surrounded with white cloth, paper, or leather, they were to remain in place until recovery or death.[30] Not all amulets derived their power from magic: many were linked with the belief of classical medicine in the healing properties of stones, which was part of the understanding of the nature of the physical world. Accordingly, miscarriage could be prevented by a *shternshis* (protective stone).[31]

Advice on dietary matters, employing ideas derived from the classical theory of the humours, also represents an important aspect of traditional medical teaching. According to the Yiddish edition of *Refa'el hamalakh*, for example, pregnant women should avoid alcoholic drinks and coffee, since they harmed the foetus. They should not eat dishes that were too bland, too fatty, or too salty, take strong medicines (especially for vomiting and purging), or use healing creams on the stomach. The book recommended, instead, taking walks and other moderate activity and avoiding anger and hot baths.[32] *Imrot shelomoh* advised a couple trying to conceive to eat light, fresh, and cool dishes: 'anything that would neither overstimulate nor chill desire'. Lean poultry—since chicken meat increases the amount of blood and semen—egg whites, mutton, and small quantities of pure white wine low in acidity and tartness should all be consumed. Goat, beef, and goose, and to a certain extent courgettes, watermelon, chives, and garlic were supposedly bad for the quality of sperm.[33] In addition, the mother's diet had a clear influence on the child's development. In order that her children should enjoy good health, a woman should be given meat and wine. If she ate fish, she could expect charming children, while consuming an *etrog* ensured they would be 'fragrant'.[34] Dietary advice can even be found in codices of Jewish law, such as *Kitsur shulḥan arukh*, where the need for caution when eating those organs which play a central part in the theory of humours (such as the heart) was stressed.[35]

The Patient

Lack of offspring in a world with no provision for maintenance in old age represented a tragedy for many families.[36] The main cause was infant and child mortality. It is hard to find accounts of Jewish life in eastern Europe from this period that do not contain moving descriptions of relatives, friends, or complete strangers suffering from the loss of offspring.[37] This problem attracted the attention of supporters of the Haskalah, and their demand to stop 'the murder of the innocent' struck a chord in people's imaginations. Specifically, this encouraged the reform of customs which in traditional circles were considered essential and sometimes even fundamental. The dangers of circumcision, one of the most important rituals of Judaism, were now highlighted. Calls were also made for the reform of traditional religious education in order not only to ensure access to rational secular knowledge but also to provide education on health and hygiene.[38] Interest in the child as the 'patient' of folk medicine had always existed, but this does not fully explain the great wealth of sources dealing with the issue.

The extent and variety of documentation of beliefs and practices regarding the care of children at this time can best be explained by examining how care for the very youngest involved parents and the adult world in general. Despite the fact that the death of a child was not unusual and affected many families more than once, it still needed to be explained. The search for an answer which could justify such a painful loss pushed people towards religion and mysticism. Within the framework of traditional Jewish society, as in other east European communities which had long preserved their traditional value systems, reality was not limited to the physical domain. Little wonder, therefore, that the death of a child was seen as the result of the parents' —and even sometimes the whole community's—moral impurity.[39] Thus parents who lost a child needed to regain God's favour. This usually involved activities that, according to rabbinic tradition, warded off death: prayer, repentance, and charitable offerings. Depending on the circumstances each of these three paths could assume an individual or a collective form, a simple one or one augmented by rich cultural ornamentation. For example, even before the birth of a child, a couple was encouraged to give to charity, to consider their sins, and to say the 'Anenu' prayer on fast days.[40] If, after its birth, a child turned out to be sickly, the parents could designate the day of its birth or another day of the week as a permanent day of fasting. In the event of problems with fasting—for instance, another pregnancy—charitable donations could act as an alternative.[41] As well as initiatives which were clearly approved of by the rabbinic authorities, the sources also urge undertaking steps of ambiguous provenance. If the parents suspected that the high mortality rate amongst their children represented a punishment by God, they could undertake the symbolic 'sale' of a child to a pious couple who were not so threatened.[42]

The days preceding important rituals (such as circumcision, the redemption of the first-born, barmitzvah, the wedding of a child) and also times perceived as transitional (such as the changing of the seasons) required individuals to seek God's protection and also led to recourse to magic. This was even more the case when the child's state of health was judged to be precarious or in danger (such as labour in the eighth month). On these occasions, recourse was made to practices inspired by the religious tradition, such as quotations from the psalms, incantations in the form of stories of biblical characters or themes, and various kabbalistic motifs: angelic names, sentences built on gematria, geometric figures (such as the shield of David), and so on. However, the sources also mention the use by Jews of practices clearly derived from the non-Jewish environment. For instance, the arrival of a child's adult teeth was symbolically associated with their ability to protect themselves from danger, and it was recommended to throw the milk teeth into the fire while chanting an appropriate formula, which was more or less identical with a practice found in German sources.[43] Often these practices were assimilated culturally and acquired Jewish symbolism. Bags containing items which were believed to ward off evil, such as garlic, salt, nails, and amber, were widely employed to protect children among the people of eastern Europe, and Jews also made use of them. Alongside the simple and extensively used form of such amulets, Hebrew and Yiddish sources provide examples of more complex ones whose preparation required kabbalistic knowledge (as they included parchments or other materials, such as almonds, with kabbalistic inscriptions).[44] In turn, slaughtering a cockerel over a sick child (an action also performed before Rosh Hashanah), which was considered by the rabbis to be a dubious practice, was sometimes undertaken with the recitation of Hebrew formulae connected to biblical texts.[45]

The practices of their non-Jewish neighbours remained a constant reference point for the Jewish population of eastern Europe. Some descriptions of children's illnesses indicate clearly that they had become integrated into the medical world of Jews who were resident in areas dominated by German culture. Hence, in the sources there are references to *munkalb* (mooncalf), an illness whose symptoms included diarrhoea, blurred vision, and yellowness of complexion, and to *wasermun*, where the sufferer takes on the appearance of a drowned man, to mention only ailments believed to be brought on by the light of the moon. There are also a large number of German-derived names for healing techniques. Similarly, there are many confirmations in the sources that Jewish–Slavonic contacts also led to the exchange of medical ideas. There are numerous examples in Jewish sources of Slavonic terminology used to describe both illnesses (*kolten* for plica polonica, a condition characterized by diffuse matting of the hair; *gostic* for rheumatism) and medical remedies (for example, the names of herbs or simple preparations). However, the most obvious contacts appear in the case of medical advice, where Jewish discussions of treatment for various ailments find their counterpart in documents produced by almost every community in eastern Europe. Jewish sources, for instance, reproduce Slavonic magical texts against diseases affecting children (such as erysipelas or fever) in Yiddish. The Slavonic understanding of spells and the Jewish understanding of the evil eye show far-reaching similarities not only in identifying the symptoms they caused but also in how they should be treated. Certainly, it is almost impossible to separate Jewish healing culture from its German and Slavonic environments.[46]

However, these were not the only methods used by Jewish parents to heal their children. They also sought to obtain earthly assistance. In the pre-modern era this meant medicine based to a great extent on the theory of the humours. Even until the twentieth century vestiges of ancient views and medical practices survived in the Jewish community, including the use of cupping glasses and inducing sweats. Their longevity was helped by the rabbis, who at various times tried to evaluate such methods of diagnosing or treating children and whose opinions survived on the strength of the authority of the written word. This was the case in advice of a dietary nature found, for example, in talmudic tractates and also in actions carried out by the ritual circumciser. Within his power lay not only the ritual itself but also the assessment of the child's condition before and after the procedure and how to respond to any problems. A guidebook for circumcisers published towards the end of the nineteenth century in Kraków describes how to distinguish minor ailments (such as a rash) from serious ones (for example, smallpox). This classification is to a great extent based on the views of Maimonides and the Talmud but was also influenced by the theory of the humours.[47]

At the beginning of the twentieth century modern medicine became an important element in the treatment of illness. In the case of life-threatening childhood illnesses, even very religious and traditionalist families (including hasidim) sought help from doctors. With each passing decade confidence in doctors and professors of medicine grew, despite the relatively high cost of their services and the fact that their definitions of illness and the role of the patient were completely different from traditional understandings.[48]

As Zbigniew Libera has argued, ideas about illness in the Slavonic world depended, to a great extent, on the age and sex of the person affected. From birth, children were held to be at risk from a great many illnesses, which was to a certain extent explained by their lack of emotional, physical, and social development, their dependence on others, and their vulnerability to external influences. Some illnesses were regarded as specific to children, whereas others did not affect them, especially in cases where protection was provided by them being unaware of the symbolic meaning of their actions.[49] Similar views are found in surviving Jewish sources, and, as with the Slavs, different treatments were sometimes used for children from those used for adults—almost always less extreme or with fewer side effects. For a bladder infection, *Refa'el hamalakh* suggested steeping two teaspoonfuls of garlic seeds in a quart of water, straining it, and drinking it every two hours: a tablespoonful for an adult and a teaspoonful for a child.[50] Boils on a child's head were to be treated using cleansed butter and vodka, and in the case of an older child, also goose grease.[51] The decision as to which method to use and whether it should be applied to a young patient was taken by the child's relatives. As in other communities of eastern Europe, Jewish parents (or other family members) decided what was good for the child, even if they did have questions for experts.

The varied collection of beliefs and practices in the Slavonic cultural landscape became an indispensable element of Jewish culture, which in turn imposed its own very particular stamp on them. The remedies were recorded in Hebrew or Yiddish, references to Elijah and Job replaced references to New Testament figures, and the remedies were linked to the cycle of the Jewish year, the synagogue liturgy, and even the customs of a given town. However, the main feature of Jewish treatments appears to be their specific focus on protecting male children. There is very little information explicitly referring to this, and there are amulets protecting young girls against Lilith; nonetheless, in the overwhelming majority of cases the sources refer to the protective powers of items traditionally worn by men, to the key significance of circumcision and barmitzvah, and to teaching a boy Jewish prayers and how to observe Jewish rituals. This finds its justification in the conviction that a young man would play a key role in the achievement of salvation. It was he who would realize in full the ideal of the Jew through marriage and performing the commandments and good deeds. Eventually he would also take care of his parents' well-being in the world to come, saying Kaddish regularly, and remembering the dead on feast days and the anniversaries of their deaths.[52]

The Healer and Methods of Healing

In the context of medical culture, the child usually appears as a passive recipient. The child is a one-dimensional figure: weak and at risk from disease and the workings of demonic forces. However, within a Jewish family, a child had a range of duties that changed with age and differed by gender. Furthermore, childhood, like old age, represents a specific period in a person's life. In the popular understanding, the child, close to both this and the other world, was not a fully fledged member of the group, yet was vested with specific features and characteristics. Demonic creatures gravely threatened the child, but the child was also more frequently in touch with them and able to placate and win them over.[53] In the pre-modern cultural imagination, children could even become the repositories of extraordinary powers, especially when their birth was accompanied by circumstances deemed to be exceptional.

Girls played a large part in medical culture. In families with many children, they were prepared for the role of caregivers by looking after their younger siblings. The work of girls was in essence an extension of the work of adult women, especially mothers. Therefore, it included shopping, tending the kitchen garden, cooking, nursing, and simple medical procedures. If grandparents were also living in the household, then they, too, would be the objects of such care. The transition from childhood to young womanhood accompanied a girl's first period and remained shrouded in secrecy. There was no public ceremony, like the barmitzvah, and only a minimal private initiation involving mother and daughter.[54] A girl entering young adulthood was seen as a eligible for marriage; however, she had to possess those abilities necessary for a future mother and mistress of a household, including taking care of individuals who were too young to look after themselves and sick members of the family, and even carrying out minor medical procedures.

Boys had a completely different role. Their influence on the success of a family was to be guaranteed by piety and knowledge gained in prayer and religious literature. While girls were taught to prepare herbs and apply bandages, aspects of the natural side of medical culture, boys were instructed in the working of the supernatural. Thus pre-emptive procedures of a supernatural character were their specific preserve. If they did not learn this knowledge from their parents, older siblings, or grandparents, they became acquainted with texts on exorcism and magical incantations from a *melamed*. As they began their education in the ḥeder, boys learned of the dangers of evil spirits and ways to counter them.[55] This was not just theoretical learning. People who needed to protect an infant from the machinations of evil forces invited ḥeder pupils and their teachers to visit them to say the appropriate prayers and sometimes also to carry out other magical actions. With time boys were introduced to the field of ethical literature, which discussed in detail the conflict of good and evil, the implications of sin for health, repentance as the road to recovery, and other matters. When they achieved adulthood they were not only able to take care of their own health but also knew what actions would ensure the safety of the other members of the family.

In the Slavonic lands, children were also seen as having access to the other world. Predestined by virtue of the time, place, or any special circumstances of their birth, they were able to attain supernatural abilities which could be drawn on later in adult life to practise traditional medicine.[56] Such beliefs were also a part of Jewish medical culture. Hasidic hagiography often emphasized that the birth of child destined to assume the role of *tsadik* (and also miracle worker) was accompanied by an extraordinary aura presaging a great future or that the actual birth itself appeared as a miraculous event (such as when the parents were very old).[57] It was usually the firstborn, however, who was meant to practise magic, or occasionally the seventh or the youngest child.

The sources also contain advice on quite prosaic ailments which it was believed children could cure. For example, for backache the sufferer was supposed to lie face down and let a first-born child walk over the spot.[58] When the actual illness was ascribed to demonic or magical sources, attempts were made to turn to supernatural powers. Thus, Jewish sources recommended putting the sufferer between the legs of a first-born, or three first-borns in turn, as a cure for the evil eye.[59] A person afflicted by a spell could be cured by having their face spat on or blown over, usually three times, by a first-born boy before his thirteenth year (this worked best after fasting).[60] The Jewish community generally preferred male children to perform these rituals. It is worth emphasizing, however, that female first-borns also had a special status: as adult women they were believed to become *opshprekherkes* (cleansers of the evil eye).

Sometimes simply being a child was sufficient to enjoy supernatural powers. Within the Jewish community, it was believed that a child who was not yet fully grown was immune to the temptations of evil forces, especially once it had survived the period of infancy during which it was most at risk from them, usually when it acquired teeth. Therefore, an innocent child was sometimes included in a party that had to deliver bad news or to counteract the dangers of misfortune or illness.[61] Pupils from a *ḥeder*—not older and undoubtedly better educated yeshiva students— were called upon to say prayers over a newborn. The Shema was believed to be able to render evil powerless, and having it recited by innocent children supposedly increased its strength.[62] Likewise, certain actions taken towards pupils who had visited the house for such a purpose, such as offering them sweets from a child's cradle, can be seen as a way of warding off demons and were dependent on the innocence of the young participants.

Pre-modern medicine saw children not only as objects of care or just young patients but also as individuals possessing skills in caring for and even curing the sick. The examples given above indicate that this could serve as a pretext to help a child negotiate its position in a group; however, as a rule, it assumed the prosaic character of gifts, such as sweets. In such circumstances the child did not seem to have any possibility of acquiring independence from the adults, who to a greater or lesser degree controlled their involvement in healing. This lack of independence brought into relief specific practices in which adults used a child instrumentally, as when people suffering from infertility were encouraged to participate in the ritual of circumcision. Playing the role of godfather or godmother allowed the afflicted person to perform a commandment and at the same time to be in contact with a child at an exceptionally holy moment which confirmed its relationship with God.[63] The woman playing the role of godmother often also bathed the child.[64] In this way, she not only performed a charitable act but also served the child at the moment of its especially strong relationship with holiness. Perhaps not surprisingly, such actions did not always cure infertility.

A very marginal yet striking set of treatments employed in Jewish medical culture were medicines derived from children. They were certainly less important than other protective or benevolent charms or medicines, above all those derived from animals, plants, and mineral materials. The sources refer to only a few of them. In the case of a fistula, an abnormal opening connecting two or more organs or spaces inside or outside the body, *Refa'el hamalakh* recommended smearing the affected spot with the excrement of a breast-fed infant.[65] It was also recommended to preserve the umbilical cord to show to the child when it began to learn (this supposedly was good for the memory) or to add it in powdered form to a drink (to improve the child's appearance).[66]

In this context I should also mention the remedies linked with the ritual of circumcision. The sources themselves, especially those actually originating in Orthodox circles, seem to be aware of the dubious character of such remedies, and at times distance themselves from them. Thus, in one remedy, a man wishing for a child should obtain from the circumciser a freshly amputated foreskin, put it on a finger of his left hand for about half an hour, and after the ceremony burn it to ashes. These should then be drunk with 'good' wine on the day of the wife's visit to the ritual bath, some in the morning, some in the afternoon, and the rest in the evening.[67] Another remedy suggested that an infertile woman should swallow a recently amputated foreskin, although this was criticized as being contrary to the laws of *kashrut*.[68] Contact after circumcision with a penis that had not yet been tainted by a discharge of sperm supposedly also helped in the case of childhood epilepsy and, in general, protected against evil (especially on the eve of the circumcision of another young patient).[69]

Reversion to Childhood

Concluding the discussion of the various forms of participation by children in east European Jewish medical culture, there is the case of adults who, motivated by a desire to maintain or regain their health, symbolically reverted to childhood. In traditional Jewish culture, a person over the age of 70 was seen as a newborn, since they had reached the allotted biblical lifespan. They could perceive their advanced age as the result of God's grace, proof of a life well spent. They could then start counting 'the acquired years' again: when a man reached the age of 83, he would symbolically have another barmitzvah.[70] Such behaviour had no legal consequences—that is to say it did not involve giving up the rights gained with maturity. Underlying this belief was, however, the deeply rooted fear of the negative consequences of provoking the Angel of Death (or impure forces) by talking of a person's advanced age.

The practice of dating one's age from the year in which one turned 70 clearly derives from a view of childhood as a period when death is rather unlikely and definitely not 'normal'. As a result, among magical remedies, there are rituals involving a second birth. Closely associated with them was the Hebrew tradition of changing one's name, especially in the case of adults, after a potentially fatal illness. Such people were seen as returning to a life free from the sins of their previous one, and, as with a newborn infant, this required a new name.[71] Symbolic participation in a second birth to ward off death is also common in rituals widely practised in eastern Europe. When a suffering person was told to go between the legs of a woman or a first-born, the symbolic meaning of this action also unambiguously referred to the moment of leaving the mother's womb.[72] In the opinion of contemporary ethnographers, actions such as putting a sick person into a stove, passing a child through a window, or carrying a sick person over a threshold should be seen in the context of renewed birth (the house–person relationship to be seen as a reflection of the mother–child relationship).[73] Despite the fact that it is hard to find anything typically Jewish in such practices, the sources record similar behaviour among east European Jews. The Jewish customs of bringing a child to a sick person or entering or leaving a house through a window should be seen as attempts to prevent death.[74] In turn, like non-Jews, Jews used the stove to aid a patient threatened by death. This seems to be linked with its central location within a household and can also be understood as the symbolic equivalent of a funeral pyre. In order to strengthen the effect it was necessary to put the sick person into a heated stove three times.[75]

Conclusion

A considerable part of the folk materials collected at the beginning of the twentieth century among east European Jews apply to children, their health and well-being. This is to a certain extent the result of interest by early ethnographers in explaining very high levels of infant mortality. It is, however, above all testimony to the care with which Jewish society surrounded the youngest generation. Surviving materials present a complicated image of the methods used to protect, diagnose, and cure children, reflecting the broad range of alternatives available. It is hard to describe this conglomerate simply as 'folk medicine', since it consists also of recommendations sanctified by the authority of classical and contemporary doctors. This medical culture was also closely in touch with those of the surrounding societies. The immediate family was still the centre of decision-making in this complex system. No external institution was able to take its place, although amongst the various types of health care that were developing there was no lack of those that called for entrusting a child to the care of an outside agency.[76]

Portraying children exclusively as passive beneficiaries of Jewish medical culture would leave a very one-sided image that fails to take into account the strong relationship of children with their family and the society in which they would grow up. It is not possible to identify any advice concerning the prenatal phase that would not at least require the involvement of the pregnant woman. As the child grew, its aid was also sought for adult patients. However, the area of freedom thus created remained limited. It was for the most part linked to the acquisition of not very significant privileges and more often was the result of the imposition on a young person of a strictly defined social role. Control over the administration of a ritual or a healing intervention remained essentially in adult hands.

Those Jewish medical practices which result from differences of religion or custom are easily observable, including those in which the principal role (passive or active) was played by children. Actions which sought to protect the community from evil forces primarily involved male children and rituals derived from the Bible, Talmud, and kabbalah which were traditionally performed only by males. In eastern Europe, Jewish society distinguished itself by its attachment to the heritage it brought from the West, although it also incorporated elements widespread among the Slavs. The traditions of classical medicine which had been assimilated by the rabbinate remained important. At the same time the development of modern medicine, which was very attractive to the Jewish elite and led to the emergence of many Jewish doctors, provided an increasingly successful challenge to the traditional Jewish medical world.

Translated from the Polish by Jarosław Garliński

Notes

1 See, inter alia, Y. Lipyets, *Sefer matamim* (Warsaw, 1890); id., *Sefer matamim heḥadash* (Warsaw, 1893/4); A. E. Hirshovitsh, *Minhagei yeshurun* (Vilna, 1898/9); A. I. Sperling, *Ta'amei haminhagim umekorei hadyni*, 4 vols. (Lwów, 1881); id., *Ta'amei haminhagim oyf ivre taytsh*, 2 vols. (Lwów, 1909).

2 See, inter alia, I. Y. Goldberg and A. A. Eisenberg, *Sefer laḥashim usegulot vegoralot umazalot* (Jerusalem, 1880/1); S. Lifshits, *Sefer haḥayim hanikra segulot yisra'el* (Munkacs, 1905); Y. Y. Rosenberg, *Refa'el hamalakh* (Piotrkov, 1911); id., *Der malekh refoel* (Przemyśl, 1913); *Shemirot usegulot niflaot* (Warsaw, 1913); *Sefer refuot* (Vienna, 1926/7).

3 e.g. S. Wilff, *Imrot shelomoh vehu ḥupat ḥatanim heḥadash* (Kraków, 1906).

4 e.g. A. Danzig, *Ḥayei adam* (Vilna, 1843); id., *Ḥokhmat adam* (Vilna, 1844); Eng. trans. in *Chochmas Adam: The Laws of Niddah / Ḥokhmat adam: hilkhot nidah*, trans. Y. Cohen (New York, 1999); S. Ganzfried, *Kitsur shulḥan arukh* (Lwów, 1884).

5 See E. Baumgarten, 'Judaism', in D. S. Browning and M. J. Bunge (eds.), *Children and Childhood in World Religions: Primary Sources and Texts* (New Brunswick, NJ, 2009), 15–81; J. R. Berkovitz, 'Judaism', in P. S. Fass, *Encyclopedia of Children and Childhood in History and Society*, 3 vols. (New York, 2004), ii. 508–11.

6 The pioneers of Polish and Polish Jewish ethnography focused on this (see esp. R. Lilientalowa, 'Dziecko żydowskie', *Materiały Antropologiczno-Archeologiczne i Etnograficzne Akademii Umiejętności w Krakowie*, 7 (1904), 141–73; Ger. trans.: R. Lilienthal, 'Das Kind bei den Juden', *Mitteilungen zur jüdischen Volkskunde*, 25 (1908), 1–24; expanded edn.: R. Lilientalowa, *Dziecko żydowskie* (Kraków, 1927); new edn. (Warsaw, 2007); H. Biegeleisen, *Matka i dziecko w zwyczajach, obrzędach i praktykach ludu polskiego* (Lwów, 1927)); postwar research has been redefined by Raphael Patai (see R. Patai, 'Jewish Folk-Cures for Barrenness', *Folklore*, 54 (1943), 117–24; id., 'Jewish Folk-Cures for Barrenness, II', *Folklore*, 56 (1945), 208–18); the motif of the child in folk healing, especially in relation to amulets, has also been addressed (e.g. M. Folmer, 'A Jewish Childbirth Amulet for a Girl', *Amsterdam Studies in Jewish Thought*, 12 (2007), 41–56); on birth, see M. Klein, *A Time to Be Born: Customs and Folklore of Jewish Birth* (Philadelphia, 1998); see also A. Jeziorkowska-Polakowska and A. Karczewska (eds.), *Żydowskie dziecko* (Lublin, 2013). This chapter is based on sources assembled during work on a doctorate devoted to Jewish 'folk medicine' (M. Tuszewicki, 'Wierzenia i praktyki lecznicze ludności żydowskiej na ziemiach polskich przełomu XIX i XX wieku', Ph.D. thesis (Jagiellonian University, 2014)) and also used in M. Tuszewicki, *Żaba pod językiem* (Kraków, 2015); Eng. trans.: *A Frog under the Tongue: Jewish Folk Medicine in Eastern Europe*, trans. J. Taylor-Kucia (Liverpool, 2021). Although my research was not focused on Jewish children, this thread ran through it.

7 BT *Nid.* 31a.

8 Wilff, *Imrot shelomoh*, 76.

9 Ibid. 63.

10 H. J. Zimmels, *Magicians, Theologians, and Doctors: Studies in Folk Medicine and Folklore as Reflected in the Rabbinical Responsa* (Northvale, NJ, 1997), 62; cf. Galen, *On Semen*, ed. and trans. P. De Lacy, Corpus Medicorum Graecorum, 5.3.1 (Berlin, 1992), II, 5: 36–9 (p. 187); Henryk Biegeleisen also mentions the belief in lying on the right side as a way of conceiving a boy amongst Jewish and Ruthenian women (Biegeleisen, *Matka i dziecko*, 29).

11 Wilff, *Imrot shelomoh*, 76.

12 Ibid. 99. Abraham Rechtman mentions that in small towns in Ukraine women working as traditional healers prided themselves on being able to influence the sex of a child, especially the first born (A. Rechtman, *Yidishe etnografye un folklor* (Buenos Aires, 1958), 294).

13 Wilff, *Imrot shelomoh*, 99. If, after her first confinement, a mother wanted to give birth to a boy, she should throw the placenta to a male dog, and to a bitch for a girl (B. W. Segel, 'Wierzenia i lecznictwo ludowe Żydów', *Lud*, 3 (1897), 49–61: 57).

14 Yoel Halpern's *Mifalot elokim* was developed on the basis of the practical kabbalah and, in addition to works such as *Toledot adam* and *Sefer zekhirah*, had for almost two centuries worked on the Jewish imagination in matters of health (Y. Halpern, *Mifalot elokim* (Żółkiew, 1726); id., *Toledot adam* (Żółkiew, 1720); Z. Simner, *Sefer zekhirah* (Hamburg, 1709)). Rosenberg cites them as his prime sources in the introduction to *Refa'el hamalakh*.

15 Rosenberg, *Refa'el hamalakh*, 39.

16 Zimmels, *Magicians, Theologians, and Doctors*, 62.

17 Sperling, *Ta'amei haminhagim oyf ivre taytsh*, i. 85.

18 Rosenberg, *Refa'el hamalakh*, 62; Lilientalowa, *Dziecko żydowskie* (2007), 20; S. Bastomski, *Bam kval: yidishe shprikhverter, vertlekh, glaykhvertlekh, rednsartn, farglaykhenishn, brokhes, vintshenishn, kloles, kharomes, simonim, zgules, zabobones, un andere* (Vilna, 1920), 109; J. Pulner, 'Obryady i povir'ya, spolucheni z vahitnoyu, porodileyu i narozhdentsem u zhydiv', *Etnografichnyi visnyk*, 8 (1929), 100–14: 108.

19 Rosenberg, *Refa'el hamalakh*, 17.

20 Lilientalowa, *Dziecko żydowskie* (2007), 20–1.

21 Ibid. 41; E. Herzog and M. Zborowski, *Life is with People: The Culture of the Shtetl* (New York, 1962), 136; J. Trachtenberg, *Jewish Magic and Superstition* (New York, 1939), 187.

22 Wilff, *Imrot shelomoh*, 40.

23 Ibid. 56; Rosenberg, *Refa'el hamalakh*, 17. It was good for conception to take place on a Friday night, since the sabbath's holiness would benefit the child (Trachtenberg, *Jewish Magic and Superstition*, 186).

24 Wilff, *Imrot shelomoh*, 54–5.

25 Y. Y. Rosenberg, *Der malekh refoel* (Przemyśl, 1913), 15; cf. R. Lilientalowa, 'Kult ciał niebieskich u starożytnych Hebrajczyków i szczątki tego kultu u współczesnego ludu żydowskiego', *Archiwum Nauk Antropologicznych*, 1/6 (1921), 1–15.

26 Rosenberg, *Refa'el hamalakh*, 42; Lipiets, *Sefer matamim*, 47.

27 *Shimush tehilim* (Kraków, 1648). This anonymous publication explained in an accessible manner practical methods for using specific passages from the Psalms. It was updated many times over the centuries (see Trachtenberg, *Jewish Magic and Superstition*, 109).

28 Rosenberg, *Refa'el hamalakh*, 62.

29 Ibid. 112.

30 See T. Schrire, *Hebrew Amulets: Their Decipherment and Interpretation* (New York, 1982).

31 Rosenberg, *Refa'el hamalakh*, 61. This stone could even be worn on the sabbath (see BT *Shab.* 66b; Ganzfried, *Kitsur shulḥan arukh*, 84: 19). Dioscorides advised tying an 'eagle

stone' (*aetites lithos*) to the shoulder and to the thigh during childbirth (Dioscorides, *De materia medica*, trans. T. A. Osbaldeston and R. P. A. Wood (Johannesburg, 2000), 5: 161 (p. 823)).

32 Rosenberg, *Der malekh refoel*, 63–4.
33 Wilff, *Imrot shelomoh*, 55–6.
34 Ibid.; see Trachtenberg, *Jewish Magic and Superstition*, 185.
35 Ganzfried, *Kitsur shulḥan arukh*, 32: 9. The restrictions on pregnant women or children eating heart, liver, or brains were based on a concern to maintain the equilibrium of the humours (see J. S. Wasilewski, 'Tabu, zakaz magiczny, nieczystość, Część II: Tabu a paradygmaty etnologii', *Etnografia Polska*, 34 (1990), 7–45).
36 Infertility was one of the most important reasons for going to see a *tsadik*. Popular hagiographies in Hebrew and Yiddish provide numerous examples of the intervention of a *tsadik* in such cases (see G. Nigal, *The Hasidic Tale* (Oxford, 2008), 114).
37 See B.-C. Bernstein, *Zikhroynes un geshtaltn* (London, 1962), 102–4; R. E. Kositsa, *Zikhroynes fun a byalistoker froy* (Los Angeles, 1964); M. Rawicz, *Mayse bukh fun mayn lebn*, 3 vols. (Buenos Aires, 1964), i. 13.
38 See, inter alia, R. Lilientalowa, *Precz z barbarzyństwem! (Rzecz o obrzezaniu)* (Warsaw, 1908). Criticism of the sanitary conditions of *ḥeder*s in which circumcisions were carried out appears frequently in accounts of life in old Jewish villages, for instance in the *yizkor* (memorial) book of Bełz (Y. Rubin (ed.), *Belz: sefer zikaron* (Tel Aviv, 1974), 315, 325).
39 Y. Zelkovitsh, 'Der toyt un zayne bagleyt-momentn in der yidisher etnografye un folklor', *Lodzer visnshaftlekhe shriftn*, 1 (1938), 149–90: 155.
40 Wilff, *Imrot shelomoh*, 98.
41 *Ets ḥayim vehu sefer kitsur shenei luḥot haberit* (Vilna, 1889), 99; Wilff, *Imrot shelomoh*, 110; Rosenberg, *Refa'el hamalakh*, 33; Lilientalowa, *Dziecko żydowskie* (2007), 70–1.
42 Wilff, *Imrot shelomoh*, 111; Rosenberg, *Refa'el hamalakh*, 18; Lipyets, *Sefer matamim*, 84. Sometimes a child was 'sold' to a community institution, for example, the burial society (Zimmels, *Magicians, Theologians, and Doctors*, 143–4).
43 E. Sosnovik, 'Materialn tsu der yidisher folksmeditsin in vaysrusland', *Yidishe filologye*, 2–3 (1924), 160–8: 168; A. Fayvushinski, 'Pruzhener folklor', in M. W. Bernstein and D. Forer (eds.), *Pinkes pruzhene, bereze, maltsh, shershev, selts: zeyer oyfkum, geshikhte un umkum* (Buenos Aires, 1958), 199–205: 203; 'Simonim un zgules', in Y. L. Kahan (ed.) *Yidisher folklor* (Vilna, 1938), 277–97: 285; cf. O. Hovorka and A. Kronfeld, *Vergleichende Volksmedizin*, 2 vols. (Stuttgart, 1908), ii. 856.
44 Rosenberg, *Segulot urefuot . . . ibergezetst oyf zhargon fun heyligen seyfer refa'el hamalakh* (Łódź, [1920?]), 26.
45 Zimmels, *Magicians, Theologians, and Doctors*, 4; cf. C. F. Plaut, *Likutei ḥaver ben ḥayim*, 11 vols. (Munkács, 1878–93), v. 8a; M. Berger, *Imrei yisra'el* (Sósfalu, 1911/12), 9a.
46 Jewish memoirs contain evidence of Christians seeking help for sick children from Jews. This was especially the case at the courts of *tsadikim* but also in terms of the widely understood concept of neighbourly assistance (see N. Blumental (ed.), *Sefer borshtshiv* (Tel Aviv, 1960), 47; Herzog and Zborowski, *Life is with People*, 172; A. Almi, *Momentn fun a lebn* (Buenos Aires, 1948), 75–6).
47 Y. Levin, *Ḥotam kodesh* (Kraków, 1892), 25b–26b; see *Shulḥan arukh*, 'Yoreh de'ah', 263.
48 The growth of faith in physicians was also helped by paediatric handbooks appearing at the start of the nineteenth century whose authors had studied at European universities, including works by Moses Mahel (Lwów) and Mateusz Studencki (Warsaw). A book by

the former published for the first time in 1821 appeared almost 100 years later in Przemyśl, entitled *Yesodot harefuah o gidul banim*, as the work of a 'famous doctor in Berlin'.

49 Z. Libera, *Medycyna ludowa: Chłopski rozsądek czy gminna fantazja?* (Wrocław, 1995), 44–5. However, inappropriate behaviour could lead to misfortune for children despite their being unaware of the implications of their actions.

50 Rosenberg, *Der malekh refoel*, 10.

51 Sperling, *Ta'amei haminhagim oyf ivre taytsh*, ii. 111.

52 Herzog and Zborowski, *Life is with People*, 317.

53 *Refa'el hamalakh* points to the presence of a demon even in children's excrement (Rosenberg, *Refa'el hamalakh*, 44). There are many Yiddish tales in which children exhibit knowledge of the realm of demons or deal with them directly (e.g. A. Levita, 'A shpatsir ibern shtetl', in id. (ed.) *Sefer zikaron kehilat breziv (bzhozov)* (n.p., 1984), 167; B. Silverman-Weinreich (ed.), *Yiddish Folktales*, trans. L. Wolf (New York, 1997), 343).

54 I. Fels, 'Zabobony lekarskie u żydów', *Wschód*, 3 (1906), 2–6: 4; Y. L. Zlotnik, 'Miminhagei yisra'el', *Reshumot*, 1 (1918), 335–77: 369.

55 Herzog and Zborowski, *Life is with People*, 91.

56 Libera, *Medycyna ludowa*, 213, 239.

57 Nigal, *The Hasidic Tale*, 125.

58 Jewish Theological Seminary, MS 9862: 'Segulot urefuot' (1913).

59 R. Lilientalowa, '"Ayn-hore"', *Yidishe filologye*, 4–6 (1924), 245–71: 260.

60 B. W. Schiffer [Segel], 'Alltagglauben und volkstümliche Heilkunde galizischer Juden', *Am Ur-Quell*, 4 (1893), 272–3: 273; id., 'Materyały do etnografii Żydów wschodnio-galicyjskich', *Zbiór Wiadomości do Antropologii Krajowej*, 17 (1894), 261–332: 319; id., 'Wierzenia i lecznictwo ludowe Żydów', 60; Lilientalowa, 'Dziecko żydowskie', 152. In his memoirs, A. Almi provided an interesting description of a child operating as a quack. Since he was a first-born son, he was taken to people's homes from an early age to deal with the evil eye. In such cases the women called for him first, and only if he was unable to help would a doctor be summoned. The *melamed* taught him a special blessing, which he recited and then spat three times in the patient's face. If he was not at home when he was required, a handkerchief was taken from his mother to lay by the head of the sick child. And because a few children did in fact recover, he acquired a reputation as a good 'go-to person' (A. Almi, *Momentn fun a lebn*, 73–6).

61 C. Chajes, 'Gleybungen un minhogim in farbindung mitn toyt', *Filologishe shriftn*, 2 (1928), 281–328: 311.

62 Lipyets, *Sefer matamim*, 47; N. Blumental, *Tsurikblikn* (Tel Aviv, 1973), 152.

63 S. An-ski, *Dos yidishe etnografishe program* (Petrograd, 1914), 36, 177.

64 I. Rivkind, *Yidishe gelt in lebnshteyger, kultur-geshikhte un folklor* (New York, 1959), 40–1; see S. Weissenberg, 'Das neugeborene Kind bei den südrussischen Juden', *Globus*, 93/6 (1908), 85–8: 87.

65 Rosenberg, *Refa'el hamalakh*, 59.

66 See Segel, 'Materyały do etnografii', 322; R. Lilientalowa, 'Przesądy żydowskie', *Wisła*, 14 (1900), 639–44: 640–1.

67 'Segulot urefuot', 27; Lilientalowa, 'Dziecko żydowskie', 148; A. Ben-Ezra, 'Minhogim', in id. (ed.), *Horodets: a geshikhte fun a shtetl* (New York, 1949), 172–6: 174.

68 Rosenberg, *Refa'el hamalakh*, 6.

69 Wilff, *Imrot shelomoh*, 107, 109.

70 G. Bin Wolf, 'Zikhronot mibeit aba', *Jeda am*, 17 (1974), 149–50: 149.

71 S. Weissenberg, 'Krankheit und Tod bei den südrussischen Juden', *Globus*, 91 (1907), 357–63: 359; Chajes, 'Gleybungen un minhogim', 296–7; Zelkovitsh, 'Der toyt un zayne bagleyt-momentn in der yidisher etnografye un folklor', 165.
72 Lilientalowa, '"Ayn-hore"', 260.
73 Libera, *Medycyna ludowa*, 185–6.
74 Lilientalowa, 'Dziecko żydowskie', 150; Bastomski, *Bam kval*, 105; J. Pulner, 'Obryady i povir'ya', 112; Chajes, 'Gleybungen un minhogim', 311; Fayvushinski, 'Pruzhener folklor', 200.
75 Lilientalowa, *Dziecko żydowskie* (2007), 64; Rosenberg, *Refa'el hamalakh*, 37; id., *Segulot urefuot*, 23; see also Libera, *Medycyna ludowa*, 34.
76 Herzog and Zborowski, *Life is with People*, 355.

Newborn Care and Survival among Jews in Early Modern Poland

ZVI ECKSTEIN AND ANAT VATURI

While there were discrepancies between Jewish law and custom and actual practice, the customs, beliefs, and norms governing post-partum breastfeeding and wet-nurse employment that were standardized as 'good' among Jews in early modern Poland favoured infant survival. In particular, the fact that Jewish religious precepts enjoined maternal breastfeeding from shortly after birth gave the newborn the benefit of the first milk, known as colostrum, which contains a range of antimicrobial elements as well as substances strengthening the immune system, of which medical knowledge only became aware in the nineteenth century. These practices thus constituted one of the factors that reduced infant and child death rates among Jews, which seem to have been lower than the corresponding rates among Christians. This contributed to the rapid rise of the Jewish population in Poland–Lithuania.

Introduction

In seventeenth-century Europe, between one-third and one-half of children born did not reach the age of 10,[1] and the estimated infant mortality rate in Poland was 350 per 1,000 live births. At the same time, child mortality among Jews was significantly lower for all ages, and, on average, from birth to 5 years old it was 23 per cent lower. According to the earliest available statistical data for the province of Posen (1819–63), during the first year of life the infant mortality rate among Jews was 27 per cent lower than among the general population.[2] Although historians have noticed this difference, they have not provided sufficient explanation for it.[3] This chapter takes up the challenge and attempts to explain the lower infant mortality rate among Jews as resulting from, among other factors, the care provided to newborns in the first twenty-eight to thirty days of life known as the neonatal period. In modern medical practice, neonatal care supports physiological processes which assist the neonate in the transition from intra-uterine to extra-uterine life. It helps to establish proper feeding and sleeping habits,[4] to avoid high-risk infections, and to recognize birth or congenital defects, and is thus pivotal to the baby's survival at least during the first year of life.[5]

This chapter outlines the major traditions and concepts that governed neonatal care among Jews in early modern Poland and discusses their impact in the light of modern medicine. It raises the hypothesis that the customs, beliefs, and norms governing post-partum breastfeeding and wet-nursing that were standardized as 'good' among Jews in early modern Poland supported infant survival and thus contributed to lower infant and child death rates.[6]

Despite this awareness of the importance of neonatal care and the wealth of scholarship on the history of childhood, these topics have aroused little scholarly interest.[7] More has been written on delivery and the almost parallel period of the new mother's life, known as the puerperium, that is, the four to six weeks during which she recovers after giving birth. Here we partially fill this scholarly lacuna and discuss the ideas that governed neonatal care among Jews in early modern Poland as they appear in the major halakhic sources and in seventeenth-century Jewish ethical guides and community rulings.[8] While acknowledging that there were discrepancies between law and norms, on the one hand, and practice, on the other,[9] the basic assumption of this research is that social and cultural norms partially shaped by religion were influential in how early modern Jews took care of their newborns. Consequently, the first two sections of this chapter lay out the traditional Jewish religious rulings that influenced early modern attitudes. In the third section, we first discuss the concepts present in early modern halakhic rulings and then adduce literary sources and information derived from legislation and from the existence and activities of community institutions related to children and their well-being.[10] Since Jews did not live in a vacuum, the study is supplemented with information from non-Jewish legislation and popular non-Jewish medical treatises. The fourth section presents some findings of modern medicine regarding infant care and mortality in order to help understand the impact of these concepts and norms on Jewish infant mortality rates. It shows that the early modern Jewish concepts were surprisingly close to modern practice, and thus, although mostly unconsciously, they aided infant survival.

Biblical and Talmudic Concepts Governing Neonatal Care

The ideal of fulfilling a child's basic physical, emotional, and intellectual needs is deeply rooted in Judaism. This is evident from biblical references to the importance of child-rearing and newborn care. The Bible imposes a commandment to procreate[11] and suggests that a family's fruitfulness is proof of God's blessing.[12]

The Bible prescribes special care for a newborn. First, it ruled that the umbilical cord should be ligatured and cut immediately after birth. Then the baby should be bathed, rubbed with salt, and wrapped in swaddling clothes: 'And as for your birth, when you were born your navel cord was not cut, and you were not bathed in water to smooth you; you were not rubbed with salt, nor were you swaddled. No one pitied you enough to do any one of these for you out of compassion for you.'[13]

Although the Bible does not specify when the first feeding of the newborn should occur, it does emphasize the importance of breastfeeding.[14] The sages interpreted the prayer of the childless Hannah as implying that the female breast had been created solely for breastfeeding.[15] The Bible views milk-producing breasts as a blessing and dry breasts as a curse.[16] It also gives priority to the infant's nutritional needs, and thus states that breastfeeding outweighs all of a woman's other domestic duties[17] and, if a woman cannot nurse her baby, that a wet nurse should be employed, and treated with respect.[18]

In the book of Genesis, circumcision of the newborn male was a sign of the covenant between God and Israel: 'And throughout the generations, every male among you shall be circumcised at the age of eight days.'[19] Although there is no explanation why the eighth day was chosen, it is likely that the stabilization of the blood-clotting mechanism that occurs from that day onwards was taken into account.

The talmudic literature followed in the footsteps of the Bible. It praises procreation and discusses a child's needs at the different stages of its development. Marriage is emphasized as the ideal, and a man who does not marry and has no children is described as committing a sin of omission. A talmudic saying from the second century about Rachel's lament over her barrenness claims that a man with no children is considered dead.[20] According to Beit Shammai, a man is obliged to have a minimum of two sons; Beit Hillel ruled that the minimum was one son and one daughter.[21]

The Mishnah lists three major principles in nurturing an infant's development as reflected in the advice given by a nanny of Abaye: personal hygiene, proper nutrition, and developmental play: 'The care and development of the infant requires first that he be bathed and anointed with oil; later, when he grows older, that he be given eggs and dairy products; and when he grows older still, that he be given the freedom to play with toys.'[22] In regard to the care of a newborn, the Talmud accepts the biblical and mishnaic approach and does not add many further details:

> We learned in the Mishnah: And one may tie the umbilical cord of a child born on the sabbath. The sages taught similarly in the Tosefta and even added to it: One may tie the umbilical cord of a child born on the sabbath. Rabbi Yosei said: One may even cut the umbilical cord. And one may insulate the placenta as a healing remedy so as to warm the newborn.[23]

This lack of pragmatic instruction can be interpreted in two ways: first, as a result of the scholastic approach of the Talmud, which is not interested in neonatal care per se but discusses it as part of other subjects, for example, observance of the sabbath;[24] second, as a testament to the prevalence of and familiarity with biblical procedures and the consequent redundancy of explanations.[25] During the rabbinic period, among both Jews and non-Jews the newborn was usually salted (to strengthen its skin) and wrapped (to straighten its limbs),[26] as described in the Bible. The Talmud treats the wrapping and binding of the newborn's head as a vital procedure and an important skill required of a good midwife.[27] While discussing the laws of the sabbath, the Talmud rules that the care of a mature newborn justifies the desecration of the sabbath,[28] except for wrapping, which, when intended to straighten out limbs deformed during delivery, should be forbidden as manipulating the spinal column.[29]

Regarding nutrition, the talmudic literature disseminates the prevailing view that it is natural for a woman to breastfeed her child[30] and discusses the qualities of breast milk, patterns of breastfeeding, and the status of the breastfeeding mother. It stresses the desirability of breastfeeding as the best possible source of nourishment in infancy and justifies even the employment of non-Jewish wet nurses, when the mother cannot breastfeed. Regarding neonatal care, the Talmud refers to the practice of giving 'children's herbs' (*asubei yanuka*) to the newborn infant in order to cause it to vomit and clean its mouth of mucus before breastfeeding.[31] While the Talmud does not prescribe a specific time for the first feeding of the newborn, it accepts the norm prevailing among contemporary Jews, which, according to Preuss, was 'for the newborn to be placed at the mother's breast immediately after birth, but in any event before twenty-four hours have elapsed, even if the navel has not yet been cut'.[32] This practice of post-partum breastfeeding was contrary to the Christian model, which was deeply influenced by the Greek physician Soranus of Ephesus (second century CE), who believed that the child should not be given the mother's breast until it was 20 days old, because the earlier milk was not healthy.[33] The reason for the Jewish approach was probably the prevailing belief that delay in relieving the mother of her milk might constitute a danger to the mother and consequently to the infant requiring her care.[34]

The Talmud prescribes that a baby should be nursed for twenty-four months. If the mother was ill or had died or was wealthy enough not to have to, then a wet nurse was to be hired. The Tosefta permit a non-Jewish wet nurse to be used, on condition that she is brought into the domain of the baby's father, 'for safety's sake'.[35] Moreover, the halakhah rules that, if possible, a wet nurse should be hired during the neonatal period before the infant is able to recognize its feeder and thus respond negatively to the change in the source of breastmilk. Acknowledging babies' attachment to the source of milk, the rabbis advised avoiding changing the nursing woman.[36] It is not clearly stated whether the danger was due to the change of milk, the risk that the baby might refuse to suck from a strange woman, or the separation from its mother and her care.[37] Consequently, it was recommended that any change or employment of a wet nurse should be done during the neonatal period.

The talmudic literature does not mention nursing from vessels. It mentions the nursing of an infant by an animal,[38] and, in extreme circumstances, even nursing from a non-kosher animal is permitted.[39] It is known that in talmudic times women expressed their milk into a glass or a bowl, but nursing in this way was considered a kind of play.[40] Women also expressed their milk into an animal horn in order to feed their babies.[41]

In talmudic times, babies were bathed and anointed with oil. They were probably placed in a small bed, in which they were rocked.[42] At night they slept with their mother.[43] Then during the day, they were carried on the bosom.[44]

Neonatal Care in Medieval Ashkenazi Communities

In medieval Ashkenazi communities, the sages continued to elaborate on the approaches found in the Bible and talmudic literature. The prevailing attitude was that the birth of a child and childcare were central to a woman's life. It was believed that a barren woman could not be happy, because a woman's role was to have children.[45] Consequently, a woman was expected to be concerned for the child's welfare during pregnancy, especially after she felt movement in her womb.[46] A man was considered pious if he had children.[47]

Although men were not present during the actual delivery, the sages did know a lot about the process of childbirth, and included it and neonatal care in their discussions of various other activities.[48] For example, they accepted the ruling that one could desecrate the sabbath in order to facilitate the birth of a fully developed foetus.[49] Thus even on the sabbath, the umbilical cord was ligatured and cut right after the birth, and the baby was bathed and rubbed with salt. Then it was wrapped in swaddling clothes,[50] but only in a way that was not intended to alter the infant's body. If swaddling was done 'to straighten the delicate limbs, which have been pressed upon and bent during delivery', it was postponed until after the sabbath.[51]

During the first days after the birth, the baby and the mother were waited on by other women.[52] If it was a boy, he was bathed by the women of the community every day, starting from the third day, in preparation for circumcision. The washing of a baby boy was even done on the sabbath but within sabbath restrictions. The woman who received the honour of washing the neonate or supervising the bath before the circumcision was usually chosen from the family.[53] After the ceremonial bath, a baby boy was beautifully dressed. He was then taken to a specially prepared synagogue where the circumcision took place right after the morning prayer.[54] As part of the ritual, the baby was given his name, publicly recognized by his father, and accepted into the Jewish community.

Medieval sources do not state clearly whether the mother was present at the circumcision or stayed at home.[55] When possible, it was customary to isolate a woman and baby during the neonatal period to avoid infection. The sources mention the first post-partum visit of the mother to the synagogue, which took place on the sabbath approximately a month after the birth and was called *shabat yetsiat hayoledet*. This event was accompanied by a ceremony known in Germany in the fourteenth century as *Hollekreish*, during which a baby girl got her name and a baby boy got his additional, non-Hebrew, name.[56]

Contemporary sources contain little information about the practice of breastfeeding in medieval Ashkenazi society. The sages followed the Bible and Talmud on the subject and mentioned them in their discussion of the parental responsibility for feeding infants, the special status of a nursing woman, the use of contraception by a nursing woman, and the employment of non-Jewish wet nurses. Their rulings varied, probably depending on time and place. Still, deducing from the frequency of wet nurses' appearance in the sources, their employment was a widespread practice, especially among wealthier families.[57] Contemporary sources reveal two additional points which most probably also influenced the care of the newborn: wet nurses were allowed to breastfeed only one baby, and parents were anxious to avoid harming the baby by changing wet nurses.[58] While, in the fourteenth-century Sephardi compendium *Zeidah laderekh*, there is the advice that after the birth of a child the mother 'should not nurse him until eight days pass, so that her milk stabilize[s]',[59] there is no such prescription in the known Ashkenazi texts.

Care for the Newborn in Early Modern Poland

Jewish society in early modern Poland generally accepted the halakhic approach to breastfeeding, care of a nursing mother, and childcare, and believed that 'raising children is essential, and much depends on it'.[60] By and large, it followed the rulings in the *Shulḥan arukh* with Rema's glosses known as the *Mapah*, which adopted the above-mentioned talmudic and medieval Ashkenazi tradition regarding neonatal care.

In addition to halakhic writings, people could learn the concepts governing childcare from the growing body of Yiddish ethical books. Whether written by representatives of the learned rabbinical elite or by less educated women, these books viewed giving birth and childcare as the central elements of a woman's life and her primary religious purpose.[61] Addressed mainly to women but also 'to men ... who cannot read and understand books in the holy tongue and the sermons delivered on the sabbath',[62] they disseminated the belief that a woman who gives birth, nurses her babies, and provides for all their needs was following the way of the Creator and was deserving of eternal life.[63] Following the recommendations of the ethical literature, women prayed to become mothers and to breastfeed,[64] and were expected to think about their pious children when conceiving them[65] and during pregnancy to 'improve herself with good deeds, and distance herself from evil deeds ... if she wants to have pious, upright children who will be raised to serve God and be God-fearing'.[66]

If the baby was born in the seventh or ninth month, it was regarded as viable and care for it started right after delivery: 'For the newborn, we take care of all of his needs. We wash him, salt him, hide the placenta so that the child will be warm, and cut the umbilical cord.'[67] The procedure of cutting the umbilical cord was not described in ethical books, as it belonged to a midwife's duties and was probably similar to the practices in the past or in the surrounding society, in which they 'cut the navel cord right after the little baby is born and three fingers away from the body, then tie it while sprinkling it with powder', usually made of local herbs.[68]

Although the *Shulḥan arukh* states that—except for immediately after the birth—in its first days the baby is not washed at all, and 'the laws regarding washing [a baby boy] are the same as the laws of washing any man', according to Rema, in Poland, the Jews followed the tradition from the time of the sages and did wash the newborn in warm water before and after circumcision as well as on the third day after that.[69] If the circumcision was scheduled for the sabbath, the water had to be heated the day before, and the bathing following the circumcision was to be performed after the end of the sabbath.[70] In addition to the halakhic rulings concerned with the ceremonial bath on the sabbath, the ethical books gave additional practical instructions, probably in view of the various methods of washing the baby prevailing in the surrounding Christian society:[71]

One should not bathe the child in water that is too hot, since it makes the child weak and sluggish. And one should not wet its head at all, because its brain is soft, and much bad,

God forbid, comes of it, so that I will not write here what, God protect us, comes of it. When one takes it out of the bath, one may wash it carefully. One should also not leave it in the bath for too long.[72]

In contemporary halakhic texts and ethical guides, one of the major issues related to neonatal care discussed at length is breastfeeding, its source and duration. The *Shulḥan arukh* advocates breastfeeding as the best source of nutrition. It does not state clearly the time of the first feeding; however, Rema's indirect comments on the pain caused by milk accumulating in a new mother's breast and the lack of recommendations to avoid nursing in the first days support the claim that the prevailing norm was to start nursing a few hours after the birth.[73] Yemima Chovav claims that in the early modern period Ashkenazi rabbis believed that the first milk was harmful and mothers were advised not to breastfeed for the first ten hours.[74] A similar time for the first feeding is recommended in *Meynekes rivko*, which advises new mothers to breastfeed their newborn after they rest for a while: 'as soon as the child is born, she must watch over the child, and be careful not to give the child to anyone else for nursing. She herself should begin the next day.'[75]

Neither in *Meynekes rivko* nor in any other contemporary source is there any discussion of the benefits of the first milk known as colostrum. Instead, the emphasis is on the advantages of early breastfeeding to the mother and on its effect on the establishment of nursing habits, the mother's future ability to breastfeed, and the infant's willingness to nurse from her. According to *Meynekes rivko*, early nursing ensures a good flow of milk. If the mother postpones breastfeeding 'her milk goes bad and becomes bitter, and then she no longer wants to nurse the child at all'. Moreover, if the mother gives in to the pain and passes the newborn to a wet nurse, her 'milk [is no longer] good but watery and bitter', and she may never nurse well.[76]

Despite having a different goal, those recommendations established a norm of feeding with colostrum, which was contrary to the prevailing Christian practice of avoiding 'the impure, thick stuff which is very unhealthy to the baby', as recommended in, among other sources, the popular sixteenth-century treatises by Stefan Falimirz and Marcin Siennik.[77] This concept of early nursing not only protected Jewish mothers from the risk of breast congestion and mastitis (milk fever)[78] but also provided their neonates with the advantages of colostrum, which was critical for the infant's proper development and survival in pre-modern times, as we will discuss in the next section.

In *Meynekes rivko*, as in the halakhic writings, the discussion of early breastfeeding is related to the practice of hiring a wet nurse. The author claims that a woman who is able to nurse the baby herself merits a good reputation, and is 'upright and straight'. However, a woman who turns to a wet nurse is undutiful and will always regret not nursing, because 'as soon as the child tastes another, it will not want to suckle from the mother again'.[79] This recommendation is based on a rather free interpretation of a ruling of the *Shulḥan arukh*, which follows the talmudic tradition[80] and claims that a child of nursing age, used to one source of milk, cannot have its nursing woman changed.[81] More precisely, it states that if the baby already knows its mother, then she cannot give it to a wet nurse, because 'the trauma of separation might cause the child physical harm'.[82] She must continue breastfeeding the baby until it is twenty-four months old:

> She may [choose to] not breastfeed it until it [is old enough that it] recognizes her, but if it recognizes her [Rema: and does not want to breastfeed from another], even if it is blind, we do not separate it [from her], because of the danger to the infant, but rather we compel her and she breastfeeds it until it is twenty-four months old. [Rema: And he pays her the hire of breastfeeding.] And some say that even another woman, if she breastfeeds a baby until it is [is old enough that it] recognizes her, we compel her [to continue] and she nurses it for hire, because of the danger to the infant.[83]

The rabbis recognized the developmental changes at different stages of childhood and were aware of the individual pace of some of the transitions. Thus, they did not set down unambiguously when the infant recognizes its source of milk and ruled it could happen around the age of two to six weeks. *Meynekes rivko* views the change of milk source as problematic in the neonatal period. This is introduced by the author to support her argument against the hiring of wet nurses, especially by rich families.

In Jewish communities in Poland–Lithuania during the early modern period, wet nurses were primarily employed when a mother died, when she could not breastfeed herself, or when she refused to breastfeed. Such 'refusal' was common among rich families that did not want to wait twenty-four months between pregnancies, which was required if the mother was breastfeeding. Those families often secured alternative sources of breastmilk during the neonatal period or even before the birth, so that the baby would not get used to the mother and she be compelled to breastfeed it.

The author of *Meynekes rivko* opposed this practice not only on ideological grounds but also by pointing to the instability of people's economic situations. She suggests that 'even if she is rich—one never knows what the future holds', and she might find herself unable to continue paying for a wet nurse but also unable to breastfeed herself. Although *Meynekes rivko* does not elaborate on this point, it can be supported with the contemporary recurrent rulings against bankrupts.[84]

Wet nurses were hired in the neonatal period if the mother was a widow and planned to remarry. According to the ruling *meineket ḥavero*, a woman nursing her child couldn't remarry until the child reached the age of twenty-four months.[85] However, if she hired a wet nurse before the baby 'knew her' and there was no need to switch the milk source, which could harm the baby's will to suck, she could marry again. As Jewish women were not permitted to employ a wet nurse on the sabbath but had to feed their baby themselves, it was difficult to find a Jewish wet nurse. Hence, although milk from a non-Jewish woman was generally deemed to be less pure, the *Shulḥan arukh* followed the earlier tradition and permitted the baby to be breastfed by a non-Jewish woman, but only in the mother's home, not the wet nurse's. Presumably when possible Jews followed this ruling and avoided sending their babies to a wet nurse's home, as practised by Christians, who were not restricted by similar religious norms.[86] Though permitted, the employment of non-Jewish wet nurses was criticized in the ethical literature, which testifies to the popularity of the practice: 'And those, who have non-Jewish wet nurses commit a great injustice, if they could have a Jewish [wet nurse]. The milk of a non-Jewish wet nurse comes from the food she eats, which is *treyf* [non-kosher], she blocks the heart of the child that drinks of her.'[87]

The Church fought against the Jewish employment of Christian wet nurses because they had to lodge in Jewish homes.[88] It denied the wet nurses Communion, and used the help of municipal authorities to impose fines on Jews who hired them: 'It is forbidden for the Jews to keep Christian servants especially Christian wet nurses and governesses under penalty of a 100 grzywna fine for the Jew and of arrest for the Catholic who served him.'[89] The Sejm and the king (probably under the influence of the Church) also introduced laws to prohibit the employment of Christian wet nurses by Jews.[90] Despite criticism and prohibitions, the Jewish authorities (which usually followed the law in order to avoid a backlash from the non-Jewish authorities) followed the halakhah and allowed the hiring of Christian wet nurses, although within limits. For example, according to the regulations of the Kraków community, in 1595 it was prohibited for a Christian female servant (including wet nurses) to be lodged in the home of a Jewish employer because of 'the confusion arising out of this'.[91] The response of the Jewish authorities testifies to the recognition of both the importance of breastfeeding and the necessity of wet nurses.[92]

The important ceremony during the neonatal period was circumcision. In the early modern period it took place either in the synagogue or at home.[93] On the sabbath before the ceremony, there was a ceremonial meal to mark the baby's first commandment (observing the sabbath). In the mid-seventeenth and eighteenth centuries (and perhaps earlier) it was customary to gather in the baby's home on the night before the circumcision in order to pray,[94] and in some places it was customary for the men to eat a meal with the mother and the baby.[95] In other places, the women had a meal together with the mother and baby. For many couples the circumcision of the first son signalled their independence and transformation into a family.[96] Community sumptuary laws testify to the importance of the ceremony and of the feasts accompanying circumcision, which were often used as a means of exhibiting social status.

During pregnancy and labour, a woman was assisted by a midwife. The midwife was also responsible for the earliest care of the newborn. The attitude of Jewish communities towards the institution of the midwife testifies to the high appreciation of the profession and, in turn, to Jewish emphasis on and investment in childcare. Midwives were licensed by the community administration. Following a successful trial period, the midwife and her family would receive authorization by the community and even tenure for a long period or even for life, as recorded in the minute book of the Jewish community council of Tiktin (Tykocin) in the early eighteenth century.[97] Big urban communities, such as Poznań, employed two or more midwives. In addition to what they received from the families they assisted, the community gave them a respectable annual salary and housing or partial payment of rent.[98]

Everyday care for a neonate included swaddling. In early modern Poland, Christian babies were usually tightly swaddled so that only the head could be seen.[99] This was done in order to avoid deforming parts of the body, to protect the baby, and to prevent it from putting things in its mouth. The material for swaddling was usually linen. However, the rich also used cotton, while the poor were advised to swaddle with used clothing.[100] Jewish sources accepted the talmudic norms and did not elaborate on the practice of swaddling. The first wrappings were probably done by the midwife. In *Meynekes rivko*, young women were advised to 'take care of the child like a shell [of an egg], because one can, God forbid, harm the child very quickly'.[101] This could testify to the awareness that swaddling could be done too tightly. According to modern research, swaddling is one of the earliest procedures that sets up communication between the adults and the baby.[102] Thus, although in pre-modern times swaddling was done as part of the care for a child's physical needs, it unconsciously exposed a neonate to its parents' attitude to childcare.

During the vulnerable post-partum period, the mother and newborn were taken care of by women from the family. The close assistance usually lasted for seven days, and when possible, the mother and the baby stayed at home for four weeks until *shabat yetsiat hayoledet*.

Jewish Infant Care in Early Modern Poland in the Light of Modern Medical Knowledge

The previous sections laid out the traditions and concepts that governed the practice and forms of parental handling that were viewed as good and necessary by the Jewish community. Actual methods might have been different, but no information is available. Still, these concepts and supporting evidence reveal what the religious elite viewed as best practice, which certainly had an impact on community practice. Today also, medical advice is not always closely followed, but it does have an impact on actual practice. The main argument of this chapter is that the religiously based Jewish rules and norms promoted practices and attitudes that modern medicine recognizes as supporting the infant's survival: breastfeeding the newborn with colostrum, isolation of the mother and the neonate, employment of home wet nurses, and not changing wet nurses.

According to modern medical knowledge, an infant is born with a passive immunity which helps it fight micro-organisms and some viruses present in the mother's body. However, to develop its own, adaptive immune system, a newborn needs, among other things, a boost of IgA antibodies. These can be found in colostrum. Concentrated and easy to digest, colostrum has as much as 20 to 40 mg/ml of IgA antibodies and contains a range of antimicrobial elements and substances that may boost the immune system: for example, the iron-binding antimicrobial protein lactoferrin, the antibacterial enzyme lactoperoxidase, and lysozyme. Moreover, colostrum contains leukocytes and growth factors that may boost neonatal intestinal development and provide a source of energy which may improve IgG absorption in the newborn and stimulate effective immune responses.[103] Before the invention of milk formula and vaccinations, it was colostrum that provided the infant with the first adaptive barrier against pathogens and certain illnesses of early infancy, especially intestinal and respiratory diseases, which often led to the infant's death.

These facts led historians to claim that in traditional societies 'a mistrust of colostrum deprived the child of important immunities and exposed its mother to the risk of milk fever':[104] we assume that a newborn nursed with colostrum had a better chance of survival than an infant left hungry or fed in other ways, and post-partum breastfeeding was one of the reasons why Jews in early modern Poland had a lower infant mortality rate than the surrounding Polish society, in which colostrum was viewed as impure and harmful and the baby was given honey for the first few days after birth instead.[105]

Modern medicine claims that, as long as the infant remains in the environment to which the mother was exposed during pregnancy, it is protected by the passive, transplacental immunity which continues for the first few weeks after birth and is conditioned by, among other things, the diseases to which its mother has been exposed and the environment she lives in.[106] Consequently, if the infant is sent away (for example, to a wet nurse in the country) where different strains of bacteria exist, then the immunity acquired from the mother cannot protect it.[107] These findings support the conclusions of historical research, that in pre-modern times sending babies away for nursing was hazardous,[108] and not only due to possible negligence by the wet nurse. In the early modern period, in western Europe, 'the pattern was not only for the rich to breed and the poor to lactate, it was also for the cities to send their children out to nurse and for the country to feed and care for them until they were two or three years old'.[109] In Poland, sending babies away was less popular than in France or Italy. Yet, as it was not forbidden by religious norms, it did occur;[110] although not usually among wealthy families, who hired live-in wet nurses and nannies, or poor farmers, who breastfed their own babies or passed them to nursing neighbours or family members.[111] Sara Matthews Grieco's observation that, in the early modern period, 'those nursed by their mothers or by a live-in wet nurse at home had a much better chance [of survival] than those sent out to nurse'[112] means that the hiring of live-in wet nurses not only allowed Jewish mothers to supervise the wet nurse (and protect their babies from negligence and non-Jewish customs and food) but also protected the newborn from exposure to a different environment, which, in turn, contributed to some degree to the difference in infant mortality rates between Jews and the surrounding Polish society.

As well as hiring live-in wet nurses, Jews confined the mother and newborn and limited their contact with visitors. According to modern medical knowledge, despite the psychological damage it can do to the mother, isolation reduces contact with germs and illnesses, improves levels of hygiene, and increases the baby's chances of survival during the high-risk neonatal period. Thus, although Jewish communities usually practised isolation for protection against 'forces of darkness', they unconsciously contributed to lower infant mortality.

In Polish society, the upper class also practised isolation for up to six weeks after birth and ended it with a ceremonial visit to the church called 'churching', which was usually followed by a feast. Resting mothers were visited only by other women, neighbours, friends, and family, who brought gifts and sometimes helped in the house. However, according to repeated Church condemnations, many such visits turned into celebrations by the women. Despite advice to mothers on diet and rules imposed by magistrates, it was often the case that too much alcohol was consumed at such gatherings.[113] According to one account: 'In the villages alcohol is given to women after delivery (a common habit), in noble houses wine or other tinctures, this sends many mothers away from this world.'[114] Isolation and churching were not practised in the countryside. There, poor women had to return early to work in the fields or leave the infant with other mothers in the family or village and seek employment as a wet nurse.

As well as hiring live-in wet nurses, not changing wet nurses has been shown to contribute to the survival of infants.[115] While Jewish writings advocated hiring a single wet nurse for two years, early modern Christian society—although aware that a change of wet nurse might influence an infant's willingness to feed—recommended switching them in cases of the wet nurse's pregnancy, menstruation, or illness. Moreover, when an infant became ill, the wet nurse's milk was blamed rather than the change of wet nurse, and again the nurse was replaced. In 1782 Teodor Tomasz Weichardt—the author of a popular guide for mothers—advised that a wet nurse should not nurse during her menstrual period, because 'babies that nursed during that time often got sick'.[116]

Conclusion

Children and childhood have been one of the central elements in the social organization of the Jewish people, and childcare is embedded in the various religious obligations of Judaism. Although understood differently, depending on time, place, and surrounding cultures, the positive attitude towards childcare remained one of the pillars of Jewish life for centuries.

This chapter has described the norms mentioned in the Bible, the Mishnah, the Talmud, their later commentaries, and early modern popular ethical guides, which prescribe how children's physical, emotional, and cognitive needs should be addressed in the first thirty days after birth. It has acknowledged their influence on the concepts and patterns prevailing in neonatal care in Jewish communities in early modern Poland.

We have emphasized that the adaptation of those norms in the Ashkenazi community of early modern Poland testifies not only to the importance of childcare in traditional society but also to the influence that religiously based norms had on attitudes towards it. Concentrating on first feeding and the hiring of wet nurses, we have shown that the concepts that the Jewish community in early modern Poland viewed positively were surprisingly close to those that modern medicine recognizes as contributing to the survival of infants. Consequently, we claim, the norms prevalent among Jews contributed to their lower infant mortality rate. To strengthen this argument, we juxtaposed those norms with attitudes dominant in non-Jewish society and showed that in light of modern medical knowledge the latter made a significant contribution to higher infant death rates.

One of the main questions arising from this study is the reasons for the differences in practices between Jews and non-Jews. Our main hypothesis follows Maristella Botticini and Zvi Eckstein,[117] and suggests that when children's education became the main religious norm among Jews during the talmudic period, Jews also began developing a unique corpus of norms and practices related to the care of infants and children and followed them throughout the subsequent centuries. The emphasis on the ability to read at an early age led the sages to follow the outcomes of early childcare practices closely. Their observations in turn provided the recommendations that most likely resulted in practices that promoted the development of high cognitive abilities at an early age. While these recommendations also influenced infant care, they also probably contributed to lower infant mortality among Jews. Clearly, the importance and methods of neonatal care in Jewish culture are not the only explanation for the low infant mortality rates observed among Jews in Poland, and therefore this analysis should be viewed as a starting point for further research.

Notes

1 N. Zemon-Davis, *Women on the Margins: Three Seventeenth-Century Lives* (Cambridge, 1995), 12, 225 n. 23.
2 M. Botticini, Z. Eckstein, and A. Vaturi, 'Child Care and Human Development: Insights from Jewish History in Central and Eastern Europe, 1500–1930', *Economic Journal*, 129 (2019), 2637–90: 2659–60.
3 G. D. Hundert, 'Approaches to the History of the Jewish Family in Early Modern Poland–Lithuania', in S. M. Cohen and P. E. Hyman (eds.), *The Jewish Family: Myths and Reality* (New York, 1986), 17–28: 19.
4 A. V. Holmes, 'Establishing Successful Breastfeeding in the Newborn Period', *Pediatric Clinics of North America*, 60 (2013), 147–68.
5 N. K. Goyal, 'The Newborn Infant', in *Nelson Textbook of Pediatrics*, ed. R. M. Kliegman, J. W. St Geme III, N. J. Blum, S. S. Shah, R. C. Tasker, and K. M. Wilson, 21st edn. (Philadelphia, 2020), 867–76.
6 This chapter is a continuation of two other publications: Botticini, Eckstein, and Vaturi, 'Child Care and Human Development'; A. Vaturi, 'Domeh akh shoneh: hanakah bekerev yehudim venotserim bemamlekhet polin-lita vehashlakhoteiha hademografiyot', *Gal-ed*, 26–7 (2021), 15–36.
7 Although Jewish scholarship on the history of childhood had a revival after the publication of Philippe Ariès's *Centuries of Childhood* (P. Ariès, *L'Enfant et la vie familiale sous l'Ancien Régime* (Paris, 1960); Eng. trans.: *Centuries of Childhood: A Social History of Family Life*, trans. R. Baldick (New York, 1962)), only a few studies concentrated on Jewish childhood in early modern eastern Europe (e.g. Hundert, 'Approaches to the History of the Jewish Family in Early Modern Poland–Lithuania'; id. 'Jewish Children and Childhood in Early Modern East Central Europe', in D. Kraemer (ed.), *The Jewish Family: Metaphor and*

Memory (New York, 1989), 18–94), and no special attention has yet been given to the neonatal phase.

8   In the early modern period more literature on how to raise and educate children appeared (see M. H. Altschuler, *Brantshpigl* (Basel, 1602 [Kraków, 1596]); 'Mosheh henokhsh altshuler, *Sefer brant shpigl* / Moses Henochs [Yerushalmi] Altshuler, *The Burning Mirror* (1596) [excerpts]', in *Early Yiddish Texts: 1100–1750*, ed. J. Frakes (Oxford, 2004), 420–31; Rivkah bat Meir Tiktiner, *Meynekes rivko* (Prague, 1609); Eng. trans.: Rivkah bat Meir, *Meneket Rivkah: A Manual of Wisdom and Piety for Jewish Women*, ed. F. von Rohden, trans. S. Spinner (Philadelphia, Pa., 2009); Isaac ben Eliakim of Posen, *Sefer lev tov* (Jerusalem, 1975 [Prague, 1620])).

9   Halakhic sources, for example, indicate what should and should not be done and thus are more prescriptive than descriptive. They do seem to reflect the norms accepted by the educated male elite.

10 For a similar methodological strategy, see E. Baumgarten, 'Judaism', in D. S. Browning and M. J. Bunge (eds.), *Children and Childhood in World Religions: Primary Sources and Texts* (New Brunswick, NJ, 2020), 15–81.

11 Gen. 1: 28; 9: 1–7.

12 Gen. 49: 25; Ps. 127: 3.

13 Ezek. 16: 4–5.

14 Gen. 49: 25.

15 1 Sam. 1: 12–17; see BT *Ber.* 31*b*.

16 Gen. 49: 22; Hos. 9: 14.

17 1 Sam. 1: 21–3; see W. M. Feldman, *The Jewish Child: Its History, Folklore, Biology and Sociology* (London, 1917), 180.

18 Exod. 2: 7, 9.

19 Gen. 17: 12.

20 Gen. 30: 1; see J. G. Schenker, 'Jewish Law (Halakha) and Reproduction', in id. (ed.), *Ethical Dilemmas in Assisted Reproductive Technologies* (Berlin, 2011), 343–62: 343.

21 Mishnah *Yev.* 6: 6.

22 Mishnah *Yoma* 78.

23 BT *Shab.* 129*b*.

24 For a discussion of the scholastic approach in rabbinic literature, see J. Rosenblum, '"Blessing of the Breast": Breastfeeding in Rabbinic Literature', *Hebrew Union College Annual*, 87 (2016), 145–77.

25 J. Preuss, *Biblical and Talmudic Medicine* (New York, 1993), 402.

26 See also BT *Shab.* 147*b*.

27 BT *Shab.* 31*a*.

28 BT *Yev.* 80*a–b*; *Shab.* 129*b*.

29 BT *Shab.* 147*b*.

30 Rashi on BT *Bekh.* 7*b*, s.v. *kol hamolid*.

31 BT *Shab.* 123*a*.

32 Preuss, *Biblical and Talmudic Medicine*, 405.

33 Soranus advised women to leave the newborn hungry for two days and then employ a wet nurse. If there was no wet nurse available, he advised giving the newborn some honey water, possibly enriched with goat's milk. See Soranus, *Gynecology*, trans. O. Temkin (Baltimore, 1956), 2: 11 (p. 89).

34 BT *Shab.* 135a; see Preuss, *Biblical and Talmudic Medicine*, 405.
35 Tosefta *Nid.* 2: 5; see Preuss, *Biblical and Talmudic Medicine*, 408.
36 BT *Ket.* 59b–60a.
37 Tosefta *Nid.* 2: 4; see E. Shochetman, 'Lemahutam shel kelalei hahalakhah besugiyat haḥzakat hayeladim', *Shenaton hamishpat ha'ivri*, 5 (1977), 286–320: 291.
38 Tosefta *BK* 8: 13.
39 BT *Ket.* 65a; see A. I. Eidelman, 'The Talmud and Human Lactation: The Cultural Basis for Increased Frequency and Duration of Breastfeeding among Orthodox Jewish Women', *Breastfeeding Medicine*, 1 (2006), 36–40: 39.
40 Tosefta *Shab.* 9: 22.
41 Tosefta *Shab.* 13: 16.
42 *Gen. Rab.* 53: 10.
43 Preuss, *Biblical and Talmudic Medicine*, 404; Feldman, *The Jewish Child*, 194.
44 Num. 11: 12.
45 This idea was present in biblical commentaries and works of poetry about the matriarchs, Sarah, Rebecca, and Rachel (see E. Baumgarten, *Imahot viyeladim: ḥayei mishpaḥah be'ashkenaz biyemei habeinayim* (Jerusalem, 2005), 42; Eng. edn.: *Mothers and Children: Jewish Family Life in Medieval Europe* (Princeton, NJ, 2004)).
46 Rashi on Gen. 49: 25.
47 Baumgarten, *Imahot viyeladim*, 51; ead., *Mothers and Children*, 28.
48 Baumgarten, *Imahot viyeladim*, 69, 73; ead., *Mothers and Children*, 42.
49 F. Levin, *Halacha, Medical Science and Technology* (New York, 1987), 3–38.
50 E. Baumgarten, '"Kakh omerot hameyaledot haḥakhamot": meyaledot umeyaledut be'ashkenaz bame'ah hashelosh-esreh', *Zion*, 65 (1999), 45–74: 67.
51 Rashi on BT *Shab.* 66b, s.v. *leterutsei sugyah*; see also Feldman, *The Jewish Child*, 176; Baumgarten, *Imahot viyeladim*, 86 n. 227; ead., *Mothers and Children*, 52 n. 169.
52 Baumgarten, *Imahot viyeladim*, 86, 156; ead., *Mothers and Children*, 53, 107.
53 See e.g. Baumgarten, 'Judaism'.
54 It was in the medieval period that the ceremony of circumcision was moved from the home to the synagogue. On the ritual of circumcision, see Baumgarten, *Imahot viyeladim*, 97–8; ead., *Mothers and Children*, 61; ead. 'Judaism', 43.
55 The obligation of circumcision is on the father, not the mother (Mishnah *Kid.* 1: 7).
56 Y. Chovav, *Alamot ahavukha* (Jerusalem, 2009), 116–17. If a baby boy did not get a vernacular name, his Hebrew name was celebrated again.
57 Baumgarten, *Imahot viyeladim*, 195, 200; ead., *Mothers and Children*, 128, 133.
58 For examples from medieval responsa, see Baumgarten, *Imahot viyeladim*, 196; ead. *Mothers and Children*, 129–30.
59 Menahem ibn Zerah, *Zeidah laderekh*, trans. J. Feldman (Warsaw, 1880), 14: 32a.
60 Rivkah bat Meir, *Meneket Rivkah*, 152.
61 This despite the fact that the commandment to procreate applied only to men (see Chovav, *Alamot ahavukha*, 154, 164; A. Fisher, 'Patur nashim mimitsvat "peru uveru"', in T. Cohen and A. Lavie (eds.), *Liheyot ishah yehudiyah*, 6 vols. (Jerusalem, 2001–13), iii. 199–212).
62 Altschuler, *Brantshpigl*, title page; see also J. Frakes, 'Introduction', in 'Mosheh henokhsh altshuler, *Sefer brant shpigl*', 420–3; E. Fram, *My Dear Daughter: Rabbi Benjamin Slonik and the Education of Jewish Women in Sixteenth-Century Poland* (Cincinnati, 2007), 10–11.
63 Altschuler, *Brantshpigl*, 170a.

64 Ibid. 125–33.
65 B. Slonik, *Seder mitsvot hanashim* (Kraków, 1585); trans. in Fram, *My Dear Daughter*, 158–60.
66 Rivkah bat Meir, *Meneket Rivkah*, 93; see also Altschuler, *Brantshpigl*, 302.
67 *Shulḥan arukh*, 'Oraḥ ḥayim', 330: 7. The rabbis were aware that a baby born in the eighth month would probably not survive, although one born in the seventh might ('For an eight-month infant or one that is possibly seven or possibly eight, we do not desecrate the sabbath unless he has grown hair and nails' (ibid.)). Even today, it is better for a premature birth to occur during the seventh month than the eighth due to the critical stage of lung development in the eighth month.
68 S. Falimirz, *O ziołach i o mocy ich* (Kraków, 1534), 34.
69 *Shulḥan arukh*, 'Oraḥ ḥayim', 331: 9. In seventeenth-century Worms, a ceremonial bath was performed three days after the circumcision and was attended by the women of the community and the wife of the rabbi (Shames Juspa, *Minhagim dikehilah kedoshah vermaisa*, ed. B. S. Hamburger and E. Zimmer, 2 vols. (Jerusalem, 1988–92), ii. 60).
70 Isaac ben Eliakim of Posen, *Sefer lev tov* (Jerusalem, 1975 [Prague, 1620]), 73.
71 According to Dorota Żołądź-Strzelczyk, some advised that it be bathed every day, although others claimed this weakened the baby. According to an eighteenth-century guide, the first bath should be prepared with one-third wine and two-thirds water, and the water should be warm. This could be repeated during the first few days in order to strengthen the child. Later on, it was advised that cold water be used. In some circles, it was believed that dirt was not dangerous and that maintaining hygienic standards was not critical in the case of babies. They even believed that urine was healthy, and therefore babies weren't changed that often (D. Żołądź-Strzelczyk, *Dziecko w dawnej Polsce* (Poznań, 2002), 102).
72 Rivkah bat Meir, *Meneket Rivkah*, 155–6.
73 Baumgarten, *Imahot viyeladim*, 200; ead., *Mothers and Children*, 133.
74 Y. Chovav, 'Childbearing', in G. D. Hundert (ed.), *YIVO Encyclopedia of Jews in Eastern Europe* (New Haven, Conn., 2008).
75 Rivkah bat Meir, *Meneket Rivkah*, 154–5.
76 Ibid.
77 Żołądź-Strzelczyk, *Dziecko w dawnej Polsce*, 120; see Falimirz, *O ziołach i o mocy ich*; M. Siennik, *Herbarz, to jest ziół tutecznych, postronnych i zamorskich opisanie* (Kraków, 1568); see also H. Biegeleisen, *Matka i dziecko w obrzędach, wierzeniach i zwyczajach ludu polskiego* (Lwów, 1927), 154. There were only a few lone voices that advised nursing with colostrum: not for its nutritional value but rather to cause the meconium (the first excrement, of material ingested in the womb) to be excreted: 'Mother's breast should be served right after some rest after the pain: that is, two hours after the delivery. Mother's milk because it is still very liquid and whey-like, is the best medicine to expel the meconium and cause bowel movements in the baby' (*Dykcyonarz powszechny medyki, chirurgii i sztuki hodowania bydląt czyli lekarz wieyski*, 9 vols. (Warsaw, 1788–93), ii. 67).
78 In Christian society, the fact that feeding babies after labour reduces the risk of milk fever was first observed and published in the mid-eighteenth century. Until then many new mothers died of it (S. F. Matthews Grieco, 'Breast-Feeding, Wet Nursing and Infant Mortality in Europe (1400–1800)', in S. F. Matthews Grieco and C. A. Corsini (eds.), *Historical Perspectives on Breast-Feeding: Two Essays* (Florence, 1991), 15–62: 52).
79 Rivkah bat Meir, *Meneket Rivkah*, 155.

80 BT *Ket.* 59b.
81 *Shulḥan arukh*, 'Even ha'ezer', 82: 5.
82 *Shulḥan arukh*, 'Even ha'ezer', 82: 1.
83 *Shulḥan arukh*, 'Even ha'ezer', 82: 5. Note Rema's addition which emphasizes the danger to the infant of changing wet nurses.
84 Both community statutes and the rulings of the Council of Four Lands against so-called *boreḥim* (bankrupts who tried to escape from the community) testify to the growing frequency of the phenomenon (see e.g. A. Jakimyszyn, *Statut krakowskiej gminy żydowskiej z roku 1595 i jego uzupełnienia* (Kraków, 2005), par. 56; *Pinkas va'ad arba aratsot: likutei takanot, ketavim ureshumot*, ed. I. Halperin (Jerusalem, 1945), 45–7, 49).
85 'A man may not marry a woman who is pregnant with the child of another man, nor a woman who is nursing the child of another man' (BT, *Yev.* 36b); 'The rabbis decreed that a man should not engage a woman who is pregnant from another, or who is nursing another [woman's child], until the infant is twenty four months old' (*Shulḥan arukh*, 'Even ha'ezer', 13:11).
86 According to Baumgarten, in medieval times also Jewish mothers did not send their babies to a wet nurse's home so as to be able to supervise the nursing (Baumgarten, *Imahot viyeladim*, 184; ead., *Mothers and Children*, 121).
87 Altschuler, *Brantshpigl*, 137.
88 For example, a resolution of the provincial synod of Piotrków in 1542 (*Decretales summorum pontificum pro Regno Poloniae et constitutiones synodorum provincialium et dioecesanarum Regni eiusdem ad summam collectae*, ed. Z. Chodyński and E. Likowski, 3 vols. (Poznań, 1869–83), iii. ch. 10).
89 J. A. Lipski, *Epistola* (Kraków, 1737), 73.
90 *Volumina legum: Leges, statuta, constitutiones et privilegia Regni Poloniae, Magni Ducatus Lithuaniae*, 10 vols. (St Petersburg, 1859–60), ii. 51 (Sejm 1565); v. 585–6 (Sejm 1678) (which specifies wet nurses among other servants); viii. 50 (Sejm 1775). For royal legislation, see *Pinkas medinat lita*, ed. S. Dubnow (Berlin, 1925), 121 no. 512.
91 Jakimyszyn, *Statut krakowskiej gminy*, par. 91: 75.
92 See also *Pinkas va'ad arba aratsot*, 483–7; on the problem of Christian wet nurses in Jewish homes, see Vaturi, 'Domeh akh shoneh'; J. Kalik, 'Christian Servants Employed by Jews in the Polish–Lithuanian Commonwealth in the 17th and 18th Centuries', *Polin*, 14 (2001), 259–70; A. Kaźmierczyk, 'The Problem of Christian Servants as Reflected in the Legal Codes of the Polish-Lithuanian Commonwealth during the Second Half of the Seventeenth-Century and in the Saxon Period', *Gal-ed*, 15–16 (1997), 23–40.
93 Baumgarten, *Imahot viyeladim*, 98; ead., *Mothers and Children*, 61.
94 Chovav, *Alamot ahavukha*, 174–5.
95 Rema on *Shulḥan arukh*, 'Oraḥ ḥayim', 640: 6.
96 Baumgarten, *Imahot viyeladim*, 133; ead., *Mothers and Children*, 85.
97 See T. Salmon-Mack, 'Birth and Birthing', in Hundert (ed.), *YIVO Encyclopedia of Jews in Eastern Europe*.
98 See the budgets of the Poznań community for 1637/8 and 1645/6 (B. D. Weinryb (ed.), *Texts and Studies in the Communal History of Polish Jewry* (New York, 1950), 57–60 (Hebrew pagination)).
99 Żołądź-Strzelczyk, *Dziecko w dawnej Polsce*, 44.
100 Ibid. 108.
101 Rivkah bat Meir, *Meneket Rivkah*, 156.

102 R. Benedict, 'Child Rearing in Certain European Countries', *American Journal of Orthopsychiatry*, 19 (1949), 342–50.
103 W. L. Hurley and P. K. Theil, 'Perspectives on Immunoglobulins in Colostrum and Milk', *Nutrients*, 3 (2011), 442–74; on the immunological qualities of colostrum and breastmilk, see J. Akre (ed.), *Infant Feeding: The Physiological Basis. Bulletin of the World Health Organization*, 67 (supp.) (1990), 31–2.
104 Matthews Grieco, 'Breast-Feeding, Wet Nursing and Infant Mortality in Europe', 52.
105 D. Musiał-Morsztyn, G. Bogdał, and B. Królak-Olejnik, 'Karmienie piersią na przestrzeni dziejów, Część I: Od starożytności do współczesności', *Pielęgniarstwo i Zdrowie Publiczne / Nursing and Public Health*, 4/1 (2014), 59–64: 62; Żołądź-Strzelczyk, *Dziecko w dawnej Polsce*, 119.
106 Matthews Grieco, 'Breast-Feeding, Wet Nursing and Infant Mortality in Europe', 43.
107 V. A. Fildes, *Breasts, Bottles and Babies: A History of Infant Feeding* (Edinburgh, 1986), 200.
108 A study of fifteenth-century Florence showed that the mortality of children sent out to nurse by their families hovered around 17.9 per cent (Matthews Grieco, 'Breast-Feeding, Wet Nursing and Infant Mortality in Europe', 42).
109 Ibid. 34; see also M. E. Wiesner, *Women and Gender in Early Modern Europe* (Cambridge, 2000), 87.
110 See the complaint by Konrad Bitschin (*c*.1400–*c*.1464) about mothers who couldn't control their sex drive and hence sent their babies to wet nurses (K. Bitschin, 'Über das Eheleben', in K. Arnold (ed.), *Kind und Gesellschaft in Mittelalter und Renaissance: Beiträge und Texte zur Geschichte der Kindheit* (Paderborn, 1980), 146–53: 151–2).
111 Żołądź-Strzelczyk, *Dziecko w dawnej Polsce*, 114; C. Kuklo, *Demografia Rzeczypospolitej przedrozbiorowej* (Warsaw, 2009), 330. In Poland, foundlings were sent to wet nurses in the countryside who were hired by the community.
112 Matthews Grieco, 'Breast-Feeding, Wet Nursing and Infant Mortality in Europe', 39.
113 Żołądź-Strzelczyk, *Dziecko w dawnej*, 73.
114 Jewish sources permitted wine for pregnant and breastfeeding woman, but not more than one cup (BT *Ket.* 60b–61a, 65a).
115 David Herlihy and Christiane Klapisch-Zuber examined the cases of a number of infants from wealthy Florentine families who were sent to wet nurses. They discovered that a number of deaths were directly related to the switching of wet nurses (D. Herlihy and C. Klapisch-Zuber, *Tuscans and Their Families. A Study of the Florentine Catasto of 1427* (New Haven, Conn., 1985), 136–48).
116 T. T. Weichardt, *Rady dla matek względem zapobieżenia różnym słabościom i chorobom, którym dzieci od urodzenia swego podlegać mogą* (Warsaw, 1782), 48–51; see also Żołądź-Strzelczyk, *Dziecko w dawnej*, 118.
117 M. Botticini and Z. Eckstein, *The Chosen Few: How Education Shaped Jewish History, 70–1492* (Princeton, NJ, 2012).

Who Nursed the Jewish Babies?
Wet-Nursing among Jews in the Late Russian Empire

EKATERINA OLESHKEVICH

> Wet-nursing in its two variants—live-in and live-out wet nurses—was widespread among the Jewish community of the tsarist empire, as it was among their non-Jewish counterparts. Of the two types of breastfeeding, the live-in variety, although more expensive, was generally preferred, particularly by the Jewish elite, since it afforded parents greater control. Less expensive and therefore resorted to by less affluent families was the practice of hiring a wet nurse who took the baby to her own home and brought it back to the parents when it had been weaned, between the ages of 1 and 2. Jewish and non-Jewish wet nurses, both in live-in and live-out variants, were employed in equal numbers by Jewish families. For women whose income was essential for the family budget or who were the sole breadwinners, hiring a wet nurse was a necessity rather than a matter of choice. As the century progressed, the perception of 'good motherhood' began to change in the tsarist empire, and increasing pressure was put on women to nurse their own children instead of hiring a wet nurse. In Jewish society, public discussion of wet-nursing had a national rather than a medical character condemning employment of non-Jewish wet nurses rather than the wet-nursing itself.

IN 1897 THE JEWISH NEWSPAPER *Hamelits* recounted a shocking story to its readers. It took place in Kremenchug (Kremenchuk). The wife of a *gevir*, a rich man, R., gave birth to a son and boarded him with a wet nurse. After a year and a half, the wet nurse weaned the baby and brought him home to his parents. The story would have ended there, if not for an alarming twist. When the boy turned 10, the former wet nurse returned to reveal a shocking secret—the boy was the son of her sister, who had given birth at the same time as R.'s wife, and the children had been switched. The husband of the wet nurse's sister had now died, and the family had decided that the real son was needed to say Kaddish for his father.[1] The newspaper does not mention the reaction of R. and his wife to this revelation, but one can imagine how appalled and angry they must have been.[2]

These days the idea of sending a newborn to live with an unknown woman for a year and a half would sound absurd to most mothers, but wet-nursing was a widespread childcare practice in Europe until the late nineteenth century. Some researchers suggest that it shows a lack of attachment to children, while others argue that it had an economic basis (maternity leave is a very recent invention).[3] They all agree, however, that wet-nursing was a common phenomenon and an important reflection of attitudes to children and relations within the family.

In the Jewish context, wet-nursing provides a fascinating insight into the relations between Jews and non-Jews, since the employment of non-Jewish wet nurses was not uncommon, which shows that Jewish families found them trustworthy enough for the task. Such proximity allowed for inter-ethnic communication and the exchange of ideas and practices.

This chapter discusses wet-nursing in the Jewish communities of the tsarist empire in the nineteenth and early twentieth centuries. I will mostly address the cases where the mothers were alive and, at least hypothetically, could nurse their babies but chose to hire a wet nurse, and will leave aside the cases where mothers died in childbirth or shortly after it. The chapter explores two variants of wet-nursing—live-in and live-out—and compares this practice among Jews and non-Jews. My first question concerns the social connotations of wet-nursing, in other words, what type of families were willing to hire a wet nurse of either kind. Then I discuss the employment of non-Jewish wet nurses in Jewish households. Finally, I examine wet-nursing in Jewish society in the framework of the discursive changes that took place in the late nineteenth century and which altered the perception of wet-nursing and the expectations of 'good' mothers. The phenomenon of wet-nursing among Jews has never received much scholarly attention, but now the situation is changing, and some new studies have been published recently.[4] None of them, however, focuses on nineteenth-century eastern Europe.

Wet-Nursing: Attitudes and Perceptions

Wet-nursing was a normal childcare practice in Europe until the nineteenth century. Wet nurses were not only employed when the mother had a medical condition or died in childbirth: often it was a matter of choice influenced by social, economic, and personal factors rather than by physical inability. Affluent mothers considered it inappropriate to their social status to breastfeed, perceiving it as more suited to animals than humans. They preferred to hire a wet nurse. Being a wet nurse was traditionally perceived as 'a low-prestige and poorly paid job',[5] and only poor women would agree to do it.

In the Mishnah, breastfeeding is listed among the duties of a married Jewish woman, but she is permitted not to breastfeed if she has two maids or the means to employ two maids.[6] These regulations were later repeated in the *Shulḥan arukh*, with the addition that if a wife came from a poor family, where a woman 'was obliged to breastfeed', and her husband was rich and could afford it, he could hire a wet nurse, because his wife 'rises with him and does not go down'.[7]

Alongside normative texts, the rabbinic responsa also affirmed that affluent women were not expected to breastfeed and mentioned women who explicitly linked their unwillingness to breastfeed with their social status.[8] The rabbis agreed, affirming that, according to the halakhah, a wealthy woman was free not to breastfeed and confirming that it was the practice of affluent women to hire a wet nurse for their babies.[9]

Obviously, maternal breastfeeding never entirely disappeared, even among the rich.[10] However, affluent mothers who were eager to breastfeed were perceived as both heroic and unconventional.[11] According to one study, if a mother in a Russian noble family chose to breastfeed, it was evidence of either financial problems or eccentricity.[12] Even in the mid-nineteenth century, when women from the Russian imperial dynasty, the Romanovs, wanted to breastfeed their babies, they encountered fierce opposition and were finally compelled to give the babies to a wet nurse.[13] There is no reason to assume that Jewish society perceived maternal breastfeeding any differently.

In the tsarist empire, the discourse on wet-nursing and maternal breastfeeding began to change in the 1870s and 1880s with active advocacy for maternal breastfeeding which was linked to the gradual medicalization of child-rearing and a general shift in the perception of childhood. Nevertheless, wet-nursing was actively practised well into the first decades of the twentieth century. Paradoxically, it encompassed an even wider social circle and began to include middle-class and poor families.[14] This seems to have been a result of the fact that wet-nursing became less popular among wealthy families. Consequently, it became more affordable for poorer social groups who sought to copy the patterns of the rich, although with a time-lag. Mid-nineteenth-century Russian doctors expressed regret that not only the aristocracy but mothers from the *meshchanstvo* (townspeople) also tended to avoid breastfeeding.[15] In 1900 a Jewish journalist who supported the new medical trends and called for maternal breastfeeding described wet-nursing as 'one of the worst abuses' of his time and complained that even the poorest Jewish mothers did not want to breastfeed.[16] In articles published during the First World War, wet-nursing was still actively being debated, and doctors called for 'a conscious and systematic' campaign against the practice.[17] Tellingly, the Jewish Ethnographic Program, the questionnaire compiled by S. An-sky and his colleagues in the early 1910s, features more questions about wet nurses than nursing mothers, which testifies to the frequency of the practice in the shtetls.[18]

There are no statistics on wet-nursing in the tsarist empire, and it is therefore impossible to measure exactly how common the practice was or to compare its frequency among Jews and non-Jews. Both Jewish and non-Jewish sources mention wet nurses constantly and routinely, indicating widespread recourse to the practice among both groups. However, the ethno-religious aspects of wet-nursing do deserve a special study, which I hope will be conducted in the future.

Live-in Wet Nurses

A live-in wet nurse was the most expensive option but also the safest, since the parents could exercise control over the nurse and her actions. Usually, the baby was nursed for a period of one or two years, depending on various factors.[19] Jewish notables, merchants, and very wealthy families, like that of Yehiel Yeshaya Trunk and Ita Yelin, hired live-in wet nurses.[20] The newborn children of hasidic rebbes often had live-in wet nurses, even in the first decade of the twentieth century.[21] Well-to-do, but not extremely rich, families also often employed live-in wet nurses.[22] For example, Miriam Shomer Zunser's maternal grandfather was a middle-class houseowner in Pinsk. His wife gave birth to twenty-four(!) children between 1834 and 1871 and never breastfed the infants but always made use of a resident wet nurse.[23] Fanny Schwarzman, whose father held a concession to supply fodder to the army and whose mother ran a dry-goods store, was also nursed by a live-in wet nurse who later became her nanny.[24] The practice was also not infrequent among the assimilated Russian-speaking Jewish intelligentsia.[25]

In Galicia, some well-to-do artisans seem to have hired live-in wet nurses.[26] Indirect evidence suggests that similar practices also existed among Jewish artisans in the tsarist empire.[27] Poor families who wanted to follow the trends of the rich 'took the last coin from their pockets and hired a wet nurse to suckle their babies'.[28] This is obviously an exaggeration, yet it demonstrates that the employment of a wet nurse ceased to be solely the privilege of the rich in the late nineteenth century.

Some mothers hired a live-in wet nurse because of a medical condition—if they could not breastfeed, did not have enough milk, or were of a delicate physical constitution. For many others, hiring a wet nurse was merely a status symbol (economic reasons will be discussed later). In the 1870s Miriam Shomer Zunser's mother hired a wet nurse instead of nursing her baby herself, despite the fact that at the time her husband Nachum Meir Schaikewitz (who would later become a famous writer under the pen-name Shomer) barely earned a living and she did not even have enough money for food. In her memoirs Zunser emphasized that 'in her most dire extremity the thought of nursing her own baby never even occurred to Dinneh [her mother]'.[29] It was social prestige and the influence of her parents' home which made Dinneh avoid breastfeeding, and the combined social factors were stronger than any economic considerations.

Jewish newspapers contained many accounts of live-in wet nurses and, in particular, the abuses linked with the practice. Articles described wet nurses who tried to kill either the baby in their charge or themselves, attempted to steal from their employers, or killed their own babies in order to secure employment as a wet nurse in a wealthy household.[30] Obviously, such abuses were not committed by all those engaged as wet nurses. Indeed, the prevalence of such accounts should rather be seen as proof that they were exceptional and that most Jewish families had satisfactory relations with their wet nurses.

There were cases where a mother breastfed her baby together with a wet nurse.[31] Sometimes the wet nurse only helped the mother when necessary and breastfed infrequently. In most cases, however, it was the mother who breastfed the baby infrequently, while the wet nurse breastfed the child most of the time.[32]

Boarding a Child Out to a Wet Nurse

Another version of wet-nursing was to hire a wet nurse who took the baby into her home and brought it back after weaning, between the ages of 1 and 2 years. This practice was widespread in Europe and was normal until the end of the eighteenth century.[33] The popularity of wet-nursing in early modern France has been described by Sara Matthews Grieco:

> Even the wives of bakers, butchers and silk weavers found it economically viable to hire a wet nurse, and many women who exercised other professions—embroiderers, market vendors, peddlers—could not afford to abandon their jobs as the money they would save by not sending their children out to nurse hardly compensated them for their lost income.[34]

It was safer to take in a wet nurse, but a live-out wet nurse was cheaper. In addition, a live-in wet nurse required a separate room, food, and even additional benefits, such as clothing.

The practice of boarding out babies existed among Jews in the Middle Ages, even if it was limited in scope,[35] and persisted until the early twentieth century. The sources from nineteenth-century eastern Europe frequently mention the practice and it seems never to have aroused surprise or severe condemnation. In other words, authors residing in different regions of eastern Europe were familiar with non-resident wet-nursing and considered it more or less normal.

Affluent Families

Babies from both affluent and poor families were boarded with wet nurses. Surprisingly, there are many cases where members of the child's family were described as *gevirim*, or merchants, which indicates a relatively high social status.[36] For example, the responsa record the story of an affluent woman living in Poland in the early 1880s who gave birth to a son. The woman's husband died soon after she gave birth, and as a widow she was described as 'rich and having many businesses'. The doctors advised her not to breastfeed, and therefore a wet nurse was hired. The nurse breastfed the baby in his mother's house three days after his circumcision and then took him to her home. After two months, the mother decided to entrust her son to a different wet nurse who lived in another city. This wet nurse breastfed the boy for one more year.[37]

Another story of a wealthy family involving a non-resident wet nurse who lived in another town was cited at the beginning of this chapter, and many others can be found in the newspapers of the time. Most of the stories end with the substitution of babies, which suggests that the employer's family enjoyed a much better social position than the wet nurse, as the reason for switching the babies was to guarantee the wet nurse's baby a better chance in life, and there would be no sense in secretly giving the baby to a family of the same social status.[38]

Apparently, the wealthy parents whose children were substituted did not visit them frequently (which was indeed complicated if the wet nurse lived in another town). Otherwise, they would have been able to recognize their offspring. This represents a less emotional and more practical attitude to babies.[39] Yet new attitudes to children were already on the way. They did not entirely end the practice of boarding babies out, but they altered it, as a story from Warsaw in 1904 proves. A local merchant, A.R., 'had to board his baby son with a wet nurse because of his wife's illness'.[40] Later, he was shocked to see his son in the arms of the wet nurse's daughter as she begged for alms, pretending he was a poor orphan. This shows, first of all, that the father was able to recognize his baby son, and so had kept a close eye on him and the care provided.[41] To achieve that, he had gone to the trouble of finding a wet nurse in Warsaw, not in a smaller town which would have been cheaper, and of paying her the exceptional sum of 12 roubles per month (twice the usual rate).

Yet A.R. had decided not to hire a live-in wet nurse. Was this on grounds of expense? Was A.R.'s wife so ill that it was impossible to have a stranger in the house? Did the family not have enough space in their apartment for the wet nurse? It is difficult to say, but it is safe to assume that A.R. was not a poor man, since he is described as a merchant in the newspaper article and was able to pay very decent wages to the wet nurse.

Some parents went even further. In the mid-1890s, the mother of future Israeli prime minister Golda Meir was employed as a live-out wet nurse and nursed the baby girl of a wealthy family in Kyiv. The girl's mother ensured that the wet nurse received a proper training in child-rearing before she started her job and sent a female specialist to teach her. After that the girl moved to live with the wet nurse's family and gradually became their favourite. Her mother came to visit every week and was happy about her daughter's health.[42] Just as in the case of A.R., this story reveals the modernized attitudes of the girl's affluent parents, who nevertheless made use of the practice of non-residential wet-nursing.

Thus, boarding a baby with a wet nurse was a valid option for affluent families including those who followed modernized child-rearing tendencies.

Poor Families

Although babies from affluent families were boarded with wet nurses, the practice was apparently more often resorted to by poorer, petit bourgeois families. Poor women needed to return to their jobs as quickly as possible, since their wages were essential to the family income.[43] Such families could not afford a live-in wet nurse, but having the mother at home with the baby was equally out of the question. Thus they had to board the baby with a nurse. Rabbi Yisrael Yehoshua Trunk of Kutno mentions in his responsa that when a mother could not breastfeed herself and could not afford a live-in wet nurse, she would frequently give the baby to a wet nurse to be suckled in the wet nurse's house.[44]

The practice of non-residential wet-nursing is at the centre of a story about a fictitious shtetl called Madmenah (dunghill) by Moshe Yosef Rudaev.[45] In Madmenah, women had two main sources of income—they either sewed stockings or took nurslings from the largest town in the province, called Levanah (moon), since they were almost always lactating. In Levanah, life is very difficult and women too have to work and to sell goods all day long. In such a city, women cannot deal with the raising of the children... Fathers are busy and do not care about the upbringing of their children ... Mothers are also busy and cannot nurse their babies and raise them. But blessed be the Creator who created not only the problem but also the solution. He created Levanah and he created Madmenah. Before one baby is born in Levanah, in Madmenah three wet nurses have already given birth.[46]

Rudaev characterizes the women who board their babies in Madmenah as 'street vendors and owners of small shops, those who trade in old clothes and all those who stand [in the market] with baskets full of fruits or fish'.[47] In other words, they are from low-income families. Rudaev's account is fictional, but nevertheless the issues he describes in a critical, realistic style seem to have been drawn from real life.[48]

A letter sent to the editor of *Nedel'naya khronika Voskhoda* from Minsk provides further support for Rudaev's description. The author mentions that many urban Jews used to board their newborns with rural wet nurses, and he ironically enquires whether this would be allowed now, in light of the new state regulations enacted in May 1882 which prohibited Jews from settling in rural areas, since a newborn who was Jewish and living with a rural wet nurse should presumably have been barred from settling in a rural area.[49]

Another example comes from Jadów, a town located about 50 kilometres east of Warsaw. The local rabbi wrote a letter to the Warsaw-based Hebrew periodical *Hatsofeh* to warn Warsaw Jews against sending their babies to wet nurses in his town, since the women there made a 'business' out of it and had been taking too many babies when they did not have enough milk. As a consequence, many babies had died.[50] His account gives the impression that many infants were sent to Jadów and that this was a normal practice for Warsaw Jews. Moreover, the fact that he decided to use a Warsaw newspaper to issue such a warning seems to confirm its frequency.

The geography of sending babies to a wet nurse can be clearly drawn from these sources. The babies were sent from a large city (Warsaw, Minsk, the fictitious Levanah) to a smaller one (Jadów, the fictious Madmenah) or to a village.[51] This phenomenon is easy to explain. Wet-nursing could function only in a society with a high birth rate, since it required a large number of lactating women. In addition, it was a sad fact that wet-nursing depended on a high infant mortality rate: if the wet nurse's own baby had died, she was more willing to look for employment as a wet nurse.[52] Wet-nursing was a low-prestige job with low wages, so a woman who had recently given birth had to be not only lactating but also poor enough to have to take the job. Women residing in smaller towns and villages were poorer and had fewer job opportunities, so the wages of a wet nurse were more attractive to them.[53] Therefore, babies were usually sent to such locations and not boarded out in the city where their parents lived. Although there were many women giving birth in Warsaw, very few of them would have been interested in being a poorly paid wet nurse, since they had many better job opportunities. If a Warsaw-based nurse was hired, she would demand higher wages than one in a village. Live-in wet nurses also usually came from smaller towns and were not permanent residents of big cities like Warsaw.[54]

Wet Nurses as a Vital Necessity

Some Jewish widows and divorcees may have preferred wet-nursing over maternal breastfeeding for halakhic reasons. According to the halakhah, a woman nursing her child could not remarry for twenty-four months, even if she had weaned the baby earlier. However, in the early modern and modern periods, rabbis tended to grant permission for remarriage to women who had not begun to breastfeed their baby. The life of a poor single mother, even with a legitimate baby, was much more difficult economically and socially than that of a married woman. Thus, some women may have chosen to pay a wet nurse instead of breastfeeding in order to be able to remarry sooner.[55] The choice of live-out wet nurse served thus as a guarantee that the mother had no possibility of breastfeeding her baby even if she suddenly desired to do so, since the infant lived somewhere else.

Yet the halakhic factor rarely seems to have been decisive, since many women, especially lower-class ones, were not aware of the prohibition of marriage within the period of twenty-four months and learned about it only when trying to remarry sooner and facing a disappointing answer from the local rabbi.[56] It was economic considerations, shared by Jewish and non-Jewish society, which played a much more crucial role. For many single mothers (widows, divorcees, and unmarried women), boarding a baby with a wet nurse was a matter of survival. Many of them (except rich widows who inherited their husband's businesses) were totally dependent upon their work, since they usually had no other source of income. Thus, they could not afford to spend much time with their babies and had to return to work or find employment immediately after giving birth. Usually they could not afford a live-in wet nurse and chose the cheaper option of non-residential wet-nursing.

Married women seeking employment as live-in wet nurses also had to give up their own infants, because it was believed that a woman could only breastfeed one baby at a time.[57] For them, boarding their baby with a wet nurse was the only way both to get a job and to secure the health of their child by at least providing them with breastmilk. For this to be possible, the wet nurse needed to board her baby with someone who charged less than what she earned as a live-in wet nurse.[58]

In his *Essay on the Ethnography of the Jewish Population in Russia*, published in 1861, Moisei Berlin described how Jewish women placed their babies with a cheaper nurse in order to be hired as a live-in wet nurse.[59] Thus this practice already existed in the late 1850s and early 1860s and continued throughout the late nineteenth and early twentieth century. From the very beginning of the emergence of Jewish newspapers in the tsarist empire, they featured many accounts of such live-in wet nurses who boarded their own babies either with a Jewish or a non-Jewish wet nurse.[60] Since such newspapers frequently engaged in sensationalism, their accounts of wet-nursing usually ended up with the baby being baptized by the nurse or abandoned by the mother. In reality, very few cases of boarding an infant had such a tragic end. As a rule, mothers kept in contact with the wet nurse and the baby, visited them, and retrieved their child after it was weaned, as can be seen in the responsa.[61] Wet nurses boarding their own babies out was not only a Jewish practice, it also occurred in Russian, Polish, and other communities. Only in the late nineteenth century did the pattern begin to change when live-in wet nurses were sometimes allowed to bring their own babies with them to the employer's house.[62]

Illegitimate children were often boarded with wet nurses, since they were an embarrassment to the mother and a constant reminder of her disgrace. Sometimes a woman pregnant with an illegitimate child went to another town to give birth and left the baby with a wet nurse there.[63] She thus had more anonymity, since in her home town people knew her, while elsewhere she could remain incognito.

Beginning in the mid-1870s, another form of childcare came into existence in the Russian empire and partly substituted for the practice of boarding babies with a wet nurse.[64] Pejoratively called 'baby farming' or 'the angel factory' (*fabrika angelov*), it was an enterprise in which someone (usually a woman) took in several babies to care for. Here, there was no wet nurse, and the infants were fed by hand. This practice appealed particularly to poor single mothers, especially of illegitimate children.[65] Such enterprises were notorious for the mortality rate among the children, which was usually not the result of malice but of malnutrition and neglect, since baby farmers themselves came from the poorest social stratum and their standards of childcare and hygiene were not especially high.[66] Jewish mothers used the services of both Jewish and non-Jewish baby farmers—their ethno-religious origin did not play an important role.[67]

Wet nurses were also hired for abandoned babies and paid by affluent local men, the local rabbi, or the community charity funds.[68] In large communities such as Vilna and Warsaw, payments to wet nurses for abandoned babies were often a permanent part of the community budget, since big cities had a greater number of orphans who could not survive without community care.[69] In the late nineteenth century, when the traditional system of charity ceased to function effectively, modern benevolent societies began to emerge to help orphans and abandoned children, making themselves partly responsible for their care and for payments to wet nurses.[70]

Live-out wet nurses were therefore used in a number of situations. Both affluent and poor families employed them when the mother could not or chose not to breastfeed. Boarding the baby out was also sometimes the only solution for single mothers, who had to return to work almost immediately after giving birth. Finally, orphans and abandoned babies were sent to wet nurses, which did give them a chance of survival.

The Wages of Wet Nurses

The wages of a live-in wet nurse amounted to approximately 60 to 120 roubles a year (5 to 10 roubles a month) in the late nineteenth century.[71] The rate was the same for both Jewish and non-Jewish wet nurses, but differed between big cities and small towns—big cities offered higher rates.[72] Even the wet nurses of the Romanovs do not seem to have earned much more. Their annual salary, which they continued to receive for the rest of their lives, ranged from 100 to 130 roubles in the late nineteenth and early twentieth century.[73] In comparison, female domestic servants in a capital city earned about 60 to 70 roubles a year, female garment workers earned 150 to 200, and female shop assistants 180 to 200.[74]

In addition to wages, a live-in wet nurse received meals, lodging, and usually clothing, which made the position more attractive. Live-in wet nurses may have grown accustomed to the good conditions in the house of their employers and demanded fine food and special consideration.[75] This problem was not exclusively Jewish; it was also frequently mentioned by Russians who employed wet nurses.[76] Some of the accounts of wet nurses demanding favours from their employers were probably true, but they were also very frequently an expression of changing attitudes towards wet-nursing, which began to depict wet nurses in a negative light.

The wages of wet nurses who lived out usually varied from 3 to 6 roubles per month.[77] In some cases, they earned up to 12 roubles a month, but this was exceptional.[78] It seems that wet nurses employed by institutions earned less than those working on an individual basis. In Warsaw, the benevolent society for aiding poor mothers and orphans spent 3,453 roubles on the wet-nursing of 170 orphans in 1903, approximately 20 roubles for each wet nurse (about 1.7 roubles per month).[79] Even if we assume that not all the babies were nursed for a whole year, the maximum rate is still 2 to 3 roubles a month. Similarly, a rural wet nurse who took a baby from the Moscow Imperial Foundling Home earned 2 roubles and 40 kopecks a month in 1863, which was considered a very low rate.[80] Towards the end of the century the payments increased, but not significantly.[81]

Jewish and Non-Jewish Wet Nurses

Employment of non-Jewish nurses, both live-in and live-out, for Jewish babies was widespread in the nineteenth century. Memoirists (even those, like Yehiel Yeshaya Trunk, from families with a distinguished rabbinical ancestry) mention Christian wet nurses who nursed them or their siblings or close relatives.[82] Newspaper articles contain many examples of non-Jewish wet nurses hired for Jewish infants.[83] The responsa describe the employment of live-in and live-out non-Jewish wet nurses too, mostly in a tone that reflects acceptance by the learned elite of this phenomenon, or at least an awareness of it.[84]

Jews were a minority in the tsarist empire, and there were many more lactating non-Jewish women than Jewish ones. Therefore, it was easier to hire a non-Jewish wet nurse, especially for those living outside the Pale, while the search for a Jewish wet nurse required particular effort. Although the law prohibited Jews from hiring Christian servants, one newspaper complained that this law was very difficult to observe, since it was next to impossible to find a Jewish wet nurse outside the Pale —where Jews needed special permission to settle—and even in Odessa, which was within the Pale.[85] A letter to the editor of *Nedel'naya khronika Voskhoda* from St Petersburg complained that if one opted for a Jewish wet nurse, it meant inviting her from the Pale several months before the baby was born in order to have enough time to process the necessary paperwork. In addition, the mother had to undergo a humiliating medical examination (conducted by 'the same doctor who examines prostitutes') to prove that she could not nurse.[86]

Within the Pale, the process of finding a Jewish wet nurse was easier, but there were still many cases of non-Jewish wet nurses employed in Jewish households. Moreover, some authors mention the special efforts undertaken by parents to find a Jewish wet nurse within the Pale, which shows that it was not easy.[87] There were always parents who required a wet nurse who could not, or who were not interested in, investing the time and effort necessary to find a Jewish one.

For many parents, the ethno-religious origin of a wet nurse was not a decisive factor. The wages, the physical condition of the nurse, and the quality of her milk were more important.[88] Wet nurses were often objectified and referred to as merchandise: the process resembled the purchase of a cow more than the employment of a person.[89] In light of this widespread attitude towards wet nurses, it is no wonder that parents were much more interested in objective characteristics than in the woman's religious beliefs.

Interestingly, in Jewish society, as in Russian and many others, there was a belief that, along with the breastmilk, the baby suckled the moral qualities of the wet nurse.[90] Nevertheless, moral considerations do not appear to have had much influence on the choice of a wet nurse and did not prevent Jewish parents from hiring non-Jewish wet nurses.[91] The wet nurse was perceived foremost as a servant with a specific practical role, not an ideologically loaded figure. If she met all the necessary physical and economic requirements and the baby seemed healthy, she was seen as suitable, regardless of her religion.

Non-Jewish wet nurses who lived out were also employed by Jewish mothers, although this practice contradicted halakhah, which allows a non-Jewish wet nurse to be taken into a Jewish house but prohibits boarding Jewish babies with non-Jewish wet nurses.[92] Nevertheless, this regulation was not always strictly observed—in central Europe in the Middle Ages some Jewish babies were placed with non-resident non-Jewish wet nurses.[93] Although it might not have been the common pattern, it continued to exist into the early modern period. *Ba'er heitev*, a commentary on the *Shulḥan arukh* written by Polish rabbis Judah ben Simeon Ashkenazi and Zechariah Mendel ben Arieh Leib in the late seventeenth and early eighteenth centuries, mentions the case of a non-Jewish woman who brought a baby to the Jewish community and claimed that 'a Jewess gave her [the baby] to nurse' in her house.[94]

The practice of entrusting Jewish babies to non-Jewish wet nurses continued throughout the nineteenth century. The letter to the editor of *Nedel'naya khronika Voskhoda* from Minsk mentioned earlier revealed that urban Jews there opted for it quite often—apparently because it was easiest and cheapest.[95] Around the same time, Rabbi Yisrael Yehoshua Trunk of Kutno wrote: 'It frequently occurs that a mother could not find a Jewish wet nurse and if she could not breastfeed herself and also could not [afford to] hire a Jewish or even a non-Jewish wet nurse who would breastfeed in the [mother's] house, she gave [her baby] to a non-Jewish wet nurse who would nurse in her own house.'[96]

Some nineteenth-century rabbis who were aware of the discrepancy between reality and halakhah attempted to resolve it in favour of live-out, non-Jewish wet nurses. They explained that previously it was prohibited to place a Jewish baby with a non-Jewish wet nurse due to the danger that this might provoke bloodshed, but this danger no longer existed, and thus it was permitted, though it was not desirable.[97] It is impossible to determine whether the rabbis indeed thought that the danger was now non-existent or had to submit to the popularity of the practice. Jewish women were also employed as live-out wet nurses for Jewish babies, like Golda Meir's mother, but the frequency is impossible to estimate in the absence of quantitative data.

Theoretically, Jewish women were prohibited from nursing non-Jewish babies, even for money. The *Shulḥan arukh* allowed it only when a Jewish woman had too much milk and suffered because of it.[98] I have not yet found any sources that explicitly mention the employment of Jewish wet nurses in non-Jewish households, and the issue needs further research.

Wet-Nursing and Ideology

In the late nineteenth century the wet nurse became an ideologically loaded figure, especially among educated middle- and upper-class people. There were still many families who perceived a wet nurse as just a servant with a particular function, but, for those inspired by new ideologies, the perception of wet nurses changed. In the national Jewish context, a non-Jewish nurse became a symbol of assimilation and of Jews forgetting or neglecting their Jewishness. In criticizing wealthy Jews and maskilim in Warsaw, Yakov Zak mentioned that when a baby was born to them, 'they take a local [Polish] woman as a wet nurse for him . . . and she will teach him to call his mother and father in her language'.[99] Shmuel Kanevski gave a similar explanation for the phenomenon of Jewish children being unable to read Hebrew: 'Their teachers and their instructors . . . were a non-Jewish wet nurse, nanny, and governess, then a non-Jewish student.'[100]

For the assimilated Jewish intelligentsia, a non-Jewish wet nurse was sometimes seen as more desirable than a Jewish one. Besides the practical ease of finding one, they were seen as a way of increasing familiarity with Russian or Polish culture, with the undeniable benefit of the infant acquiring fluent, accentless Russian or Polish.[101] For nationally minded parents, however, the employment of a Jewish wet nurse became an important principle. Yehiel Mikhel Pines, a proto-Zionist who was later active in Palestine, and his wife put much effort into finding a Jewish wet nurse for their newborn baby in Mogilev in 1879. About two years later, when the family was preparing to move to the Land of Israel, they searched for a Jewish nanny to go with them, but could not find one who wanted to accompany them on their journey, and therefore had to sacrifice their principles and hire a Russian woman.[102]

A decade later, a Jewish woman residing in Moscow and writing under the pseudonym Bat Amram produced a manifesto on education for nationally minded

Jewish mothers which also alluded to this topic. She complained that it was a widespread practice among Jewish women to employ 'Moabite and Ammonite wet nurses from the villages'.[103] What was wrong with these nurses? The foreign culture they planted in the hearts of the babies they looked after. The main object of her attack was the non-Jewish lullabies sung by wet nurses that promoted values alien to a Jewish child, which she considered totally inappropriate. She conceded that the wet nurses were not solely to blame: the lullabies, written by Mikhail Lermontov, the famous Russian poet, which, she claimed, 'many educated [Jewish] mothers sing to their children', were no less inappropriate than the songs sung by uneducated non-Jewish wet nurses.

The choice of pseudonym reflects the point of view of the author. Bat Amram is a reference to Miriam, Moses' sister. When Pharaoh's daughter found Moses in the bullrushes and assumed that he was a Hebrew child, Miriam approached her and suggested she get a Hebrew woman to nurse the baby. The princess agreed and Miriam brought her mother to nurse baby Moses.[104] Just as Miriam brought a Hebrew woman to nurse Moses, so the author sought to bring Jewish mothers back to their Jewish identity.[105] This parallel almost demands that the nineteenth-century Bat Amram would attempt to persuade mothers to breastfeed their babies themselves instead of hiring a wet nurse of any kind—as ended up happening with Moses' mother. However, there is no reference to maternal breastfeeding in the article, in contrast to contemporary Russian discussions, where authors opposed wet-nursing in general, regardless of the origin of the wet nurse.

The Changing Discourse: Wet-Nursing and Maternal Breastfeeding

The discourse on breastfeeding was changing in the 1870s and 1880s, and wet-nursing became an actively debated issue.[106] Doctors had more and more influence in childcare issues, adding to the medicalization of childhood, and they actively advocated maternal breastfeeding instead of wet-nursing.[107] The authors of childcare manuals followed the newest trends in paediatrics and proclaimed breastfeeding to be the sacred duty of every mother.[108] These developments, along with the changing discourse on childhood and motherhood, created a new image of the mother, who was expected to be inseparable from her baby. Central European mothers faced the change earlier, while mothers in the tsarist empire encountered it only towards the middle of the nineteenth century.

In the new medicalized discourse of childhood, wet nurses were tolerated only if the mother had a medical condition that prevented her from breastfeeding. Childcare manuals still discussed wet-nursing but accepted the practice only in situations where no other solution was possible. However, judging by the length of the sections in these manuals on how to choose a proper wet nurse, the practice was still popular, and was employed not only out of necessity but as a matter of choice.[109]

Nonetheless, this new medicalized discourse had a major impact, and employing a wet nurse ceased to be the norm and began to require some justification. From the mid-nineteenth century, mothers who did not breastfeed tended to claim poor health or a delicate physical constitution and cited the advice of doctors prohibiting them from breastfeeding. In other words, the wish of the woman was not enough to hire a wet nurse—medical reasons were needed to justify it. Yet medical reasons were sometimes only a pretext to avoid breastfeeding, and many doctors accused mothers of not really trying.[110]

Towards the end of the century, Jewish women also began to feel the need to justify themselves medically for having recourse to a wet nurse. East European responsa feature numerous questions about the mothers of newborns. When confronted with a situation in which a baby was breastfed by a wet nurse, the enquiring rabbi often listed the medical conditions of the mother and referred to the opinions of doctors who prohibited her from breastfeeding because it would endanger her health and the health of the baby. In some cases, apparently, the danger was real; in others, it was merely the woman's personal preference which required a medical opinion as a necessary support in the context of the new medicalized discourse. Rabbis obtained this information from the women or their immediate family who had approached them with a halakhic question. This reveals that the women themselves felt the necessity of a medical justification for employing a wet nurse even when seeking advice from a rabbi rather than a doctor.[111]

However, the responsa are a problematic source in this regard. They all deal with the issue of whether a widow or a divorcee with a baby was permitted to remarry within the period of twenty-four months when she was supposed to be breastfeeding her baby.[112] According to the halakhah, such marriages were prohibited, since it was believed that they could harm the infant, as the mother might stop breastfeeding because of her new husband's desire for her to become pregnant, which would spoil the milk.[113] Nevertheless, when a baby was breastfed by a wet nurse, the mother could obtain permission to remarry within the twenty-four-month period.

Mothers thus had their own agenda. Their goal was to prove that they could not breastfeed the baby for medical reasons. This would mean that if they married within the twenty-four-month period, there was no chance that they would be depriving their baby of milk, and thus should be allowed to marry. Even so, the arguments deployed do provide a glimpse into what was considered a plausible reason for hiring a wet nurse.

Surprisingly, in Jewish discourse on childcare, the call for maternal breastfeeding seems to have been less strong than in Russian or Polish society. Jewish newspapers introduced new columns on childcare where doctors gave medical advice to mothers, but there was no active discussion of why maternal breastfeeding should be regarded as preferable to wet-nursing.[114] The authors of articles on wet-nursing usually had nothing against the practice itself. What concerned them was the ethno-religious origin of the wet nurses. They were worried that many wet nurses nursing Jewish babies were not Jewish. The fact that many Jewish babies were not nursed by their own mothers was of less concern.

Conclusion

Since almost no studies have been conducted on wet-nursing among Jews, especially in eastern Europe, this chapter has aimed to break new ground in describing the different forms of wet-nursing practised by Jews in the Russian empire and to discuss the main social, economic, and ideological issues related to the practice. Wet-nursing was widespread among Jews in the Russian empire and employed by very different categories of families—by rich and poor, by those who lived in shtetls and those in big cities outside the Pale, by those who spoke Russian or Polish on a daily basis and those who knew no other language than Yiddish. Jewish babies were nursed by both Jewish and non-Jewish wet nurses, both in their own homes and in the homes of the wet nurses, although boarding out Jewish babies with non-Jewish wet nurses was explicitly prohibited by halakhah. The decision as to whether to hire a Jewish or non-Jewish wet nurse was based on availability, the remuneration demanded, physical condition, and quality of milk. From the end of the nineteenth century, ideological considerations also began to play a role. The acculturated Jewish intelligentsia, whether Russified or Polonized, preferred to hire non-Jewish wet nurses in order to expose their babies to native speakers of the local language immediately after birth. Nationally minded Jewish parents, for their part, invested considerable effort in finding a Jewish wet nurse who would nourish the baby not only with her milk but also with the Jewish spirit.

As a first step in the research on wet-nursing among Jews in eastern Europe, this chapter has posed more questions than it is able to answer. It is to be hoped that future research will address these questions and contribute to our understanding of the Jewish family, the way it functioned and the changes it underwent in the process of modernization.

Notes

I would like to dedicate this chapter to my father, Valery Oleshkevich, who passed away while I was working on it. May he rest in peace. For comments, suggestions, and discussions, I am grateful to Vladimir Levin and Uriel Gellman. Many thanks to Annette Ezekiel Kogan for language editing. This study would not have been possible without the National Library of Israel's JPRESS: The Historic Jewish Press Project and the Bar Ilan Responsa Project. I am deeply grateful to their developers.

1 Evidently, the wet nurse and her family decided to switch the babies in an attempt to provide their child with a better life in a wealthy household. R.'s son was raised in the house of the wet nurse's sister. The story does not say explicitly how he had fared, but apparently he was in good health.
2 S. Byhovsky, 'Be'artsenu: krementshuk', *Hamelits*, 13 / 25 Feb. 1897, pp. 2–3.
3 For a historical survey of wet-nursing in Europe, see V. A. Fildes, *Wet Nursing: A History from Antiquity to the Present* (Oxford, 1988); S. F. Matthews Grieco and C. A. Corsini (eds.), *Historical Perspectives on Breastfeeding: Two Essays* (Florence, 1991); on wet-nursing among European Jews in the Middle Ages, see E. Baumgarten, *Mothers and Children: Jewish Family Life in Medieval Europe* (Princeton, NJ, 2004), 119–53; S. Emanuel, 'Hameineket

hanotserit biyemei habeinayim: halakhah vehistoryah', *Zion*, 73 (2008), 21–40; on wet-nursing in early modern Florence, see C. Klapisch-Zuber, *Women, Family and the Ritual in Renaissance Italy*, trans. L. Cochraine (Chicago, 1987), 132–64; for France, see G. D. Sussman, *Selling Mothers' Milk: The Wet-Nursing Business in France, 1715–1914* (Urbana, Ill., 1982); for America, see J. L. Golden, *A Social History of Wet Nursing in America: From Breast to Bottle* (Cambridge, 1996); on wet-nursing as a sign of lack of attachment to the child, see E. Shorter, *The Making of the Modern Family* (New York, 1977), 168–204.

4 M. Botticini, Z. Eckstein, and A. Vaturi, 'Child Care and Human Development: Insights from Jewish History in Central and Eastern Europe, 1500–1930', *Economic Journal*, 129 (2019), 2637–90; A. Vaturi, 'Domeh akh shoneh: hanakah bekerev yehudim venotserim bemamlekhet polin-lita vehashlakhoteiha hademografiyot', *Gal-ed*, 26–7 (2021), 15–36; for a compendium of sources, see E. Bashan, *Hahanakah vehamenikah behalakhah uveminhagei yisra'el* (Lod, 2014).

5 S. F. Matthews Grieco, 'Breast-Feeding, Wet Nursing and Infant Mortality in Europe (1400–1800)', in Matthews Grieco and Corsini, *Historical Perspectives on Breastfeeding*, 15–62: 34.

6 Mishnah *Ket.* 5: 5; *Shulḥan arukh*, 'Even ha'ezer', 80: 8.

7 *Shulḥan arukh*, 'Even ha'ezer', 82: 3.

8 A. S. Koidonover, *She'elot uteshuvot emunat shemu'el* (Lemberg, 1885), fo. 3ᵛ (*siman* 2); Y. M. Ornstein, *Yeshuot ya'akov* (Piotrków, 1906), 95 ('Even ha'ezer', *siman* 21); S. M. Shvadron, *She'elot uteshuvot maharsham, ḥelek alef* (Jerusalem, 1972), 119 (*siman* 99).

9 C. Halberstam, *Divrei ḥayim*, 3 vols. (New York, 2002), ii. 63–5 ('Even ha'ezer', *ḥelek alef*, *siman* 19); 242–4 ('Even ha'ezer', *ḥelek beit*, *siman* 44); Kluger, *Ha'elef lekha shelomoh*, 34 of third pagination ('Even ha'ezer', *siman* 59).

10 See e.g. Y. L. B. Katzenelson, *Mah shera'u einai veshamu oznai* (Jerusalem, 1947), 4; L. Trotsky, *My Life: An Attempt at an Autobiography* (New York, 1970), 2; P. Rakovska, *My Life as a Radical Jewish Woman: Memoirs of a Zionist Feminist in Poland*, ed. P. Hyman (Bloomington, Ind., 2002), 22.

11 For medieval and early modern examples, see Matthews Grieco, 'Breast-Feeding, Wet Nursing and Infant Mortality in Europe', 26.

12 A. V. Belova, 'Period grudnogo vskarmlivaniya kak element dvoryanskogo rodil'nogo obryada v XVIII – seredine XIX v.', *Smolenskii meditsinskii al'manakh*, 4 (2016), 129–37: 132.

13 N. A. Mitsyuk and N. L. Pushkareva, 'Vnedrenie praktiki samostoyatel'nogo grudnogo vskarmlivaniya v vysshikh sloyakh rossiiskogo obshchestva XIX veka', *Vestnik Smolenskoi gosudarstvennoi meditsinskoi akademii*, 15/4 (2016), 182–91: 183. The first tsarina who breastfed her infant was Alexandra Fedorovna, the wife of Nicolas II. In 1895 she tried to breastfeed her firstborn baby daughter, Olga. It did not work out, but later she breastfed her only son and male heir, Alexei (b. 1904).

14 On the same situation among Russians, see N. A. Mitsyuk, 'Materinstvo u dvoryanok tsentral'noi Rossii vo vtoroi polovine XIX – nachale XX v.: istoriko-antropologicheskii i etnokul'turnyi aspekty', habilitation thesis (Institute of Anthropology and Ethnography, Russian Academy of Sciences, 2016), 570.

15 D. L. Ransel, *Village Mothers: Three Generations of Change in Russia and Tataria* (Bloomington, Ind., 2000), 26–7.

16 Nathan, 'Be'artsenu: varshah', *Hamelits*, 21 Dec. 1899 / 2 Jan. 1900, p. 2; see also Y. A. Grossberger, 'Ma'amarei mada', *Hamelits*, 16/29 May 1900, p. 3.

17 Z. O. Michnik, 'Ob estestvennom i iskusstvennom vskarmlivanii grudnykh detei', *Okhrana materinstva i mladenchestva*, 2 (1916), 35–56: 47; see also V. P. Gerasimovich,

'Kormilichnyi promysel i mery zakonodatel'noi ego regulirovki', *Okhrana materinstva i mladenchestva*, 6 (1917), 469–80.

18 S. An-sky, *The Jewish Ethnographic Program*, in N. Deutsch, *The Jewish Dark Continent: Life and Death in the Russian Pale of Settlement* (Cambridge, Mass., 2011), 103–314: 133–7.

19 The length of the breastfeeding period needs a separate study—some women considered one year enough, while others thought that it should be two. My impression is that ideas on the length of the breastfeeding period depended on a large number of factors, many of which were highly individual. For some insights and interesting, though disputable, conclusions, see Botticini, Eckstein, and Vaturi, 'Child Care and Human Development', 2675–6; for sources on the issue from various Jewish groups, see Bashan, *Hahanakah vehamenikah behalakhah uveminhagei yisra'el*, 23–39.

20 'Ḥadashim labekarim', *Hamelits*, 20 July / 1 Aug. 1861, pp. 803–4: 803; 'Moda'ah', *Hamelits*, 1/13 Nov. 1878, pp. 355–6; 'Ḥadashot beyisra'el', *Hatsefirah*, 3/15 Nov. 1886, pp. 1–2; Yehiel Yeshaya Trunk, *Poyln: zikhroynes un bilder*, 7 vols. (New York, 1944–53), ii. 13, 17–18; I. Yelin, *Letse'etsa'ai: zikhronot*, 2 vols. (Jerusalem, 1979), i. 21, 29.

21 Y. Twersky, *Heḥatser hapenimit: korot mishpaḥah* (Tel Aviv, 1954), 13, 195; I. Kalish, *A rebishe heym in amolikn poyln* (Tel Aviv, 1963), 39–40; Eng. trans.: 'Life in a Hassidic Court in Russian Poland toward the End of the 19th and the Early 20th Centuries', *YIVO Annual of Jewish Social Science*, 13 (1965), 264–78: 268–9; Heb. edn.: *Etmoli* (Tel Aviv, 1970). The children of Rebbe Israel of Ruzhin had wet nurses, including non-Jewish ones (see D. Assaf, *The Regal Way: The Life and Times of Rabbi Israel of Ruzhin* (Stanford, Calif., 2002), 274, 282; Y. Halevi Weber, *Nishmat kol ḥai* (Kolomea, 1904), 4). There is not much information available about wet nurses at other hasidic courts, but it is plausible that other hasidic rebbes employed them as well.

22 See e.g. Ben-Ir, 'Mibeit hamishpat', *Hayom*, 13/25 May 1886, p. 3; M.R.R.Y., 'Mikhtevei soferim', *Hayom*, 11/23 Nov. 1886, p. 1; Y. Zak, 'Ma'asim bekhol yom', *Hamelits*, 8/20 July 1888, pp. 1567–71; 'Mikrementshuk', *Hamelits*, 22 Feb. / 3 Mar. 1889, p. 2; S. Belkin, 'Be'artsenu: svisloḥ', *Hamelits*, 29 Nov. / 11 Dec. 1896, pp. 3–4; Nathan, 'Be'artsenu: varshah' (21 Dec. 1899 / 2 Jan. 1900).

23 M. S. Zunser, *Yesterday: A Memoir of a Russian Jewish Family* (New York, 1939), 27.

24 F. Schwarzman, *Moya sud'ba: Vospominaniya*, 2 vols. (Paris, 1964–6), i. 24.

25 Dushegubets, letter to the editor, *Nedel'naya khronika Voskhoda*, 13/25 Mar. 1883, pp. 242–3; Trotsky, *My Life*, 60, 63.

26 See e.g. 'Nefutsot yehudah', *Hamagid leyisra'el*, 30 Jan. 1902, pp. 56–7: 56.

27 According to ChaeRan Freeze young women who gave birth found employment as wet nurses both in 'affluent and working-class families', including one who was hired by a butcher's family (C. Y. Freeze, 'Lilith's Midwives: Jewish Newborn Child Murder in Nineteenth-Century Vilna', *Jewish Social Studies*, 16/2 (2010), 1–27: 17).

28 Nathan, 'Be'artsenu: varshah' (21 Dec. 1899 / 2 Jan. 1900).

29 Zunser, *Yesterday*, 118.

30 See e.g. A.Y.S., Slutsk, 'Ḥadashot shonot: konstantinograd', *Hamagid*, 11 Nov. 1874, p. 391; 'Moda'ah'; M.R.R.Y., 'Mikhtevei soferim'; 'Mikrementshuk'.

31 See A. S. Friedberg, 'Segulah le'ayin ra'ah (zikhronot miyemei hane'urim)', *Hamelits*, 20 Feb. / 3 Mar. 1896, pp. 2–3; A. Bornstein, *Avnei nezer*, 'Even ha'ezer', *ḥelek alef* (Piotrków, [1920s?]), 96–7 (*simanim* 48–9); Y. Y. Schmelkes, *Beit yitsḥak*, 'Even ha'ezer', *ḥelek rishon vesheni* (Jerusalem, 1983), fo. 44ᵛ (*ḥelek rishon, siman* 58); H. Volozhiner, Hillel Fried, and E. Fried, *Ḥut hameshulash* (New York, 1965), 170–2 (*ḥelek gimel, siman* 8); Y. A. Halevi

Ettinger, *Mahari halevi, ḥelek rishon vesheni* (Lemberg, 1893), fo. 87 (*ḥelek rishon, siman* 161); Shvadron, *She'elot uteshuvot maharsham, ḥelek alef*, 119–20 (*siman* 99).

32 Sometimes, when the baby resided with a wet nurse, the mother may have come to visit and suckled the baby then (see e.g. Schmelkes, *Beit yitsḥak*, 'Even ha'ezer', ḥelek rishon vesheni, fo. 44ᵛ (*ḥelek rishon, siman* 58); Ettinger, *Mahari halevi, ḥelek rishon vesheni*, fo. 87 (*ḥelek rishon, siman* 161)).

33 See e.g. Klapisch-Zuber, *Women, Family and the Ritual in Renaissance Italy*; Matthews Grieco and Corsini, *Historical Perspectives on Breastfeeding*; Shorter, *The Making of the Modern Family*, 168–204.

34 Matthews Grieco, 'Breast-Feeding, Wet Nursing and Infant Mortality in Europe', 34.

35 On medieval Jewish babies permanently or temporarily residing in the houses of their Christian wet nurses, see Baumgarten, *Mothers and Children*, 139–44; Emanuel, 'Hameineket hanotserit biyemei habeinayim', 37–8.

36 It seems that affluent Russian families also boarded babies out (see e.g. E. L. Sklovskii, *K voprosu o bor'be s detskoi smertnost'yu (ob ustroistve konsul'tatsii dlya grudnykh detei* (Kyiv, 1906), 3). Nevertheless, no study has been made of the subject.

37 Schmelkes, *Beit yitsḥak*, 'Even ha'ezer', ḥelek rishon vesheni, fo. 44ᵛ (*ḥelek rishon, siman* 58). For a similar Galician case from the mid-nineteenth century, see Halberstam, *Divrei ḥayim*, ii. 62–3 ('Even ha'ezer', ḥelek alef, siman 18).

38 See 'Ḥadashot shonot', *Hayom*, 22 Dec. 1887 / 3 Jan. 1888, p. 3; Mesaper haḥalom, 'Be'artsenu: vilnah', *Hamelits*, 26 Aug. / 7 Sept. 1898, pp. 4–5.

39 On pre-modern versus modern attitudes towards children in Jewish society, see E. Oleshkevich, 'Images of Parenthood in the Traditional and Modernized Jewish Family in the Russian Empire', *Pardes*, 26 (2020), 123–39.

40 'Yediot mekomiyot', *Hatsofeh*, 23 Apr. / 6 May 1904, p. 408.

41 See also *Everyday Jewish Life in Imperial Russia: Select Documents, 1772–1914*, ed. C. Y. Freeze and J. M. Harris (Waltham, Mass., 2013), 243–4.

42 S. Korngold, *Zikhroynes* (Tel Aviv, 1970), 28–9; G. Meir, *My Life* (London, 1977), 4.

43 On Jewish women as breadwinners, see S. Stampfer, *Families, Rabbis and Education: Traditional Jewish Society in Nineteenth-Century Eastern Europe* (Oxford, 2014), 121–41; C. Y. Freeze, *Jewish Marriage and Divorce in Imperial Russia* (Hanover, NH, 2002), 35, 63–70.

44 Yisrael Yehoshua Trunk, *Yeshuot malko* (New York, 1958), 66–7 of third pagination ('Even ha'ezer', siman 17).

45 M. Y. Rudaev, 'Kegamul alei imo: zikhronot me'ir moladti', *Hatsefirah*, 21 July / 3 Aug. 1902, p. 2; 22 July / 4 Aug. 1902, p. 2; 23 July / 5 Aug. 1902, pp. 2–3.

46 Rudaev, 'Kegamul alei imo' (22 July / 4 Aug. 1902).

47 Ibid.

48 In central Europe, such endeavours aroused much criticism and were actively debated in the press. I have not found such an active discussion in the Jewish press, which may mean that the practice of boarding babies out to wet nurses was not as widespread as it was in central Europe. For European polemics on the issue, see Fildes, *Wet Nursing*, 196–9.

49 A. Mashk., letter to the editor, *Nedel'naya khronika Voskhoda*, 4 Dec. 1882, p. 1344.

50 'Yediot mekomiyot', *Hatsofeh*, 30 June / 13 July 1903, p. 649; for a similar story about orphan babies dispatched to wet nurses, see P.B.P., 'Ma'asim bekhol yom. be'artsenu: vilnah', *Hamelits*, 2/14 July 1887, pp. 1551–3.

51 The same is true for some of the stories about children switched at birth: for a family from Vilna whose wet nurse resided in a small town, see Mesaper haḥalom, 'Be'artsenu: vilnah';

for a Jewish baby from Batumi, Georgia, boarded out in a village, see 'Nefutsot yehudah: merusyah', *Hamagid leyisra'el*, 12 Aug. 1897, p. 255. In central Europe, the geography of wet-nursing functioned in the same way for the same reasons (see Fildes, *Wet Nursing* 229–34; Matthews Grieco, 'Breast-Feeding, Wet Nursing and Infant Mortality in Europe', 33–4).

52 On birth rates and infant mortality rates in eastern Europe and a comparison between Jews and non-Jews, see Botticini, Eckstein, and Vaturi, 'Child Care and Human Development', 2653–63.

53 Nineteenth-century Russian doctors were also aware of this (see S. F. Voyutsky, 'Zhestokii obychai', *Vrach*, 19 (1897), 545–6: 545; D. M. Glagolev, *K voprosy o kormilitsakh* (Moscow, 1896), 7).

54 This was the typical geography of the wet-nursing business in central Europe as well (see e.g. Shorter, *The Making of the Modern Family*, 176–81; Matthews Grieco, 'Breast-Feeding, Wet Nursing and Infant Mortality in Europe', 33–4). For the same reason, orphanages gave babies out to rural wet nurses. For detailed analysis of the economic position of women ready to accept the job, see D. L. Ransel, *Mothers of Misery: Child Abandonment in Russia* (Princeton, NJ, 2014), 222–55.

55 I have found one responsum which explicitly stated that a divorced woman gave her baby to a wet nurse in order to remarry sooner (Y. S. Nathanson, *Sho'el umeshiv*, ḥelek alef (New York, 1980), fos. 13ᵛ–14ʳ (*siman* 24)). Many others may not have been so honest about their motives, or else their reasons were more complex, involving economic and medical factors not only halakhic ones.

56 See e.g. Kluger, *Ha'elef lekha shelomoh*, 38 of third pagination ('Even ha'ezer', *siman* 59).

57 Fildes, *Wet Nursing*, 190–3.

58 For the motivations of women looking for work as a live-in wet nurse and their socio-economic profile, see Ransel, *Mothers of Misery*, 222–55.

59 M. Berlin, *Ocherk etnografii evreiskogo narodonaseleniya v Rossii* (St Petersburg, 1861), 41.

60 See e.g. 'Ḥadashim labekarim'; 'Hanose'aḥ', *Hamelits*, 18/25 June 1863, pp. 334–5; 'Mah yomeru haberiyot bemikhtevei ha'et?', *Hamelits*, 18 Feb./2 Mar. 1885, pp. 224–5; 'Mah yomeru haberiyot bemikhtevei ha'et?', *Hamelits*, 20 May/1 June 1885, pp. 595–7; 'Ma'asim bekhol yom: varshah', *Hamelits*, 4 / 16 Mar. 1885, p. 287; 'Mikrementshuk'.

61 See e.g. Bornstein, *Avnei nezer*, 'Even ha'ezer', ḥelek alef, 96 (*siman* 48); Schmelkes, *Beit yitsḥak*, 'Even ha'ezer', ḥelek rishon vesheni, fo. 44ᵛ (*ḥelek rishon, siman* 58); M. M. Schneersohn, *Tsemaḥ tsedek*, 'Even ha'ezer', ḥelek beit vegimel (New York, 1995), 7 of second pagination (*siman* 336).

62 See Mitsyuk, 'Materinstvo u dvoryanok tsentral'noi Rossii', 574–5.

63 See e.g. S. M. Shvadron, *She'elot uteshuvot maharsham*, ḥelek dalet–heh (Jerusalem, 1974), fo. 8 (*ḥelek dalet, siman* 13); Kluger, *Ha'elef lekha shelomoh*, 23–4 of third pagination ('Even ha'ezer', *siman* 38); M. T. Tenenbaum, *Divrei malki'el*, vol. 7 (Jerusalem, 1976), 36–7 (*siman* 31). For some more examples from nineteenth-century Vilna, see Freeze, 'Lilith's Midwives'.

64 The practice first came to light in Great Britain in the mid-1860s.

65 On baby farming in the Russian empire, see E. Oleshkevich, 'Conflicting Norms, Female Solidarity and Childcare: Baby Farming in the Western Lands of Late Imperial Russia' (forthcoming).

66 For cases of baby-farming involving Jews, see 'Z sądu', *Kurjer Warszawski*, 25 May/6 June 1882, p. 5; 'Mah yomeru haberiyot bemikhtevei ha'et?', 20 May / 1 June 1885; 'Nowa Szyfersowa', *Kurjer Warszawski*, morning edn., 18/30 Aug. 1889, p. 2; X., 'Morderczynie dzieci',

Słowo, 23 June / 5 July 1890, p. 2; Negus, 'Morzenie dzieci głodem', *Kurjer Warszawski*, morning edn., 5/17 Mar. 1891, p. 3; 'Bemikhtevei ha'et', *Hamelits*, 10/22 Mar. 1891, p. 2.

67 Some non-Jewish baby farmers were reported to take predominantly Jewish babies into their care (see e.g. 'Mah yomeru haberiyot bemikhtevei ha'et?' (20 May/1 June 1885); 'W Berdychowie', *Kurjer Lwowski*, 23 June 1893, p. 4); others baptized Jewish babies immediately after receiving them (both cases I have come across took place in Łódź) (see 'Fabrykantka aniołków', *Kurjer Poranny*, 22 Jan./3 Feb. 1897, p. 4; 'Łódź: Zbrodnie', *Kurjer Poranny*, 3/16 Oct. 1902, p. 3).

68 For payments from the charity funds, see e.g. 'Hanose'ah'; for wealthy local men paying a wet nurse, see B. N. Hasofer, 'Ma'asim bekhol yom: kishinev', *Hamelits*, 2/14 July 1884, pp. 847–8; Egoz, 'Meḥayei varshah', *Hamelits*, 7/20 Feb. 1903, p. 2; for a rabbi, see 'Miplonsk', *Hatsefirah*, 27 Jan./8 Feb. 1887, p. 4; Nekudah, 'Ma'asim bekhol yom: be'artsenu: moskvi', *Hamelits*, 29 Nov./11 Dec. 1889, p. 2; 'Mikaydanov', *Hamelits*, 4/16 June 1892, p. 3. On the Jewish charity system in eastern Europe, see N. M. Meir, *Stepchildren of the Shtetl: The Destitute, Disabled, and Mad of Jewish Eastern Europe, 1800–1939* (Stanford, Calif., 2020).

69 As it was, for example, in Vilna in the 1820s (see M. Zalkin, '"Hakatsavim pareku ol": me'afyenim umegamot bife'ilut ma'arekhet harevaḥah bikehilat vilnah bereshit hame'ah hatesha esreh', in I. Bartal, Y. Fridlander, H. Turniansky, D. Asaf, A. Holzman, and S. Feiner (eds.), *Mivilnah liyerushalayim: meḥkarim betoledoteihem uvetarbutam shel yehudei mizraḥ eiropah mugashim liprofesor shemu'el verses* (Jerusalem, 2002), 25–42: 27). On problems encountered by this system in the late nineteenth century, see P.B.P., 'Ma'asim bekhol yom', 1552.

70 See e.g. N. Ha'izre'eli, 'Mikhtevei soferim: minsk', *Hayom*, 17 Jan./1 Feb. 1887, p. 2; S. G. Kanevski, 'Lema'an tinokot shel beit raban', *Hatsefirah*, 25 Apr./7 May 1888, p. 3; Y. Zak, 'Ma'asim bekhol yom', *Hamelits*, 16/28 June 1888, pp. 1373–5; Y. L. Davidovich, 'Ezrat soferim: lishe'elat harabanim be'odesah: alef', *Hamelits*, 28 Oct./9 Nov. 1890, pp. 1–2; Hatsofeh, 'Be'artsenu: kovno', *Hamelits*, 30 Dec. 1894/11 Jan. 1895, pp. 2–3; N. 'Be'artsenu: minsk', *Hamelits*, 19/31 July 1898, p. 5.

71 Ben-Ir, 'Mibeit hamishpat'; 'Be'artsenu', *Hamelits*, 21 Oct. / 3 Nov. 1901, p. 3.

72 In 1897 a Russian doctor, S. F. Voyutsky, who seems to have been working in a small town, mentioned a rate of 60 to 70 roubles per year (Voyutsky, 'Zhestokii obychai', 545). Natalia Mitsyuk mentioned rates of between 60 and 120 roubles (Mitsyuk, 'Materinstvo u dvoryanok tsentral'noi Rossii', 585).

73 I. Zimin, *Povsednevnaya zhizn' Rossiiskogo imperatorskogo dvora: Detskii mir imperatorskikh rezidentsii. Byt monarkhov i ikh okruzhenie* (Moscow, 2010), 50–1, 54–6.

74 R. L. Glickman, *Russian Factory Women: Workplace and Society, 1880–1914* (Berkeley, Calif., 1986), 61–7.

75 See e.g. 'Nefutsot yehudah'; Berlin, *Ocherk etnografii evreiskogo narodonaseleniya v Rossii*, 41.

76 See A. V. Belova, *'Chetyre vozrasta zhenshchiny': Povsednevnaya zhizn' russkoi provintsial'noi dvoryanki XVIII–serediny XIX v.* (St Petersburg, 2010), 423–4; Mitsyuk, 'Materinstvo u dvoryanok tsentral'noi Rossii', 580–1, 585–6. For similar stories from Europe, see Fildes, *Wet Nursing*, 194.

77 For 3 roubles per month, see M.V., 'Hayoledot ha'aniyot be'irenu', *Hatsefirah*, 18 Sept./ 1 Oct. 1900, pp. 854–5; Egoz, 'Meḥayei varshah'; for 5 roubles per month, see Hasofer, 'Ma'asim bekhol yom'; 'Miplonsk'; Rudaev, 'Kegamul alei imo' (22 July/4 Aug. 1902); for

6 to 6½ roubles per month, see A. Korrus, 'Ma'asim bekhol yom: S—y', *Hamelits*, 10/22 Jan. 1883, pp. 40–1; *Everyday Jewish Life in Imperial Russia*, 244. The maximum salaries I found were 8 roubles a month ('Mikaydanov') and an exceptional 12 roubles a month, more than twice the regular rate ('Yedi'ot mekomiyot' (23 Apr./6 May 1904)). Interestingly, a similar rate was charged by baby farmers (see E. Oleshkevich, 'Conflicting Norms, Female Solidarity and Childcare: Baby Farming in the Western Lands of Late Imperial Russia').

78 See e.g. 'Yediot mekomiyot' (23 Apr. /6 May 1904).

79 'Yediot mekomiyot', *Hatsofeh*, 20 May/2 June 1904, p. 511; see also 'Telegramot shel hatsefirah', *Hatsefirah*, 21 Jan./3 Feb. 1904, p. 3.

80 'Istoricheskii ocherk vospitaniia pitomtsev v derevniakh', in *Materialy dlya istorii Imperatorskogo Moskovskogo vospitatel'nogo doma* (Moscow, 1914), 95–131: 117.

81 For more on the St Petersburg and Moscow foundling homes, see Ransel, *Mothers of Misery*.

82 See e.g. Schwarzman, *Moya sud'ba*, i. 24; Yehiel Yeshaya Trunk, *Poyln*, ii. 13, 17; E. Yakhnina, 'Ya – poslednyaya…', in *Iz arkhiva sem'i Tsederbaum* (Moscow, 2008), 308, 312; O. Dymow, *Vos ikh gedenk (zikhroynes)*, 2 vols. (New York, 1943–4), i. 11.

83 See A.Y.S, Slutsk, 'Ḥadashot shonot'; M.R.R.Y., 'Mikhtevei soferim'; Zak, 'Ma'asim bekhol yom' (8/20 July 1888), 1569; 'Nefutsot yehudah: merusiya'; Nathan, 'Be'artsenu: varshah', *Hamelits*, 15/28 Sept. 1900, pp. 2–3. For Galician cases, see 'Estreikh', *Ivri anokhi*, 7 Feb. 1868, p. 122; 'Nefutsot yehudah'.

84 See A. Bornstein, *Avnei nezer*, 'Yoreh de'ah', ḥelek beit (Piotrków, 1924), 162–3 (*siman* 342); Yisrael Yehoshua Trunk, *Yeshuot malko*, 65–7 of third pagination ('Even ha'ezer', *simanim* 15, 17).

85 'Kategor vesanegor', *Hamelits*, 25 Mar./6 Apr. 1879, p. 265; see also 'Mah yomeru haberiyot bimikhtevei ha'et?', *Hamelits*, 21 Mar./2 Apr. 1883, p. 364.

86 Dushegubets, letter to the editor.

87 e.g. Yelin, *Letse'etsa'ai*, i. 21.

88 Since antiquity, there were many criteria on how to choose a proper wet nurse and how to check the quality of the breastmilk (see Fildes, *Wet Nursing*, 18–23; Mitsyuk, 'Materinstvo u dvoryanok tsentral'noi Rossii', 571–6).

89 On the objectivization of wet nurses, see Mitsyuk, 'Materinstvo u dvoryanok tsentral'noi Rossii', 577–80.

90 This belief was widespread among Jews and non-Jews from antiquity to the early twentieth century (see Fildes, *Wet Nursing*, 33–4, 42, 73, 91, 205–6).

91 A similar situation could be found in America and in Asia where European families hired mostly native or African-American wet nurses (see Fildes, *Wet Nursing*, 205–6). As in eastern Europe, moral considerations did not play a large role, although such people certainly did not feel that the local or African-American population lacked negative qualities.

92 *Shulḥan arukh*, 'Yoreh de'ah', 154: 1.

93 Emanuel, 'Hameineket hanotserit biyemei habeinayim', 37–8.

94 *Ba'er heitev* on *Shulḥan arukh*, 'Even ha'ezer', 4: 43.

95 Mashk., letter to the editor.

96 Yisrael Yehoshua Trunk, *Yeshuot malko*, 66–7 of third pagination ('Even ha'ezer', *siman* 17).

97 See ibid. 65–6 ('Even ha'ezer', *siman* 16); Shvadron, *She'elot uteshuvot maharsham*, ḥelek dalet–heh, fo. 22 (*ḥelek dalet, siman* 33). Shvadron attributed this ruling to Yom Tov Asevilli (1260–1330).

98 *Shulḥan arukh*, 'Yoreh de'ah', 154: 2.
99 Zak, 'Ma'asim bekhol yom' (8/20 July 1888), 1569.
100 Kanevski, 'Lema'an tinokot shel beit raban'.
101 See e.g. Dushegubets, letter to the editor; see also S. A. Grant, *The Russian Nanny, Real and Imagined: History, Culture, Mythology* (Washington DC, 2012), 59.
102 See Yelin, *Letse'etsa'ai*, i. 21, 27.
103 Bat Amram, 'Ezrat soferim: ḥinukh hayeladim', *Hamelits*, 20 Nov. / 2 Dec. 1890, p. 3.
104 Exod. 2: 5–9. I am grateful to Uriel Gellman who drew my attention to this connotation of the pseudonym.
105 Bat Amram dealt extensively with the national education of Jewish children (see also Bat Amram, 'Em habanim', *Hamelits*, 18 Feb. / 1 Mar. 1892, pp. 1–2).
106 See N. Chernyaeva, 'Childcare Manuals and Construction of Motherhood in Russia, 1890–1990', Ph.D. thesis (University of Iowa, 2009), 57–81; Mitsyuk and Pushkareva, 'Vnedrenie praktiki samostoyatel'nogo grudnogo vskarmlivaniya v vysshikh sloyakh rossiiskogo'; N. A. Mitsyuk, 'Zarozhdenie ideologii "soznatel'nogo materinstva" v rossiiskom obschchestve na rubezhe XIX – nachala XX vekov', *Smolenskii meditsinskii al'manakh*, 4 (2016), 168–75.
107 Actually, intellectuals have attempted to persuade mothers to breastfeed their babies instead of hiring a wet nurse since antiquity. The attempts proved successful only in the nineteenth century.
108 Chernyaeva, 'Childcare Manuals and Construction of Motherhood in Russia', 69.
109 Ibid. 70.
110 See Mitsyuk and Pushkareva, 'Vnedrenie praktiki samostoyatel'nogo grudnogo vskarmlivaniya v vysshikh sloyakh rossiiskogo', esp. pp. 187–9.
111 For such responsa from the Russian empire, see e.g. Volozhiner, Fried, and Fried, *Ḥut hameshulash*, 170–2 (*ḥelek gimel, siman* 8); N. T. Y. Berlin, *Meshiv davar* (Jerusalem, 1968), 43–4 of fourth pagination (*ḥelek dalet, siman* 19). Many more such responsa stem from Galician cities (see e.g. Meir ben Aaron Judah Arik, *Imrei yosher*, 2 vols. (Munkacs, 1913), i. fo. 95 (*ḥelek alef, siman* 184); Halberstam, *Divrei ḥayim*, ii. 62–3 ('Even ha'ezer', *ḥelek alef, siman* 18); A. L. Horowitz, *Harei besamim* (Jerusalem, 1984), 135–40 ('Even ha'ezer', *siman* 64); Ettinger, *Mahari halevi, ḥelek rishon vesheni*, fo. 88 (*ḥelek rishon, siman* 163)).
112 For more on the development of halakhic discourse on the topic, see A. Gurman, *Gilgulah shel halakhah: isur nisu'ei me'uberet umeineket* (Jerusalem, 2020).
113 The belief that pregnancy spoils breastmilk was common in ancient times (see Fildes, *Wet Nursing*, 8–9); it continued in the Middle Ages, among Jews as well as Christians (see Baumgarten, *Mothers and Children*, 125); and still exists. On its current circulation among Turkish women, see P. Ergenekon-Ozelci, N. Elmaci, M. Ertem, and G. Saka, 'Breastfeeding Beliefs and Practices among Migrant Mothers in Slums of Diyarbakir, Turkey, 2001', *European Journal of Public Health*, 16 (2006), 143–8. Another similar belief, which is still widespread, is that breastfeeding while pregnant harms the foetus.
114 For advocacy of maternal breastfeeding, see e.g. Ben-Zama, 'Higayon selah', *Maḥazikei hadat*, 5 Oct. 1886, p. 4; Dr. V, 'Kalkalat hayeladim, 3', *Hatsefirah*, 1/13 Aug. 1897, p. 864; Dr. Volb…, 'Kalkalat hayeladim, 4', *Hatsefirah*, 17/29 Aug. 1897, p. 929; 'Varshah', *Hatsefirah*, 30 Oct./12 Nov. 1900, p. 969.

TOZ Summer Camps
Modern Welfare for Weak and Exhausted Jewish Children in Poland, 1924–1939

RAKEFET ZALASHIK

In interwar Poland, what was regarded as a more scientific approach to children's health care became increasing popular. In this environment, the Towarzystwo Ochrony Zdrowia Ludności Żydowskiej sought to improve the physical state of poor Jewish children. Initially TOZ summer colonies were established by local Jewish organizations in eastern Europe with the support of the American Jewish Distribution Committee, with the goal of providing emergency aid during and immediately after the First World War. This aim was superseded by that of providing long-term facilities which would contribute to the improvement in the health of the Jews by implementing preventative and social medicine, including the provision of hygienic living conditions, better nutrition, and the encouragement of physical exercise. The colonies and semi-colonies established by the organization thus came to play an important role in the lives of the children and their parents and emerged as an important institution for the Jews in interwar Poland, who sought to safeguard the health of their young generation without significant governmental support.

Introduction

The numbers we have provided show most clearly the enormous medical and social significance of the TOZ camps for the weak and exhausted child of the Jewish poor, for the juvenile inhabitant of basements and attics. The camps give the child an opportunity to rest, gain strength, and enjoyment of life under the beneficial influence of country air (or suburban air in the day camps), sunshine, supervised nutrition, and properly organized educational, medical, and hygienic care.[1]

This is how the Jewish physician Lejb Wulman, who served as the medical director of the American Jewish Joint Distribution Committee (JDC) for Poland from 1921 to 1923 and later became the director of TOZ (Towarzystwo Ochrony Zdrowia Ludności Żydowskiej; Society for the Protection of the Health of the Jewish People), described the first fifteen years of TOZ in a report published in Warsaw in 1937. The report appeared in both Polish and Yiddish, so that it would reach both Jews and non-Jewish Poles involved in caring for the welfare of the local Jewish communities in Poland. Wulman devoted a whole chapter of the report to the summer camps and day camps run by TOZ.

This chapter examines those camps, which flourished in Poland during the interwar period, hosting thousands of children from the ages of 4 to 16. They were supported by TOZ and the JDC, and their establishment was possible because of the new political and legal framework of the Second Polish Republic. Reconstructing their history has a wider significance and sheds light on the intersection of public health, welfare, culture, and politics. In particular, it serves as an example of how transnational Jewish organizations undertook civic initiatives to improve the health of local Jewish communities through field work and politics. It also provides insights into how medical services were provided for minorities in a multi-ethnic society and into child welfare in the Second Polish Republic.[2]

I argue that the TOZ camps ought to be understood less as part of the camping and youth-movement culture which evolved in the context of nation-state building from the end of the nineteenth century and which was also a feature of the various Jewish political movements in the first decades of the twentieth century. Rather, they should be seen as part of a new approach to child welfare that saw as legitimate the intervention of external agents in family life to aid children. It was thus part of the way Polish Jews coped with their community's social needs in the light of the decline of the role of the *kehilah* in the provision of Jewish welfare and its replacement by non-governmental organizations such as TOZ and CENTOS (Centralne Towarzystwo Opieki nad Sierotami; Central Society for the Care of Orphans) in Poland and OZE (Obshchestvo Zdravookhraneniya Evreev; Society for the Protection of the Health of the Jews) in Russia. In Poland this was possible because of the formal legal equality which the Jews had achieved with Polish independence.[3]

Summer Camps and Nation-Building Projects

The establishment of summer camps in the countryside for poor and often unwell urban children was part of the movement from the end of the nineteenth century supported by philanthropists in Europe and in the United States to improve the physical health, hygiene, and even the moral behaviour of such children.[4] The rationale was that children were healthier when raised in rural areas rather than in crowded cities. In some cases, it was linked with exploring nature as part of modern nation-building which attempted to establish primordial connections with the landscape and the nation's soil, as in the case of the German youth movement Wandervogel and the Polish Krajoznawstwo, which sought to foster better acquaintance with the different regions of the country.[5]

There are extensive studies of summer camps as cultural and political phenomena in the history of Jewish communities, and these have highlighted the differences and particularities of these institutions.[6] Although initially the creation of summer camps for Jewish children in North America served a similar aim to those in eastern Europe —to be a refuge from congested slums and to improve physical health—such camps quickly became a vehicle for assimilation into the American mainstream, offering American sport, folklore, and other activities in a Jewish cultural setting as a way of responding to the growing xenophobia which viewed Jews as a danger to American culture and values.[7] Later, when most Jewish children in the United States did not attend Jewish schools, summer camps were a means to foster Jewish education and awaken interest in Judaism in children who were assimilated into the American environment.[8] In addition, political summer camps were established for children who joined youth movements, such as the Zionist Habonim, and for those who attended the 'red diaper' summer camps of progressive left-wing American Jews.[9]

Studies of the summer camps of Jewish youth organizations in Poland associated with the Bund, such as Tsukunft, have demonstrated that these became a means to foster a Jewish connection with nature and the Polish landscape and to politicize and create a 'new socialist individual'; in parallel, they also challenged the stereotype of the weak urban Jew.[10] Sotsyalistishe Kinder Farband, the Bundist children's movement, operated summer camps in deliberately challenging conditions to compete with the activities of the Zionist and communist movements and to imbue those who attended them with Bundist values.[11] Camps organized by the Bundist women's association, Yidishe Arbeter Froy Organizatsye, sought to provide childcare during the summer holidays for working women. As long as it had the financial resources to do so, the organization ran half-day camps in towns for the children of working Jewish women.[12] In addition, the religious traditionalists established summer camps in the interwar period where the genders were separated.[13] Other summer camps for Jewish children in Poland were linked to sport associations, such as the Jewish Women's Sports Association in Poland (Zrzeszenie Żydowskich Kobiecych Stowarzyszeń Sportowych w Polsce) founded in 1928 to organize summer camps for Jewish girls in order to propagate among them a love of participation in sport.[14]

Health and Nation-Building

In the first half of the twentieth century health became a central concern and played a significant role in the formation and reconceptualization of nations. It not only served to integrate and exclude peoples and groups, define borders, and forge identities, but was also seen as a means to underpin the political and social system.[15] In the period after the First World War health policy became a means for governments, non-governmental agencies, and international health organizations to rebuild and rejuvenate communities and nations.[16] The changing political and geographical contexts of the interwar era, the social dislocation, the demographic trauma, and the humanitarian crisis which these caused brought the issue of minority health rights to the fore both in long-established European states and in those which gained their independence after 1918.[17] One of these ethnic minorities was the Jews of eastern Europe.

During the First World War, and especially in its aftermath, Poland became the focus for the health concerns of international health organizations, mainly because of the large numbers of refugees from Russia who were spreading disease. Thus Poland functioned as a cordon sanitaire to prevent typhus moving westwards, with five Polish medical quarantine stations established by American officers in the east of the country which could vet Russian and Polish refugees heading west.[18] These measures contributed to halting the spread of typhus, and Poland could thus claim that it had regained its place as the 'bulwark of the West', protecting Europe from the 'threatening' East.[19] Poland's central geographical location, bordering what would later become the Soviet Union, turned it into an 'ideal' space for the implementation of public-health interventions by agencies such as the International Health Division founded by the Rockefeller Foundation, the League of Nations, and the American Red Cross.[20] They invested resources and sent healthcare workers to Poland to improve the health situation, prevent epidemics, and establish a humanitarian presence.[21] Preventative medicine and the creation of a solid public-health infrastructure based on contemporary American models were the goals of these agencies, as they attempted to impose a new social and political order. Europe in general, and Poland in particular, became a laboratory in which American methods of welfare, social work, nursing, public health, urban reform, and medicine were tested alongside new philosophies and practices.[22] However, the implementation of American 'reformist' ideals[23] in the emerging area of public-health policy within the newly established state was not a smooth process. It involved adaptation, negotiation with local agents, and in some cases resentment from the recipients.[24]

Jews and Health

The preoccupation with health among Jews in interwar Poland has to be understood as part of an earlier discourse dating back to the mid-nineteenth century, in which physicians contributed to the marginalization of Jews by demonstrating 'scientifically' their 'otherness'. Both Jewish and non-Jewish physicians claimed that Jews as a group suffered from certain pathologies because of their 'racial attributes'. In particular, it was believed that the Jewish 'race' was undergoing a process of physiological degeneration: weak nerves, late marriage, and low fertility rates were adduced to document this.[25]

Most Jewish physicians in Europe in the first decades of the twentieth century accepted or internalized the argument of Jewish degeneration.[26] In general, they explained it as the result of the harsh conditions in which Jews had been forced to live and in which they were still living. It was these conditions which had led to the weak physical constitution and fragile nervous system from which Jews were alleged to suffer.[27] Others took a more positive view and sought to prove that the Jewish 'race' was more resilient than the non-Jewish population to some diseases, such as tuberculosis.[28] In any event, what was perceived as the physical and mental degeneration of the Jewish people was seen as a national and social problem.

Whereas during the nineteenth century both 'eastern' and 'western' Jews were held to be suffering from pathologies, at the end of the century it was east European Jews, who continued to suffer from persecution and harsh political, economic, and social conditions, who were the focus of reform.[29] The improvement of the health of the Jews of eastern Europe, expressed as a political imperative regardless of ideology, was considered vital.[30] Health was becoming a means not only for promoting Jewish political rights as a minority but also for strengthening the Jews' potential development as a nation. Thus, the desire to improve the state of health of the Jews aimed also to render them worthy of acceptance as equals in the eyes of other peoples.

TOZ Activity among Polish Jews

As one of the largest minorities in Poland, constituting almost 10.5 per cent of the general population,[31] Jews experienced a major crisis during the First World War which manifested itself in further impoverishment, uprooting, and epidemics, and which exacerbated the already poor state of their health before the war.[32] This was especially the case with children, who were particularly vulnerable.[33] Moreover, the antisemitic atmosphere and the wave of pogroms in 1918 and 1919 in Poland on the eve of independence[34] spurred the JDC to provide aid to the local Jews.[35]

The common interests of the JDC and TOZ in the face of the crisis confronting the Jewish population of eastern Europe during the First World War created an alliance between the two organizations. This led to an interaction in which ideas, people, and technologies were transferred westwards and eastwards, influencing and transforming both organizations.[36] Formally, this activity was possible because of the abolition of earlier legal restrictions in accordance with the Polish Constitution of 1921 and especially Article 110, which granted Polish citizens who belonged to national, linguistic, or religious minorities the same rights as other citizens to establish, maintain, and manage, at their own cost, charitable facilities.[37] Article 113 allowed them to deploy funds for scientific and charitable purposes, as long as such actions did not conflict with the laws of the state.[38] Although in 1923 the Polish government demanded that all international welfare organizations—including the JDC—leave the country, this was not in fact implemented. In 1919 the US State Department had made it a condition that JDC aid in Poland should also be made available to non-Jewish Poles. This was now done, and the JDC was able to continue its operations in the country.[39]

TOZ was active in Poland from 1921, working in the field of preventative medicine and hygiene. Supported by the JDC, it launched public-health campaigns, disseminated information on good sanitary and dietary practices, ran clinics for mothers and mothers-to-be and nurseries, and set up numerous other medical institutions.[40] In many ways, TOZ's ideas about social medicine, shared by the JDC, were revolutionary for east European Jewish communities, which led to considerable resistance in adopting them.[41] Nevertheless, TOZ did succeed in positioning itself as a non-partisan group and was thus able to co-operate with the different Jewish social sectors active in interwar Poland. The persuasive force of TOZ resulted from its use of scientific rhetoric and its concentration on local initiatives to improve the health of different Jewish communities. This tactic was a powerful tool for introducing new ideas in places where previously individual physicians had been less successful in changing health practices. TOZ attempted to take action against contagious diseases and against those health problems that were believed to predominate among Jews because of their 'racial' attributes. It also provided information on good hygienic practices and the prevention of disease through public-health campaigns and education, targeting Jewish refugees, city and village inhabitants, and orphaned children.[42]

The Centrality of Jewish Children in Welfare Work

Although the initial aim of the JDC was to provide immediate help through local organizations, its involvement and presence soon became permanent. In the light of the need for medical care for 40,000 Jewish children in Poland at the beginning of the 1920s,[43] childcare activities there expanded and included school hygiene programmes; clinics to monitor children's mental and physical development and provide counselling, pregnancy follow-ups, and vaccinations; walk-in clinics, where mothers could get advice on how to raise their children; mobile clinics for schoolchildren, where dentists, nurses, and doctors checked their development, nutrition, and for diseases such as trachoma, tuberculosis, and ringworm; and summer and day camps. The JDC understood child health as an all-encompassing concept which included not only medical care but also the provision of adequate nourishment, hygiene, and physical conditions. The goal was to raise a healthier generation of Jewish children despite their devastated environment.[44]

Since the welfare organizations in the new Polish state were segregated and the Jewish community wished to have control of its children's health because of its lack of trust in government welfare bodies, Jewish non-governmental organizations such as TOZ and CENTOS provided such services with little financial support or involvement from the Polish government.[45] These organizations represented a new form of welfare and philanthropy which corresponded with the legally equal status of Jews in Poland, embodying both opportunities and challenges for Jewish agencies.

In the light of the miserable state of health of Jewish children and because of these organizations' commitment to reformist visions, it is no wonder that the first public-health campaign in Poland undertaken by TOZ (at this stage still known as OZE) and the JDC in 1922 sought to combat favus among Jewish children.[46] Favus, a fungal infection of the scalp, was seen as a typical 'Jewish disease' related to poverty and backwardness, and linked with Jews in the derogatory expression *Żyd parchaty* (scabby Jew), which was a common pejorative way of referring to Jews in Poland and part of their 'otherness' in Polish Catholic culture.[47] Jewish children in eastern Europe suffered from very high rates of this disease, which left scars on their scalps.[48] Four years after the successful favus campaign, in 1926 TOZ became a central organization for the health care of Jewish children in Poland. By then it was already active in thirty-six cities in Poland, with ninety-one medical facilities, as well as providing sports education, patrols to supervise the hygienic condition of Jewish neighbourhoods, day care for children, dental services, pharmacies, and the summer and day camps.[49]

TOZ Summer Camps

Summer camps for impoverished urban children were an important part of the health programme of the JDC. In the years 1914 to 1916 they were set up for Jewish refugees in Russia by OZE and Evreiskii Komitet Pomoshchi Zhertvam Voiny (the Jewish Committee for Aid to Refugees).[50] The first summer camps in Poland for

Table 1 Development of TOZ summer camps

Year	Number of summer camps	Number of children attending
1924	7	1,745
1925	10	1,796
1926	15	3,134
1927	18	3,690
1928	24	3,954
1929	22	3,588
1930	28	5,015
1931	28	4,636
1932	25	5,045
1933	25	4,992
1934	27	5,286
1935	29	6,154
1936	29	6,867
Total		55,902

Source: Wulman, *Na straży zdrowia ludu żydowskiego*, 38.

Jewish children were established by the JDC in the summer of 1919 and accommodated 25,000 children.[51] From 1921 TOZ took over JDC activities in Poland, including long-term plans for summer camps, where children could escape their urban slum conditions.[52] These camps aimed to temporarily counteract the deplorable living conditions of poor and ill Jewish children by offering ample nutrition, fresh air, and physical activity.[53] More specifically, the establishment of the TOZ summer camps was justified on the grounds that 'it is clear that the care provided to children by TOZ during school hours cannot produce the desired results if it is not extended, at least in part, into the summer months'.[54]

It took until 1924 for the first seven camps operated by TOZ to be opened. On 13 May 1924 a report in the Yiddish newspaper *Haynt*, 'What is Going on in Warsaw', included an announcement of the establishment of TOZ camps for 'weak children' near Danzig. They were to open on 1 June.[55] In that year 1,745 children were enrolled.[56] Very quickly the summer camps became one of the most important aspects of TOZ's work and expanded steadily,[57] so that by 1936 there were twenty-nine summer camps providing care for 6,867 children (see Table 1).[58] TOZ also established camps for treatment and recuperation. There were four of these which accommodated a few hundred sick orphans each summer supervised by specialist physicians and located in Ciechocinek.[59]

Finance

Summer camps were expensive to run. Suitable premises had to be rented, staff had to be paid, and the accommodation and activities of the children had to be financed.

Although initially the JDC planned to withdraw its economic involvement in long-term activities on behalf of Jewish children in Poland in the hope that TOZ's summer camps would be supported by Jewish *Landsmanshaftn* in the US,[60] it found itself obliged to provide considerable financial support for children's summer camps, providing between 40 and 70 per cent of their budgets.[61]

After the First World War the social welfare system in Poland was still in its infancy. It was based on the Social Welfare Law of August 1923, under which the Ministry of Labour and Social Welfare imposed on local authorities the obligation of providing and financing social welfare.[62] This was to be organized by social welfare committees created at the municipal level, in municipalities with more than 5,000 residents, or at the district level.[63] The Polish state did subsidize TOZ summer camps, but only to a limited degree. In a discussion in the Polish Sejm in December 1928 on the budget of the Ministry of Labour and Welfare for the year 1928/9, Hersz Luzer Heller, a member of the Zionist Socialist group Hitachdut, accused the Ministry of Labour and Welfare of providing Jewish organizations with only a minimum government subsidy. In his words: 'It is completely unacceptable and unheard of that within this modest budget and in a purely social field, Jews should be discriminated against—the same Jews who, by their own efforts, have created and, to this day, maintained dozens of social institutions.'[64] He then mentioned TOZ explicitly and the important work it was undertaking among Jewish children who otherwise would have been a burden on the Polish welfare system. He also specifically mentioned the summer camps and the varying extent to which they were subsidized: 'The subsidies for summer camps are as follows: for a Polish child 6 zlotys, and for a Jewish child a mere fifth of this, because it is only 1.30 zlotys.'[65]

Had more resources been available, the number of summer camps could have been greater. TOZ activists estimated that between 40 and 60 per cent of the children who wanted to attend summer camps and had the approval of the TOZ school physician to do so could not be accommodated.[66] To deal with this problem TOZ created day camps. These were located in towns, and provided children with meals and outdoor activities under the medical, hygienic, and educational supervision of TOZ during the day, the children returning to their parents' home in the evening. Between 1926 and 1936, 46,760 Jewish children attended these day camps (see Table 2).[67] As was the case with the summer camps, not all those who wanted a place could be accommodated, and those admitted amounted to less than 60 per cent of those who sought places.[68]

According to Wulman's report of 1937, 37 per cent of the annual cost of operating the summer camps, which amounted to 3.5 million zlotys, came from the contributions of parents, 13 per cent from the central TOZ office, and the remainder from local authorities, Jewish local organizations of self-government, health insurance, and money raised at special supportive events. Day camps cost approximately 1 million zlotys annually to run: 19.1 per cent came from parents' contributions, 22.8 per cent from the central TOZ office, and the remainder from local branches (14.1 per cent), local government (13.5 per cent), and money from gatherings and events (13.1 per

Table 2 Development of TOZ day camps

Year	Number of day camps	Number of children attending
1926	18	3,909
1927	28	4,130
1928	25	3,679
1929	22	2,839
1930	22	3,627
1931	18	2,918
1932	19	3,083
1933	23	4,093
1934	24	5,142
1935	27	5,991
1936	31	7,349
Total		55,902

Source: Wulman, *Na straży zdrowia ludu żydowskiego*, 40.

cent).[69] The report does not mention financial support from the JDC for TOZ summer camps and day camps, although this was the main source of funding for TOZ activity in general and childcare in particular.[70]

Because of the impact of the Great Depression in Poland, TOZ summer camps experienced a crisis between 1932 and 1934 which led to a decline in the number of children admitted.[71] At this time the cost of keeping a child in a summer camp for four weeks was 60 zlotys and in a day camp 15 zlotys. A successful fundraising campaign for TOZ summer camps headed by Gershon Lewin in 1937 succeeded in raising 400,000 zlotys. This was sufficient to finance the admission of 16,000 Jewish children into the organization's summer camps and day camps.[72]

Who Attended TOZ's Summer Camps?

TOZ's activities were part of modern philanthropy, which, in contrast to traditional religious charity, is perceived as an investment that will lead the beneficiaries to a self-sustaining future. Modern philanthropy bases its operation on surveys, statistics, and data on the social problems it wishes address in order to evaluate the investment needed and its impact.[73] Accordingly, TOZ gathered data on the functioning of its camps. An analysis of the available socio-demographic data on the children who attended the camps shows who they were, what their social and economic profile was, and the differences between those who attended summer camps and those who attended day camps.

Children aged 6 to 16 were eligible to attend TOZ's summer camps, but in practice the majority were aged between 8 and 12. Children from this age group were old enough to stay away from home for a period of four weeks and were usually too young to work during the summer holidays. Moreover, the figures show that, although TOZ summer camps provided for all the needs of the children, even the poorest parents were not willing to send younger children to a camp far away from their homes for a whole month.[74]

Places in TOZ day camps—which were located in towns, because they included only activities and nutrition during the day, with no accommodation—were offered to younger children from the age of 4. However, the majority of the children who enrolled in them were aged between 6 and 10. Less than 10 per cent were under the age of 6 (see Table 3). The gender distribution did not vary much between summer camps and day camps. The attendees at the summer camps were 51.3 per cent boys and 48.7 per cent girls and at the day camps 49 per cent boys and 51 per cent girls.[75]

The TOZ camps were meant to improve the physical state of the poor and sick Jewish children in the Polish towns and cities. The data collected by TOZ shows that the majority of the children (58 per cent) who attended the summer camps were under-nourished and that 46 per cent were in a poor physical state as a result of malnutrition and disease and were not well developed physically.[76] Forty per cent of the children suffered from anaemia, 44.3 per cent suffered from enlarged lymph glands, and 13.2 per cent had constant fever, which usually indicated the presence of an infection.[77] The physical condition of the children who attended day camps was even worse. The impact of attending TOZ summer camps was positive and the children gained between 2 and 4 kilograms on average over the four weeks they spent in them, which probably represented between 10 and 25 per cent of their initial weight.

Clearly the children who attended the camps came mainly from the poor strata of the Jewish population. Data on the social background of the children was collected by TOZ. Eighty-seven per cent of children who attended TOZ summer camps went to

Table 3 Ages of children attending TOZ summer camps and day camps

Age group	Summer camps N	Summer camps %	Day camps N	Day camps %
4–6	–	–	4,558	9.7
6–8	9,279	16.6	12,212	26.1
8–10	16,069	28.7	13,657	29.2
10–12	15,581	27.9	10,940	23.5
12–14	12,459	22.3	5,539	11.5
14–16	2,515	4.5	–	–
Totals[a]	55,903	100.0	46,906	100.0

Source: Wulman, *Na straży zdrowia ludu żydowskiego*, 40.

[a] The discrepancies between the totals in Table 3 and in Tables 1, 2, and 4 are a result of how the data was originally collected.

Table 4 Parental occupation of children attending TOZ summer camps and day camps

Parental occupation	Summer camps N	%	Day camps N	%
Craftsmen	14,252	25.5	13,655	29.2
Workers	11,414	20.4	8,502	18.2
Tradesmen and small merchants	12,226	21.9	7,667	16.4
Shop workers	3,014	5.4	1,882	4,0
Free professions	1,934	3.5	1,079	2.3
Unspecified	2,804	5.0	3,003	6.4
Unemployed	565	0.1	7,724	16.6
Child orphans	4,587	8.2	3,248	6.9
Totals	55,902	100.0	46,760	100.0

Source: Wulman, *Na straży zdrowia ludu żydowskiego*, 45.

Jewish schools or Zionist schools such as Tarbut. Ten per cent did not attend school. Around 2.5 per cent came from orphanages, and 1 per cent were working children who had to support their family. Around 75 per cent of the parents of children who attended TOZ camps were craftsmen, workers, tradesmen, and small merchants. Around 16 per cent of parents of children in the day camps were unemployed, in comparison to 0.1 per cent of parents of children who attended summer camps. The disadvantaged background of the children is clearly revealed in Table 4.

Activities in the Summer Camps and Day Camps

In the reports on the camps, not much written evidence is available on the actual activities of the children: records concentrate on the budget, personnel, the children's backgrounds, and their physical condition before and after attendance. In addition, there are no memoirs of caregivers or of children who attended the summer camps. What do exist are mainly photo albums and single pictures that give a vivid image of the way these camps functioned on a daily basis (see Figures 1–3).

TOZ summer camps offered freedom to impoverished Jewish children, who were able to get away from their parents and their often harsh living conditions in crowded cities. Living in nature, undertaking physical activity on a daily basis, scouting, dancing, swimming, attending costume balls, and spending their days mainly with their peers without worries were part of the experience of the attendees. As a result, it seems that the children who participated in TOZ summer camps developed a loyalty to and appreciation of TOZ. The camps were bilingual, and TOZ used both Polish and Yiddish in its published and unpublished materials, reflecting to a certain extent the situation in which Polish Jews were living in the interwar period (see Figures 4 and 5). TOZ personnel involved the children in the daily routine of the camp and gave them a feeling of responsibility.

The summer camps and day camps were thus an important part of TOZ's attempts to care for Jewish children, and a source of pride. They also received public attention and were perceived as a success both for the Jewish minority in Poland and for TOZ. The daily Jewish press reported in detail on the activities of summer camps and the opening of such camps in new locations.[78] A particularly festive occasion was the naming of a summer camp after Dr Tsemach Shabad, a pioneer in providing health care to Jewish children, by TOZ activists on his seventieth birthday.

The camps were also the subject of research. In May 1938 TOZ devoted a whole conference in Warsaw to the fifteen years since the establishment of the first summer

Figure 1 TOZ day camp
YIVO Archive, New York, RG 120/yarg120p06754

Figure 2 TOZ summer camp, Ostróg, 1938
YIVO Archive, RG 335.7, Box 8, folder 307, 11

Figure 3 TOZ summer camp, Pośpieszka suburb, Vilna, 1920s
YIVO Archive, RG 120/yarg120poalbum31_p001

Figure 4 Invitation to the opening of a new building at TOZ children's summer camp, Vilna, in Polish (n.d.)
YIVO Archive, RG 28/P/997

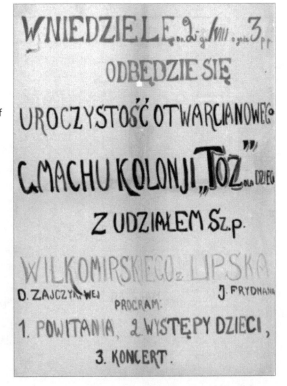

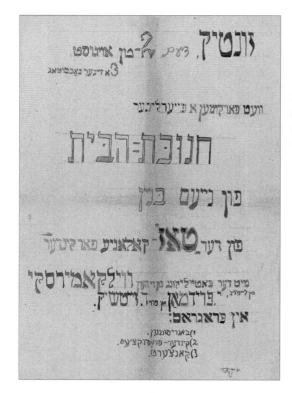

Figure 5 Invitation to the opening of a new building at TOZ children's summer camp, Vilna, in Yiddish (n.d.) YIVO Archive, RG 28/P/999

camp. Sixty-seven teachers, physicians, nurses, and others involved in the camps from forty-two cities and towns participated. Dr Schwalbe of Łódź gave a lecture on summer camps and day camps, Dr Yurin of Lwów described 'a few preventive measures undertaken in preparation of summer camps', Dr Greenwald of Warsaw talked about 'medical-hygienic inspection in the camps', and Dr Thorsh analysed 'preventive action against contagious diseases on the camps'. Other lectures discussed the educational work in the camps. The lectures were followed by discussions. In the summer of 1938 TOZ aimed at opening eighty summer and day camps.[79] However, this plan to expand the camps' operation was not realized because of the more pressing need to feed thousands of Jewish children who were suffering extreme deprivation, and later because of the outbreak of the Second World War.

Conclusion

This chapter has sought to analyse the activity of TOZ summer camps and day camps for Jewish children in the interwar period as a case study of the attempt to provide health care for minorities in a multi-ethnic society. The history of TOZ summer facilities for Jewish children highlights the challenges faced by the Jewish minority in Poland. The community strove to be integrated into the general society as equal citizens and believed they were entitled to an equal share of welfare provision. At the same time, Jewish activists also had to rely on non-governmental funds and logistics to provide assistance to the Jewish community—especially children—a situation which was the result both of institutional discrimination against Jews and of the desire to keep Jewish education and welfare under Jewish control.

Initially TOZ summer camps were established by local Jewish organizations in eastern Europe supported by the JDC, with the goal of providing emergency aid during and immediately after the First World War. This was superseded by the aim of providing long-term facilities which would contribute to the improvement in the health of Jews by implementing preventative and social medicine, including the provision of hygienic living conditions, better nutrition, and the encouragement of physical exercise. In this framework, Jewish children were the focus of attention, both as one of the most vulnerable groups and as the future of the Jewish people. Because of the poverty and difficult conditions in which the majority of them lived, the rationale of summer camps was that it was not enough to provide aid during the school year and that the summer months should be used to improve the children's physical and mental state.

TOZ's summer camps played a significant part in the lives of those Jewish children who came from deprived socio-economic backgrounds and were lucky enough to attend them. In addition, the setting up of summer camps was central to the mission of TOZ and a source of pride to its activists. In summer 2007 in New York, I interviewed Mira Jedwabnik Van Doren, the daughter of Dr David Jedwabnik, a Jewish physician and one of the leaders of the TOZ branch in Vilna.[80] She told me that the last thing her family did prior to their departure for a visit to New York on 31 August 1939—a visit from which they never returned—was to attend a performance prepared by Jewish children to mark the end of the summer camp in Vilna. Watching the performance on the last day of the summer, a day before the outbreak of the Second World War, symbolized for her the essence of the work of TOZ in Vilna. It was also a joyful moment which seemed to presage an optimistic future for these Jewish children and for Polish Jewry as a whole, a future that was never to be realized.

Notes

1 L. Wulman, *Na straży zdrowia ludu żydowskiego (15 lat TOZ-u.)* (Warsaw, 1937), 37; see also id., *Af der vakh fun yidishn folksgezunt: 15 yor 'TOZ'* (Warsaw, 1937).

2 Very little has been written on the role of Jewish welfare organizations in Poland as part of the emerging Polish welfare system. This issue is discussed in Z. Cutter and E. Sadowska, 'Opieka nad ludnością II Rzeczypospolitej ze szczególnym uwzględnieniem mniejszości żydowskiej', in S. Walasek (ed.), *Opieka nad dziećmi i młodzieżą: Studia z dziejów oświaty w XX wieku* (Warsaw, 2008), 91–115.

3 S. Martin, 'How to House a Child: Providing Homes for Jewish Children in Interwar Poland', *East European Jewish Affairs*, 45 (2015), 26–41: 27–8.

4 See J. C. Albisetti, 'Sending City Children to the Country: Vacations in "Nature" ca. 1870–1900', *Paedagogica Historica*, 56 (2020), 70–84.

5 R. Kahane, *The Origins of Postmodern Youth: Informal Youth Movements in a Comparative Perspective* (Berlin, 1997), ch. 4; K. R. Mazurski, 'Kształtowanie postaw przez polskie krajoznawstwo', in M. K. Leniartek (ed.), *Autokreacja poprzez turystykę* (Wrocław, 2010), 259–74.

6 On the Polish Jewish case, see S. Kassow, 'Travel and Local History as a National Mission: Polish Jews and the *Landkentenish* Movement in the 1920s and 1930s', in J. Brauch, A. Lipphardt, and A. Nocke (eds.), *Jewish Topographies: Visions of Space, Traditions of Place* (Farnham, Surr., 2008), 241–64; on Jewish revisionism in Poland and the Polish landscape and patriotism, see D. Kupfert Heller, *Jabotinsky's Children: Polish Jews and the Rise of Right-Wing Zionism* (Princeton, NJ, 2018), 148–50.

7 N. Mykoff, 'A Jewish Season: Ethnic-American Culture at Children's Summer Camp 1918–1941', Ph.D. thesis (New York University, 2002), 71–8.

8 D. Issacman, 'Jewish Summer Camps in the United States and Canada, 1900–1969', D.Ed. thesis (Dropsie College, 1970), 39.

9 D. Breslau (ed.), *Adventure in Pioneering: The Story of 25 Years of Habonim Camping* (New York, 1957); P. Mishler, *Raising Reds: The Young Pioneers, Radical Summer Camps, and Communist Political Culture in the United States* (New York, 1999).

10 M. Kozłowska, 'Wandering Jews: Camping Culture and Jewish Socialist Youth in Interwar Poland', *Jewish Culture and History*, 16 (2015), 242–53: 243.

11 J. Jacobs, *Bundist Counterculture in Interwar Poland* (Syracuse, NY, 2009), 44.

12 D. Blatman, 'National-Minority Policy, Bundist Social Organizations, and Jewish Women in Interwar Poland', in Z Gitelman (ed.), *The Emergence of Modern Jewish Politics: Bundism and Zionism in Eastern Europe* (Pittsburgh, Pa., 2003), 54–70: 61.

13 G. Dynner, 'Replenishing the "Fountain of Judaism": Traditionalist Jewish Education in Interwar Poland', *Jewish History*, 31 (2018), 249–50.

14 J. Banbula, 'Interwar Jewish Women Sports Clubs in Warsaw', *Israel Affairs*, 26 (2020), 273–81: 273.

15 I. Borowy and W. D. Gruner, 'Introduction', in eid. (eds.), *Facing Illness in Troubled Times: Health in Europe in the Interwar years, 1918–1939* (Frankfurt am Main, 2005), 1–2: 1.

16 See e.g. ibid. On the League of Nations' health activities, see I. Borowy, *Coming to Terms with World Health: The League of Nations Health Organization 1921–1946* (Oxford, 2005).

17 N. Davidovitch and R. Zalashik, 'Scientific Medicine and the Politics of Public Health: Minorities in Interwar Eastern Europe', *Science in Context*, 32 (2019), 1–4: 1.

18 M. A. Balinska, 'The Rockefeller Foundation and the National Institute of Hygiene, Poland, 1918–45', in *Studies in History and Philosophy of Science*, Part C: *Studies in History and Philosophy of Biological and Biomedical Sciences*, 31 (2000), 419–32: 422; ead., 'Le Typhus: Une maladie idéologisée', *La Revue du practician*, 55 (2005), 1619–21: 1620; P. Weindling, *Epidemics and Genocide in Eastern Europe, 1890–1945* (Oxford, 2003), 148.

19 Balinska, 'Le Typhus'.

20 Balinska, 'The Rockefeller Foundation and the National Institute of Hygiene'.

21 Borowy, *Coming to Terms with World Health*, 11–13; P. Weindling, *Health, Race and German Politics between National Unification and Nazism, 1870–1945* (Cambridge, 1993), 163–6, 168–70; id., *International Health Organisations and Movement, 1918–1939* (Cambridge, 1995), 45–6; id., *Epidemics and Genocide in Eastern Europe, 1890–1945* (Oxford, 2003), 364–5; Balinska, 'The Rockefeller Foundation and the National Institute of Hygiene', 90–2. On American humanitarian involvement in Poland after the First World War, see S. Kuźma-Markowska, *Dziecko, rodzina i płeć w amerykańskich inicjatywach humanitarnych i filantropijnych w II Rzeczypospolitej* (Warsaw, 2018), 168–77.

22 See E. M. Ozer and C. E. Irwin Jr., 'Adolescent and Young Adult Health: From Basic Health Status to Clinical Interventions', in R. M. Lerner and L. Steinberg (eds.), *Handbook of Adolescent Psychology* (Hoboken, NJ, 2009), 618–41.

23 The classic historical account of the Progressive Era (1896–1916) in the US and the role of experts is still R. H. Wiebe, *The Search for Order 1877–1920* (New York, 1967). On the rise of the 'new public health' at that time, see B. Gutmann Rosenkrantz, *Public Health and the State: Changing Views in Massachusetts, 1842–1936* (Cambridge, Mass., 1972); on specific public health issues, such as bacteriology or occupational health, and their influence on the American public, see R. R. Tomes, *Apocalypse Then: American Intellectuals and the Vietnam War, 1954–1975* (New York, 1998).

24 The importation of American public health practices to other countries, including the resistance to such moves, is now widely documented (see e.g. A.-E. Birn and A. Solórzano, 'Public Health Policy Paradoxes: Science and Politics in the Rockefeller Foundation's Hookworm Campaign in Mexico in the 1920s', *Social Science and Medicine*, 49 (1999), 1197–213; M. Cueto and S. Palmer, *Medicine and Public Health in Latin America: A History* (Cambridge, 2014)).

25 M. Hart, *Social Science and the Politics of Modern Jewish Identity* (Palo Alto, Calif., 2000), 101–7.

26 On Max Nordau, see T. S. Presner, *Muscular Judaism: The Jewish Body and the Politics of Regeneration* (London, 2010), ch. 3; on Polish racial discourse, see K. Uzarczyk,'"Moses als Eugeniker?" The Reception of Eugenic Ideas in Jewish Medical Circles in Interwar Poland', in M. Turda and P. Weindling (eds.), *'Blood and Homeland': Eugenics and Racial Nationalism in Central and Southeast Europe, 1900–1940* (Budapest, 2007), 283–98.

27 See J. Efron, *Jewish Doctors and Race Science in Fin-de-Siècle Europe* (New Haven, Conn., 1994). On the Polish context, see E. Bauer, '"Polishing" the Jewish Masses: Personal Hygiene, Public Health, and Jews in *Fin de Siècle* Warsaw', *Jewish History*, 35 (2021), 179–203.

28 See e.g. G. Lewin, 'Rola czynnika rasowego w większej odporności Żydów przeciw gruźlicy', in *Księga pamiątkowa Pierwszego Krajowego Zjazdu Lekarskiego 'TOZU', 24–25 czerwca 1928 roku* (Warsaw, 1929), 19–27.

29 See e.g. Bauer, '"Polishing" the Jewish Masses'.

30 Hart, *Social Science and the Politics of Modern Jewish Identity*, 108–12.

31 S. Rudnicki, 'Jews in Poland between the Two World Wars', *Shofar*, 29/3 (2011), 4–23: 6.

32 On the health of east European Jews before the war, see A. Rosental, 'Zur Charakteristik des Gesundheitszustandes der jüdischen Bevölkerung Osteuropas', *'OSE': Weltkonferenz für jüdischen Gesundheitsschutz, Berlin, 27.–31. August 1923* (Berlin, 1923), 4–5; on conditions in Poland during the war, see K. Sierakowska, *Śmierć, wygnanie, głód w dokumentach osobistych: Ziemie polskie w latach Wielkiej Wojny 1914–1918* (Warsaw, 2015); on Jewish children after the First World War and new institutes for their care, see N. Meir, 'From Communal Charity to National Welfare: Jewish Orphanages in Eastern Europe before and after World War I', *East European Jewish Affairs*, 39 (2009), 19–34: 26–7; S. Martin, 'How to House a Child', 26.

33 A. Kotik, 'Di velt milkhome un poyln', *Folksgezunt*, 1923, nos. 2–3, pp. 6–7.

34 Y. Lifshitz, 'Hapogromim bepolin bashanim 1918–1919: va'adat moregentau umisrad haḥuts ha'amerikani', *Zion*, 23–4 (1958–9), 66–97: 66–7.

35 In some cases Polish officials and clerks were hostile to JDC officials because of antisemitism (see J. Shaikowsky, 'Pe'ulot hasa'ad shel yahadut artsot-haberit liyehudei polin, 1918–1923', *Zion*, 34 (1969), 219–60: 220–1).

36 On JDC health initiatives, see R. Zalashik, 'Medical Welfare in Interwar Europe: The Collaboration between AJDC and OZE-TOZ Organizations', in A. Patt, A. Grossmann, L. G. Levi, and M. S. Mandel (eds.), *The JDC at 100: A Century of Humanitarianism* (Detroit, 2019), 21–39; J. D. Golden, '"Show that you are really alive": Sara-Zofia Syrkin-Binsztejnowa's Emergency Medical Relief and Public Health Work in Early Interwar Poland and the Warsaw Ghetto', *Medizinhistorisches Journal*, 53 (2018), 125–62: 135.

37 Cutter and Sadowska, 'Opieka nad ludnością II Rzeczypospolitej ze szczególnym uwzględnieniem mniejszości żydowskiej', 91.

38 Ibid. 92.

39 See Shaikowsky, 'Pe'ulot hasa'ad shel yahadut artsot-haberit liyehudei polin', 245–6.

40 See R. Zalashik, 'The Anti-Favus Campaign in Poland: Jewish Social Medicine', *Polin*, 27 (2015), 369–84.

41 For example, encouraging children to play outside, criticizing the lack of physical education and the material conditions of many Jewish schools and ḥeders, and expanding the involvement of medical professionals in schools and families (see N. Davidovich and R. Zalashik, '"Air, sun, water": Ideology and Activities of OZE (Society for the Preservation of the Health of the Jewish Population) during the Interwar Period', *Dynamis*, 28 (2008), 127–49).

42 Ibid. 128.

43 Jewish Telegraphic Agency, '40,000 Children in Poland Seen Needing Medical Care', *Jewish Daily Bulletin*, 18 June 1935, p. 4.

44 J. Granick, *International Jewish Humanitarianism in the Age of the Great War* (Cambridge, 2021), 223.

45 On CENTOS, see S. Martin, 'A History of CENTOS', in *For the Good of the Nation: Institutions for Jewish Children in Interwar Poland. A Documentary History*, ed. and trans. S. Martin (Boston, Mass., 2017), 1–59; Golden, '"Show that you are really alive"', 127.

46 K.A., 'Favus (parekh) un der kamf kegn', *Folksgezunt*, 1923, no. 1, p. 22; 'Vegn oystratn di krankeyt "parekh" bay yidn', *Folksgezunt*, 1923, no. 2–3, p. 1; see also Zalashik, 'The Anti-Favus Campaign in Poland'; Granick, *International Jewish Humanitarianism in the Age of the Great War*, 181–2.

47 M. Brzezina, *Polszczyzna Żydów* (Kraków, 1986); A. Pufelska, *Die 'Judäo-Kommune': Ein Feindbild in Polen. Das polnische Selbstverständnis im Schatten des Antisemitismus 1939–1948* (Paderborn, 2007), 38–9; J. Tuwim, 'Poeta zazdrości pewnemu literatowi', *Szpilki*, 1937, no. 5, p. 2. On favus as a social disease, see Zalashik, 'The Anti-Favus Campaign in Poland'; Davidovitch and Zalashik, '"Air, sun, water"'.

48 3,000 cases of favus in Warsaw, 2,000 in Congress Poland, 2,000 in Białystok, 2,500 in Vilna, 4,500 in Kaunas, 1,500 in Kraków, 2,000 in Lwów, and 2,000 in Brześć Litewski (Brest) (JDC Archives, NY, New York Office 1921–9132, RG 4.25, series 4 'Poland: DR. J. J. Golub Collection of Medical-Sanitary Files', G67: report of Medical Commission Conference, Warsaw, 5 Dec. 1921, pp. 12–13; Verband für Gesundheitsschutz der Juden (OSE) (ed.), *Die Entstehung der Gesellschaft OSE und ihre ersten Massnahmen* (Berlin 1925), 12–14).

49 L. Wulman, *Pięć lat działalności TOZ-u: 1922–1926* (Warsaw, 1927), 57–8; 'Mipe'ulot toz bepolin', *Davar*, 22 Aug. 1926, p. 2.

50 Granick, *International Jewish Humanitarianism in the Age of the Great War*, 187.

51 Ibid. 181.

52 Davidovitch and Zalashik, '"Air, sun, water"'.

53 Wulman, *Na straży zdrowia ludu żydowskiego*, 44.

54 Ibid. 38.
55 'Kolonyes fun "toz" far shvakhe kinder', *Haynt*, 13 May 1924, p. 3.
56 The first Jewish children's camp was established by the Jewish paediatrician Anna Braude-Heller near Warsaw (see Granick, *International Jewish Humanitarianism in the Age of the Great War*, 222). On Braude-Heller, see A. Witkowska-Krych, 'Anna Braude-Heller, Seen from a Distance', *Nashim*, 36 (2020), 117–32.
57 Wulman, *Na straży zdrowia ludu żydowskiego*, 38.
58 Ibid. 39.
59 *Odbudowa i Samopomoc. Zjednoczony Komitet przy Towarzystwach: 'CENTOS', 'JEAS', 'ORT' i 'TOZ'* (Warsaw, 1931/2), 8.
60 On the intervention of small Jewish *Landsmanschaften* in Jewish needs and politics in Poland, see R. Kobrin, 'Polish Jewry, American Jewish Immigrant Philanthropy, and the Crisis of 1929', in H. Diner and G. Estraikh (eds.), *1929: Mapping the Jewish World* (New York, 2013), 73–92: 76–7.
61 Davidovitch and Zalashik, '"Air, sun, water"'; see also L. Lestchnisky, 'Economic Aspects of Jewish Community Organization in Independent Poland', *Jewish Social Studies*, 9 (1947), 319–38: 337.
62 K. Chaczko, '"Polska w soczewce": Ewolucja i modernizacja systemu opieki/pomocy społecznej w perspektywie instytucjonalnej', *Rocznik Administracji Publicznej*, 2 (2016), 353–72: 354.
63 Ibid. 355.
64 'Preliminarz budżetowy na r. 1928/29', *Sprawozdanie stenograficzne z 19 posiedzenia Sejmu Rzeczypospolitej z dnia 8 czerwca 1928 roku* (Warsaw, 1928), 3–40: 8.
65 Ibid. Heller's speech was mentioned in a telegram sent to the JDC in the US (Jewish Telegraphic Agency, 'Complains Government Subsidies Discriminate Against Jewish Groups', *Jewish Daily Bullection*, 12 June 1928, p. 1).
66 Wulman, *Na straży zdrowia ludu żydowskiego*, 38, 43.
67 Ibid. 41.
68 Ibid. 40.
69 Ibid. 44.
70 Granick, *International Jewish Humanitarianism in the Age of the Great War*, 228.
71 Wulman, *Na straży zdrowia ludu żydowskiego*, 38.
72 '400,000 zlotes hat "toz" oysgegebn af der zomer-kolonyes aktsye', *Haynt*, 26 Oct. 1937, p. 5.
73 Davidovitch and Zalashik, '"Air, sun, water"'.
74 Wulman, *Na straży zdrowia ludu żydowskiego*, 41.
75 Ibid.
76 Ibid. 38.
77 Ibid. 44.
78 See e.g. '"Toz" kolonyes far kinder bay kuzmir', *Haynt*, 7 May 1934, p. 7; '"Toz" aroysgeshikt di ershte 200 kinder af di zomer kolonyes', *Haynt*, 3 June 1935, p. 5.
79 'Konferenz fun "toz" in poyln vegn di zomer kolonyes un halb kolonyes', *Haynt*, 4 May 1938, p. 5.
80 See A. Lipphardt, 'Die Vilner Überlebenden in New York', in ead., *Vilne. Die Juden aus Vilnius nach dem Holocaust: Eine transnationale Beziehungsgeschichte* (Paderborn, 2010), 165–86.

3. THE EDUCATIONAL EXPERIENCE

What Kind of Self Can a Pupil's Letter Reveal?

The Tarbut School in Nowy Dwór, 1934–1935

DAVID ASSAF AND YAEL DARR

A rare collection of some ninety letters written between 1934 and 1935 by boys and girls who studied in the Tarbut primary school in Nowy Dwór Mazowiecki, approximately 35 kilometres north-west of Warsaw, provides a unique insight into the social and emotional life of children who attended Hebrew-language elementary schools in Poland between the two world wars. The letters were part of a classroom project for pupils to write to pen pals in Palestine, an established practice in the Tarbut institutions in Poland, intended both to train pupils in Hebrew writing and to create a living connection with the Yishuv. Most were addressed to the school's director, Zvi Plesser, on the eve of his departure for Palestine. They reveal not only loyalty to the school and to Plesser himself, but also the deep and complex relations between the pupils and teachers and the torn and divided selves of the pupils, who are far from possessing the confident Zionist identity the school sought to impart.

THIS CHAPTER focuses on the private lives of Jewish children who studied in Hebrew elementary schools in Poland between the world wars. Their social and emotional lives—as individuals and as a collective—are revealed through a rare collection of ego-documents, some ninety letters written in Hebrew between 1934 and 1935 by boys and girls who attended the Tarbut elementary school in the town of Nowy Dwór Mazowiecki, approximately 35 kilometres north-west of Warsaw.[1] A close reading of these letters allows a glimpse into their culture, inner worlds, and complex self-identities.

Children's Letters as Ego-Documents: A Methodological Note

The study of childhood in general, and Jewish childhood in eastern Europe in particular, very often includes testimonies and memories of adults who reconstruct and recount their childhood from the perspective of a later time. Very few sources are authentic child ego-documents, that is, documents produced at the time by children, who, consciously or unconsciously, reveal their 'I' or 'self'. This self might be readily apparent or restrained, even repressed, and needing to be extracted cautiously from the text.[2] Such documents are highly sought after by historians of childhood, as they are extremely rare. This is primarily because children do not tend to reveal their personalities and inner worlds through writing but rather through speech or actions. Moreover, even when children do produce ego-documents, such as personal letters, diaries, or school compositions, few are preserved, since, unlike adults, children lack awareness of the historical value of preservation and documentation.

With regard to first-hand knowledge about the world of Jewish children in Poland between the world wars, documents of this kind are rarer still due to the destruction of European Jewry and its cultural and material treasures in the Holocaust. The little that has survived are the voices of young adults, who naturally were more expressive, critical, and already equipped with religious, national, class, and political worldviews. The prime example of this is the approximately 350 surviving autobiographies of young Jews aged 16 to 22 from Poland from the three competitions initiated by YIVO between the wars (1932, 1934, 1939), a small selection of which have been comprehensively discussed elsewhere.[3] There are also the reflections of adults about their childhood experiences and schooling in Poland, especially those written after and against the background of the Holocaust, in Mandatory Palestine, later the State of Israel, and other pre- and post-war emigration destinations.[4]

Hence, at the centre of this chapter is an extraordinary collection of ego-documents of young Jewish children in Poland, primary-school boys and girls up to the age of 11, which reveal their personal and collective identities at the time. These letters contain a wealth of information mainly because the writers corresponded candidly with their recipients, and their writings reflect not only their childish personalities but also the knowledge and values inculcated in them by adults. The letters also reveal the children's day-to-day routine at school, their relationships with their teachers and their perception of the teaching profession, internalized gender roles, and the multi-lingual reality in which they grew up. They provide details of the children's families, and of their relationships with their parents and siblings and with the broader non-Jewish environment. Finally, they shed light on how children spent their free time, what games they played, what books they read, what plays they saw, what songs they sang, how they celebrated their holidays, and what their hopes were for the future.

The letters were written as part of a Tarbut project. For the Tarbut institutions in Poland, writing letters to pen pals in Palestine not only gave the pupils practice in writing in Hebrew but also created a living connection with their overseas peers. Letters arriving from Palestine were read aloud in the classroom and published in the children's school newspapers. This didactic method was discussed at a conference of teachers and graduates of the Vilna Tarbut Teachers' Seminary held in Vilna in December 1932, and one of the resolutions stated:

The conference recognizes the great educational and learning value of the exchange of letters between the children of the diaspora and the children in the Land of Israel and obliges all graduates to make every effort to create this connection. The conference expresses its hope that the JNF [Jewish National Fund] bureau will continue to act as an intermediary for this connection and turn to the teachers in the Land of Israel with a request to assist in the formation of these important connections.[5]

The resolution also clearly reflects the expectation of the JNF in Poland (whose offices were in Warsaw) to serve as an intermediary between the Tarbut schools and teachers in Palestine. The teachers in Palestine were expected to locate pupils who would participate in the pen-pal project. There is quite a bit of evidence for this project. A year later, in December 1933, a special pedagogical conference of Tarbut teachers for the JNF convened in Warsaw, where the curriculum for the network's elementary schools was discussed. Among other topics suggested for teaching in the fifth grade was 'pen-pal correspondence'.[6] Similarly, teachers' conferences were held in Palestine in which the connection between the schools there and the Hebrew schools in the diaspora was raised. Thus, for example, at the third JNF Conference of Teachers and Kindergarten Teachers in Palestine, which met in Jerusalem in December 1933, various ways were discussed regarding how to strengthen the bond between local children and the children of the diaspora. 'Correspondence through letters with the children of the Land of Israel', wrote the Zionist activist Abraham Levinson in 1935, 'arouses in the hearts of the pupils a genuine connection to everything that happens in the Land of Israel'.[7]

For Tarbut teachers, the letter exchange had a dual pedagogical effect: to assist in teaching Hebrew as a modern secular language and to ground the children's connection to the Land of Israel. In addition, writing a letter and sending it to Palestine was a kind of Zionist ritual: a symbolic act that had the power to connect potential Zionists with those who were living the dream.

Care is required when viewing this correspondence as ego-documents. School is not a natural setting for the expression of a child's 'self', as it involves an unequal inter-generational discourse dictated by adult teachers to a class, which at its base is a collective framework inherently tending to obscure individuality. Furthermore, children are usually strongly influenced by the school's ethos and values and consciously or unconsciously strive to identify with the governing principles. In terms of a classroom letter-writing project, this is expressed in an attempt to please the teachers who might be reviewing the letters before they are sent. Moreover, in the Tarbut pupils' letters to Palestine, the very writing in Hebrew carried a dividing and hierarchical dimension, as the recipient was often assumed to be fluent in a high-level Hebrew, while the writer was still taking their first steps. The personal element in the letters is therefore somewhat elusive. In addition to the hierarchical aspect, the writers were not familiar with the formal rules of letter-writing, nor with writing models, nor with the technique of writing itself. It is therefore dangerous to assume that a blatant violation of traditional codes of writing is necessarily an informed decision with subversive intent.

Moreover, another methodological difficulty faced by researchers of schoolchildren's letters as ego-documents is the danger of being patronizing, whether this is research patronage, which tries to interpret retrospectively, in a 'holistic' and detached way, a correspondence, the duration of which the parties to it were unaware of, or adult patronage, which tries to interpret schoolchildren's writings as 'immature', 'unskilled', 'innocent', or 'lacking'. Methodological efforts are needed to coax the child's self from the page. Yet we believe that ample personal space remains for learning about the intimate and emotional worlds of the young writers, as a group and as individuals. From careful and close reading of the letters, we will suggest that they present not only lofty praise of the school, its teachers, and its ideology but also deep and complex relations between pupils and teachers and a torn or divided self rather than a decisive Zionist ego.

The Corpus from Nowy Dwór

Twenty-one boys and thirteen girls wrote the letters from the Tarbut school in Nowy Dwór. Most were in fifth grade, apparently the highest grade in the school that year, 1934/5. The writers were therefore around the ages of 10 or 11, and most had attended the school since its founding in autumn 1930.

Some of the children wrote more than one letter, and a few of the letters were collectively written. Most were addressed to the school's director Zvi Plesser, who was also the children's teacher. Many of the letters were gathered together into a farewell album that was presented to Plesser at a banquet in his honour in November 1934, on the eve of his departure for Palestine. Some were mailed to him after he was already settled there. A few more were addressed to children in Palestine, who became pen pals through Plesser's mediation and encouragement.

This corpus of letters was found by Mr Erez Lev in a box in his parents' home in Israel. Plesser had kept the letters for many years and apparently passed them on to Joseph Shimkovitch, Lev's maternal grandfather, who was among the members of the public committee that had prepared the Nowy Dwór memorial book.[8] Plesser himself contributed an article to the book describing the history of the Tarbut school in the town, in which he also referred to the correspondence with his pupils.[9]

Plesser and the rest of the school's teachers were not known to be distinguished pedagogues, and as for the pupils, the majority perished in the Holocaust a few years later. Their letters tell primarily individual stories. Reading them together, as a collection, they reveal the world of Jewish children in Poland who attended Hebrew and Zionist educational institutions between the two world wars, of which the Tarbut network was the most prominent.

The Tarbut School in Nowy Dwór

In the early 1930s Nowy Dwór was a small town with a pronounced Jewish character —a typical shtetl.[10] It had a large synagogue, a Jewish cemetery, and renowned rabbis. The Jewish community included hasidim, mitnagedim, Zionists, Bundists, communists, and other factions. Modern secular culture flourished alongside traditional religious life, with public libraries, sports associations, and youth movements;

music and theatre circles; schools that taught in Polish, Hebrew, and Yiddish; and a vibrant political life, in which some of the children participated enthusiastically.

Between the wars, the Jews of Nowy Dwór experienced deprivation and poverty. Many made a living from petty trade; various crafts, most notably tailoring; and peddling. From 1918 to 1926 various anti-Jewish discriminatory acts introduced by successive governments and local administrations dominated by Roman Dmowski's National Democracy movement (Endecja) harshly affected the Jews' daily life. The lower-middle class was especially hard hit by the so-called 'Grabski laws' of 1924. After 1926, with the ousting of the Endecja by Józef Piłsudski in a coup d'état, rightwing anti-Jewish sentiment increased in the town and young Polish activists took to the streets. From the Great Depression of 1929 until the Second World War, Poland in general and Nowy Dwór in particular saw a rise of ideological radical antisemitism and anti-Jewish physical violence, which reached its peak in the years 1935 to 1937.[11]

Zvi Plesser recalled the mid-1930s and the ever-present feeling of terror on the Jewish street in Nowy Dwór:

The very air was filled with the poison of intense loathing ... The newspapers were full of reports of riots against the Jews. Here and there, in various towns, there were many attacks on the Jews on market days. Not far from Nowy Dwór, the Polish government set up a Polish youth camp in order to employ them in various development projects. There was incitement against the Jews in the camp. Every evening, when these boys would show up in town, they would search for the Jews and beat them. They also smashed the windows of Jewish shops. The fear in the town was great and every morning the children would come with stories about the antics of the youth camp. The Jewish youth organizations in the town began to discuss the need to organize in order to defend themselves against these youths in the future. Hitler's influence across Poland was felt day after day, and all this strengthened my desire to hurry and emigrate to the Land of Israel.[12]

This tense atmosphere, which combined economic and political crises, climaxed with the death of Marshal Piłsudski in May 1935.[13]

Those years also witnessed the growth of the Tarbut movement and many new schools were set up throughout Poland. A Joint Distribution Committee report from 1936 counted 44,780 students in 269 Tarbut schools in Poland, making Tarbut the second largest Jewish educational network (after Horev, the ultra-Orthodox school network associated with Agudat Israel).[14] The Tarbut school in Nowy Dwór was founded in the summer of 1930 by an active and energetic 'parents' committee', and opened its doors in the academic year 1930/1.[15] Zvi Plesser, appointed by the Tarbut Central Committee in Warsaw as the school's principal, came to the town in 1932 as a 23-year-old graduate of the Tarbut Teachers' Seminary in Vilna. He, like many others in his class at the seminary, hoped to realize what he had learned by introducing a new Hebrew spirit into what he considered a 'typical Polish town of the times'.[16]

The school was located in a rented building, which in Plesser's mind did not have the proper infrastructure for a modern school:

The accommodations of the Tarbut school were extremely unsatisfactory. The school was housed in a two-room rental on the second floor, with two smaller rooms in the courtyard. We didn't have a teachers' room at all. Our staff meetings took place in a room of the Sholem Aleichem Public Library, among the bookshelves, where I also met with parents in my role as the school principal.[17]

Many of the pupils came from impoverished families, and some exhibited a bitterness that reflected profound social tensions. For example, Eliezer Ravitzky complained that enthusiastic yet poor Zionists were forced to remain in Poland while the rich and well-connected were able to emigrate to Palestine:

It is winter now, here in the *golah*.[18] Things are very bad for us, especially for me and my entire household, because my father is sick. And the teacher has known about our situation for a long time, so I will write about something new. All the well-off of Nowy Dwór take their wealth and travel to the Land of Israel to preserve their riches. They aren't going there to build the Land of Israel, like the teacher, only to hold on to their money. Only we, the poor, remain here in the *golah*, and with them my father, and my brothers and sisters, who want to work, but for whom? They would like to go to the Land of Israel, and would work hard, because they would know whom they were working for. They would understand that the more they work, the better it will be for them . . . I can also inform the teacher that I'm already paying [tuition] like all the rich.[19]

Apart from the school's primary role of educating children, it also fulfilled a social and cultural function for the town's Zionist families, not only those whose children attended the school. The school held extracurricular cultural activities, mainly sabbath and holiday gatherings, which fostered social cohesion through topics such as current events and issues related to modern Hebrew literature and life in Palestine. The school promoted the Zionist movement's secular nationalist ideals, but it was not anti-religious.[20] Once or twice a year (around Hanukah, Purim, or at the end of the school year), there would be a 'children's ball', which included plays in Hebrew put on by the pupils, and exhibitions of their work from vocational training courses, in which the school paraded its commitment to the values of self-sufficiency and skilled labour.[21] The culmination of the educational activity was during summer break, when the students and some of the teachers would leave for one of the nearby villages for a month-long summer camp. They would rent a suitable house and hire a local villager to cook their meals. All the activities in the *moshavah*—as the camp was called—were conducted entirely in Hebrew and closely connected to issues regarding Palestine. This activity, in Plesser's words, was 'to enable the children to experience something of the life in the Land of Israel'.[22]

The Hebrew language united the school's community and differentiated it from the outside surroundings, as Yiddish was the everyday language of most Polish Jews, and Polish the language of the public, non-Jewish domain. In a letter to a female pen pal in Palestine, Eliezer Ravitzky explained this tri-lingual framework:

We have many lessons, mainly in Hebrew. In our school everyone speaks Hebrew, but there are children from a Polish school who speak Polish . . . If they understand that they need this language, then they will learn Hebrew. Here, in Poland, it's like this: when I get up in the morning, I speak to my mother in Yiddish, in school in Hebrew, and with a Polish child in Polish.[23]

The very fact that he writes about this in Hebrew makes him unique in his own eyes, and sets him apart from other members of his household, from the Polish street, and from the Jewish pupils who do not attend Hebrew schools, and identifies him as Zionist. However, as we will point out later, this information also betrays a deep internal divide between himself—a boy living in a multi-lingual reality—and his pen pal in Palestine who, in his mind, speaks Hebrew all day—at home, in school, and on the street.

All this transformed the school into an exterritorial space, an imagined micro Land of Israel and alternative community, offering the children an escape from the depressing poverty at home and humiliating antisemitism on the street. Writing letters in Hebrew to recipients in Palestine was intended to strengthen the sense of belonging to this alternative community.

Pupil–Teacher Relations and the Expression of Emotion

Writing the letters to Plesser presumably took place in the classroom under the guidance of one of the teachers. The reading of the letters from the Land of Israel was also a collective classroom event rather than the intimate experience customary with personal correspondence. A letter written by Yisrael Lerich, probably in 1935, reveals something about the nature of the letters that arrived from Palestine—which unfortunately have not been preserved—and how they were read in the classroom:

Dear Teacher,

We received your letter with great joy. And while the teacher read the letter to us, we were happy that we were receiving letters from children in the Land of Israel and from you. In their letters, they always wrote about their considerable toil and their communal life. And when I heard this, I knew that they are giving fruit to the Land of Israel and to the Jewish People, and I desired also to move to the Land of Israel . . . and to work with them together and to live with them together.[24]

This suggests that the correspondence from the children in Palestine through Plesser's mediation was quite formulaic and not at all personal. In contrast, in the letters the children wrote to Plesser himself, the personal eclipsed the formal and they seem to have been written with relative freedom. The unrestrained relationship between writer and recipient, without the intervention of an adult, is evident in the letters in the farewell album, which exhibit a variety of writing styles and no corrections of the frequent mistakes in spelling, syntax, and vocabulary.

The same is true also of the content: the children's letters express an array of emotions for their teacher, who was realizing the aspiration towards which the school had educated them, and ranged from warm love, admiration, and hope of meeting again in the Jewish homeland to envy and even anger, frustration, and despair.

The Class as an Alternative Family

The progressive teaching method practised in the Tarbut schools viewed the teacher–pupil relationship as a reflection of the family, with the teacher as a parental figure (and sometimes even a parental substitute) and the pupils as siblings.[25] Within this context, the pedagogical model instituted in Tarbut enabled different relationships between teachers and pupils and among the pupils themselves. The letters show that Plesser maintained a hierarchical yet very warm and sincere relationship with his pupils.

The heartfelt and close connection to the teacher is apparent in the valedictions of some of the letters: 'Written by the teacher's loving pupil, Fried, Gavriel',[26] 'The teacher's favourite pupil, Moshe Kofman',[27] or 'From me, your dear pupil, Ravitzky, Eliezer'.[28] Some students signed their letters with affectionate nicknames, some probably given by the teacher himself: 'The Rascal',[29] 'Snake',[30] 'The Horse',[31] 'Flea'.[32] The nicknames indicate an intimate classroom dynamic that would have been incomprehensible to an outsider, a familial kinship nurtured over years of learning together as a group.

Many of the pupils expressed their concern that the new teacher replacing Plesser would not know how to maintain this kinship. Yisrael Lerich's letter in the farewell album reveals how painfully this was felt, vacillating between the personal and the collective—which were not always distinguished. In the first lines, he presented his personal frustrations and feelings of loss, but then moved on to a communal lament about the teacher, who had left 'us' behind:

I am writing in this notebook a letter to the teacher. And when I start to write, my hand shakes when I feel that this dear and good teacher is leaving us and emigrating to the Land of Israel . . . On the one hand, I am happy that the teacher is emigrating to build the Jewish homeland, and, on the other hand, I am not satisfied that this dear teacher, who gave us knowledge and wisdom for two years, is now leaving us; and if a new teacher comes he will ruin everything that you did with us.[33]

Despite the farewell album's celebratory format and the letter's formal heading, 'Letter to Teacher Zvi Plesser Who is Emigrating to the Land of Israel', Lerich did not begin with the bright side—the teacher's emigration—but rather with his sense of despair in the face of the teacher's departure. The feeling of loss is akin to a death. It is personal but also familial: a new teacher would not be able to fill the gap and sustain the family bond and 'will destroy everything'.

Furthermore, the image of the teacher's potential new class in Palestine aroused feelings of rivalry: 'I think that in the Land of Israel the teacher will have other good children. But I ask the teacher that when he is in the Land of Israel with the other children, that he will not forget us, by writing letters to us.'[34] Note that Lerich chose the word 'children' rather than 'pupils'.

Like him, many of the children (especially the boys) refer to Plesser as a father. Eliezer Ravitzky expresses this directly and indirectly. It is worth noting the rising tones of his letter, a signal of the freedom he took when expressing his emotions:

> I can inform the teacher that I was very happy to receive greetings from you. And I read, but I was very disappointed, why didn't I receive a whole letter, so I had more to read? Because every word of the teacher is sacred and precious to me. So far, I have always sent letters to the teacher with all the other children, and I do not understand why the teacher did not receive mine. But now that I was able to get the teacher's address, I'm writing a letter. And when I take the pen in hand, and when I start writing a letter to the teacher, tears come to my eyes. And when I start to remember, then I am reminded that the teacher was not just a teacher, but a father, a beloved father. And when the teacher went away, it was as if they had taken away my right hand, and as if they had taken away my whole life. Because the teacher was a father, a dear father to the son. And I miss my teacher now... And when in the morning, when I come to school, I think I will meet the teacher. But when I just open the door I see a strange teacher. So I stand in one place and I can't move from the spot. Because it's all a fantasy. Yet, I think I will come to the Land of Israel, and then I will be able to give the teacher thanks at the gates of Zion, though the teacher knows that I'm the son of a worker, and my father has no money to spare, so I may not be able to come to the Land of Israel and to build it.... Thus, I end my letter, and I send it from far, far away, from the *golah*. Farewell! Farewell! Farewell! From me, your pupil, who will always remember you.[35]

Some of the pupils recalled with nostalgia the warm, family-like ties created between them and Plesser in the summer camps where they spent several weeks with him away from home. Moshe Gurecki wrote:

> And if I remember the things the teacher did for us then it is difficult to part from the teacher. When I remembered the *moshavah*, when the teacher was with us much better than a father, and many more wonderful things the teacher did for us. So it's really hard to say goodbye to the teacher.[36]

Gavriel Fried similarly wrote: 'I remember how the teacher was with me in the *moshavah* and raised me. How wonderful it was for me then.'[37] In the absence of parents and family, it was easy for the children to imagine their class as a warm family and Plesser as a beloved parent. Now, upon his departure, these warm recollections of the *moshavah* triggered in the children a sense of bereavement.

Demands for Reciprocity and Accountability

The close ties between Plesser and his pupils were also expressed in their pleas for reciprocity in their relationships. This is evident in the letters written by the girls, who often choose to equate Plesser with a beau. Rivka Don likens Plesser to a loved one who has forgotten her:

> We received letters from the teacher, but the teacher did not mention me. I think the teacher has forgotten me already. I did not forget the teacher. I always remember the teacher. For example, whenever the new teacher Skurnick stands beside the table, I imagine how the teacher sits alongside the table. And the [new] teacher twirls his hair just like the teacher used to. I always think about it and always say to myself, that a teacher

like the one we had we will not have again. I will never forget the teacher for all my life. I am keeping the photos I have with the teacher as a keepsake.[38]

And in another letter she writes:

I was very happy when the teacher told us that there is a letter from the teacher. How good it was for me when I saw the teacher. It is very sad for us without the teacher . . . It's very hard for me to forget the teacher. I sincerely ask the teacher, that the teacher be so good as to send me a letter about how he is. I have a great favour to ask of the teacher, to have his picture taken and send me a photo. How much I longed to see the teacher's face. It's hard for me to finish my letter.[39]

Esther Zucker chastised Plesser like an inattentive lover for not replying to her letters:

My dear and precious teacher, I am very angry with the teacher because he has not responded. I realize that the teacher may not have had time, or it is not permitted to send so many letters, because the post office would not allow it, and this is why you write to another child. I don't want more, just two [personal] words as well, and then I would forget my anger. I am done, and I go on to my main points . . . a warm and huge kiss, be a pioneer forever, good health.[40]

In some letters, pupils allowed themselves to criticize their teacher, as if they were his equals. For example, Yosef 'Snake' was not satisfied with Plesser's decision to live in a big city:

I heard that the teacher is already teaching in Tel Aviv. I didn't think the teacher would go to the city, I thought the teacher would go to a village and work the land. This too is work, but it is not as beloved as working the land. When I come to the Land of Israel I will come to the teacher, and we will drink and eat together.[41]

Yisrael Lerich scolds Plesser for not having done enough as the class's representative to the JNF. In his description of his peers' efforts to raise money for the JNF, he holds Plesser accountable for his promise:

I ask one thing of the teacher. Has the teacher fulfilled what he said he would? . . . Because what the teacher always promised, he fulfilled. The teacher said he would meet with Mr Ussishkin [head of the JNF] and tell him about our work for the JNF. And if the teacher has not yet been, then I ask him that he fulfil this promise.[42]

All these examples are clearly a way of defusing the school's generational roles: the children are the ones demanding that the grown-up keep his promises to them.

The attempt to moderate the teacher–pupil pedagogical hierarchy is quite striking when the matter of corporal punishment, a practice in which the teacher's dominance translates into actual physical violence, is raised in the letters. It may be that the family model of the school occasionally permitted the practice—which was still prevalent in many Jewish homes—in Plesser's classroom.[43]

Addressing corporal punishment in their letters reveals the pupils' mixed feelings about it. Most expressed an understanding of an educational motive and justified it, even asking the teacher for forgiveness, as if he were a loving father who did not spare the rod for the greater good of those in his care. Yisrael Lerich wrote at the end of his letter: 'But we won't pay attention to the fact that the teacher hit us. I think that the teacher didn't hit without reason, but because he wanted us to learn, for this the teacher hit us.'[44] Note that Lerich used the plural, as if he were speaking also for his classmates.

For Mordechai Lanzman, physical punishment was a personal act, part of the father–son relationship he had with his teacher and likewise the pardon he asked of the teacher:

I want to write a few words. The teacher was more dear to me than my life. Every slap I got from the teacher was more precious to me than a kiss, because it was for my own good, so that I will study better, it was all for me. And every time I got a two,[45] I wanted to be angry with the teacher, but then I remembered that I am the sinner, I am the bad one. I ask the teacher to forgive me for the sins I have committed. I feel that they are many. The teacher is emigrating to the Land of Israel, to the land of the Jews, there the teacher will build it, grow it. My heart aches when I remind myself that this good teacher will no longer teach us.[46]

Yehoshua Dulz worried that the teacher's conscience was plagued by the physical punishment he inflicted and sought to free Plesser and himself from the burden of the memory:

And I say to my teacher, it is possible that during these years I may have committed sins against the teacher or done a bad thing. I ask the teacher to forgive me for my misdeeds. Then the teacher will travel clean to his country and work, and I will be clean here as well. And we will not become strangers, only the teacher will write letters to us and we to the teacher.[47]

Moshe Kofman presented physical punishment as an educational defect, as a weakness, but forgave Plesser because of his other virtues as a teacher. For him, forgiveness was a means to open a new page, for the benefit of a common future in Palestine:

And even though I was beaten, and not only me, but many pupils, the teacher gave me so much knowledge and wisdom. So I have to say goodbye to the teacher, it is very hard for me to part. But this is nothing. Being in the *golah* is the worst thing. The teacher will travel to our land, and when I finish school and I will go to the treasured land and will work with the teacher and we will dance with all our brothers on the soil of the Land of Israel.[48]

The children's understanding transformed corporal punishment from a means of intimidation into a necessary, mutually accepted reprimand. In doing so, they marked themselves as the teacher's colleagues, not just in the Zionist ideology taught in the school but also in the educational practice. Yet the criticism, direct and indirect, also indicates an open wound. Their asking for and offering forgiveness seeks to clear the personal and collective memory from the aggressive and polarizing act. In the pupils' eyes, forgiveness is the mature approach towards reconciliation and clears up any misunderstandings that may have strained the teacher–pupil relationship in the past, and will allow for an exchange of letters in the future, and perhaps someday reunion in Palestine. Until then, the teacher will become a kind of representative for them there, as their equal.

Divided Self-Identity

In an attempt to exhibit their knowledge as well as their ideological partnership with their teacher, the pupils often used the Zionist ideological terms *golah*, *galut*, and 'Land of Israel' when addressing the two locations of correspondence. The children's 'here' and 'there' are described in terms of iconic contrasts: 'here' in Poland, it is cold and dark, 'there' in Palestine, it is warm and sunny; 'here' they eat bland potatoes, 'there' they gobble up sweet oranges; 'here' it is nearly impossible to earn a living, 'there' abundant physical labour is for the having; 'here', the public domain is dangerous, 'there' one can travel the country freely; 'here' Hebrew is only spoken by the Zionists, 'there' everyone speaks Hebrew. These binary dichotomies elucidate the internalizing of the idyllic images of Palestine and rejection of the *galut* inculcated in the pupils by the educational system, which conformed to the spirit of Zionist education practised at the time in Palestine, where rejection of the *galut* was a fundamental principle.[49]

A typical example of this dichotomous view appears in a letter written by Yosef 'Snake':

I am sorry for not being able to sit with the teacher and feast with my teacher on oranges. There it is sunny and warm, and here white snow is falling. The frost rises up the window. Cold outside. We get around on skates and sleds. There, there is none of that. There the sun is shining and the grapevines are blooming. There it is the exact opposite. Oh! I miss the Land of Israel. Had I wings, I would fly to the kind teacher.[50]

The fantasy about eating oranges also appears in Yisrael Lerich's letter, which attributes to Palestine the properties of life and growth, while the 'here' from where he sends his letter embodies the exact opposite:

From what the teacher and the children report in their letters, I think that in the Land of Israel they gobble oranges like potatoes here, and that the pioneering work is immense, as is the work in the fields and the orchards, and the Hebrew language rings throughout the land ... Over here it's cold. It's snowing and windy. Nothing here is alive, because there are no birds always singing to cheer us up. We are not happy here, and nature is not as it should be.[51]

The pejorative words *golah* and *galut* that replace the neutral word 'Poland' are thus charged with irony. What signifies a distant, dispersed, and transient existence in Zionist ideology as taught to the children in Palestine is, for the children in Poland, their concrete and daily 'here'. Thus, while writing denigratingly about their life in Poland, the pupils' letters reveal a clear pattern of self-deprecation, as those who are physically in exile. Their collective identity as Zionists ironically negates their identities as individuals living in Poland with no other option.

Many of the children translate the tension between the Zionist self and the Polish self into a strong sentiment of jealousy of their teacher who was lucky enough to emigrate to Palestine, along with the hope of joining him in the near future. Yisrael Lerich bravely describes this miserable situation:

> But now, when I see that the teacher is going to the land of milk and honey, I have the greatest envy in the world. The dear teacher is going to the Land of Israel, where he will certainly come to no harm. They will not beat the teacher, they will not say about him: 'Jew, go away!' But I and the rest of the Jews are not safe as the teacher is safe in the Land of Israel. The teacher is certain he will have work there, and we are not so certain.[52]

This valiant attitude also comes across in a letter written in the singular but signed by four boys:

> My teacher, you have left us in a foreign land that is not ours. It's bad for us here. But what to do, I think we still haven't lost hope. But you, my teacher, have rid yourself of this *galut*. Good for you. Whatever you hoped for—you have realized. You sit under your vine and do your pleasant work, and earn your sacred coins. My teacher, I heard your head hurt, but it's nothing. After all, the teacher has emigrated to the Land of Israel. We grow day by day, and we need still to see your face again, because I despair of sitting in this *galut* already, and what will I do? . . . It is cold outside. Snow is falling. And therefore, it is not good for us in the *golah* and therefore our hopes are not lost yet. I have no time. I want to do my homework.[53]

The tension between the desire to assimilate the Zionist 'I', which negates the *galut*, and the reality that demands solidarity with the Jews living in Poland is also evident in Zvi Greenshpan's letter:

> My dear teacher, you are now in the Land of Israel and I am now in the *golah*. It's hard for me to tell the teacher and to write about our life in the *golah*. Wherever we go, they beat us, and call us names. I do not want to write to the teacher the name they call us, because the teacher already knows the name . . . Now, I send greetings to the children who are in the Land of Israel, in our homeland, and perhaps we will meet one day in the Land of Israel.[54]

All these passages hint at the pupils' sense of a divided self: at school, they feel like Zionist pioneers, while at home and in the street, they live a frustrating and difficult life. The letters that travel from 'here' to 'there' and back unite the two spaces and as such are a sublimation of this complex concept of self. Writing a letter is therefore a dramatic moment that generates an inner clash between the two parts of the self, but also their painful integration. The letters thus encode the internal struggle between the children's unique Zionist self, which in their fantasy world lives in Palestine like their teacher, and their Jewish Polish self, which is jealous and even angry with the teacher who has managed to realize the dream and, by doing so, left his pupils behind. To assess this divided and torn ego, a more moderate and less decisive perspective on the concept of diaspora rejection in Zionist thinking is called for.

The children's sense of being part of an exclusive group, of 'being chosen', also characterized pupils of other secular Jewish schools in Poland (especially that of TSYSHO, the socialist-Yiddishist network) and Zionist and non-Zionist political parties and youth movements, such as the Bund and the communists. All felt chosen to bring radical change to the life of the Jews. Thus, while subjectively feeling drastically different from their peers, Tarbut school pupils were more similar to other members of their generation than they were able to admit.[55]

Conclusion

This chapter has dealt with the subjective aspect of the corpus of pupils' letters from Nowy Dwór—the young letter-writers' emotional worlds and complex self-identities. In addition, it underscores the research potential inherent in the genre of 'pupils' letters' as ego-documents, despite the fact that in many cases this genre is dictated from above, by teachers or parents.

The Nowy Dwór corpus holds within it rich possibilities for other areas of research on the life of east European Jews between the wars: Jewish education; Jewish child culture; Zionism; and the Hebrew language, its development and instruction. This research would strongly benefit from many such ego-documents, as this collection is not the only one. It is part of a pen-pal culture initiated in other Tarbut schools in which Hebrew letters like these made their way to Palestine and today might be found in archives or private collections.

An example is the correspondence from another Tarbut elementary school in Baranowicze (Baranavichy).[56] There, too, the pupils prepared a farewell album for the school principal, Ze'ev Lerman (Livne), who emigrated to Palestine in 1936. The album was presented to him at a party held in honour of his departure, with dozens of greetings written in Hebrew by the school's sixth- and seventh-grade pupils, accompanied by their personal photographs. Lerman himself specifically referred to the correspondence between the teachers and pupils who emigrated to Palestine and the pupils who remained at the school: 'The school has a close relationship with the Land of Israel... The immigrants, among them pupils, exchanged letters with the school. The letters from the Land of Israel were read in the classrooms and caused a great commotion.'[57]

Another example is five fifth-grade pupils' letters from the Zawiercie elementary school, written to pen pals in Palestine in late 1937. They were addressed to 'Dear Friends' and were written collectively on the same day (8 November), making it clear that they were part of a teacher-initiated classroom writing project. One of the letter-writers, Rachel Mintz, even commented that the teacher had read aloud to them in the classroom a letter received from Palestine to which the children responded in their letters: 'The teacher read us your letter. We received your letter in the summer but there was no time to answer because there were holidays.'[58]

Four letters written by children from Tarbut schools in Równe (Rivne) and nearby Ludwipol (Sosnove), Kleck (Kletsk), and Brzostowica Wielka (Vyalikaya Berastavitsa), dating from 1935 and the end of 1936, also testify to the widespread pen-pal custom of Tarbut schools in Poland. A. Rivlin, a representative of the JNF liaison bureau, sent three of the letters to a school in Nahalal on 16 December 1936 with a covering form letter with the date, the name of the school in Poland from where the letters were sent, and the name of the school in Palestine that received them. There is no doubt that there were many form letters like this attached to letters written in Poland that were gathered and distributed through the JNF liaison bureau.[59]

Finally, we cannot ignore what we know, and what the young Nowy Dwór letter-writers could not have ever imagined. Most of the children who wrote the letters were murdered a few years later in the Holocaust, never realizing their dream of emigrating to Palestine. This lends a tragic dimension to this collection of letters. Throughout our research, we had to remind ourselves repeatedly to interpret the letters only in the context of the time when they were written. We offer our conclusions as a modest memorial to those children and to a world that is no more.

Notes

This chapter is a product of ongoing research on letters written by Hebrew school pupils in interwar Poland, supported by the Israel Science Foundation (no. 300/19). The original letters are preserved in the archive of the Goldstein-Goren Diaspora Research Center at Tel Aviv University, file A38, and will be published in a critical edition by Magnes Press. The numbers of the letters relate to this forthcoming edition. We would like to thank Kamil Kijek for his close reading of this chapter and his thoughtful comments.

1 The complete social history of Tarbut has yet to be written. Although it was founded in April 1917 in Russia, the core of its activity was in interwar Poland where it was formally established in January 1922 (see A. Levinson, *Hatenuah ha'ivrit bagolah* (Warsaw, 1935); H. S. Kazdan, *Di geshikhte fun yidishn shulvezn in umophengikn poyln* (Mexico City, 1947), 409–44; E. Indelman, 'Tarbut bepolin, mekorah vegidulah, ḥazonah vekhilyonah', in Z. Scharfstein (ed.), *Haḥinukh vehatarbut ha'ivrit be'eiropah bein shetei milḥamot ha'olam* (New York, 1957), 107–33; N. Plantovski [Pniel], *Letoledot mosedot haḥinukh shel tarbut bepolin* (Jerusalem, 1946); S. Rozenhak, 'Hatenuah ha'ivrit vetarbut', in I. Gruenbaum (ed.), *Entsiklopedyah shel galuyot: varshah*, vol. i (Jerusalem, 1953), 142–55; J. Taitelbaum, 'Haḥinukh hatikhoni hayehudi bepolin bein shetei milḥamot ha'olam', Ph.D. thesis (Tel Aviv University, 1994), 159–254; K. Kijek, 'Was it Possible to Avoid "Hebrew Assimilation"? Hebraism, Polonization, and Tarbut Schools in the Last Decade of Interwar Poland', *Jewish Social Studies*, 21/2 (2016), 105–41).

2 See R. Decker, *Childhood, Memory and Autobiography in Holland from the Golden Age to Romanticism* (Basingstoke, Hants., 2000), ch. 2; P. Summerfield, *Histories of the Self: Personal Narratives and Historical Practice* (London, 2018). Brill has published the series Egodocuments and History since 2009. To date twelve volumes have been published.

3 *Awakening Lives: Autobiographies of Jewish Youth in Poland before the Holocaust*, ed. J. Shandler (New Haven, Conn., 2002); *Ostatnie pokolenie: Autobiografie polskiej młodzieży żydowskiej okresu międzywojennego*, ed. A. Cała (Warsaw, 2003; *Alilot ne'urim: otobiyografiyot shel benei no'ar yehudim mipolin bein shetei milḥamot ha'olam*, ed. I. Bassok (Tel

Aviv, 2011)), including two especially important autobiographies of former Tarbut pupils: 'Hanzi' (pp. 155–95) and 'Im ein kesef, ein torah' (pp. 701–30). On the educational system for Polish Jews in the interwar period, see I. Bassok and A. Novershtern, 'Ma'arkhot haḥinukh liyehudei polin bein shetei milḥamot ha'olam', in *Alilot ne'urim*, 731–68; on Tarbut, see ibid. 758–60.

4 For example, the children's book by Benjamin Tene (B. Tene, *Korot kitah aḥat* (Tel Aviv, 1977)) and in hundreds of autobiographies, book-length memoirs, and both short and long recollections printed in the *yizkor* (memorial) books of communities destroyed in the Holocaust.

5 'Kinus hayovel shel haseminaryon lemorim "tarbut"', *Tarbut: yediot hava'ad hamerkazi shel histadrut tarbut bepolin*, 25 Feb. 1933, pp. 6–7.

6 Levinson, *Hatenuah ha'ivrit bagolah*, 307–8, 317.

7 Ibid. 316–17. For more on the importance of correspondence as a pedagogical tool, see 'Al kishrei gomelim bein yaldei hagolah uvein yaldei ha'arets', *Ofakim*, 1/1 (May 1932), 28–30; M. Raziel, 'Kesharim bein yaldei hagolah veyaldei ha'arets', *Ofakim*, 1/1 (May 1932), 78; Y. Oheli, 'Emtsa'i ḥashuv leḥinukh tsiyoni', *Ofakim*, 1/4 (Dec. 1932), 195–6; Z. Zohar, *Darkhei ḥinukhenu* (Jerusalem, 1933), 81–2.

8 *Pinkas novy dvor*, ed. A. Shamri and D. First (Tel Aviv, 1965).

9 Z. Plesser, 'Beit hasefer "tarbut"', in *Pinkas novy dvor*, 146–52.

10 In 1931 there were 9,386 people living in Nowy Dwór; 3,961 of them were Jews (42 per cent). On the eve of the Second World War there were approximately 10,150 people living in the town. See D. B. First, 'Novy dvor un ir yidisher yishuv', in *Pinkas novy dvor*, 19–44: 25; 'Nowy Dwór', in A. Wein (ed.), *Pinkas hakehilot: polin*, vol. iv: *Varshah vehagalil*, 298–303; D. Bielecka, 'Społeczność żydowska w Nowym Dworze Mazowieckim w latach 1918–1939', *Rocznik Mazowiecki*, 14 (2002), 99–114.

11 This can be inferred from reports published in the contemporary Yiddish and Hebrew press. For example, on the desecration of the Jewish cemetery and shattering of dozens of tombstones (*Haynt*, 23 Oct. 1929, p. 1; *Der moment*, 24 Oct. 1929, p. 5; *Davar*, 24 Oct. 1929, p. 1); on the shattering of all the windows in a synagogue (*Do'ar hayom*, 17 Feb. 1936, p. 5); on the desecration of the cemetery and the breaking of windows in the home of the local rabbi (*Haaretz*, 26 Mar. 1939, p. 6); on the expulsion of Jewish peddlers from the markets (*Haaretz*, 16 July 1936, p. 2). For a general description of anti-Jewish economic and other discrimination, antisemitism, and anti-Jewish violence throughout the interwar period, see E. Mendelsohn, *The Jews of East Central Europe* (Bloomington, Ind., 1987), ch. 1; on the worsening situation in the 1930s, see E. Melzer, *No Way Out: The Politics of Polish Jewry, 1935–1939* (Cincinnati, 1997). For a case study of the role of opponents of the Endecja in rising anti-Jewish violence in Polish provincial areas like Mińsk Mazowiecki, from the Great Depression of 1929 until the pogroms of 1935 to 1937, see K. Kijek, 'The Road to Przytyk: Agitation and the Sociotechnique of Violence in the Kielce Region, 1931–1936', *Gal-ed*, 26–7 (2021), 59–102.

12 Plesser, 'Beit hasefer "tarbut"', 148–9.

13 For more on the dilemma of the Jewish situation in interwar Poland, which pitted the rising threat of ethno-nationalism and antisemitism against the many opportunities for development of various institutions and a modern, pluralistic Jewish national culture (both, secular and religious), see E. Mendelsohn, 'Interwar Poland: Good for the Jews or Bad for the Jews?', in C. Abramsky, M. Jachimczyk, and A. Polonsky (eds.), *The Jews in Poland* (Oxford, 1986), 130–9.

14 S. Rozenhak, 'Al ma'arekhet haḥinukh hayehudi bepolin bein shetei milḥamot ha'olam', in

I. Halperin (ed.), *Beit yisra'el bepolin*, 2 vols. (Jerusalem, 1948–54), ii. 154; Basok, *Alilot ne'urim*, 736–40. Other data suggests a lower number (see Levinson, *Hatenuah ha'ivrit bagolah*, 369; Kazdan, *Di geshikhte fun yidishn shulvezn in umophengikn poyln*, 429–34; Rozenhak, 'Al ma'arekhet haḥinukh hayehudi bepolin', 150–1; N. Pniel, *Perakim betoledot haḥinukh ha'ivri* (Tel Aviv, 1981), 111–12, 119–20; Taitelbaum, *Haḥinukh hatikhoni*, 66–7, 161–72).

15 J. Shimkovitch, 'Di tsiyonistishe yugnt-bavegung', in *Pinkas novy dvor*, 201–7: 207. The first report of a Tarbut school in Nowy Dwór was published in the newspaper *Haynt* ('Menahalei batei hasefer shel "tarbut"', *Haynt*, 17 Oct. 1930, p. 2). According to Poland's Compulsory Education Act of 1921, a private elementary school (as all Tarbut schools were) had to have seven grades for ages 7 to 14, but the government allowed for the law's gradual implementation. In 1937 the school in Nowy Dwór already had seven full grades. About 200 pupils studied in the school during the nine years it operated until it closed in 1939.

16 Plesser, 'Beit hasefer "tarbut"', 146.

17 Ibid. 147. This was not unusual: most Jewish schools in Poland were in rented buildings (see Rozenhak, 'Al ma'arekhet haḥinukh hayehudi bepolin', 144).

18 In their letters, the children did not always differentiate between *golah* (diaspora), meaning Jews living outside of their homeland, and *galut* (exile), the existential state of Jewish life in the non-Zionist space, which also carries a religious burden of guilt. The distinction between the two concepts is important against the background of the concept of rejection of the exile in Zionist thinking.

19 Eliezer Ravitzky, letter to Zvi Plesser, Palestine, [Mar. 1935] (letter no. 34) .

20 For a discussion of the relations and tensions between tradition and secularism in Tarbut schools, see Kazdan, *Di geshikhte fun yidishn shulvezn in umophengikn poyln*, 414–18; M. Eisenstein, *Jewish Schools in Poland, 1919–1939: Their Philosophy and Development* (New York, 1950), 40, 42, 44; S. Frost, *Schooling as a Socio-Political Expression: Jewish Education in Interwar Poland* (Jerusalem, 1998), 74–8, 128.

21 A. Bar-El, 'Ha'amlanut baḥinukh hatsiyoni bagolah', *Ma'of uma'aseh*, 6 (2000), 239–52.

22 Plesser, 'Beit hasefer "tarbut"', 147.

23 Eliezer Ravitzky, letter to Lea Vosbshag, Palestine, [1935] (letter no. 90).

24 Yisrael Lerich, letter to Zvi Plesser, Palestine, [1935] (letter no. 76).

25 On pedagogical trends in Polish state and private schools between the wars, which ranged from conservatism and nationalism to the liberal and democratic ideology of the 'new pedagogy' influenced by the ideas of John Dewey, see F. W. Araszkiewicz, *Ideały wychowawcze Drugiej Rzeczypospolitej* (Warsaw, 1978). The modern Jewish schools, especially the secular ones, were influenced by the new liberal pedagogy (see H. Ormian, *Hamaḥshavah haḥinukhit shel yahadut polanyah le'or hasifrut hapedagogit vehapsikhologit* (Tel Aviv, 1939), 119, 123, 151; Frost, *Schooling*, 108, 129–31; J. Sobczak, 'Nowe wychowanie' *w polskiej pedagogice okresu Drugiej Rzeczypospolitej (1918–1939)* (Bydgoszcz, 1998), 366).

26 Gavriel Fried, letter to Zvi Plesser [1934] (letter no. 12).

27 Moshe Kofman, letter to Zvi Plesser [1934] (letter no. 13).

28 Eliezer Ravitzky, letter to Zvi Plesser, Palestine (letter no. 34).

29 Elazar Tsiz, letters to Zvi Plesser, Palestine, 8 Mar. 1935, [1935] (letters nos. 39, 66).

30 Yosef Nahash, letters to Zvi Plesser 1934, [Mar. 1935], [1935] (letters nos. 2, 36, 72); Shmuel Shafir and Yosef Nahash, letter to Zvi Plesser, Palestine, [1935] (letter no. 59).

31 Zvi Finkelstein, letters to Zvi Plesser, Palestine, [10 Mar.] 1935, [1935] (letters nos. 45, 64).

32 Gavriel Fried, letter to Zvi Plesser, Palestine, [1935] (letter no. 63).

33 Yisrael Lerich, letter to Zvi Plesser [1934] (letter no. 3).

34 Ibid.
35 Eliezer Ravitzky, letter to Zvi Plesser, Palestine, [31 Mar. 1935] (letter no. 81).
36 Moshe Gurecki, letter to Zvi Plesser, [1934] (letter no. 22).
37 Gavriel Fried, letter to Zvi Plesser, Palestine, 8 Mar. 1935 (letter no. 38).
38 Rivka Don, letter to Zvi Plesser, Palestine, [Mar. 1935] (letter no. 52).
39 Rivka Don, letter to Zvi Plesser, Palestine, [1935] (letter no. 86).
40 Esther Zucker, letter to Zvi Plesser, Palestine, [Mar. 1935] (letter no. 48).
41 Yosef Nahash, letter to Zvi Plesser, [Mar. 1935] (letter no. 36).
42 Yisrael Lerich, letter to Zvi Plesser, [1935] (letter no. 76).
43 Corporal punishment was perceived as outdated and unacceptable in both Polish and Jewish modern liberal schools and, among Jews, as a negative remnant of the ḥeder. There were, of course, gaps between educational theory and everyday reality, especially against the background of violent daily life. Of course, children who were taught at home or at old-fashioned schools were also beaten.
44 Yisrael Lerich, letter to Zvi Plesser, [1934] (letter no. 3).
45 Lanzman probably means a second round of slaps.
46 Mordechai Lanzman, letter to Zvi Plesser, [1934] (letter no. 10).
47 Yehoshua Dulz, letter to Zvi Plesser, 25 Oct. 1934 (letter no. 17).
48 Moshe Kofman, letter to Zvi Plesser [1934] (letter no. 13).
49 See A. Shapira, 'Le'an halkhah shelilat hagalut?', *Alpayim*, 25 (2003), 9–54; E. Schweid, 'The Rejection of the Diaspora in Zionist Thought: Two Approaches', in J. Reinharz and A. Shapira (eds.), *Essential Papers on Zionism* (New York, 1995), 133–60.
50 Yosef Nahash, letter to Zvi Plesser, [1935] (letter no. 72).
51 Yisrael Lerich, letter to Zvi Plesser, [1935] (letter no. 76).
52 Yisrael Lerich, letter to Zvi Plesser, [1934] (letter no. 3).
53 Dov Sushinsky, Eliezer Ravitzky, Yehoshua Dulz, and Yisrael Lerich, letter to Zvi Plesser, Palestine, 13 Dec. 1934 (letter no. 58).
54 Zvi Greenshpan, letter to Zvi Plesser, Palestine, [Dec. 1934] (letter no. 56).
55 See K. Kijek, 'Haradikalism hapoliti shel hano'ar bashtetl bein milḥamot ha'olam', *Yalkut moreshet*, 92–3 (2013), 20–59.
56 Aviezer Yellin Archive of Jewish Education in Israel and the Diaspora, Tel Aviv University, Ze'ev Livne (Lerman) file.
57 Ze'ev Livne (Lerman), 'Mosedot haḥinukh bebaranovits', *Baranovits: sefer zikaron* (Tel Aviv, 1953), 179–96: 192.
58 Goldstein-Goren Diaspora Research Center, Tel Aviv University, A38-1: Rachel Mintz, letter to pen pals, Palestine, 8 Nov. 1937. The letters were preserved for decades by the former director of an unknown educational institute in Haifa whose pupils, presumably, had corresponded with pen pals in Poland. They were set to be auctioned in 2019, but this raised a public outcry in Israel, and the Tel Aviv District Court eventually prevented their sale. After long deliberations between the seller, Dudi Zilbershlag, and descendants of one of the girls who wrote the letters, the seller agreed to donate them for research purposes. On 2 November 2021 they were given to the authors of this chapter, who deposited them in the archive of the Goldstein-Goren Diaspora Research Center at Tel Aviv University, under the signature A38-1.
59 These were also offered for sale and eventually made $100 (see 'Lot 180: "Mikhtavim mibatei sefer ivriyim be'eiropah leveit hasefer benahalal, shenot ha-30–40"' (19 Dec. 2019): Bidspirit website, visited 2 Apr. 2022).

State Schools as Polish–Jewish Contact Zones

The Case of Tarnów

AGNIESZKA WIERZCHOLSKA

The minutes of the teachers' councils (Rady Pedagogiczne) of two schools in Tarnów in former Galicia illustrate the difficulties Jewish children faced in Polish primary schools. Located in a predominantly Jewish, working-class part of this mid-sized town (with a population of around 55,000, about 45 per cent of which was Jewish), the Czacki and Staszic schools were intended to foster Polish acculturation. While the Czacki school ostensibly supported inclusivity, its teachers categorized Jewish students as problematic because of their poor level of Polish, failure to attend school on Saturday (Polish schools had a six-day week), and what they saw as unruly behaviour. Their presence was seen as deleterious to the educational opportunities of their Catholic classmates. In the Staszic school, integration was more successfully pursued, since the teachers, though aware of these difficulties, sought solutions that addressed the needs of the Jewish students.

THE GREAT MAJORITY OF JEWS in the Second Polish Republic were urban—to be more precise, 76 per cent of the Jewish population lived in towns. In contrast, 78 per cent of the non-Jewish Polish population lived in the countryside.[1] Cities thus became important areas of interaction and exchange between the Jewish and non-Jewish populations. In an essay of 2017, the literary anthropologist Eugenia Prokop-Janiec called for greater use in the study of Polish–Jewish relations of the concept of 'contact zones' employed in postcolonial studies.[2] She defined these as zones in which exchange, co-operation, and negotiation, as well as confrontation and violence, occur. In addition, the asymmetry and hierarchy of power relations become visible when these contact zones are closely analysed.

In the interwar years state elementary schools became important spaces of interaction between Jewish and non-Jewish students. Most Jewish children in the Second Republic—about 80 per cent—attended Polish state schools.[3] At the same time, school was an institution of the nationalizing state, in which the next generation was to be educated 'towards the nation' in the culture of the ethnic Polish majority population. So what did the interaction space of a classroom in a state school look like in everyday life?

So far, research on this topic has mostly analysed state schools either from the perspective of the policies of the state[4] or on the basis of the autobiographical writings of Jewish students.[5] In this chapter, I turn to a hitherto little-researched set of sources relating to Polish–Jewish relations: the minutes of teachers' meetings at two state schools in Tarnów. Tarnów was a middle-sized town in Western Galicia, about 80 kilometres east of Kraków. Before the Second World War it had a population of around 55,000, of whom approximately 45 per cent were Jewish.[6] The town's social make-up was diverse: it had a large industrial base with a growing number of trade unions and workers' parties, a significant intelligentsia, and a stratum of well-to-do businessmen. Both primary schools analysed in this chapter were located in the poorer, mostly working-class Grabówka district, which had a high percentage of Yiddish-speaking Jews: around 77 per cent of the population. Both schools, the Tadeusz Czacki and Stanisław Staszic primary schools, have preserved the minutes of their teachers' meetings—the Czacki school from 1925 to 1939 and the Staszic school from 1925 to 1950—and have deposited these documents in the municipal archives. They provide insight into the teachers' views on the students. These minutes were regularly read by an outside school inspector, who annotated them. His comments appear in red. The authors of the minutes were well aware that their discussions were vetted by a higher authority. I will discuss the limitations of this type of source in more detail below. Where possible, I supplement the official documents with the recollections of former students.

The question of whether and in what way state schools in the Second Polish Republic sought to foster the acculturation of Jewish children has been widely discussed in historical research.[7] Celia Heller sees the state schools as successful 'agents of acculturation' that achieved a far-reaching Polonization of Jewish children.[8] Recently, Kamil Kijek has provided a more complex picture of this process in his study based on autobiographies of young people. Because they were educated in public schools, many Jews of the younger generation identified with the symbolic universe of the Polish nation (its images, heroes, historical narratives), but at the same time they were denied full participation in this Polish 'imagined community' (imagined, one might add, in ethno-national categories).[9] As a result, many, according to Kijek, turned to Jewish movements, and some to radical groups.[10] Analysis of the language employed by teachers in relation to multi-ethnic classes and the attitudes this reveals contributes important new insights into this issue.

School education played an essential role in the nationalization project of the Second Polish Republic. When the Polish state was re-established, one of its first tasks was to create a single educational system in the territories that had previously been ruled by the three partitioning powers. In this context, schools not only took on an educational role in the narrow sense (ensuring the literacy of the population and the teaching of Polish) but were also supposed to promote patriotic education as an instrument of the newly created state, and thus contribute to the cultural unification of the country through a standardized Polish education. On the one hand, school education was to serve democratization and educate the broad strata of the population to become responsible citizens; on the other hand, it was to strengthen the 'national spirit'.[11] However, the conceptions of the nation of the different Polish political groups differed, so that in the course of arguments over the design of school education it ultimately became clear that the 'dispute over the school . . . was at the same time a dispute over the "correct" concept of the nation', as Stephanie Zloch put it.[12] In addition, the Minority Treaty which Poland signed with the Allied and Associated Powers at Versailles in June 1919, which protected the rights of minorities, stipulated that such groups should be taught in their native language. The school of the Second Republic was thus set contradictory goals: it was to create a democratic school education for all, to educate 'towards' the Polish nation, and at the same time to establish a diversified system which would cater to the needs of the various minorities in the state. The tension between the nation-state and the nationality-state, between the idea of civic citizenship and the primacy of the ethnically defined Polish nation, affected the debate on school policy and found its echo in the classroom.[13]

In the Second Republic, education was compulsory from 7 to 14, that is, from the first to the seventh year. As early as 1918/19, a seven-year period of compulsory and free elementary education was introduced.[14] This primary school gave entry to secondary schools, and after the reforms of education minister Janusz Jędrzejewicz in 1932, provided for a four-year gymnasium and a two-year lyceum.[15] According to the Minority Treaty, the Polish state was obliged in ethnically heterogeneous regions to create schools where children of primary-school age could be taught in a language other than Polish. Polish was, however, a compulsory subject at these schools.[16] Most of those state schools in which instruction was given in a language other than Polish (mostly Ukrainian) were eventually converted into bilingual, so-called 'Utraquist', schools. Yiddish never had the status of a minority language, and thus in the Second Polish Republic there were no bilingual state schools teaching in Yiddish.[17] Furthermore, the question of whether Yiddish or Hebrew was or should be *the* language of Polish Jewry was disputed within the Jewish community.[18] As a 'compromise' with the demands of the Jewish minority, state schools were set up in which teaching was only in Polish, but where the free day fell on Saturday and not on Sunday (Polish schools had a six-day week). These schools were called *szabasówki*. They could not be located near a Catholic place of worship, so as not to interfere with the religious practice of Christians.[19] The popularity of these schools declined with time, and they were almost completely abolished in the early 1930s.[20]

A private Jewish school network developed alongside the state school system, which allowed children to receive a Jewish education. What Jewish education was and what it was supposed to achieve were matters of dispute and were evaluated differently by the various Jewish groups. Most of these were politically engaged (the Bund, the Zionists, Mizrachi, and others), and the private Jewish school sector was thus extremely politicized and diverse. Private Jewish schooling filled a gap, as state institutions largely failed to address the educational needs of minorities. In the words of Stephanie Zloch, 'dealing with multi-ethnicity [in the school system] was literally privatized'.[21]

Going to School Together: Elementary Schools

Elementary schools became important spaces of interaction between Jewish and non-Jewish pupils. They were free, and only very few families could afford to send their children to a private Jewish school. In addition, some parents wanted their children to acquire a good knowledge of Polish.[22] Jewish leaders, however, complained that attending state schools led to the total assimilation of Jews and alienated the children from Judaism. The debate about the right school for Jewish children also took place in the Jewish press.[23] Some parents decided to have their children educated in a state school but also sent them to a private Jewish school. Gizela Fudem of Tarnów, for example, attended both the Bais Yaakov School and the state Saint Jadwiga School.[24] In the latter, the proportion of Jewish pupils was between 50 and 70 per cent.[25]

In Tarnów there was a total of ten public elementary schools, separated into boys' and girls' schools, in which there were 4,461 pupils in 1938/9; 754 children attended private schools.[26] The Staszic and Czacki schools were for boys; in the latter, girls were also listed in a separate section of the class registers.[27] They were probably taught separately from a certain point on. The minutes of the teachers' meetings which have been preserved concern only the school for boys.

Both the Czacki and the Staszic schools were located on the outskirts of the working-class Grabówka area, a poor neighbourhood in which a high proportion of the residents were Jewish. The Czacki school was located in the south of Grabówka. Of its nearly 500 students, about half were Jewish, and for most of them Yiddish was their mother tongue.[28] The Staszic school was located north-west of Grabówka. Just over 400 students studied there, almost half of whom were Jewish, although that percentage dropped to 33 per cent in the 1938/9 school year.[29] The majority of children (Jewish and non-Jewish) in both schools came from very poor backgrounds. As in a microcosm, the problems of state elementary schools in the Second Polish Republic were highlighted in these classrooms. These were to be schools for all, in which the poorest classes were to be included in the process of democratization and educated towards the Polish nation. At the same time, they were to be schools that included minorities in this process, but which, in practice, left little room for being different from the Catholic Polish majority. How did the teachers deal with this?

How Teachers Wrote about Jewish Students in the Czacki School

The teachers of the Czacki school regarded the students as highly problematic. They were undernourished and hardly any had shoes or suitable winter clothing, so that a wave of illness regularly affected the student body at the onset of winter. The teachers repeatedly complained that the parents hardly cared for their offspring and that the students were not looked after properly at home, and about a lack of hygiene.[30] Some children had to earn money or help their family.[31] Many students came from homes considered to be 'uneducated'. (This, however, did not include religious education or knowledge of Yiddish or Hebrew.) At the same time, the school had no capacity for in-depth support: class sizes varied between forty-five and sixty-five students.[32]

Reading the minutes of the teachers' meetings at the Czacki school, a picture emerges that it was above all the Jewish students who were causing problems, failing to master the subject matter of the curriculum, coming to school late, being conspicuously unclean, and behaving badly. According to the teachers, the overall standard of the school was so poor because 50 per cent of the children were Jewish.[33] When a school inspector paid his first visit, the headmaster stood up solemnly and asked 'that our work not be judged too harshly and that the inspector should take into account that in our school we have about 50 per cent Israelites who speak poor Polish and that the whole student body comes mainly from a poorer working-class background'.[34] With regard to the Jewish students, the teachers of the Czacki school discussed three principal issues at length: their lack of knowledge of Polish, their failure to attend school on Saturdays, and their bad behaviour.

Repeatedly, the teachers complained that the Jewish children spoke little or no Polish when they started school. The question of language was a recurring issue at almost all the teachers' meetings when teachers reported on their classroom experience. Although the problem diminished somewhat in the upper years as children acquired Polish, it never completely disappeared. 'Great difficulties', lamented one teacher, 'continue to be encountered in written essays because of the large number of Jews (thirty-two out of forty-nine students) who write the way they pronounce, but in fact mispronounce many words. They cannot be taught correct pronunciation because outside school these students speak only Yiddish.'[35] The two months of summer vacation would further deprive them of the opportunity to improve their Polish. The teachers also complained that Jewish children spoke Yiddish among themselves during breaks.[36] The poor level of Polish among Jewish students was explained by their laziness: 'Jews, in particular, read badly, whether because of carelessness or laziness or perhaps because of the great trouble they have in learning the language. This has a negative effect on Catholic children.'[37]

In those towns where, as in Tarnów, there was no *szabasówka*, Jewish children had the right to be exempted from classes on Saturdays.[38] Consequently, in the Czacki school half of the student body was absent on Saturdays. Sometimes Jewish students missed even two days of classes, because some courses were taught in the afternoon, and in winter Jewish children did not come to school on Fridays afternoons, after the sabbath had begun.[39] The frequent absence of Jewish students worsened the statistics. The low number of attendees on Fridays and Saturdays made the school appear to be full of truants. Eventually, teachers moved to submitting two sets of attendance statistics to the school inspector: one for a five-day week (excluding Saturdays) and an overall attendance list for the full week.[40] Again and again the Jewish teacher of religion, Jakób Wachtel, was asked to influence Jewish parents so that the children would speak Polish at home and appear at school on Saturdays.[41] Wachtel, although patently anxious to prove his loyalty, pointed out that such a request of a Jewish teacher of religion would force him into a difficult position: even though he himself was in favour of students going to school on Saturdays and also taught on Saturdays, he felt he could not be asked as a teacher of religion to say to the students: 'You should go to school on Saturdays.' At the same time he asserted that he had never said and would never say that Jewish students should not come to school on Saturday.[42]

Some boys took advantage of the fact that they were allowed to be absent on the sabbath, but, rather than attending synagogue, preferred to spend the morning playing football. Eventually some were caught, leading to them being very poorly regarded. This was discussed at the teachers' meetings, and reinforced the stance of those teachers who already held the opinion that the Jewish children attended school as they pleased: 'They attend school according to their whim . . . according to what they want to do.'[43]

Complaints about the behaviour of Jews occurred more frequently from 1935/6 onwards.[44] When the teachers criticized students' bad behaviour, they emphasized that it was mainly Jews: 'It was noted that Jewish students were most often late.'[45] In another minute, a teacher reported: 'The frequent lateness of individual students, especially Jews, is unpleasantly noticeable. Here I turn to Mr Wachtel with the heartfelt request that he should discuss the subject in religious studies class.'[46] Repeatedly Wachtel was called upon to solve problems of various kinds during his religious studies classes. In this way, the difficulties were externalized as it were, as a 'Jewish problem' to be solved 'among the Jews'. Thus: 'Mr Otwinowski turned to Mr Wachtel with a request to influence Jewish students, because their behaviour is worse than that of the Catholics. The former organize brawls and write obscene words and sentences.'[47] The minutes also record the following observations about the behaviour of Jewish students: 'Brawls often take place in class, and especially among the Jewish students';[48] 'the students who misbehave are usually Jews';[49] and 'there are also pupils who manifest conspicuous features of mental underdevelopment, especially Jews who do not know the Polish language, the children of the slum in the neighbourhood.'[50]

Non-Jewish children—who also came from poor families—were much less likely to be written about in pejorative terms in the minutes of the teachers' meetings, with the exception of a few from rural areas, though still not with the same frequency. Jewish students were presented exclusively as a problem in the teachers' meetings. Reading the minutes gives the impression that this way of seeing and speaking intensified during the 1930s, especially as the bad behaviour of Jews was increasingly criticized from 1935 on. In the Czacki school, which had to cope with a complex set of challenges, Jews were seen as the main problem, onto whom all other difficulties were projected.

Similar Problems, Different Solutions: The First Years of the Staszic School

Although the student body of the Staszic school, like that of the Czacki school, was composed of the poorer social strata of the Grabówka district and was also ethnically mixed, the attitude of the teachers was, rather, one of understanding and support—at least until 1934, when Adolf Zarzycki was the headmaster. Minutes of teachers' meetings repeatedly described the poverty of all the pupils. Parents 'lacked funds for clothing and shoes'.[51] Often the children came to class barefoot. These negative accounts of the pupils' homes were constantly repeated in the minutes, but at the same time action was taken on the part of the school. From 1930 it organized free lunches for the children, initially for forty students: by 1933, 300 children were benefiting.[52] In the same year the school bought twenty-four pairs of shoes; two years later it provided its pupils with 140 pairs of shoes.[53] Since parents often had no money to buy school books and other educational materials, the school directorate also sought funding from outside parties. For the Jewish children, it turned to the *kehilah*: 'The school directorate received a positive answer from the Jewish community that textbooks would be loaned for the entire school year for poor children of the Mosaic faith.'[54]

The problem of the non-attendance of Jewish students on Saturdays was quickly solved. When the teachers complained in 1925 that Jewish children were absent on Saturdays, the school inspector wrote in red pen underneath: 'Calculate average attendance excluding Saturdays.'[55] After that, hardly any other complaints about absences on Saturdays appeared—quite different from the dispute at the Czacki school, which lasted for years. Reference was also made to the fact that 'teaching in September and October is made more difficult because there are many Jewish children and that is the time of Jewish holidays'.[56] According to the minutes,

> The teacher Wojcikówna, who teaches the first year, says that because of the high percentage of Jews (58 per cent Jews and 42 per cent Catholics) and the Jewish holidays, which fall in September and October, the subject matter could not be completed, but she hopes that this will now be made up in November, when attendance figures are better.[57]

Here a teacher merely explained why she was not progressing with her subject as planned. The absence of Jewish students was not framed as a problem of the Jews but rather one the teachers needed to deal with. Moreover, they were also accustomed to dealing with the issue. In the early summer months the high attendance rate at school was even mentioned in a positive way: 'Attendance was good: 93 to 94 per cent.'[58]

The lack of Polish-language skills among Jewish students was also a constant topic of discussion at the Staszic teachers' meetings. The level of Polish instruction was so poor because 60 per cent of the student body was Jewish, the headmaster admitted, but at the same time he gave 'a number of suggestions and advice' on how teachers could remedy this deficiency.[59] One teacher complained: 'In this class, 64 per cent of the children are of the Mosaic faith, and have a poor command of the language of instruction, which makes the work difficult for the teachers and for the children.'[60] Another teacher explained the poor level of Polish as follows:

We have a high percentage of Jews in the school and that from the poorest classes. These children hear the Polish language only at school, at home they use the jargon [Yiddish], and even at school they often speak among themselves in Yiddish. This should be ruthlessly combated, and the jargon should be forbidden in school. This must be strictly observed.[61]

Another teacher complained:

The Jews, who make up 35 per cent of the class, have a poor level of Polish, which is reflected in their written essays. In order to remedy this deficiency, the topics chosen for the written essays in Polish classes should be as accessible as possible, involving topics that interest the children and which evoke a number of impressions, ideas, and memories in them.[62]

Although one teacher reported pejoratively that 'Jews [declaim] in a comical way because of a lack of language skills', the overall impression from the minutes of the teachers' meetings in the Staszic school are that the teachers were making an effort to support the children in learning Polish through interesting essay topics, increasing motivation, and various methods suggested by the headmaster.[63] According to the minutes, 'Teaching Polish is a priority, as the language is important for other subjects as well. Serious deficiencies among Jewish youth—here, everything must be done so that the Polish language is raised to a high level.'[64]

In response, the headmaster purchased an additional and new textbook for Polish for classes with a high percentage of Jewish students.[65] The teachers demanded that extra teachers be hired.[66] When in the 1929 school year the first class numbered sixty-three students, 'of whom over 60 per cent [were] Jews with no knowledge of Polish, who sometimes even do not understand the teacher, the teachers requested, for the good of the class, the creation of a parallel class and the assignment of an additional teacher'.[67] This request was granted, and class 1A was created, with only non-Jewish students, and class 1B with only Jewish students. After three months, the progress of class 1B was evaluated: 'Reading is better than in class 1A. Dictation turned out well. They are doing better in maths than class 1A. The pronunciation of the class 1B (Jewish) students leaves much to be desired; however, this is not the fault of the teacher.'[68]

Praise and acknowledgement of the Jewish students were not absent from the minutes of the Staszic school (in contrast to those of the Czacki school). In addition, the headmaster complained several times about a teacher who neglected his teaching duties. In his second class the following conditions prevailed:

The learning of the Polish language has not proved to be very positive. Of the forty-five present, four could not read at all and nine only very poorly, and these were all Catholics. One can explain this in such a way that the Jews have an innate thirst for knowledge and were able to help themselves, while the Catholics were not able to do so, they lack the attentive supervision of the teacher.[69]

There are thus some positive evaluations of Jewish students in the minutes of the Staszic school, even if this did involve attributing essentialist characteristics to them. With regard to the prizes awarded at the end of the school year, teachers were sensitive to religious differences among the student body. They decided 'to buy books (prayer books for Catholics and novels for Jews) and distribute them in the lower classes, while in the higher classes a book on the history of Tarnów was given to the best students'.[70]

Negative evaluations of Jewish students were certainly also found in the minutes of the Staszic school, but their behaviour was not explained solely by their Jewishness or, as in the Czacki school, by their laziness and carelessness, but often by reference to their difficult economic and social circumstances:

The teachers work with zeal and strive not only for the education of the children but also for their good upbringing, which is sometimes a challenge in our school. We are dealing with probably the worst element in Tarnów, a large proportion of which are Jews, especially from the poorest classes, whose home education leaves much to be desired.[71]

The students' writing is described as 'deficient . . . because of the high percentage of Jews and also because of the uneducated background of most of the children of this school'.[72] At no point in the minutes is the Jewish religious studies teacher, Jakób Wachtel, who also taught in the Staszic school, called upon to influence the Jewish students during his classes, as was often the case in the Czacki school.

In contrast to those at the Czacki school, the teaching staff of the Staszic school, at least while Zarzycki was headmaster, saw it as their responsibility to confront the challenges of a multi-ethnic school in an area with serious social problems. The staff considered ways to support Jewish students, among them with additional books, teachers, and parallel classes. There is a marked contrast between the ways in which the conflict between a national state and one which attempted to find a place for the minorities, above all the Jews, was played out in the classrooms of the Staszic and Czacki schools. At the Staszic school, attempts were made to assist the scholarly integration of Jewish children, while the minutes of the teachers' meetings at the Czacki school give the impression of a divide between the titular nation in a nationalizing state and the 'Others', who were perceived as deficient, undisciplined, and, because of their often inadequate command of Polish, intellectually underdeveloped. This was the discursive framework in which the teachers discussed their Jewish students during the teachers' meetings. Jewish students were largely left to handle the task of acculturation into Polish language and culture, which was, after all, a prerequisite for successful participation in the classroom, on their own. The challenges of a multi-ethnic state were externalized onto the Jews. In the Staszic school, by contrast, these 'Others' were understood as part of a (difficult) school community who needed to be supported in learning Polish. What caused the difference? Certainly, the general political situation could have contributed to the different atmosphere in the two schools. However, the personality of the headmaster probably also played a significant role in shaping the teachers' attitudes towards the students. The headmaster could steer the teachers in one direction or another and set standards. I will return to both aspects subsequently.

Patriotism, Nation, and Religion in Primary Schools

Perhaps because there was no independent Polish state between 1795 and 1918, for many Poles there was a big difference between *państwo* (state) and *naród* (nation). The nation was understood as ethnically Polish and religiously Catholic. However, the Polish–Lithuanian Commonwealth had been home to many nations, cultures, and religions and prided itself on its diversity and tolerance. After Poland regained independence there were roughly two points of view. One, held by Piłsudski and his followers in the Sanacja movement, saw Poland as a state with many nationalities and many religions. The other saw Poland as a nation primarily of ethnic Poles, and all others were really 'guests'. Until Piłsudski's death in 1935, the first point of view was clearly dominant; after his death the second gradually gained ground.

In 1930 a teacher at the Czacki school wrote in the minutes: 'We educate our children in a patriotic spirit, that is, in loyalty to the Polish state, not only *ex officio* but out of deep conviction.'[73] The school inspector underlined '*ex officio*' in bright red and added a large exclamation mark and a question mark in the margin. What is most remarkable in this quotation however, is the use of the terms 'patriotic' and 'state' and the absence of the term 'national'. In the understanding of the Sanacja regime, loyalty to the state was in 1930 at the centre of schools' educational mission. The official language of the minutes at this time clearly rejects a purely ethno-national approach. The slogan *upaństwowienie* (alignment with or adherence to the state) is also reflected in the schools, at least at the official level in the minutes of the teachers' meetings. According to Sanacja, the state was to be an integrating force for society, and all citizens were to work for the common good, that is, for the state. However, this also meant that pupils should be educated to that end—in other words, schools should make their contribution to the process of *upaństwowienie*. The 'patriotic' spirit of the students was mobilized, in various ways, including celebrations of the state and its leaders—presidential name days; anniversaries of their deaths; appointments, such as that of Edward Śmigły-Rydz to the post of general inspector of the army in May 1935; and Polish Constitutions.[74] As Dorota Wojtas has shown, school reformers and the Ministry of Education from the late 1920s, and under Janusz Jędrzejewicz from 1931 to 1934, were concerned that state education—that is, education to create loyal citizens—should find its way into classrooms and into the emotional experience of pupils.[75] Only once did a teacher at the Czacki school complain that Jewish children would not sing the Polish anthem. However, a few months later, a teacher reported that the Jewish children were very much in favour of singing patriotic songs, although a few did not yet know the words because they had been absent at the beginning of the year.[76] In the following years no further complaints of this type can be found in the minutes of the teachers' meetings.

The state-oriented language of the minutes shifted somewhat over the years: as early as 1933 the minutes of the Czacki school assert: 'Education for *państwowość* [statehood] goes hand in hand with *edukacja narodowa* [national education].'[77] In the same year, it was emphasized that Polish should serve as the guiding culture, to be taught to children through Polish literature.[78] This emphasis on both national and state aspects of education can be traced back to the *Guidelines for Authors of School Curricula* published in 1932.[79] Until the outbreak of the Second World War, in the language of the Czacki school teachers' meetings, *państwowość* remained the core concept rather than *edukacja narodowa*. However, how this was actually implemented in the classrooms, especially when teachers tended to have a pejorative opinion of their Jewish students and when the gap between those belonging to what was seen as the 'titular nation' and the 'Others' was very palpable, is questionable.

The minutes of the Staszic school provide more detailed information on how patriotism was to be strengthened in the classroom. As in the Czacki school, the concept of *państwowo-obywatelska* (civic)[80] education dominated in the years 1926 to 1931: 'The goal of the school and the teacher is to direct the youngsters so that they grow up to be decent and obedient citizens.'[81] The children were to be transformed into citizens rather than 'good Poles', a significant difference of emphasis in the teaching of civic values. In 1931 the headmaster opened the assembly of the teachers with the following words: 'We will overcome all difficulties, because we know that we are working for our state—or society—and for a better future.'[82] The concept of *upaństwowienie*, which was paired with that of *uobywatelnienie* (making a citizen of someone), which saw as its goal the strengthening of the consciousness of the civic principle, appeared in the minutes as late as 1934, where it was claimed that the goal was 'to influence the pupils even more strongly in the spirit of civic education and *upaństwowienie*. Emphasize the need for all citizens to live and work together.'[83]

However, from 1932 onwards the concept of civic education was accompanied by that of national education in the concept of *narodowo-państwowa* (national-state) education, and the two ideas were increasingly merged. This concept was to be taught to the children through various rituals, and integrated into the school day as follows: 'To consolidate the collective, *narodowo-państwowa* consciousness, the youngsters should take vows and oaths in a choral setting to create an uplifted mood during the festivities.'[84] In each class, the teacher was to come up with 'a farewell formula with patriotic content, which all the children would recite at the end of class after praying and before leaving school.'[85] In addition, beginning in 1932, children in the lower years were required to recite Władysław Bełza's 'Katechizm polskiego dziecka' ('Catechism of the Polish Child'), a poem current today that begins with the words, 'Who are you? A little Pole. What is your sign? A white eagle.'[86] Prayer and the Catholic faith were increasingly integrated into the practice of national-patriotic education in schools. The very title of 'Katechizm polskiego dziecka' points to this amalgamation of Roman Catholic religion, nation, and education. Every child was to be inculcated with 'the love of his mother tongue—of God and fatherland'.[87]

How were the Jewish children supposed to see themselves as part of this group, when the mother tongue referred to was exclusively Polish, when it was not their religion that was clearly being invoked in the reference to God? 'I am a Pole...' soon became the motto of the first and second classes, which all children were expected to recite at the beginning of class. Celia Heller summed up the situation as follows, using Bełza's poem as an example: 'The exalted world of Polishness unfolded to Jewish children like a magic castle: to glance at, to admire, but seldom, if ever, to enter fully.'[88] This simultaneous identification by Jewish students with 'Polishness' combined with their exclusion from a community understood in ethno-national terms is what the historian Kamil Kijek called, following Bourdieu's terminology, the symbolic violence of the dominant majority society towards Jewish children, of which the latter were not always aware.[89] The notion of civic patriotism continued to be present in the minuted discussions, but being Polish was at the same time filled with meanings that were increasingly aimed at ethno-national (and not civic) belonging—coupled with identification with the Roman Catholic faith.

The Catholic Church was very present in the school day. Catholic religious instruction was given by a priest who came to the schools. Prayers were said at the beginning of lessons; very probably crucifixes hung in the classrooms. William Celnik, a Jewish survivor from Tarnów, whose teacher of religion had been Jakób Wachtel, recounted that during Christian prayers in elementary schools, Jewish children folded their hands together (he imitated the gesture in the interview) but did not cross themselves.[90] In 1932 the minutes of the Czacki school mentioned that the graduation ceremony was held in Tarnów Cathedral. What this meant for the Jewish student body, whether they held separate ceremonies, the minutes do not say.[91] Wachtel finally intervened, and in 1933 requested of the Czacki school directorate that all school ceremonies be held in such a way that students of the Jewish faith could also participate.[92] Apparently, it had become necessary to point out that Jews were being excluded from the celebrations.

The state schools attended by Jewish students offered Jewish religious instruction —usually twice, later four times, a week.[93] At the Staszic school, Jewish religious instruction always took place on Mondays and Fridays.[94] In 1918 a state seminary for teachers of the Jewish religion was founded, as the state wanted to exert its influence on what was taught in religion classes. A total of 300 teachers were trained in the seminary before the outbreak of the Second World War. Since many of them were employed by private Jewish schools, the public schools continued to lack state-trained teachers who could provide Jewish religious instruction.[95] At the same time, Jewish religious authorities complained that religious instruction in the state schools left much to be desired.[96] Under his signature, Wachtel described himself as 'graduate teacher of the Jewish religion'.[97] Whether he was a graduate of the state teachers' seminary is unknown. In addition to the Staszic and Czacki schools, he also taught religion at the First Kazimierz Brodziński Gymnasium in Tarnów. In the annual reports of this school, he gave a detailed insight into how he was instructing the children. In addition to imparting knowledge of religion (the Pentateuch with commentaries, the books of the prophets and psalms, the five scrolls, and preparing the high-school children for barmitzvah), the lessons dealt with the history and literature of Polish Jewry and the history and geography of the 'Promised Land'.[98] In his official report, Wachtel also emphasized loyalty to the state: 'All years were also taught about their duty to the fatherland, the president of the republic and the government. In the services on the occasion of state holidays all pupils of all years took part.'[99] Although religious diversity in a classroom must have been the norm in such towns as Tarnów, certainly something experienced on a daily basis by the children of the town, the pressure of the Catholic Polish majority society must also have been strongly felt in class groups.

Jews and Catholics: The Language of the Minutes of the Teachers' Meetings

In 1926 a teacher wrote in the minutes of the Czacki school: 'The level of teaching would be better if there were fewer Jews [żydki], many of whom do not know or understand Polish.'[100] The school inspector marked in red the word żydki, which was a pejorative way of referring to Jews (as opposed to the neutral word żydzi). Presumably there was some discussion about what term should be used, because żydki subsequently disappeared from the minutes. Teachers now wrote either of Israelites or of Jewish and Catholic students. The dichotomies 'Jews versus Poles' or 'Jewish versus Polish' students did not appear in the language of the minutes in either the Czacki or the Staszic school. Religious difference was emphasized, which was in keeping with the discourse of upaństwowienie.

In addition, in the minutes, the Polish word żydzi was written in lower-case letters. In Polish, the noun denoting an affiliation to a nation or nationality is written with a capital (Polacy, Francuzi), while the noun denoting religious affiliation is written in lower-case letters (katolicy, ewangelicy). Thus, the lower-case word 'jew' in Polish marked religious difference, but not a national Jewish affiliation. (In other contexts, however, the word 'jew' in Polish was also written in lower-case letters to mark the pejorative attitude of the writer.) The use of the lower case is also ambivalent, because many Jews certainly felt that they belonged to the Jewish nation. Nevertheless, in the discourse of the state elementary schools, such as the Staszic and Czacki schools, a distinction was initially made according to religious affiliation. Ludwik Garmada, in his interview for the Shoah Foundation, recalled that the schools spoke of Catholic and Jewish pupils, thus linguistically emphasizing religious (and not ethno-national) differences.[101] It was only in June 1936 that Żydzi was capitalized for the first time in the minutes of a meeting at the Czacki school, but subsequently this occurred only sporadically. Increasingly, however, lower-case żydzi disappeared, and from the school year 1936/7 onwards 'Jews' was written almost exclusively with a capital. In 1938 the word żydki appeared again, but it was used by a teacher who had only recently been hired. It was not repeated a second time.[102] Whether there were ministry guidelines on the use of language in state schools is not known. What is clear, however, is that the Czacki and Staszic schools were concerned about what today we would call politically correct language. Although even after 1936 the dichotomy *Polacy/Żydzi* cannot be found in the minutes and the Catholic pupils were never referred to simply as 'the Poles' *tout court*, at least the use of the capital in the word 'Jews' at the Czacki school revealed a small shift. In official usage, students were not divided into 'Poles' and 'Others' in ethno-nationally defined categories, but rather their religious differences were emphasized. For many Jews of the time, this terminology was significant. 'Everyone was considered Polish', Ludwik Garmada recalled of his schooldays.[103] For him, being a Pole was an open category that included him as a Jew. At the same time, however, as explained above, the attitude of the teachers and the practice in the schools testified to the fact that—despite the general avoidance of ethnic language—'being Polish' was increasingly thought of and understood in ethno-national and exclusive categories.

Pedagogical Concepts in Primary Schools

Adolf Zarzycki was the headmaster of the Staszic school until 1934. Under his aegis, the staff endeavoured to support all its students. This attitude went hand in hand with modern pedagogical concepts. The headmaster required that the lessons should be as interactive as possible: the teachers should not only offer top-down teaching[104] but use methods 'to mobilize the greatest possible activity of the children'.[105] During Polish classes teachers should encourage the performance of short plays and the recitation of texts.[106] The students should be encouraged to reach solutions to problems on their own and the teacher should act primarily as a guide.[107] Teachers should always try to arouse children's interest in their subject.[108] Children, the headmaster urged, should not be treated coolly from above but with warmth and affection.[109] A large red 'Yes!' was written by the school inspector alongside this admonition. A system of student self-government was also established in the school.

At the Czacki school, the treatment of the student body, which was considered 'difficult', changed when a new headmaster, Józef Cierniak, took over in 1933. Under his aegis, the principle of 'democratization' found its way into the pedagogical concepts employed in the school, which, however, did not lead to an improved attitude towards Jews. When, in the first school year of his tenure, a teacher complained about the poor performance of a class with over fifty students, Cierniak replied that a class teacher was responsible for the performance of the class and should try to influence each child in a positive way. It was important, he said, to investigate where the bad habits came from, to familiarize oneself with the child's environment, to learn about the conditions in which they lived, and then to apply appropriate educational methods. However, another teacher added that, because of the large number of students in one class, these methods could hardly be applied.[110] Another example of Cierniak's new pedagogy is found in the same minutes: the priest who provided Catholic religious instruction complained that the children—mostly Jews, he said —behaved so badly because they received no punishment. He suggested that the parents be called into the school so that they could carry out the physical punishment of the children in the headmaster's office. The new headmaster strongly opposed these measures.[111] From 1936 Cierniak also introduced 'autodidactic' training for the teachers: they were to work out how a subject should be taught on the basis of pedagogical journals and present their findings as a paper to the other teachers during the teachers' meetings.[112] Although the new headmaster did not change the basic tone towards the Jewish students, more emphasis was placed on the fact that the children, from the first year onwards, should be encouraged to be articulate. Especially in the early stages of school, it was important to motivate as many children as possible to express themselves.[113] In the case of Jews, teachers had to pay special attention and 'make an unceasing effort to strengthen the ability of all students to express themselves, to formulate their own thoughts, to express feelings and needs'.[114] A system of student self-government was set up and was particularly attractive to pupils in higher classes, who demonstrated a desire to organize themselves autonomously.[115] Unfortunately, no documents relating to the student self-government have survived.

However, despite these changes, complaints about the Jewish students did not cease, and even intensified after 1935. Cierniak himself was a supporter of Obóz Zjednoczenia Narodowego, a pro-government group founded in February 1937. In March 1939 he ran for the city council on the nationalist list and won a seat in the Grabówka district. His efforts to 'democratize' the school system did not include the Jews as equals.

At the Staszic school, in August 1934 Adolf Zarzycki was replaced as the headmaster by Wojciech Mazurkiewicz, who ran the school until the outbreak of war. Politically, Mazurkiewicz was on the right and openly expressed his suspicion of socialist parties. This was bound to cause tension, to say the least, in a school located in a working-class district. He even explicitly warned that students who attended a summer camp organized by the Polish Socialist Party were 'demoralizing' others by behaving in an 'anti-state and anti-religious way'.[116] With the change of headmaster, Jews were no longer explicitly mentioned in the Staszic school's minutes, with one exception: in February 1939 a Jewish student was expelled for insulting the religious feelings of his Catholic fellow students.[117] Did this mean that under the new headmaster, Mazurkiewicz, no distinction was made between Jewish and non-Jewish children? An examination of the general situation of Jewish students in Tarnów in the late 1930s suggests, rather, a serious worsening of their position.

The Late 1930s and the Harassment of Jewish Students

After Piłsudski's death in 1935 the political situation in Poland shifted dramatically to the right. Not only did the concept of ethno-nationally defined Poland prevail, but antisemitic policies, violent attacks on Jews, exclusion from economic and institutional positions, and open discrimination proliferated. This was also palpable for Polish youth and children in schools. In December 1936 an incident occurred at the Czacki school which was extensively discussed at the teachers' meeting. A Jewish student in the seventh year stayed away from class and instead went for a walk with some girls in Strzelecki Park. A class from the Mikołaj Kopernik primary public school was taking a field trip there at the same time, and an argument broke out. The boy from the Czacki school defended the girls from the verbal attacks of the Kopernik students and reproached the teacher for their bad behaviour. The teacher replied: 'Only a Jew would behave as you are doing.' The boy responded by saying: 'If it weren't for us Jews, you Poles would all perish.'[118] This episode shows how quickly in 1936 ethnic categories were employed to explain behaviour and hostility that had nothing essentially to do with ethnicity. The conflict between a truant student and an offended teacher was articulated in ethnic terms. By the end of the year such ethnic stereotyping was happening on a daily basis, without thinking, in all groups (from children to teachers), in trivial situations, in the park and at school.

Children and young people liked to spend their free time in the park, but in the late 1930s increased hostility towards Jews meant that they no longer dared to frequent it. The incident of the Czacki student should be seen in this context of growing everyday antisemitism. Jacob Gastwirth remembers Strzelecki Park as follows: 'We went there frequently, especially on Saturdays ... Shortly before the war, we were afraid to be beaten up. So we either went in large groups or we didn't go at all.'[119] When Joe Hershkowitz was asked about antisemitism before the war in his interview for the Shoah Foundation, he said he did not initially experience it himself:

Not until the last year or two before the war. You could see it in the park, when you went to the park ... There were certain places we liked to go on Saturday afternoon, we were afraid to go, because mostly the students were the ones who started fights ... We were limited in the places to which we could go ... It was getting scary.[120]

Jewish girls reported hearing antisemitic and sexist comments in the park: 'Precz z Żydami, Żydóweczki z nami [Away with the Jews, Jewish girls stay with us]'.[121]

In 1937, when the problem of antisemitism in the city was openly discussed in the city council, the anti-Jewish attitude in schools was brought up. The city councillors complained that teachers insulted children with expressions such as *ścierwo żydowskie* (Jewish scoundrel).[122] In October 1937 an article appeared in *Tygodnik Żydowski* reporting that the Staszic school planned to introduce 'ghetto benches', similar to those in universities, on which Jewish students would sit separately from their non-Jewish classmates.[123] However, in the minutes of the Staszic teachers' meeting for this period there is no mention of any such proposal. This is precisely the period under Mazurkiewicz when the Jews completely disappeared from the minutes. Markus Ender had spent the first six years of his elementary school education at the Baron Hirsch School, a private Jewish school, and switched to the Staszic school in 1937. In his interview with the Shoah Foundation, he complained of the antisemitic atmosphere there: 'the principal was very antisemite, [a] very big antisemite, so much that we have in our grade, in our class, we have Jews sitting separate and Gentiles sitting separate. This was the only school in the city there is separation between those two, Jews and Gentile.'[124] Although this separation of the student body was not mentioned at all in the minutes of the teachers' meetings, at least two sources record antisemitism at the Staszic school. Here the limitations of the minutes of the schoolteachers' meeting become apparent. They reflect the teachers' view of the students, but only what was acceptable to the school inspector found its way into the minutes. There was a controlling authority, and the authors of the minutes were aware of this.

Conclusion

This chapter has examined the schools of a Polish Jewish town as spaces of interaction between Poles and Jews from the perspective of the teachers. The political struggle over whether Poland was to be a national state or a state of nationalities extended into the classroom. Various developments, some contradictory, took place simultaneously. Thus, in the official language of the minutes, a school could uphold the principle of a civic understanding of belonging and emphasize religious rather than ethno-national differences between the students. At the same time, Jewish students were perceived by the teachers as 'Others', and more so as deficient 'Others'. The minutes of the Staszic school, at least under Adolf Zarzycki, show that the teaching staff were eager to support their pupils, including the Jewish ones. However, from 1932 onwards, national education towards 'Poland' increasingly found its way into the classroom. Civic education now merged with the ethno-national principle of 'being Polish'. By the late 1930s former students describe the new headmaster of the Staszic school as being openly antisemitic.

In November 1939 the first teachers' meeting of the school year was held at the Czacki school. By then the war had begun and Tarnów was occupied by German troops. The headmaster, Józef Cierniak, gave instructions to the committee: history, geography, and singing classes were to be banned immediately. No more badges were to be worn, all maps showing the former border, all historical portraits, all pictures that had anything to do with Polish history were to be removed and kept under lock and key. Political topics were no longer to be discussed in class.[125] And one more thing had changed in the school, which was not explicitly discussed at the meeting: Jewish students—according to the orders of the German occupiers—were no longer allowed to attend. The Czacki school was closed in August 1940, and only reopened in 1945.

Notes

1 *Atlas historii Żydów polskich*, ed. W. Sienkiewicz (Warsaw, 2010), 253.
2 E. Prokop-Janiec, 'Kontakt i konflikt: polsko-żydowska *contact zone*', *Tematy i Konteksty*, 12/7 (2017), 58–72.
3 The figures varied greatly by region: in Lwów, Kraków, and Tarnopol the proportion was 90 per cent or more (see G. Bacon, 'National Revival, Ongoing Acculturation: Jewish Education in Interwar Poland', *Jahrbuch des Simon-Dubnow-Instituts*, 1 (2002), 71–92: 76).
4 See D. Wojtas, *Learning to Become Polish: Education, National Identity and Citizenship in Interwar Poland, 1918–1939* (Cologne, 2009); S. Zloch, *Polnischer Nationalismus: Politik und Gesellschaft zwischen den beiden Weltkriegen* (Cologne, 2010).

5 See E. Prokop-Janiec, *Pogranicze polsko-żydowskie: Topografie i teksty* (Kraków, 2013), 47–75; K. Kijek, *Dzieci modernizmu: Świadomość, kultura i socjalizacja młodzieży żydowskiej w II Rzeczypospolitej* (Wrocław, 2017).
6 *Rocznik statystyczny GUS* (Warsaw, 1939).
7 C. Heller, *On the Edge of Destruction: Jews of Poland between the Two World Wars* (New York, 1977); A. Landau-Czajka, *Syn będzie Lech… : Asymilacja Żydów w Polsce międzywojennej* (Warsaw, 2006); Kijek, *Dzieci modernizmu*.
8 Heller, *On the Edge of Destruction*, 224–7.
9 On 'imagined communities', see B. Anderson, *Imagined Communities: Reflections on the Origin and Spread of Nationalism*, new edn. (London, 2016).
10 Kijek, *Dzieci modernizmu*; id., 'Between a Love of Poland, Symbolic Violence, and Antisemitism: The Idiosyncratic Effects of the State Education System on Young Jews in Interwar Poland', *Polin*, 30 (2018), 237–64: 252–4.
11 See Zloch, *Polnischer Nationalismus*, 213–14.
12 Ibid. 210.
13 On the debates on school policy, see Wojtas, *Learning to Become Polish*.
14 Zloch, *Polnischer Nationalismus*, 214.
15 Until 1932 the school system was not uniform. For the situation in Galicia and the Tarnów district, see Z. Ruta, *Szkolnictwo powszechne w okręgu szkolnym krakowskim w latach 1918–1939* (Wrocław, 1980).
16 Minority Protection Treaty between the Main Allied and Associated Powers and Poland. Versailles, 28 June 1919, art 9.
17 Zloch, *Polnischer Nationalismus*, 248–9.
18 See Heller, *On the Edge of Destruction*, 220.
19 'Rozporządzenie Ministra Wyznań Religijnych i Oświecenia Publicznego, 22.02.1923, w sprawie nauki w szkołach powszechnych, do których uczęszcza młodzież wyznania mojżeszowego', *Dziennik Urzędowy*, 1923, no. 4, pp. 35–7: 36.
20 Bacon, 'National Revival, Ongoing Acculturation', 85; J. Tomaszewski, 'Niepodległa Rzeczpospolita', in id. (ed.), *Najnowsze dzieje Żydów w Polsce* (Warsaw, 1993), 143–272: 243; Heller, *On the Edge of Destruction*, 221.
21 Zloch, *Polnischer Nationalismus*, 251.
22 On parents' motives for sending their children to state schools, see Kijek, 'Between a Love of Poland, Symbolic Violence, and Antisemitism', 242–3.
23 See Bacon, 'National Revival, Ongoing Acculturation', 86–9; Prokop-Janiec *Pogranicze polsko-żydowskie*, 56.
24 University of Southern California Shoah Foundation, Los Angeles, Visual History Archive (hereafter VHA), interview 7896: Gizela Fudem (23 Oct. 1995; Pol.); see also interview 7291: Chana Bloch (1 Oct. 1995; Eng.).
25 See the class registers of Saint Jadwiga School (Archiwum Narodowe w Krakowie Oddział w Tarnowie (hereafter ANKOT), 33/373: Szkoła Powszechna im. Królowej Jadwigi w Tarnowie (1911–43)).
26 Ruta, *Szkolnictwo powszechne w okręgu szkolnym krakowskim*, 558.
27 ANKOT, 33/363/0/-/21: Metryka szkolna (1921–34).
28 Ruta, *Szkolnictwo powszechne w okręgu szkolnym krakowskim*, 558; on the proportion of Jewish pupils, see ANKOT, 33/363/0/-/3: Księgi Protokołów Rady Pedagogicznej [Czacki school] (1930–49).

29 1935/6: 422 pupils, of whom 48 per cent were Jewish; 1938/9: 412 pupils, of whom 33 per cent were Jewish children (ANKOT 33/370/0/-/34–39: Księgi ocen (1935–1940)).
30 Księgi Protokołów Rady Pedagogicznej [Czacki school] (1930–49), 30 Mar. 1936; 22 Mar., 3 Apr. 1937 (fos. 167, 202–3).
31 Księgi Protokołów Rady Pedagogicznej [Czacki school] (1930–49), 22 Mar., 3 Apr., 15 June 1937; 17 Dec. 1938 (fos. 202–3, 209, 286–7).
32 Księgi Protokołów Rady Pedagogicznej [Czacki school] (1930–49), 24 Oct. 1933 (fo. 82).
33 Księgi Protokołów Rady Pedagogicznej [Czacki school] (1930–49), 20 Apr. 1931 (fo. 30).
34 Księgi Protokołów Rady Pedagogicznej [Czacki school] (1930–49), 6 May 1931 (fo. 30).
35 Księgi Protokołów Rady Pedagogicznej [Czacki school] (1930–49), 31 Mar. 1938 (fo. 245).
36 Księgi Protokołów Rady Pedagogicznej [Czacki school] (1930–49), 22 June 1932 (fo. 43).
37 Księgi Protokołów Rady Pedagogicznej [Czacki school] (1930–49), 16 Dec, 1932 (fo. 61).
38 'Rozporządzenie Ministra Wyznań Religijnych i Oświecenia Publicznego, 22.02.1923', 37.
39 Księgi Protokołów Rady Pedagogicznej [Czacki school] (1930–49), 31 Mar. 1938 (fo. 245).
40 Księgi Protokołów Rady Pedagogicznej [Czacki school] (1930–49), 3 Sept. 1937 (fo. 223).
41 Księgi Protokołów Rady Pedagogicznej [Czacki school] (1930–49), 20 Apr., 22 June 1931; 26 Mar. 1934; 30 Mar., 18 Dec. 1936; 31 Mar. 1938; 24 Feb. 1939 (fos. 17–19, 32, 102–3, 162–3, 192, 194–5, 259, 303).
42 Księgi Protokołów Rady Pedagogicznej [Czacki school] (1930–49), 20 Apr., 22 June 1931 (fos. 17, 32).
43 Księgi Protokołów Rady Pedagogicznej [Czacki school] (1930–49), 20 Apr. 1931 (fos. 17–18).
44 Księgi Protokołów Rady Pedagogicznej [Czacki school] (1930–49), 10 Dec. 1935; 30 Mar., 18 Dec. 1936 21 Oct 1937 (fos. 165, 192–5, 226).
45 Księgi Protokołów Rady Pedagogicznej [Czacki school] (1930–49), 24 Apr. 1939 (fo. 306).
46 Księgi Protokołów Rady Pedagogicznej [Czacki school] (1930–49), 18 Dec. 1936 (fo. 191).
47 Ibid. (fo. 195).
48 Ibid. (fo. 192).
49 Księgi Protokołów Rady Pedagogicznej [Czacki school] (1930–49), 2 Mar. 1934 (fos. 102–3).
50 Księgi Protokołów Rady Pedagogicznej [Czacki school] (1930–49), 10 Dec. 1935 (fo. 152).
51 ANKOT, 33/370/0/-/2: Księgi Protokołów Rady Pedagogicznej [Staszic school] (1925–35), 30 Oct. 1930 (fo. 122); see also 4 Sept. 1928; 16 Apr. 1932 (fos. 73, 151–2).
52 Księgi Protokołów Rady Pedagogicznej [Staszic school] (1925–35), 24 Jan. 1931; 1 Apr. 1933 (fos. 128–9, 177).
53 Księgi Protokołów Rady Pedagogicznej [Staszic school] (1925–35), 1 Apr. 1933; 7 June 1935 (fos. 177, 257).
54 Księgi Protokołów Rady Pedagogicznej [Staszic school] (1925–35), 10 Nov. 1926 (fo. 23).
55 Księgi Protokołów Rady Pedagogicznej [Staszic school] (1925–35), 5 Nov. 1925 (fo. 3).
56 Księgi Protokołów Rady Pedagogicznej [Staszic school] (1925–35), 21 Oct. 1933 (fo. 198).
57 Księgi Protokołów Rady Pedagogicznej [Staszic school] (1925–35), 10 Nov. 1927 (fos. 46–7).
58 Księgi Protokołów Rady Pedagogicznej [Staszic school] (1925–35), 22 June 1931 (fo. 134).
59 Księgi Protokołów Rady Pedagogicznej [Staszic school] (1925–35), 19 Nov. 1932 (fo. 168).
60 Księgi Protokołów Rady Pedagogicznej [Staszic school] (1925–35), 26 Jan. 1929 (fo. 81).
61 Księgi Protokołów Rady Pedagogicznej [Staszic school] (1925–35), 21 Oct. 1933 (fo. 199).

62 Księgi Protokołów Rady Pedagogicznej [Staszic school] (1925–35), 30 Oct 1930 (fo. 123).
63 Księgi Protokołów Rady Pedagogicznej [Staszic school] (1925–35), 19 Dec. 1928 (fo. 73).
64 Księgi Protokołów Rady Pedagogicznej [Staszic school] (1925–35), 16 Dec. 1933 (fo. 210).
65 This was S. Szober, C. Niewiadomska, and C. Bogucka, *Nauka pisowni we wzorach i ćwiczeniach: Zeszyt 1 B* (Warsaw, 1929); Księgi Protokołów Rady Pedagogicznej [Staszic school] (1925–35), 15 Sept. 1931 (fo. 140); see also 21 Nov. 1931 (fo. 144).
66 Księgi Protokołów Rady Pedagogicznej [Staszic school] (1925–35), 4 Sept. 1928 (fo. 68b).
67 Księgi Protokołów Rady Pedagogicznej [Staszic school] (1925–35), 19 Dec. 1929 (fo. 100).
68 Księgi Protokołów Rady Pedagogicznej [Staszic school] (1925–35), 31 Mar. 1930 (fo. 104).
69 Księgi Protokołów Rady Pedagogicznej [Staszic school] (1925–35), 20 Dec. 1926 (fo. 27).
70 Księgi Protokołów Rady Pedagogicznej [Staszic school] (1925–35), 30 June 1930 (fo. 110).
71 Księgi Protokołów Rady Pedagogicznej [Staszic school] (1925–35), 28 Mar. 1931 (fos. 130–1).
72 Księgi Protokołów Rady Pedagogicznej [Staszic school] (1925–35), 16 Apr. 1932 (fo. 153).
73 Księgi Protokołów Rady Pedagogicznej [Czacki school] (1930–49), 10 Mar. 1930 (fo. 92).
74 Księgi Protokołów Rady Pedagogicznej [Czacki school] (1930–49), 15 June 1937 (fos. 211–19); ANKOT, 33/363/0/-/55: Kronika Szkoły (1913–76), 1934/5 (fo. 22).
75 Wojtas, *Learning to Become Polish*, 110–82.
76 Księgi Protokołów Rady Pedagogicznej [Czacki school] (1930–49), 15 Nov. 1929; 25 Jan. 1930 (fos. 84–5).
77 Księgi Protokołów Rady Pedagogicznej [Czacki school] (1930–49), 23 Sept. 1933 (fo. 75).
78 Księgi Protokołów Rady Pedagogicznej [Czacki school] (1930–49), 4 June 1934 (fo. 115).
79 *Wytyczne dla autorów programów szkół ogólnokształcących: Szkoła powszechna III stopnia i gimnazjum* (Warsaw, 1932); see Wojtas, *Learning to Become Polish*, 148–63.
80 See Księgi Protokołów Rady Pedagogicznej [Staszic school] (1925–35), 10 Nov. 1926; 15 Feb., 13 Sept. 1932 (fos. 22, 147, 162).
81 Księgi Protokołów Rady Pedagogicznej [Staszic school] (1925–35), 31 Mar. 1930 (fo. 109).
82 Księgi Protokołów Rady Pedagogicznej [Staszic school] (1925–35), 15 Sept. 1931 (fo. 139).
83 Księgi Protokołów Rady Pedagogicznej [Staszic school] (1925–35), 24 Mar. 1934 (fo. 221).
84 Księgi Protokołów Rady Pedagogicznej [Staszic school] (1925–35), 15 Feb. 1932 (fo. 148).
85 Księgi Protokołów Rady Pedagogicznej [Staszic school] (1925–35), 13 Sept. 1932 (fo. 162).
86 See Księgi Protokołów Rady Pedagogicznej [Staszic school] (1925–35), 13 Sept. 1932; 1 Apr. 1933 (fos. 162, 180).
87 Księgi Protokołów Rady Pedagogicznej [Staszic school] (1925–35), 29 Oct. 1932 (fos. 163–4).
88 Heller, *On the Edge of Destruction*, 225.
89 Kijek, 'Between a Love of Poland, Symbolic Violence, and Antisemitism', 252–3.
90 VHA, interview 1712: William Celnik (24 Mar. 1995; Eng.).
91 Księgi Protokołów Rady Pedagogicznej [Czacki school] (1930–49), 22 June 1932 (fo. 43).
92 Księgi Protokołów Rady Pedagogicznej [Czacki school] (1930–49), 24 Oct. 1933 (fo. 82).
93 Bacon, 'National Revival, Ongoing Acculturation', 87; on Jewish religious education in public schools, see S. Martin, 'Between Church and State: Jewish Religious Instruction in Public Schools in the Second Polish Republic', *Polin*, 30 (2018), 265–82.
94 Księgi Protokołów Rady Pedagogicznej [Staszic school] (1925–35), 6 Sept. 1927 (fo. 42).
95 Bacon, 'National Revival, Ongoing Acculturation', 87.

96 Ibid. 86.
97 *Sprawozdanie Dyrekcji Państwowego Gimnazjum im. Kazimierza Brodzińskiego w Tarnowie za rok 1930–1931* (Tarnów, 1931), 18.
98 Ibid. 17–18.
99 Ibid. 17.
100 Księgi Protokołów Rady Pedagogicznej [Czacki school] (1930–49), 23 Jan. 1926 (fo. 15).
101 VHA, interview 7329: Ludwik Garmada (5 Dec. 1995; Pol.).
102 Księgi Protokołów Rady Pedagogicznej [Czacki school] (1930–49), 7 Oct., 17 Dec. 1938 (fos. 273, 286–7).
103 Ludwik Garmada, VHA interview.
104 Księgi Protokołów Rady Pedagogicznej [Staszic school] (1925–35), 11 May 1926 (fo. 12).
105 Księgi Protokołów Rady Pedagogicznej [Staszic school] (1925–35), 9 Jan. 1928 (fo. 49).
106 Ibid. (fo. 50).
107 Księgi Protokołów Rady Pedagogicznej [Staszic school] (1925–35), 28 Mar. 1931 (fo. 131).
108 Księgi Protokołów Rady Pedagogicznej [Staszic school] (1925–35), 9 Jan. 1927 (fo. 31).
109 Ibid.
110 Księgi Protokołów Rady Pedagogicznej [Czacki school] (1930–49), 26 Mar. 1934 (fos. 100–1).
111 Ibid.
112 The school subscribed to *Śpiew w Szkole*, *Wychowanie Fizyczne*, *Ruch Pedagogiczny*, and *Praca Szkolna* (Księgi Protokołów Rady Pedagogicznej [Czacki school] (1930–49), 26 Sept. 1936 (fo. 187)).
113 Księgi Protokołów Rady Pedagogicznej [Czacki school] (1930–49), 12 June 1936 (fos. 171–2).
114 Księgi Protokołów Rady Pedagogicznej [Czacki school] (1930–49), 24 Feb. 1939 (fo. 303).
115 Ibid. (fos. 306–8).
116 ANKOT, 33/370/0/-/3: Księgi Protokołów Rady Pedagogicznej [Staszic school] (1935–1950), 13 June 1938 (fos. 58–9).
117 Księgi Protokołów Rady Pedagogicznej [Staszic school] (1935–1950), 23 Feb. 1939 (fo. 68).
118 Księgi Protokołów Rady Pedagogicznej [Czacki school] (1930–49), 18 Dec. 1936 (fo. 192).
119 VHA, interview 19034: Jacob Gastwirth (29 Aug. 1996; Eng.).
120 VHA, interview 8723: Joe Hershkowitz (13 Nov. 1995; Eng.).
121 VHA, interview 5343: Yetta Brand (8 Sept. 1995; Eng.); see also I. Burstein (dir.), *Unfinished Talk: The Jewish Community of Tarnow*, documentary (Nathan Beyrak, 1988).
122 ANKOT 33/1c, fos. 67–8: Dyskusja szczegółowa nad preliminarzem budżetowym, 22 Mar. 1937.
123 'Posiedzenie Rady Miejskiej', *Tygodnik Żydowski*, 15 Oct. 1937, pp. 1–2.
124 VHA, interview 43669: Markus Ender (23 July 1998; Eng.).
125 Księgi Protokołów Rady Pedagogicznej [Czacki school] (1930–49), 11 Nov. 1939 (fos. 326–39).

Working Children and Young People as Seen by Contributors to *Mały Przegląd*

ANNA LANDAU-CZAJKA

The letters sent to *Mały Przegląd*, the popular Polish-language supplement of the Jewish daily *Nasz Przegląd* intended for young people and published in Warsaw from the second half of the 1920s, provide a unique picture of Jewish child labour at this time. Child contributors give a largely hostile picture of the effect of work on their lives. They describe the negative impact that such labour, both in their homes and outside, had on their ability to pursue long-term education, and say how they were compelled to assume parental duties in relation to younger siblings. Perceiving their situation as an injustice, they decry their lack of opportunity. Attitudes changed in the 1930s, when adolescents begin to express anger at being unable to attend secondary school. A large number of the letters express regret for what their authors see as a lost childhood, although an exception is made for work in Palestine or in preparation for leaving Poland.

Introduction

Mały Przegląd (Warsaw, 1926–39), the Friday supplement to the Polish-language *Nasz Przegląd*, was the only publication of its type in Poland.[1] It was aimed at young Jewish readers and, apart from its earliest issues, almost exclusively published pieces written by its readers. Its editorial board was also composed of readers of the paper. Janusz Korczak (Henryk Goldszmit), its founder and first editor-in-chief, expected letters on the daily life, school, home, friends, and personal observations of its readers, and he also required that they write only the truth.[2] As a result, *Mały Przegląd* is an invaluable source for studying the youngest generation in the Second Polish Republic—mainly Jewish but also some Poles who had no links with the Jewish community—although it was not the only paper in interwar Poland geared towards Jewish children.[3] The pieces published in *Mały Przegląd* were subjective accounts written not by journalists but by children and young people. Therefore, they are not always factually accurate and do not contain certain details that might be expected: a young person might complain about a boring job without mentioning what they actually did; note that they dropped out of school without mentioning at what stage; or describe a trip without mentioning where they actually went; and so on.

Most of the pieces also lack context: the writers' names are not given, nor are any details of their actual age, social background, or family situation. They were published anonymously, giving only a name or nom de plume and a street, for writers from Warsaw, or a town in other cases. Contributions also came from further afield (see Figure 1). Occasionally the age of the writer was given, or their school year.

Many pieces were written under the influence of recent experiences and are filled with emotion. As a rule, they dealt with current events, rarely referring to more distant experiences. Pieces written by regular contributors tended to be longer but were not reflections on personal experiences.

Mały Przegląd appeared for fifteen years, and during that time its core concept—with the exception of its commitment to being written and edited by its readers—evolved, as did its editorial board. After Korczak's departure in 1930 and his replacement by Igor Newerly, *Mały Przegląd* gradually became directed more at adolescents, devoting relatively little space to its youngest readers. This too changed, and in 1936, at a general meeting with Korczak himself present, it was decided to return to being a publication primarily for children. Yet in its final years *Mały Przegląd* bore little resemblance to how it looked when Korczak was editor. There were far more long reports, articles, and memoirs, while letters were relegated to a single section, and sometimes only one long letter on personal matters was published. The greatest number of pieces on working young people thus appeared in the first half of the 1930s, especially at the start of the Great Depression, when many parents lost their jobs and young people were struggling to find work. If a lot of letters were received, they would be included a special section called 'Lives of Young Working People'. However, irrespective of the period and the paper's vision, young workers, trades-people, and apprentices probably found very little in the publication about or for them.

In November 1935 *Mały Przegląd* published a very interesting critical piece by M.H., responding to a proposal by a female reader that the paper should officially transform itself into a publication for schoolchildren, since there was almost nothing in it written by young people in employment. In response to the original letter, the editors had justified themselves by stating that this was neither their intention nor their fault: they simply received few letters from such readers. However, M.H. strongly maintained that this was not the case. A lack of letters was not the problem; rather, it was the selection of subjects and an unwillingness to publish letters from young people who were working, as opposed to studying. He argued that perhaps *Mały Przegląd* did not want to print letters that were too pessimistic and that it was definitely opposed to publishing 'ideological letters'. Meanwhile young workers, especially during the Depression, did not have the 'balanced' opinions that the editors liked and were attached to their, often deeply held, right- or left-wing views. 'Can such young people, convinced that only their ideas are correct, publish in a publication such as *Mały Przegląd* which stresses its freedom from ideology?'[4] There was no doubt, at least in his mind, that contributions from young working people were in some way being censored. Not everything could be published in the paper, which was after all simply a supplement to *Nasz Przegląd* and was not as fully open to every opinion as it maintained. It is difficult to establish unambiguously what the truth was, but, taking into account that letters were trimmed or altered, and that more than one contributor complained that too strong a left-wing ideology was unwelcome, M.H. was correct, at least in part. This is doubtless one of the reasons why there was a dearth of information on working young people.

Figure 1 Geographical distribution of contributors to *Mały Przegląd*
Mały Przegląd, 12 Oct. 1934, p. 1

There is, however, another, no less important, reason: *Nasz Przegląd* was not just a Polish-language publication with Zionist sympathies[5] but was aimed at people who were acculturated and educated, more for readers from the middle class than for the poor. Among the readers of *Mały Przegląd*, for the most part residents of Warsaw,[6] there were almost none from Orthodox or even very traditional families.[7] In order to write a letter to *Mały Przegląd*, one not only needed the money for an envelope and a stamp (not all that common among the poorest members of the Jewish community) but one also had to know Polish in order to read the paper and to be able to write a letter in that language.[8] Korczak rejected the idea of printing letters in languages other than Polish, although, as he himself wrote, many readers had requested this: for example, proposing the publication of letters in Yiddish, but using Latin letters.[9] He replied: 'It has recently been suggested to the editor of *Mały Przegląd* that in addition to Polish we should publish in Yiddish, Hebrew, Esperanto, and now even in French. We cannot turn the paper into a tower of Babel.'[10] Furthermore, the contributors were for the most part either children from acculturated families or who went to Polish schools and had intellectual ambitions. They dreamed more of education and access to university than of going out to work at an early age.

The paper's archive went up in flames during the Second World War, and the letters themselves have not survived. Most of the contributors also almost certainly perished. What remains is what was published in Mały Przegląd. The paper did not impose a rigid editorial line, although analysis of its contents, including the letters it published expressing controversial views, shows clearly that an editorial policy did exist: not only in the choice of subjects for competitions or topics for discussion but also in the selection of letters and the changes that were made to them. Initially, in 1926 and 1927, Korczak did sometimes comment on a letter, but later they were printed without any editorial remarks. However, there can be no doubt that the letters were not only edited and mistakes corrected, but that the contents themselves were sometimes modified, and what appeared in print was not necessarily a faithful reflection of the writers' views. Occasionally the same letter was printed more than once, sometimes in a longer form, sometimes a shorter one. Sometimes the main thrust of each version was quite different. Complaints by children about their letters being altered were also published. Not all of the hundreds of letters sent in were published, although it is not known whether those that reflected *Nasz Przegląd*'s Zionist sympathies were given preferential treatment. It was often claimed that there was no censorship, that the decision whether to publish or reject a piece lay with the editorial board, and that what was printed was what contributors had sent in,[11] but it is not known whether this applied only to longer articles or to letters to the editor as well.[12]

Children and young people working is a very complex subject. In the Second Polish Republic, paid employment was allowed from the age of 15, although this prohibition was not strictly enforced, particularly since compulsory schooling ended a year earlier.[13] Many families' financial situation was such that going out to work was essential not just for young people but also for children, even if it was against the law. Very often nannies and 'maids-of-all-work' were younger than 15. The neighbours' 14-year-old servant, who took care of the house and of two small children, was, as one correspondent wrote, 'a very small and a very poor girl. She has no mother and is constantly telling me just how happy she was when her dear mother was still alive.'[14]

Key here is the definition of 'work'. Help around the house, or even assuming most of the domestic responsibilities, is not the same as work outside the house. In the first case often very small children were involved, in the second case, mainly older children and adolescents. However, both involved monotonous daily tasks and often too much responsibility, and had similar consequences: dropping out of full-time education and feeling that life was meaningless. This was mentioned largely by children in towns; it was less of an issue in the country.

Children Working

Children working and dropping out of, or being withdrawn from, school was always seen in a negative light by the youthful contributors. This was true of those who wrote about their own conditions and of those who had only observed such situations. During the first years of *Mały Przegląd*'s existence it carried reports by adults which included interviews with children who were working. Their work was the result of circumstances, such as those of 10-year-old Jankiel (Janek), who sold sweets after school because his father could no longer work following an accident. He and his elder brother would stand for whole afternoons, whatever the weather, in front of a cinema in Warsaw selling chocolates. Jankiel had just started Year 1 and in the morning was too tired to learn, which distressed him dreadfully. His elder brother had also lost an opportunity to improve his situation: he had been apprenticed to a shoemaker, but had had to abandon it. Selling sweets was risky, because the police chased them, dragged them down to the police station, and at best took a bribe. The boy dreamed of finishing five years of school and of becoming a tailor, but did not feel that he would achieve his goals.[15] The article was written from the point of view of an adult, deeply sympathizing with the child (as did many of his adult customers), but with no commentary, even on the illegality of employing children younger than 15.

Most dramatic were the letters written by the youngest children, who had not even had the opportunity to finish compulsory primary school since they had been needed at home, or had had to go out to earn money. In the 1920s children often finished their schooling after four or five years in order to start earning. In 1927 a letter from a 12-year-old was published, who, orphaned of her father, had had to stay at home after finishing Year 2 in order to bring up her younger siblings and to help in the home. The impossibility of continuing her education was for her a greater tragedy than poverty or even the loss of her father.[16] Another contributor, Ewa, 'went out to work after finishing four years and the only solace in her life is a book and the unsullied beauty of nature'.[17] Unfortunately, no reason is given why she had to drop out of school or where she obtained her books. Such letters testify to the fact that school attendance was poorly enforced in the 1920s and no institutions were concerned with children not attending school. Children were not afraid to write about this and did not see it as breaking the law, while the editors, even when Korczak was in charge, did not react to this kind of information with its obvious implication that the law was being broken.

Children also helped their parents at work, usually in a shop, often during the school holidays. Those contributors who did not have to drop out of school in order to work in the family business were usually proud of the fact; those who did saw it as cruelty and injustice. A pupil in Year 6 asked the editors for advice: he was a good pupil, but his parents wanted to take him out of school not because they were short of money but because they needed him to work in their shop, which they felt was not bringing in enough. 'I need to go to school', wrote the boy. He was considering running away from home, but he did not want to hurt his parents, he only wanted to convince them; and thus he had turned to *Mały Przegląd*.[18] However, given that *Mały Przegląd* at that time did not print replies, it is not known whether they gave him any advice.

At the start of the 1930s *Mały Przegląd* published several letters on the subject of children working, children who ought still to have been in school. The contributors felt, on the one hand, that child labour should be illegal; on the other, they understood the need for it and were angry that the police pursued working children if their parents had no money and there was nothing else they could do except try to earn some.[19]

A typical example is a letter from a girl, the eldest in her family. While the father had been alive, her parents had taken care of her, she had had no domestic obligations and had even received presents. After her father's death, new responsibilities were imposed on her: not only was there no one taking care of her, but after school she had to take care of her younger sister and the house.[20] This motif of having suddenly to grow up after the death of a parent appeared very frequently on the pages of *Mały Przegląd*. It affected the oldest children in a family and only children, irrespective of age and sex (although more often girls than boys). However, towards the end of the 1930s, even in such difficult circumstances, children, as far as can be judged from the letters published in *Mały Przegląd*, continued to go to school. There were far fewer letters from children who had been withdrawn from primary school and sent out to work, which did not mean, however, that such things did not happen. According to one letter:

Szlamek works at the carpenter's for over twelve hours a day. He was pulled out of Year 4. He dreams about studying, about school and about his friends. If only God were to take pity on him and send him back to school, where one forgets about everything, about home, about one's parents, one's siblings, about the endlessly annoyed master craftsman. That would be bliss![21]

The discussion about children working was not limited to Poland. The need for young children to contribute to the family income was also perceived as a serious problem by contributors living in Palestine. In one letter a girl from Tel Aviv described a little newspaper seller whom she had seen on the streets. He was small, wearing torn shoes, frozen. He lived in a single room with his father, mother, and two siblings, two others having died.

I forgot about the most important tenant, who had been filling all the free space in that cramped room—poverty. It is claimed that all are doing well in Palestine but anyone who thinks that would be making a big mistake. While the sort of poverty that exists in Poland and other countries is not in evidence, and no one here is starving, even here there are exploited people, reminiscent of the poor worker in Poland.[22]

The objection to children being compelled to go out to work thus did not depend on location and was always seen as an injustice, depriving the very youngest of their childhood and exploiting them. However, it is difficult to decide whether this account was not somewhat exaggerated. Frozen, working children constantly appear in accounts from Poland. It would appear that the cliché of poverty, hunger, and cold has here been rather reflexively used when referring to the far warmer climate of Palestine.

However, what is striking is the fact that the youngest children saw not only full-time work or helping their parents at work as injustice and exploitation but also carrying out domestic chores, which were often described as excessive. A great many children were unhappy at the fact that they had to take care of their younger siblings in their free time. One wrote: 'My little brother is 5 years old, my youngest sister and brother are 3 years old each and they bother me the most. When I want to sleep in the morning, as early as 6 o'clock they wake me up; Miecio is crying that he would like a piece of cake and Wandzia some pears.'[23]

The children emphasized that this obligation was too onerous for them, which might, paradoxically, prove that it was not that widespread, at least among the contributors to *Mały Przegląd*. It was presented not as a normal part of their childhood but as an exceptional demand on the part of their parents. Some of their parents, doubtless the wealthier ones, also clearly did not consider looking after younger siblings a normal task. 'Rózia is 7 and teaches Frania, who is 6, for which Frania's mummy pays 50 grosze a month.'[24] Not an enormous sum but one that points to the 'unusual' task of educating a younger sister.

Although care of younger children was not only time-consuming but also stressful for children, complaints focused not so much on the associated responsibility as on having to justify how they carried out the obligation of childcare. Older children were responsible for the younger children's behaviour, but were not, in fact, the ones bringing them up. 'The younger children constantly torment our lives. If my little sister kicks up a fuss, they immediately say: "That's your doing, she learned that from you." If the little fellow doesn't want to eat, immediately there are accusations: "See what you've taught him." How are we to blame?'[25]

Demanding excessive help at home was seen by the contributors to *Mały Przegląd* as an injustice that parents were inflicting on their children. In one letter a little girl, who had been accepted into the Dom Sierot orphanage, decidedly preferred it to her own home: 'At home I had too much work to do, I scrubbed the floors, I peeled the potatoes, while here we don't have that much work: I only have to clean under the stoves with a small brush every day.'[26]

An older contributor from Warsaw, describing the fate of poor families, emphasized in particular daughters having to help at home at the expense of their schooling:

Ten-year-old girls already work at home. They often have to leave school. Later the headmistress says there is no room for such lazy children. Initially the mother is anxious, then she thinks: 'Good, at least I'll have her at home all day long. She wouldn't have become a doctor anyway. What's the point of all that effort?' Thereafter the little girl completely takes over the running of the household.[27]

Girls were more likely than boys to be obliged to assume the burden of running the household and taking care of the smaller children. This reflects the belief that such tasks were more suited to girls and that education was not essential in their case. A young woman was to get married, therefore domestic skills were more valuable than finishing school. Boys had to earn money and thus had to master a trade.

However, it was not only physical work that contributors to *Mały Przegląd* saw as unsuitable for children. One article described the life of a 13-year-old hasidic boy who was exceptionally highly valued by his community and spent his whole day either studying or visiting people's houses. 'It crosses no one's mind that he ought to be protected from a serious nervous collapse. Not a bit of it; they wear out the boy day and night. They shower him with questions, he quotes and explains for them. He visits the rabbis and has complicated discussions with them.'[28] The writer claimed with sorrow that he was loved by the neighbours and hasidim from other towns and that everyone wanted to invite him round to offer him food and listen to him, but no one bothered about his physical or mental well-being. 'What will be your fate, Alteru, child of Jewish poverty? Will you finally get sick from overtaxing your brain and from an excess of early experiences? Or will they one day turn you into a legend: "A long, long time ago lived the great Rabbi Alteru, wealthy and happy"?'[29] The writer was in no doubt that he was not describing a religious genius but an abused child, denied school and typical childish occupations. This was no miracle-working rabbi but a child deprived of his childhood, a victim of religious fanaticism.

Contributors to *Mały Przegląd* were interested only in the problems of Jewish children, which automatically meant that in Poland they were almost exclusively children living in urban areas. Both in Poland and in Palestine, those writing about the work of Jewish children in the countryside did so in the context of *hakhsharot* or kibbutzim, that is, those farms that were preparing Jews to work in the Land of Israel, never on normal farms. On the kibbutzim, work was always seen as worthy of praise and was never excessive, nor was it at the expense of schoolwork.

Young People

During the 1920s and even later young people working were not seen as anything out of the ordinary. Not all youngsters either wanted to or were able to stay at school after the end of compulsory schooling at 14, and for them work was the only option.[30] It was their working conditions, not their age, that concerned the contributors to *Mały Przegląd*. One wrote: 'Pay . . . is seen as charity. On payday a boy like that comes last. The money, which he receives honestly, is not enough to support him, the results of which are pitiful. Employers should treat youngsters working for them better, take care of their health and look to their needs.'[31]

The pages of *Mały Przegląd* reveal how during the 1930s attitudes to work by young children were changing. A growing number of the working young were clearly frustrated by their inability to continue on to secondary school, just as in the 1920s it had been children who had been unable to finish primary school who expressed their discontent. Sufficient numbers of places in primary schools and a change in social attitudes resulted in young people beginning to see completing six or seven years as the absolute norm, and their ambitions now rose. Secondary school or trade school were no longer just dreams but something to which they felt they had a right. When Lejzor from Gęsia Street in Warsaw in 1937 entitled part of his report 'No School', he was no longer writing about children in employment, but about 15- or 16-year-olds who had completed seven years of schooling and had been unable to continue.[32]

In 1937, a very poor girl whose parents were unemployed and could not afford to eat, and who earned money to go to school and to pay the admissions fee by collecting bottles, was worried that after she had completed seven years of school her mother would not want to send her to trade school.[33] Another girl, who had had to assist her father in the shop two years before her school-leaving examination, was deeply unhappy, not that she would fail the examination (she had a tutor and was trying to prepare for the examination), but that her school friends knew much more than she did.[34]

It was observed with growing regularity that education was a prerequisite not only for finding a better job but for finding any job at all, and continuing schooling provided better prospects than unqualified paid work. There were almost no letters in which young people rejoiced at ending their schooling and at the opportunity to earn money working. Fourteen-year-olds finishing primary school had no chance of rewarding, well-paid, and legal work. 'Whenever I think that I shan't see school anymore, I'm filled with fear. Oh, if only I could choose between school and work! If only I could decide my own fate.'[35] In the same issue another female Year 7 graduate described the problems that young people leaving school had finding a job:

Everywhere they are looking for people with education and experience and I have neither education nor experience. After all I've only completed seven years. What did they give me? Have they taught me how to live, or some trade? No. I have been shown how to calculate angles and triangles, I have been told who lived 200, 500, even 1,000 years ago, and I have been taught to read, write, and count. That is too little, decidedly too little.[36]

Additionally, many employers were unwilling to break the law and hire children younger than 15.[37]

However, a few contributors, all young boys, wrote to *Mały Przegląd* to say they were happy at the thought of leaving school, at least initially. A pupil in Year 5 at secondary school, whose parents were no longer able to pay the fees, did not much protest at leaving school, and boasted to his friends that he was starting a new life:

To have some money! To go to the cinema! To cock a snook at algebra and schoolmasters! . . . I go to the beach in the pleasant knowledge that my friends are in school 'swotting' their German until steam comes out of their ears, trembling before an assignment and the end of the school year, while I'm just having a good yawn and sunning myself.[38]

But the pleasure lasted only a short time: after the holidays he had to start work in a warehouse, and it turned out that his life had changed completely. He became active in the trade union and saw his friends far less frequently. Above all, after the death of his father he became the family's breadwinner. Subsequently he lost his job, and only then did he realize that, without schooling, he had no qualifications and that independent reading was not the same as systematic study, and he greatly lamented his lost opportunities.

During the Great Depression between 1930 and 1935, *Mały Przegląd* received letters from many young people who hated their work but at the same time were afraid of losing it. A young boy, a secondary-school graduate, after much searching found a rather miserable position. On the one hand, he was unhappy at having to carry out tasks far beneath his qualifications; on the other, he was glad that he had a job at all. 'The life of a general dogsbody: cleaner of spittoons, general cleaner, postman and delivery boy, waiter at lunch. I was ashamed and embarrassed, yet, remembering the recent past, I willingly devoted myself to the job. The pay was low . . . Work had become a habit, even an addiction.'[39] Another boy describing his search for work and potential employers' demands wrote: 'young people talk a lot about exploitation; what can one do though, if, despite unions and appropriate laws, one cannot find work?'[40]

The motif of a wasted childhood, adolescence, or even a whole life was a recurring theme. Pola, a seamstress, 'had her childhood miserably shortened. Life has laid its heavy hand on her head and said "come". "Come", said the machine, "I shall teach you mindlessness and resignation."'[41]

Letters printed in the 'Lives of Young Working People' section contain hardly any mention of job satisfaction apart from the pleasure of being able to contribute to household expenses. A young boy, working as a nightwatchman at a yard, wrote in a letter under the memorable title 'Youth behind Bars': 'At times I am close to despair. Why do I have to sit in a three-room facility? Why could I not attend evening classes? But that's how it is. I tell myself, if I don't earn money how shall I support myself?'[42] An 'errand boy' from a shoe shop saw his work and future in a similarly hopeless fashion. His boss was demanding and unpleasant, and the sales staff (among whom he had relatives) treated him badly.[43] Many contributors had a deep sense of the hopelessness of their fate; furthermore, they did not believe it could change—hard work; lack of schooling, free time, and money; isolation from those who lived better in the centre of the town was not just their present, but, they were convinced, it was their future too. As a young worker in a factory in Białystok that dyed cloth wrote: 'tomorrow, the day after tomorrow, and always will be the same'.[44]

Those contributors (admittedly few in number) whose friends were also working were less likely to feel humiliated by their circumstances and saw things somewhat less pessimistically. They were not happy with their lot, but they were not ashamed of it. In their case it was working conditions and pay rather than the actual fact of working that aroused dissatisfaction. In 1930 an article by Froim—who had first worked in a jeweller's shop and then at a printer's, and who had been attending evening classes—was published. Froim needed to earn money, so he did not complain at the idea of work, but the issue was that he was being exploited; while on probation he had not been paid, and everything indicated that after a month or six weeks of unpaid 'on-the-job training' employers simply let people go and took on the next free worker.[45] A girl from a tailor's shop complained that the eight-hour day was not observed and that she worked longer hours.[46] Benek, who worked in a women's clothing store, complained that the owner's wife continually required services from him and that he had learned nothing; the designer gave him a scrap of cloth and told him to sew without showing him much more. Furthermore, he was earning less than his friends. In addition, such work, unlike school, simply dumbed him down and did not encourage development. In his view, 'when a man runs down a hill, once he is at the bottom, for a time he keeps on running until he stops. That's what happened to me. After leaving school I still thought that I was a pupil, that I was moving forwards, until I noticed that I was in a rut.'[47]

There can be no doubt that for many young workers the problem was not the work itself, but the awareness of the lack of prospects. As soon as such prospects appeared, the work also became more interesting. A young girl forced for lack of money to seek employment with a seamstress was initially ashamed of her work. This passed when she found a school she could attend: 'I am now only too happy to work; I leave home at nine, work till three with a lunch break, then again till six. From my workplace I go to an evening class for workers . . . I want to continue my studies; therefore, I work with redoubled energy in order to earn and save up for further education.'[48]

Analysis of the letters sent in by young workers produces a reasonably clear pattern: those in traditional Jewish professions, such as trade, complained about their fate the most. It is not easy to find anyone who was happy there, perhaps with the exception of one writer, who complained only of the month-long holiday, during which he was dreadfully bored and in fact went into the shop and read Tolstoy. He greeted the end of his holiday and his return to work with relief. 'At last, I could go back to work. I was awaiting this with pleasure since my holiday had got stale and I was bored.'[49] Those letter-writers who were afraid that they might have to drop out of school were afraid precisely of having to go and work as salespeople and be hounded by the shop owner and have to kowtow to the customers.

Those who had completed trade school and obtained a qualification were much more enthusiastic about their work. Some of them were happy with their jobs and did not feel that they had been deprived of prospects and were on a mindless treadmill. However, these youngsters had not encountered one of the most important causes of frustration, interrupted education; they were usually slightly older, and more of their peers had jobs.

There were also letters in which employment was depicted as satisfying and enriching. As a rule, in these cases the jobs were relatively prestigious and interesting and, above all, somewhat atypical for first jobs and outside the stereotypical Jewish trades.[50] A young nurse in a hospital in Vilna, who wrote about a difficult night shift was at the same time decidedly satisfied with her profession. However, she was undoubtedly educated, and, at 17, proud to be the youngest nurse in the hospital.[51]

Satisfied too was a primary school graduate, who had managed to obtain a post as a trainee dental technician. He was happy, since he found the profession interesting and also as having good financial prospects.[52] A 16-year-old who installed radios in people's homes complained of the ignorance and lack of basic knowledge of his customers, but was proud at the same time of the fact that he was a specialist in his field and knew far more than the wealthy grown-ups who needed his help with their radio receivers. However, he also emphasized that his youth was a handicap in his work, since the owners of new radio receivers simply could not believe that he knew more than they did.[53] A courier for the editorial office of an unidentified publication wrote with satisfaction of his work and of the people with whom he came into contact, although he did complain about his hours of work, which often ended around midnight.[54]

However, there was one exception: work on a *hakhsharah* was seen as the fulfilment of a dream, of finding one's own place on the land. Although, of course, there were not many letters about Jews working on farms, they are marked by a decidedly different tone. Tilling the land and taking care of animals fired the enthusiasm of young people. Even accidents at work were treated with humour. Although Icie lost a finger in a threshing machine, he laughed that he could do more with half a finger missing than others with whole hands.[55] Students at agricultural college worked the most enthusiastically. 'There's nothing like taking a horse into the field ... After all we are running the whole school farm by ourselves', the students reported with pride. Their pleasure was not accidental. The author of the piece remarks that 'it makes us think about a spiritual spring, the rebirth of the Jewish nation'.[56] It is surely no accident that in the supplement to *Nasz Przegląd*, which was sympathetic towards Zionism, agricultural work, which was highly valued in Palestine and for which Zionist organizations were preparing young Jews, was even more valued by those writing in to *Mały Przegląd*.

Another group of working youngsters were the numerous secondary-school pupils who provided tutoring for students younger than themselves (although the youngest tutor was barely 10 years old herself[57]) or who were struggling. This group felt in no way excluded from the school environment or worse off than other pupils. Tutoring was temporary work, was not full-time, was connected to schoolwork, and did not deprive them of school status. Yet even they complained of a great many difficulties and problems. Above all, they worried about the low pay and of their pay being withheld on the slightest pretext: parents avoided paying, put it off for another day, or linked it to the child's progress. According to one correspondent:

After three weeks my 'little one' was making progress; her mother was pleased with me. I impatiently awaited my first payday. They paid punctually. The problems began with the second payment. I would go round, ask and threaten. I received my walking papers with the second salary. The parents clearly thought that their daughter now knew enough.[58]

The same girl also complained of 'thick pupils' and their unpleasant parents, who trivialized her work.

He was an older boy, but so lazy and deeply stupid that he could not get out of Year 4. He was in deep trouble with his Polish. He initially would come round, but not a day passed that he was not late and had not done his homework... One time I arrived for the class, but he ran off to the stadium. I asked the parents what they thought of this. It turned out that they were on his side. The father even said: 'You need to come an additional time.'[59]

An article appeared in 1938 summing up the experiences of girls working as tutors. It includes numerous complaints about parents who were unwilling to pay for lessons.

Perhaps these ladies do not understand that while teaching their children we must pay for our own schooling? We need the money. It appears from the accounts of my friends that sometimes, even for two or three months, they go round to collect back pay. The ladies are very surprised that the young ladies are so insistent on getting paid.[60]

This group also contained youngsters who were not poor, who were not working to support themselves or to pay for their education, but who provided private tuition because they wanted to have a little pocket money. As a rule, they felt that teaching others would help them with their own schoolwork. Giving private lessons provided a sense of satisfaction when their pupil began to receive better marks, and the parents of poorer pupils treated them with respect.[61] This motif did not change over time. In 1929 a schoolgirl who was giving private lessons to the daughter of a cobbler wrote how politely she was treated in this house, that the parents would interrupt a meal in order to free up the table for study, and that the cobbler conscientiously tried to pay even if the sum involved was only 50 grosze but was more than he could afford. 'Later', she wrote, 'giving other private lessons, I came to the conclusion that poor people understood much better the need to pay promptly.'[62] In the 1938 article mentioned earlier, summing up the experiences of professional contributors to *Mały Przegląd*, one of the few girls who was happy was the one who gave private lessons to the children of the janitor: he at least understood that she was not wealthy and that every penny counted.[63] It is hard to state, on the basis of so few accounts, whether in fact poor parents were always more pleasant and paid on time. It is possible that this was true; it is also possible that the tutors appreciated the efforts of poor people more (the cobbler was also often unable to pay the full amount, but he made an effort). However, they do not write of conscientious, wealthy employers and mention only those incidents when such people did not pay even though it was not a problem for them, because they saw such behaviour as scandalous.

Things were different for those who had to give private lessons in order to pay for their own schooling or to contribute to domestic expenses. In this case, too many hours spent teaching others meant that when they sat down to their own studies, they were tired and did not have enough time to do them properly. 'I have pupils with whom I work daily up to 10:30. You can doubtless imagine how tired I am after these lessons. If only I could then go to bed... but I must still do my own homework in history, English, mathematics. I won't get my maths done, because I don't have the book and at that time I can't go round to a friend.'[64]

An evolution in views is clearly visible. While in the 1920s 15- and 16-year-olds working aroused no surprise or indignation, in the 1930s working by those of school age was no longer seen as something normal by the young people themselves, and began, at least in certain parts of society, to be seen in a negative light. A growing number of adults believed that a young person's place was in school. The young worker in the dye factory, already quoted, recalled with irony the opinion of a doctor, who claimed that 'young whippersnappers like myself... needed schooling and not a factory, and that I should now go to the countryside. How odd it is that someone could be so clever and so stupid.'[65] Admittedly the writer of the letter saw the doctor as naive, but it also testifies to a change in people's view of young people working.

Also relevant was the prestige that contributors to *Mały Przegląd* accorded to study as opposed to work. In the 1920s young people in full-time education were viewed more positively by their peers than young people in employment. Both the students and the workers saw this. In cases where the need to work led to dropping out of education, employment and financial help for the family were no cause for pride; on the contrary, former pupils were ashamed that they were no longer in full-time education while their friends were. A girl who had been working for two years in a shop encountered her former friends on the street and tried to slip by unnoticed, feeling in some way guilty for the fact that she was no longer at school.[66] This fear was not unjustified—old school friends treated their peers in work as inferior and broke off contact with them.[67] In a report on the alumnae club of a Warsaw primary school it was clear that the girls, who even two months earlier had been classmates, had already split into two groups. 'The newly minted secondary-school girls with badges on their berets are cheerfully discussing their successes of the first day at school. And the other group—candidates for the workforce—sit sad and thoughtful.'[68] According to the same account things were even worse at subsequent meetings. The secondary-school girls talked about their studies and school dances, while the girls who had gone to work felt even more isolated. Eventually the club folded. In 1929 a secondary-school pupil admitted: 'A schoolboy or schoolgirl has something indefinably better than his or her friends who are in the workforce. No attention is paid to the fact that those in employment often exceed them in experience, stature, and even intelligence. The fact that they are not going to school is enough to label them as morally inferior.'[69]

Only one article, and that during the Great Depression, stigmatized the ambition of girls choosing schooling and studies over work, even if they did not have the means to do so. The owner of a small tailor's shop in Łódź was looking for finishers but could not find any. The report ends with a telling conclusion:

Silly Szlojme. He did not know that these sad young women preferred to study without a penny to their name than to go to some cramped little room to finish off sweaters... Indeed as a philosopher he understood many things but this he could not grasp. Until one day the female supervisor explained things to him. 'Today, you see, young women want to be doctors, or produce medicines. So clever and ... so stupid. They're ashamed of going to work.'[70]

Finding a job, earning money for themselves and their family, especially during the Depression, was the highest goal for many young people, especially given how hard it was to find work because of the high levels of unemployment.[71] Traces of this can be found in *Mały Przegląd*, but the subject nearly always crops up in a similar context. Paid employment is always being sought by someone other than the contributor, some poor boy or girl met quite by chance or a school friend—when that person finds work, they are happy and when they do not, they are sad and lose heart. This reveals little about job satisfaction or a real desire to find employment by the young people described, but it tells us a great deal about the contributors, who were still in school and who believed that in such a situation poor young people should be pleased to find paid employment.

However, contributors to *Mały Przegląd* were not representative of Jewish children and adolescents in the interwar period. Above all, those who wrote to the paper were ambitious, and at the start of the 1930s more serious articles began to appear, letters not just from children about daily life but also from those who had developed their own ideas on many subjects and were willing and able to clothe them in words. Writing to *Mały Przegląd* implied a certain commitment to the paper's values: secularism, ambivalence towards Orthodoxy and sympathy for Zionism, concerns about complex social problems, and a commitment to action. It was hardly strange, then, that the young letter-writers dreamed of further education, of learning more about the world, or of choosing their own life path, and the pages of *Mały Przegląd* were filled, for the most part, with letters which stressed the importance of formal and informal education even if it came at the cost of a lower standard of living. In reality, outside the world of *Mały Przegląd*, doubtless not all nor even a majority of children and young people saw completing secondary education as their most important goal in life. There can be no doubt that young people brought up in less modern, more traditional and religious environments were more likely to accept going out to work early, earning money, financial independence, and choosing this on their own, having no desire to continue their studies nor to leave for Palestine.[72]

'We won't leave, although we can, and no one is forcing us to go out to work'

The letters of working contributors reveal an interesting fact. Although most of them complained of tedium, boredom, and hopelessness, only a few claimed that hard physical work was destroying their health or was beyond them. This may be chance, or efforts may have been made not to overburden young people in the workplace, or it could simply be a result of which pieces were selected for publication. One young man, who complained of missing school and the hopelessness of life, wrote nothing that was contrary to the ideas of Zionism: preparing children and young people for hard physical labour in the Land of Israel. After arriving in Palestine, they did not go to work on a kibbutz but enrolled in school. The correspondents had no intention of working, only of studying; however, this did not affect Zionist propaganda—

promoting work on a kibbutz, the study of Hebrew, and emigration from Poland. Letters from members of Zionist youth organizations (above all, although not exclusively, Hashomer Hatsa'ir) endlessly repeated that Jewish children needed to prepare themselves for hard work in Palestine, in factories and on the land, and that education was not essential and would, on the whole, not be useful there. Letters suggesting that work was physically too hard for children and young people would have spoilt this narrative. A difficult and unsatisfying job is, of course, easier if it is seen as a means to an end rather than as an endless struggle to get by. Performing menial tasks because of poverty was more life-sapping than performing them as part of the Zionist project. This did not mean that contributors did not complain about the work they did, but they did not consider that they were being exploited or that their childhood had been stolen from them. It was seen as a passport to a better life in their own homeland, not the start of a hopeless existence in the diaspora.

Readers of one of the first issues of Mały Przegląd were taught how a young Jew should behave, although the writer of these guidelines was clearly an adult. 'We want Jewish young people to become accustomed to work, to respect work and the worker. Our comrades in Palestine are working and are not sitting idly around.'[73] One of the girls compared her school, home, and 'normal' summer camps with the 'tough' Zionist ones (most probably organized by Hashomer Hatsa'ir), emphasizing precisely that there the participants were taught about hard work, which she saw in a positive light.

We follow orders all the time, and no one does what they want . . . Two different worlds. Two polar opposites. Here—orders and duty, there—the will of the individual and freedom. Yet here there is honesty, there—artificiality. Here—glorious communal work, there —striving for personal comfort. Here, content, there—nothing. Here—the dignity of work, there—pleasure and comfort.[74]

Members of kibbutzim in Poland wrote enthusiastically of their work. 'We work nine morgen of agricultural land, one morgen of vegetable garden and we also tend the trees. We have an animate and an inanimate inventory. We enjoy the work very much.'[75]

Not only work on the farm but also work in a factory was satisfying. 'In my granny's factory *ḥalutsim* [pioneers] are working. They are learning to work so as to be useful people in Palestine. When they finish working, they dance and sing. They have a communal kitchen and they live as friends. They want to leave for Palestine as soon as possible.'[76]

According to the pieces published in Mały Przegląd, young Jews in Palestine saw things similarly. Initially, contributors from Palestine depicted it as a normal country with children going to school rather than working. However, this needed to be qualified. In reports from the kibbutz of Ein Harod it is clear that children were involved in work from their earliest years. Six-year-olds were not just tending gardens, but were also dreaming of growing up as quickly as possible and starting to work in the fields, which in their eyes was a cause for pride. The daily schedule was arranged so that work did not clash with studies, but where they could not combine them, work took precedence, for without it the community could not survive. In that case young people took turns at carrying out the difficult tasks. Moszełe, who delivered food to the camp, complained that he was missing many classes and was waiting for his monthly rota to end.[77]

Even small children in the kibbutzim were fascinated with working on the land. In their reports from trips to Palestine, they saw the most important event not as visiting or admiring the countryside but as the moment when the children were allowed to do adult jobs.

We besieged the farmers; we grabbed their mules and began ploughing on our own. Chezi, Uri, Josek, Ruth and Joseph from Geva hung their clothes on the ends of the mules' yokes just like fellahin. There were twelve ploughs and a single seeding machine. There were not enough ploughs for us, so those who could not hold the reins took either a whip or a handle of the plough.[78]

Other children during the course of the two-week school holidays were so busy on the kibbutz that they often did not come in for meals. They were building a pond, which was to contain water for irrigation, but they had been promised that they would be able to swim in it, hence the work on it was attractive.[79] What in Poland would have been considered too tiring for them was not so in Palestine. However, it has to be said that in reality the irregular, unregulated work of poor children in Poland was one thing, while work on kibbutzim was something else, integrated as it was with the rhythm of the day and linked with their schooling. Starting in 1933 there was a change. In letters from Palestine children and young people working became more prominent.

Was the work on kibbutzim depicted as satisfying only because of ideology? Definitely not. Above all it was because it was the result of a free choice. It was seen as work for oneself from which in later life one would be able to draw material and emotional benefits, not as exploitation. It was important too that the young people working in Palestine also studied. They did not always go to school, but in addition to work they had Hebrew lessons, talks, meetings, and discussions. Even if the work was very tiring, as a great many people complained, diversions, such as dances and parties, and the possibility of personal development awaited them after work.

The depictions of young people's working lives in *Mały Przegląd* are full of contradictions. On the one hand, they are definitely critical, showing early entry into the workforce as the end of any ambitions, making it impossible to continue education, and exposure to endless exhaustion and a lack of time for pleasure and normal life. On the other hand, it was accepted that even young children should work in Palestine, where work was everyone's greatest ambition, where exhaustion was satisfying, and yet time was also found for pleasure. Unfortunately, it is impossible to say if this really was the general opinion of contributors to the paper or whether, consciously or otherwise, letters were chosen that reflected the view of the editors, who were themselves mostly adolescents. *Mały Przegląd* was meant to show a world in which young people actually lived, not a world portrayed according to a specific political line directed to the young.[80] It appears, however, that in the case of young people and children working, ideology, at least to some extent, did have an influence on what appeared in its pages.

Mały Przegląd is such a specific source that it is difficult to compare its contents with other accounts, autobiographies, and memoirs. Its pages contain the spontaneous outpourings of children and young people from age cohorts that do not usually leave written records. Memoirs and autobiographies are generally written years later by older people and are laden with years of experience and knowledge of the consequences of choices or events that took place during childhood and adolescence. There is, however, an extensive autobiographical literature written by young Jewish people for the YIVO competitions of 1932, 1934, and 1939.[81] The competition laid down very specific topics to be tackled, and the entries were also written with the chance of winning a prize. There are also the letters written by pupils of the Hebrew-language school system Tarbut, which are described in this volume by David Assaf and Yael Darr.[82] These, however, are fewer in number. As a result, it does seem that *Mały Przegląd* remains the only extensive record left by at least some of the youngest citizens of the Second Polish Republic.

Translated from the Polish by Jarosław Garliński

Notes

1 On *Mały Przegląd*, see A. Landau-Czajka, *Wielki 'Mały Przegląd': Społeczeństwo i życie codzienne w II Rzeczypospolitej w oczach korespondentów 'Małego Przeglądu'* (Warsaw, 2018).
2 See ibid.
3 See A. Bar-El, *Bein ha'etsim hayerakrakim: itonut yeladim beyidish bepolin 1918–1939* (Jerusalem, 2006).
4 M.H., Lublin, 'O młodzieży pracującej', *Mały Przegląd*, 22 Nov. 1935, p. 2.
5 That was undoubtedly the case during the first years of *Mały Przegląd*'s existence, proof of which was letters on the subject of youth organizations: almost all those published were by members of Hashomer Hatsa'ir.
6 The two other major Polish-language Jewish dailies, the Lwów *Chwila* and the Kraków *Nowy Dziennik*, had their own supplements: *Chwilka dla Dzieci i Młodzieży* and *Dzienniczek dla Dzieci i Młodzieży*. They were never as popular as *Mały Przegląd*, but they did have a large local readership.
7 See Landau-Czajka, *Wielki 'Mały Przegląd'*, 297.
8 In the publication's early years, when Korczak still printed his own responses to letters, he would criticize contributors for orthographical mistakes. For instance, he scolded a contributor for misspelling *pożytek* (benefit) in one of the first numbers ('Odpowiedzi redakcji', *Mały Przegląd*, 5 Nov. 1926, n.p.). Requiring correct Polish from children who were still learning the language frightened off in particular those who spoke Polish badly, for not only did they make mistakes but they also could not ask anyone in their family to check their work for them.
9 'List Lutka z Paryża', *Mały Przegląd*, 7 Jan. 1927, p. 6.

10 Editorial response to 'List Lutka z Paryża'. A real problem was also Korczak's poor knowledge of Yiddish. According to Agnieszka Witkowska-Krych of the Institute of Polish Culture at the University of Warsaw and the Jewish Historical Institute:

> Korczak (at the time Goldszmit) definitely did not learn Yiddish as a child... Little Goldszmit in his school/schools studied Russian, learned Latin and Greek at grammar [secondary] school (his Latin was the same he later encountered during his medical studies), he also used German and French, and later had a 'smattering' of English. After the age of 50 he also mastered around 200 Hebrew words, but, unfortunately, it is unknown whether he was able to write anything. He was also able to pray a little in Hebrew (someone recalled that in the ghetto he would recite the Haggadah with his children and sing Hebrew songs, although he could do this either from memory, or by reading a text that had been transcribed into the Latin alphabet).
>
> In terms of Yiddish the situation was probably that, knowing German and working for a time in the Bersohn and Bauman Hospital as well as at the Dom Sierot [orphanage] to which from time to time came children speaking (initially) only Yiddish, he understood what they were trying to tell him, and he was able in some way to communicate with them. There is no proof, however, that he ever studied Yiddish systematically. In the orphanage the children very quickly 'switched' to Polish, even though many of them went to Jewish schools and on Saturdays would visit their Yiddish-speaking families. The fact is that in the Yiddish publication *Dos Kind* several pieces by Korczak appeared, but they had doubtless been translated by someone else. Furthermore... Korczak's knowledge of Yiddish was less rather than more advanced and, if indeed it existed, was used only for verbal communication, also not necessarily at the highest level. In this context also problematic is the word 'knew': did it mean that he achieved fluency, or that he managed to get something out, possibly the answer to a simple question, confusing Yiddish with the German he had learnt years before? (A. Witkowska-Krych, private correspondence, 24 June 2020).

11 See *O Małym Przeglądzie po latach: Materiały ze spotkania korespondentów i czytelników*, ed. A. Wernik (Warsaw, 1989).

12 See A. Landau-Czajka, 'Czasopisma jako źródła badań nad społeczeństwem: Osobliwy przypadek "Małego Przeglądu"', *Roczniki Dziejów Społecznych i Gospodarczych*, 78 (2017), 267–82.

13 'Dekret Naczelnika Państwa z 7 lutego 1919 r. o obowiązku szkolnym, zatwierdzony przez Sejm Ustawodawczy 22 lipca 1919 r.', *Dziennik Ustaw*, 1919, no. 14, item 147. 'Paid employment of children younger than 15 years of age... is prohibited' (Constitution of the Republic of Poland, 17 Mar. 1921, art. 103; see also S. Mauersberg, 'Wykonywanie obowiązku szkolnego w niepodległej Polsce (1918–1939)', *Rozprawy z Dziejów Oświaty*, 37 (1996), 155–76). Schooling in the Second Polish Republic was compulsory between the ages of 7 and 14.

14 Syma, Zamość, 'Nasz dom i jego mieszkańcy', *Mały Przegląd*, 27 Dec. 1935, p. 6.

15 Jawan, near Nalewki Street, 'Sześć za dziesiątkę (Wywiad Małego Przeglądu)', *Mały Przegląd*, 28 Jan. 1927, p. 6.

16 Alinka, 'Nauka to światło', *Mały Przegląd*, 23 Sept. 1927, p. 7.

17 'Z kraju', *Mały Przegląd*, 6 Jan. 1928, p. 7.

18 'Bez szkoły', *Mały Przegląd*, 7 Oct. 1927, p. 7.

19 'Bez szkoły', *Mały Przegląd*, 6 Nov. 1931, p. 1.

20 H.C., 'Już jestem duża', *Mały Przegląd*, 27 Jan. 1939, p. 4.

21 'Marzą-myślą', *Mały Przegląd*, 23 Sept. 1938, p. 4.

22 Rachel, Tel-Aviv, 'Z listów z Palestyny: Gazeciarz', *Mały Przegląd*, 21 May 1937, p. 3.
23 'Wiadomości bieżące', *Mały Przegląd*, 13(15?) Oct. 1926, p. 7.
24 'Z kraju', *Mały Przegląd*, 4 Jan. 1928, p. 7.
25 Mineczka, Otwock, 'Źle z małemi', *Mały Przegląd*, 19 Oct. 1928, p. 7.
26 'Fajga opowiada', *Mały Przegląd*, 11 Dec. 1936, p. 4.
27 'O rodzicach: Basia, Niezamożni', *Mały Przegląd*, 17 Mar. 1933, p. 3.
28 Reporter Szlamek (Year 6), 'Alteru', *Mały Przegląd*, 6 Sept. 1935, p. 3.
29 Ibid.
30 Proof that growing attention was being paid to young people in employment is the absence of this category in earlier statistical yearbooks (e.g. *Rocznik Statystyki Rzeczypospolitej Polskiej – 1920–21* (Warsaw, 1921) or *Mały Rocznik Statystyczny 1930* (Warsaw, 1930). However, it appears in *Mały Rocznik Statystyczny 1938* (Warsaw, 1938), 263). In 1931 4.1 out of 1,000 workers in heavy and medium industry were youngsters; in 1938 it was 3.5.
31 Balbina, Ogrodowa Street, 'Praca małoletnich', *Mały Przegląd*, 25 Jan. 1929, p. 2.
32 Lejzor, Gęsia Street, 'Idziemy w nowy rok szkolny', *Mały Przegląd*, 10 Sept. 1937, p. 1.
33 Bronia, Radom, 'Ircia', *Mały Przegląd*, 26 Feb. 1937, p. 3.
34 'Bez szkoły', *Mały Przegląd*, 7 Oct. 1927, p. 7.
35 Ada, Franciszkańska Street, 'Skończyłam', *Mały Przegląd*, 1 July 1932, p. 1.
36 Renia, Sierakowska Street, 'Co teraz pocznę?' *Mały Przegląd*, 1 July 1932, p. 1.
37 On how far the experience of contributors to *Mały Przegląd* differed from what was officially recommended and how far their working conditions conformed to the various laws and decrees, see A. Jarosz-Nojszewska, 'Ochrona pracy młodocianych w II Rzeczypospolitej', *Od kwestii robotniczej do nowoczesnej kwestii socjalnej: Studia z polskiej polityki społecznej XX i XXI wieku*, 2 (2014), 56–70.
38 Mik, 'Po szkole', *Mały Przegląd*, 9 Sept. 1932, p. 4.
39 Leon G-RG, 'Ręce do sprzedania', *Mały Przegląd*, 3 Feb. 1933, p. 2.
40 Moniek, Piekarska Street, 'W poszukiwaniu posady', *Mały Przegląd*, 14 Jan. 1930, p. 3.
41 Regina Kwiatkowska, 'Pola szyje trykotaże', *Mały Przegląd*, 26 Apr. 1935, p. 3.
42 'Młodość za kratą', *Mały Przegląd*, 8 Apr. 1938, p. 2.
43 Sewek, Franciszkańska Street, 'Chłopak na posyłki', *Mały Przegląd*, 21 May 1937, p. 2.
44 C.T., Białystok, 'W farbiarni', *Mały Przegląd*, 27 Dec. 1935, p. 4.
45 Froim, 'Z pamiętnika Froima', *Mały Przegląd*, 17 Jan. 1930, p. 3.
46 Fela, 'Przy pracy', *Mały Przegląd*, 7 Feb. 1930, p. 3.
47 B. Awner, 'Bez szkoły', *Mały Przegląd* 18 June 1937, p. 2.
48 K-T-Ś, Krasnystaw, 'W pracowni krawieckiej', *Mały Przegląd*, 29 Apr. 1932, p. 2.
49 ES-JOT, 'Urlop', *Mały Przegląd*, 29 Apr. 1932, p. 2.
50 Jerzy Tomaszewski, writing about the period after 1929, claimed that 'around 37 per cent of Jews supported themselves by business and related trades (above all running small retail shops). Almost 15 per cent were tailors or cobblers. Almost 60 per cent of the whole community were minor businessmen (with their families) who had no paid employees (J. Tomaszewski, *Żydzi w II Rzeczypospolitej* (Warsaw, 2016), 201). Jakub Appenszlak, the editor-in-chief of *Nasz Przegląd*, maintained that Jews' involvement in trade was detrimental to the nation's future and warped the social fabric. 'In the diaspora every Jew lives to some extent at the expense of our race's business genius. We're all merchants: this is a deadly state of affairs even for such a par excellence trading organism as are the Jews' (J. Appenszlak, 'Dziennik podróży do Palestyny', *Nasz Przegląd*, 12 May 1925, p. 4).
51 Mirjam, 'Nocny dyżur: Z pamiętnika najmłodszej siostry', *Mały Przegląd*, 5 June 1936, p. 1.

52 Samek, Pańska Street, 'U technika dentystycznego', *Mały Przegląd*, 29 Apr. 1932, p. 2.
53 Chaim, 'Monter', *Mały Przegląd*, 6 Dec. 1935, p. 3.
54 Chaim Basok, Vilna, 'W pogoni za ogłoszeniami', *Mały Przegląd*, 23 Dec. 1938, p. 3.
55 Ida Monter, 'Nasze gospodarstwo', *Mały Przegląd*, 10 Jan. 1930, p. 3.
56 Ż.S., Żytomierz, 'Reportaż ze szkoły rolniczej', *Mały Przegląd*, 7 Apr. 1939, p. 2.
57 Młoda nauczycielka, 'Moja karjera korepetytorska', *Mały Przegląd*, 25 Jan. 1929, pp. 2–3.
58 Eńcia, Łomża, 'Udzielam lekcji', *Mały Przegląd*, 1 Oct. 1937, p. 2.
59 Ibid.
60 Trzydziestka, 'My już zarabiamy', *Mały Przegląd*, 8 Apr. 1938, p. 1.
61 Młoda nauczycielka, 'Moja karjera korepetytorska', *Mały Przegląd*, 25 Jan. 1929, p. 3.
62 Ibid.
63 Trzydziestka, 'My już zarabiamy'.
64 Jehuda Waserman, 'Doba mojego życia (dokończenie)', *Mały Przegląd*, 13 Jan. 1939, p. 2.
65 C.T., 'W farbiarni'.
66 Fira, 'Ten dzień', *Mały Przegląd*, 27 June 1930, p. 2.
67 Leon, Śliska Street, 'Pożegnanie ze szkołą', *Mały Przegląd*, 16 Jan. 1931, pp. 1–2.
68 'Joter, 'Klub abiturientek', *Mały Przegląd*, 25 June 1937, p. 1.
69 Izrael, 'Młodzież, która pracuje', *Mały Przegląd*, 25 Jan. 1929, p. 2.
70 Regina, Łódź, 'Szlojme szuka wykańczarki', *Mały Przegląd*, 23 Mar. 1934, p. 3.
71 'The Great Depression led to an enormous rise in unemployment. The percentage of unemployed in Poland at that time exceeded 43 per cent' (A. Jarosz-Nojszewska, 'Bezrobocie w Polsce w latach 1918–2018', *Kwartalnik Kolegium Ekonomiczno-Społecznego Studia i Prace / Szkoła Główna Handlowa*, 2018, no. 3, pp. 101–19: 106).
72 For the process of modernization among young Jews, see K. Kijek, *Dzieci modernizmu: Świadomość, kultura i socjalizacja polityczna młodzieży żydowskiej w II Rzeczypospolitej* (Wrocław, 2017).
73 Jawan, 'O szomrach', *Mały Przegląd*, 24 Dec. 1926, p. 6.
74 Róża, Mylna Street, 'Dwa światy', *Mały Przegląd*, 16 Aug. 1935, p. 1.
75 'Sobotni poranek', *Mały Przegląd*, 5 Aug. 1927, p. 6.
76 Hela, Przedbórz, 'Braterskie współżycie', *Mały Przegląd*, 3 Nov. 1933, p. 4.
77 Mordechaj, Kibbutz Ein Charod, Palestine, 'Ukłon od dzieci z Ejn-Charodu', *Mały Przegląd*, 22 Apr. 1927, p. 7.
78 Chezi, 'O świcie', *Mały Przegląd*, 12 May 1933, p. 3.
79 Ibid.
80 e.g. J. Halperin, *Tajemniczy rycerz*, Biblioteka Palestyńska dla Dzieci, supplement to *Mały Przegląd* (Warsaw, n.d.).
81 See *Awakening Lives: Autobiographies of Jewish Youth in Poland before the Holocaust*, ed. J. Shandler (New Haven, Conn., 2002); *Ostatnie pokolenie: Autobiografie polskiej młodzieży żydowskiej okresu międzywojennego*, ed. A. Cała (Warsaw, 2003); *Alilot ne'urim: otobiyografiyot shel benei no'ar yehudim mipolin bein shetei milḥamot ha'olam*, ed. I. Bassok (Tel Aviv, 2011); see also Kijek, *Dzieci modernizmu*, 108–17.
82 D. Assaf and Y. Darr, 'What Kind of Self Can a Pupil's Letter Reveal? The Tarbut School in Nowy Dwór, 1934–1935', this volume.

Through Their Own Eyes
Jewish Youngsters Describe Their Holidays in Interwar Poland

ULA MADEJ-KRUPITSKI

> Travel to different parts of the country became a favourite activity for young Jews in interwar Poland. They have described their experiences of vacationing in a number of settings—spontaneous or organized, with family members and among their peers. Vacationing offered Jewish children unique opportunities to experience Polish landscapes and culture, to reflect on social and gender norms, and to be socialized into various political ideologies. Among those who participated in these experiences were children and adolescents from large urban environments and middle-sized towns, those who could afford visits to splendid spa towns or trips to fashionable Zakopane and the Baltic coast, and those for whom a subsidized visit to nearby countryside or forest was their first chance to move out of a largely Jewish environment.

My entire body was joyous in anticipation of the holidays.
S. J., Jewish schoolboy from Warsaw, March 1928

Introduction

In the scholarship on the history of Polish Jewry, age as a category of analysis has yet to receive adequate consideration. That there are so few histories of Jewish childhood in Poland is unfortunate, and has been recognized as such for quite some time. As Gershon Hundert pointed out over three decades ago, a systematic study of the experience of children and adolescents would undoubtedly lead to some major revisions in how Jewish societies of the past are understood.[1] Yet while a few recent works have made significant and insightful strides towards placing Jewish youngsters at the centre of their stories,[2] this approach still remains undervalued, especially in comparison with the larger historiography that favours more conventional subjects. Certainly, concentrating on children offers various advantages for the better conceptualization of broader topics pertaining to key issues in any given society at any given time period. But this methodological choice seems particularly urgent in order to fully account for the first few decades of the twentieth century. Beyond doubt, between the wars Polish Jewry paid particular attention to its youngest members. Not only were children and adolescents numerically significant among the Jewish population in Poland,[3] but for that generation, their development, experiences, and future trajectories occupied a remarkably critical part of their world-view, especially compared with previous ones. Strikingly, among the adults who cared for, wrote, spoke, and worried about the Jewish children of the 1920s and 1930s, regardless of their ideological and political preferences, a nationalist context seemed pervasive. The Polish language Jewish monthly *Dziecko* put it plainly in the summer of 1932: 'the child is the nation's future'.[4]

The focus on Jewish children in Poland was manifest in child-rearing manuals;[5] advice columns in Yiddish and Polish in the daily press;[6] children's periodicals;[7] children's literature; child and youth groups; school, summer, and winter camps; and activities provided for children across the religious and political spectrum.[8] Many of these initiatives should be seen, at least in part, as a consequence of the democratizing and technological changes of the time. Children were now increasingly not only the subject of books and magazines but also their consumers.[9] These wide-ranging initiatives for, and increasingly by, children and adolescents epitomize the particular consideration and scrutiny that children began to receive. On the one hand, this attention can be viewed as a form of child empowerment, while on the other it can be seen as a way of exerting control over them, their choices, and their world-views.

Furthermore, what clearly separates the first decades of the twentieth century from earlier periods is the unprecedented access to children's voices. Diaries, autobiographies, essays and letters printed in national and local newspapers, and summer camp bulletins and newsletters all feature the largely unmediated experiences of Jewish children and adolescents, usually described and interpreted in their own voices.[10]

The extent of children's agency began to grow substantially. Not only did they narrate their own experiences, but increasingly children were able to shape new projects and activities. In the context of the Polish Jewry of the 1920s and 1930s, one undertaking that encapsulates this fresh potential particularly vividly was the 'Great Children's Beauty Contest' announced in March 1930 by the Polish-language Jewish daily *Nasz Przegląd*.[11] The goal of the contest was to select 'the most beautiful Jewish children in Poland' out of 'the enchanting parade of stunning children's faces'.[12] Between March and June, over 800 black and white photos depicting Jewish girls and boys up to the age of 10 poured into the editorial office. From all over the country, hopeful parents, and at times the contestants themselves, carefully selected staged photos. Many photos featured children wearing school uniform, others were in festive clothing, or in the case of newborns, simply naked, while a few participants even modelled traditional Polish folk outfits.[13] Many held toys, but cigarettes and tennis rackets were nearly equally popular props.[14] Among the hundreds of contestants was the grandson of the Zionist activist and Hebrew author Nahum Sokolow and the future philosopher Zygmunt Bauman.[15] What makes this enterprise utterly remarkable though is not just the vast interest it generated but the fact that the contest was initiated by the children themselves. The children, inspired by Polish and European beauty pageants, and above all by the Miss Judaea competition of 1929, pleaded that an equivalent contest for Jewish children had to be organized.[16] Why?

Because 'not everything should only be for adults', Janeczka from Miodowa Street in Warsaw noted,[17] or because 'children are also beautiful', according to Jaś from Złota Street.[18] Finally Różka and Estusia chimed in to sum up the ultimate goal of this project, 'so everyone will see how beautiful the young Jewish generation is'[19] (see Figure 1).

Taking its cue from this contest and interwar Jewry more broadly, this chapter pays close attention to the voices of children and adolescents themselves. It draws upon a variety of children's materials: from the autobiographies written for the YIVO contests in the 1930s[20] to post-war memoirs, but especially notes, essays, and letters written by Jewish youngsters which were printed in summer-camp newsletters or published in local and national magazines for young readers throughout the interwar period. Among the published narratives, those that appeared on the pages of *Mały Przegląd* deserve special acknowledgement.[21] This weekly supplement to *Nasz Przegląd* was not only directed towards children but was edited by its own readers, with the core of its content constituting letters and notes written by young correspondents from across the country. The editorial board, headed until 1930 by the acclaimed physician and pedagogue Janusz Korczak, urged the child authors to 'write how they speak . . . without lofty phrases' or help from adults, to express what they saw and thought.[22] Even though some of these impressions may pose methodological dilemmas for historians, since usually only the first name and place of residence of the authors were supplied, the sheer number of these accounts outweighs some of these concerns.[23]

This chapter examines one aspect of the lives of Polish Jewish children: holidays and leisure travel. The choice to focus on holidays may seem arbitrary, but it is not accidental. Leisure travel gained enormous popularity among the Jews of Poland during the first three decades of the twentieth century. Until then the notion of leisure was unfamiliar to the majority of Polish Jews, especially traditional Jews, who considered it inherently un-Jewish. Through social and economic developments and, above all, various agents who promoted recreational activities, by the mid-1920s Polish Jews began to embrace tourism in large numbers.[24] Therefore, especially among the youngest generation, going on holiday was a common experience for the diverse groups that made up Polish Jewry and, as such, affords an invaluable opportunity to capture their joys, struggles, and mundane day-to-day activities, regardless of levels of religiosity, linguistic preference, or political affiliation. This is not to say, however, that all Jewish youngsters experienced holidays equally or that they all had access to leisure travel. Yet, by focusing on holidays, several undervalued facets of the Polish Jewish experience assume more prominence. Certainly, in this case, social class and gender account for the varied opportunities and perspectives, hitherto largely ignored in the historiography (see Figures 2–7).

For those children and adolescents who came of age in the 1920s and 1930s, holidays and travelling constituted an experience and practice upon which they reflected often, frequently describing their encounters as life-changing. This was especially the case given that their parents and grandparents either had not travelled for leisure

Figure 1 Submissions for the Great Children's Beauty Contest
Nasz Przegląd, 16 May 1930, p. 5

Figure 2 Nusia and Ina Szyfman, near Gdynia
Beit Lohamei Hagetaot Archive, 49722

Figure 3 Felicja Berland and her mother Sara, Krynica, 1920s. The Berland family ran a bakery in Chełm (see F. Berland Hyatt, *Close Calls: Memoirs of a Survivor* (Washington DC, 2000))
YIVO Archives, New York, RG 120, Poland, f. 427.06

Figure 4 Pupils from the Hebrew school in Mława during a trip in Gdynia, May 1935
Beit Lohamei Hagetaot Archive, 33260

Figure 5 Pupils from the Jewish gymnasium in Warsaw visiting Zakopane, June 1935
United States Holocaust Memorial Museum, Washington DC, photo. no. 29029

Figure 6 Jewish boys from Łódź at a summer camp, c.1934–8

United States Holocaust Memorial Museum, photo. no. 61623

Figure 7 Talmud Torah summer camp, Rabka
Central Archive for the History of the Jewish People, Jerusalem, JDC/Ph 151

themselves or had begun to do so only very recently. Moreover, even though summer or winter breaks, school excursions, overnight camps, or resort stays might be associated with idyllic settings and exhilarating adventures, the narratives of Jewish children in interwar Poland are far from one-sided, idealistic, or nostalgic. Rather, they present a spectrum of experiences: some particularly cherished, others traumatic. In these reflections, holidays are unique moments of time, cultural constructs that lend themselves to unexpected encounters with nature and the landscape and with other individuals: children and adults, Jewish and not.

In addition to insights into the period, the focus on holidays provides first-hand comments on a wide variety of destinations. In particular, places outside the large urban centres of Warsaw, Łódź, Kraków, Vilna, and Lwów acquire a notable prominence, in contrast to the bulk of the existing historiography.

Significantly, the focus on holidays and leisure travel not only reveals this new activity through the eyes of Jewish children but provides a unique lens to capture their impressions of interwar Poland, which continue to be contested by historians.[25] Moreover, in my view, observations from the youngest Jewish generation complement and at times contrast with the more familiar adult-centred perspectives. Unlike their adult equivalents, reflections by the youngest children were less bound by or were completely free of ideological influences.[26]

The Significance of Holidays

For the majority of children and adolescents, summer and winter breaks and the associated prospects of travelling, whether accompanied by family, friends, or fellow members of various organizations, constituted the most highly anticipated time of the year. In this regard, Jewish youngsters who grew up in the Second Polish Republic were no different.

In June 1934 a schoolgirl named Tusia expressed an overwhelming desire to explore places beyond her native Będzin. Her dramatically titled short story 'Will I Go or Not Go?' provides an insight into the emotional torment she was undergoing in the weeks leading up to summer.[27] Her uncertainty and anticipation loomed so large that Tusia dreamed day and night about the clean sand on the beach and the sound of the waves, and at one point she even heard the voice of Mother Nature addressing her directly. Tusia's agony ended at last with her mother's promise that the family could afford to send her to a summer camp after all. 'Hurray, I'm going!' Tusia screamed.

Autobiographies, letters, and articles in the press spotlight similar sentiments with considerable frequency. H. Weissblumówna, a student at the Jewish gymnasium in Stanisławów, noted in January 1933 that her sole dream was to travel. The school trip around the country, taking in Kraków, Katowice, Sosnowiec, Gdynia, Puck, and Warsaw, she asserted with joy, satisfied this longing at least 'in part'.[28] Some Jewish children and adolescents made broader observations, like the young man born in 1914 who signed the autobiography he submitted to the YIVO contest in 1934 with the initials G.J. He maintained that this desire to travel was not only a common characteristic of his entire generation but that it was particularly pronounced along gender lines as well. G.J. noted 'all girls wanted to travel, and I began to resent them for that'.[29] Just a couple of pages prior to this probably embellished statement, he seemingly contradicted the notion that these ambitions were mainly prevalent among females, as he dedicated a significant amount of space to a description of the two-month-long trek across the country he participated in during the late 1920s. This group escapade made a lasting impression on him, one that he summed up with a new awareness, declaring 'I love Polish nature. I only got to know it during that trip across the villages and towns.'[30]

The widespread interest in going on holiday among Jewish children and adolescents had a variety of causes. Some were inspired by their peers, schoolmates, or fellow members of youth organizations. Nearly all were also heavily influenced by their parents' approach to leisure travel. Naturally, these attitudes varied significantly, depending on social class and, at times, level of religiosity. For those from the upper and middle classes, their first experiences of going on holiday often took place in one of the spa towns or summer or winter breaks in the suburbs of the big cities or the countryside. Usually accompanied by their mothers, children would spend six to eight weeks in one of these places, while their fathers would remain in the city and join them occasionally on weekends.[31] Spending about two months in one of these tourist destinations, despite their rising popularity, remained a luxury during the interwar period. Among the working mothers of comfortable households, guesthouses specially for children were an increasingly attractive option.[32] Classified advertisements in the Polish Jewish press from women offering to look after several children in one of the holiday destinations for a month or two suggest that there was a certain, rather small, group who could manage such an expense.[33] Those with family members in rural areas and spa towns, not surprisingly, were able to enjoy the surroundings without the heavy financial burden of paying for accommodation. By the 1930s this was quite a common phenomenon, given the significant number of Jewish-owned inns, hotels, and lodgings. Many others sought less expensive accommodation by simply renting rooms from peasants in the countryside, where running barefoot, swimming, sun-bathing, and even voluntary work in the host's fields during the harvest grew into a highly anticipated form of recreation and joy.[34]

Yet for others even these less pricey options were beyond their reach. Economic status was decisive. *Di kinder-velt*, a Yiddish magazine associated with the socialist Po'alei Tsiyon party and directed at the children of the working classes, illustrates this dynamic well. Its editors frequently stressed that only a small number of its readers could afford to spend the upcoming summer 'playing in the fields and forests', while the majority of 'us, workers' children . . . will remain in the narrow streets and dirty courtyards'.[35] 'The capitalist order' was to blame for this sad state of affairs, while calls for change and equal access to leisure activities were voiced repeatedly.[36] Moreover, *Di kinder-velt* shared a conviction that children possessed a rare ability to recognize and, more importantly, denounce social injustice.[37] The voices of many Jewish youngsters seem to support this notion. Mietek from Warsaw wrote to *Mały Przegląd* with a passionate plea, stating: 'Let us remember that everyone has equal rights to sun and air!'[38] He desperately tried to make a case for a fund that would allow children from impoverished families to attend summer camps.

For some of the children, the new awareness of social inequality was sparked or deepened precisely during their own holidays. When Szaja from Częstochowa was visiting Kamińsk in the summer of 1938, he was shaken by an encounter with starving, orphaned children, who inhabited a small hut in the nearby forest. Szaja not only ran back home to tell his mother about this experience so that he could return to the hut right away with some provisions, but it dominated his account of the holiday, where he urged his readers to be more empathetic and to provide aid for all poor children.[39]

Lena Jurand, born in Przemyśl in 1917, who spent every July between 1927 and 1935 in Szczawnica, recalled a similar experience. When she and her father arrived in the resort, they had a chance meeting with a Jewish family with two children who also came to Szczawnica for the season but struggled to make ends meet. In her interview for the United States Holocaust Memorial Museum, Lena recalled saying to her father: 'I don't understand, if they are so poor, why do they go to a summer resort?' She continued her account stating that it 'was a logical question, but he was enraged. He says, "You mean to tell me that only the wealthy can have good air and good water? We have to do something about it", he decided.'[40] Thereafter, Lena and her father began to raise money to help them. The 14-year-old Lena, outfitted in her newest pink chiffon dress and a festive hairdo, gave a piano concert, which generated the necessary funds.[41]

Unlike Lena's father or Szaja's mother, a significant number of Jewish parents did not embrace going on holiday. For many, economic concerns were the main obstacle. Yet for others, scepticism was fuelled by additional concerns and anxieties, especially among religiously observant parents. They frequently correlated excursions, going on holiday, or even taking a stroll in the city park with 'the plague of heresy that could ambush' their children.[42] With assimilation already increasing in late nineteenth-century Galicia, many of them were convinced that girls and young women were at particular risk. This fear peaked after two teenage girls of the Sandz hasidic dynasty not only left their traditional lifestyle but sued their families for financial support in order to attend university.[43] The story was widely reported in the Jewish as well as the general press, causing a particularly intense reaction among hasidic parents. For many of them, extreme preventative measures had to be implemented. The answer they looked for was rooted in the Talmud, which advised that in a time of a plague one should 'remain indoors'.[44] Many Orthodox teenage girls were actually prohibited from spending time outdoors unaccompanied by their parents, their siblings, or their husbands.

Even in the interwar period, adolescents from particularly observant families often struggled to obtain their parents' permission to participate in school excursions or summer camps, which were usually run by Jewish youth groups. Some of these concerns were rooted in the fear that their offspring would be exposed to secular ideologies, such as Zionism or Bundism. In her autobiography submitted to the YIVO contest in 1934, a girl born near Czernowitz to a family of ritual slaughterers and Torah scholars shared a noteworthy story. Using the pseudonym Yidishe Meydl (Jewish Girl), she remarked that she was hoping to go with a friend of hers to a summer camp organized by the Yiddish school union in Vyzhenka, a picturesque village in Bukovina. Her parents' reaction was typical of the prevailing attitude: 'Travel to Vyzhenka to eat *treyf* [non-kosher]?'[45] Despite this strong opposition, Yidishe Meydl finished her autobiography with a hint of optimism: 'I hope that I will push through and go, despite the obstacles.'[46] For some parents, the fear of diverging from tradition was coupled with concerns about their children's safety. Yet many were also opposed to excursions and summer camps, because an activity such as taking a hike in the woods or visiting a royal castle was not necessarily something that had occurred to them. In the traditional *ḥeder*, which their fathers and grandfathers attended, such practices were not part of the curriculum. Anecdotal evidence and folk stories often refer to an actual fear of the outdoors or of leaving the city or town boundaries, as such things could easily take a dangerous turn. All these considerations meant that banning children from recreational activities was not uncommon. Nineteen-year-old J., a resident of Stanisławów and member of Hashomer Hatsa'ir, recalled his past experiences: 'When my peers struggled at home to get permission to participate in excursions and camps, in our home it was all natural. We weren't refused any pleasures, mainly because of mother, who set the tone of our family life.'[47] During the 1920s and 1930s a range of Jewish organizations sought to appeal to these parents by launching a pro-tourism campaign in the Yiddish press, conducting school visits, and making pitches at *kehilah* meetings.[48]

The strong desire among Jewish children to go on holiday was ubiquitous, despite, or perhaps in some cases because of, their parents' lack of understanding and approval. Certainly, many of them did not want to miss out on the summer and winter adventures experienced by their peers, classmates, and fellow youth-group members. But camaraderie or even peer pressure, influential as they can be, especially at a young age, seem to have been just two of many impetuses that drove the youngsters' thirst for travel. Diverse individuals and groups issued explicit endorsements which targeted children. Many of them, such as Janusz Korczak, led by example. Every summer, *Mały Przegląd* would stop publishing as Korczak headed to a summer destination, usually not only to rest but also to lead a summer camp.[49] In his writings on holidays and leisure, whether in the magazine or other publications, he frequently stressed striving for appropriately balanced activities. As he put it, '[you should have] a reading room on one side, sand and a forest on the other'.[50] Korczak and *Mały Przegląd* mostly influenced assimilated, Polish-speaking, middle-class children and adolescents, but those who grew up in more traditional or even religious homes received analogous messages concerning excursions and summer camps from elsewhere. Sarah Schenirer, the founder of the revolutionary Bais Yaakov schools for Orthodox girls, drew on her personal experiences of travelling. Describing a trip to Zakopane in 1912, she wrote: 'The impression the view of the Tatra Mountains made on me is inexpressible. Once again, I've begun to admire the might of God ... What am I, compared with these mighty mountains, that the Eternal should so constantly remember me?'[51] Her long hikes by lakes such as Morskie Oko and Czarny Staw were marked by adoration of the astonishing landscapes but even more so by prayers expressing her deep gratitude. As she states repeatedly in her Polish diary, nowhere else did she feel such a sense of awe as on a mountain peak, in a lush forest, or by a stunning waterfall. As Naomi Seidman convincingly argues, Bais Yaakov schools, and Sarah Schenirer herself, undertook a deliberate effort to make leisure travel accessible to observant women.[52] From the outset, Bais Yaakov incorporated hikes, summer camps, and trips to the country, allowing Jewish girls not only to admire the beauty of nature and landscapes without their fathers, brothers, or husbands but also to experience new and much-appreciated freedoms.

Encountering the 'Other'

Travelling to different places occasioned new encounters and perceptions, many of which were often recalled and reflected upon in personal narratives. Sixteen-year-old Leyzer, a native of Vilna, reflected upon his stay in Druskienniki years earlier. He was only 3 years old at the time but assured his readers that 'he remembered this himself':

In the summer of 1925 I went to Druskienniki with my aunt, uncle, and grandmother. We had a wonderful time there ... Marshal Piłsudski was actually holidaying in Druskienniki at the time. Twice a week he invited children to his villa for an afternoon snack ... Since I was the youngest in the room, the marshal asked me to sit on his lap ... A few Jewish scouts stopped by the villa asking for donations towards the Jewish National Fund. The marshal gave them a certain amount and wished them well in fighting for a homeland, just like he and his compatriots had done. I enjoyed that a lot.[53]

This description is not without ambiguity. The all-too-familiar trope of Jewish citizens being told by the head of their country of residence that they should feel free to 'go and create their own homeland', just as he and his compatriots had done, has ringing overtones of exclusion. Yet, from Leyzer's perspective, the glass was not half empty but half full. To him it was evidence that even Piłsudski supported the Zionist cause, and Leyzer himself was a witness to it.

Although this personal interaction with the country's leader made a monumental impression on Leyzer, it was not the only encounter he reflected upon. When he arrived in Łódź, he noted: 'I saw hasidim for the very first time. I always thought that a hasid was born with a beard, since I never saw one without one. They were very savage, Asiatic-like ... They looked like Indians.'[54] Leyzer's observation was not unique. Olek Abramowicz, who grew up in Poznań, recalled that, while heading for a holiday in Krynica with his mother, they had to change trains in Kraków, and it was there on the platform that he saw, for the very first time, hasidic Jews. As he recounted later, he ran to his mother to tell her 'about these strange people, who were wearing "saucepans" on their heads'.[55] Janina Bauman, who like Leyzer and Olek grew up in a rather secular and Polonized home, had a similar experience one summer. In the diary that she wrote while in the Warsaw ghetto, she reflected on spending the summer months of her childhood in the family villa located in the suburbs along the railway line from Warsaw.[56] She fondly depicted the wonderful gardens full of fruit and flowers, and the fields and forests, where she spent the happiest times every year, but she also remembered encountering pious Jews for the first time while grocery shopping in the marketplace. Her reaction to mothers wearing 'sloppy wigs' and men with long beards was particularly significant. Janina contemplated: 'I was afraid of them, and perhaps even looked down on them ... But mostly I was dumbstruck: do *we* and *they* have anything in common, apart from the label "Jews"?'[57]

While Olek from Poznań probably did not have much chance of meeting hasidic Jews in his home town, for some of the other authors, such as Leyzer, who grew up in Vilna, and Janina from Warsaw, it is hard to believe that they had never seen them before. But that is beside the point. What matters here is the story they wanted to tell: the perception of other Jews that they considered radically different from themselves and that it took a long journey for them to encounter. Some of the travellers valued these personal interactions more than anything else they experienced or saw.

More broadly, these interactions point to the significant gap between the acculturated, secularized Jews from large cities and those who continued to lead a traditional Jewish lifestyle, especially in the small shtetls. When in the summer of 1929 two young 'reporters' from *Mały Przegląd* decided to 'see the province' and headed northeast of Warsaw, they were struck by a variety of memorable encounters: with drunken peasants in the local tavern who argued amongst themselves about grocery prices, or with Polish soldiers who asserted that they were simply 'too young' to actually be journalists.[58] But what particularly shaped their experience in the small towns was how different the sabbath was in comparison to what they were used to. 'Silence. Closed stores. Jews are returning from *shuls* and rushing home for *chulent*' they summed up.[59] The very fact that the two reporters appeared hatless and carried walking sticks caused 'general shock and indignation'.[60] Yet perhaps what is most noteworthy about this narrative is the fact that they genuinely had no idea why everyone stared at them, and it took an explicit explanation from some of Ostrów's Jews for them 'to understand their customs'. Still, despite the initial discomfort, they were fed so much 'excellent *chulent* that [they] could have easily fasted for three subsequent days'.[61]

Of no less consequence were encounters with nature and new, unfamiliar landscapes. For some, such as F.B. from Bereza Kartuska, son of a poor, Yiddish-speaking shoemaker, even a seemingly ordinary excursion to a forest was monumental.[62] The urban middle-class Jewish children found the country and its inhabitants curious and alluring. Stories about running around barefoot, sleeping in barns on bales of hay, and observing the daily activities in the fields appeared frequently in the Polish-language Jewish children's magazines. Janka from Warsaw had for a very long time 'dreamed about potatoes baked in the campfire, just like herdsmen make'. Finally, while on holiday, an opportunity arose to try some. She admitted that she had no clue about the technicalities involved and almost started a fire with her friends instead. While the potatoes did not quite come out right, she proudly asserted that nevertheless her dream had been fulfilled.[63] For G.W., a family picnic in the countryside during Shavuot was the first opportunity for similar observations. He recalled a village near Siedlce: 'I saw how beautiful it was there: meadows, fields of grain, gardens, orchards, small low houses with thatched roofs, a well in almost every yard— these were the charms of the peasants' home life.' A Christian man whom he knew had a swing in his yard: 'I played with the children there swinging with them for a long time. At noon Mother could barely tear me away, and we went home.'[64]

For many, if not all, Polish citizens at the time, seeing the sea was the most cherished of travel treasures, but when Kuba described his summer adventures in *Mały Przegląd* he disclosed other priorities: 'I liked the [Baltic] Sea very much, but in Józefów [a small village] I had good pals.'[65] Many, like him, headed yearly to the same destination, hoping to meet their holiday friends again. Mania from Warsaw also emphasized the new young acquaintances she had made. It was during her winter holiday in nearby Otwock that she had made many friends. Significantly, though, some of them introduced her to two boys, which led to a breakthrough observation. Mania remarked, 'I was convinced that boys are basically sacred—but only when I began to chat with them and play with them, I realized—they are as human as us girls.'[66] Some of these encounters, especially with other children, made a lasting impression, at times leading to friendships or even romantic connections. A 15-year-old girl recalled one of her first ventures into that realm with the following: '[I was 8 at the time] and away for the summer, with one of my relatives. Because all of my girlfriends had crushes on boys, I was trying to convince myself that I liked one boy as well. After a short while, I realized it was silly, and gave up on it.'[67] As is to be expected, for some Jewish adolescents, these chance encounters on holiday sometimes turned into proper romantic relationships, which certainly enhanced their summer experience.[68] Yet the details of how these unfolded were often vague. Frequently, the young authors only alluded to these experiences or instead chose to describe how their 'friend' couldn't forget a girl or a boy they met during their summer holidays.[69]

While most of the Jewish holidaymakers returned to their homes to reminisce about the exciting, positive encounters they had experienced at these destinations, some had less pleasant recollections. When 15-year-old H.C. from Kołomyja wrote her autobiography for the YIVO contest in 1939, she recalled various aspects of her summer adventures in the acclaimed spa towns as well as her long-anticipated visit to Kraków. 'One time, when I was visiting the National Museum by myself, I heard a voice behind my back: "This Jewess also imposes herself here!" It made me feel awfully sad.'[70] Perhaps H.C.'s pain was amplified due to the location of the incident, Kraków's National Museum. Her autobiography, written in flawless Polish, captures her deep emotional connection to Polish culture and, in particular, her nearly obsessive admiration of Polish literature. This offhand but overt remark that her presence was not welcome in this particular museum of all places possibly meant more than just unpleasant humiliation, but was, rather, a reminder that acceptance of her as fully Polish was quite possibly a pipe-dream. Tellingly, H.C. made two brief remarks about this unpleasant encounter: she noted that she wasn't 'used to such things', but, 'despite that, [she] enjoyed this trip and would gladly go back there again'.[71] Her brief conclusion and terse dismissal of this encounter allude to a certain level of powerlessness on her part, or to her ability to repress the unpleasant.

Among the many examples of the antisemitism that young Jewish holidaymakers experienced, such as name-calling or the throwing of stones or sticks, especially at organized Jewish groups, what stands out is the context in which many of these incidents occurred.[72] The majority of them took place at popular tourist destinations. Significantly though, those characterized as most consequential and hurtful unfolded not only in lush forests or on rocky hiking trails but within particular types of spaces. When, in June 1939, schoolboy Dadek wrote to *Mały Przegląd* to share his recollections of the previous summer spent in the Beskid mountains, his narrative strove to balance his genuine excitement and fondness for Polish landscapes and summer freedoms with the dreadful memories of the unpleasant encounters that made him 'beg God that the holidays would finally end'.[73] Tellingly, it was while Dadek, along with a group of other Jewish children, was sightseeing at the church in Żywiec that a group of Polish scouts began verbally harassing them. The fact that these Jewish youngsters included a church in their itinerary might seem a bit surprising, yet other sources indicate that this was not particularly exceptional.[74] However, they were mainly interested in the history and architecture of the churches, and the visit expressed a general curiosity rather than any interest in assimilation.

Jewish Summer Camps

Summer camps aiming to improve the health of young Jews in the Polish lands were first introduced in the 1880s.[75] Jewish associations in Warsaw, Lwów, and Kraków began to arrange overnight camps for children from impoverished families on a regular basis within the next decade. In part, these projects were motivated by a consciousness of exclusion, since at the time general initiatives were usually available only to Christian children. Originally, these were small-scale enterprises: for instance, in the first years of its existence, Kraków's association sent on average fifty children a year to a well-known and conveniently located spa town, Rabka. Thanks to increased funding, by the mid-1930s that number had risen to 700.[76] The number of 'fresh-air camps' for Jewish youngsters peaked in the 1920s and 1930s. Various agencies endorsed and supported such activities, with the Society for the Protection of the Health of the Jewish People and the American Jewish Joint Distribution Committee leading the charge.[77] The latter seemed to somewhat overstate its role, suggesting in its publications that it introduced the idea in the mid-1920s, and it 'soon developed into a permanent local activity'.[78] A close look at the financial reports reveals that even though the Joint Distribution Committee's subsidies for summer camps were distributed across the religious and ideological spectrum, they constituted no more than 10 per cent of the cost of these summer activities.[79] Above all, it was the effort of Polish Jews themselves that facilitated overnight camps. By the mid-1930s the scale of the endeavour was impressive, with over 37,000 children attending camps each summer. Their parents covered half of the cost, while donations collected locally—and shrinking state and municipal subsidies—made up the rest.[80]

The widespread enthusiasm for summer camps was not limited to those who sought health benefits, and included politicized youth movements such as Tsukunft, Betar, Stern, and various groups who were preparing Jews to emigrate to the Land of Israel and live on kibbutzim. Though they disagreed strongly, at times even violently, on any number of aspects concerning the Jewish future—where it would take place; what language(s) Jews would speak there; and what role, if any, they imagined for Judaism itself[81]—they all agreed on one thing: hiking in Zakopane, kayaking on the Vistula, and summer and winter camps across the country were all equally appealing. The reasons behind this varied. Many group leaders, such as the author of Betar's camp manual, saw in summer camps a unique opportunity to create 'a small society where life will be based on the established movement's principles and where... those values will no longer be [just] theoretical concepts, but reality'.[82] For others, such as E. Meshtshinski, who was writing in the early 1930s, it was the role summer camps played in strengthening the body which would come in particularly handy later in life, especially in the case of military service.[83] Or finally, for those where a religious upbringing and lifestyle were a priority, summer camps and trips to the country had yet another goal, to facilitate a time and place where young pupils could feel God's presence most powerfully.[84] Many of these aims, of course, were not mutually exclusive. The camp manuals of all the groups—the political right, left, and those aspiring to remain apolitical; the religious and the secular—their ideological differences notwithstanding, reveal that they were dedicated to regulating and fashioning the leisure time of their youngest members and sympathizers.[85]

Correspondingly, the narratives about summer camps by children and young people highlighted certain universal experiences. Lusia's comment could serve as an emblematic statement for nearly all campers: 'Life in the summer camp was one long arc of joy.'[86] In the summer of 1939, 15-year-old B.B. took a similar observation a step further, by declaring that a month spent at an overnight camp was 'hitherto the most enjoyable and beautiful time of [his] life.'[87] The young protagonists enjoyed the outdoors, especially those, like 11-year-old Mendele from an observant home, for whom a summer camp with over 230 boys attending *ḥeder* was their very first opportunity to see the countryside.[88] In their recollections, campers frequently underscored the companionship, games, sport and leisure activities; the many small and big adventures they were part of; and, above all, the 'carefree environment'.[89] Some, such as Chaimek from Łódź, kept assuring their parents that they 'eat and drink a lot ... and the camp counsellor is good, [because] she doesn't hit us and doesn't even yell'.[90] Many kept meticulous journals, acted in the camp theatres, or wrote for the camp newsletters. Such handwritten 'publications' featured and commented on all the major activities of a given group. For instance, an overnight camp in a small village near Zakopane in July 1939 produced over fifty pages of jokes and long satirical pieces.[91] The young authors ridiculed the allegedly 'fresh mountain air' by conducting 'tests for air pollution'[92] and instructed fellow campers on how to persuade Jewish parents to allow their children to attend future summer camps. The recommended strategies featured flattery, namely casually telling the parents of another prospective camper that 'they must be related' to some noteworthy individual. Here specifically they suggested using the acclaimed historian Majer Bałaban or Sigmund Freud.[93] The approach, they suggest, would work especially well if the parents did not quite know who these two were but still confirmed kinship with them. They even provided ideas from Freud that they could use to further emphasize the importance of attending the camp.[94]

Along with these commonalities, there were also crucial differences. Especially among attendees of camps with an explicit ideological thrust, certain environments and contexts acquired new meanings. In the summer of 1933, not far from Nowy Sącz amid the picturesque Beskid mountains, members of Hanoar Hatsioni set up camp after a long day of hiking. As one of the campers recalled: underneath the night sky,

while the campfire was blazing brightly, branches crackled, and, in the background, we heard the forest's hum—we were lying in our tent, covered with blankets and kept contemplating our home, the Land of Israel. Images of our future life in the Palestinian land passed before our eyes. But this picture was slowly slipping away, covered with the fog of *galut* [diaspora].[95]

Members of Hanoar Haivri Akiba, in order to receive scout merits, were expected not only to pass a Level-1 Hebrew test, be familiar with 'Jewish history until the Crusades', and 'know perfectly the geography of Palestine', but also to pass practical tests of topography, locating and following hiking trails during excursions across Poland.[96] The young proponents of these Zionist movements may have marvelled at the lush spruce and beech forests, creeks, and mountains, but to them these east European landscapes were supposed to be mere canvases, preparing them to live in distant deserts, among the exotic palm trees and ancient stones of the Land of Israel.[97] Even the youngest camp attendees internalized these directives. For some of them, it may have been close to a seamless shift, but many others wrestled with how to reconcile the two drastically different scenarios, one representing the present and the other a yearned-for, even if unattainable, future. Often, they described their visions as daydreams or otherworldly experiences, almost impossible to comprehend 'for those who weren't there', as these feelings were uniquely intensified by late-night settings, songs, speeches, and an intense sense of camaraderie.[98] The campfire rituals were of course not limited to Zionist camps, and aimed to play a similar role in transmitting a variety of other messages. The participants at the Bundist Tsukunft's camps heard a different narrative about the Polish countryside. In accordance with the movement's main principles of *doykayt* (addressing the concrete problems faced by Jews in the present) and socialism, camp leaders encouraged the young attendees to get to know the local environment and especially its peasant inhabitants and, in order to build new lasting connections along class lines, to volunteer to help them on their farms.[99] Upon returning home, the young Jewish campers recalled these events and encounters. Frequently they were more than just fond memories, helping to solidify loyalty to the organization and deepening ideological commitments.

Moreover, for many of the youngsters, a few weeks spent away from their families and their mundane surroundings led to important lifestyle changes. For instance, H.Z. confessed that it took an overnight camp for him to finally 'discard his *tefilin* into the bottom of his backpack' and to 'end this unnecessary charade'.[100] Here, unlike at home, this decision was not impeded by his father but rather precipitated by his new friends, who were 'fellow adolescent atheists'.[101] His experience was not unique. Various Jewish groups held excursions on Saturdays that featured campfires, setting up tents, handling money, and other activities that are forbidden on the sabbath. As expected, such an approach had its supporters but also outspoken critics, even within the same network of organizations.[102] Naturally, Orthodox organizations sought to renew or deepen prayer and religious values at the overnight camps they arranged.[103] Meanwhile, G.C., a young man who as a boy had prayed in the Gerer synagogue, became inspired by Zionism and socialism and joined the Zionist youth movement Gordonia, crediting an overnight camp for this development.[104] It was there in picturesque Skała that he not only 'fell in love at first sight with the mountains' but, above all, found the time and space allowed for necessary reflection. In his free time, G.C. put a blanket over his shoulders and wandered deep into the forest, away from everybody. 'I sat there for hours', he reminisced, 'and thought about my current situation and my immediate future. As a result of all my thinking, I came to the conclusion that I had to find productive work which would make it possible to support myself and my household.'[105] Others, like R.M., a 16-year-old girl who attended a Tsukunft summer camp, instead of searching for solitude, used this time to bond with her peers. In her case, though, it was with one teenage boy from another part of the country in particular, whom she kept missing long after returning to her home town of Białystok.[106]

Conclusion

The various examples in this chapter of the holiday culture of Jewish youngsters in interwar Poland, whether spontaneous or organized, whether in the company of their families or their peers, are taken from accounts by diverse participants, such as the girl from an upper-class Warsaw family who loved spending summers in the countryside, because she was finally allowed to do things which were deemed 'insufficiently proper' back in the city,[107] or the Yiddish-speaking boy from an impoverished background, for whom an overnight summer camp was the first opportunity to appreciate the Polish language. There, unlike at home where he associated it with the caretaker of a building who was always cursing, he heard it anew while surrounded by the Polish countryside, the language becoming an expression that flowed from him as 'naturally and harmoniously as the joyful Polish meadows'.[108] Among thousands of others were children and adolescents from large urban environments and middle-sized towns, those who could afford visits to splendid spa towns or trips to fashionable Zakopane and the Baltic coast, and those for whom a subsidized visit to the nearby countryside was the first chance finally to step 'out of the ghetto and to get to know the wide world', as the pages of the *Lubliner togblat* passionately called on the youngsters to do.[109]

As the young protagonists themselves relate, for many of them these new leisure experiences provoked profound emotions and even life-changing decisions. Undeniably, for a majority of them, holidays were joyful, hopeful, and highly anticipated events. Yet at the same time Jewish children and adolescents navigated the complex reality of the 1920s and 1930s, and even on holiday they faced various challenges. Taken together, their diverse experiences highlight many of the deep-seated contradictions of interwar Polish Jewish reality. On the one hand, Jewish children and adolescents clearly constituted a generation marked by rapid Polonization; on the other, ethnic distinctiveness and exclusion were pronounced. Unlike their parents and grandparents, many of them not only had first-hand exposure to the Polish school system,[110] but, thanks to excursions and overnight camps, they visited places, saw historical monuments, and interacted with ethnic Poles, all radically different experiences from those which they were used to at home. Making sense of these perceptions was frequently a complex process, and many of them continued to reflect upon their adventures for years, sometimes into their adolescence and even adulthood.

In a time of increasing economic and political distress, further amplified by growing antisemitism, there should be little doubt that many Jewish youngsters shared the sentiment expressed in the summer of 1939 by a Jewish schoolboy from Katowice, who said that 'holidays are meant to [help us] forget about sadness and unpleasantries'.[111] While many of the holidaymakers certainly hoped for temporary relief from their day-to-day worries, their own voices vividly demonstrate that their embrace of leisure travel was not a mere act of escapism. Instead, I suggest that, for Polish Jewish youngsters, going on holiday was not only a clear indication of lives fully lived but also a source of inspiration, empowerment, and profound personal growth. Their own narratives recounting the numerous journeys which were published in national and local magazines fulfilled a similar task. They demonstrate that even those of a very tender age had a certain level of agency to assert their place in the ever-changing, if uncertain, Polish Jewish world.

Notes

I would like to thank Natalia Aleksiun; John Efron; Naomi Seidman; the participants of Leisure History(ies): The Significance of Summer in the Biography international workshop organized by the German Historical Institute in Warsaw and Vilnius in June 2021, among them in particular Ruth Leiserowitz; and the two anonymous reviewers for their comments on the earlier drafts of this chapter.

1 G. D. Hundert, 'Jewish Children and Childhood in Early Modern East Central Europe', in D. Kraemer (ed.), *The Jewish Family: Metaphor and Memory* (New York, 1989), 81–94: 90.
2 Some of the most significant contributions include I. Bassok, *Teḥiyat hane'urim: mishpaḥah veḥinukh beyahadut polin bein milḥamot ha'olam* (Jerusalem, 2015); id., 'Darkhei ḥinukh bamishpaḥah hayehudit bepolin bein milḥamot ha'olam: nisayon behistoryah antropologit', *Gal-ed*, 24 (2015), 75–106; K. Kijek, *Dzieci modernizmu: Świadomość, kultura i socjalizacja polityczna młodzieży żydowskiej w II Rzeczypospolitej* (Wrocław, 2017); A. Bar-El, 'Jewish Children's Periodicals in Poland between the Two World Wars—in Three Languages', *Rocznik Historii Prasy Polskiej*, 16/1 (2013), 5–48; A. Szyba, '"Czy można zniszczyć kopiec mrówek?" Nauka przyrody w szkołach Centralnej Żydowskiej Organizacji Szkolnej (1921–1939): Teoria i praktyka', *Kwartalnik Historii Żydów*, 268 (2018), 743–61; E. Nachmany Gafny, *Dividing Hearts: The Removal of Jewish Children from Gentile Families in Poland in the Immediate Post Holocaust Years* (Jerusalem, 2009); J. Sliwa, *Jewish Childhood in Kraków: A Microhistory of the Holocaust* (New Brunswick, NJ, 2021); J. Michlic (ed.), *Jewish Families in Europe: 1939–Present: History, Representation, and Memory* (Waltham, Mass., 2017); A. Helman (ed.), *No Small Matter: Features of Jewish Childhood* (Oxford, 2021); H. Datner-Śpiewak, 'Instytucje opieki nad dzieckiem i szkoły powszechne Centralnego Komitetu Żydowskiego w Polsce w latach 1945–1946', *Biuletyn Żydowskiego Instytutu Historycznego*, 119 (1981), 37–51; S. Martin,' Jewish Youth Between Tradition and Assimilation: Exploring Polish Jewish Identity in Interwar Krakow', *Polish Review*, 46/4 (2001), 461–77; id., 'How to House a Child: Providing Homes for Jewish Children in Interwar Poland', *East European Jewish Affairs*, 45 (2005), 26–41.
3 By 1934 there were nearly 600,000 school-age Jewish children (see J. Marcus, *Social and Political History of the Jews in Poland 1919–1939* (Berlin, 1983), 149). That is more than the entire Jewish community of Germany at the time. In Kraków in autumn 1939, out of 64,000 Jews, a third were children (see J. Michlic, 'Mapping the History of Child Holocaust Survivors', in Helman (ed.), *No Small Matter*, 79–102: 84).
4 Dr M. Peker, 'Dzieci w mieście', *Dziecko*, June–July 1932, p. 3. This is not unique to Poland, of course. For an excellent example of the heightened focus and competing claims on children perceived as collective property and its consequences, see T. Zara, *Kidnapped Souls: National Indifference and the Battle for Children in the Bohemian Lands, 1900–1948* (Ithaca, NY, 2008); see also A. Griffante, *Children, Poverty and Nationalism in Lithuania, 1900–1940* (Cham, 2019); M. Venken and D. Stola (eds.), *Borderland Studies Meets Child Studies: A European Encounter* (Frankfurt am Main, 2017).
5 Particularly noteworthy is the work of the ethnographer and folklorist Regina Lilientalowa (1877–1924) (see R. Lilientalowa, 'Dziecko żydowskie', *Materyały Antropologiczno-Archeologiczne i Etnograficzne Akademii Umiejętności w Krakowie*, 7 (1904), 141–73; Ger. trans.: R. Lilienthal, 'Das Kind bei den Juden', *Mitteilungen zur jüdischen Volkskunde*, 25 (1908), 1–24; expanded edn.: R. Lilientalowa,, *Dziecko żydowskie* (Kraków, 1927); new edn. (Warsaw, 2007)).
6 See the journal *Folks-gezunt* (Warsaw, 1923–40); 'Men muz shoyn zorgn faran kind', *Vohliner nayes*, 21 May 1937, p. 3.
7 *Chwilka*, the first Jewish magazine for children in Polish appeared in Lwów in 1925. As many as eighty-six additional titles just in Polish appeared until 1939. See A. Landau-Czajka, 'Not Just *Mały Przegląd*: The Ideals and Educational Values Expressed in Jewish Polish-Language Journals for Children and Young Adults', in A. Polonsky, H. Węgrzynek, and A. Żbikowski (eds.), *New Directions in the History of the Jews in the Polish Lands* (Boston, Mass., 2018), 338–55. For an overview of Yiddish and Hebrew magazines, see Bar-El, 'Jewish Children's Periodicals in Poland between the Two World Wars'.

8 Naturally, some of these initiatives pre-date the 1920s nor were they exclusive to the Polish lands.
9 P. S. Fass, 'Introduction', in Helman (ed.), *No Small Matter*, 3–5: 4.
10 The level of editorial interference, usually by adults, differed greatly, as did the detail and background information provided by the authors and the spontaneity of the writings. Therefore, these sources can pose methodological challenges. For a discussion of similar considerations in the German context, see N. Stargardt, 'German Childhoods: The Making of a Historiography', *German History*, 1 (1998), 1–15.
11 'Wielki konkurs piękności dzieci: Rewja urody dziecka żydowskiego', *Nasz Przegląd*, 23 Mar. 1930, p. 12. The contest not only closely resembled the 1929 Miss Judaea beauty pageant but to a certain extent was explicitly patterned upon it. Unlike the case of Miss Judaea, however, no particular criteria or selection committee had been established. Instead, the winners were picked solely based on votes from the general public, with a special write-in ballot printed in *Nasz Przegląd*. Twenty-five children from each age category (0–3 years, 3–6 years, and 6–10 years) were chosen and awarded prizes. The first set of photographs appeared in *Nasz Przegląd*, 25 Mar. 1930, p. 5; the last in *Nasz Przegląd*, 1 June 1930, p. 11; the results were announced in 'Wyniki konkursu piękności dzieci', *Nasz Przegląd*, 15 July 1930, p. 4. For more on Miss Judaea, see E. Plach, 'Introducing Miss Judea 1929: The Politics of Beauty, Race, and Zionism in Inter-War Poland', *Polin*, 20 (2008), 368–91.
12 'Wielki konkurs piękności dzieci: Rewja urody dziecka żydowskiego'.
13 See e.g. *Nasz Przegląd*, 19 Apr. 1930, p. 9; *Nasz Przegląd*, 16 May 1930, p. 5.
14 See e.g. *Nasz Przegląd*, 25 May 1930, p. 11.
15 For Józio Raczkowski, Nahum Sokolow's grandson, 5 years old, see *Nasz Przegląd*, 1 June 1930, p. 11; for Zygmunt Bauman, 5 years old, see *Nasz Przegląd*, 2 Apr. 1930, p. 8; see also I. Wagner, 'Zdjęcie z konkursu piękności i inne dokumenty osobiste: O pracy badawczej i poszukiwaniu znaczeń "czarnych dziur" – na przykładzie rekonstrukcji biografii Zygmunta Baumana', *Autobiografia. Literatura. Kultura. Media*, 1/14 (2020), 145–67.
16 The call was issued on the pages of *Mały Przegląd*. As Anna Landau-Czajka has observed, *Mały Przegląd* encouraged children to question or even challenge the authority of adults. Children were invited to make informed, conscious decisions about whether they should be following and upholding resolutions made by adults. See Landau-Czajka, 'Not Just *Mały Przegląd*', 353.
17 Janeczka, Miodowa Street, 'Wszystko dla dorosłych', *Mały Przegląd*, 21 Mar. 1930, p. 1.
18 Jaś, Złota Street, 'I chłopcy', *Mały Przegląd*, 21 Mar. 1930, p. 1.
19 Różka and Estusia, 'Z całej Polski', *Mały Przegląd*, 21 Mar. 1930, p. 1. For children's requests for the contest, see 'Konkurs Dużego Przeglądu na najładniejsze dziecko żydowskie', *Mały Przegląd*, 21 Mar. 1930, pp. 1–2. A few of the youngsters specifically opposed the idea. Among the arguments they raised, two resonated the most, namely 'why should we imitate adults?' (Frania, 'Przeciwnicy Konkursu', *Mały Przegląd*, 21 Mar. 1930, p. 1) and 'beauty is not a merit . . . instead there should be a contest of diligence, patience' (Felek, 'Przeciwnicy Konkursu', *Mały Przegląd*, 21 Mar. 1930, p. 1). However, the editorial board of *Nasz Przegląd* dismissed this scepticism, asserting that these malcontents should not be taking it so seriously. See 'Wielki konkurs piękności dzieci: Rewja urody dziecka żydowskiego'.
20 The autobiographies were submitted by young people for three competitions in 1932, 1934, and 1939. The primary goal of the contests was to gain an in-depth understanding of the social and cultural processes at work within the Polish Jewish society of the interwar period. See *Awakening Lives: Autobiographies of Jewish Youth in Poland before the Holocaust*,

ed. J. Shandler (New Haven, Conn., 2002); *Ostatnie pokolenie: Autobiografie polskiej młodzieży żydowskiej okresu międzywojennego*, ed. A. Cała (Warsaw, 2003); *Alilot ne'urim: otobiyografiyot shel benei no'ar yehudim mipolin bein shetei milḥamot ha'olam*, ed. I. Bassok (Tel Aviv, 2011). Max Weinreich, one of the founding directors of YIVO and the contest's originator, believed that writing an autobiography could serve as a compensation mechanism that could enhance the self-confidence of young Polish Jews, who were experiencing particularly severe pressures, especially economic hardship and antisemitism. In 1935 Weinreich published research based on the findings (M. Weinreich, *Der veg tsu unzer yugnt: yesoydes, metodn, problemen fun yidisher yugnt forshung* (Vilna, 1935); M. Weinreich, 'Studjum o młodzieży żydowskiej', *Przeglądu Socjologicznego*, 3 (1935), 30–82). See also I. Bassok, 'Lishe'elat erkhan hahistori shel otobiyografiyot benei no'ar me'osef yivo', *Mada'ei yahadut*, 44 (2007), 137–64; K. Kijek, *Dzieci modernizmu: Świadomość, kultura i socjalizacja młodzieży żydowskiej w II Rzeczypospolitej* (Wrocław, 2017); id., 'Was It Possible to Avoid Hebrew Assimilation? Hebraism, Polonization, and the Zionist Tarbut School System in the Last Decade of Interwar Poland', *Jewish Social Studies*, 21/2 (2016), 105–41; M. Klingsberg, *Child and Adolescent Behavior under Stress: An Analytical Topical Guide to a Collection of Autobiographies of Jewish Young Men and Women in Poland (1932–1939)* (New York, 1965); M. Moseley, 'Life, Literature: Autobiographies of Jewish Youth in Interwar Poland', *Jewish Social Studies*, 7/1 (2003), 1–51.

21 *Mały Przegląd* was established by Janusz Korczak in 1926, and its circulation soon reached 50,000. Józef Hen, who would later become an illustrious writer, sent his first contribution to *Mały Przegląd* when he was 8 years old and was one of many Jewish children who wrote letters and reports for the paper. On average, the editorial office received about 4,000 letters a year. See A. Witkowska-Krych, 'Budowanie od podstaw: "Mały Przegląd" jako nowatorski, systematyczny i wieloletni projekt pedagogiczno-społeczny', *Almanach Muzealny*, 8 (2014), 167–89.

22 'Przypisek redakcji', *Mały Przegląd*, 8 June 1928, p. 2.

23 On the benefits and disadvantages of using *Mały Przegląd* as a source, see A. Landau-Czajka, 'Czasopisma jako źródła do badań nad społeczeństwem: Osobliwy przypadek "Małego Przeglądu"', *Rocznik Dziejów Społecznych i Gospodarczych*, 78 (2017), 267–82.

24 On how Polish Jews embraced travelling, see S. Kassow, 'Travel and Local History as a National Mission: Polish Jews and the Landkentenish Movement in the 1920s and 1930s', in J. Brauch, A. Lipphardt, and A. Nocke (eds.), *Jewish Topographies: Visions of Space, Traditions of Place* (Aldershot, 2008), 241–64; M. Silber 'Lirot o lo lirot: tiyulim beshalosh safot bevilnah bashanot ha-30 hame'uḥarot', *Zmanim*, 125 (2014), 58–67; see also my forthcoming book with the tentative title *Mapping Jewish Poland: Leisure Travel and Identity in the Interwar Period*.

25 Ezra Mendelsohn eloquently fleshed out the main arguments (see E. Mendelsohn, 'Interwar Poland: Good for the Jews or Bad for the Jews?', in C. Abramsky, M. Jachimczyk, and A. Polonsky (eds.), *The Jews in Poland* (Oxford, 1986), 130–40). Historians continue to disagree about the Jewish experience in the Second Polish Republic (see E. Melzer, *No Way Out: The Politics of Polish Jewry, 1935–1939* (Cincinnati, 1997); A. Landau-Czajka, *Syn będzie Lech...: Asymilacja Żydów w Polsce międzywojennej* (Warsaw, 2006); P. Brykczynski, *Primed for Violence: Murder, Antisemitism, and Democratic Politics in Interwar Poland* (Madison, Wis., 2018); B. Wasserstein, *On the Eve: The Jews of Europe before the Second World War* (New York, 2012)).

26 Naturally, the same cannot be said about the adolescent members of Poland's politicized Jewish groups.

27 Tusia, Będzin, 'Wyjadę, czy nie wyjadę?', *Mały Przegląd*, 15 June 1934, p. 3.
28 H. Weissblumówna, Stanisławów, 'Nasza wycieczka do Gdyni', *Świt*, Jan. 1933, p. 5.
29 YIVO Archives, New York, RG 4 (Autobiographies of Jewish Youth in Poland) Autobiography, 3505: G.J. (Pol./Yid., 1934), 30.
30 Ibid. 29.
31 The phenomena of spa towns being visited mainly by women can be observed at the beginning of the twentieth century (see e.g. *Podręcznik statystyki Galicyi*, ed. T. Pilat, iii/1 (Lwów, 1908); for social commentary, see e.g. Lustige Pesimist, 'Lebn zol di datshe', *Haynt*, 19 June 1931, p. 8; M. Kipnis, 'A Tog in Ciechocinek', *Haynt*, 24 Aug. 1934, p. 8; S. Faygenboym, 'Fun der serye: tsurik fun datshe', *Haynt*, 16 Sept. 1927, p. 8; M. Nadelman, *Undzer expres*, 20 Sept. 1929, p. 12; 'Żona na willegiaturze, a mąż w mieście', *Ewa*, 3 June 1928, p. 9).
32 H. Griesówna, 'Światła i cienie pensjonatów dla dzieci', *Ewa*, 22 June 1930, p. 2; 'Zdrojowiska', *Nowy Dziennik*, 30 May 1932, p. 16.
33 See e.g. 'Letniska', *Nasz Przegląd*, 3 June 1926, p. 8.
34 YIVO Archives, RG 4, Autobiography 3722: Kubuś (Pol., 1932), 12–13.
35 'Tsum sof fun shul-yor', *Di kinder-velt*, May–June 1930, p. 2.
36 Ibid.
37 'Lomir lernen-zingendik un shpilendik', *Di kinder-velt*, June 1928, pp. 1–2.
38 Mietek, Muranowska, 'Prawo do słońca', *Mały Przegląd*, 27 Apr. 1934, p. 1.
39 Szaja, Częstochowa, 'W Kamińsku', *Mały Przegląd*, 17 May 1929, p. 1.
40 United States Holocaust Memorial Museum, Washington DC, 1998.A.0176: Lena Jurand, oral history interview (15 Aug. 1998; Eng.) 10.
41 Ibid. 10–11.
42 T. Y. Gutentag (Tavyomi), *Ḥokhmat hanashim* (Piotrkow, 1926), 24; cited in N. Seidman, *Sarah Schenirer and the Bais Yaakov Movement: A Revolution in the Name of Tradition* (London, 2019), 58.
43 On one of the girls, Anna Kluger, see R. Manekin, 'Mashehu ḥadash legamrei', *Masekhet*, 2 (2004), 63–85: 82–3; ead., *The Rebellion of the Daughters: Jewish Women Runaways in Habsburg Galicia* (Princeton, NJ, 2020), 135–65.
44 See Gutentag, *Ḥokhmat hanashim*, 24.
45 YIVO Archives, RG 4, Autobiography 3682A: R.A. (Yid., 1934), 42.
46 Ibid. 43.
47 YIVO Archives, RG 4, Autobiography 3735: J. (Pol., 1934), 13.
48 'Rodzice i wycieczki szkolne', *Ewa*, 1 July 1928, p. 10.
49 J. Korczak, 'Pożegnanie', *Mały Przegląd*, 1 July 1927, p. 1.
50 Ibid.
51 S. Schenirer, 'Appendix A: From the Diary', trans. U. Madej-Krupitski, in Seidman, *Sarah Schenirer and the Bais Yaakov Movement*, 369–80: 380; see also Sarah Schenirer's diary (Wrocław University); *'Żydówką być to rzecz niemała': Pisma autobiograficzne Sary Szenirer*, ed. D. Dekert and J. Lisek (Warsaw, forthcoming).
52 Seidman, *Sarah Schenirer and the Bais Yaakov Movement*, 79.
53 YIVO Archives, RG 4, Autobiography 3630: Leyzer (Pol., 1939), 3–4. The comprehensive study of Józef Piłsudski's attitudes towards the Jews has yet to be written. On the one hand, historians have emphasized that Polish Jews perceived Piłsudski as a strong leader and upholder of their civic rights; on the other, he did not acknowledge the national rights of Polish Jewry. Natalia Aleksiun correctly states that Piłsudski was 'not antagonistic towards

Jews and . . . included them in the conception of Polish citizenship as long as they remained politically loyal and committed to the Polish national cause' (N. Aleksiun, 'Regards from My Shtetl: Polish Jews Write to Piłsudski, 1933–1935', *Polish Review*, 56 (2011), 57–71: 70). On the ambivalent attitudes of Piłsudski and the Polish Socialist Party towards Jews, see e.g. P. Shwartz, *Yuzeph pilsudski zayn batsiung tsu der yidn-frage un zayn kampf kegn bund: 1893–1905* (Warsaw, 1936); see also J. D. Zimmerman, *Józef Piłsudski Founding Father of Modern Poland* (Cambridge, Mass., 2022).

54 YIVO Archives, RG 4: Autobiography 3630, Leyzer, 8–9.
55 See Z. Pakuła, *Siwe kamienie: Wielkopolscy Żydzi* (Poznań, 1998), 181–4.
56 A train line connecting Warsaw and neighbouring villages such as Miedzeszyn, Falenica, Józefów, and Michalin was built in 1910. Given the close proximity and easy commute, it was an extremely popular leisure destination for Warsaw's Jews. See M. Olkuśnik, *Wyjechać z miasta: Mieszkańcy Warszawy wobec podróży, turystyki i wypoczynku na przełomie XIX i XX wieku* (Warsaw, 2015); R. Lewandowski, *Kronenberg, Andriolli i wilegiatura, czyli podwarszawskie letniska linii otwockiej* (Józefów, 2012).
57 J. Bauman, *Zima o poranku: Opowieść dziewczynki z warszawskiego getta* (Kraków, 1989), 9–10.
58 'Reporterzy Harry i Norris w podróży', *Mały Przegląd*, 16 Aug. 1929, p. 2.
59 'Reporterzy Harry i Norris w podróży', *Mały Przegląd*, 23 Aug. 1929, p. 2.
60 Ibid.
61 Ibid.
62 YIVO Archives, RG 4, Autobiography 3823: F.B. (Yid., 1933), 10.
63 Janka, Walicowa, 'Pieczone kartofle', *Mały Przegląd*, 16 June 1933, p. 3.
64 'G.W.', in *Awakening Lives*, 296–320: 298; see YIVO Archives, RG 4, Autobiography 3713: 'G.W.' (Yid., 1939), 7.
65 Kuba, Józefowie, 'Wakacje zeszłego roku', *Mały Przegląd*, 17 May 1929, p. 1.
66 Mania, Prague, 'W Otwocku', *Mały Przegląd*, 17 May 1929, p. 2.
67 YIVO Archives, RG 4, Autobiography 3815: B.B. (Pol., 1939), 24.
68 YIVO Archives, RG 4, Autobiography 3505: G.J., 29.
69 Jerzy Zichy, 'W Tatrach', *Mały Przegląd*, 2 June 1933, p. 3.
70 YIVO Archives, RG 4, Autobiography 3817: H.C. (Pol., 1939), 37–8.
71 Ibid.
72 Heniek, 'W Urlach: Antysemitizm', *Mały Przegląd*, 1 June 1928, p. 3.
73 Dadek, Nowolipie, 'Niech będzie dobrze i spokojnie…', *Mały Przegląd*, 23 June 1939, p. 4.
74 For other examples of Jewish children taking an interest in churches and monasteries, see e.g. 'Reporterzy Harry i Norris w podróży', *Mały Przegląd*, 9 Aug. 1929, p. 2. Moreover, the first and probably only Yiddish travel guide to Poland, by the Vilna-based physician Hirsch Matz, described 115 locales over 370 pages. Matz included detailed recommendations for spending time in these destinations, featuring walking tours in nearby forests, mountains, old towns, castle ruins, and occasionally even churches. See, for example, his note about the 'splendid church in Żółkiew' (H. Matz, *Kurorter un turistik in poylen* (Warsaw, 1935), 104).
75 A. Maślak-Maciejewska, 'Ku poprawie zdrowia i "utrzymaniu duszy dziecięcej w atmosferze słonecznej i radosnej" – lecznicza kolonia wakacyjna dla dzieci żydowskich w Rabce (1890–1939)', *Studia Historyczne*, 2015, no. 3, pp. 349–66.
76 Ibid. 357.
77 See L. Vulman, *Tsen yor yidishe gezuntshutz-arbet in poyln: tsum 10-yorikn yubiley fun 'toz'*

(Warsaw, 1933), 18; Y. Bauer, *My Brother's Keeper: A History of the American Jewish Joint Distribution Committee, 1929–1939* (Philadelphia, Pa., 1974).

78 Central Archive for the History of the Jewish People, Jerusalem, JDC/Ph 123–152: 'Child Care Activities in Poland: Summer Colonies Initiated and Supported by the A.J.D.C.', [5].
79 Ibid. [8, 32].
80 Municipal and governmental subsidies amounted to around 10 per cent of the total cost (ibid. [147–8]).
81 On Jewish youth movements in interwar Poland, see e.g. I. Bassok, 'Jewish Youth Movements in Poland between the Wars as Heirs of the Kehilah', *Polin*, 30 (2018), 299–320; D. Kupfert Heller, *Jabotinsky's Children: Polish Jews and the Rise of Right-Wing Zionism* (Princeton, NJ, 2018); J. Jacobs, *Bundist Counterculture in Interwar Poland* (New York, 2009); M. Kozłowska, *Świetlana przyszłość? Żydowski Związek Młodzieżowy Cukunft wobec wyzwań międzywojennej Polski* (Kraków, 2016).
82 Betar, *Oyfn lager un oysflug* (Warsaw, 1937), 4.
83 E. Meshtshinski, *Pyonyer, hit dayn gezunt* (Moscow, 1932), 19.
84 Seidman, *Sarah Schenirer and the Bais Yaakov Movement*, 125.
85 See *Instruktsye far vanderungen* (Vilna, 1927); *Instruktsyes vegn zumer-lagern un vanderungen* (Warsaw, 1935); L. Khain, *Vi azoy darf men pravn turitsik* (Warsaw, c.1938); I. Kornblit, *Onvayzungen un eytzes far onfanger-nartler* (Warsaw, 1938); Edwin, 'Ze śpiewem i plecakiem, jak i dokąd?', *Mały Przegląd*, 5 May 1933, pp. 2–3.
86 Lusia, Częstochowa, 'Miłe wspomnienia', *Mały Przegląd*, 9 June 1933, p. 4.
87 YIVO Archives, RG 4, Autobiography 3815: B.B., 27.
88 Mendele, 230 Chłopców, Michalin, 'Kolonje letnie: Wycieczki', *Mały Przegląd*, 8 June 1928, p. 1.
89 YIVO Archives, RG 4, Autobiography 3660: Z.F. (Pol., 1935), 26.
90 Chaimek, 'Trzy listy do rodziców z kolonji', *Mały Przegląd*, 12 Aug. 1927, p. 1.
91 Archiwum Żydowskiego Instytutu Historycznego, Warsaw, 809: *Iton hituli*, July 1939.
92 Ibid. 38.
93 Ibid. 10–11.
94 Ibid. 6–11.
95 A. 'Nocna wycieczka', *Itonejnu*, 15 June 1933, p. 7.
96 Szimszon, 'Warunki II. Próby Skautowej', *Diwrej Akiba*, 28 May 1937, p. 555.
97 Daniel Heller made a similar point concerning Betar; however, this way of thinking applied to all Polish Zionists (see Heller, *Jabotinsky's Children*, 151–4).
98 YIVO Archives, RG 4, Autobiography 3815: B.B., 29–33.
99 M. Kozłowska, 'Wandering Jews: Camping Culture and Jewish Socialist Youth in Interwar Poland', *Jewish Culture and History*, 16 (2015), 42–53: 47.
100 YIVO Archives, RG 4: Autobiography 3654, H.Z. (Pol., 1934), 16.
101 Ibid.
102 'Wieści z ruchu', *Diwrej Akiba*, 28 May 1937, pp. 547–50.
103 For more on religious initiatives and the young, see G. Bacon, 'To Enlist the Enthusiasm of the Young: Orthodox Jewish Non-Political Responses to the Challenges of Interwar Poland', *Polin*, 33 (2021), 285–308.
104 YIVO Archives, RG 4: Autobiography 3707: G.C. (Yid., 1939); YIVO Archives, RG 4: Autobiography 3707: G.C. (Yid., 1939); 'The Stormer', in *Awakening Lives*, 226–62.
105 Ibid. 242.

106 YIVO Archives, RG 4: Autobiography 3541: R.M. (Yid., 1939), 28–9.
107 Jadzia, 'Wakacje roku zeszłego', *Mały Przegląd*, 17 May 1929, p. 2.
108 J. Korczak, *Na koloniach letnich: Mośki, Joski i Srule* (Warsaw, 1946), 54.
109 S. Sholzou, 'Turistik un landkentenish bay unz, yidn', *Lubliner togblat*, 20 Oct. 1933, p. 4.
110 By 1934 as many as 84 per cent of Jewish children attended state schools, although there were significant regional differences (see K. Kijek, 'Between a Love of Poland, Symbolic Violence, and Antisemitism: The Idiosyncratic Effects of the State Education System on Young Jews in Interwar Poland', *Polin*, 30 (2018), 237–64: 241–2).
111 Marcin Wiener, Katowice, 'Ostatni dzwonek szkolny', *Mały Przegląd*, 23 June 1939, p. 1.

Autograph Books of Polish Jewish Schoolgirls as Historical Documents

NATALIA ALEKSIUN

The autograph books and the inscriptions in them collected by teenage Jewish girls during the Second World War shed significant light on the persistence of a culture in which Polish poetry continued to be cited in the midst of the Soviet and Nazi occupations. The ritual of collecting such inscriptions was an integral part of attending a Polish school, and offered an inclusive space for inter-ethnic friendships. In the context of the Second World War, these autograph books help us construct a more nuanced picture of the childhood of young Jews before and during the occupation. They provide a sense of both biographical continuity and the new context of dramatically reduced social interaction. They show both how pre-war conventional tropes survived in the new conditions and how these were also adversely affected by the conditions of Nazi rule. They are a remarkable testament to those who survived, and to those who perished.

IN FEBRUARY 1945, several months after the Soviets liberated Borysław (Boryslav) in Eastern Galicia, Danuta Bodwińska reproduced a poem, 'For the New Year', in the autograph book that belonged to Irena Koretz, her Jewish classmate.[1] Written by the neo-Romantic poet Władysław Bełza, whose verses had long been part of the literary canon in Polish schools,[2] it implored its readers:

> We should keep ourselves far from what is pompous,
> From what caresses our ears with an empty sound.
> Let us love what is bright and reasonable,
> What is deep and full of meaning.[3]

Along with this universal message about making moral choices, Danuta placed her commemorative citation in the context of the occupations, loss, and destruction, dedicating it to 'lovely and cute Irenka during the time of war'.[4] The citation was accompanied by a colourful picture of a boy and girl at play wearing festive clothes, accompanied by toys and a dog (Figure 1). The poem cited by Danuta is one of more than a dozen literary texts, many of them accompanied by drawings and collages, included in Irena's autograph book. Adolescent girls and boys, teachers, and family members dedicated them to her, a teenage Polish Jewish refugee from Warsaw, who started collecting autographs in Lwów (Lviv) in February 1940, continued in Borysław during the Soviet and German occupations and after the liberation, and then following her family's relocation to Kraków as part of the post-war repatriation of Polish citizens.[5] Danuta's note is one of a handful of dedications that explicitly mention the war and allude to the dramatic experiences of the owner of the autograph book, her family, and friends.

Figure 1 Irena Koretz, autograph book, [7]
United States Holocaust Memorial Museum, Washington DC, 1995.A.1064

Autograph books like Irena's reflect a practice that had been current among young people, Jewish and non-Jewish, in Poland before autumn 1939 and which continued after the outbreak of the war.[6] They include anonymous literary exhortations and fragments of poems by well-known authors whose work had been studied and learnt by heart in schools.[7] These tokens of shared experience were built on a centuries-long tradition that harked back to early modern Europe. In sixteenth-century German universities, students used autograph books to collect signatures on graduation and kept them as a sentimental memento of college life. Increasingly, students and scholars carried such books with them as they moved between universities, as was the common practice in the German lands. They sought to record the good wishes of fellow students, teachers, and colleagues and therefore provide themselves with academic credentials, depending upon who had signed them and what had been written. In doing so, they also chronicled their academic peregrinations and encounters far from home. By the seventeenth century autograph books had become current outside universities too, with entries inscribed by noteworthy acquaintances and famous personalities. In particular, they mapped out social relations of importance to their owners. They were filled with inscriptions, which consisted of a dedication, a citation, maxim, or the writer's original text, and a signature, followed by the date and place. Both their format and content were only slightly personalized. Autograph books circulated in salons, which were increasingly held by women, incorporating the genres of rhymed compliments and panegyrics. 'They constituted a sort of written materialization of salon sociability, giving a convenient pretext for conversation.'[8] Popular in the nineteenth century, by the twentieth century autograph books had lost their appeal among their adult audience and become part of adolescent school culture.[9]

This chapter analyses the autograph books that Polish Jewish teenagers put together during the Second World War, under the Soviet and German occupations. I consider the social context and internal chronology of the texts and drawings. Taking Bożena Keff's study of Jewish poetry written by young authors during the Holocaust as a point of departure, I discuss the choice of texts cited and the personal inscriptions. I also examine the tension between self-expression and the role played by customary formulas.[10]

I will focus on two autograph books created by two Jewish teenagers who survived the Holocaust in Eastern Galicia: Irena Koretz and Klara Szwarc (Schwarz).[11] These autograph books, which include signatures, poems, and drawings by their classmates, relatives, and friends in Lwów, Borysław, Żółkiew (Zhovkva), and Kraków, document their friendships and help to map out relationships among Jewish teenagers, their non-Jewish classmates, their teachers, and their family members before, during, and after the war. Irena's and Klara's autograph books supplement and contextualize their other personal accounts: diaries, memoirs, and oral testimonies. These do not mention their autograph books or describe how they collected signatures or what the autograph books meant for them. However, Irena's and Klara's bonds often feature indirectly. In her brief memoir and wartime notes, Irena reflected on the centrality of her friendships. She repeatedly mentions close friends, and alludes to her affectionate relationship with her elder sister. Klara's wartime diary describes cramped living conditions, meagre food supplies, frequent threats of discovery, and the death of her sister. Over the many months of being confined in a small hiding place, the subject of friendship disappears almost completely from view. Klara returned to the subject of her friends in her post-war recollections. The practice of keeping autograph books was hardly unique to Jewish adolescents, so these personal Holocaust documents raise questions: is there a distinctively *Jewish* content to Irena's and Klara's autograph books? How did their content and style reflect their interrupted childhoods? Do they constitute a unique type of Holocaust ego-document which offers insights into coming of age during the Soviet and German occupations?

The Making of the Autograph Books

Irena Koretz was born in January 1928, in Borysław, to a family who originally came from Tarnów.[12] In 1920 her father Józef was listed as a second lieutenant in the Polish army, and later he worked as a general manager for an international plumbing company, while her mother Rozalia (née Müller) was a homemaker.[13] Together with her elder sister Olga, Irena was raised in Warsaw, where she enrolled in the Zofia Kurmanowa school, a private school attended mostly by non-Jewish children. The family left their home at 49 Mokotowska Street on 6 September 1939, fleeing east, and by October had arrived in Lwów, where her mother's relatives lived.[14] In the spring of 1940, after her father received an offer of employment in a branch of the plumbing firm he worked for, the family relocated again, settling in Borysław, which at this time had a Jewish community of about 13,000. Following the outbreak of the German–Soviet war, the town was occupied by the Germans on 1 July 1941. The Koretzes survived the pogrom which took place on 2 July 1941, shortly after the arrival of the Germans, and escaped capture during several round-ups—in November 1941 and August, October, and November 1942. Irena and her mother relied on Olga's friend Ewa Fedorow and her parents, who lived on the outskirts of Borysław. By the spring of 1943 the Koretzes had moved to the local labour camp which had been established in Mraźnica in October 1942, and where the remaining Jews of Borysław enjoyed a degree of security.[15] In mid-February 1943, 600 Jews from the city's workshops and sawmill and Jews from the ghetto deemed unfit for labour were shot at the slaughterhouse. The Jews remaining in the ghetto were murdered when it was liquidated on 2 June 1943. Those interned in the camp feared it would be liquidated as well, and alarming rumours grew strong in the early spring of 1944. In March 1944 Irena bid goodbye to her remaining friends and went into hiding.[16] She survived hidden by a local family on the outskirts of Borysław together with her mother, and later on also with her sister and father. They were liberated on 7 August 1944.[17]

Klara Szwarc was born in Żółkiew in 1926. The daughter of Majer Berisz (Meir) Szwarc and Sara (Salka; née Reitzfeld), she grew up in a relatively affluent family who owned an oil-pressing factory. She attended a primary school in her home town and the Jewish Tarbut school. During the Soviet occupation of Żółkiew, when the Jewish population increased to some 5,000 due to the influx of refugees, her family struggled as their enterprise was nationalized. Her father was able to avoid arrest, and Klara attended a Soviet public school. Shortly after the arrival of the Germans on 29 June 1941, a pogrom took place and the local synagogue was set on fire. During the German occupation Klara studied in a small underground group of students set up on her mother's initiative. She became active in the sanitary commission organized by Pepka Fisz, which provided medical assistance to Jews and took care of those who had been injured jumping from the trains taking them to the Bełżec death camp that passed close to Żółkiew. Her family evaded capture during the round-ups in March and November 1942. When the ghetto was established in December 1942, her father decided they would not move there but hide instead. Together with her parents and her younger sister, Mania, Klara hid in a bunker prepared by members of the Melman and Patrontasch families in a house taken over by Walenty Beck, who together with his wife and daughter took care of them. Encouraged by her mother, she wrote a diary while in hiding. Klara and her parents survived, but her sister fled the bunker during a fire, was betrayed and murdered.[18] Klara and her parents emerged from hiding when the Soviets liberated Żółkiew on 23 July 1944.

Neither Klara nor Irena mentions autograph books in their wartime diaries or post-war memoirs, and neither reflects on the meaning of the practice. It seems they must have been familiar with it in the context of school. In a conversation with me, Irena called her autograph book, usually described in Polish as a *sztambuch*, a *pamiętnik* (memoir). She did not recall any particular inspiration for commencing it: 'I started it. No sooner did we leave Warsaw [than] we found ourselves in Lwów. I started the *pamiętnik* there. I don't know how. I don't know how [it happened], nobody gave me the idea.'[19] She began it on 5 February 1940 with the formal title 'Memoir of Irka Koretz' and a conventional admonition:

> Who sincerely wishes to do so,
> should inscribe a remembrance.
> Who does not know what to write,
> is asked at least not to tear a page out.[20]

She signed it with a drawing of a duckling, her nickname among her friends.[21] Irena's friends signed her autograph book during the Soviet and German occupations until the spring of 1944, then in Borysław after liberation and later in Kraków. The first to leave an inscription was her sister Olga, who did so on 11 February 1940. Olga situated this in her contemporary condition of being a refugee, stating that the note was inscribed 'unfortunately in Lwów rather than in Warsaw'.[22]

By contrast, Klara's autograph book starts shortly before the war, in July 1939, but lasts only until December 1941 and thus ends during the German occupation. She seems to have ceased collecting autographs before the third round-up in her home town when her family went into hiding. She did not collect signatures in either Żółkiew, after the arrival of the Soviet army, or Legnica in Lower Silesia, where her family settled briefly after repatriation.

In both autograph books, throughout the Soviet and German occupations the inscriptions remain formulaic, true to the genre, which mixes personal and public spheres. While most friends wrote their inscriptions and drew decorations individually, they were aware of the fact that these would be read by others.[23] The wartime reality did not change the rules of collecting: the pages do not follow a chronological order, but their sequence can be reconstructed since most of them are dated. Nor did the war change the literary or visual repertoire: short poems, dedications, and illustrations.

Envisioning a Worthy Life

On 4 July 1939 J. Handlowa wrote in Klara's autograph book the earliest dated maxim: 'One gets to know oneself not by pondering, but by doing. Try to fulfil your duty and you will know your value.'[24] Although no attribution is provided, this citation comes from Johann Wolfgang Goethe, the most influential representative of nineteenth-century German literature and precursor of Romanticism.[25] Indeed, many poems dedicated to Klara and Irena were written by the Romantic poets, whose verses played an important role in Polish formal education. Particularly favoured were poems by Adam Mickiewicz, who was cited by both teachers and classmates.[26] In February 1940 a teacher, Izabella Kosińska, inscribed an aphorism by Mickiewicz in Klara's autograph book:

> In words, we see only desire
> In action, strength
> It's harder to live the day well
> Than to write a book.[27]

In October 1940 Rózia Post cited Mickiewicz for 'dear Klara':

> 'Why', asked the boy, 'do I need these
> Triangles, quadrilaterals, circles, parabolas?'
> 'That they are necessary', said the sage, 'you must believe;
> You'll understand when you start measuring the world.'[28]

A couple of weeks later a Jewish classmate by the name of U. Farbówna inscribed another fragment of Mickiewicz's, quoting his poetic drama *Forefathers' Eve* to the effect that one should live to serve one's fellow human beings.[29] Romantic poetry provided many examples of moralizing calls to pursue self-improvement, self-realization, and self-discovery. A Polish classmate of Irena's advised her: 'Look at the world with clarity and overcome difficulties with your will.'[30] Another inscription in Irena's autograph book, probably written by an adult, read: 'Deeds testify to a person's worth. Keep on increasing yours.'[31] Eścia Sochaczewska inscribed a poem she erroneously attributed to the Polish pre-Romantic poet, literary critic, and translator Kazimierz Brodziński:

> Life is a task, not a reward
> We must redeem the prize of life with smoke,
> Life is a fight, but not a freedom
> Only victory is decorated with laurel.[32]

Irena's autograph book includes a similar quotation: 'Life is a struggle; the world is a battlefield.' The writer, Zygmunt Stein, wished her victory. While the text could have been understood in universal terms, the illustration was chillingly contemporary: a plane dropping a bomb (Figure 2).[33]

Equally popular was the poetry of Adam Asnyk. In Klara's autograph book, her friend Hemerling cited his poem 'The Echo of the Cradle', conveying the importance of the beauty of the soul and eternal love.[34] In spring 1940 a teacher cited a poem by Józef Ignacy Kraszewski:

> Even if your soul is thirsty and hungry,
> Do not drink the chalice of life to the bottom,
> Lest you turn the desired into the accursed—
> There are bitter dregs at the bottom of every cup![35]

This, like many other citations, was inscribed without identifying the author.[36]

Figure 2 Irena Koretz, autograph book, [54]
United States Holocaust Memorial Museum, 1995.A.1064

On the pages of Klara's and Irena's autograph books, it is difficult to see a clear change in source material or even of tone during the Soviet occupation. Possibly one exception is the appearance of Pushkin in Russian, written by Klara's new teacher.[37] The outbreak of the German–Soviet war, the German arrival in Eastern Galicia, and the occupation of its cities accompanied by a wave of anti-Jewish violence are also imperceptible. For example, on 5 September 1941, two months after a pogrom in Borysław in which hundreds of Jews were brutally murdered and many more wounded, A. Ziller cited a poem ascribed to Pushkin as a keepsake for 'Irena', whose name was represented by a drawing of a duck:

> It has always been so,
> Because this is how the world has been created,
> Many are learned, but few wise:
> One has scores of acquaintances, but only few friends.[38]

In late October 1941, several months after the arrival of the Germans in Żółkiew, a friend of Klara's inscribed a verse from Mickiewicz: 'Others enrich themselves with study and money. You must arrive at wisdom through your own work.'[39] An adult, probably a teacher, reminded Klara that 'immortality is born through grey daily labour'.[40]

The second most important aspect of the literary quotations was the references to the centrality of memory—as having the highest of values—and of one's friends. This is reflected in the quotation Marceli (Martek) Egert chose for Irena in the summer of 1940:

> Treasure every beauty on earth
> Let your heart be touched by it.
> But remember above all
> The most beautiful soul![41]

In summer 1940 Anita Lauf wrote in Irena's autograph book that friendship was eternal and resisted ageing and decline.[42] Neither friends nor teachers seem to allude to the ever-present chaos, hardship, and fear. Some citations, however, take the form of formulaic verses that underscore the importance of memory in the face of transience.[43]

When seeking to leave a record of themselves, some young people did not cite poetry or share advice, but simply inscribed their name.[44] While this could seem rather trivial or banal in peacetime and could be a result of time constraints or a weaker emotional bond with the owner of the book, during the war and occupation even a plain inscription gained additional meaning. It was part of the convention of the genre that entries in autograph books were to be read in the future, but the Jewish teenagers who collected signatures in Borysław and Żółkiew could hardly rely on having a future. Yet, in defiance or denial, Karol Randmesser, who wrote in Irena's autograph book only the simple words 'As a memento', did so in August 1943, shortly after the liquidation of the ghetto.[45] Most of Irena's and Klara's friends implored the addressees to remember them in the future, to resist the passage of time.[46] Thus in May 1941, in Żółkiew, a Jewish colleague of Klara's, Rachela Löwenkron, cited a poem about memory by Mickiewicz:

> Blessed are those who drown in your memory,
> Like the coral or the pearl,
> Which the Baltic water will keep in its pure womb.
> Their azure colour,
> They will keep forever.
> But I, like a small pebble,
> Do not glow like corals, nor with the grace of a pearl,
> I would like to play for at least one moment in this wave,
> Before I am forgotten and fall into the oblivion of sand.[47]

Following the liquidation of the ghetto in Borysław, J. Kriegel, living in the labour camp in the town, dedicated to Irena verses about the slow vanishing of the material and psychological worlds:

> Everything in the world slowly wanes
> Memories of happiness and pain
> Everything passes away as fate decrees
> Only memory remains.[48]

While he did not mention the recent tragic events, his text probably referred to the raw emotions and sense of powerlessness following the destruction of the vast majority of Borysław's Jews. Inscriptions about memory were particularly poignant in the last weeks and days before the labour camp was liquidated, as many of the remaining Jews feared the worst and hoped to survive by going into hiding.[49]

Apart from aphorisms referring to memory, maxims pertaining to ethical behaviour predominate among the citations, usually anonymous. In Irena's autograph book, her Lwów classmate Olga Infeld advised her:

> May God be your hope
> And virtue, your heart
> Your happiness, the happiness of others
> And your adornment, simplicity.[50]

Her teacher Stefania Matuszewska advised Klara:

> Have a soul of hardened steel,
> A treasure in your breast, have a heart of gold,
> And in every word, in every smile, in every gaze, simplicity.[51]

Friends inscribed citations that underscored the meaning of comradeship in the face of transience.

> Nothing in the world is constant
> Time is breaking and tearing everything apart...
> Only one thing is powerful and permanent:
> The weak link of friendship.[52]

Berta Mittelmann implored Klara to be happy; to have few desires; and few, but genuine, friends.[53] Testifying to the continuity of literary tropes, the same quotation was cited after the war in Irena's autograph book.[54]

Friendship is an important theme of autograph books. In April 1941 Bronia Wolf wrote in Klara's autograph book, calling her a 'beloved colleague'.[55] New bonds were celebrated on the pages of Irena's, as she moved from Warsaw to Lwów and then to Borysław.[56] In March 1944 in Borysław, Runa Wienerówna wrote in it:

> Always remember, in the midst of the dark paths of life,
> That while people are not watching, God always does.[57]

The inscriptions that focus on the future may seem formulaic, but at this time of utter uncertainty they were also a proof of resilience and hope. The message of seizing the moment was particularly poignant when, in the summer of 1943, Gerta Bloch inscribed in Irena's autograph book:

> From spring days, happy years, happy memories,
> A bouquet of roses.
> The world smiles at you
> With the beautiful colour of fragrant roses
> So collect them when the time comes
> Because the roses bloom only once.[58]

Gender shaped the contents of the autograph books and participation in the practice of writing in them. The vast majority of inscriptions whose writers can be identified are by female classmates and teachers. Autograph books circulated among friends, family members, and teachers and were, therefore, a public platform, which constrained emotional expression. Within socially acceptable norms, some friends—female and male—alluded to love and desire. One advised Klara to be careful with jokes in order not to lose her heart.[59] One of the most direct was the advice given to Irena by Wuna Eisenstain to 'love boys as much as chance offers'.[60] In May 1943 J. Bander drew a heart bearing his and Irena's initials and jested: 'Love without reciprocity is like a garden without flowers, a tram without passengers, and Kulparków [a psychiatric hospital in Lwów] without lunatics' (Figure 3).[61] An undated inscription probably written by an adult advised Irena to 'strive for excellence, edify her brain and knowledge' if she wanted to be appreciated by 'boys'.[62] In Klara's autograph book only a handful of inscriptions seem openly frivolous: one is dedicated 'to Klara with beautiful legs from nameless with braids'.[63] The grammatical form identified the author as female. Klara's autograph book also contains a poem dedicated to her by a teenage boy. Accompanied by the drawing of a swan[64] and titled 'Sadness', it expressed his desire to write a love poem. 'I wanted to write it on your body, so that beautiful words became living flesh.'[65] Last but not least, in Irena's autograph book Ludwik Hirsz wrote a playful rhyme in June 1943, on the eve of the final liquidation of the Borysław ghetto.[66]

Emotional Communities

The autograph books shed light on the cultural world of these teenagers but also on the centrality of their emotional bonds to their daily lives under occupation.[67] They provided a platform not only for discussing friendship and for veiled courtship and flirtation but also for establishing emotional communities: friends and acquaintances who shared networks of feeling. Autograph books attest to communities delineated by

> what these communities (and the individuals within them) define and assess as valuable or harmful to them (for it is about such things that people express emotions); the emotions that they value, devalue, or ignore; the nature of the affective bonds between people that they recognize; and the modes of emotional expression that they expect, encourage, tolerate, and deplore.[68]

Initially, these emotional communities were centred on school, where they solidified but also shifted and shrank in the course of the war, first as a result of the flight, then

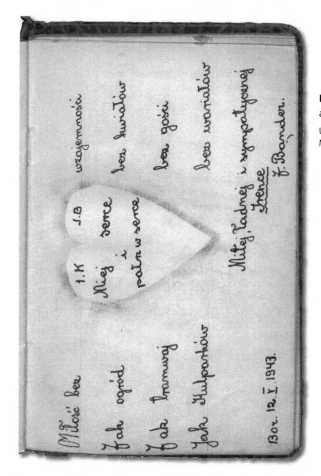

Figure 3 Irena Koretz, autograph book, [45]

United States Holocaust Memorial Museum, 1995.A.1064

because of Soviet arrests and deportations, and subsequently because of German persecution and the mass murder of Jews. The dynamic emotional communities to which Klara and Irena belonged can be reconstructed from the pages of their autograph books. The picture is further complicated by comparing what is found in these autograph books with how Irena and Klara describe their respective circles of friends in their diaries, memoirs, and oral interviews.

For Irena's parents the move from Lwów to Borysław was a return to a familiar community. This helped their daughters to create new circles of friends which dovetailed with alliances from the new Soviet school. Irena recalled in her diary that her parents

> rekindled old friendships with people whose children became my friends. Among them was the Kessler family, who rented us a room in their house. The Teichers lived next door. Their comfortable house became my second home. Daughters Janka and Niuta, and Ewa Kessler and Romek Engelberg became my closest friends. We went to the same primary school and spent time together after classes. We shared secrets and laughter, played in the

park and celebrated birthdays. We were inseparable. Despite the difficulties of being away from our home in Warsaw, life seemed almost normal. In this period of innocence, unaware of what was to come, I was happy.[69]

Janka and Niuta (Renata) Teicher, Ewa Kessler, and Romek Engelberg all wrote in her autograph book.[70] Irena's autograph book also has entries from both Jewish and non-Jewish friends, collected during the Soviet occupation.[71]

Born and raised in Żółkiew, Klara initially continued to be surrounded by friends from before the war. Because of the status of her family and because their home was outside the largely Jewish centre of the town, she had been a popular companion among her non-Jewish classmates who also lived in the area. Indeed, Klara recalled having had mostly non-Jewish friends: 'I happened to have a lot of Polish friends because your friends were the ones that went with you to school and walked with you from school.'[72] Not only did she walk to school with non-Jewish colleagues from the outskirts of Żółkiew, she also recalled being invited to their homes to see decorated Christmas trees.[73] In her autograph book there are both Jewish and non-Jewish friends. One, Janina Wesołowska, identified herself as a Year 6 student on 18 April 1941 and drew an image of a boy stealing cherries from a girl, accompanied by birds and flowers (Figure 4).[74]

Despite her many non-Jewish colleagues, Klara's closest friends were three Jewish girls: Giza Landau, Genya Astman, who was her second cousin, and Klara Letzer. During the Soviet occupation they met in school and at political events organized for the pupils and their families.[75] As in Irena's case, Klara's closest friends wrote in her autograph book. But Irena's and Klara's autograph books also include inscriptions by those outside their inner circles, who wrote and dedicated drawings and poetic references. Their friends and acquaintances could hardly comment in the autograph books on the arrests of family members or their efforts to navigate the Soviet economic system. However, other accounts, such as memoirs and oral interviews, provide additional insights into how friendships and family ties ensured that the individuals involved could be trusted, which proved very important during the Soviet occupation. Klara's father bartered oil for food brought by the peasants, which was in turn exchanged for other necessities at the store owned by the father of her friend Genya. Because of their shrewdness in operating in the conditions of the Soviet economy and local relationships of trust, the family never lacked food.[76]

During the Soviet occupation, the circle of friends began to experience losses. The autograph books gloss over the disappearance of close friends, although this is noted in Klara's diary. In her words: 'Friend after friend and their families disappeared in the middle of the night.'[77] In addition, she spotted her classmates' clothes 'on the Russian daughters [of Soviet officials] and saw Russian sons playing with the toys of their little brothers. My friend Sonia Maresky, from Silesia, was one of the first to be deported with a hundred other Jewish refugees from Austria and the west.'[78] In spring 1941 Klara received a letter describing the brutal conditions of exile and work in the coalmines. According to this, such workers usually died within a year. Klara recalled

Figure 4 Klara Szwarc, autograph book, [45]

United States Holocaust Memorial Museum, 1994.95.3

that the friend ended the letter with a grim forewarning 'When this war is over only the *kurhany*, the mass graves, will be a witness that there once was a people there.'[79]

After the arrival of the Germans, inscriptions in the autograph books did not change in content or form. Friendships continued to provide an important point of emotional reference and a framework for communal initiatives. Some friends were trusted enough to be involved in dangerous endeavours such as underground schooling. Klara recalled that in autumn 1941 her mother organized such a school for her own daughters and their friends: Giza, Genya, Klara, and Lipka: 'We met in a different house every day for our safety. We studied Hebrew with Gershon Taffet, mathematics with a famous university professor from Warsaw who had fled to Żółkiew. We even had Latin. I don't think any of us studied harder in our lives then we did in those months.'[80]

With some of her friends she began to work with Pepka Fisz and the sanitary commission: 'Girls are helping her and I join in as well. I accompany her to dress the wounds, I collect clothes and food. The Judenrat (Jewish council) gives us some money. I spend most of the day away from home (in the hospital or in the town), and

I fear being surprised by a round-up, I could be left alone with nowhere to run.'[81] They assisted the sick in Żółkiew and helped Jews who had jumped from deportation trains. As Klara noted, 'some jumpers had been told to try their luck near Żółkiew because they had heard about the hunchbacked nurse who was as good as any doctor at setting bones. We learned to make splints and bandage clean wounds.'[82] Among the friends who worked with Klara were Genya Astman and Hela Ornstein.[83] Most of them left inscriptions in Klara's autograph book that reflect their social and cultural milieu.

As their circle shrank, Jewish friends clung to one another. Klara described the times as 'grim', as her father was trying to find a hiding place for the family: 'I took refuge with my girlfriend whenever I could. Giza Landau lived several streets away, and it was too dangerous for her to come and visit. But Genya, Libka, Muschka, and Klara Letzer were nearby and still alive. One day at Genya's house, we realized that we were the last of our group.'[84]

In Borysław, in the midst of news about round-ups and deportations, the youngsters in the camp, as Irena noted, 'lived intensely, as if each day could be our last. We formed strong friendships and built brief intense relationships. We shared almost every aspect of our daily lives, including the struggle to survive. We laughed and we loved and talked of the day we would be free.'[85] Her father and elder sister worked for a German oil company. When they left the labour camp, Irena and her mother were hidden in a hayloft by the Fedorows. In the spring of 1944, with the Russians approaching, Irena reflected on her family's plan to leave the camp and go into hiding and seemed reconciled to her fate. But on the following day she seemed much more emotional, describing the panic engulfing the camp and her own sense of living 'in agony' and walking around 'feeling crazy'. She thought about her sick friend Dozia Weiler. They spent the day together, and were joined by other friends, Wuna and Dolek. When another friend, Julek, left to go into hiding, the remaining friends gathered to say goodbye.[86] Shortly before her own departure, on 29 March, Irena met again with her friends and walked around with Zygo and Wuna: 'All we talked about was who was leaving and when. Let it all end soon!'[87] she wrote in her diary. On the following day the news of the impending evacuation intensified. Irena drew emotional strength from her father and her friends: 'Wuna came over in the afternoon in the midst of last-minute preparations for hiding with the Fedorows. Wuna was also going into hiding as we said a tearful goodbye. Will our paths ever meet again? Maybe after the war. I said goodbye to Dozia. Almighty God, help us meet again after the war.'[88] As Irena and her mother made their escape on 31 March, her friends were 'waving goodbye from a distance. "Farewell, we'll meet again soon, after the war".' Dolek walked with her and gave her 'a little brooch as a souvenir and asked me not to forget him. I will never forget you! How can I? It was almost dusk when we reached the house. We didn't even say goodbye. He just kissed me. We said goodbye to Daddy. He went back to camp, where he and Olga will stay for now.'[89] Irena's emotional horizon shrank once she went into hiding together with her mother, but she continued to think about her friends.[90]

Klara's and Irena's relationships with their non-Jewish classmates did not survive the stresses of the war. The withering of bonds with non-Jews is not immediately visible on the pages of their autograph books. However, after the arrival of the Germans, there are no further inscriptions by non-Jews, with one exception. On 14 March 1944, when Jews remaining in the camp frantically prepared to flee and hide, Irena's non-Jewish friend Włodek Milewski asked her to remember him. The circumstances of this inscription are not clear: he may have entered the camp to see his Jewish friends.[91] In their diaries, memoirs, and oral interviews, Klara and Irena comment on their sense of betrayal by their former friends. Klara recalled: 'I was a nice Polish girl. And then the Hitlerites came and all my Polish friends turned away from me. It hurt, but that was before they started killing me.'[92] In particular, she stressed that during the German occupation fewer and fewer classmates acknowledged her on the streets of Żółkiew. In particular, she recalled that none came to offer help or express sympathy.[93] Klara also remembers the death of her friend Helena Freymann, who was killed when she stepped out of her house without an armband:

A Pole, someone whom she smiled at whenever she saw him and who had known her family for years, pointed her out to a soldier who was not even SS. He simply took out his pistol and shot her as if he were lighting a cigarette. She had forgotten her armband. This happened right down the block from our house one day after the edict was imposed. In this way we learned that the Pole or Ukrainian who might turn us in would not be a stranger. They would know us. Their children would be our classmates, their fathers would know our fathers, and their grandfathers would have known our grandfathers. I suppose, in the end, it made no difference if you were betrayed by a friend or an enemy. It really only meant that your heart might break a little more in the moment before you felt the bullet.[94]

In her memoir, Klara also recalled an encounter with a boy who called her a 'dirty Jew' on the street, as she was going to a studio to have her picture taken. Terrified, she gave up and returned home.[95] She does not provide the names of those who betrayed her trust. Later, she reflected on her and her sister's fate, so different from that of their non-Jewish friends. On 11 July 1944, less than two weeks before the arrival of the Soviet army, Klara noted bitterly that this would have been Mania's second birthday since her death:

For what? What did she do to anyone? Why is there no space for her on earth, unlike for her friends, because they are Aryans? I at times see through the window and it breaks my heart. I simply cannot comprehend that she is gone, I still see her full of life. She used to stand as if glued to the curtain and looked outside. I saw how much she was eager to live.[96]

Aftermath

There were few reunions with friends after the liberation of Żółkiew and Borysław. Klara, who no longer collected signatures in her autograph book, movingly described one such unexpected return to Żółkiew. Her mother had thrown open the back door, and, standing on the steps, like two ghosts risen from a grave, were Giza Landau and her mother. I ran down the stairs and embraced her. Klara Letzer, Genya Astman and so many others were all gone. To find a friend, alive, flesh and blood with smiles and tears at the sight of me, was a miracle. We brought them inside and Giza told us a Russian soldier had given them a ride to Żółkiew to see what remained of their lives. When they walked by our homes, Giza wanted to knock, but her mother said not to. It was too much to think that we were alive.[97]

She also recalled a new friend, Nina:

A little older than me, sweet and very serious. Everybody knew that her father was a colonel and the ranking officer in Żółkiew. Consequently, she was fawned over like a Russian princess by any adult who knew who her father was. But she didn't care. We never said much to each other at gymnasium, but I considered her a schoolfriend although I never saw her outside the classroom.[98]

Irena also returned to school in liberated Borysław. One survivor, Nina Fleischer, left a simple signature in her autograph book 'as a memento' in February 1945.[99] Another teenage survivor, Blanka Lieber, wrote for 'the most beloved and sweetest Irka' leaving a blank space for a drawing.[100] Yet another returned to the much-loved repertoire of Polish literary quotes and cited the poet Wincenty Pol.[101] Irena's autograph book might suggest that her school life returned to the familiar routine. However, within a few months her parents decided to move west and settle in Kraków. While there, Irena continued to collect signatures of new colleagues, including non-Jewish ones.[102] In March 1946, ahead of Irena and her family's emigration from Poland, a friend, Tolek Manskleid, hoped to be remembered. He also alluded to their shared background in Eastern Galicia.[103] One of the last inscriptions, in July 1946, was by Marta Weitzman, 'in memory of days spent pleasantly together':

> Do not look for happiness far away
> behind a seventh mountain and river
> or in the void wilderness
> but look for it in your own soul.
> Seek happiness not in the crowd
> which will sully and tarnish you.[104]

Conclusion

Autograph books constitute a unique historical source, reflecting a practice that was an important part of coming of age in Poland. As such, they also provide a remarkable insight into Jewish childhood before, during, and after the Holocaust in a variety of contexts.[105] With their formulaic nature, repetitiveness, and predictability, autograph books echo community and family norms and expectations and the literary canon taught in Polish schools and internalized by students. They also offer insights into the Polish cultural canon: poems and maxims that were known by heart and circulated among children; texts and images they were expected to memorize and repeat.[106] Klara's and Irena's autograph books provide invaluable glimpses of these practices in the context of the Holocaust. They suggest that their cohort of friends continued to rely on the familiar literary references and formulas. Analysing poems written during the Holocaust by young Polish Jews, Bożena Keff found them deeply moving because 'they are the most naked, and they give access directly to how a child or teenager experiences and sees the situation, without any correction, linguistic or literary'.[107] Similarly, autograph books reflect a poignant tension between the past experiences of children and their continued existence in the difficult present. Irena's and Klara's friends may have lacked a model for their inscriptions in the midst of persecution and destruction or continued to rely on the familiar quotations and drawings as an act of defiance. At the same time, autograph books are intimate personal documents reconstructing relationships at school and beyond which define the boundaries of an emotional community.[108] They map out networks of social contacts, reflecting a degree of intimacy among classmates and teachers. Read together, they illuminate the social contexts of the schoolchildren from their school space to their life beyond the school walls.

The two autograph books discussed in this chapter shed light on ways of expressing friendship and the prevalent literary and visual canons in pre-war Poland. In the historical context of the Second World War, they provide a more nuanced picture of Jewish childhoods before and during the occupation. They contribute to a sense both of biographical continuity and of the new context of dramatically reduced social interaction. At a time of fear, vulnerability, and powerlessness, keeping autograph books was a practice offering young Polish Jews a bridge between their childhood before the war and experiences during the occupation.

Yet these autograph books are more than just documents describing the social experience of the Holocaust. In her memoir, Klara recalled that she and her friends tried to find a way to create a material token of their bond, well aware of how little control they had over their individual fates:

We had already lost so many friends, and we were discussing which one of us would be next to die. We mourned the fact that we had nothing, not one photo, to remember our friends by. We decided to go to Mr Domański and get our picture taken to have something by which to remember each other. We wanted a token of our friendship to survive the war, even if we didn't.[109]

They must have had the picture taken, as Klara's papers, preserved in the United States Holocaust Memorial Museum, include a photograph showing five teenagers embracing. While in hiding, she wrote in Polish on the back of it: 'Letzter Klara, Astman Genia, Sochaczewska Eścia, Czaczkes Lieba, Eidelheit Muszka. Not one of them left. All fell victim to the Hitlerite murderers.'[110] Miraculously both Irena Koretz and Klara Szwarc survived, as did their autograph books. The signatures, drawings, and literary quotations preserved in them record the reactions of their friends, both Jewish and non-Jewish, to the Nazi and Soviet occupations. They show how pre-war conventional tropes survived in the changed conditions and how these were also sometimes reflected in the inscriptions. They are a remarkable testament both of those who survived and of those who perished.

Notes

The first draft of this chapter, 'Z żydowskiego sztambucha – dzienniki młodych Żydówek', was presented at the conference Zapisywanie wojny: Dzienniki z lat 1939–1945, at Warsaw University, Institute of Polish Literature, 7–8 June 2021. The author would like to thank Katharina Friedla, Agnieszka Ilwicka-Karuna, Magdalena Szkwarek, and Karolina Szymaniak for their comments on the earlier version of this text.

1 Irena Peritz (née Koretz), email to author, 18 Apr. 2022.
2 See W. Bełza, *Katechizm polskiego dziecka* (Lwów, 1901).
3 United States Holocaust Memorial Museum, Washington DC (hereafter USHMM), 1995.A.1064, 'Irena Peritz Papers', Series 1: Danuta Bodwińska (Borysław, 3 Feb. 1945), in Irena Koretz, autograph book, 1940–6, [6]; see W. Bełza, 'Na Rok Nowy...', in *Poradnik Teatrów i Chórów Włościańskich*, 1913, no. 1, p. 1.
4 Danuta Bodwińska, in Irena Koretz, autograph book, [7]. Another direct reference to the war was made by Salek Linhard, who signed Irena's autograph book: 'As a memento of a friend from the war years' (Salek Linhard (10 June 1943), ibid. [32]). Salek survived the Holocaust ('Betzalel Salek Linhard': Yad Vashem website, 'Central Database of Shoah Victims' Names', visited 6 June 2022).
5 On the repatriation of Polish citizens after the war, see G. Hryciuk, *Przemiany narodowościowe i ludnościowe w Galicji Wschodniej i na Wołyniu w latach 1931–1948* (Toruń, 2005).
6 See F. Sielicki, *Folklor dziecięcy i młodzieżowy na Wilejszczyźnie w okresie międzywojennym* (Wrocław, 1992). I would like to thank Magdalena Szkwarek, who allowed me to see a family autograph book that belonged to her great-aunt Antonina Szyszko (née Milewska) containing friends' signatures collected between 1933 and 1938 in Borysław. It included similar literary references and tropes.
7 On the school literary canon, see J. Marchewa, *Nauczanie literatury w szkole średniej w latach 1918–1939: Koncepcje i podręczniki* (Warsaw, 1990); L. Jazownik, *Teoria kształcenia literackiego w latach 1918–1939: Antologia*, 2 vols. (Zielona Góra, 2001), i. 267–335; T. Jaroszuk, *Humanistyka nowych czasów: Szkolna edukacja humanistyczna w Polsce Odrodzonej (1918–1939)* (Olsztyn, 2011).
8 A. Sikora, 'Sztambuch', in G. Godlewski, A. Karpowicz, M. Rakoczy, and P. Rodak (eds.), *Od aforyzmu do zinu: Gatunki twórczości słownej* (Warsaw, 2014), 462–73: 466; see also E. Kotarski, 'O imionnikach XVI i XVII wieku', in H. Dziechcińska (ed.), *Staropolska kultura rękopisu* (Warsaw, 1990). For a collection of autograph books, see Princeton University Library, Mudd Manuscript Library, AC040, 'Autograph Book Collection, 1825–1884 (Bulk 1848–1882)'.
9 Sikora, 'Sztambuch', 469; see S. Wasylewski, *Sztambuch: Skarbnica romantyzmu* (Lwów, 1921); A. Biernacki, *Sztambuch romantyczny* (Kraków, 1994). For a source of possible inscriptions to use, see *La Nouvelle Corbeille de fleurs ou recueil complet de compliments pour le jour de l'an, de bouquets pour les fêtes de famille, de félicitations et couplets pour les anniversaires etc., ainsi qu'un choix de vers pour les albums* (Lwów, 1844). Autograph books have remained an important source for scholars interested in youth culture (see R. Shapira and H. Herzog, 'Understanding Youth Culture through Autograph Books: The Israeli Case', *Journal of American Folklore*, 97 (1984), 442–60).

10 *Tango łez śpiewajcie muzy: Poetyckie dokumenty Holokaustu*, ed. B. Keff (Warsaw, 2012).
11 Irena Koretz, autograph book; USHMM, 1994.95.3, 'Clara Kramer [née Klara Szwarc] Papers', Series 2: Klara Szwarc, autograph book, 1940–1.
12 Z. Bernhardt and N. Altman, 'List of Forced Laborers in Borysław and Drohobycz' (2004): JewishGen website, visited 30 May 2022.
13 See *Wykaz oficerów, którzy nadesłali swe karty kwalifikacyjne, do Wydziału prac przygotowawczych, dla Komisji Weryfikacyjnej przy Departamencie Personalnym Ministerstwa Spraw Wojskowych* (Warsaw, 1920); *Sprawozdanie z I-go Zjazdu Ogrzewników Polskich 1936 r.* (Warsaw, 1939). Irena Peritz, interview with author, 13 Jan. 2022.
14 USHMM, 1995.A.1064, Series 3: Irena Peritz, 'Irena's Diary: My Wartime Memories' (2004), 7–8.
15 Ibid. 9–10.
16 Ibid. 10–11, 17–18.
17 For a concise history of the Holocaust in Borysław, see A. Kruglov, M. McConnell, and M. Dean, 'Borysław', in United States Memorial Holocaust Museum, *Encyclopedia of Camps and Ghettos, 1933–1945*, ii: *Ghettos in German-Occupied Eastern Europe*, ed. M. Dean and M. Hecker (Bloomington, Ind., 2012), 755–7.
18 USHMM, 'Clara Kramer Papers'; 1993.A.0088.13: Clara Kramer, oral history interview (1982; Eng.); University of Southern California Shoah Foundation, Los Angeles, Visual History Archive, interview 37123: Clara Kramer (28 Dec. 1997; Eng.); C. Kramer and S. Glantz, *Clara's War: One Girl's Story of Survival* (New York, 2009); C. Kramer, *Tyleśmy już przeszli: Dziennik pisany w bunkrze (Żółkiew 1942–1944)*, ed. A. Wylegała (Warsaw, 2017), 40–1. For a brief history of the Holocaust in Żółkiew, see A. Kruglov and M. McConnell, 'Żółkiew', in United States Memorial Holocaust Museum, *Encyclopedia of Camps and Ghettos, 1933–1945*, ii. 852–3.
19 Irena Peritz, interview with author.
20 Irena Koretz, autograph book, [4–5].
21 Ibid. [5]. Her friend Binka Haberman left a signature and a drawing for 'kaczula [duckling] Irusia' (Binka Haberman (Borysław, 17 Feb.) 1941, ibid. 29). Mala Rosenberg dedicated her signature 'For a memento for darling Kaczulińska', playfully turning the nickname into a typical Polish family name (Mala Rosenberg (10 June 1943), ibid. 33).
22 Olga Koretz (11 Feb. 1940), ibid. 11.
23 'Those writing in an autograph book were aware of the fact that it was not a place for a spontaneous expression or intimate confessions' (Sikora, 'Sztambuch', 465).
24 J. Handlowa (4 July 1939), in Klara Szwarc, autograph book, [5].
25 J. W. Goethe, 'Betrachtungen im Sinne der Wanderer', in *Maximen und Reflexionen* (Berlin, 2016), 545–73: 545.
26 See M. Gajak-Toczek, 'Twórczość Adama Mickiewicza w podręcznikach Franciszka Próchnickiego dla szkół ludowych i wydziałowych', in B. Gala-Milczarek, A. Klimas, and A. Kowalkiewicz-Kulesza (eds.), *Wiek XIX na lekcjach języka polskiego: Literatura – język – kultura – historia* (Siedlce, 2020), 49–67.
27 'To the sweetest student for a memento' (Izabella Kosińska (Żółkiew, 5 Feb. 1940), in Klara Szwarc, autograph book, [37]; see A. Mickiewicz, 'Słowo i czyn', in *Poezje* (Lwów, 1929), 438).
28 'To dear Klara, as a memento' (Rózia Post (Żółkiew, 3 Oct. 1940), in Klara Szwarc, autograph book, [15]; see A. Mickiewicz, 'Praktyka', in *Poezye Adama Mickiewicza*, ed. P.

Chmielowski, 4 vols. (Kraków, 1899), i. 284). Rózia Post was probably the daughter of Josef (Markus) Post, a merchant and store-owner in Żółkiew. She had a younger sister. The entire family perished in 1943. Her father was a member of the local elite, arrested when the Germans demanded a levy from the community. Rózia was born in 1926 and was murdered at the age of 17. The testimony was submitted by a survivor, Miriam Zobel Haller, in 2010 ('Rozia Post': Yad Vashem website, 'Central Database of Shoah Victims' Names', visited 7 June 2022).

29 U. Farbówna (11 Nov. 1940), in Klara Szwarc, autograph book, [23].
30 'To lovely Ireczka, something to remember me by' (Irena Sowówna (13 Feb. 1941), in Irena Koretz, autograph book, [73]).
31 Unsigned (Borysław, 12 Oct. 1943), ibid. [72].
32 'As a memento for pleasant Klara' (Eścia Sochaczewska (Żółkiew, 28 Oct. 1940), in Klara Szwarc, autograph book, [51]). The quotation is from Karol Antoniewicz, a Polish Armenian Jesuit and missionary (K. Antoniewicz, 'Kto w życia wiośnie nadzieją się łudzi', in *Poezye Karola Antoniewicza*, ed. K. Jan Badeni, vol. 1 (Kraków, 1899), 142).
33 'To a lovely friend, as a wartime memento' (Zygmunt Stein (Borysław, 6 Dec. 1942), in Irena Koretz, autograph book, [54]). This seems to be the only illustration that broke the routine of idyllic images in both autograph books.
34 'Always faithful to you' (Hemerling (Żółkiew, 27 Jan. 1941), in Klara Szwarc, autograph book, [17]; see A. Asnyk, 'Echo kołyski', in *Wybór poezyj*, ed. E. Kucharski (Kraków, 1926), 33–4).
35 'To my student' (Olga Pazowska (Żółkiew, 1 Apr. 1940), ibid. [25]); see J. I. Kraszewski, 'Chociażby dusza była spragniona...', in *Poezye i urywki prozą* (Warsaw, 1912), 85.
36 Klara Szwarc, autograph book, [31]. Klara's sister called on her to 'go through life performing good deeds for others' (Mania Szwarc (Żółkiew 12 Apr. 1940), ibid.). An inscription written by a teacher implored Klara to trust her strength and to follow a straight path. (ibid. [29]).
37 'All's ephemeral, all will pass; what has passed, shall dearer be' (Sonia Sandowicz (16 Sept. 1940), in Klara Szwarc, autograph book, [35]; see A. Pushkin, 'If You Find that Life Deceives You', trans. N. Derkatch and D. Derkatch (n.d.): Pushkin Literary Society of South Australia website, visited 2 July 2022).
38 'To lovely [duck], for a souvenir' (A. Ziller (Borysław, 5 Sept. 1941), in Irena Koretz, autograph book, [15]), Anatol Ziller was born in 1927. He was captured and imprisoned first in Płaszów and later Mauthausen ('Anatol Ziller': Yad Vashem website, 'Central Database of Shoah Victims' Names', visited 7 June 2022). According to Szkwarek, he was a friend of her uncle, Włodzimierz Milewski, who helped him during the German occupation and brought food to him in a bunker in the forest (see M. Szkwarek, 'List z getta', *Kurier Galicyjski*, 28 Jan. – 14 Feb. 2011, p. 7).
39 'To dearly loved Klara' (G.L. (Żółkiew 23 Oct. 1941), in Klara Szwarc, autograph book, [27]).
40 T. Kołodziej (2 Feb. 1942), ibid. [7].
41 'To lovely Irka, as a memento' (Martek Egert (Borysław, 23 Aug. 1940), in Irena Koretz autograph book, [13]). According to his sister Lidia's testimony, Martek was murdered in Lwów ('Marceli Egert': Yad Vashem website, 'Central Database of Shoah Victims' Names', visited 7 June 2022).
42 'To dear Irenka, for a memento' (Anita Lauf (Borysław, 11 July 1940), in Klara Szwarc, autograph book, [71]). Lauf was a native of Vienna and survived the Holocaust ('Anita

Lauf': Yad Vashem website, 'Central Database of Shoah Victims' Names', visited 7 June 2022).

43 'To a lovely friend, as a memento' (Frydzia Siebert (Żółkiew, 6 May 1940), in Klara Szwarc, autograph book, [21]; see 'Frida Zibert': Yad Vashem website, 'Central Database of Shoah Victims' Names', visited 7 June 2022).

44 'To very beloved Klara' (Janina Wesołowska (Class VIb, 19 Apr. 1941), in Klara Szwarc, autograph book, [45]; see also ibid. [12–13]).

45 Karol Randmesser (Aug. 1943), in Irena Koretz, autograph book, [33].

46 'After you leave the school and step into the world, do not forget dear Irena, our shared school years of youth' (Janina Teicher (Borysław, 21 Apr. 1940), ibid. [68–9]). Her inscription was accompanied by a colourful collage of two birds. See also: 'When you forget about me among [other] people and the world, may this verse rekindle in you a memory of me. For dear Klara' (Alicja M. Hemmerling (Żółkiew, 25 Apr. 1941), in Klara Szwarc, autograph book, [42]).

47 'As a memento' (R. Löwenkron (21 May 1941), in Klara Szwarc, autograph book, [57]; see 'W imionniku (Nad morzem Baltyckiem)', in *Poezye Adama Mickiewicza*, i. 194). Rachela lived on Turyniecka Street in Żółkiew ('Rachela Löwenkron': Yad Vashem website, 'Central Database of Shoah Victims' Names', visited 7 June 2022).

48 'To dear Duck, as a memento' (J. Kriegel (Borysław 1 Sept. 1943), Irena Koretz autograph book, [14]). The grammatical form identifies the author as male.

49 See Sydcia (Sydonia) Twyesschorr ('Borysław koszary', 1 Mar. 1944), in Irena Koretz, autograph book, [66]. Sydcia survived Płaszów and Auschwitz and was liberated in Lichtewerden subcamp in Czechoslovakia ('Sidonia Tviashor': Yad Vashem website, 'Central Database of Shoah Victims' Names', visited 7 June 2022).

50 'To cherished Irka asking to be remembered' (Olga Infeld (Lwów, 8 Feb. 1940), in Irena Koretz, autograph book, [23]).

51 'To my pupil' (Stefania Matuszewska (Żółkiew, 1 Feb. 1940), in Klara Szwarc, autograph book, [43]).

52 'As a memento, to darling Klara' (Klara Letzter (Class VIb, Żółkiew, 27 Oct. 1940), ibid. [53]). The quotation seems to contain a mistake as it describes friendship as 'weak', against the logic of the verse.

53 'Have few wishes, which will make you happy, and few friends, but real ones. To lovely Klara as a memento' (Mittelmann Berta (Żółkiew, 5 Nov. 1940), ibid. [39]). Berta erroneously ascribed the quotation to the popular Polish writer Henryk Sienkiewicz.

54 'To my sweet darling Irenka' (Lucy Fertig (Kraków, 20 Juny 1946), in Irena Koretz, autograph book, [70]).

55 'As a souvenir for my beloved colleague' (Bronia Wolf (Żółkiew, 20 (30?) Apr. 1941), in Klara Szwarc, autograph book, [50]). The signature was accompanied by a drawing of a bouquet of flowers.

56 'To a girlfriend from Warsaw, whom I only met in Borysław' (Janina Teicher, in Irena Koretz, autograph book, [68]).

57 'For the friendly and much-loved Irenka' (Runa Wienerówna (Borysław, 13 Mar. 1944), ibid. [25]).

58 'To sweet Irka, as memento' (Gerta Bloch (29 July 1943), ibid. [9]). The date, however, could be 1941.

59 'Be careful with jokes | Because sometimes the joke will change | You can lose your heart by joking | And not everyone is worthy of heart. To a dear friend for a memento' (Tylda (31 Jan. 1941), in Klara Szwarc, autograph book, [33]).

60 Wuna Eisenstain (Borysław, 7 Oct. 1941), in Irena Koretz, autograph book, [37].
61 'To nice, pretty, and friendly Irenka' (J. Bander (Borysław, 12 May 1943), ibid. [45]).
62 'Asking to remember him' (Halerski Henryk (n.d.), ibid. [24]). He also stated that he would write 'from his heart' rather than 'repeating clichés in abundance here'.
63 Klara Szwarc, autograph book, [59]. The inscription was not dated but was accompanied by a drawing of a fashionable-looking female wearing an elaborate hat.
64 Ibid. [49]. The drawing bears the date 23 December 1941.
65 'To beloved Klara' (Lonek (23 Dec. 1941), ibid. 47–8).
66 'Diddly dee, diddly dum | Here I am in your book. To darling Irka, as a memento' (Ludwik Hirsz (10 June 1943), in Irena Koretz, autograph book, [32]).
67 B. Rosenwein, 'Problems and Methods in the History of Emotions', *Passions in Context*, 1 (2010), 1–32: 1.
68 Ibid. 11.
69 Irena Peritz, 'Irena's Diary', 8. Romek was taken to Bełżec with his mother before spring 1943 (Irena Peritz, interview with author).
70 Ewa Kessler wrote a moralizing piece about achieving happiness by making others happy, which she accompanied by an elaborate illustration of the Brothers Grimm fairy tale about Hansel and Gretel (Ewa Kessler (14 Apr. 1940), in Irena Koretz, autograph book, [38–9]). Renata Teicher wished her friend a 'sweet, nice, and happy life' (Renata Teicher (Borysław, 21 Apr. 1940), ibid. [64–5]). She also drew a child in festive clothes playing on a drum. Romek Engelberg drew a Mickey Mouse and scribbled a verse about life being a sword with many dents and calling on his friend 'Kaczula' to 'love, win and suffer' (Romek Engelberg (Borysław, 7 Apr. 1941), ibid. [46]).
71 'To a dear girlfriend, as a memento' (Aleksandra Ważna (Borysław, 13 May 1940), ibid. [43]). Aleksandra drew a page-size image of a peaceful sunset in the winter countryside.
72 Clara Kramer, USHMM oral history interview, part 1, 05:07–05:17 mins.
73 Clara Kramer, Visual History Archive interview, tape 1, 15:30–15:37 mins.
74 Janina Wesołowska (18 Apr. 1941, Żółkiew), in Klara Szwarc, autograph book, [45].
75 Kramer and Glantz, *Clara's War*, 20.
76 Ibid. 25.
77 Ibid. 23. Recalling the circumstances of the arrests, she wrote: 'Either they were accused of having too much money, or being Polish loyalists. Or they might be intellectuals, whose minds might dare question what the communists were doing in Żółkiew. Or they might have simply voiced their opposition to communism once twenty years ago in a café conversation. The reason didn't make any difference, the result was always the same' (ibid. 23–4).
78 Ibid. 24.
79 Ibid. 33.
80 Ibid. 48.
81 Kramer, *Tyleśmy już przeszli*, 39.
82 Ibid. 51.
83 Ibid. In his pioneering study of the Holocaust in Żółkiew, Gerszon Taffet mentioned Jewish girls who selflessly collaborated with the sanitary commission: Klara Letzter, Mundzia Degen, and Klara Szwarc. Only Klara Szwarc survived (G. Taffet, *Zagłada Żydów żółkiewskich* (Warsaw, 2019), 46).
84 Ibid. 52. Bronia's name was listed by her sister, Charlota Kahane, who also listed her

brother Leopold ('Bronia Wolf'; 'Leopold Wolf': Yad Vashem website, 'Central Database of Shoah Victims' Names', visited 7 June 2022).

85 Irena Peritz, 'Irena's Diary', 10.
86 On 26 March 1944 Irena noted in her diary: 'The Russians are approaching fast. We have to make a decision about our next move. Everybody is scattering to go into hiding. We will be leaving the camp any day now. Daddy has found a hiding place. I am frightened. I am young; life is ahead of me. I would like to live to see better times with all my loved ones. Everything is in God's hands. Keep us in your care. I know that I cannot escape my fate' (ibid.). 'Whatever must happen, will happen' (ibid. 17).
87 Ibid.
88 Ibid. 18.
89 Ibid. 19.
90 'It was a year ago today that I met Janek [Bander]. A whole year! I remember it as if it were yesterday. He was on the swing and I approached him. Janek, do you remember that?' (ibid. 22–3).
91 'If one day in a free moment you gaze at this page, remember my name, if you hold it worthy of memory' (Włodek Milewski (Bor[ysław], 14 Mar. 1944), in Irena Koretz, autograph book, [16]).
92 See 'Book TV: Clara Kramer, "Clara's War"' (21 Oct. 2009): YouTube website, visited 30 May 2022.
93 A. Wylegała, 'Wprowadzenie', in Kramer, *Tyleśmy już przeszli*, 9–30: 17.
94 Kramer and Glantz, *Clara's War*, 44.
95 Ibid. 52.
96 Kramer, *Tyleśmy już przeszli*, 198.
97 Kramer and Glantz, *Clara's War*, 309.
98 Ibid. 316.
99 'To darling Irusia, as a memento' (Nina Fleicherówna (Borysław, 15 Feb. 1945), in Irena Koretz, autograph book, [28]).
100 Blanka Lieber (Borysław, 22 May 1945), ibid. [62].
101 'Man will fly like a bird through youth. He is a ploughman through life. To darling Irka' (Janka Landau (Borysław, 1 Feb. 1945), ibid. [36]; citing W. Pol, 'Improwizacja', in *Klejnoty poezyi polskiej wybrane z dzieł najznakomitszych dawnych i nowoczesnych poetów* (Warsaw, 1882), 259).
102 See several inscriptions made on 2 February 1946 (Irena Koretz, autograph book, [56]). On teaching literature in Polish schools after the war, see M. Sienko, *Polonistyka szkolna w gorsecie ideologii: Dyskusje wokół wychowania literackiego w latach 1944–1989* (Kraków, 2002), 11–48.
103 Tolek Manskleid (Kraków, 20 Mar. 1946), in Irena Koretz, autograph book, [67]). He referred to 'our *batiar* three', using a term that denoted Lwów subculture. Anatol Manskleid appears on the list of Jews in Borysław during the German occupation ('Anatol Manskleid': Yad Vashem website, 'Central Database of Shoah Victims' Names', visited 7 June 2022).
104 Marta Weitzman (Kraków, 16 Mar. 1946), in Irena Koretz, autograph book, [21].
105 Autograph books collected before the Holocaust or on the eve of emigration or flight also provide important historical insights (see 'Janów: Book of Autographs, 1913 to 1920': JewishGen website, visited 30 May 2022; D. Levy, *The Year of Goodbyes: A True Story of Friendship, Family and Farewells* (New York, 2010)).

106 I am grateful to Katherina Friedla for drawing my attention to the autograph book of Jewish teenager Gucia Yakubowicz from the Klettendorf (Klecina) labour camp in Breslau (Wrocław), covering the years 1942 and 1943. It contains more than a dozen inscriptions in Polish by Jewish female inmates (Ghetto Fighters' House Archive, Lohamei Hageta'ot, 625: Klattendorf camp: memorial book (1942–3), 625).

107 B. Keff, 'Tango łez śpiewajcie muzy, czyli czym jest zawartość tej książki', in *Tango łez śpiewajcie muzy*, 11–26: 19.

108 Rosenwein, 'Problems and Methods in the History of Emotions', 1.

109 Kramer and Glantz, *Clara's War*, 52.

110 USHMM, 1994.95.3, Series 4, nos. 1–2: Clara Kramer's childhood friends, 1940–1.

From Relief to Emancipation
Cecylia Klaftenowa's Vision for Jewish Girls in Interwar Lwów

SARAH ELLEN ZARROW

> Cecylia Klaftenowa, director of the Szkoła Zawodowa Żeńska Towarzystwa Warsztatów Rękodzielniczych dla Dziewcząt Żydowskich, the Women's Vocational School of the Association of Handicraft Workshops for Jewish Girls, in interwar Lwów, had ambitious plans for the Jewish girls who made up its student body. Her aim was not only to give her pupils an academic education but also to produce a cohort of independent women with practical skills. This vision was closely connected to the broader project of the productivization of Polish Jewry, understood as an emancipatory project which would also include girls from impoverished homes. By and large, Klaftenowa's students viewed their participation in her great experiment in similar terms. Embedded in the material culture of the region, the school thus constituted a successful model for interwar Poland.

> Tens and hundreds of pedestrians pass by the three-storey building on 9 Piekarska Street daily. Some look at the school coldly and indifferently, while others smile calmly at the thought that 'something' is happening there, that some kind of interesting process is taking place. But we do not fall into either category. We enter after a few moments and see for ourselves what's happening there, how this interesting process takes place.
>
> Albina Rosenblatt, in
> *Rocznik jubileuszowy Związku dla Szerzenia Wykształcenia Zawodowego wśród Żydów w Małopolsce 'Wuzet'* (1937)

THE 'INTERESTING PROCESS' referred to was the work of Cecylia Klaftenowa. In the imposing building at 9 Piekarska Street, a short distance from the main square of Lwów (Lviv), Klaftenowa directed the Szkoła Zawodowa Żeńska Towarzystwa Warsztatów Rękodzielniczych dla Dziewcząt Żydowskich, the Women's Vocational School of the Association of Handicraft Workshops for Jewish Girls (the TWR school). The students at the school, Jewish girls and young women from Lwów and the surrounding region, constituted a great experiment in women's education in interwar Poland, as part of a vision for a new Polish Jewish society. Klaftenowa wished to create a cohort of Polish Jewish women not reliant upon men for material support or for the interpretation of Jewish life and artistic expression. By and large, the students viewed their participation in Klaftenowa's great experiment in similar terms. The belief that 'schools penetrate society', that young people would lead Poland, and Poland's Jews, into a new future, pervaded the school's ethos, as exemplified by its curriculum and its attitudes towards the students' training and growth.[1] The blend of ideologies of productivization, independence, and autonomy for students and women, a cross-class orientation, and a Polish Jewish civic nationalism formed the basis for more than an 'interesting process'. Klaftenowa was inspired by the idea of the 'productivization' of the Jewish population, turning it into a goal for Jewish women in particular, in order to help them liberate themselves both from 'unproductive' labour and from their economic reliance on fathers and husbands.

This chapter explores Cecylia Klaftenowa's views on women, work, and the purpose of women's education in the reborn Second Polish Republic. I ask what role she intended the school to play in Polish Jewish—and Polish civic—society. What was the purpose of educating young women in both a secondary-school curriculum and practical vocational training? What was the relationship, in Klaftenowa's eyes, between the work of the school and broader Polish Jewish society? What was the relationship of the school to similar initiatives to teach Jews—men and women—trades? I argue that the TWR school functioned as a laboratory, with its students as its subjects. Klaftenowa aimed to transform Jewish society in Poland, especially its Jewish women, one class at a time. Klaftenowa's school eventually became the model for other schools belonging to a network known as WUZET (Związek dla Szerzenia Wykształcenia Zawodowego wśród Żydów w Małopolsce; the Society for the Promotion of Vocational Education among Jews in Lesser Poland), which opened co-educational and boys' schools in addition to girls' schools.

Unfortunately, the TWR school students' voices are by and large lost to contemporary scholars, although some accounts of life at the school survive in oral history testimonies. It is probable that the students who appear in the school's official publications were featured precisely because they had positive things to say about their educational environment. The schools' own publications—yearbooks and reports on activities—necessarily paint only a partial picture. Cecylia Klaftenowa's own essays and reports about herself and about the TWR school give further insight into the ideological underpinnings of the school's programne, while official reports also help develop a more comprehensive picture of its workings.

Cecylia Klaftenowa's Early Work

Klaftenowa's own social background undoubtedly influenced both her decision to enter charitable work and also the specific direction that that charitable work took. As a general rule, women took the lead in organizing war-relief efforts, especially those having to do with spheres gendered feminine: soup kitchens, children's relief, and care for other women and girls. These activities were viewed as an appropriate activity for middle-class women especially. Marion Kaplan has noted that women's voluntary work helped solidify middle-class status for Jewish families. Furthermore, welfare work often led into social work.[2] Involvement in relief activities was both a civic effort, a way that women could serve on the 'home front' of the war, and an ethno-national activity that solidified group cohesion.[3]

Klaftenowa was born Cecylia Beigel in Tarnopol (Ternopil), Galicia in 1881,[4] and it does not appear that she came from a monied family.[5] Her sickly father raised her after her mother died in the first year of Cecylia's life. At the age of 15, she left home for Lwów, where she worked as a private tutor. She then entered the Państwowe Seminarium Nauczycielskie Żeńskie (State Female Teachers' Seminary) followed by the University of Lwów in 1902, where she studied natural sciences and humanities. She later entered the Zoological Institute under the direction of zoologist and Darwinist Józef Nussbaum-Hilarowicz, who also came from a Jewish background, and worked as his assistant from 1907 until 1920. She received her doctorate in December 1913, with a dissertation on the regeneration of olfactory organs in bony fish.[6] While working as Nussbaum-Hilarowicz's assistant, she sat for and passed her teaching examination and taught natural sciences at a number of schools in Lwów. In the meantime, she married engineer Aleksander Klaften, who died in a mine accident a few months later in the early 1910s. She never remarried. Klaftenowa's ideological commitments probably stemmed from her personal experience with parental illness and death, the early death of her husband, and her relief work.

Klaftenowa's charitable work seems to have first begun with war-relief efforts in 1915, when she helped found the first Jewish Relief Committee in Lwów: Klaftenowa herself managed the soup kitchen. She soon opened a shelter for abandoned and orphaned children at 6 Piekarska Street, donated by Cecylia Wechsler, and helped establish the Central Committee to Care for Jewish War Orphans in Galicia (Centralny Komitet Opieki nad Żydowskimi Sierotami Wojennymi w Galicji) in 1916; in 1918 she was chosen to lead the organization. The organization ran orphanages and summer camps and provided medical care for the thousands of Jewish children impoverished and orphaned by the war. In April 1915, during the Russian occupation of Lwów, 'under the most primitive of conditions', Klaftenowa also founded craft workshops for girls.[7] Beginning in twelve rooms loaned by a community member at 23 Sykstuska Street (Doroshenka Street), these workshops received initial funding from the American Jewish Joint Distribution Committee (JDC). A year later, in April 1916, the workshops were officially organized as the Association of Handicraft Workshops for Jewish Girls in Lwów. The mayor of Lwów, Tadeusz Rutowski, promised to provide assistance for the school from the city council after a subvention had been obtained from the Jewish Rescue Committee.[8] Other funds from the Vienna-based Society for the Rescue of Abandoned Jewish Children in Galicia and Bukovina were used to pay for clothing.[9] At first, the workshops focused on dressmaking, using fourteen sewing machines that Klaftenowa had managed to borrow.[10] In November 1918 the school had to close temporarily and then reopened with reduced hours, because of the Polish–Ukrainian war and the pogrom in Lwów in November 1918. By 1919 it had resumed normal operations, moving into the orphanage building at 6 Piekarska Street.

The workshops had been immediately popular, and, as the Russian occupation regime had forbidden most schooling, there had been 'enormous pressure' to open a new school after the end of war.[11] In 1919, with additional funding from the JDC,

Klaftenowa formed the TWR school out of the workshops at 9 Piekarska Street: the association purchased the building for 600,000 Polish marks. The renowned architect Józef Awin volunteered to remodel the building, adding an extra storey between 1922 and 1926; the total cost was 100,000 zlotys for the extra floor, which the JDC subsidized.[12] The new addition featured the name of the school in large letters, visible to everyone who passed by.[13]

Vocational Training in Interwar Poland: Goals and Politics of Jewish Work

Klaftenowa expressed concern over what she considered to be the low numbers of working women in Galicia. Citing figures from Józef Tenenbaum, a representative from Eastern Galicia in the Jewish delegation to the Paris Peace Conference, she wrote in 1927 that before the First World War, only 22 per cent of Jewish women in Galicia worked, as opposed to 43 per cent worldwide.[14] She expressed further consternation that fully half of those employed worked in trade—considered a typically Jewish occupation and looked down on as 'unproductive'[15]—although she also noted that after the war there were 'undoubtedly significant changes in the participation of Jewish women in productive work'.[16] Klaftenowa preferred that all women, regardless of class, learn a trade. She stressed the 'unhealthy' economic character of Jewish society from the end of the eighteenth century, where Jews were concentrated in larger towns and in only a few lines of work, 'creating an atmosphere of hostility and mistrust, which often turned into persecution of Jews, harassment from authorities, and contempt on the part of society'.[17] The belief that Jewish occupational structures were flawed, and especially the idea that some professions were 'unproductive' and did not contribute to society, fitted squarely within the maskilic (Jewish Enlightenment) goals of ameliorating the 'dysfunctional' Jewish occupational structure and of schooling that was 'productive'.[18]

For Klaftenowa, making Jewish women productive had two purposes: the inherent value of work and the economic liberation of women. She approached labour with the idea of the moral good that comes from a hard day's work. She once commented that she herself did not grow tired from hard work, since to stop working for rest would mean reflecting on all that had not been, or had not been fully, accomplished.[19] She wrote: 'To give light and value to women of every family means to renew and strengthen the deepest foundations of society and of the nation' and that, within Jewish society, working women (supporting their husbands' Torah study) provided 'the main foundation and soul of a family, the greatest holiness of Judaism'.[20] Although European Jews often embraced the idea of women working in order to support their families, Klaftenowa did not view women taking on the family's financial burden while their husbands devoted themselves to the study of holy texts in a wholly positive light. She questioned whether such a life, passed down over the generations, could be truly fulfilling, asking: 'Do we often meet a truly happy woman? Can a father—even if he provided his daughter with his entire fortune—

secure her future?'²¹ Klaftenowa believed that, rather than wealth, the greatest gift parents could give a daughter was a set of practical skills.

Of contemporary women, Klaftenowa wrote:

In the dedication of today's woman to independence one finds not only the external struggle for existence in conditions of misery and coercion but also a great internal force in which each takes on the burden of responsible work in order also to have a place in real life and in everything that life creates, with the dignity of the folk and with moral values.²²

Linking the liberation of women to both economic independence and to a life filled with the dignity of work and a concomitant contribution to society was a thread that runs throughout Klaftenowa's writing in publications such as *Przegląd Społeczny*, the monthly publication of CENTOS (Centralne Towarzystwo Opieki nad Sierotami; the Central Society for the Care of [Jewish] Orphans). She noted in an interview that she had at first considered herself a 'naturalist' not a social worker, and indeed had an antipathy to social work. However, the existence of a group of women in pre-1914 Lwów dedicated to 'emancipation' seems to have steered her in the direction of social work for social change.²³

Although in 1930 she claimed that she did not involve herself in political work, she observed to an interviewer that as a scientist she believed in evolution (presumably, of society and of women's representation in community structures).²⁴ She was involved in multiple political initiatives. In 1934 she ran for the city council as part of the Jewish bloc and was elected to represent the fourth electoral district of Lwów.²⁵

Klaftenowa's concern for children, especially Jewish girls, did not extend only to the lower classes.²⁶ Throughout the school's operation, she was deeply concerned that few students from the middle and upper classes had enrolled in her school: in the school year 1935/6, for example, only 1.6 per cent of students had fathers in white-collar professions, and another 11 per cent had fathers working in private and state firms. The rest were children of craftsmen and tradesmen, Jewish community professionals, labourers, and farmers.²⁷ She understood this as a problem which originated with their parents, who may have felt that financial security could come from marriage or from inherited wealth, regardless of occupation, and may have looked down on manual work as something only poorer families relied upon. Certainly, the school's origins in social welfare and war relief would not burnish its image among wealthier Jewish families as an appropriate place for their daughters. Klaftenowa's desire to provide a vocational education for Eastern Galicia's Jewish upper classes as well as its poor makes clear that the school's mission was one of economic liberation rather than economic empowerment. If the school did not serve all strata of Jewish society, it could not fulfil its mission of fashioning a new Polish Jewish woman, reliant neither on familial wealth nor charity.

Klaftenowa saw paid work as a way to ameliorate the economic, and therefore social, situation arising from women's reliance on their fathers, and later husbands, for money. A 1919 report on the school's first years of activity excoriated the general public (presumably, those who had the means to help) for not realizing the importance of occupational training for girls, which led to their 'current fatal position'.[28] In Klaftenowa's words:

The situation of these women has revealed one of the gravest errors in the upbringing of young Jewish women in committed families, that often in situations when relations are barely tolerable they do not teach girls any concrete trade, do not prepare them for any defined occupation, putting them on the road of life with so-called general education . . . without any specialized training.[29]

In contrast to a general trend of education for girls, which began with girls from the wealthiest families, Klaftenowa had to convince well-to-do families of the value of particular types of education for their daughters (with only limited success).[30]

It is instructive to contrast the TWR school with other schools for Jewish girls that focused on domestic arts, which shared some characteristics with it but which were driven by different ideological underpinnings. Fears of the 'white slave trade', and of the poverty of Poland and Galicia in particular, compelled west European Jewish activists to establish new Jewish schools to combat both poverty and prostitution. Activists such as Bertha Pappenheim also believed that young women had an 'underdeveloped desire to work',[31] and there was an overlap between local anti-prostitution organizations and the leadership of the TWR school. Róża Melcerowa, for example, a member of the Sejm and president of the Lwów Jewish Society for the Protection of Girls and Women, was also a leader of the Women's International Zionist Organization, to which Klaftenowa belonged (Melcerowa was herself an orphan).[32] Although Klaftenowa was involved in activities to combat prostitution, TWR school materials conspicuously lacked any implicit or explicit anti-prostitution message.[33]

From a German or an American perspective, training east European girls in practical skills, particularly of a domestic character, was not always intended to promote their emancipation. The various schools in Germany and the United States that educated east Europeans in domestic arts generally aimed to create servants for the wealthier (generally German or German-origin) Jews, or else good middle-class housewives. Nancy Sinkoff has written about the efforts of the Clara de Hirsch Home for Working Girls in New York City to produce homemakers and 'good' domestic workers. Although the school's own board stated its purpose as training women to be 'self-supporting', as Sinkoff noted: 'Self-support was not the only priority on the agenda of German Jewish female reformers . . . They had internalized the nineteenth-century ideas of middle-class American womanhood and sought to inculcate those values in their East European charges.'[34]

In contrast, the TWR school's one-year course, the closest thing the school offered to a curriculum for domestic work, provided young women with the domestic skills needed for middle-class living but also with a greater 'scientific' approach to household management than courses for domestic help would have offered. Students took courses in the theory of home economics, food chemistry, decorating, cleaning, ironing, sewing, washing, shopping, general hygiene, children's hygiene, home finance, winter provision, commodities, first aid, social science, home aesthetics, and home bookkeeping.[35] Franciszka Lapterowa, writing about the 'modern housewife', discussed not merely recipes (of which she included a few), but also Taylorism (the idea of streamlining work processes and eliminating waste), the *Journal of Home Economics* (which sought to bring efficiencies and scientific research into household management), and work by Helena H. Richards (Ellen Henrietta Swallow Richards) at the Massachusetts Institute of Technology.[36] Richards, an industrial safety engineer and the first woman to receive a degree from the institute, also introduced the study of chemistry into nutrition.[37] Notably, Richards also believed that women's work in the home should be included in studies of the economy as a vital contributing force.[38] It is probable that this one-year course, attended by middle-class women, would also be a source of revenue for the school.

The Curriculum

The curriculum of the TWR school blended vocational education, Judaic studies, and general education. Both Judaic studies and vocational education had at their heart the idea of 'mastery', mastery in order to give students the tools to change the course of their lives, whether in Poland, Palestine, or elsewhere. The curriculum stemmed from Cecylia Klaftenowa's own brand of Zionism and related commitments to Hebrew-language education and education in Jewish history, and emphasized the school's ideal of blending 'Jewish' and 'Polish' subjects. The Jewish history course emphasized Jewish history in Poland, with a particular stress on its 'highlights', positive aspects of which students might be proud. In the early years of the school's existence, Majer Bałaban offered lectures in Jewish history, and on Saturdays the girls attended supplementary lectures or went on field trips to local sites of Jewish history.[39] Students at the school, therefore, were taught Jewish history in much the same way as Bałaban's university students, using local history and monuments as a starting point for examining the Jewish past in the Polish lands.[40]

Klaftenowa did not emphasize the Jewish character of the school in her letters to the JDC or her interviews, and the importance of a particularly Jewish schooling does not come across in her writing on women's education. Nevertheless, a (non-Jewish) school inspector, Ludwik Misky, praised the school particularly for its 'eminently religious and national Jewish character'.[41] He compared Klaftenowa, whom he called 'an indefatigable Jewish activist ... the soul of raising the level of didactic and material development of the school', with Eliza Fraenklowa, the director of the Ognisko Pracy school in Kraków. The school in Lwów inculcated, according to him, a Zionist spirit 'in a mild form, rather more contemplative than militant, that one can feel at every step', as opposed to what Misky termed the 'anti-Zionist' Kraków school.[42]

The passion Misky expressed for the Jewish nature of the school and Klaftenowa's apparent disregard for that aspect of it present a puzzle for the historian trying to ascertain the relative weight of ideological factors in the school's creation and operation. Klaftenowa's only references to Judaism and Jewish tradition in her own words are to the place of women historically in Jewish economic life and a few nods to biblical sources. It was of course not unusual to connect the charitable purpose of the school—providing for young women's education—to the Jewish community, and the school's history in the orphanage and shelter underscores this connection. It was perhaps Klaftenowa's Zionist leanings, though she did not write at length about her convictions, which led her to emphasize Jewish subjects and Jewish artistic traditions in the school. Certainly, successful girls might emigrate, as did the most famous alumna of the TWR school, Stryj-born American textile designer Pola Stout.

Misky's admiration for the 'mild' Zionism of Klaftenowa's school can be read in the broader context of the new cultural expressions available to Jews in the early 1920s as a 'national minority'. A few short years later, Klaftenowa helped found the Union of Jewish Women in Lwów, alongside figures, such as Ada Reichenstein, who were also involved in the orphanage and in various Jewish cultural and artistic endeavours across the city. It was this organization that founded, in 1929, a local branch of the Women's International Zionist Organization, in which Klaftenowa became quite active.

The school's curriculum included Jewish and Polish history and Hebrew language through literature. The school's twentieth-anniversary yearbook blended the history of Poland with the history—mainly biblical and rabbinic—of the Jewish people. The calendar included in the yearbook began on 1 September, the first day of school, and included the months and days of the Hebrew calendar alongside the civic calendar. Quotes from Józef Piłsudski, *Pirkei avot*, Hillel, Hayim Nahman Bialik, and the Constitution of the Second Polish Republic appeared interspersed throughout.[43]

In the school's third year, Jewish education included lessons on the Jewish national movement, including the thought of Leon Pinsker, Theodor Herzl, Ahad Ha'am, and Peretz Smolenskin; Jewish creativity, including the works of Bialik, Shaul Tchernichowsky, Mendele Moyker Sforim, Isaac Leib Peretz, Shalom Asch, and Sholem Aleichem; and Jewish points of view on aspects of the First World War, including the Balfour Declaration, the Treaty of Versailles (which established minority rights in Poland), the San Remo Declaration (which established the mandate system in former Ottoman areas), the resurrection of Poland after the war, and Józef Piłsudski as the leader of the struggle for Polish liberation. All of these topics share a sense of Jewish history as a history of political power: the 'high points' of Jewish life in the Polish lands. One student, enrolled in the co-educational WUZET school in Stanisławów, saw an opportunity for learning about the Jewish past (where Jews were 'farmers and craftspeople') before the coming of antisemites like 'Khmelnytsky and Petlyura' which would strengthen Jews against 'becoming martyrs to the Endeks' sticks'.[44]

Although the language of instruction at the TWR school and of its publications was Polish, Klaftenowa believed in the importance of Yiddish-speaking teachers and Yiddish-language outreach work. Speaking Yiddish, Klaftenowa wrote, would assist with contact between schools and students' families, 'to whom the teacher must speak in their language, with respect for their way of thinking'.[45] Knowing Yiddish, additionally, would help teachers understand the 'categories of thinking' of parents.⁴⁶ As some families only ate kosher food, the school's kitchen was also kosher, but sabbath activities were not compulsory.⁴⁷

Klaftenowa hoped to reach the children of Yiddish-speakers in order to make Polish Jewish society more productive and to move Polish Jewish women from a position of dependence on men to one of self-sufficiency and mastery. If the various strata of Polish Jewish society could attend school together, so much the better. Klaftenowa considered this a self-evident good, demonstrated by the demand of young Jews for the type of education offered by WUZET schools:

If the daughter of a former innkeeper, not having money for a train ticket, travels a few dozen kilometres on foot to Lwów to vocational school; if the son of a ritual slaughterer sleeps in an attic, enduring hunger and cold, in order to gather the strength to finish artisan schooling; if among the young representatives of artisanship in Małopolska are also daughters of lawyers, industrialists, rabbis, who went on to vocational school after finishing middle school, then this fact speaks for itself.⁴⁸

Klaftenowa's use of Yiddish does seem to have conveyed her message to its intended audience. A Yiddish account of WUZET's general meeting described Klaftenowa's bold ideas about the changes necessary to form 'an ideal foundation' for Jewish life in Poland. When she suggested, in her speech, that the current foundations of religious education, home life, and general studies were inadequate to ameliorate women's situation, she seems to have been met with agreement.⁴⁹

Beyond Vocational Education

Rather than merely blending technical training with academic subjects, Klaftenowa's school included particular Jewish traditions of craft into the curriculum and made the school into a space for the display of the girls' handiwork. Folk motifs seem, from multiple reports, to have infused the entire curriculum. The architect Artur Stahl used 'Jewish folk motifs drawn mainly from Jewish fabrics and embroideries and from cemetery tombstones' in his course, emphasizing vernacular Jewish folk art and local traditions, in line with tendencies from the Viennese Secession movement to draw on folkloric and historical motifs and the movement in Lwów which sought to inspire a new interest in Jewish art, particularly in its Galician variety.⁵⁰

The school's arts curriculum also drew from the Arts and Crafts and Bauhaus schools. Emphasis was placed on original work rather than reproductions, even as courses prepared students to work with machines. (A focus on original work was a hallmark of Arts and Crafts and Bauhaus, each responding to mechanization and routinization, even as, especially within Bauhaus, mass production was also a goal of student training.⁵¹) In a woodworking workshop, the (female) teacher noted the importance of spontaneous artistic creation: 'Of course we have designs that our students and draughtsmen have planned, but it often happens that the hands themselves, like the fingers of a musician, play some new motif that then moves onto the paper.'[52] Drawing classes started with letter forms, much as Bauhaus stressed simple forms as the first step in drawing.[53]

One student, writing about his experience at the WUZET school in Stanisławów, described how the theoretical aspect of his training enhanced the hands-on vocational training. The first half of the first year was spent learning the science of materials, and all of the workshops began with drawing by hand—also features of the Bauhaus curriculum.[54] Daily, he spent five hours in hands-on workshops and three hours on theory. He wrote: 'I thought that [theoretical study] was completely useless, but I changed my mind about that. I realized that vocational training without theory isn't worth anything. Both of these things are so closely linked, that one without the other simply can't exist.'[55]

Art Nouveau influences can also be seen in the arts curriculum of the TWR school. Those involved with the school were certainly familiar with the Bezalel School of Arts and Crafts in Jerusalem: the 1937 yearbook included a eulogy for Bezalel's founder, Borys Schatz, who died in 1932.[56] Bezalel drew inspiration from biblical imagery and stories, incorporated local Middle Eastern influences, and expressed them through Art Nouveau. The TWR school also used biblical imagery and incorporated local Galician influences.[57] Students at the TWR school were involved in the creation of truly new works of art: one article noted that the works produced 'are not copies of contemporary patterns, but rather original manifestations of Jewish native art: whether it is in Torah covers, kilims, or frames, we see original entwinement of letters of the Hebrew alphabet with motifs from the initials of old books and motifs from prayer shawls'.[58]

The school building provided a space that was ideal for display as well as for instruction. An article in the Kraków daily *Nowy Dziennik* mentioned the 'broad, light rooms' and the 'neat and airy work rooms'.[59] These characteristics conformed with widely held beliefs about the health benefits of light and air at the time. The Bauhaus school in Dessau, for example, although it was very different in appearance from Klaftenowa's school, also boasted light-filled workspaces and large windows to allow cross-breezes. Józef Awin, who had remodelled the school's building, was also a proponent of the healthy building. For Awin, healthy Jewish architecture was a move away from east European vernacular Jewish architecture towards buildings that did not suggest a diaspora existence. Borrowing ideas from Max Nordau's concept of 'healthy traditions', Awin deplored the use of folk motifs in architecture.[60]

Ludwik Misky also noted both the high quality and Jewish character of the work of the girls at the school. He wrote that the displays of 'national costumes, decorative motifs, antique embroideries and textiles, bronzes and tapestries' were housed in vitrines, creating 'collections of museum quality'.[61] As an artist himself, active in the Galician artistic sphere, Misky understood the importance of display and the equal importance of having high-quality work to display. Other WUZET schools featured dedicated exhibition rooms: the one in Stanisławów had an 'attractive, extensive' exhibition room, where 'every branch of [its] vocational work is well-represented'.[62] Students took pride in the exhibits, 'the fruits of our own labour', which they mounted themselves, 'just as we turn iron into hammers'.[63] Exhibits of student work were to demonstrate that 'we can create . . . we understand our task . . . we are not parasites, but rather artisans and creators. We answer to society, which cares for us.'[64]

Arts instructors sought to revive Jewish art forms thought to have been lost in the war. Discussing the art of gold-weaving for synagogue tapestries, Klaftenowa lamented that, before the First World War, Małopolska was known for its craftsmanship, work which 'stemmed from piety but not from schooled hands'.[65] She hoped to inject skill and a modernist sensibility into traditional crafts, noting that students at 'Jewish vocational schools, which cultivate knowledge of Jewish heritage and are familiar with religious motifs, not only learn the value of folk art but incorporate these motifs into modern creations—whether for the goal of sacred art, or for use in daily life'.[66] In this way, they were entrusted both with reviving beautiful local Jewish art traditions and with transforming them into something quite new.

Those involved with the school prided themselves on the high quality of the work produced and its marketability. Working with master instructors, especially those trained abroad or domestically in artisan workshops, was considered of the utmost importance. In the interwar period, most crafts teachers in the former Galicia had no pedagogical background.[67] Antonia Fleck-Kesslerowa, the school's commodities science teacher and arts workshops director, wrote of the idea of a studio which could fulfil orders for wedding dresses, fine linens, gold-threaded synagogue vestments, and other delicate work. She placed special emphasis on the idea of the customer and the order for the students: 'The commission, its importance, and the responsibility for its fulfilment inspires in the students a feeling of the weightiness of the work, and raises its importance in their eyes, not as "preparation for life"—as is often said [but as part of life itself]'.[68] Students' work, even before graduation, was expected to be on a par with work produced in Viennese ateliers, and students would go to local ateliers for advice.[69]

The TWR school building on Piekarska Street also housed 'an artistic workshop for synagogue decorations' called Rimon.[70] Rimon produced banners for a number of Lwów's Jewish organizations, especially professional organizations. The training school, another sub-faculty of the TWR school, served as an intermediary between the TWR school itself and the private workshops.[71] Rimon provided the perfect extension for the school's work and a place for its graduates to find employment. 'The school, nurturing knowledge of Jewish monuments and familiarizing the schoolgirls with their motifs related to religious worship, not only teaches understanding of the value of Jewish art based on these motifs but incorporates them into modern creations of the same ornamentation.'[72]

The workshops and the school, therefore, worked hand in hand with the academic and practical aspects of art creation and used Jewish sources to provide further inspiration for 'forging a better tomorrow'.[73] The purpose of the atelier atmosphere and the Rimon studio was to transform Jewish art for the modern world. Fleck-Kesslerowa wrote about an exhibit of domestic crafts as 'defin[ing] . . . the artistic tradition of the Jewish family table in a new contemporary form'.[74] Evidently, this also fulfilled a perceived need on the part of customers. One correspondent writing for the Jewish women's weekly *Ewa* noted: 'For this resurrection of the artistic tradition of the Jewish family table in a new modern form, we, Jewish women, are especially grateful to the leadership of the school.'[75]

The TWR school also expected students to produce their own work for sale, and to participate in the marketing and selling of it. When she visited the school, Albina Rosenblatt expressed surprise that it had customers but was informed by a teacher, 'of course there are customers!'[76] Students from the school won a silver medal at the Len Polski (Polish flax) fair in Warsaw in 1934. At this fair, Jadwiga Beck, wife of Polish foreign minister Józef Beck, known for her elegance, was 'delighted' by a dress made at the TWR school and opened the exhibition wearing it.[77] Students' works were shown at an exhibition in the United States sponsored by the JDC. Within Poland, students displayed their wares at an exhibition of products from girls' professional schools sponsored by the Ministry of Religious Denominations and Public Enlightenment in 1924, at a fair sponsored by the Lwów school council in 1928, and at the National Exhibition in Poznań in 1929. WUZET took student products to the World Congress of Jewish Women in Hamburg in 1929 and the Tarnopol Regional Exhibition in 1931. This public activity served a dual purpose. For students and their families, exhibiting and selling work reinforced the idea that the school's vocational programme was effective, turning them into master artisans whose work had value on the open market; and, for the school, the fairs served as a source of revenue and publicity.

All of this activity was made possible by the structures of student governance. Each class had its own committee modelled on that of the local Jewish community, with a head, secretary, and treasurer, which organized activities. Fryderyka Rotenstreichowa, geography and civics teacher and adviser for the student government, noted that 'the influence of the teachers on the system of self-government can be observed even outside the realm of the classroom'.[78] Second-hand accounts from students, filtered through Albina Rosenblatt on her visit to the school, indicate that they appreciated the autonomy the school offered them. She noted that a banner with Stefan Żeromski's admonition 'Piękno życia jest tylko w pracy' (A beautiful life is only obtained through work) hung in one of the light-filled classrooms she visited.[79] Here, 'work' did not refer only to the crafts students were learning but also to the workshop they ran collectively.

In 1924 students formed the Self-Help Circle and operated a shop in the school building from which supplies could be purchased.[80] Those who talked to Rosenblatt told her that their classroom experience created a 'natural self-governing community', with executive officers and their own newspapers which were distributed in the wider school community.[81] They printed both one-offs for school holidays and periodicals: *Pobudka*, *Nasz Dom*, and *Nasz Świat*. One student from a WUZET vocational school in Lwów related in the student publication *Echo Szkolne* how they came to the realization that the newspaper was the best source of information about society: 'Now I cannot manage without looking at the newspaper.'[82]

Supplementing the curriculum was a full programme of events and excursions. The 1931/2 year alone featured a synagogue service to mark the beginning of the school year and celebrations of both Jewish and Polish cultural and historical events. The students visited the Panorama Racławicka in Lwów, commemorating the Battle of Racławice in 1794, and attended programmes marking Poland's independence, a memorial service for Education Minister Sławomir Czerwiński, and a celebration of the name day of President Ignacy Mościcki. They also attended a film evening, had an excursion to the theatre to see a production of Adam Mickiewicz's *Pan Tadeusz*, listened to a radio broadcast by ethnographer Giza Frankel about her work on lace, and took trips to an exhibition of works by Artur Szyk, a morning gala marking the 600th anniversary of the battle of Płowce between the Poles and the Teutonic Knights, and the Eleventh Eastern Trade Fair. The school was also visited by the renowned Hebrew poet Hayim Nahman Bialik.[83] The extracurricular programme's breadth—from religious services to cultural activities related to Jewish art and artists, to civic patriotic events—was characteristic of the curriculum as a whole.

Conclusion

The sudden end of the TWR school and the WUZET network prevents a full evaluation of their impact. The network of schools established by Klaftenowa and WUZET reveals how different ideological commitments—to women's liberation, to productivity, to Zionism, and to Polish patriotism—intersected and informed each other, and they cannot be easily separated. The WUZET network was perhaps the only Jewish educational organization in Poland that grew in the 1930s, with new schools opening until 1939, still committed to educating orphans.[84] The Ministry of Religious Denominations and Public Enlightenment claimed that students had no trouble finding work and often went on to head their own schools,[85] no doubt a result of the work the school's staff did to keep students informed of job openings.[86]

Much like Marcus Braude's Society of Jewish Secondary Schools founded in 1912 in Łódź, which aimed to create a generation of Polish Jews committed to Jewish causes and also fully Polish, and Sarah Schenirer's Bais Yaakov schools founded in 1917, which combined religious studies with vocational training,[87] Klaftenowa brought together different currents in modern educational practice with the no less ambitious goal of transforming Polish Jewish society. Functioning as a laboratory, the TWR schools and other schools in the WUZET network fashioned new Polish Jewish women, with Jewish historical and artistic awareness and pride, Polish patriotic sensibilities, and the skills for economic liberation.

Cecylia Klaftenowa met with wide acclaim for her work. Her fiftieth birthday was honoured with scholarships in her name,[88] she undertook a speaking tour of the United States, and she received Poland's second-highest civilian honour, the Order of Polonia Restituta. A memorial book lauded her as a 'great woman'.[89] Klaftenowa's vision for a revitalization of Polish Jewish society that began with young women and included women from all strata of Polish Jewry was probably shared by the majority of pupils at the TWR school and at WUZET schools enthusiastic about 'forging a better tomorrow'.[90]

Notes

Research for this chapter was made possible thanks to a Fellowship by the European Holocaust Research Infrastructure (EHRI). Research and preliminary writing was made possible thanks to a guest fellowship at the Leibniz Institute for Jewish History and Culture—Simon Dubnow. Many thanks to Natalia Aleksiun and the two anonymous reviewers for their suggestions for improving this chapter.

1 'W roku jubileuszowym: Od T.W.R. do Związku "Wuzet"', in *Rocznik jubileuszowy Związku dla Szerzenia Wykształcenia Zawodowego wśród Żydów w Małopolsce 'Wuzet' oraz kalendarz na rok 1937–5697* (Lwów, 1937), 78–86: 78.

2 M. A. Kaplan, *The Making of the Jewish Middle Class: Women, Family, and Identity in Imperial Germany* (New York, 1991), ch. 7.

3 For an analysis of relief efforts as patriotic activity, see M. Rozenblit, *Reconstructing a National Identity: The Jews of Habsburg Austria during World War I* (New York, 2001), ch. 3.

4 See H. Stachel, 'Klaften Cecylia Dr.', *Almanach Żydowski* (Lwów, 1937), 515–16; M. Łapot, 'Cecylia Klaften (1881–194?): Pionierka żydowskiego szkolnictwa zawodowego we Lwowie i w Małopolsce w okresie międzywojennym', *Polsko-Ukraiński Rocznik*, 13 (2011), 357–67; K. Rędziński, 'Żydowskie szkolnictwo zawodowe w Małopolsce (1918–1939)', *Prace Naukowe Akademii im. Jana Długosza w Częstochowie: Pedagogika*, 15 (2006), 159–72.

5 One news item from 1938 claimed that Klaftenowa funded the schools she founded with family money; however, this is not borne out by the published financial records (see D. Klotts, 'Speaking of Women', *The Sentinel*, 14 Apr. 1938, p. 17).

6 The percentage of women earning doctorates increased in Polish universities, starting in the late nineteenth century (see J. Suchmiel, 'Emancypacja naukowa kobiet w uniwersytetach w Krakowie i we Lwowie do roku 1939', *Prace Naukowe Akademii im. Jana Długosza w Częstochowie: Pedagogika*, 13 (2004), 115–23: 115, 121–2). Although she received her doctorate in Lwów, Klaftenowa's dissertation was published in Kraków (see *Rocznik Akademii Umiejętności w Krakowie rok 1913/1914* (Kraków, 1914), 44, 114).

7 C. Klaftenowa, 'Jak młodzież żyje', in *Rocznik jubileuszowy Związku dla Szerzenia Wykształcenia Zawodowego wśród Żydów w Małopolsce*, 164–7: 167.

8 R. Romantsov, 'Polityka władz polskich wobec żydowskiego szkolnictwa zawodowego we Lwowie 1919–1939', *Wschód Europy*, 3/1 (2017), 97–119: 97.

9 Klaftenowa, 'Jak młodzież żyje', 167.

10 For the most complete treatment of the workshops including details of the loans, see Romantsov, 'Polityka władz polskich wobec żydowskiego szkolnictwa zawodowego we Lwowie'.

11 See ibid. 109.

12 See S. R. Kravtsov, 'Józef Awin on Jewish Art and Architecture', in J. Malinowski, R. Piątkowska, and T. Sztyma-Knasiecka (eds.), *Jewish Artists and Central-Eastern Europe: Art Centers—Identity—Heritage from the 19th Century to the Second World War* (Warsaw, 2010), 131–45: 132, 140.

13 Towarzystwo Warsztatów Rękodzielniczych dla Dziewcząt Żydowskich we Lwowie, *Z działalności T.W.R.: Sprawozdanie za lata 1915–1932* (Lwów, 1932), cover.

14 See C. Klaftenowa, 'O zawodowe wykształcenie kobiety', *Przegląd Społeczny*, Nov. 1927, pp. 21–6: 23.

15 Ibid.
16 Ibid.
17 C. Klaftenowa, 'Zagadnienie produktywizacji i szkolnictwo zawodowe wśród Żydów', *Miesięcznik Żydowski*, 8 (July–Aug. 1931), 123–35: 124.
18 M. Wodziński, 'Good Maskilim and Bad Assimilationists, or Toward a New Historiography of the Haskalah in Poland', *Jewish Social Studies*, NS 10/3 (2004), 87–122; M. Zalkin, *Modernizing Jewish Education in Nineteenth Century Eastern Europe: The School as the Shrine of the Jewish Enlightenment* (Leiden, 2016), 109.
19 R. Auerbach, 'W gościnie u "ziomków" b. Galicji: Wywiad z p. Dr C. Klaftenową po jej powrocie z Ameryki', *Nowy Dziennik*, 2 June 1938, p. 10.
20 Klaftenowa, 'O zawodowe wykształcenie kobiety', 23.
21 Ibid. 22.
22 Ibid.
23 A. [P. Appenszlak?], '"Z niemi na czele…": (Rozmowa z p. dr. Cecylją Klaftenową)', *Ewa*, 19 Oct. 1930, p. 2; see also C. Klaftenowa, 'Opiekun ubogich – opiekun społeczny', *Przegląd Społeczny*, Oct. 1929, pp. 364–72: 366.
24 See A., '"Z niemi na czele…"'.
25 The Jewish bloc was comprised of the General Zionists, the Mizrachi movement, the Revisionists, assimilationists, and representatives of economic organizations (see E. Yones, *Smoke in the Sand: The Jews of Lvov in the War Years, 1939–1934* (Jerusalem, 2006), 32).
26 Klaftenowa, 'O zawodowe wykształcenie kobiety', 23.
27 'W roku jubileuszowym. Od T. W. R. do Związku "WUZET"', in *Rocznik jubileuszowy Związku dla Szerzenia Wykształcenia Zawodowego wśród Żydów w Małopolsce*, 78–86: 79; cited in Rędziński, 'Żydowskie szkolnictwo zawodowe w Małopolsce', 161.
28 'Słowo wstępne', in *I. Sprawozdanie Towarzystwa Warsztatów Rękodzielniczych dla dziewcząt żydowskich we Lwowie za lata 1915, 1916, 1917, i 1918* (Lwów, 1919), 1–6: 2.
29 Ibid. 4.
30 Adler, *In Her Hands*, 62–77, 94. One student at the TWR school noted in an interview that she found the school's atmosphere 'very exclusive', contrary to what Klaftenowa's own writings indicate (see University of Southern California Shoah Foundation, Los Angeles, Visual History Archive, interview 6871: Irena Bryk (30 Sept. 1995; Pol.)).
31 'Kronika', *Nowe Słowo*, 15 May 1903, pp. 224–7: 224–5; quoted in K. Stauter Halstead, *The Devil's Chain: Prostitution and Social Control in Partitioned Poland* (Ithaca, NY, 2015), 209–10 n. 50; see also Pappenheim's publications from her visits to Galicia (P. Berthold [B. Pappenheim], *Zur Judenfrage in Galizien* (Frankfurt am Main, 1900); ead., *Zur Lage der jüdischen Bevölkerung in Galizien. Reise-Eindrücke und Vorschläge zur Besserung der Verhältnisse* (Frankfurt am Main, 1904)).
32 See E. J. Bristow, *Prostitution and Prejudice: The Jewish Fight against White Slavery 1870–1939* (New York, 1983), 290; A. Leszczawski-Schwerk, 'Dynamics of Democratization and Nationalization: The Significance of Women's Suffrage and Women's Political Participation in Parliament in the Second Polish Republic', *Nationalities Papers*, 46 (2018), 809–22.
33 See W. Wierzbieniec, 'Zakres i formy aktywności kobiet w żydowskich gminach wyznaniowych na terenie byłej Galicji (1918–1939)', in J. Hoff (ed.), *Kobiety i kultura religijna: Specyficzne cechy religijności kobiet w Polsce* (Rzeszów, 2006), 196–219: 209.
34 N. B. Sinkoff, 'Educating for "Proper" Jewish Womanhood: A Case Study in Domesticity and Vocational Training, 1897–1926', *American Jewish History*, 77 (1987–8), 572–99: 573–4.
35 'Szkoła gospodarstwa domowego T.W.R.', *Rocznik jubileuszowy Związku dla Szerzenia Wykształcenia Zawodowego wśród Żydów w Małopolsce*, 100–1: 100.

36 F. Lapterowa, 'Nowoczesna pani domu', *Rocznik jubileuszowy Związku dla Szerzenia Wykształcenia Zawodowego wśród Żydów w Małopolsce*, 236–8.
37 H. J. Mozans, *Woman in Science* (London, 1913), 217. Interestingly, many aspects of Richards' life parallel Klaftenowa's, including their work in soup kitchens and their marriages to mining engineers.
38 B. Richardson, 'Ellen Swallow Richards: "Humanistic Oekologist", "Applied Sociologist", and the Founding of Sociology', *American Sociologist*, 33/3 (2002), 21–58.
39 'Warsztaty jako akcya "Sekcyi Ochronek i Warsztatów Żydowskiego Komitetu Ratunkowego" w latach 1915 i 1916', I. *Sprawozdanie Towarzystwa Warsztatów Rękodzielniczych dla dziewcząt żydowskich we Lwowie*, 6–12: 11.
40 See N. Aleksiun, *Conscious History: Polish Jewish Historians before the Holocaust* (Liverpool, 2021).
41 Tsentral'nyi derzhavnyi istorychnyi arkhiv Ukrayiny, Lviv, f. 179, op. 4, spr. 1545: 'Sprawozdanie z wizytacji Prywatnej Szkoły Zawodowej Żeńskiej Żydowskiego Towarzystwa Warsztatów Rękodzielniczych we Lwowie' (23 June 1923), 2.
42 Ibid.
43 'Kalendarz', *Rocznik jubileuszowy Związku dla Szerzenia Wykształcenia Zawodowego wśród Żydów w Małopolsce*, 12–64.
44 M. Hundert, 'Unzer shul', in *Jednodniówka z okazji 5-lecia 'Wuzetu': 1933–1938* (Stanisławów, 1938), 2.
45 C. Klaftenowa, 'Zagadnienie przewarstwienia, a żeńskie szkolnictwo zawodowe', in *Towarzystwo Warsztatów Rękodzielniczych dla Dziewcząt Żydowskich we Lwowie, Z działalności T.W.R.*, pp. iii–xxii: xix.
46 Ibid.
47 Ibid., p. xii. The school continued to function as an orphanage as well, hence the weekend activities and full kitchen facilities for students.
48 Ibid., p. ix.
49 'Iberboyen funem yesod!', *Eyntogblat gevidmet der general-farzamlung fun 'wuzet'* (Kolomeja, 1938), 1. For figures on the professions of the parents of students at the school, see Klaftenowa, 'Zagadnienie przewarstwienia, a żeńskie szkolnictwo zawodowe', p. xii.
50 'Sprawozdanie z wizytacji Prywatnej Szkoły Zawodowej Żeńskiej Żydowskiego Towarzystwa Warsztatów Rękodzielniczych we Lwowie', 2.
51 See M. Franciscono, *Walter Gropius and the Creation of the Bauhaus in Weimar: The Ideals and Artistic Theories of its Founding Years* (Urbana, Ill., 1971); E. Cumming and W. Kaplan, *The Arts and Crafts Movement* (London, 2004).
52 A. Rosenblatt, '"Dla życia—przez życie": Godzina z uczennicami Szkoły Zawodowej T.W.R.', in *Rocznik jubileuszowy Związku dla Szerzenia Wykształcenia Zawodowego wśród Żydów w Małopolsce*, 93–9: 99.
53 Getty Research Institute, 'Principles and Curriculum' (n.d.): Getty website, 'Exhibitions and Events', 'Online Exhibitions', 'Bauhaus: Building the New Artist', 'History', visited 20 Apr. 2022.
54 'Warsztat i klasa', *Jednodniówka propagandowa Wuzetu, Związku dla Szerzenia Wykształcenia Zawodowego wśród Żydów w Małopolsce* (Stanisławów, 1936), 2.
55 Ibid.
56 L. Sch., 'Twórca Becalelu', in *Rocznik jubileuszowy Związku dla Szerzenia Wykształcenia Zawodowego wśród Żydów w Małopolsce*, 219–20: 219.
57 N. Shilo Cohen, 'The "Hebrew Style" of Bezalel, 1906–1929', *Journal of Decorative and Propaganda Arts*, 20 (1994), 140–63.

58 'W żydowskiej szkole zawodowej dla dziewcząt we Lwowie', *Nowy Dziennik*, 29 Sept. 1928, p. 10.
59 Ibid.
60 Kravtsov, 'Józef Awin on Jewish Art and Architecture', 135.
61 'Sprawozdanie z wizytacji Prywatnej Szkoły Zawodowej Żeńskiej Żydowskiego Towarzystwa Warsztatów Rękodzielniczych we Lwowie', 3.
62 'Nasza wystawa', *Jednodniówka propagandowa Wuzetu, Związku dla Szerzenia Wykształcenia Zawodowego wśród Żydów w Małopolsce*, 2.
63 'O wystawie prac', in *Rocznik jubileuszowy Związku dla Szerzenia Wykształcenia Zawodowego wśród Żydów w Małopolsce*, 194–5.
64 Ibid. 194.
65 Klaftenowa, 'Zagadnienie przewarstwienia, a żeńskie szkolnictwo zawodowe', p. xix.
66 Ibid.
67 Rędziński, 'Żydowskie szkolnictwo zawodowe w Małopolsce', 160.
68 A. Fleck-Kesslerowa, 'Z pracowni szkolnej', in Towarzystwo Warsztatów Rękodzielniczych dla Dziewcząt Żydowskich we Lwowie, *Z działalności T.W.R.*, 53–7.
69 Ibid. 53–4.
70 *Rocznik jubileuszowy Związku dla Szerzenia Wykształcenia Zawodowego wśród Żydów w Małopolsce*, 6.
71 'Przeciwwskazania do wyboru zawodu', *Rocznik jubileuszowy Związku dla Szerzenia Wykształcenia Zawodowego wśród Żydów w Małopolsce*, 150.
72 'Rimon', *Rocznik jubileuszowy Związku dla Szerzenia Wykształcenia Zawodowego wśród Żydów w Małopolsce*, 221–3: 222.
73 'Z kuźni lepszego jutra', *Rocznik jubileuszowy Związku dla Szerzenia Wykształcenia Zawodowego wśród Żydów w Małopolsce*, 93–135.
74 Fleck-Kesslerowa, 'Z pracowni szkolnej', 55.
75 Z.R., 'Żydowska sztuka stosowana w rękach kobiet (Korespondencja własna 'Ewy')', *Ewa*, 26 July 1931, p. 2.
76 Rosenblatt, '"Dla życia—przez życie"', 94.
77 Ibid. 99.
78 F. Rotenstreichowa, 'Nieco o samorządzie uczniowskim', in Towarzystwo Warsztatów Rękodzielniczych dla Dziewcząt Żydowskich we Lwowie, *Z działalności T.W.R.*, 67–91: 69.
79 Rosenblatt, '"Dla życia—przez życie"', 93.
80 'Koło Samopomocy Szkolnej uczennic Szkoły Zawod. Żeńskiej T.W.R.', *Rocznik jubileuszowy Związku dla Szerzenia Wykształcenia Zawodowego wśród Żydów w Małopolsce*, 187–8: 187.
81 Rosenblatt, '"Dla życia—przez życie"', 94.
82 L.R., 'Prasa w moim życiu', *Rocznik jubileuszowy Związku dla Szerzenia Wykształcenia Zawodowego wśród Żydów w Małopolsce*, 193–4: 194.
83 'Z kroniki szkolnej', in Towarzystwo Warsztatów Rękodzielniczych dla Dziewcząt Żydowskich we Lwowie, *Z działalności T.W.R.*, 102–5: 103.
84 Orphans accounted for 40 per cent of the student body in the new schools (see Romantsov, 'Polityka władz polskich wobec żydowskiego szkolnictwa zawodowego we Lwowie', 116).
85 Ibid. 117.
86 On the work placement programme, see S. Herzer-Fischlerowa, 'Szukamy pracy', *Rocznik*

jubileuszowy Związku dla Szerzenia Wykształcenia Zawodowego wśród Żydów w Małopolsce, 201–2: 201.

87 See N. Aleksiun, 'Marcus Braude and the Making of the Future Jewish Elite in Poland', in M. Galas and S. Ronen (eds.), *A Romantic Polish-Jew: Ozjasz Thon from Various Perspectives* (Kraków, 2015), 151–68; N. Seidman, 'Legitimizing the Revolution: Sarah Schenirer and the Rhetoric of Torah Study for Girls', in A. Polonsky, H. Węgrzynek, and A. Żbikowski (eds.), *New Directions in the History of the Jews in the Polish Lands* (Boston, Mass., 2018), 356–65.

88 L.A., 'Hołd zasłudze: W dniu 50-lecia dr. Cecylji Klaftenowej', *Nowy Dziennik*, 14 Feb. 1931, p. 8.

89 B. Felsenstein (Tzimeles), 'Beit hasefer miktso'i levanot', in M. Gelber and Y. Ben-Shem (eds.), *Sefer zolkiv* (Jerusalem, 1969), 401–4: 404.

90 'Z kuźni lepszego jutra'.

4. CHILDREN AND TRAUMA, 1914–1947

Zionist Care and Education for Galician Refugee Children in Austria during the First World War

JAN RYBAK

In 1914, Russian advances led to between 340,000 and 600,000 refugees either fleeing or being expelled from Galicia. About half were Jewish, many of whom were children. The need to care for them was a major preoccupation of the Jewish leadership in Vienna and Prague. In these relief activities, a key role was taken by the Zionists, who saw such action as not only necessary to aid suffering Jews but also as a way to broaden their influence within the Jewish community. Throughout the war the Zionist activists invested considerable resources in providing rescue and assistance for Jewish refugee children from Galicia, whom they saw as potential future pillars of the nation, and in creating institutions in which these children would be educated in a modern and progressive manner.

THE WAR arrived in Vienna in September 1914. Erna Segal, who had moved there from Lemberg (Lviv) some years earlier, recalled in her memoirs:

One day, Vienna was caught by a new scare. People were standing in every street, telling each other in an agitated way that the *Nordbahn* train station, where only weeks earlier the troops had been sent off, was crammed with thousands of refugees from Galicia. Nobody knew what to do with those people, the refugees themselves knew it the least.[1]

Just weeks earlier at that very train station cheering crowds had seen off the troops on their way to the front, expecting a swift victory over the Russian and Serbian armies. Shocking generals and civilians alike, within a few weeks Habsburg troops were dealt a serious blow on the eastern front and were forced to retreat from northern Bukovina and much of Eastern Galicia and to abandon Lemberg, the regional capital.[2] In the chaos of retreat in late August and early September, hundreds of thousands of civilians moved westwards, either fleeing the Russian advance or being deported or evacuated by the authorities.[3] Of the estimated 340,000 to 600,000 refugees—about half of them Jewish[4]—only a minority found themselves in the hastily erected refugee camps, segregated by language and religion, the largest of which was located in Nikolsburg (Mikulov) in southern Moravia.[5] Eager to avoid the miserable conditions in the camps,[6] most refugees made their way to the major urban centres of the western empire, arriving in their tens of thousands in Vienna, Prague, and Budapest.[7]

Jewish activists in the various cities rushed to their aid. For many, as Marsha Rozenblit has shown, this was a means to simultaneously assert Austrian patriotism and Jewish national and community solidarity.[8] In Vienna and Prague, Zionists were at the forefront of organizing relief for the refugees. They responded, on the one side, to pressure from the wider society for everyone to do their 'patriotic' duty, and, on the other, from the Jewish community to alleviate the suffering of fellow Jews.[9] In doing so, they also concentrated their efforts on one of the few forms of political activity that was still permissible under the conditions of an increasingly restrictive wartime regime. As Robert Stricker, the leading figure of the Zionist party in Western Austria,[10] stated: 'Our [relief] activities are due to the urgency that stems from the extreme distress amongst the refugees from Galicia and Bukovina and the need to help. We emphasize that it is our organization [that is helping] since we have to legitimize our special activities before the public and before Zionist circles.'[11] For Zionist activists, relief efforts for Jewish refugees were not only motivated by the desire to help their suffering brethren but were also seen as a means to broaden their influence, win the respect and support of the Jewish people, and prove that they were in fact the leaders of the nation.[12]

As David Rechter has shown, such community or nationally organized welfare and relief work for refugees contributed profoundly to 'the increasing salience and temporary ascendancy of ideologies of nationalism and ethnic self-determination'.[13] This chapter centres on one crucial aspect of this process—the care for refugee children. Assuming responsibility for the Jewish nation required the Zionists first and foremost to care for the safety and well-being of the nation's future—the children. They were particularly vulnerable: many had lost their parents, either directly due to the fighting or in the chaos of the retreat, and many others could not be cared for by their destitute families and required urgent support.

The Zionists, of course, were not the only ones who rushed to help Jewish children affected by the war. Jewish community boards, the Orthodox Agudat Israel party, liberal philanthropists, and local women's groups were all involved in numerous ways.[14] In these efforts, the Galician Jewish refugee children came to be a marker for differing conceptions of Jewish responses to the crisis of war and flight and of the future of the people. All of these movements in one way or another were concerned with keeping the children within the Jewish fold. Agudat Israel, for example, described its work for refugee children in Vienna as a means to 'preserve them for Judaism, while, at the same time, to educate them to tidiness and protect them from neglect'[15] through newly established *ḥeder*s.

This chapter focuses specifically on the childcare work of Zionist activists in the two Habsburg Austrian urban centres of Vienna and Prague during the war and their ideas about the Jewish nation and its children. It shows how their work to protect, support, and educate Jewish refugee children was part of their larger efforts of transforming the community and raising a new generation to become pillars of national revival. In the imagination of Zionist activists—mirroring their counterparts in other national movements in the region—children were at the heart of national rebirth.[16]

As a call for donations by the Jewish National Fund, an institution originally established in 1901 to collect money for the purchase of land in Palestine, stated: 'The rescue of the Jewish children is a great national mission. The Jewish children are the most valuable national fund our Jewish nation has, and we cannot shy away from any difficulty or obstacle in order to fulfil this holy duty.'[17] The elevation of the Jewish children of war-torn Europe to a position equalling, or even surpassing, that of the Land of Israel as the nation's 'most valuable national fund' and making their rescue and recovery the cornerstone of the national project reflects the Zionists' specific conceptions of Jewish national revival and children's role in it. This not only mirrored similar projects by other nationalists[18] but also demonstrates how, as Michael Berkowitz, Tatjana Lichtenstein, Joshua Shanes, and others have shown, the Zionist project entailed much more than 'return' to the Land of Israel and was concerned with transforming Jews' lived realities in Europe.[19] In these efforts, Zionists' wartime work to 'save' the Jewish refugee children reflects several key aspects of Zionist history: crucially, the way in which they imagined the Jewish nation's revival, the children's place in it, and the way they wanted to achieve it.

Protecting the Nation's Children

As refugees streamed into Vienna, Zionist activists there were confronted with a dual problem. First of all, while the state invested considerable sums and the city administration organized large-scale relief efforts led by the liberal Jewish city councillor Rudolf Schwarz-Hiller, they fell far short of what was required.[20] Second, while the board of the Viennese Jewish community similarly engaged in large-scale welfare and relief work—including for children, by establishing a school, financially supporting associations dedicated to their care, and providing facilities for Hebrew-language classes—this was also considered inadequate by the Zionist movement.[21] Zionists argued that the community board completely failed to live up to the responsibility it had towards the people. However, it is probable that no institution would have been capable of adequately responding to the crisis, given its immensity and the scarcity of resources. The Zionists' critique therefore essentially centred not on the quantity of the relief provided but on its quality and purpose; and, by arguing over the form of relief work, they raised the question of who should lead the community in times of crisis.[22] Through their own—supposedly more efficient—efforts, activists strove to become the leaders of the Jewish people: 'The Jewish refugees instinctively realize where they can find fraternal help, where they will receive heart-felt advice and support: with all their great and small sorrows, they turn to us Zionists.'[23]

Similarly in Prague, local relief committees and Jewish institutions were overwhelmed by the pressures of the refugee crisis, and Zionist activists decried what they perceived as the inactivity of the official community leadership and the inefficiency of community responses, which were 'handled by the community boards in a miserable way'.[24] They concluded that the responsibility for organizing relief for refugees, including children, lay with themselves, both to make up for the failure of the traditional community leadership and as a means to win support amongst the refugees and the local Jewish population. Activists in Prague hoped that they would eventually be able to 'organize all refugee relief in Bohemia under the Zionist banner'.[25] By doing so, 'not the community boards but we would . . . become the representatives of the Jewish people'.[26] In the eyes of Zionist activists in Prague and Vienna, relief work implied a national mission and was part of their efforts to gain hegemony within the community.[27] At the heart of this project were the children from war-torn eastern Europe, who needed to be protected from neglect and starvation and at the same time cared for and prepared for the future. For this purpose, Zionists in Vienna and Prague established orphanages, kindergartens, and schools that catered to both their physical and spiritual needs.

The need for such institutions came with the social crisis and the sense that existing welfare institutions, as well as public schools, kindergartens, and orphanages, had proved insufficient.[28] The situation of orphans was most pressing, in many ways a crisis within the larger crisis. Not all such children were orphans in the literal sense. Some still had at least one parent, but who was unable to provide for them and depended on support for their care.[29] For nationalist activists, childcare and relief was much more than attending to urgent material needs. It was an effort to save and raise the nation's children. 'Saving', in this sense, had a dual meaning: aside from the immediate threats of hunger, disease, violence, and neglect, Zionists believed that the failure to raise Jewish children in the national spirit would mean 'losing' them. A proposal for the establishment of orphanages in Vienna, probably drafted in 1917, summarized the problem. According to the authors, this was necessary since the Jewish community lacked adequate infrastructure to care for all the orphans and the existing alternatives were highly problematic. The city's orphanages were in poor condition and Jewish children were confronted with hatred and prejudice:

> The [city's] orphanage is an old monastery, a grey building in which the children live. It is only a transitional institution and therefore not well maintained. The rooms are insufficient, as are the supervisors and caregivers, who see it as their task to silence the children by beating and shouting. Here, a particular martyrdom begins for the Jewish child. Nobody will call him by his name, he is only 'the Jew', if this name is mercifully thrown at him and not combined with other insults. And there is no child, however miserable, abandoned, and pitiful he may be, who would not feel superior to the child that he can call 'the Jew'.[30]

The only alternative provided by the Viennese city administration was not much better. The municipality and various Jewish and non-Jewish philanthropic organizations tried to find foster parents for abandoned or orphaned children, but, since apparently few Jewish families would accept a refugee orphan, they would have to be assigned to Christian families.[31] There, the Zionists feared the children would not only be mistreated or neglected—while the foster parents collected money from the municipality—but the nation would also be danger of losing them.

> Amongst those people [foster parents], who are at best from the upper layers of the proletariat, there is no tolerance or respect for other races and faiths . . . In most cases, what is

supposed to be most valuable to a child is taken from it: its consciousness of belonging to its people is turned into a mockery, a ridicule, a curse.[32]

The fear that if a child were raised by members of another nation it could be lost was a common feature amongst nationalists—Jewish or not—everywhere.[33] Beyond traditional Jewish fears of conversion, activists believed that, in what they saw as the largely secular, modern environment of the West, the danger that Jewish children would lose their connection to their people was particularly high. In Prague, where activist and writer Max Brod taught in a Zionist school for Jewish refugee children, he was involved in numerous debates over the extent to which girls should be taught the Jewish religion. His colleague Alfred Engel, the director of the school, had initially insisted that girls should only be taught the bare minimum about religious rituals, as had been customary. Of how he responded, Brod wrote: 'With all my eloquence I explained to him the dangers of defection in [this] alien, western environment. Here [it] is not as in the East with its concentrated Jewries. "If your daughters do not know anything about Judaism, what will keep them from abandoning us?"'[34]

Of course, this fear of abandonment and loss was not confined to young east European Jews in the West, as Rachel Manekin has shown.[35] This particular conceptualization and the methods employed relate to the specific ideas 'western' Zionists had about east European Jews. Complementing the fear of loss of identity and belonging was an idealization of east European Jewry in general and the east European Jewish child in particular.[36] In 1915 Brod wrote a poem about the refugee girls he taught in Prague, capturing what he believed to be their national spirit and the teleological mission that guided his educational efforts. Even though their homes had been destroyed, with father looking back to Galicia and mother crying, the spirit of the girls remained unbroken, as they gazed upon the wide world and into a better future.

School for Galician Refugee Children

The world stands on the breath of schoolchildren
They stream in, they sit here,
On their benches, four by four,
And sway their virtuous heads.
You good girls, don't you know,
The raider is breaking into your home!
How will you get home?
The good girls, they do not bother

. . . .

The great map is put up,
Their gaze is steered far away
And colourful images float before them.
You flower-girls, mother cries
Gentle father curses the enemy.

> The flower-girls, they listen together.
> No, flowers would have already withered,
> Plucked from their roots.
> Yet, you blossom with strength and brightness,
> While all around the world tears itself apart,
> Fed by a higher power,
> You live and prepare yourselves.
> You brave girls: you are the spirit![37]

Establishing Institutions

With the influx of Jewish refugees from Galicia, Zionist activists began establishing institutions that would address their situation, especially that of the children.[38] Setting up and maintaining such institutions, raising funds, finding volunteers to work in them, and developing them into the ideal spaces for raising 'pillars of the nation' occupied much of the energies and resources of Zionist activists. Activists reported that by the autumn of 1914 all their energies were bound up in work for the refugees, which had become the centrepiece of their work during the war.[39] As one proposal explained:

> Outside Vienna, a children's colony could be established, in which those who are abandoned, expelled, and tormented could find a bright home . . . They would have their play and workspaces, their teachers and counsellors. They would receive the physical and spiritual care and education they need, they would be protected from brutality and ignorance, which has hampered and misdirected their physical and spiritual development. From the poorest and sickest, from the most miserable and most depressed, strong, happy, and proud pillars of our people would be formed.[40]

In the mindset of Zionist childcare and welfare activists, the purpose of the institution was not only to save the children from physical harm and to care for them. Their accommodation in such institutions would also be an essential part of a process of collective regeneration. From these children, activists imagined, a new, healthy, and nationally conscious generation would be formed.

In October 1914 Zionists established a kindergarten for refugee children in Vienna.[41] The local Zionist press praised the institution and its efforts in the fields of pedagogy and spiritual revival: 'Thanks to the proficient kindergarten teacher, who has been educated in Palestine, the little ones are speaking and singing equally well in Yiddish, German, and Hebrew.'[42] Founded by Erna Patak and supported by the Zionist Women's Association, the Kindergarten of the Zionist Central Committee, as it was called, remained relatively small, supervising, clothing, feeding, and educating forty children initially, later expanding to eighty.[43] Zionists attributed great national importance to the institution, and managerial decisions, especially regarding pedagogical matters, were taken by the party leadership itself.[44] In their representation of the institution and its goals, they emphasized its transformative effect on the children and its regenerative, national spirit:

One has to have seen the joy and happiness, shining from the children's eyes, of those poorest of the poor, when a visitor comes and they have the chance to give to him from their rich poverty—and they love to give. The songs in Hebrew, German, and Yiddish resound bright and rhythmical. One listens in amazement to the Jewish fairy tales and everywhere, one can see and feel the great and strong intelligence of the Jewish children . . . They are well cared for and fed, happy and healthy, and, until the furthest future, their stay in Vienna in these dreadful times will be nothing but a series of happy memories.[45]

While the children flourished, thanks to the conditions in the kindergarten, the emphasis on their poverty connected them to a concept of purity. This was part of many German-speaking Viennese Zionists' essentialist and idealized views of east European Jewry. They were often portrayed as the 'real', unassimilated Jewish nation. It was believed that they were connected to their roots, hardened, and proud.[46]

Thus, children's education was simultaneously 'the fulfilment of a "national requirement" and a social and patriotic task'.[47] While the number of those cared for in the kindergarten in Vienna remained limited—mainly due to lack of funds—it gained significant symbolic importance. The kindergarten children also participated in Zionist political activities and political rituals, demonstrating both Jewish-national and Austrian-patriotic allegiances at Hanukah and for the emperor's birthday, when Erna Patak personally handed over a collection of poems of praise by the children.[48]

Patak, like Robert Stricker, had been born in Brünn (Brno). However, many of the Viennese Zionists, as well as a significant part of the Jewish community itself, had originally come from Galicia.[49] Due to the war and the flight of many Galician Zionist activists westwards, even more Galicians became active in Zionist circles in the western centres of the empire.[50] Many of them were involved in relief and educational activities, despite their precarious situation and the simmering tensions between themselves and some of the more established activists—especially in Vienna—who claimed for themselves the leading role in all national political affairs.[51] Many groups in Vienna, Zionists and non-Zionists alike,[52] saw the Galician Jewish refugee children as naive and pious, the bearers of a pure, unadulterated Judaism, and felt it to be the duty of supposedly more enlightened activists and communities in the West to rescue, guide, and raise them.[53] This image of the children and the work with them was the basis for all of their manifold visions for the renewal of Jewish society.

For Zionists, the dual task of the physical and spiritual renewal of the Jewish children was central to their childcare and relief efforts throughout the region, leading them to create safe and healthy physical spaces for the children and often connecting them with nature.[54] In many respects this reflected the activists' awareness of contemporary ideas about children's developmental processes and needs. Simultaneously they responded to fundamental questions about the formation of a modern, nationally defined Jewish identity. The insistence on the progressive character of childcare, the openness and brightness of the spaces in which it occurred, and the kindness of the caretakers and teachers reflected the rejection of the *ḥeder*, the traditional institution of Jewish children's education, especially those from eastern Europe.[55]

There existed a dialectical relation between the idealization of east European Jewry, on the one hand, and the vision of their progressive transformation on the other. For the activists, Zionist kindergartens and schools should strive to create the 'new Jew' or, as they were instructed at a 1918 youth conference in Vienna: 'Do not allow the ḥeder to be resurrected, create in its stead true educational institutions, modern Jewish kindergartens into which sun, air, and light stream and from which our children will emerge strengthened in body and spirit.'[56]

In Prague, Zionist activists won the support of the Jewish community board for the establishment of the school for refugee children discussed above.[57] While the Jewish community provided the facilities and covered a large part of the expenses, Zionists also engaged in fundraising activities for the institution, to which they also attributed great national significance.[58] In fact, their efforts to build the school, and several smaller institutions in other cities and towns throughout Bohemia, were remarkably successful.[59] By Passover 1915 its director, Alfred Engel, claimed that over 1,300 students were enrolled; other sources speak of even higher numbers.[60] Similarly to those in Vienna, refugee children attending the school participated in the political activities of the Zionist movement, for example by organizing special commemorative celebrations on the anniversary of Theodor Herzl's death.[61] The school was part of a network of educational institutions in Prague and the wider region catering specifically for refugee children that had been set up by various activists in coordination with the local Jewish community boards and philanthropic organizations, sometimes even with public funding, which illustrates the extent to which activists attained responsibility for the people and significantly extended their role beyond party political contexts.[62]

Such institutions, of which the Zionist school was by far the biggest, won recognition and support from the government, which allowed activists to institutionalize their efforts not only in community and national contexts, but also in the imperial one.[63] The school offered classes in general subjects (such as German, Hebrew, mathematics, and history) and vocational training. The latter courses, such as cooking, vegetable gardening, handicrafts, and carpentry, were strictly segregated by gender, with boys being trained in traditionally male professions and girls gaining experience in fields deemed appropriate for them—such as the forty girls of the cooking and housekeeping course providing meals for the children at the school.[64] In the eyes of the activists and educators running the school, its purpose was to bring east European Jewish children into contact with the best and most advanced knowledge and practices of nationally conscious western Jewry. Reports on the school's activities highlighted the idea of liberating the supposedly 'ignorant'—although 'pure'—Galician children from the supposed backwardness of their origins and allowing them to fulfil their potential, not only for themselves but for the nation.[65] In August 1915 the school simultaneously celebrated the end of the first school year and bade farewell to a number of students who would return to newly reconquered East Galicia. The ceremony gave Alfred Engel the opportunity to articulate the school's mission:

He declared that he happily gave so much time and effort for the management of the school, which gave him nothing but joy and inner satisfaction, because he was aware of having accomplished educational work for the nation, and requested the children to work on themselves in the national spirit, following the inspiration of this school after they returned to their homes. The simple celebrations ended with the singing of the 'Hatikvah'.[66]

Education for 'National Rebirth'

The war had a profound impact not only on the organization of Jewish childcare and education but also on the content and methods of education. Zionists needed to work out for themselves what they wanted to teach children and how they wanted to teach it. Throughout the region, childcare and educational activists often employed modern pedagogical methods.[67] This was part of a broader phenomenon within Jewish society, as traditional teaching methods, curriculums, and the question of independent Jewish educational institutions were heavily debated, reflecting a wider sense of urgency to transform Jewish education.[68] In a Zionist context, this included a marked tendency towards teaching subjects considered to be of national importance, such as the Hebrew language and Jewish history, and efforts to professionalize pedagogy.

In late 1916 Zionist activists opened a Hebrew-language school for children aged 5 to 9 in Vienna. In many respects, it built on the efforts of the kindergarten, since 'at a tender age the children shall become accustomed to the language of their people, so they shall learn to love it from earliest childhood on, so that it should fill their souls with its sweet sound. They shall learn Hebrew so that they become true and upright Jews—as far as the *galut* [exile] allows for this.'[69] The following year Moses Rath published a new and greatly expanded edition of his Hebrew-language textbook *Sefat amenu*, praised as the 'first practical method for learning the Hebrew language',[70] which would go through several editions in the years afterwards.[71]

In order to promote children's education, activists began addressing the question of pedagogical methods and the best way to educate children and shape their minds for the future. One of the most prominent voices in this debate was Siegfried (Selig) Bernfeld. Born in Lemberg in 1892, he joined the Zionist Central Committee for Western Austria in 1917 at the age of 25 and became an important youth leader in wartime Vienna.[72] In two articles published in the Viennese Zionist *Jüdische Zeitung* in early 1917, he outlined what he considered to be the necessities of Jewish education in the face of a rapidly changing world. His starting point was a critique of traditional Jewish religious instruction in public schools, which he believed estranged young Jews more than it connected them to Judaism. Due to its inability to inspire students and to convey a deeper understanding, it would eventually strengthen assimilationist tendencies.[73] Jewish education, he believed, required a complete overhaul. Teachers not only needed to be able to inspire the children and teach them a love for the subject, but should also define themselves more as historians and sociologists than as mere teachers of religion.[74] In addition to building independent Zionist kindergartens and schools, Bernfeld believed that assuming responsibility for the entire Jewish people meant nationalizing the whole Jewish educational system. 'The foremost task of Zionism', he wrote a few months later, was 'to create Jewish teachers for the existing Jewish educational system in order to reconstruct and complete it as a Jewish national educational system'.[75]

Of course, this aroused protests from political opponents, who insisted that 'the Jewish child must not become a guinea pig!'[76] Such a backlash, and their open critique of established educational norms and institutions, required Bernfeld and his colleagues to concentrate first and foremost on training teachers. Their idea was to develop an empire-wide Jewish national pedagogical movement, since 'in the coming times, every people will care for its own wellbeing'. For this reason, an organization 'based on our idea of national rebirth' was necessary to protect the children from outside influences and from 'the ḥeder, which harms the child body and soul'.[77] To this end, in September 1917, the Viennese Zionists established a seminar focusing particularly on the Hebrew language, Jewish culture and history, and the teaching of pedagogical methods.[78]

A year later, the Working Group for Jewish Education was established by Bernfeld and some of the others who had participated in the seminar. It established contacts and partnerships throughout the country, which persisted beyond the war and the dissolution of the Habsburg empire.[79] Its pedagogical approach focused on children's self-determination, self-organization, and the connection of formal education with agricultural and vocational training to overcome the barrier between intellectual and physical labour.[80] In autumn 1918 a kindergarten and a pedagogical institute for the training of kindergarten teachers and Hebrew-language teachers were established.[81] The plans were grand. Very much in the spirit of the fundamental changes that swept through the region in 1918, Bernfeld and his colleagues hoped to build an entirely new network of kindergartens, schools, orphanages, boarding schools, and summer camps. These would not only meet the highest and most modern pedagogical standards but also involve communal living on the premises. In particular, their early plans for the new educational network—reflecting their own biographies to an extent—strongly emphasized the unity between 'eastern' and 'western' Jewry, insisting on the necessity of building such institutions in Galicia and Bukovina, as well as in the West, and of bringing together Viennese Jewish children and Galician refugee children and thereby 'rescuing' Galician children from the ḥeder and Viennese children from assimilation.[82]

The Jewish pedagogical courses offered in Vienna are well documented in the archives and offer insights into the modern pedagogical thinking of the activists. Their content shows a strong focus on Jewish history, culture, literature, and ethics, as well as didactics and pedagogical methods.[83] These courses, which sought a 'blending of general and Jewish knowledge with pedagogical knowledge and skills',[84] were headed by Bernfeld. Over three-quarters of the 194 participants were female and between 18 and 30 years old, most of them apparently from a well-educated bourgeois background.[85] Two reports survive from teachers who taught these courses—

one on Hebrew and the other on ancient Jewish history. Both strongly emphasize the role of dialogue with the students as opposed to lecturing, and both record a particularly warm and friendly relationship between teachers and participants.[86]

A draft concept for a future elementary school reveals a pedagogical focus on three key elements: the teaching of younger children by their older peers, the breaking of the barrier between formal knowledge and experience with nature and practical (work) skills, and the connection of these with a nationalist ethos. The draft stressed the importance of pupils' self-awareness, the fostering of autodidactic abilities, the connection between formal and practical aspects, and learning not because they were told to by the teacher but because of their own drive and motivation.[87] This can be seen in the report by the teacher who taught Hebrew: 'Before I approached the children with words that are foreign to them and [feeling that] to repeat them would be uninteresting, I thought it appropriate to first speak with them about the concept of language in general and the Hebrew language in particular.'[88] This was in stark contrast to the traditional way of learning Hebrew, especially in the *ḥeder*, which primarily consisted of repetition and rote learning. Such methods were rejected here, and the teacher sought to involve the children:

Who of you understands Yiddish, who Polish, who Hungarian, who German? So, all of you understand German, Polish only two, Yiddish five, Hungarian one. You can see that not all people and not all children speak the same way. Out there, not in Vienna, there are many children who speak completely differently to you and if you come to them and tell them something, they will not understand you. Why is that? The children's response: 'Because they speak a different language.' There are many different languages. Which languages do you know? The children begin to name several languages: German, Polish, Hebrew, English as well. Why does one learn a different language? The children's response: 'To understand the children who speak a different language.'[89]

The implicit question was, of course, Who should we want to speak with? Which children should we aim to understand?

And do you know which language we will learn? The children joyfully: 'Hebrew!' Yes, correct, but why do we learn the Hebrew language and not another one? The children's responses vary. The majority know it but cannot express it. It only becomes clear that in the land where many Jews live (one shouts out that this land is called Palestine) and where we all want to go, [people] speak like this. But if we go there and do not understand Hebrew then we cannot speak with the Jews who live there, can neither say anything nor understand what they want to say. That is why we need to learn the Hebrew language.[90]

Conclusion

The joy of the children, many of whom were war refugees from Galicia, was a key element in how educational activists perceived and represented them. This common theme, as observed earlier in regard to the kindergarten of the Zionist Central Committee in Vienna and the Zionist school in Prague, reflects a number of key elements of the activists' understanding of national education and care and the role of the children themselves. First of all, the kindergartens and schools were seen in marked contrast to the traditional *ḥeder*, and activists believed that this would emancipate the refugee children from their supposedly backward traditions and lead them to a progressive future. Secondly, it responded to the wish of many—especially parents, but also members of the wider community—to create a safe and joyful space for the children in the surrounding misery caused by war and flight. The national movement, embodied by the Zionist school and kindergarten, thereby represented a haven of safety and well-being for the children. Thirdly, the value attached to children's joy in learning suggests an inner drive by the children themselves to appropriate the knowledge and skills offered by their educators. In the imagination of the activists, this expressed the natural instinct of the children as the future of the Jewish nation.

This need not necessarily have reflected children's lived reality, and, since hardly any sources by those who went through these experiences exist, it is difficult to contrast it with their perception of the developments. However, the efforts of the Zionists—and many others—in this period were a key aspect of the profound transformations in Jewish social and political life throughout eastern Europe that would have long-lasting consequences. The wider national educational mission and the new pedagogical methods, which reflected a different understanding of the child in society, continued after the war. Siegfried Bernfeld's approaches, including the kindergarten, came to be seen as an exemplary case of modern education, studied widely and beyond the circles of Jewish educational activists.[91] Similarly, activists in Prague, by then the capital of Czechoslovakia, built on the experience and prestige they gained through their educational work during the war to work on a complete 'nationalization' of the new state's Jewish educational system.[92]

The pedagogical models employed by activists such as Bernfeld reflect their wider understanding of the world and the tasks they saw for the Jewish national movement. Positive, friendly relations between teachers and students, older children helping to teach their younger peers, and the connection of intellectual and physical education were part of wider ideas of developing Jewish national solidarity and self-reliance. While Bernfeld and many other activists envisioned this new form of education and care for all young Jews in Europe, the main group they addressed was the refugee children. This was not only because of their urgent material needs in an alien and often hostile environment, but also because of their idealization as the 'pillars of the nation' in the imagination of many activists. Taking care of them meant assuming responsibility for the people itself and for shaping its future.

Notes

1 Leo Baeck Institute, New York, ME-295: E. Segal, 'You Shall Never Forget' (1956), 16–17.
2 C. Mick, *Lemberg, Lwów, L'viv, 1914–1941: Violence and Ethnicity in a Contested City* (West Lafayette, Ind., 2016), 19–20.
3 B. Hoffmann-Holter, *'Abreisendmachung': Jüdische Kriegsflüchtlinge in Wien, 1914–1923*

(Vienna, 1995), 23–30; D. Rechter, *The Jews of Vienna and the First World War* (Oxford, 2008), 67–74; M. L. Rozenblit, *Reconstructing a National Identity: The Jews of Habsburg Austria during World War I* (Oxford, 2001), 66–7.

4 Hoffmann-Holter, 'Abreisendmachung', 29–30.

5 P. Judson, *The Habsburg Empire: A New History* (Cambridge, Mass., 2016), 410–15; W. Mentzel, 'Kriegserfahrungen von Flüchtlingen aus dem Nordosten der Monarchie während des Ersten Weltkriegs', in B. Bachinger and W. Dornik (eds.), *Jenseits des Schützengrabens. Der Erste Weltkrieg im Osten: Erfahrungen–Wahrnehmungen–Kontext* (Innsbruck, 2013), 359–90.

6 On conditions in the camps, see esp. Central Archives for the History of the Jewish People, Jerusalem (hereafter CAHJP), CS 191, Moritz Lewin collection.

7 C. Morelon, 'L'Arrivée des réfugiés Galicie en Bohême pendant la Première Guerre mondiale: Rencontre problématiques et limites du patriotism autrichien', *Histoire@Politique*, 28/1 (2016), 5–18; R. Klein-Pejšová, 'The Budapest Jewish Community's Galician October', in M. L. Rozenblit and J. Karp (eds.), *World War I and the Jews: Conflict and Transformation in Europe, the Middle East, and America* (New York, 2017), 112–30; Rechter, *The Jews of Vienna and the First World War*, 69–71.

8 Rozenblit, *Reconstructing a National Identity*, 59–80.

9 Ibid.; Rechter, *The Jews of Vienna and the First World War*, 83–90. Central Zionist Archives, Jerusalem (hereafter CZA), Z3 779: Zionistisches Distriktbureau für Böhmen in Prag, letter to L. Herrmann, 1 Sept. 1914; Z3 840: A. Hantke, letter to Zionistisches Zentralbüro für Westösterreich, 25 Sept. 1914.

10 The Zionist movement in Habsburg Austria was organized into three separate, albeit closely connected, organizations: Galicia, Bukovina, and 'Western Austria', which comprised local organizations in Bohemia, Moravia, Silesia, and the German-speaking lands that would later make up the Republic of Austria, including the capital Vienna (A. Gaisbauer, *Davidstern und Doppeladler: Zionismus und jüdischer Nationalismus in Österreich, 1882–1918* (Vienna, 1988), 244–368).

11 CZA Z3 840: R. Stricker, letter to Zionististisches Central-Bureau Berlin, 19 Sept. 1914.

12 CZA, Z3 814: A. Hantke, letter to Z. Bickels, 11 Nov. 1915; Z3 779: Zionistisches Distriktkomitee für Böhmen in Prag, letter to L. Herrmann, 1 Sept. 1914; S. Kaznelson, letter to L. Herrmann, 14 Dec. 1914. For the broader, regional context, see J. Rybak, *Everyday Zionism in East-Central Europe: Nation-Building in War and Revolution, 1914–1920* (Oxford, 2021), 60–86.

13 D. Rechter, 'Galicia in Vienna: Jewish Refugees in the First World War', *Austrian History Yearbook*, 28 (1997), 113–30: 113.

14 Ibid. 121–2; Rozenblit, *Reconstructing a National Identity*, 70–2; see also 'Ein Heim für Flüchtlingskinder', *Jüdische Korrespondenz*, 17 Feb. 1916, p. 3; R.U., 'Hietzinger Frauenverein zum Schutze armer, verlassener Kinder', *Die Wahrheit*, 28 May 1915, p. 8; 'Verein Kinderheim', *Die Wahrheit*, 6 Apr. 1916, pp. 5–6; 'Leopoldstädter Kinderschutz', *Dr. Bloch's Österreichische Wochenschrift*, 18 Dec. 1914, p. 884; 'I. Generalversammlung des Vereins zur Rettung verlassener jüdischer Kinder Galiziens und der Bukowina', *Dr. Bloch's Österreichische Wochenschrift*, 30 Mar. 1917, pp. 195–200. One of the most significant aid networks in Vienna was initiated by Anitta Müller. She was a Zionist and her efforts undoubtedly raised Zionism's profile in the city, but—unlike other efforts—it was not organized in a party political context. See D. J. Hecht, '"Meine Pflicht zu verstehen und zuerst den Juden zu dienen": Anitta Müller-Cohen (1890–1962)', in S. Hering (ed.), *Jüdische Wohlfahrt im*

Spiegel von Biographien (Frankfurt am Main, 2007), 307–19; id., *Zwischen Feminismus und Zionismus: Die Biografie einer Wiener Jüdin. Anitta Müller-Cohen (1890–1962)* (Vienna, 2008); Rechter, *The Jews of Vienna and the First World War*, 85, 88; Rozenblit, *Reconstructing a National Identity*, 72.

15 Ben-Amitai, 'Die "Agudas Jisroel" in Wien', *Jüdische Korrespondenz*, 21 Dec. 1916, p. 2.
16 T. Zahra, *Kidnapped Souls: National Indifference and the Battle for Children in the Bohemian Lands, 1900–1948* (Ithaca, NY, 2008), 3–5.
17 CZA, L6 103: Jewish National Fund, memorandum on Jewish children's relief work (1917(?)).
18 Zahra, *Kidnapped Souls*.
19 M. Berkowitz, *Western Jewry and the Zionist Project, 1914–1933* (Cambridge, 1997); T. Lichtenstein, *Zionists in Interwar Czechoslovakia: Minority Nationalism and the Politics of Belonging* (Bloomington, Ind., 2016); J. Shanes, *Diaspora Nationalism and Jewish Identity in Habsburg Galicia* (Cambridge, 2012).
20 Gemeinde Wien, *Ein Jahr Kriegsfürsorge der Gemeinde Wien* (Vienna, 1915), 95–6; Rechter, *The Jews of Vienna and the First World War*, 75–8, Rozenblit, *Reconstructing a National Identity*, 67; Hoffmann-Holter, 'Abreisendmachung', 41–52.
21 CAHJP, A/W 357, box 2c: M. Kanitz, 'Bericht über die Flüchtlingsschule II, Malzgasse 16 erstattet am Ende des Schuljahres 1914/15' (July 1915); A/W 71.15: Präsidium der Israelitischen Kultusgemeinde Wien, 'Protokoll der Plenar-Sitzung vom 14. März 1915'; A/W 71.16: Präsidium der Israelitischen Kultusgemeinde Wien, 'Protokoll der Plenar-Sitzung vom 30. April 1916'; A/W 357.1: Israelitische Kultusgemeinde Wien, 'Referatsbogen 5197/1914' (10 Dec. 1914).
22 'Die galizischen Flüchtlinge und die Wiener Kultusgemeinde', *Jüdische Zeitung*, 9 Oct. 1914, p. 1; 'Die Flüchtlingsfürsorge ist eine jüdische Pflicht', *Jüdische Zeitung*, 25 Dec. 1914, p. 1.
23 'Unsere Tätigkeit für die Flüchtlinge bei der Regierung', *Jüdische Zeitung*, 30 Oct. 1914, p. 2.
24 CZA, Z3 779: Zionistisches Distriktkomitee für Böhmen in Prag, letter to L. Herrmann, 1 Sept. 1914; see also 'Die Flüchtlingsfürsorge', *Selbstwehr*, 29 Dec. 1914, p. 1. On refugee relief in Bohemia, see K. Habartová, 'Jewish Refugees from Galicia and Bukovina in East Bohemia during World War I in the Light of the Documents of the State Administration', *Judaica Bohemiae*, 43 (2007/8), 149–54.
25 CZA, Z3 779: Zionistisches Distriktkomitee für Böhmen in Prag, letter to Zionistisches Actions-Commité, 6 Dec. 1914.
26 CZA, Z3 779: Siegmund Kaznelson, letter to L. Herrmann, 14 Dec. 1914.
27 As could be seen throughout the region (see Rybak, *Everyday Zionism*, 60–98).
28 A problem observed by everyone involved (see e.g. 'Schulaktion für Flüchtlingskinder aus Galizien und Bukowina', *Die Wahrheit*, 9 July 1915, pp. 6–7; L. Körner, 'Die Betreuung und Erziehung der Flüchtlingswaisen eine der dringendsten und wichtigsten Aufgaben der Kriegsfürsorge', *Dr. Bloch's Österreichische Wochenschrift*, 10 Dec. 1915, pp. 894–5).
29 The community board, for instance, informed mothers and legal guardians that they could register their 'war orphans' for accommodation in an orphanage ('Jüdische Kriegswaisen', *Jüdische Korrespondenz*, 10 Aug. 1916, p. 4).
30 CAHJP, AU 166: 'Schaffet Kinderkolonien für Verlassene Jüdische Kinder' (1917(?)).
31 Ibid.; 'Aufruf zur Meldung von Jüdischen Familien, welche Pflegekinder übernehmen wollen', *Dr. Bloch's Österreichische Wochenschrift*, 7 July 1916, pp. 454–5; 'Wer adoptiert elternlose Waisen?', *Neue Nationalzeitung*, 19 Feb. 1915, p. 34.

32 'Schaffet Kinderkolonien für Verlassene Jüdische Kinder'.
33 P. M. Judson, *Guardians of the Nation: Activists on the Language Frontiers of Imperial Austria* (Cambridge, Mass., 2006), 3; T. Zahra, 'Reclaiming Children for the Nation: Germanization, National Ascription, and Democracy in the Bohemian Lands, 1900–1945', *Central European History*, 37 (2004), 499–540.
34 M. Brod, *Streitbares Leben, 1884–1968* (Munich, 1969), 231. Note the phrasing 'as in the East with its concentrated Jewries' ('wie im Osten mit seinen konzentriert wohnenden Judenschaften'). Brod chose to use not only the plural but also the possessive determiner *seinen*, suggesting the East's possession and control of its Jewries.
35 R. Manekin, *The Rebellion of the Daughters: Jewish Women Runaways in Habsburg Galicia* (Princeton, NJ, 2020).
36 For the German case, see S. E. Aschheim, *Brothers and Strangers: The East European Jew in German and German-Jewish Consciousness, 1800–1923* (Madison, Wis., 1982); J. Wertheimer, *Unwelcome Strangers: East European Jews in Imperial Germany* (New York, 1987).
37 M. Brod, 'Schule für Galizische Flüchtlingskinder', in id., *Das gelobte Land: Ein Buch der Schmerzen und Hoffnungen*, 3rd edn. (Leipzig, 1917), 19–20. The poem was published in *Jüdische Zeitung* and *Selbstwehr* on 4 June 1915. In his memoirs Brod did not print the second verse of the poem (which I have also left out here) and claimed that it was dedicated to the Galician Jewish refugee girls he had taught (Brod, *Streitbares Leben*, 232). As a matter of fact, it had been dedicated to the school's director 'Prof. A[lfred] Engel, the ingenious philanthropist and organizer' (ibid. 20). The epigraph is from BT *Shab*. 119*b* where the 'breath of schoolchildren' refers to their reciting of the Torah.
38 There is a notable difference between the approach of Zionists in Vienna and Prague, who concentrated on building institutions in their cities, and those welfare activists and philanthropists from Orthodox backgrounds, who concentrated on supporting institutions in Galicia itself after the region was retaken by the Austrian army, often attracting financial support from non-Jewish donors. See e.g. 'Hilfe für unsere Kriegswaisen', *Jüdische Korrespondenz*, 16 Mar. 1916, p. 1; 'Rettet die verlassenen Kinder Galiziens', *Jüdische Korrespondenz*, 27 Apr. 1916, pp. 1–2; 'Jüdische Kriegswaisenfürsorge in Galizien', *Jüdische Korrespondenz*, 1 June 1916, pp. 1–2; 'Große Sitzung für die Aktion zur Rettung verlassener Kinder Galiziens', *Jüdische Korrespondenz*, 23 Nov. 1916, p. 3; 'Rettet die verlassenen jüdischen Kinder Galiziens', *Die Wahrheit*, 21 Apr. 1916, pp. 1–2; S. Fleischer, 'Eine Aktion für die galizischen Kriegswaisen', *Dr. Bloch's Österreichische Wochenschrift*, 9 June 1916, pp. 390–1.
39 CZA, Z3 840–1: Zionistisches Zentralkomitee für Westösterreich, letters to Zionistisches Central-Bureau, Berlin, 10, 29 Oct. 1914; Z3 780: Zionistisches Distriktkomitee für Böhmen in Prag, 'Zirkular an alle Vereine und Vertrauensmänner' [early 1915]; Z3 842: Leo Herrmann, letter to Martin Rosenblüth, 23 Apr. 1915.
40 'Schaffet Kinderkolonien für Verlassene Jüdische Kinder'.
41 'Unser Hilfswerk für die Flüchtlinge', *Jüdische Zeitung*, 9 Oct. 1914, p. 2.
42 'Das Hilfswerk der Wiener Zionisten für die Kriegsflüchtlinge', *Jüdische Zeitung*, 4 Apr. 1916, p. 9.
43 CAHJP, A/W 248.5: Zionistisches Zentralkomitee für Westösterreich, 'Das Hilfswerk der Wiener Zionisten für die Kriegsflüchtlinge 1914/1916'.
44 'Unsere Hilfsaktion: Der Kinderhort', *Jüdische Zeitung*, 26 Feb. 1915, p. 2.
45 Ibid.
46 See, for example, Otto Abele's description of his encounters with eastern Jews (O. Abeles, 'Ostjuden', *Jüdische Zeitung*, 14 Apr. 1916, pp. 5–6).

47 'Die Fürsorge für die Waisen der jüdischen Kriegsopfer', *Jüdische Zeitung*, 21 Jan. 1916, p. 1.
48 'Chanukafeier im Kinderhort des Zionistischen Zentralkomitees', *Jüdische Zeitung*, 1 Jan. 1915, p. 3; 'Zionistischer Kinderhort', *Jüdische Zeitung*, 27 Oct. 1915, p. 3; 'Makkabäerfeier des jüdischen Kinderhortes', *Jüdische Zeitung*, 29 Dec. 1916, p. 4; 'Kleine Chronik', *Neue Freie Presse*, 10 Sept. 1915, p. 10.
49 R. Wistrich, *The Jews of Vienna in the Age of Franz Joseph* (Oxford, 1989), 347–80; K. Hödl, *Als Bettler in der Leopoldstadt: Galizische Juden auf dem Weg nach Wien* (Vienna, 1994); id., 'Galician Jewish Migration to Vienna', *Polin*, 12 (1999), 147–63; A. G. Rabinbach, 'The Migration of Galician Jews to Vienna, 1857–1880', *Austrian History Yearbook*, 11 (1975), 43–54; M. Rozenblit, 'A Note on Galician Jewish Migration to Vienna', *Austrian History Yearbook*, 19 (1983), 143–52; id., *The Jews of Vienna, 1867–1914: Assimilation and Identity* (Albany, NY, 1983), 40–5; id., 'Jewish Immigrants in Vienna before the First World War', *Aschkenas: Zeitschrift für Geschichte und Kultur der Juden*, 17 (2007), 35–53.
50 Galician Zionists in Vienna tried to convince the refugees to join the Galician Zionist Organization, thus transferring 'Galician' Zionist work westwards (see CZA, Z3 507: Zionistisches Central-Bureau Berlin, letter to Leon Reich, 31 Dec. 1914).
51 e.g. CZA Z3 507: Victor Jacobson, letter to Leon Reich, 18 Oct. 1915; Z3 519: Adolf Stand, letter to Zionistisches Zentralkomitee für Westösterreich, 11 Sept. 1916; Arthur Hantke, letters to Adolf Stand, 15, 18 Sept. 1916; Z3 841: 'Protokoll über die ordentliche Sitzung des G. A. des Z. K.' (4 Feb. 1915); Z3 842: Leo Herrmann, letter to Martin Rosenblüth, 23 Apr. 1915; Z3 520: W., letter to Robert Stricker, 31 Dec. 1914.
52 Rechter, *The Jews of Vienna and the First World War*, 72–3.
53 e.g. 'Kinderheim in Laa', *Die Wahrheit*, 30 June 1916, pp. 5–6; R. Ritter v. Schwarz-Hiller, 'Jüdische Kinder aus dem Osten', *Die Wahrheit*, 4 Oct. 1918, pp. 5–6; 'Ein Besuch im Heim für Flüchtlingskinder', *Dr. Bloch's Österreichische Wochenschrift*, 16 Apr. 1915, p. 300.
54 CZA, L6 108: report on Zionist children's relief work in Poland [Sept. 1917(?)]; L6 109: Schobach and B. Epstein, report on the Jewish summer colonies near Vilna (1918).
55 e.g. J. Kimmel, 'In den Kindergarten oder zurück in den Cheder?', *Dr Bloch's Österreichische Wochenschrift*, 17 May 1918, p. 299.
56 'In den Kindergarten oder zurück in den Cheder?', *Jüdische Zeitung*, 17 May 1918, p. 3.
57 Rozenblit, *Reconstructing a National Identity*, 71 n. 104.
58 CZA, Z3 781: Zionistischer Distriktverband für Böhmen in Prag, 'Rechenschaftsbericht vom 12. Dezember 1915 bis 30. September 1916' (Oct. 1916); Z3 783: Zionistischer Distriktverband für Böhmen in Prag, 'Arbeitsbericht des zionistischen Distriktkomitees für Böhmen für die Monate November, Dezember, Jänner und Feber' (1918).
59 M. Frankl, M. Niedhammer, and I. Koeltzsch, 'Contested Equality: Jews in the Bohemian Lands, 1861–1917', in K. Čapková and H. J. Kieval (eds.), *Prague and Beyond: Jews in the Bohemian Lands* (Philadelphia, Pa., 2021), 120–56: 154.
60 'Unsere Flüchtlingsschule in Prag', *Selbstwehr*, 21 May 1915, pp. 4–5; 'Schulkanzlei zur Errichtung von Notschulen in Böhmen', *Prager Tagblatt*, 25 Mar. 1916, p. 8.
61 'Herzlfeier der Flüchtlingsschule in Prag', *Selbstwehr*, 9 July 1915, p. 8.
62 'Notschule für Flüchtlinge in Prag', *Prager Tagblatt*, 3 Sept. 1916, p. 6; 'Herrn Prof. Alfred Engel', *Prager Tagblatt*, 25 Mar. 1916, p. 7.
63 'Das Schulwerk für die jüdischen Flüchtlinge', *Selbstwehr*, 30 July 1915, pp. 1–2.
64 Ibid.; 'Graf Schönborn in der jüdischen Haushaltungsschule für Flüchtlinge', *Selbstwehr*, 16 July 1915, p. 6.
65 'Die jüdische Schulkanzlei in Prag', *Selbstwehr*, 7 Jan. 1916, p. 7.

66 'Abschiedsfeier in der Prager Flüchtlingsschule', *Selbstwehr*, 13 Aug. 1915, p. 7.
67 e.g. Report on Zionist children's relief work in Poland.
68 See, for example, the lively debate in the columns of the religious weekly paper *Die Wahrheit* over the reform of Jewish religious education in public schools (S. Brod, 'Methode eines praktischen Religionsunterrichtes and öffentlichen Schulen', *Die Wahrheit*, 7 Apr. 1916, pp. 4–5; R.L., 'Eine "neue Methode" des Religionsunterrichtes', *Die Wahrheit*, 12 May 1916, p. 3; 'Jüdische Erziehung', *Die Wahrheit*, 6 Oct. 1916, pp. 4–6; A. Fried, 'Errichtet jüdische Volksschulen!', *Die Wahrheit*, 19 Oct. 1917, p. 5; R.O., 'Die kommende Schulerneuerung in Oesterreich', *Die Wahrheit*, 18 May 1917, pp. 4–6).
69 'Unserer Kinder Sprache', *Jüdische Zeitung*, 25 Oct. 1916, p. 1.
70 'Ein modernes hebräisches Lehrbuch', *Jüdische Zeitung*, 9 Mar. 1917, p. 2.
71 M. Rath, *Sefat amenu: sefer lehora'at halashon ha'ivrit, didukah vesifrutah levateisefer ulemitlamedim / Lehrbuch der hebräischen Sprache für Schul- und Selbstunterricht, mit Schlüssel und Wortverzeichnis* (Vienna, 1917).
72 Rechter, *The Jews of Vienna and the First World War*, 105–19. Bernfeld eventually became one of the most influential scholars and practitioners in the field of anti-authoritarian education and an early proponent of Freudo-Marxism (P. Dudek, *'Er war halt genialer als die anderen': Biografische Annäherungen an Siegfried Bernfeld* (Gießen, 2012)).
73 S. Bernfeld, 'Vom Religionsunterricht an den Mittelschulen I', *Jüdische Zeitung*, 5 Jan. 1917, pp. 1–2.
74 S. Bernfeld, 'Vom Religionsunterricht an den Mittelschulen II', *Jüdische Zeitung*, 12 Jan. 1917, pp. 1–2.
75 S. Bernfeld, 'Jüdische Lehrer!', *Jüdische Zeitung*, 28 Sept. 1917, p. 3.
76 V.b.I., 'Jüdische Kindergärten', *Die Wahrheit*, 12 July 1918, p. 4.
77 YIVO Archives, New York, RG 6, folder 19: J. Kimmel, 'Die Notwendigkeit einer gesamtösterreichischen Organisation zwecks der Fürsorge für die vorschulpflichtige Jugend (Osterreichische Juedische Kindergarten-Aktion)' (1918).
78 'Jüdisch-pädagogische Kurse', *Jüdische Zeitung*, 5 Sept. 1917, p. 3.
79 YIVO Archives, RG 6, folder 15: S. Stammeier, letter to S. Bernfeld [1918]; S. Stamler, letter to S. Bernfeld, 17 June 1918; J. Weiner, letter to Arbeitskreis für Jüdische Erziehung, 9 Jan. 1919; E. Kohn, letter to S. Bernfeld, 15 June 1918; S. Bernfeld, letter to E. Kohn, 10 July 1918.
80 YIVO Archives, RG 6, folder 16: 'Konstituierende Besprechung des Arbeitskreises für jüdische Erziehung' (1 Dec. 1918).
81 YIVO Archives, RG 6, folder 15: Arbeitskreis für Jüdische Erziehung, circular no. 1 (June 1918); RG 6, folder 19: Arbeitskreis für Jüdische Erziehung, Kindergartenkommission, minutes of meeting, 17 June 1918; A. Müller, letter to Arbeitskreis für Jüdische Erziehung, 20 Nov. 1917.
82 Kimmel, 'Die Notwendigkeit einer gesamtösterreichischen Organisation zwecks der Fürsorge für die vorschulpflichtige Jugend'.
83 YIVO Archives, RG 6, folder 22: Jüdisch-Pädagogische Kurse, 'Kursplan 1917/18'.
84 Ibid.
85 YIVO Archives, RG 6, folder 22: Jüdisch-Pädagogische Kurse, 'Liste der Kursteilnehmer 1917/18'.
86 YIVO Archives, RG 6, folder 2: S. Krauss, letter to S. Bernfeld, 3 Aug. 1918; RG 6, folder 22: V. Aptowitzer, report on teaching (n.d.).
87 YIVO Archives, RG 6, folder 86: S. Bernfeld, 'Einige Gesichtspunkte für eine zu gründende jüdische Elementarschule' (1918).

88 YIVO Archives, RG 6, folder 86: 'Meine ersten Hebräisch-Stunden in der jüdischen Volksschule in Wien' (1918/19).
89 Ibid.
90 Ibid.
91 D. Barth, *Kinderheim Baumgarten: Siegfried Bernfelds 'Versuch mit neuer Erziehung' aus psychoanalytischer und soziologischer Sicht* (Gießen, 2010); E. Lappin, 'Pädagoge, Psychoanalytiker, Psychologe und Marxist: Siegfried Bernfeld 1892–1953', in Hering (ed.), *Jüdische Wohlfahrt im Spiegel von Biographien*, 84–101.
92 Lichtenstein, *Zionists in Interwar Czechoslovakia*, 190–225.

Jewish Children Seeking Help from Catholic Institutions in Kraków during the Holocaust

JOANNA SLIWA

One of the few refuges available to Jews seeking to survive on the 'Aryan' side during the Nazi occupation was provided by Catholic institutions. In Kraków, those who found their way to a convent differed in age, status, and whether they were accompanied by a parent, all of which factors, particularly their views on baptism and conversion, had a major impact on their experience. The children's own accounts and institutional documentation shed considerable light on the delicate balance between Jewish children, their family members, and members of the clergy, above all the nuns who looked after them. They elucidate the crucial role that luck, timing, connections, and assumptions played in shaping the survival strategies of children and the adults who acted on their behalf. Jewish children emerge in this documentation not merely as appendages to their parents but as historical actors with shared experiences and diverse personal narratives.

P RACTISE SELF-CONTROL. Avoid the urge to succeed in class and especially in maths. Demonstrate through your behaviour and speech that you are not a Jew.'[1] Equipped with these lessons on how to forestall possible suspicions about her Jewish identity, Halina Leiman (after the war Janina Ecker), 11 years old in 1944, was brought to the boarding school of the Congregation of the Sisters of Saint Felix of Cantalice (Felician nuns) in Staniątki, 29 kilometres from Kraków. The nuns had moved there after the German administration requisitioned their building in the city. In her testimony, recorded in 2013, Halina explained how she felt at that time: 'I was a bit afraid of the nuns. I had never seen them before. I had had nothing to do with them before.'[2] Halina entered this new environment when a non-Jewish Polish couple, Józefa and Tadeusz Latawiec, felt they could no longer shelter her in Kraków. Their Polish neighbours had become anxious about the presence of a Jewish girl in their midst, and the Latawiecs feared denunciation.[3] A German decree of 15 October 1941 had threatened anyone who assisted Jews and any Jews found on the 'Aryan' side of a city with the death penalty.

Halina's experiences during the Holocaust serve as a point of departure for a discussion of what Jewish childhood meant on the 'Aryan' side for children who, in their formative years, sought help from Catholic institutions. Although the notions of aid and rescue are central, and this chapter examines them, it moves beyond the standard descriptions that tend to concentrate on rescuers and on assessing the extent and scale of rescue efforts. Instead, the focus is on Jewish children and the survival strategies they and the adults acting on their behalf employed. The individual stories by and about children that are at the centre of this investigation demonstrate the crucial role of luck, timing, connections, and people's assumptions in shaping children's modes of survival on the 'Aryan' side. The following questions frame my enquiry: How and when did children reach Catholic institutions? What were their experiences before their arrival? How did they navigate the new environment of organized Catholic life? What happened to the children who left Catholic-run centres?

Some Jewish children exercised a measure of agency, albeit highly restricted, in their efforts to survive. While still very young, they were suddenly not only expected but also forced to make independent decisions and assume behaviours consistent with those traditionally expected of adolescents and adults. While dependent on adults, lay and religious, at every step of the way, children were now required to exhibit ingenuity, boldness, compliance, and perseverance. Failure to do so could lead to exposing not only themselves but also their guardians and others to danger and even death. Thus, children became actively involved in shaping their survival strategies while in hiding and living under assumed identities.

Of course, not all Jewish children possessed even a fraction of agency in forging their survival strategies. Those who were still babies and toddlers without any knowledge or memory of their Jewish identity knew only the nuns or foster parents who raised them as Polish Catholics. Others, who reached Catholic institutions with their mothers or caretakers, relied on them. However, the stories of how they wound up in Catholic institutions also illuminate the responses of adults to the plight of Jewish children.

The topic of Jewish children hidden in convents in German-occupied Poland is not new, but it has not been exhaustively investigated. General information has appeared, starting with the earliest works about the Holocaust in Poland. The first major attempt at a comprehensive study of the topic, by Ewa Kurek-Lesik, still remains important, since it provides accounts of several rescuers and young rescuees that would otherwise be unknown.[4] Many convents have published histories of their order with descriptions of the nuns' wartime activities, including providing aid to Jews. References to the rescue of children are also included in works on rescuers and rescue.[5] Studies of Jewish children in German-occupied Poland contain information about children's experiences while hiding in convents. They evaluate both the nuns' wartime actions and the post-war contexts in which Jewish children were reclaimed from Catholic institutions.[6] Key information about children's experiences in hiding is also to be found in personal testimonies, among them immediate post-war and later accounts, memoirs, and oral history interviews. These present individual recollections filtered through the distance of time from the events described, the analyses of wartime situations, and post-war experiences. Still missing from the scholarship are in-depth studies of the activities of the Catholic Church and its institutions (convents, monasteries, congregations of priests, and individual churches) and their responses to the plight of Jews.[7] There is also little research on the experiences of Jews, including Jewish children, who received help in and from Catholic institutions throughout Poland.

This chapter concentrates on one city, Kraków. During the Second World War, Kraków was both the seat of the German-created Kraków district and the capital of the General Government. Hundreds of German officials, soldiers, and businessmen came to the town to implement Nazi policy in relation to eastern Europe and to the Jews. With the ubiquitous presence of Germans and the aggressive steps taken to Germanize the city and cleanse it of Jews, Kraków was a dangerous place for a Jew of any age to hide. Between May and November 1940 the governor of the General Government ordered the expulsion of Jews from Kraków, with the exception of those deemed essential because of the work they performed. In March 1941 the head of the Kraków district established a ghetto in the Podgórze section of Kraków, outside the traditional Jewish quarter, for approximately 11,000 Jews (that number had increased to about 25,000 by December 1941). In March 1943 the German authorities dismantled the ghetto, killed some Jews there, deported others to killing centres, and confined the remainder in camps.

Yet throughout the existence of the ghetto and after its liquidation, Jewish children managed to reach the 'Aryan' side to hide or to live under a false identity on the streets, in private homes, and in Catholic institutions. Such survival strategies were marked by serious difficulties in Kraków, a medium-sized city where people were acquainted with each other through school and social and work ties. The nearly 60,000 Jews in Kraków before the war, who comprised about 26 per cent of the city's population, were relatively well integrated into the larger population through language and education. According to the census of 1931, the percentage of Jews who used Polish was the third highest in Polish cities.[8] Jews lived side by side with their non-Jewish neighbours; even Kazimierz, the historic Jewish quarter, had a sizeable non-Jewish population. Jewish children attended state schools, a Hebrew school where the language of instruction was mainly Polish, and Catholic schools. Kraków was home to important Jewish religious institutions, well-respected individuals, and the whole gamut of Jewish parties. In addition, Kraków—with an archdiocese, churches dotting the city, and many female and male Catholic orders and the networks they created—was also a spiritual centre for Catholics.

Thus, Kraków is a good starting point to examine how the numerous members of the local social networks and the many institutions of the Catholic Church responded to the plight of the youngest Jewish victims of Nazi persecution. As a case study, the city illuminates the paths that led Jewish children to seek help from Catholic institutions, how these children fared in Catholic 'safe havens', and the scope and extent of the children's agency in the process.

The documentation for this study is derived both from Catholic institutional records and from the narratives of child survivors. In 2012 and 2013 I contacted twenty-two convents and twenty-one monasteries and congregations of priests that had operated in Kraków during the Second World War. I also viewed wartime documents related to Jews at Kraków's Metropolitan Curia. All of these archives are private and not readily accessible. Out of the forty-three religious institutions that I contacted, ten responded that their institution assisted Jewish children, sixteen stated that they did not possess information about such activities or claimed that their archives were too disorderly to be consulted, and nine replied that their institution did not aid Jews (although the rescue efforts which some of them engaged in emerge from accounts of child survivors). The remaining eight did not respond. Out of the ten convents and monasteries that responded affirmatively, seven invited me to view their archives. I am grateful to those nuns, monks, and priests who welcomed me into their homes and shared with me precious archival documents and other information indispensable for this study.

The wartime documentation in these institutions is fragmentary. The dangers that Catholic institutions faced during the war (and also afterwards under the communist regime) forced some to destroy their records. Others used coded language in their documents. Some decided not to keep written records during the war. In the case of convents, usually only the mother superior and a few trusted nuns knew about a child's Jewish origin. Information about the wartime activities of individual nuns and of religious institutions often comes in the form of articles and books written by nuns, and from post-war questionnaires and written accounts. In only a few cases were wartime records available, among them registration books, a chronicle about children's lives, letters from Jewish children, and documents and photographs that belonged to the children. The recollections of child survivors—among them oral testimonies that I recorded and those that I accessed through archival depositories, memoirs, interviews, and immediate post-war testimonies—are crucial for my analysis, as they describe individual memories, feelings, thoughts, behaviour, and actions that can only be provided by direct participants in the events.

In order to understand the environment into which the Jewish children entered, it is important to reflect briefly on the structure and situation of institutional Catholic life in Kraków between 1939 and 1945.[9] Kraków became the centre of Catholicism in German-occupied Poland when Archbishop Adam Stefan Sapieha assumed the role of informal spiritual leader of the Church following the flight to France in September 1939 of the Primate, August Hlond. As such, Sapieha was in contact with Pope Pius XII. Despite his position, Sapieha did not broach the subject of the persecution of Jews or Jewish converts to Catholicism in his correspondence with the Pope. Partial evidence suggests that he did intercede on behalf of converts with the office of the Governor General. The lack of an official stance from the Church in German-occupied Poland on the persecution of Jews stemmed mainly from pre-war teachings on the Jews that emphasized their otherness, and from the well-documented anti-Judaism and antisemitism of a number of leading and rank-and-file members of the clergy. Fear of Nazi retaliation and a desire to limit Nazi encroachment into the Church's activities were also factors.

If Sapieha's voice was not heard in defence of Jews and Jewish converts, his firm position on behalf of Catholic Poles and the Church echoed forcefully. A respected informal adviser and authority for the board of the Main Welfare Council (Rada Główna Opiekuńcza; RGO), an umbrella social welfare organization for non-Jewish Poles in the General Government approved by the German authorities in May 1940, Sapieha was engaged in a host of relief efforts for Kraków's population. He also played an important role in supporting convents. The German authorities were well aware of the fact that the Church enjoyed great esteem, and, while attempting to undermine its power and persecuting the clergy, they attempted to use its influence to impose Nazi policies on the Poles. This did not turn out as planned. For many Catholic Poles the Church continued to serve as a centre of spiritual life and resistance, and many clergy themselves participated in the activities of the Polish underground, for which some suffered punishment from the German administration. They engaged, too, in other resistance endeavours. Officially, all priests were subject to the Church hierarchy based in Kraków. However, without clear directions from the top about how to proceed with the baptism of known or suspected Jewish children brought in by their non-Jewish caretakers, some priests acted independently.

While priests were bound by the authority of their superiors and, ultimately, of the archbishop, nuns and monks answered on a day-to-day basis to their monastic superiors in the main convents and monastery houses located in Poland or in Rome. Before the war, nuns, in particular, created a network of social welfare, childcare, educational, and medical facilities, often several in one city. No two congregations were the same: they differed in their histories, missions, and spiritual aims; in dress, rules, and customs; and in size, wealth, and charitable endeavours. What united them all was the experience of deprivation at the onset of and during the war—damage to buildings, requisitioning of property, depletion of assets, loss of equipment, disruption of communication channels, and forced dispersion. They were all confronted with intimidation by Polish informants and harassment by German authorities. Faced with these challenges, convents mustered all their resources, and often co-operated with one another to fulfil their religious obligation to engage in works of charity. They continued to deliver assistance to those in need and focused especially on children. Naturally, they responded to the plight of Polish Catholic children. Overseeing children meant not only caring for them and feeding them but also instilling the Catholic faith.

Jewish children, too, found their way into convents. The story of Halina Leiman cited at the beginning of this chapter demonstrates how convents operated in the context of war, oppression, and insufficient resources. It also illuminates the connections among civilian welfare and rescue networks, the Polish underground, religious institutions, and individuals that allowed a small number of Jewish children to find temporary and permanent refuge in Kraków and in a convent's regional home close to the city. Halina's story elucidates, too, some of the survival strategies that children learned and adopted. Luck, timing, kinship, and people's attitudes were key in her path to the convent.

Halina Leiman entered the Felician nuns' boarding school as Janina Baran, a false name that she had acquired through the underground contacts of her rescuer,

Tadeusz Latawiec, a Home Army soldier. This he did to deceive his neighbours, whose vocal suspicions endangered the child, Tadeusz, and his wife Józefa. Halina was 10 years old when she was taken in by the Latawiecs, and old enough to understand the danger, follow directions, and become accustomed to the need to change places of residence. In autumn 1940, when the German authorities expelled the Jews from Kraków, Halina, her mother, and her brother (her father and elder brother, as was the case with many Jewish men from the city, had fled to Lwów (Lviv)), moved to a village outside Kraków. She was displaced again at the beginning of August 1942 when a German decree ordered the Jews in her village to move into the ghetto in the town of Wieliczka. At the end of August the Germans liquidated the ghetto. Thanks to an accidental encounter, Halina evaded the round-up. The Latawiecs, who had been her parents' pre-war tenants in Kraków, happened to be in Wieliczka at that time and, after her mother pleaded with them, took her back to Kraków.

At the Latawiecs' apartment on Zyblikiewicza Street, close to the city centre, Halina learned to adopt an assumed identity—that of the Latawiecs' half-orphaned niece. She spoke Polish and did not have stereotypically Semitic features. However, by spring 1943, after the Germans had liquidated the Kraków ghetto, the presence of a strange girl who stayed at home and did not attend school aroused questions. Thus, Halina became skilled at making herself invisible and often changed the hiding places that the Latawiecs arranged for her. It was in this context, after being unable to calm their neighbours, that Tadeusz acquired the genuine birth certificate of a deceased girl for Halina. She moved with Józefa to Borek Fałęcki, a suburb of Kraków. There, Halina pretended to be stricken with polio. A confrontation with a Polish policeman forced her to reveal her identity. This precipitated the Latawiecs' decision to seek a more permanent and safer hiding place for her.

Following several unsuccessful attempts to find a hiding place, Halina ended up in the boarding school of the Felician nuns, an option that Józefa Latawiec learned of from the RGO. Until September 1942, when the German authorities prohibited her from engaging in social welfare activities, the RGO's department for the care of children and youth, which oversaw all childcare institutions, was run by Róża Łubieńska. In 1939 or 1940 Łubieńska, who was a member of the Polish aristocracy and as such had extensive connections, including to Archbishop Sapieha, began to place Jewish children in homes operated by convents. Although by 1944 Łubieńska was no longer formally involved in the RGO, the networks she fostered with convents were sustained. Thus, the RGO directed Halina to a convent outside the city. The Felician nuns themselves had suffered displacement when the German authorities requisitioned the convent's building at Kopernika Street in Kraków in April 1943. After a short stay with the Sisters of Mercy of St Vincent de Paul on Piekarska Street, three Felician nuns moved to the Order of St Benedict in Staniątki, outside Kraków, in July 1943.[10] Before taking Halina there, Józefa had the girl baptized at the church of the Congregation of the Mission in Kraków. Of the eighteen girls sheltering at Staniątki, five were Jewish. All survived the war.[11]

While Halina remained in a single convent until liberation, other Jewish children had more tortuous journeys, being moved between two or more convents. Arrival at a convent usually followed a period of hiding which had become too dangerous because of the constant threat of denunciation. It was also believed that a convent-run centre would be a congenial hiding place and conducive to a child's well-being. In 1942 Barbara Metzendorf entered a nursery run by the Felician nuns through an acquaintance of her father: 'I had it good there', she recalled, 'but after a short time, the nursery was dissolved and the children were taken by women from charitable associations.'[12] A countess, her father's acquaintance, took her in. Although she was well treated, Barbara's health deteriorated, and to help her recuperate, the countess decided to place her with the Dominican Sisters of the Immaculate Conception in the Zwierzyniec district of Kraków.

Barbara's assessment of these nuns was far from positive. 'The nuns did not exude Christian love', she stated bluntly. 'They related well to children from the countryside who came to the nursery and brought in food: milk, butter, eggs.' It is unclear from Barbara's testimony if there were other children like her who stayed at the convent for a prolonged period. Although only 7 years old at the time, she appears to have been privy to the arrangements that had been made for her: 'Because no one paid for me, [the nuns] were very cruel; they ordered me to work beyond my abilities on the farm, grazing cows.'[13] Payment seems to have been important for the Dominican nuns. This is understandable: in a situation of limited financial reserves and scarce food, any outside contribution was enormously helpful. It is unclear if Barbara or the nuns received foodstuffs or money for Barbara's farm work or if sending Barbara to work in the fields was a measure to protect the child from curious neighbours or a German raid. Barbara, a young child raised in the city, had no experience of farm work. In addition, she was sick and weak and unable to perform her tasks. As a result, she stated, she was punished with beatings by the farmer and with starvation and hours-long prayer recitations by the nuns. After about two months, she returned to the countess. She realized that in order not to discourage the countess from providing her with shelter, she could not disclose what she had endured in the convent, as the countess was a patroness of the convent.

While money may not have been a requisite for sheltering Jewish children in most convents, it was essential for some. It was certainly required at the Felician boarding school where Halina Leiman lived. She was treated well, but the Latawiecs paid for her upkeep. When money ceased coming for Alicja Taubenfeld and Lena Gross, the mother superior expelled them.[14] The girls returned to the boarding school when their guardian secured payments through the Council to Aid Jews, Żegota, a Polish Jewish group providing assistance to Jews established in Warsaw in December 1942 by representatives of the Polish underground. Its branch in Kraków was set up in March 1943 on the eve of the liquidation of the Kraków ghetto.

While Halina, Alicja, and Lena, after being shuffled between private homes, were able to find shelter in a convent just outside Kraków, other children followed a reverse path—to religious institutions in Kraków through pre-war connections, transfer from convents in eastern Poland, or chance. Convents placed children within their own network or in centres operated by other orders because of overcrowding, safety concerns, lack of resources, or the confiscation of buildings. The transfer of children resulted from careful planning or in response to an urgent situation. Timing was also important.

One example is the transfer of 7-year-old Irena Jabłońska to Kraków from Brody in Eastern Galicia. In winter 1943, as the front neared Brody, the Polish Care Committee, a local arm of the RGO, transferred Irena (whose real name was Sara Warszawiak, and who was known as Sara Avinun after the war) to the Congregation of the Sisters of the Third Order of St Francis (the Albertine nuns) in Kraków. She arrived at the orphanage having already learned the need to hide, to make herself inconspicuous, to accept uncertainty, and to devise quick survival tactics.[15]

Sara had fled to Brody with her parents and brother after an earlier escape from Biłgoraj to Lwów in autumn 1939. With the establishment of a ghetto in Brody in winter 1942, Sara's parents placed her with two non-Jewish Ukrainian women. While with them, she learned Christian prayers and dutifully maintained a muted existence. However, when the money for her upkeep ceased after her parents had been deported, Sara endured a series of painful experiences, including denunciation, being forced into the ghetto, and sexual abuse. In a post-war memoir, she explained how she felt then: 'I must have forgotten how to scream a long time ago, because I always needed to hide, conceal my existence, not be revealed.'[16] Her survival strategy became non-defiance and heeding strangers' instructions. One such stranger, a pre-war acquaintance of her father's, provided Sara with a new name and a cover story before taking her to a convent.

Scarred by the violent interactions that she had experienced, grappling with the loss of her loved ones, and feeling utterly helpless, Sara was forced to navigate a new environment. Understanding the gravity of her situation, and having learned Catholic prayers, she blended in. She reflected in her memoir that it was while in the convent that she realized that her agency lay in what she chose to say and not to say and in the need to become a careful observer and follower.[17]

Sara brought the survival strategies that she had learned and followed in Brody with her and practised them in the Albertine orphanage on Podbrzezie Street in Kraków.[18] At the time many children lived there, children from Warsaw, the Kraków area, and eastern Poland, like Sara.[19] This meant that she did not particularly stand out. Nor, as she recalled, were the nuns interested in her or, for that matter, the other children. As she explained, 'the orphanage's main efforts were directed at reducing the number of children there because of the unbearable overcrowding'.[20] One way in which the nuns attempted to solve the problem was through holding events that resembled markets: 'People, mainly women, would enter the hall, observe the children, sometimes pick a child, scrutinize him, talk to him, and if they liked the "merchandise", they would begin the long bureaucratic procedure until they received the child.'[21] A nun from the Congregation of the Ursulines of the Agonizing Heart of Jesus recalled the procedure: 'Often, people who wanted to adopt children came to the orphanage. Perhaps they looked for children who could serve as substitutes for offspring they had lost or for those they never had. Perhaps they were motivated by the noble idea of raising an abandoned, poor, Polish child.'[22] The children who entered the convent as orphans were deemed suitable for adoption. For the nuns, the departure of a child meant that they could accept a newcomer; the departure of a child of Jewish or uncertain background also meant they were a little bit safer.

For the nuns, it was a particular challenge to find placements for boys. When anti-Jewish actions intensified in Kraków in the summer and autumn of 1942, a smartly dressed Jewish boy of about 2 years of age was brought to the Ursulines by his father. He had no papers on him and, apart from a nickname, could not say anything about himself. The child drew the attention of the women who visited the convent, and a foster family took him in. 'We were happy that he was in good hands; the family wanted to adopt a child', one of the nuns stated in a post-war account.[23] The nuns found out that the boy was Jewish when his father returned to the convent in 1945. The boy had never been circumcised, as that would have exposed his identity. Some parents chose not to follow this practice to increase their sons' chances of survival on the 'Aryan' side.

Older boys, for their part, devised stratagems to conceal their circumcision. Given the lack of other options, Zygmunt Weinreb, 8 years old in summer 1943, approached the Albertine monastery in the Dąbie district of Kraków. The head of the monastery suspected that Zygmunt, who introduced himself as Czesław Bojdak, was Jewish. He instructed the boy to bathe in his underwear so that his peers would not guess his origins. However, the other boys did discover that he was Jewish and he spent the rest of the war hidden in his teacher's home.[24]

There was a clear danger for those who took obviously Jewish boys from a nunnery or monastery. Older girls, who could work for those who took them in, stood a better chance. They often sought to win over the 'client'. Sara Avinun avoided attention until one day, a woman—who turned out to be Julia Pilch, the young wife of the elderly professor Jan Pilch—noticed the huddled and obviously ill child. Sara desperately wanted to be taken by Julia, and eventually she was. For five months, until May 1944, Sara stayed inside the Pilch's apartment on Rakowiecka Street, where she was able to recuperate from her various ailments. She received instructions that, as usual, she accepted and followed. To assuage possible questions and suspicions, Sara claimed to be the couple's daughter. Eager for safety and family, she took on that role happily. The Pilchs enrolled Sara in a primary school and she soon received a certificate that declared her to be a Polish Catholic. She was beginning to experience the childhood of which she had been deprived.

Jan suspected that there was more to Sara's story, and pressured her to reveal the true situation. Feeling at ease with the Pilchs, Sara sensed an opportunity to release the burden that she had been carrying. In her case, revealing her true identity did not much affect her relationship with her foster parents. They continued to treat her well. Children sometimes admitted the truth to their caretakers or to others in their surroundings when they were forced to do so but also when they let their guard down. An inadvertent slip, the use of the wrong word, could also expose a Jewish child.

Baptism, and even conversion to Catholicism, validated a child's non-Jewish identity. Children who were baptized could not only participate in the sacraments but also, in the case of boys, actively take part in Mass and thus present themselves as proper Catholics. Some served as altar boys with the knowledge of the priests or monks, who were often those who had prepared them for and carried out their baptism. The Society of St Francis de Sales provided cover for at least one Jewish boy. Shlomo Grzywacz, who used the false name Marek Kaczyński (after the war Shlomo Gazit), came to Kraków from Warsaw, and lived with a foster family. He was around 10 years old in 1944, when he served as an altar boy at their church.[25]

The baptism and conversion of young Jewish children during the Holocaust continues to cause controversy. It should be stressed that ensuring that Jewish children could pass as Catholics was a matter of life and death while the child was sheltered and posing as a non-Jew in a convent or in a foster home. For members of the Catholic Church, proselytizing was a mission. Children 8 years old and over were eligible to receive the sacrament of Communion. For them to receive it without being baptized would be sacrilege. In addition, the void created by unreachable, missing, desperate, or dead parents and adult caretakers was seen by some Catholics as an opportunity to offer their form of salvation to Jewish children. Canon law permits conditional baptism of children who are in mortal danger, regardless of their parents' religion.[26] The German authorities for their part forbade the baptism of Jews in October 1942. Nevertheless, until 1944 nuns and priests sent written requests to the curia for permission to baptize children, and these were usually granted the same day.

For children old enough to know that they were Jewish, baptism did not automatically signify the adoption of Catholicism. However, on the basis of the post-war recollections of older child survivors and their attitudes towards the religion they credited with their protection and ultimately their survival, baptism usually did mean conversion. If some children were pressured into baptism, others felt compelled to follow their guardians' instructions, and still others requested to be baptized out of gratitude to the nuns. Often, baptism resulted from a combination of factors that included a feeling that it was expected, that it would reinforce an aid-giver's resolve to continue to provide shelter, and that it would strengthen the child's ability to pass as a non-Jew.[27]

Some Jewish children began to exhibit religious fervour as a way of blending in, to earn the favour of a nun or foster parent, to acquire a feeling of safety, or in reaction to a major upheaval in their lives. Fourteen-year-old Anna Karim arrived at the Order of the Sisters of the Holy Family of Nazareth on Warszawska Street in April 1941, introducing herself as Anna Badowska.[28] She claimed she had been brought there by an elder sister. Anna Antończyk, a non-Jewish charge of the convent, wrote a post-war account about her own experiences and the help the nuns provided to two Jewish girls. News of the death of her sister had greatly affected Anna Karim, who may have suffered a nervous breakdown and even attempted to take her own life. Afterwards, Antończyk recalled, Anna became more religious and 'with great effort tried to help others in need as much as she could', including taking food to forced labourers in Olsza, in the north-east of Kraków.[29]

Before the war, the Sisters of Nazareth had devoted themselves to the education of children and young people. As a consequence, their convent, like a number of others, already had the infrastructure and experience to provide shelter and care for girls. Religious institutions of this type were obvious places for adults looking for a haven for Jewish children. This is why Monika Goldwasser ended up in the Ursuline convent. She was 7 months old when, in August 1942, the Germans liquidated the open ghetto in Myślenice, 31 kilometres from Kraków. Her parents—who were later murdered—managed to hand Monika over to a non-Jewish family. From them, she was brought to the convent in Kraków (where her parents had lived before they were expelled in 1940) with a card that stated her name, date of birth, and the names of her parents. The nuns took care of Monika, who was in very poor health. She did not stay at the convent for long. In autumn 1942 Maksymilian Kamiński visited the Ursulines. The mother superior asked him to take at least one child. Perhaps she knew Kamiński sufficiently well to trust him with the truth about the baby's origin. He and his wife Anna agreed to take Monika, renaming her Łucja. However, Monika could not live openly, as the Kamińskis were afraid of discovery. Thus, she stayed with her adoptive mother in hiding throughout the war.[30] Children as young as Monika had no agency of their own: they were completely reliant on adults.

Although most children were on their own and had to rely on strangers, occasionally Jewish children came to a convent with a parent or guardian. Teresa Abrahamowicz arrived with her mother, Janina, at the Order of the Holy Spirit de Saxia on Szpitalna Street in Kraków as part of a group of eight Jews whom a Jesuit priest named Ferdynand Machay was preparing for conversion. Sister Emanuela Kalb, herself a Jewish convert to Catholicism and an experienced educator, was given the task of teaching them the catechism.[31]

However, neither Father Machay nor any of the other priests was willing to provide baptismal certificates with false names. Sister Emanuela found the birth certificate of a deceased nun of about the same age as Janina and bought a blank birth certificate for Teresa and persuaded the Jesuits to fill it in. Mother and daughter survived the war thanks to Sister Emanuela. The nuns helped Janina and Teresa 'in great secrecy, because none of us would have received approval for such action.'[32]

In addition to those Jewish children whose names and histories were recorded, the archives contain information about anonymous children. Such information is significant because it describes a religious institution's role in assisting children, among them Jewish children; how and when children reached Catholic institutions; and what happened to them. Although the details needed to piece together individual trajectories are missing, the bigger picture that nevertheless emerges is again how luck, timing, connections, and the expectation of being sheltered shaped the survival strategies of children and the adults acting on their behalf.

The scantiest documentation is that about very young children, especially those abandoned outside a convent. The mode of arrival, the absence of identification, and often a child's physical appearance made it clear that he or she was Jewish. When a girl with obviously dyed blonde hair was left at the kindergarten of the Sisters of the

Most Holy Soul of Christ in the Azory district of Kraków, the nuns became suspicious. Dyeing hair was one of the strategies used to disguise a Jewish child's identity. When no one had come for the girl by evening, the nuns arranged for her to be adopted.[33]

Orphans, abandoned and neglected children, and those whose parents or guardians were unable to care for them found their way to Catholic institutions. In August 1942 the Ursulines were compelled by a German order to close their Home for Displaced Children. Róża Łubieńska managed to transfer the convent to a building of the former Jewish hospital for infectious diseases at Rękawka Street that had been part of the ghetto before the Germans reduced its area after the June 1942 deportation. The new home sheltered children of various backgrounds and ages, and with behavioural and emotional problems. There were not enough nuns to care for them and not enough space to accommodate them. Yet the nuns attempted to create a semblance of a home for the displaced children, one in which they were looked after, where they learned, played, and were taught 'first and foremost to love God'.[34] While about half of the thirty charges were Jewish, the nuns attempted to instil Catholic routines and beliefs in all of them. This was regarded as of the utmost importance, both to fulfil the convent's mission and to provide cover for the children.

During the second round-up in the ghetto in October 1942 and its liquidation in March 1943, the nuns continued to accept Jewish children who managed to escape. Alexander Rosner, about 7 years old in autumn 1942, claimed in his post-war oral testimony that no one instructed him how to react during a raid in the ghetto. All he could remember was that he ventured outside one day. He ended up at a back entrance of the Ursuline convent. Two nuns greeted him and gave him chocolate. He recalled feeling calm and falling asleep. The nuns were reluctant to let him go, realizing the danger that awaited him in the ghetto. Still, he returned, to the surprise of his parents.[35] Other children, once they arrived at the convent, stayed there.

Temporary or prolonged stays at a convent were beset with challenges. The story of Anita Kempler and her brother Bernhard demonstrates that being a religious institution did not protect a convent from German harassment. Their story also shows the extent to which the German authorities learned about convents sheltering Jewish children from non-Jewish Poles, including residents of shelters operated by convents. The Kempler siblings escaped from the liquidated Kraków ghetto as part of a prearranged plan. With their pre-war nanny, Franciszka Ziemiańska, they made for the Albertine convent on Krakowska Street. Nine-year-old Anita and 7-year-old Bernhard were already experienced in pretending to be their nanny's children, as they had done so until the threat of denunciation from Polish neighbours compelled them to move to the ghetto. Both were well versed in Catholic ritual. However, Anita needed to disguise her 'Semitic' features—she used a bandage to cover part of her face, claiming she had an eye complaint. Bernhard masqueraded as a girl. The siblings and their nanny managed to maintain their disguise until December 1943, when German officers, responding to a denunciation, forcibly entered the convent. Five Jews hiding there, including the Kempler siblings, were taken to the Montelupich prison and from there to the Płaszów camp.[36] Ultimately, as this story shows, the fate of Jewish children most often rested with their persecutors, regardless of the survival strategies they adopted.

Space does not allow me to discuss all the individual and collective stories of Jewish children, both known and anonymous, who received help from and in Catholic religious institutions in Kraków. On the basis of the available documentation, fewer than 100 Jewish children passed through the convents and monasteries in the city. The number of those who were baptized by individual priests is unknown. Such figures are necessary to gauge the character and extent of the help that members of the Catholic Church in Kraków provided to Jewish children. More importantly, the stories presented in this chapter illuminate how members of Catholic institutions acted during the Second World War, what challenges they faced, and how they responded to the Nazi persecution of the Jews. This was an unprecedented situation, and it was difficult for Jewish children to reach Catholic institutions on their own. Most of those who succeeded in doing so approached these institutions, both within and outside the city, between autumn 1942 and 1944: just before, during, and after major round-ups in a ghetto; in response to the advancing war front; and following the Warsaw uprising.

The stories of Jewish children who sought help from Catholic institutions elucidate the crucial role that luck, timing, connections, and people's assumptions played in shaping the survival strategies that children, and adults acting on their behalf, employed on the 'Aryan' side. These stories have a number of common features—the loss of childhood, displacement, the constant threat of denunciation from non-Jewish Polish neighbours, the need to assume new roles and take on new identities. What emerges from them are the types and scope of children's own agency, however constrained. Jewish children emerge here not merely as appendages to their parents, but as historical actors with shared experiences and diverse personal narratives.

Notes

1 Janina Ecker [née Halina Leiman], oral testimony, recorded by author, Israel, 5 May 2013.
2 Ibid.
3 Ibid.; see also 'Yanina Ecker' (n.d.): Muzeum Historyczne Miasta Krakowa website, 'Ocalić od zapomnienia', visited 21 Apr. 2022; 'Nina E.', in E. Kurek, *Dzieci żydowskie w klasztorach: Udział żeńskich zgromadzeń zakonnych w akcji ratowania dzieci żydowskich w Polsce w latach 1939–1945* (Znak, 1992), 215–22; United States Holocaust Memorial Museum, 2011.389.1, Janina Ecker Collection.
4 See E. Kurek-Lesik, *Gdy klasztor znaczył życie: Udział żeńskich zgromadzeń zakonnych w akcji ratowania dzieci żydowskich w Polsce w latach 1939–1945* (Kraków, 1992), 3rd edn. (Poznań, 2012); Eng. edn.: *Your Life is Worth Mine: How Polish Nuns Saved Hundreds of Jewish Children in German-Occupied Poland, 1939–1945* (New York, 1997).
5 See J. Leociak, *Ratowanie: Opowieści Polaków i Żydów* (Kraków, 2018), 139–256.
6 See N. Bogner, *At the Mercy of Strangers: The Rescue of Jewish Children with Assumed Identities in Poland* (Jerusalem, 2009); E. Nachmany Gafny, *Dividing Hearts: The Removal of*

Jewish Children from Gentile Families in Poland in the Immediate Post Holocaust Years (Jerusalem, 2009).

7 For an attempt to address that lacuna by sketching the wartime rescue of Jews by the Catholic Church in Kraków, see M. Grądzka, 'Kościół katolicki w okupowanym Krakowie w pomocy Żydom: Zarys problematyki badawczej', in Ł. Klimek (ed.), *Kościół krakowski 1939–1945* (Kraków, 2014), 125–54.

8 The 1931 census identified nationality based on language and religion (*Drugi powszechny spis ludności z dn. 9.XII.1931 r.: Miasto Kraków* (Warsaw, 1937), 13).

9 Research on the Church and religious life in German-occupied Poland tends to focus on the persecution of the clergy, attacks on Catholic values and way of life, and efforts to resist the Nazis (see B. Przybyszewski, 'Dzieje kościelne Krakowa w czasie okupacji 1939–1945', *Chrześcijanin w Świecie*, 83 (1979), 24–42; B. Noszczak (ed.), *W matni: Kościół na ziemiach polskich w latach II wojny światowej* (Warsaw, 2011); Klimek (ed.), *Kościół krakowski*). For a critical assessment of the Church's teachings and role before and during the war, see D. Libionka, 'Polska hierarchia kościelna wobec eksterminacji Żydów – próba krytycznego ujęcia', *Zagłada Żydów: Studia i Materiały*, 5 (2009), 19–69; J. Leociak, *Młyny boże: Zapiski o Kościele i Zagładzie* (Wołowiec, 2018).

10 M. P. Lenart, *Prowincja Krakowska Niepokalanego Serca Najświętszej Maryi Panny Zgromadzenia Sióstr Felicjanek*, vol. ii, pt. 2 (Kraków, 2000), 291.

11 By 1946, when this list was drawn up, Halina was already back with the Latawiecs. The convent also accepted children who were brought there after liberation (Archiwum Żydowskiego Instytutu Historycznego, Warsaw (hereafter AŻIH), 303/IX/652: 'Wykaz imienny dzieci znajdujących się w polskich rodzinach' (1946), 9–10).

12 AŻIH, 301/4268: Barbara Metzendorf, testimony to the Central Jewish Historical Commission (6 Feb. 1949), 2.

13 Ibid. 3.

14 See also 'Klepacka, Maria', in *The Encyclopedia of the Righteous Among the Nations: Rescuers of Jews during the Holocaust. Poland*, ed. S. Bender and S. Krakowski, 2 vols. (Jerusalem, 2004), ii. 350.

15 S. Avinun, *Rising from the Abyss: An Adult's Struggle with Her Trauma as a Child in the Holocaust* (Hod Hasharon, 2005), 69–84; see also AŻIH, 301/431: Sara Warszawiak, testimony to the Central Jewish Historical Commission (26 June 1945).

16 Avinun, *Rising from the Abyss*, 92.

17 Ibid. 94–8.

18 The Felician nuns also operated this institution (Lenart, *Prowincja Krakowska Niepokalanego Serca Najświętszej Maryi Panny Zgromadzenia Sióstr Felicjanek*, 49).

19 Among the children were charges of the Congregation of the Sisters of Mercy of Saint Vincent de Paul (A. Dzierżak, S. Motyka, W. Bomba, and J. Dukała (eds.), *Zgromadzenie Sióstr Miłosierdzia św. Wincentego a Paulo w Polsce (1652–2002)*, 2 vols. (Kraków, 2002–12), ii. 282).

20 Avinun, *Rising from the Abyss*, 101.

21 Ibid.

22 Archiwum Zakonu Sióstr Urszulanek Unii Rzymskiej, Kraków, 211/C-III-24: M. B. Dzieniakowska, 'Placówki wojenne SS. Urszulanek w Krakowie (1955)', 48.

23 Archiwum Zakonu Sióstr Urszulanek Unii Rzymskiej, R. 260: Sister Wiktoria Walczyńska, testimony (15 Feb. 1985).

24 AŻIH, 301/406: Zygmunt Weinreb, testimony to the Central Jewish Historical Commission (8 May 1945).

25 YIVO Archive, New York, RG 120, Poland 1939–45, Dembniki: Shmerke Kaczerginski, 'Yidishe oygn' (n.d.). I would like to thank Alan Silberstein for introducing this source to me.
26 *The Code of Canon Law: Latin–English Edition* (Washington DC, 1983), cann. 864–71.
27 See S. Vromen, *Hidden Children of the Holocaust: Belgian Nuns and Their Daring Rescue of Young Jews from the Nazis* (Oxford, 2008), 13–18.
28 'Anna Karim': United States Holocaust Memorial Museum website, 'Holocaust Survivors and Victims Database', visited 22 Apr. 2022; Archiwum Zgromadzenia Sióstr Najświętszej Rodziny z Nazaretu, Kraków: 'Papiery wysyłane do Op[ieki] Sp[ołecznej] Oddział Opieki na[d] uchodźcami i wysiedlonymi' (Oct. 1941), entry 94.
29 After Anna graduated from primary school, she was drafted for forced labour in Germany, which one of the nuns managed to postpone, and, instead, she worked as a courier for the German Security Police (Archiwum Zgromadzenia Sióstr Najświętszej Rodziny z Nazaretu: Anna Antończyk, testimony, (2008)).
30 M. Szczepaniak, '"Jej wzrok przyciągnęło zwłaszcza jedno dziecko": Historia rodziny Kamińskich' (Feb. 2017): Polin: Polish Righteous website, 'Stories of Rescue', visited 22 Apr. 2022; Eng. trans.: '"The Expression on the Face of One Particular Child Drew Attention": The Story of the Kamiński Family', trans. A. Rajcher (Feb. 2017): Polin: Polish Righteous website, 'Stories of Rescue', visited 22 Apr. 2022; see also Polin Museum of the History of Polish Jews, 'Poles Who Rescued Jews during the Holocaust', oral history interview 254: Monika Goldwasser (11 Aug. 2016; Pol.).
31 Sister Emanuela provided a list of Jews who were baptized and received false certificates, including the baptismal name, the parish where it took place, sometimes the priest who performed the sacrament, and the number of the certificate (Archiwum Zgromadzenia Sióstr Kanoniczek Ducha Świętego De Saxia, Kraków, Ap.Z37,1, fo. 119: Sister Emanuela (Maria Magdalena) Kalb, questionnaire (n.d.)).
32 Ibid.
33 Sister Paulina Wilk, correspondence with author, 30 Jan. 2013.
34 Dzieniakowska, 'Placówki wojenne SS. Urszulanek w Krakowie', 43.
35 University of Southern California Shoah Foundation, Los Angeles, Visual History Archive, interview 1017: Alexander Rosner (16 Feb. 1995; Eng.).
36 University of Southern California Shoah Foundation, Visual History Archive, interview 33193: Bernhard Kempler (12 Sept. 1997; Eng.); A. Lobel [née Kempler], *No Pretty Pictures: A Child of War* (Sydney, 2008). In *No Pretty Pictures*, Lobel referred to the convent as the Bernardine convent (from the name of the founder of the Albertine female order).

'It was easier with a child than without'
Creating and Caring for Polish Jewish Families in the Wartime Soviet Union, 1939–1946

SARAH A. CRAMSEY

> More Polish Jews survived the Holocaust inside the Soviet Union than outside it. Research on this group has grown rapidly in recent years but has overlooked one significant aspect: Polish Jewish families expanded systematically and vigorously across the Soviet Union in the 1940s. The presence and needs of the youngest members within this remnant greatly impacted their caretakers, both biological and circumstantial, as well as the institutions providing for them. Drawing on oral testimonies, archival documents, and interviews, this chapter suggests that studies which prioritize the perspective of the 'family' require a slight but poignant corrective. Caretaking mattered, even during this extraordinary time. Children, toddlers, and babies, and the largely invisible work they require from conception to puberty, are central to the histories told about this group, the largest part of Polish Jews to survive the war.

IN THE FIRST HALF OF 1946, roughly 150,000 Polish Jews left multiple locations across the Soviet Union and moved back towards Poland, the country of which they were citizens, on government-funded repatriation trains.[1] Most of them —residents of the eastern territories of the Second Polish Republic ceded to the Soviet Union under the terms of the 1939 Molotov–Ribbentrop Pact and refugees from elsewhere in Poland—had been deported by the Soviets in 1940 and 1941 alongside hundreds of thousands of other Polish citizens.[2] Then, after the Nazis invaded the Soviet Union and an amnesty for Polish citizens was announced as part of the larger realignment of the Allied Powers in the summer of 1941, a majority of them found themselves in central Asia and lived there for half a decade.[3] In spite of the hardships, more Polish Jews survived the Holocaust inside the Soviet Union than outside it, and they constituted a significant remnant of post-war Polish Jewry.[4] Research on this group tends to consider them as individuals,[5] yet, more often than not, they experienced their exile in the Soviet Union as members of growing families.[6]

Many of them attributed their survival to their families in general and to the youngest members of them in particular. For example, Regina Lender (b. 1919, Warsaw) 'was always with [her] family' and found strength within that unit, which grew over time. The Lender–Młynek–Platkowski clan crossed the river Bug in 1939 with seven members and one more on the way.[7] Moving back towards Polish territory in 1946, Helen Fenster (b. 1920, Rawa Mazowiecka) recalled that she 'was carrying a baby and nobody bothered [her]'.[8] She was, in fact, also pregnant. Toba Schachter (b. 1917, Tomaszów Lubelski) recalled that 'it was easier with a child than without'.[9] Toba gave birth to her daughter in Semipalatinsk, where she lived alongside roughly 2,000 Polish Jews and 4,000 non-Jewish Polish citizens. These three voices align with others captured in scores of recorded testimonies describing the visible and invisible work required to create and sustain families before, during, and after this group's exile in the Soviet Union.[10]

Of course, this is not surprising. Stories about those displaced by military combat, occupation, forced migrations, or even climate change are often stories about (planned and unplanned) pregnancies, (sometimes precarious) childbirths, and the constant care which necessarily follows.[11] And yet refugees' accounts rarely mention starting a family and the care provided by parents, doctors, midwives, neighbours, childcare providers, and other family members during uprooted times.[12] Further, while childbearing and child-rearing are timeless enterprises, deep lacunae remain around these subjects generally, as well as during the Holocaust and the Second World War.[13]

These lacunae persist despite recent contributions to the historiography of Polish Jews in the wartime Soviet Union, which have vividly outlined the sheer scale of the calamities they experienced and their role in reshaping Jewish culture and society in Poland and elsewhere after the war. Specifically, scholars have examined the influence of familial realities and networks on decisions to seek refuge elsewhere, the institutions created for Jewish children in post-war Poland, and the post-war 'baby boom' amongst Polish Jews in the displaced persons camps.[14] As my research demonstrates, however, babies were, in fact, 'booming' during the war for Polish citizens, and Jews specifically, in the Soviet Union.

Archival documentation clearly demonstrates that Polish Jewish families in the Soviet Union grew dramatically between 1939 and 1946. Roughly 1,000 of the Polish Jews who returned from central Asia and other locations across the Soviet Union during the first half of 1946 submitted detailed data, which was compiled in a registry produced by the Union of Warsaw Jews in Szczecin in June 1946.[15] This data shows that the Polish Jews returning from central Asia included a sizeable number of young couples, who had reproduced at an above-average rate during the war.[16] Roughly a third of these parents had more than one child during the war, and a handful had three. Overall, a quarter of the Polish Jews who found themselves in Szczecin in 1946 were under the age of 7, and one in eight was under the age of 2.

These statistics are generalizable to all Polish repatriates from the Soviet Union. Historians have estimated that children under 18 constituted nearly one-third of all the Polish citizens who had returned to Polish soil by mid-1946, and roughly 20 per cent of all returnees were under the age of 14.[17] Demographic tables from the 1940s collected and preserved by the central office of the Union of Polish Patriots (Związek Patriotów Polskich; ZPP) in Moscow divide the population of Polish citizens in the Soviet Union by ethnic background, gender, and age (from 0–7, 8–14, 15 and above). These records include statistics from scores of places.[18] In November 1945, to offer one example, the ZPP office in Kuibyshev counted 2,347 Polish citizens (813 Poles and 1,534 Jews; 1,047 men and 617 women), including 426 school-age pupils and 263 children under 7.[19] The presence of so many young people, toddlers, and babies exerted considerable demands on their caregivers, and their experiences should be understood in this context.[20]

Essentially, a focus on growing families demands a recalibration of how the Polish Jewish experience in the 1940s is understood. Accordingly, this chapter offers three broad insights. First, even during the time of the Holocaust couples had and raised children.[21] The story of the Polish Jews in the Soviet Union highlights how the topics of sex, pregnancy, terminations, childbirth, parenthood, and child-rearing belong to the larger history of the Holocaust overall. Related to this point, the growing families required caregivers ranging from Soviet medical workers with obstetric skills to local Uzbek midwives and deported non-Jewish women with knowledge of child-rearing.[22] Other scholars have examined the relationships between Jews and non-Jews and between Polish citizens, 'locals', and other evacuees.[23] I will look at some of these relationships below, but for now let me suggest that relationships built around families had a profound intimacy that often bridged religion, language, citizenship, and sense of ethnic belonging.

Secondly, the presence of so many young children weighed heavily on a family's calculus. When asked why she went back to Poland, Jenny Balsam (b. 1916, Łódź) repeated 'Why?' with a slight look of disbelief on her face: 'Why, I was born there! I wanted to go back and find my family!'[24] And she did find a sister when she returned. Focusing on families problematizes how ideological frameworks such as (anti-)socialism, (anti-)communism, nationalism, Zionism, and antisemitism were connected with wartime and post-war decisions about where to go. It also requires a reassessment of the violent, chaotic, and shifting milieu of post-war Poland, why one-third of all Polish Jews who survived the war remained in Poland after 1946, and why many who claimed Zionist leanings chose destinations besides Mandate Palestine.[25] Decisions to leave (or to stay in) the Soviet Union in the first half of 1946 or to leave (or to stay in) post-war Poland need to be recast in light of familial circumstances.[26]

And thirdly, it is necessary to account for the (often scant) documentation that remains.[27] By default, the 'invisible' work of changing nappies, soothing a restless baby, and cleaning the stained clothes of a gregarious toddler leaves little archival evidence. And yet stories of births and private moments of family life are passed down in most families and often retold with great frequency. These stories often contain more than just a kernel of truth despite the passage of decades.[28] Most of the evidence in this chapter is derived from seventy-five video testimonies, a handful of interviews with children born in the 1940s, and autobiographies. The remaining evidence largely originates from the archive of the ZPP. By combining archival documentation with warm, human voices, I explore different aspects of the experiences of these growing families, from marriage and fertility to birth control, toddler-rearing, and the materiality of early childhood during a time of scarcity.

'And this was our wedding in the forest': Marriage in a Time of War

Frania (b. 1918, Warsaw) was 'very far from married' in September 1939.[29] She and Pinkas Oberklaid were in the early throes of courtship when, on the second day of the war, Pinkas came to her parents' house. He asked Frania to join him as he planned to flee Warsaw. She told him: 'No, my place is with my family.' Later that autumn, 'out of nowhere', Pinkas reappeared. In the weeks since his departure, he had set up a temporary home in Brześć Litewski (Brest) with his sister and brother-in-law. He asked Frania again to join him. Frania's mother made one condition: they 'should have a ḥupah [marriage canopy]'. After the wedding in November 1939, they left Warsaw. Jenny Balsam's mother made the same condition. She and her fiancé, Max, married in her family's apartment in Łódź. When asked if she wore a wedding dress or went on a 'honeymoon', Balsam stared at her interviewer in disbelief: 'Oh darling, no.'[30] On the same day that new laws required them to wear a Star of David on their clothing, they and another couple left town.

Other weddings were seemingly rushed as well.[31] Toba Schachter married her army-enlisted husband in 1939. They had met in a kibbutz but had no concrete plans to marry until war forced a decision.[32] Other newlyweds left their homes with their immediate biological family rather than their spouses. Regina Lender's parents fled alongside her and witnessed her marriage in a registry office on the road. The wedding took place because her husband 'wanted very much to get married, because he loved me'. If not for the war, she admitted, they might not have married as her father did not like her husband. She told the interviewer about the bare-bones ceremony with a wry smile, noting that her husband was 'always complaining that he didn't have a piece of cake'.[33]

Family was also present at the November 1939 wedding of Esther Berkowitz (b. 1917, Wieluń). Her mother, who insisted on the marriage before the two fled, joined Esther's future brother- and father-in-law and a rabbi under a sheet which served as a makeshift ḥupah at a restaurant in Łódź. She wore 'whatever I had on myself, something on my head . . . and I have no pictures . . . Oh God!'[34] The video of her interview captured her laughter.

Marriages also occurred all across the Soviet Union. Helen Fenster married twice, first to David in Taganrog (Russia) in 1940 and five years later to Isaak in Akkul (Uzbekistan), after her first husband died and her first daughter was born.[35] Before her wedding by a Bukharan rabbi in 1944, Tema Abel (b. 1921, Tomaszów Lubelski) went to the ritual bath in Tashkent. Their friends threw a party afterwards.[36] A thousand kilometres to the north-east, Fela (b. 1922, Warsaw) and Yeshayahu Platkowski married at the official Soviet marriage bureau in Balkhash one year later.[37] Platkowski's reflections on his wedding day included an anecdote about their wedding night. It was spent in 'a barrack with the sister, her husband, mother, father, younger brother and me . . . can you imagine?'[38]

After half a century one couple, Bronia (b. 1916, Łódź) and Jacob Zisfain (b. 1917, Krasnosielc), spoke with exceptional warmth about their marriage. The two met in Siberia where they were assigned to the same work party chopping down trees. Bronia was injured, and Jacob cared for her during her three-month convalescence. Afterwards, in 1941, Jacob approached her with a direct proposal, saying: 'You are alone and I am alone . . . I don't know how many years we will be here. Let's get married.'[39] Bronia accepted. Jacob went to the camp commander, but since they were not Soviet citizens the commander would not marry them. Jacob decided that they would 'marry in the Jewish way', and found a rabbi in the camp who knew his family.[40] As Bronia recalled, the rabbi suggested holding the ceremony on the evening of 8 March, International Women's Day, when all the Russians would be drunk. The rabbi fashioned his *talit* into a *ḥupah* and wrote their marriage contract by hand.[41] Afterwards Jacob revealed a bottle of vodka he had procured and asked a colleague from Warsaw to 'play a Jewish march' on his harmonica. Back at the barracks, Bronia and Jacob drank a *leḥayim* with their friends. And this, a beaming Jakob summarized five decades later, 'was our wedding in the forest'.[42]

'It was like a messiah was born': Birth in Extreme Circumstances

A general impression of expectant mothers, nervous fathers, and frequent births materializes from the documents surveyed for this chapter. For the population of 1,000 Warsaw Jews who registered in Szczecin after their repatriation, three babies on average were born each month from September 1939 to March 1946.[43] Helen Goldberg (b. 1910, Nowy Dwór) went to Soviet-occupied Baranowicze in autumn 1939, because her husband had returned for her after his own flight there in the first days of the war.[44] Thinking the war would last six weeks at most, they left Nowy Dwór and Helen's parents, stopped in Warsaw to see Helen's aunt, and then moved by overstuffed train to the border. There, new camps had formed, housing thousands of refugees. Helen remembered children being born in appalling conditions. At the time she herself was pregnant. It would be the first of three pregnancies she experienced during the war.

After her wedding in Lviv, Esther Berkowitz eventually made it to Kowel with her husband. There, she 'got pregnant right away'. Laughing, she clarified, those 'must be the words, I don't know . . . Oh, I shouldn't have said that.'[45] Soon after, they were arrested as Polish citizens and taken to cattle trucks. Her narrative swerves unexpectedly.

One little thing, I cannot forget. They [the Soviets] still had a little heart . . . When they saw that I was pregnant and that I was crying that I couldn't sleep on the floor, on the hard floor on the train. I asked to go back and get my pillow and my bed . . . and you know they done that for me, and they sent a truck with a driver and I loaded up what I could.

Surprises continue as she recalls a second train trip in September 1940 from their first labour camp to the city of Asbest. On the long journey she was startled to find her family doctor from Wieluń travelling with his family. At some point, her waters broke, and she and her husband were removed from the train, which continued onwards. They were taken to a hospital in Nowosibirsk, where she delivered a son, Daniel. Unlike her sisters in Poland before the war who ate chicken soup and remained in bed for eight days after birth, the nurses gave Esther water and food and discharged her after three days. As they boarded another train, her baby was wearing nappies that Esther had fashioned from her own bed sheet.

Like Esther, Frances Hertzberg (b. 1917, Warsaw) was 23 years old when she gave birth in 1940 with the help of a 19-year-old nurse who assisted deportees in a Siberian labour camp.[46] 'She came to me when I had pain . . . She said not to breathe . . . She teached us a little bit.'[47] Some women well into their twenties did not know they were pregnant after months without menstruation. Riva Frenkel's (b. 1918, Pułtusk) periods stopped twice during the war, so when she missed four cycles in 1944, she imagined an abeyance in ovulation, not a pregnancy.[48] Her daughter was born in a Kazakh village near Kurgan five months later. The staff at a large clinic in Chimkent (Shymkent) informed Rachel Koplowicz (b. 1915, Łódź) that the lump she felt in her stomach was not a tumour but a baby. Like Frances and Esther, Rachel noted her own naivety. She too did not know that labour began with contractions or 'when the pain comes and when the pain goes'.[49] However, her son Jackie was a 'beautiful, beautiful boy'.

The birth of a boy like Jackie required recourse to ritual. Rachel relied on an unnamed Russian midwife to track down a *mohel* and arrange for his circumcision. Proud of her son and of her ability to uphold Jewish practice 'even in Russia', Rachel took him to be photographed professionally in Lenger Ugol a few weeks after his birth in 1944. Five decades later, nearing the end of a 2-hour, 20-minute interview conducted in the Bronx, she shared the image with posterity. There, held in front of the camera at a tilted angle, was a picture of her naked son. Knitted booties covered his toes, some kind of plant sat behind him, a lacy cloth separated his bare bottom from the table and natural light streamed in from his left. Matter-of-factly, she introduced it: 'This is a picture of my three-month old son, circumcised. I wanted proof to send to my parents that I circumcised my son.'[50]

Rachel recalled that it was difficult to arrange for the picture. Despite this, she was not the only one to describe such an image. Another survivor living 2,000 kilometres away, Jenny Balsam, recalled that she had a picture made by the *mohel* after her son was born.[51] However, some Polish Jewish parents decided to forgo circumcision altogether. Frances Hertzberg prayed to have a daughter so that she would not have to arrange a circumcision ceremony.[52] Her son's birth was celebrated with a *minyan*, the coming together of ten adult men, but without the full circumcision ritual.[53]

Births and the ceremonies accompanying them were often glorious moments that brought joy in otherwise joyless times. The simple wonder that babies inspire extended far beyond the biological parents. A community consolidated itself around Sarah Marenfeld (b. 1921, Ciechanowiec) when she gave birth to her daughter Rachel in a barracks in Arkhangelsk in 1943. The commandant of the labour camp ordered a horse and wagon to take her to the hospital, gave them a private barracks upon their return, and visited her and the baby every day. A woman used her own sweater to make booties. They threw a party for her, and 'everyone gave something.'[54] She recalls that everyone cried: 'Everyone was so happy that a child was born.' And the 12-pound baby Rachel was 'such a beautiful child, everybody came to see her. It was like a messiah was born.'

Finally, Frania Oberklaid remembered her first pregnancy fondly: 'My friends, the people would ask me, the girls who didn't know about pregnancy asked me to describe it, and it was beautiful.'[55] Of course, she 'wasn't happy having a baby in those circumstances, but it was a beautiful feeling, and it's hard to explain, but I did explain it to them'. However, her labour was unexpectedly difficult, and the baby only lived for five weeks. Pregnant again in 1945, she refused to have the baby in a small place, which led the couple to move to Chimkent. If she had registered with the local branch of the ZPP, details about her background, age, labour productivity, and fertility would have been included in the reports sent to Moscow.[56]

Tema Abel wanted to have her first baby on Polish soil. A friend who worked for Polski Punkt, a system connecting Polish citizens and supported by the ZPP, suggested that she return with a transport departing from Turkestan on 1 April 1946 rather than on a later one from Tashkent where she lived. However: 'It left later, so [she] had the baby on the train.'[57] There was a medical car on the train with three beds, but there were gaps between the boards that made up the car's roof: 'Snow started falling' on her, but Tema 'didn't feel pain because [she] was so cold'. She had no blankets, no nappies, not a shirt. The baby was born and she kept him under her arm, wrapped in a towel. Her husband 'ripped up a sheet and those were [her] nappies', and the ladies in her car 'sewed him a shirt, they ripped up sheets'. They celebrated with a ritual circumcision in Łódź after threats of violence prevented their repatriation to the Recovered Territories.[58] From the outbreak of war to collective and individual returns half a decade later, childbirth punctuated the lives of Polish Jews in the Soviet Union. So too, it follows, did attempts to prevent pregnancies and threats to maternal health.

'You can't have a child in war': Fateful Fertility Choices

Between 1939 and 1945 Ethel Karp (b. 1919, Chełm) became pregnant three times. She had a miscarriage once, live births twice, serious thoughts about having an abortion twice, and attempted to end her third pregnancy more than once. In 1940 Ethel, who was three months pregnant, and her husband, Gecel, went to a hospital in Równe (Rivne) after being detained at NKVD headquarters in a nearby town. There the trauma of the interrogation caused Ethel to miscarry. Less than a year later Ethel and Gecel moved eastwards to Dzhambul. There, she voluntarily sought abortions in 1943 and 1945. Her second pregnancy was 'fine', but she 'didn't want to have the baby. I didn't have food, I didn't have nothing, I slept on a cement floor . . . Why do you think I had to try this? It bothers me all the time. So I went to the doctor', she continued, 'and I said do something to me. So he said, "You have 2,000 roubles?" I said, "No." He said, "You will have a baby." So I had a baby.'[59] This unwanted baby became Ethel's only family after her husband was arrested by the NKVD for a second time.[60]

But even the love of her daughter could not soften the stark reality that Ethel and many other parents faced: 'it was hard to raise a baby.'[61] Just a year and half later, a third pregnancy forced a deeper reckoning with this reality. Unable to afford an abortion, she took water from the well: 'This would help me because it's heavy. One woman gave me from the drug store pills, and I become deaf and I couldn't move, very weak and then I took a glass of vodka and pepper and I warm up and drink this and it didn't help.' In attempting to end her pregnancy she almost 'killed herself'. When Dora was born on the night of Yom Kippur in 1945, she was 'not so healthy, she needed medical attention for a few years . . . but she was so beautiful, she was so gorgeous'.[62] Ethel's honesty about the steps she took to prevent her pregnancies is brutal but real. Her husband seems to have been absent from her decision-making and the birth. Although he was in prison for some of this period, that does not fully explain his absence from her recollections, nor did it prevent them from conceiving more than once.

Like Ethel Karp, Gusta Besser (b. 1916, Brody) became pregnant three times during the war years. She was separated from her husband in 1941 when her brother urged her to leave Kyiv as the Nazis launched their attack on the Soviet Union. Before boarding a train heading east with her mother, she visited a doctor who told that he would perform an abortion: 'You can't', he instructed her, 'have a child in war.' The worsening situation prevented her from getting to the hospital. Instead, she boarded the train with her mother and her young son Wolfbehr. On the train, 'the blood started to come out a bit and they took me with my son to the hospital'. She suffered a miscarriage, in a hospital not far from the railway line between Kyiv and Rostov. Within a year Wolfbehr became ill on yet another train trip from Rostov to Astrakhan. At a station, he was taken 'upstairs for a check up' and, after a day or two, he died. Within two years, she lost her unborn baby, her first child, and, as she later learned, her first husband.[63]

Pregnancies, both unwanted and wanted, compromised the mother's health. Freda Gruen almost lost her life due to a botched abortion in Karaganda in 1943. Without medication or transfusable blood, the procedure led to dangerous complications, and the doctors suggested that she be moved to a single room 'to die'. Lucky for Freda, 'three other women, Russian women' intervened and told the doctors 'we will take care of her'. That night, in the care of these women, Freda received a comforting message from her mother in a dream: 'It will be OK.'[64]

Genia Bikel (b. 1910, Warsaw) had a much more positive experience with her doctor. She suffered extreme bloating in her stomach and immense pain and was taken to hospital. When she arrived, she appeared to be dead, and her body was taken to the morgue, where a hospital worker discovered a pulse. At this point, she came under the care of her 'guardian angel', Doctor Yavanova. Genia had had an ectopic pregnancy, and Yavanova operated on her uterus and fallopian tubes for hours to repair the damage. Her life was saved, but Genia feared she would not be able to have any more children. Yavanova told her 'I don't know if you can have children, but I will do all in the world that I can do.' After nine months under her care, Genia became pregnant again. Yavanova did not reveal the news to Genia or her husband for three months to spare them disappointment. In January 1946 her baby, Dina, arrived, just six weeks before they boarded the train to Poland.[65] In a final gesture of kindness, Yavanova gave Genia some nappies and blankets in advance of their journey alongside twenty-nine other families.

Nappy Trouble: Baby Things in a Time of Scarcity

Babies born to Polish Jewish parents who survived the Second World War in the Soviet Union often accrued things randomly. When Frances Hertzberg gave birth to her baby in a work settlement named Basharovo near Arkhangelsk in 1940, the baby remained naked for two weeks after its birth. There was nowhere, she recalled, to buy anything. She and her husband relied on packages sent from his parents in Janów Poleski, a small town near Pinsk in Soviet-occupied Poland, and a package from a cousin in Arkhangelsk.[66] The parents sent 'garlic, some fat from pigs' and the cousin sent two shirts, which Frances used to 'make something for [her] baby'.[67] For her child, born in 1944, Riva Frenkel had 'nice clothes' sent by relatives in Palestine which she later shipped back to Poland.[68] As the war went on, parents and children remember packages containing foodstuffs from American relatives (Marlene Kreitenberg (b. 1937, near Warsaw)), the Polish government-in-exile (Riva Frenkel), the Polish Red Cross (Miriam Storch (b. 1926, Zamość)), and the ZPP.[69]

The mail did not provide for everyone, however, and when Ethel Karp's daughter Dina was born she had no nappies, no clothes for her child, and only one dress for herself. She covered herself with a towel when she washed her solitary garment, and her baby slept, at least at first, on a chair. For her daughter's first Passover in 1944, she traded her own brown bread for milk and meat, and an Uzbek woman, presumably a neighbour, gave her a little flour. 'I'm telling you', she said, 'it was a holiday.'[70] Different economic circumstances unfolded 200 kilometres to the west in Chimkent: Rachel Koplowicz bought her son a cot at the city market with money earned by her husband making uniforms for the Red Army.[71] Those without money had to sell precious personal goods. Freda Walzman's (b. 1915, Dąbrowa) nightgown bought a month's worth of food on the black market in Dzambul.[72]

Nappies were in constant demand but not always in constant supply. References to them, or more precisely the lack of them, populate stories of travel, as parents were forcibly deported eastwards in 1940 and 1941, as they travelled towards central Asia after the amnesty in 1941, and when they travelled back to Poland in late 1945 or 1946. A handful of parents remember special areas in train stations designated for children, especially babies, with hot (and therefore sterilized) water. Esther Berkowitz, who went into labour on a train moving east in 1940 and returned by train to Poland in

1946 with a month-old baby, recalled the frequency of special places in stations to 'wash nappies and bathe the child'. 'Wherever you travelled', she continued, you could dry nappies, stay overnight, because 'the Russians always tried to make the babies feel comfortable'.[73] More than five decades after these events, the mundane details of pampered baby bottoms and the struggle to contain their infants' natural and constant output remained in the memories of Polish Jews living in Australia, North America, and Israel.[74]

Breastmilk Trouble

Breastfeeding appears easy, but it is decidedly not. It demands good nutrition for the mother, a good latch and a strong suck from the baby (premature babies might find difficulties with both), nipples toughened by experience, patience before the milk 'comes in' (often several days after birth), and advice from those who have breastfed in the past. Polish Jewish mothers scattered throughout the wartime Soviet Union often learned about breastfeeding from a variety of caregivers outside their family. More than one-third of all mothers included in this research mentioned breastfeeding at some point. In 1943 a female Kazakh neighbour near Dzhambul told Freda Walzman to breastfeed her son for as long as possible, which she did for more than two years. She recalls breastfeeding other children as well.[75] A Jewish paediatrician had similar advice for Rachel Koplowicz. He told her to breastfeed her son until she was somewhere she could comfortably eat.[76] She also recalled breastfeeding other children on her journey back to Poland in 1946.

Ruzena Berler (b. 1910, Przemyśl) wove her own story about Soviet trains, breastfeeding, and the collective female struggle to nourish their children. In February 1940 she and her three-month-old daughter, Olga, were 'stuffed like herrings' in a goods wagon with other young women and children (aged 6 months to 12 years) heading eastwards from Przemyśl. A small heater in their wagon (the only such device on the entire train as far as she could tell) staved off the cold and darkness outside. She remembered that 'it was good . . . to warm something for the children on top of the stove; every day they brought us water'.[77] On the fourth day of what would become a month-long journey, her child refused her breast. 'I squeezed my breast and I saw that I had no more milk . . . afraid that I would die with my child, it was a tragedy, I was out of my mind.' The other women noticed that another mother in the car had boxes of powdered milk and jars of marmalade for her son and convinced her to share the food with everyone including Ruzena. From then on, all the children received a spoonful of marmalade daily, and Olga had enough milk for the rest of the journey.

Frances Hertzberg's son became severely ill after they travelled from Arkhangelsk to Tashkent in 1941. The family survived in a labour camp on preserved cranberries collected from the forest around the camp. They had no meat or milk. Her husband had sporadic opportunities to barter for smoked meat and bread, but the consequences for her son's health compounded. With the baby near death, she called a doctor who said: 'Your baby is starving; if I tell you to go to the hospital he won't be alive ... keep him and (feed) him every fifteen minutes.'[78] With a mixture of breast and cows' milk, Frances and her brother's wife fed the baby throughout that night and the following nights.

Breastfeeding could have unforeseen positive consequences. When Rose Horowitz (b. 1926, Pułtusk) was detained by the NKVD in 1944, her mother brought Rose's young child to the prison and insisted that Rose be released lest the baby die. Even she was surprised at the speed of her release.[79]

Mothers were willing to try nearly anything to keep their babies fed. After giving birth to her son Harry in Siberia near the end of 1944, Doris Abersteld (b. 1920, Tomaszów Lubelski) learned from 'locals' to squeeze lemons into her son's bottles to increase his vitamin intake.[80] Rita Perlmutter's (b. 1918, Bodzanów) baby needed food too. Rita joined her parents in Kizel at the end of 1945 and, in her mother's view, looked like a monkey because she was so thin. A doctor told Rita that she wasn't producing enough milk. However, her sister-in-law had a 2-year-old son. Rita sent her 3,000 roubles, and the sister-in-law came to live with them, where presumably she served as a wet nurse in exchange for food, shelter, and medical help for her own child.[81] The relationship between the women soured; however, all these stories reveal the importance of family, neighbours, and even strangers in feeding a child in wartime. Sometimes even that was not enough. Nina Lubenfeld (b. 1920, Warsaw) watched her sister's baby die of hunger and easily summoned the memory decades later in her video testimony.[82]

The Constant Caregiving was the Hardest Part

Miriam Storch admitted that the wartime experience in Tashkent was hard, not for the obvious reasons but because the adults 'had constantly to take care of children'.[83] Her circle in Tashkent included thirty families, and each had three or four children. There were five in her own family, which hailed from Zamość. Storch remembered the young children 'helping out as much as possible'. Especially in the Soviet Union, where food was linked to work, childcare proved an absolute necessity. Polish Jewish parents enlisted older children like Miriam and older women to provide care, found ways to stay at home with their children, and relied on a system of orphanages, schools, clubs, and day-homes established by the ZPP.

In 1940 and 1941 Polish citizens deported to forced labour camps in Siberia and elsewhere arrived to find few facilities for children. On the farm she initially worked at in Rostov, Gusta Besser remembered twenty people living in one room and leaving the babies behind while they went off to work.[84] Ruzena Berler noted that three women from her group stayed behind and watched the children as the others worked in the Ural Mountains.[85] Bertha Schattner (b. 1899, Jarosław) travelled east with her three children. Along the way, she became a widow and thus a single mother. When she worked, her children 'ran through the woods'.[86] Babysitting, Rose Horowitz recalled, did not really exist in those days: 'We didn't know anything about it', she admitted on behalf of her contemporaries who hailed from a society built on inter-generational care and populated with homemaking mothers. This did not prevent Rose from helping a mother look after her baby once she herself turned 14, as she needed the extra food.[87] Other Polish Jewish women worked as caregivers too. Esther Berkowitz, for example, babysat the children of a hospital worker when her son Danny fell ill with typhus.[88] Three months after childbirth, Sara Marenfeld employed an 80-year-old Jewish woman named Lampe to look after her daughter.[89] Experience as a parent or caregiver for young children proved, yet again, to be a useful skill.

As Miriam Storch mentioned, older children often had to care for the younger ones. Jean Schriebman watched the children while her parents worked.[90] Rena Harari (b. 1936) learned to clean her sister's tracheotomy hole.[91] Those mothers fortunate enough to have other family members around, including Esther Berkowitz, Regina Lender, Gusta Besser, and Toba Schachter, benefited from their help. Toba Schachter even admitted that, after she returned to Poland, she 'did not know how to feed her daughter' because her mother had been wholly responsible for doing so.[92] Some mothers stopped working after they had children. Bronia Zisfain and Ethel Karp took care of their children and most probably helped others in the community.[93] There are very few references to stay-at-home fathers in the testimonies, but the grandfathers of Esther Berkowitz's and Regina Lender's children played active roles in their upbringing.[94]

Many single mothers lacked the support of other family members. When her husband joined the Anders Army, Fela Karmoil (b. 1917, Łódź) was left alone with her son in Kazakhstan.[95] She took him with her to her job mixing cement every day until he was 2½. At that point, she trekked to a kindergarten and begged the teacher to take him. Constant work in the ambulance corps led Ruzena Berler to seek more systematic care for her daughter from her own mother in Lviv.[96] One of the women deported with her made plans to return to Lviv with her own son, and Ruzena considered sending her daughter with her but changed her mind. Eventually, she found a woman named Anastasia, who was 'too old to do anything', and they agreed that Anastasia would care for the child in return for food and money. Later the daughter stayed in children's homes in Yefremow and Czernowitz as Ruzena served with the Czech army. The memory of the more personal arrangement with Anastasia remained particularly strong: a picture of the daughter with her beloved caregiver remained in her possession until the day she gave her testimony in California half a century later.

Growing Up: Circumstantial Families and Institutional Support

Together Anastasia, Ruzena, and Olga constituted a circumstantial family brought together by the realities of exile in the Soviet Union. All Polish citizens in Soviet exile encountered new living spaces, from temporary apartments on the eastern side of the Bug to barracks across a variety of labour camps, which they were often required to share. After the opening of the eastern front and the general amnesty, a majority of them moved towards central Asia, where they found a different variety of living spaces: yurts shared with Kazakh families, rented or bought mud huts on collective farms (sometimes shared with other deportees), workers' housing complexes, private apartments in cities and towns, ZPP orphanages, and (least fortunately) parks, train stations, or under the sky of the central Asian steppe. All of these arrangements tended to create circumstantial families.

Pauline B. (b. 1925, Luboml) and her sister rented space from a Russian woman, and they became 'like her children'.[97] She cooked and cleaned for them and let them share her bed while she slept on the stove. They all survived the war together. Jean Schreibman's (b. 1928, Rejowiec) mother took in Polish Jews from her home town of Rejowiec.[98] One of the men she sheltered would become Jean's husband after the war. People teased her 'mother that she was raising her son-in-law'. Paula Blum's (b. 1929, Chorzów) mother took in two young Polish Jewish men who had knocked on their door on the Kazahk farm asking for help. One of them intervened when a neighbour, a Kazakh Muslim boy, came into their mud hut and tried to harass her.[99] In some instances, orphanages offered housing for employees and their families. Zlota Gloger's sister found work and housing at an orphanage for both herself and her son.[100] Between their time on the farm and the acquisition of their apartment, Hannah Wolkun's (b. 1938, Luboml) mother worked in an orphanage in the northern Kazakh city of Kustanai (Kostanay).[101] They lived at the orphanage, and Russian and Polish women cared for Hannah and her younger sister during her mother's shifts.

Archival documents from more than 100 settlements across the Soviet Union show that the ZPP supported a vast network of institutions dedicated to children.[102] In smaller Russian settlements such as Kirov, the list of deportees included 1,155 Poles, 481 Jews, and 481 Ukrainians, including 1,338 children under the age of 16. Two children's homes, one housing 77 children and the second housing 75, supported this predominantly young population.[103] In the Uzbek city of Fergana, the ZPP worked to clothe children in the orphanage in advance of the winter of 1944. By providing shoes and shirts, the ZPP helped prepare the children to travel to school as well.[104] In 1945 a ZPP-sponsored exhibition, 'Polish Emigration in Kyrgyzstan from 1941 to 1945', counted 299 schools and 29 orphanages across 91 different settlements, from big cities like Tashkent to smaller villages like Lenger Ugol.[105] There were ten different sections in the exhibition, which included photographic evidence of cultural activities, including one on the life of a soldier, one on Polish–Soviet relations, and one on the 'care of children and young people'.[106] Testimonies from wartime orphans such as Beatrice Sussman (b. 1933, Krzywicze) confirm what the archive illustrates: some families were destroyed while others were created.[107] Thousands of Polish Jewish children populated orphanages in the Soviet Union, attended schools in exile, and moved on to care homes in Poland after repatriation.[108]

Alongside a network of systematic childcare, the ZPP supported institutions providing educational opportunities for those of school age and above.[109] In the district of Semipalatinsk, for example, the ZPP funded a home for sixty children, a school in the city that taught 330 children, a day-care centre in Ayagoz, and even Polish classes for those enrolled in Russian schools.[110] In Samarkand in Uzbekistan, fifty-four schools served 825 students out of a population of 9,200 Polish citizens by the end of 1945.[111] Every third person in this area was a member of the ZPP, which had fifteen offices and 141 'circles' of ZPP members across twenty-three localities in the greater Samarkand region. In Samarkand itself, roughly 20 per cent of the Polish deportee population of 10,467 was under the age of 16, thus justifying a children's home for 100, a school for more than 1,000 spread across two buildings that also served as a boarding house for 663 people, and a night school for young adults. To serve the teachers in Dzhalal-Abad and south-western Kyrgyzstan, the ZPP sponsored a school board, organized conferences for instructors without pedagogical training, arranged joint meetings of the teachers' collective with the ZPP board, and provided teaching demonstrations.[112] The ZPP also supported adult-education initiatives, Polish conversation groups, and a wide array of cultural programmes to entertain Polish citizens far from home. For almost three years, the ZPP offered both Jewish and non-Jewish children and adults access to many aspects of Polish culture.

For some interviewees, being a Polish citizen in Soviet exile heightened their sense of Polishness. Freda Walzman spoke Polish with her son, 'so he could have the language, hoping we would live there again'.[113] Frania Oberklaid also wanted to live in Poland again. She grew up on Muranowska Street in Warsaw and recalled her deep love for Poland and the Polish language, and sang a song from her childhood choir during her interview.[114] Toba Schachter recalled how the Russians around her categorized her as Polish because she spoke the language so fluently.

One of the ZPP's cultural programmes had a particularly extensive reach in the spring of 1945. In places such as Chkalovsk, Chimkent, and Tashkent, ZPP affiliates hosted events commemorating the second anniversary of the Warsaw ghetto uprising, including presentations of music and poetry in Polish and Yiddish. Praise was heaped on the leaders of the ghetto fighters alongside other Polish revolutionary heroes throughout history, and the inclusion of a distinctively Jewish narrative in the broader Polish wartime experience was called for.[115] Implicitly, these events can be seen as a Soviet-based expression of *żydowska polskość*, 'Jewish Polishness', to use a term coined by the journalist Jakub Appenszlak in 1946 during his own exile in New York City.[116] Pictures of the event in Tashkent show numerous children, the youngest Polish citizens, in the packed auditorium.

Conclusion: A 'Caregiving' Turn in Holocaust Studies

Some events divide time and how it is remembered. Events like the establishment of states, the outbreak of wars, the uncovering of genocides almost always force witnesses and historians to create a decisive 'before' and 'after'. On a much smaller and more intimate scale, the experience of starting a family divides the life of the parents into before and after as well. Traces of this division are often evident when these tales are told, even years later. The period after the arrival of the child, the days spent caring for it, take on a unique rhythm that can appear monotonous: feeding, soothing, cleaning, changing nappies. This has led to a truism that circulates amongst exhausted parents and caregivers alike: the days are long but the years are short. Children hurtle forwards on their own trajectories. In their wake, they leave shifting priorities, changes in perspective, and almost no remnant of the collective work required to keep them alive, other than themselves.

The voices and documents discussed in this chapter reveal an under-represented but significant aspect of the lives and memories of the Polish exiles in the Soviet Union. The testimonies of Toba, Helen, and Regina, and the archival holdings which complement them, demand a reassessment of how members of this group decided where to go, what they felt about belonging, and how they survived severe conditions and remembered their exile. The evidence presented here suggests that other studies which prioritize the perspective of the family require a slight but poignant corrective.[117] Polish Jewish families grew vigorously throughout the Soviet Union in the 1940s. Children, toddlers, babies, and all the care they required from conception to puberty should punctuate their histories. Natalia Aleksiun has recently written about the 'familial turn' in Holocaust studies.[118] At this juncture, I would like to suggest the pressing need for a related yet more precise turn, a 'caregiving turn', one that situates thoughtful observers alongside makeshift *ḥupot*, swollen bellies, starving wails, bottoms wrapped in improvised nappies, exhausted parents, Polish-language school curriculums, and the seemingly invisible work of experienced but circumstantial caregivers.

In conclusion, there is much to write about the starting of families and the raising of children amongst those displaced from their homes in general and amongst the Polish Jews who survived the Second World War in the Soviet Union particularly. As demonstrated here, this emphasis illuminates the significant difficulties they faced during this period, shows how a particular generation spawned a subsequent generation during its wartime exile, and offers new insight into complex topics such as belonging, religious observance, and cultural inheritance. Finally, the lens of the growing family adds another viewpoint to recent studies of this group, who for many decades seemed to exist outside the standard canon of Holocaust historiography and the experiences of those who survived the war in Nazi-occupied or Nazi-aligned Europe. Their distinctive experience was, to quote Frania Oberklaid, simultaneously 'a tragedy and not a tragedy'.[119] The range of this distinctive experience was often dictated by the smallest humans in its midst.

Notes

1 According to Mark Edele and Wanda Warlik, at least 145,000 and maybe as many as 163,000 Polish Jews returned to Poland at the war's end (M. Edele and W. Warlik, 'Saved by Stalin? Trajectories of Polish Jews in the Soviet Second World War', in A. Grossmann, S. Fitzpatrick, and M. Edele (eds.), *Shelter from the Holocaust: Rethinking Jewish Survival in the Soviet Union* (Detroit, 2017), 95–131). These numbers remain best estimates. On the repatriation of Polish Jewish citizens from the Soviet Union specifically, see E. R. Adler, *Survival on the Margins: Polish Jewish Refugees in the Wartime Soviet Union* (Cambridge,

Mass., 2021), 218–38; M. Nesselrodt, *Dem Holocaust entkommen: Polnische Juden in der Sowjetunion, 1939–1946* (Berlin, 2019), 246–58; A. Kaganovitch, 'Stalin's Great Power Politics, the Return of Jewish Refugees to Poland, and Continued Migration to Palestine, 1944–1946', *Holocaust and Genocide Studies*, 26 (2012), 59–94; D. Sula, 'Z ZSRR na Dolny Śląsk: Przesiedlenie i repatriacja polskich Żydów w latach 1945–1947', in L. Zessin-Jurek and K. Friedla (eds.), *Syberiada Żydów polskich: Losy uchodźców z Zagłady* (Warsaw, 2020), 561–88: 580–2. On the repatriation of Polish citizens more generally, see K. Jolluck, *Exile and Identity: Polish Women in the Soviet Union during the Second World War* (Pittsburgh, Pa., 2002), 279–86; K. Sword, *Deportation and Exile: Poles in the Soviet Union, 1939–48* (London, 1994), ch. 7; K. Kersten, *Repatriacja ludności polskiej po II wojnie światowej: Studium historyczne* (Wrocław, 1974); T. Bugaj, *Dzieci polskie w ZSRR i ich repatriacja 1939–1952* (Jelenia Góra, 1982); A. Głowacki, *Ocalić i repatriować: Opieka nad ludnością polską w głębi terytorium ZSRR (1943–1946)* (Łódź, 1994).

2 The opening of the NKVD archives has made possible more accurate figures for these deportations. The archives of the Military Convoys Department of the NKVD suggest that the deportations of February 1940 involved between 139,000 and 143,000 people; that of April 1940 around 61,000; that of June 1940, 75,000; and that of May–June 1941 between 34,000 and 44,000 (of whom nearly 18,000 came from Lithuania). This would give a total of between 309,000 and 323,000. The records of the Department of Labour and Special Camps of the NKVD give a figure between 315,000 and 325,000. To these figures should be added those resettled from border regions, who may have numbered around 138,000. See A. Gurjanow, 'Cztery deportacje 1940–41', *Karta*, 12 (1994), 114–36; Z. S. Siemaszko, 'The Mass Deportations of the Polish Population to the USSR, 1940–1941', in K. Sword (ed.), *The Soviet Takeover of the Polish Eastern Provinces, 1939–41* (London, 1991), 217–35: 235. Laura Jockusch and Tamar Lewinsky outlined the range of estimates for these deportees (see L. Jockusch and T. Lewinsky, 'Paradise Lost? Postwar Memory of Polish Jewish Survival in the Soviet Union', *Holocaust and Genocide Studies*, 24 (2010), 373–99: 393 n. 2). Eliyana Adler and Natalia Aleksiun estimated that '300,000 Jews fled the areas recently occupied by the Germans for those now under Soviet control' in 1939 (E. R. Adler and N. Aleksiun, 'Seeking Relative Safety: The Flight of Polish Jews to the East in the Autumn of 1939', *Yad Vashem Studies*, 46 (2018), 41–71: 41). On the movement between and within occupied spheres, especially early in the war, see E. R. Adler, 'Hrubieszów at the Crossroads: Polish Jews Navigate the German and Soviet Occupations', *Holocaust and Genocide Studies*, 28 (2014), 1–30.

3 See Sword, *Deportation and Exile*, ch. 2.

4 A. Stankowski, 'How Many Polish Jews Survived the Holocaust?', in F. Tych and M. Adamczyk-Garbowska (eds.), *Jewish Presence in Absence: The Aftermath of the Holocaust in Poland, 1944–2010* (Jerusalem, 2012), 205–16.

5 See Zessin-Jurek and Friedla (eds.), *Syberiada Żydów polskich*; Grossmann, Fitzpatrick, and Edele (eds.), *Shelter from the Holocaust*; Nesselrodt, *Dem Holocaust entkommen*; N. Belsky, 'Encounters in the East: Evacuees in the Soviet Hinterland During the Second World War', Ph.D. thesis (University of Chicago, 2015); Jockusch and Lewinsky, 'Paradise Lost?'; Adler, *Survival on the Margins*; see also Y. Litvak, *Pelitim yehudim mipolin biverit hamo'atsot: 1939–1946* (Jerusalem, 1988).

6 Adler and Aleksiun explored the influence of family relations on the decision to flee and the recollections of it (Adler and Aleksiun, 'Seeking Relative Safety', 42). Adler discussed pregnancy, childbirth, and the role of the family more generally but placed little emphasis on growing wartime families (Adler, *Survival on the Margins*).

7 University of Southern California Shoah Foundation, Los Angeles, Visual History Archive (hereafter VHA), interview 41133: Regina Lender (19 Feb. 1998; Eng.).
8 VHA, interview 37881: Helen Fenster (2 Feb. 1998; Eng.).
9 VHA, interview 12346: Toba Schachter (22 Feb. 1996; Eng.).
10 This chapter uses testimonies from the University of Southern California's Shoah Foundation (over 50,000 interviews), the Fortunoff Video Archive for Holocaust Testimonies at Yale University (over 30,000 testimonies), and personal interviews with the author. Other video and written testimonies are housed at the Phillip Maisel Testimonies Project at Melbourne's Jewish Holocaust Centre, Yad Vashem in Israel, McGill University's Video Archives in Montreal, the Hoover Institution at Stanford University, and the Central Jewish Historical Commission at the Jewish Historical Institute in Warsaw.
11 See T. Zahra, *The Lost Children: Reconstructing Europe's Families after World War II* (Cambridge, Mass., 2012); C. Wunsch and L. Pearce, *Documents of Judean Exiles and West Semites in Babylonia in the Collection of David Sofer* (Bethesda, Md., 2014); W. Pearlman, *We Crossed a Bridge and It Trembled: Voices from Syria* (New York, 2018). For the Polish context, see J. B. Michlic, 'What Does a Child Remember? Recollection of the War and the Early Postwar Period among Child Survivors from Poland', in ead. (ed.), *Jewish Families in Europe, 1939–Present: History, Representation, and Memory* (Waltham, Mass., 2017), 153–72; A. Cichopek-Garaj, 'Agency and Displacement of Ethnic Polish and Jewish Families After World War II', *Polish American Studies*, 78/1 (2021), 60–82; E. Stańczyk, *Commemorating the Children of World War II in Poland: Combative Remembrance* (London, 2019); R. Fodor, 'The Impact of the Nazi Occupation of Poland on the Jewish Mother–Child Relationship', *YIVO Annual of Jewish Social Science*, 11 (1956–7), 270–85.
12 P. Gatrell, 'Refugees: What's Wrong with History?', *Journal of Refugee Studies*, 30 (2017), 170–89; D. Stone, 'Refugees Then and Now: Memory, History and Politics in the Long Twentieth Century. An Introduction', *Patterns of Prejudice*, 52 (2018), 101–6. The families were not necessarily biological (see N. Aleksiun, 'On Jews in Hiding and the Making of Surrogate Families', in E. R. Adler and K. Čapková (eds.), *Jewish and Romani Families in the Holocaust and its Aftermath* (East Rutherford, NJ, 2020), 85–100).
13 As Naomi Seidman suggested almost three decades ago, 'we still have not come to terms with the Holocaust in the history of the Jewish body', pregnant or otherwise (N. Seidman, 'Carnal Knowledge: Sex and the Body', *Jewish Social Studies*, NS 1/1 (1994), 115–46: 129; see also M. Benjamin, *The Obligated Self: Maternal Subjectivity and Jewish Thought* (Bloomington, Ind., 2018); E. Baumgarten, *Mothers and Children: Jewish Family Life in Medieval Europe* (Princeton, NJ, 2004); D. Aranoff, 'Mother's Milk: Child-Rearing and the Production of Jewish Culture', *Journal of Jewish Identities*, 12 (2019), 1–17). On the Holocaust specifically, see Michlic, 'What Does a Child Remember?'; D. Ofer, 'Cohesion and Rupture: The Jewish Family in the East European Ghettos during the Holocaust', in P. Y. Medding (ed.), *Coping with Life and Death: Jewish Families in the Twentieth Century* (Oxford, 1998), 144–65; ead., 'Motherhood under Siege', in E. Hertzog (ed.), *Life, Death and Sacrifice: Women and Family in the Holocaust* (Jerusalem, 2008), 41–67; on a different group of Polish Jewish children who were evacuated from the Soviet Union via Iran, see M. Dekel, *Tehran Children: A Holocaust Refugee Odyssey* (New York, 2019).
14 See Adler and Aleksiun, 'Seeking Relative Safety'; H. Datner-Śpiewak, 'Instytucje opieki nad dzieckiem i szkoły powszechne Centralnego Komitetu Żydów Polskich w latach 1945–1946', *Biuletyn Żydowskiego Instytutu Historycznego*, 119 (1981), 37–51; J. B. Michlic, 'The Raw Memory of War: Early Postwar Testimonies of Children in Dom Dziecka in Otwock', *Yad Vashem Studies*, 37 (2009), 11–52; A. Grossmann, *Jews, Germans, and Allies: Close Encounters in Occupied Germany* (Princeton, NJ, 2007).

15 Archiwum Państwowe w Szczecinie, 65/317/0/5/915, 'Sprawozdania sytuacyjne – miasto Szczecin 1946–1947', 2 'Wydział Repatriacji': 'Lista Zrzeszenia Żydów Warszawskich w Szczecinie' [after June 1946].

16 On Polish deportees in Osh and Kyrgyzstan, see A. Głowacki (ed.), *Obywatele polscy w Kirgizji: Wybór dokumentów (1941–1946)* (Warsaw, 2010).

17 For the number under the age of 18, see D. Boćkowski, 'Repatriacja dzieci polskich z głębi ZSRR w latach 1945–1952', *Studia z Dziejów Rosji i Europy Środkowo-Wschodniej* 1994 (29), pp. 99–108: 102; for the number under 14, see Michlic, 'What Does a Child Remember?', 155; for 202,332 Polish repatriates (Jews and non-Jews) and the 52,332 children up to the age of 16 who constituted 26 per cent of them, see A. Korzon, 'Przesiedlona ludność polska w ZSRR w latach 1941–1946', Ph.D. thesis (University of Warsaw, 1967), 4–7.

18 Ukrainians and Belarusians appear less often than Poles and Jews in this data, which is spread out over dozens of archival files and does not always correspond to the same period of time. For example, in Nowosibirsk between 1944 and 1946 there were 2,695 Polish citizens: 173 Poles, 1,253 Jews, 945 Ukrainians, and 324 Belorussians; 227 children were under 7; and 270 were between 7 and 16. The percentage of children is lower but still significant. See Archiwum Akt Nowych, Warsaw (hereafter AAN), 2/130/0/-/149, 'Położenie ludności polskiej i działalność ZPP w obwodzie Nowysibirsk', 1944–46: report (n.d.).

19 AAN, 2/130/0/-/134, 'Położenie ludności polskiej i działalność ZPP w obwodzie Kujbyszew: Sprawozdania', 1945–6, 130: 'Sprawozdanie zarządu obwodowego ZPP w Kujbyszewie' (1 Nov. 1945).

20 For testimonies from the children, see the journal edited by Israel Kaplan: *Fun letstn khurbn: tsaytshrift far geshihkte fun yidishn lebn beysn natsi-rezhim* (1946–8); *Dzieci oskarżają*, ed. M. Hochberg-Mariańska and N. Grüss (Kraków, 1947); expanded edn.: *Dzieci żydowskie oskarżają*, ed. M. Hochberg-Mariańska and N. Grüss (Warsaw, 1993); B. Tenenbaum, *Ehad me'ir ushenayim mimishpaḥah* (Merhavia, 1947); for the testimonies of 861 Polish Jewish children who left the Soviet Union for Iran along with members of the Anders Army, see H. Grynberg, *Dzieci Syjonu* (Warsaw, 1994); Eng. trans.: *Children of Zion*, trans. J. Mitchell (Evanston, Ill., 1997).

21 See also N. Aleksiun, 'A Familial Turn in Holocaust Scholarship?', in D. Nešťáková, K. Grosse-Sommer, B. Klacsmann, and J. Drábik (eds.), *If This Is a Woman: Studies on Women and Gender in the Holocaust* (Newton, Mass., 2021).

22 On maternal care in central Asia, see P. Michaels, *Curative Powers: Medicine and Empire in Stalin's Soviet Central Asia* (Pittsburgh, Pa., 2003).

23 See C. Shaw, 'Friendship under Lock and Key: The Soviet Central Asian Border, 1918–34', *Central Asian Survey*, 30 (2011), 331–48; Belsky, 'Encounters in the East'; Nesselrodt, *Dem Holocaust entkommen*; E. R. Adler, 'The Miracle of Hanukkah and Other Orthodox Tales of Survival in Soviet Exile During World War II', *Dapim*, 32 (2018), 155–71; ead., *Survival on the Margins*; for an alternative interpretation of this encounter with 'Others', see Jolluck, *Exile and Identity*, 183–278; on the evacuation of Soviet citizens, including some Polish Jews who took Soviet citizenship, see R. Manley, *To the Tashkent Station: Evacuation und Survival in the Soviet Union at War* (Ithaca, NY, 2009).

24 VHA, interview 16041: Jenny Balsam (5 June 1996; Eng.).

25 On Jewish life in post-war Poland, see Y. Bauer, *Flight and Rescue: Brichah* (New York, 1970); D. Engel, *Bein shiḥrur liveriḥah: nitsolei hasho'ah bepolin vehama'avak al hanhagatam, 1944–1946* (Tel Aviv, 1996); id., 'The Reconstruction of Jewish Communal Institutions in Postwar Poland: The Origins of the Central Committee of Polish Jews, 1944–1945', *East European Politics and Societies*, 10 (1996), 85–107; id., 'Patterns of Anti-Jewish Violence in

Poland, 1944–1946', *Yad Vashem Studies*, 26 (1998), 43–85; N. Aleksiun, *Dokąd dalej? Ruch syjonistyczny w Polsce (1944–1950)* (Warsaw, 2002); M. Shore, *Caviar and Ashes: A Warsaw Generation's Life and Death in Marxism, 1918–1968* (New Haven, Conn., 2006); J. T. Gross, *Fear: Anti-Semitism in Poland after Auschwitz. An Essay in Historical Interpretation* (New York, 2006); S. Redlich, *Life in Transit: Jews in Postwar Łódź, 1945–1950* (Newton, Mass., 2010); A. Cichopek-Gajraj, *Beyond Violence: Jewish Survivors in Poland and Slovakia, 1944–48* (Cambridge, 2014); K. Person, *Dipisi: Żydzi polscy w amerykańskiej i brytyjskiej strefach okupacyjnych Niemiec, 1945–1948* (Warsaw, 2019); K. Kijek, 'Aliens in the Land of Piast: The Polonization of Lower Silesia and Its Jewish Community in the Years 1945–1950', in T. Grill (ed.), *Jews and Germans in Eastern Europe: Shared and Comparative Histories* (Oldenburg, 2018), 234–55.

26 Post-war conditions held special challenges for young and growing families. First, the Nazis had instituted racial categories within civil law and daily life, decimated the Polish intelligentsia, annihilated the Jewish population, and created circumstances in which significant numbers of 'ethnic' Polish people killed Polish Jews (sometimes their neighbours). Second, the shifting of Poland's borders and Allied-endorsed policies of population transfer changed cities, villages, and the countryside. Severe housing crises ensued in some places, homes sat empty in others, and medium and small shtetls had ceased to exist. Third, violence and antisemitism were rampant. In their testimonies, Polish Jews who returned from the Soviet Union often compared this 'new' antisemitic violence unfavourably with the kindness of their pre-war Polish Christian neighbours and their neighbours in the Soviet Union. Repatriation trains returned to the Recovered Territories and encountered the wake of armies, power vacuums, and the expulsion of millions of ethnic Germans. See M. Zaremba, 'The "War Syndrome": World War II and Polish Society', in S.-L. Hoffmann, S. Kott, P. Romijn, and O. Wieviorka (eds.), *Seeking Peace in the Wake of War: Europe, 1943–1947* (Amsterdam, 2015), 27–62.

27 On the use of oral testimonies in Jewish history, see J. Shandler, *Holocaust Memory in the Digital Age: Survivors' Stories and New Media Practices* (Stanford, Calif., 2017); C. Browning, *Remembering Survival: Inside a Nazi Slave-Labour Camp* (New York, 2011); E. R. Adler, 'Crossing Over: Exploring the Borders of Holocaust Testimony', in Grossmann, Fitzpatrick, and Edele (eds.), *Shelter from the Holocaust*, 247–74; A. Shternshis, *Soviet and Kosher: Jewish Popular Culture in the Soviet Union, 1923–1939* (Bloomington, Ind., 2006); S. Kaplan, *Children in the Holocaust: Dealing with Affects and Memory Images in Trauma and Generational Linking* (Uppsala, 2002); D. Baranowski, *Ich bin die Stimme der sechs Millionen: Das Videoarchiv im Ort der Information* (Berlin, 2009); A. Wieviorka, *L'Ère du témoin* (Paris, 1998).

28 S. Alexievich, *The Unwomanly Face of War: An Oral History of Women in World War II*, trans. R. Pevear and L. Volokhonsky (New York, 2017), 5.

29 VHA, interview 32765: Frania Oberklaid (19 June 1997; Eng.).

30 Jenny Balsam, VHA interview.

31 Aleksiun and Adler are correct to note that 'although the decisions may have been rushed—and certainly no one could have imagined what the coming months would bring—at least some Polish Jews did not act out of panic but from a tactical calculation based on knowledge of what support they could count on in their native regions. Once again family was at the fore' (Adler and Aleksiun, 'Seeking Relative Safety', 70). In these cases, however, the new family of the husband and wife took precedence over the families left behind.

32 Toba Schachter, VHA interview.

33 Regina Lender, VHA interview.
34 Fortunoff Video Archive for Holocaust Testimonies, Yale University, New Haven, Conn. (hereafter FVA), HVT 1400: Esther J., testimony (26 Oct. 1989; Eng.).
35 Helen Fenster, VHA interview.
36 VHA, interview 14584: Tema Abel (26 Apr. 1996; Eng.).
37 VHA, interview 33606: Fela Platkowski (2 July 1997; Eng.).
38 VHA, interview 33611: Yeshayahu Platkowski (2 July 1997; Eng.).
39 VHA, interview 6943: Jacob Zisfain (19 Sept. 1995; Eng.).
40 VHA, interview 6910: Bronia Zisfain (19 Sept. 1995; Eng.).
41 On religious observance in the labour camps, see Adler, *Survival on the Margins*, 138–42.
42 Jacob Zisfain, VHA interview.
43 'Lista Zrzeszenia Żydów Warszawskich w Szczecinie'.
44 VHA, interview 21131: Helen Goldberg (17 Oct. 1996; Eng.).
45 Esther J., FVA testimony.
46 Not all labour camps in the Soviet Union had medical staff. For pregnancy in the labour camps, see A. Applebaum, *Gulag: A History* (New York, 2003), 474–94.
47 VHA, interview 10420: Frances Hertzberg (20 Dec. 1995; Eng.).
48 VHA, interview 26568: Riva Frenkel (16 Feb. 1997; Eng.).
49 VHA, interview 28262: Rachel Koplowicz (17 Apr. 1997; Eng.).
50 Ibid.
51 Jenny Balsam, VHA interview.
52 Frances Hertzberg, VHA interview.
53 On rituals amongst Jewish deportees in the Soviet Union and their legacies, see K. Friedla, '"Kiedy szabat stał się niedzielą…": Życie religijne i społeczne polskich Żydów w ZSRR podczas II wojny światowej', in Zessin-Jurek and Friedla (eds.), *Syberiada Żydów polskich*, 437–72; Adler, 'The Miracle of Hanukkah and Other Orthodox Tales of Survival in Soviet Exile During World War II'. Friedla writes about relationships and encounters between the religious Jews from Poland and those from the Soviet Union, mostly Bukharan Jews. On the relationships between Soviet Jews and Polish Jews, see N. Belsky, 'Fraught Friendships: Soviet Jews and Polish Jews on the Soviet Home Front', in Grossmann, Fitzpatrick, and Edele (eds.), *Shelter from the Holocaust*, 161–84.
54 VHA, interview 3569: Sarah Marenfeld (27 July 1995; Eng.).
55 Frania Oberklaid, VHA interview.
56 AAN 2/130/0/-/1845, 'Zarząd Rejonowy w Chawaście: Korepondencja, protokoły posiedzeń i zebrań ludności polskiej, sprawozdania, spisy', 1944–5: report (30 May 1945).
57 Tema Abel, VHA interview.
58 Other male children born in post-war Poland had their own postnatal ceremonies. Fanny Eisenberg gave birth at home in Wrocław immediately after her repatriation, as she was afraid to give birth in the hospital. They had a circumcision ceremony for sixty friends afterwards (VHA, interview 15468: Fanny Eisenberg (22 May 1996; Eng.)).
59 Helen Fenster remembered similar thoughts; her husband David fell ill and died when she 'was already pregnant, although I didn't want it, there wasn't the room, there wasn't the place, but I couldn't do anything about it' (Helen Fenster, VHA interview).
60 VHA, interview 32621: Ethel Karp (4 Sept. 1997; Eng.).
61 Ibid.
62 Ibid. Fanny Eisenberg recalled: 'I was afraid, I didn't want to have more children because

I didn't know where we were going to be . . . I went to the doctor and I took pills and it didn't help, thank God, it didn't help. And I had my daughter and I'm so proud of her' (Fanny Eisenberg, VHA interview).

63 VHA, interview 35287: Gusta Besser (15 Aug. 1997; Eng.).
64 Freda Gruen, VHA interview.
65 VHA, interview 19882: Genia Bikel (3 Oct. 1996; Eng.).
66 The mail was contingent on the war and relations between states. On relief packages from non-governmental Jewish organizations, see A. Grossmann, 'Jewish Refugees in Soviet Central Asia, Iran, and India: Lost Memories of Displacement, Trauma, and Rescue', in Grossmann, Fitzpatrick, and Edele (eds.), *Shelter from the Holocaust*, 185–218. She writes that 'by 1944 some 10,000 packages a month were making their way on Red Army trucks from Tehran to the Iran–Soviet Union border and then onwards by various routes for delivery throughout Central Asia. Remarkably, JDC records indicate that between 80 and 90 percent of 230,000 parcels shipped from Tehran "reached their destinations"' (ibid. 199).
67 Frances Hertzberg, VHA interview.
68 Riva Frenkel, VHA, interview.
69 VHA, interview 38: Marlene Kreitenberg (1 Aug. 1994; Eng.); Riva Frenkel, VHA interview; VHA, interview 13311: Miriam Lewent [née Storch] (15 Mar. 1996; Eng.).
70 Ethel Karp, VHA interview.
71 Rachel Koplowicz, VHA interview.
72 VHA, interview 16127: Freda Walzman (13 June 1996; Eng.).
73 VHA, interview 44088: Esther Berkowitz (6 Aug. 1998; Eng.).
74 Problems with nappies continued in post-war Poland, as Mayer Zaks (b. 1912, Piotrków) and Samuel Alban (b. 1912, Tarnów) attest. Zaks recorded the number of nappies he changed on a clandestine trip to occupied Germany from Silesia (FVA, HVT 561: Mayer Z., testimony (19 May 1985; Eng.)). Samuel Alban complained that the escape organization Bericha provided 'few nappies' to the parents walking for miles with their children at night to cross the Czechoslovakian border (VHA, interview 6112: Samuel Alban, testimony (30 Aug. 1995; Eng.)).
75 Freda Walzman, VHA interview.
76 Rachel Koplowicz, VHA interview.
77 VHA, interview 1207: Ruzena Berler (7 Mar. 1995; Eng.). Roughly a dozen other testimonies mention the daily allowance of hot water, from either the locomotive's boiler or the station itself.
78 Frances Hertzberg, VHA interview.
79 VHA, interview 41620: Rose Horowitz (27 May 1998; Eng.).
80 FVA, HVT 2590: Doris U., testimony (17 June 1993; Eng.).
81 VHA, interview 44318: Rita Perelmuter (21 May 1998; Eng.).
82 VHA, interview 29597: Nina Lubenfeld (23 Mar. 1997; Eng.).
83 Miriam Lewent, VHA interview.
84 Gusta Besser, VHA interview.
85 Ruzena Berler, VHA interview.
86 VHA, interview 29013: Bertha Schattner (11 May 1997; Eng.).
87 Rose Horowitz, VHA interview.
88 Esther Berkowitz, VHA interview.

89 Sarah Marenfeld, VHA interview.
90 Miriam Lewent, VHA interview.
91 Rena Harari, interview with author, 18 Apr. 2020.
92 Toba Schachter, VHA interview.
93 Bronia Zisfain, VHA interview; Ethel Karp, VHA interview.
94 Esther Berkowitz, VHA interview; Regina Lender, VHA interview; see also M. Kaplan, 'Did Gender Matter during the Holocaust?', *Jewish Social Studies*, 24/2 (2019), 37–56.
95 VHA, interview 1106: Fela Karmoil (22 Feb. 1995; Eng.). On Polish Jews in the Anders Army and its implications for families, see Goldlust, 'A Different Silence', 55–64; Grossmann, 'Jewish Refugees in Soviet Central Asia, Iran, and India'; Nesselrodt, *Dem Holocaust entkommen*, 202–11; Adler, *Survival on the Margins*, 148–211.
96 Ruzena Berler, VHA interview.
97 FVA, HVT 4420: Pauline B., testimony (28 Sept. 2008; Eng.).
98 FVA, HVT 1331: Jean S., testimony (29 Oct. 1989; Eng.).
99 VHA, interview 38469: Paula Blum, testimony (8 Dec. 1997; Eng.).
100 Ibid.
101 VHA, interview 39372: Hannah Wolkun (18 Feb. 1988; Eng.).
102 A network of similar entities preceded those sponsored by the ZPP. After the Sikorski–Maisky agreement, the Polish government-in-exile established an embassy in the Soviet Union, which oversaw the creation of over 400 welfare institutions such as orphanages and children's homes (eighty-three according to official estimates) across Soviet territory (see Adler, *Survival on the Margins*, 200–5).
103 AAN, 2/130/0/-/123, 'Położenie ludności polskiej i działalność ZPP w obwodzie Kirów', 1945–6: 'Sprawozdanie z działalności obwodowego zarządu ZPP w Kirowie' (1 May 1945).
104 AAN, 2/130/0/-/91, 'Położenie ludności polskiej i działalność ZPP w obwodzie Fergana', 1943–4: 'Sprawozdanie z działalności obwodowego zarządu ZPP w Ferganie' (9 Nov. 1944).
105 AAN, 2/130/0/-/861, 'Wystawa na temat "Emigracja polska w ZSRR w latach 1941–1945" – położenie i stan organizacyjny ludności polskiej', 1945.
106 AAN, 2/130/0/-/859, 'Wystawa i album na temat: "Emigracja polska w ZSRR w latach 1941–1945"; Plany, instrukcje, korespondencja', 1945: 'Plan ekspozycyjny wystawy "Emigracja Polska w ZSRR w latach 1941–1945"'.
107 FVA, HVT 72: Beatrice S., testimony (12 May 1982; Eng.).
108 This commitment to organized care continued in the children's homes set up by the Central Committee of Jews in Poland after the exiles returned to Poland in 1946 (see J. B. Michlic, 'The Raw Memory of War'; ead., 'The Children Accuse, 1946: Between Exclusion From and Inclusion Into the Holocaust Canon', in K. Ruchniewicz and J. Zinnecker (eds.), *Zwischen Zwangsarbeit, Holocaust und Vertreibung: Polnische, jüdische und deutsche Kindheiten im besetzten Polen* (Munich, 2003); see also Datner-Śpiewak, 'Instytucje opieki nad dzieckiem i szkoły powszechne Centralnego Komitetu Żydów Polskich w latach 1945–1946'; I. Kowalska, 'Kartoteka TOZ z lat 1946–47 (Żydowskie dzieci uratowane z Holocaustu)', *Biuletyn Żydowskiego Instytutu Historycznego*, 175–8 (1995–6), 97–106; B. Cohen, 'The Children's Voice: Postwar Collections of Testimonies from Child Survivors of the Holocaust', *Holocaust and Genocide Studies*, 21 (2007), 73–95).
109 On schooling in labour camps, see Adler, *Survival on the Margins*, 137–8.

110 AAN, 2/130/0/-/162, 'Położenie ludności polskiej i działalność ZPP w obwodzie Semipałatyńsk', 1944–6: 'Sprawozdanie z działalności obwodowego zarządu ZPP w Semipałatyńsku' (n.d.).

111 AAN, 2/130/0/-/158, 'Położenie ludności polskiej i działalność ZPP w obwodzie Samarkanda', 1944–6: 'Sprawozdanie z działalności Zarządu Obwodowego ZPP w Samarkandzie za czerwiec-lipiec 1945'.

112 AAN, 2/130/0/-/88, 'Położenie ludności polskiej i działalność ZPP w obwodzie Dżałał-Abad', 1944–5: 'Sprawozdanie z działalności Zarządu Obwodowego ZPP w Dżałał-Abadzie za IV kwartał 1945 roku'. Military families serving in the Polish Armed Forces in the USSR and other military formations benefited from the school and youth system supported by the ZPP (see AAN, 2/130/0/-/88: 'Sprawozdanie Zarządu Obwodowego ZPP w Dżałał-Abadzie za kwiecień 1944').

113 Freda Walzman, VHA interview.

114 Frania Oberklaid, VHA interview.

115 AAN, 2/130/0/-/80, 'Położenie ludności polskiej i działalność ZPP w obwodzie Czkałow: Sprawozdania, protokoły, rezolucje, korespondencja zarządu obwodowego i zarządów lokalnych, 1944–1946': 'Sprawozdanie' (20 Apr. 1945); 2/130/0/-/174, 'Położenie ludności polskiej i działalność ZPP w Turkiestanie: Sprawozdania, protokoły, rezolucje, korespondencja zarządu międzyrejonowego i zarządów lokalnych, zaświadczenia', 1945–6': 'Sprawozdanie' (n.d.); 2/130/0/-/172, 'Położenie ludności polskiej i działalność ZPP w obwodzie Taszkient: Sprawozdania, protokoły, rezolucje, korespondencja zarządu obwodowego i zarządów lokalnych, zaświadczenia', 1944–6': 'Wstrząsająca tragedja żydostwa polskiego' (n.d.).

116 See K. Steffen, *Jüdische Polonität: Ethnizität und Nation im Spiegel der polnischsprachigen jüdischen Presse 1918–1939* (Göttingen, 2004).

117 See Adler, *Survival on the Margins*, 282.

118 Aleksiun, 'A Familial Turn in Holocaust Scholarship?'

119 Frania Oberklaid, VHA interview.

Voices of Soviet Jewish Children Documenting the Second World War

ANNA SHTERNSHIS

> The material collected in 1945 by the ethnomusicologist Moisey Beregovsky (1892–1961) and his team from the Folklore Section of the Department for the Study of Jewish Culture at the Ukrainian Academy of Science in Kyiv provides a poignant account of the sufferings of children in Romanian-occupied Transnistria during the Second World War. They are not primarily survivor accounts but rather Yiddish-language songs, stories, jokes, and folklore that circulated during the war. In all, the team interviewed hundreds of survivors, and collected 263 original songs. At least one-third of those they interviewed were under 18 in 1945. The project was believed to be lost, but was rediscovered in 1990 in the basement of the Ukrainian National Library in Kyiv. One part of the collection concerns children and adolescents who survived in the Bershad ghetto in the Vinnitsa region, which was one of the largest in the area, and some of whose survivors could still be interviewed in the 1990s. In all, twenty-six songs from this ghetto have been preserved.

ON 20 AUGUST 1945 the ethnomusicologist Moisey Beregovsky (1892–1961) arrived in Bratslav, a small town in the Vinnitsa region of south-western Ukraine. He and his team from the Folklore Section of the Department for the Study of Jewish Culture at the Ukrainian Academy of Science in Kyiv were seeking survivors of the Nazi occupation. This was part of a series of folkloric expeditions Beregovsky and his team undertook; however, their goal was not specifically to document survivors' stories but to collect and publish Yiddish-language songs, stories, jokes, and folklore that had circulated during the war. In Bratslav, they met a 10-year-old girl who sang a song she had learned in Pechora, a nearby Romanian-run concentration camp. The simple lyrics sung by the child moved the collectors to tears.

> *My Mother's Grave*
>
> I leave behind my mother's grave.
> 'Mama, I won't return to you again.
> 'Oh mama, who will wake me up?
> 'Oh mama, who will tuck me in?'
>
> 'The morning star will wake you.
> 'The rainbow will cover you.
> 'I roam around, like the sheep in the field.
> 'Yet I can never arrive at any shore.'
>
> I never saw my mother again.
> They drove her to [her death]; to the other side.

But the bitter suffering will soon come to an end.
The enemy will be surrounded and defeated.[1]

The song evokes the deep sadness and horrific experiences of Jewish children orphaned during the war in the part of eastern Europe under Romanian occupation. In September 1940 a right-wing military government seized power in Romania and shortly afterwards allied itself with Adolf Hitler's Germany. The following June the Romanian regime joined in fully in the German invasion of the Soviet Union, taking Bessarabia and northern Bukovina in present-day Ukraine and occupying a region of Ukraine between the Dniester and the Southern Bug, a region dubbed Transnistria. Between 250,000 and 300,000 Jews were killed during the occupation, and between 130,000 and 150,000 survived.[2]

Beregovsky had led the Folklore Section since 1936. A graduate of both the Kyiv and Petrograd conservatories, he obtained his doctorate in music from the Moscow State Tchaikovsky Conservatory in 1944, with the first dissertation in the world to be fully devoted to Jewish instrumental folk music.

Along with his colleagues—linguist Ruvim Lerner, folklorists Hine Shargorodskaya and Ida Shaykes, and poet Sholem Kupershmidt—he went to Pechora, Bershad, Shargorod, Bratslav, Tulchin, Zhabokrich, Vinnitsa, Chernovitz, and several other towns in Ukraine. They interviewed hundreds of survivors, producing pages of ethnographic notes, including their names, ages, and where they had survived the war. They recorded 263 original songs, and asked the participants to write down the words of some of them.[3] The audio recordings, professional transcripts, and participants' handwritten materials constitute an extremely rare collection of the direct voices of Jews who survived the Holocaust in Transnistria. At least one-third of the interviewees were under the age of 18.

Until 1990 Beregovsky's project was believed lost, because the materials were confiscated following his arrest in 1950 and were never returned to him or to the Ukrainian Academy of Science.[4] They were stored initially in the KGB archive and then quietly transferred to the restricted access section of the Ukrainian National Library. They were rediscovered in 1990, when all the restricted Yiddish-language collections in the basement of the library were transferred to the newly created Institute for the Study of the Orient, soon renamed the Judaica Department.[5] Lyudmila Sholokhova published the first partial catalogue with some of these documents in 2001.[6]

The Beregovsky collection is the only large deposit to contain notes and recordings of folk poetry and music documenting Jewish experiences in the Soviet Union during the Second World War.[7] Sources of similar magnitude exist for the Warsaw ghetto, thanks to the work of Emanuel Ringelblum,[8] the Vilna ghetto, thanks to Shmerke Katcherginsky, the Łódź ghetto, and some other places.[9] Beregovsky's collection has not yet been discussed in the context of the history of the Holocaust in the Soviet Union, and this chapter is a first attempt to introduce these materials as crucial historical sources for the Holocaust in Transnistria.[10]

I focus mainly on children and young adults who survived the Bershad ghetto, south of the town where Beregovsky recorded the 10-year-old girl. I chose Bershad for three reasons. First, it was one of the largest ghettos in Transnistria, and it existed for over two and a half years, from September 1941 to April 1944. Second, the youngest of its 2,000 survivors, who lived into the 1990s, were able either to write their memoirs or to be interviewed about their experiences, which provides context for the songs. Third, Beregovsky and his colleagues recorded twenty-six songs in Bershad, and there is therefore a variety of examples of Yiddish music that can be both dated and placed, providing an opportunity to investigate which historical events the songs reflected or commemorated.

Before the war Bershad had a Jewish majority. According to the Soviet census of 1939, 73 per cent of the population was Jewish: 4,271 residents.[11] Axis forces occupied the town on 29 July 1941, five weeks after Germany invaded the USSR. During the intervening weeks, some Jews managed to escape eastwards, and men eligible for military service were drafted into the Red Army. Approximately 2,500 Jews remained. In September 1941 Romanian authorities took over the town's administration and established a Jewish ghetto, which encompassed 337 houses.[12] The ghetto was not fenced in, but leaving the area was punishable by death. The Jewish population grew as a result of deportations from other places: in October and November 1941 around 15,000 Jews from the Romanian regions of Bessarabia and Bukovina were forced into the ghetto; in December 1941 they were joined by several thousand Jews from Berezovca Județ county, including around 1,500 from Balta (although about 500 of them were soon returned) and around 500 from the village of Peschanaia. Gradually, the Bershad ghetto became one of the largest in Transnistria. By autumn 1941 25,000 people were living there.[13]

Approximately 3,000 Jews died from overwork, lack of food, and cold, and were buried in mass graves by Romanian and German troops in the weeks before the Soviet Army reached Bershad on 14 March 1944.[14] On that day 9,200 ghetto inmates remained alive, including 2,200 local Jews. Some of the survivors returned to Romania, others stayed in Bershad, others were drafted into the Red Army. Many people searched desperately for living relatives, and most were confronted with the news that their relatives were dead. The year between Bershad's liberation and the end of the war was filled with the joy of survival, grief over agonizing loss, recovery from illness, and learning how to deal with the Soviet authorities. It was during this period that Moisey Beregovsky and his team of researchers arrived in search of survivors and their Yiddish songs.

Beregovsky and two members of his team reached Bershad on 7 August 1945, and stayed until 15 August. 'Local Jews were not sent away, a few people were sent to Nikolaev to build bridges', he wrote in his notes.[15] During the week the delegation met twenty people and collected thirty-six songs. Twenty-three pieces were recorded with a phonograph, the rest by hand, with musical notation where possible.

Little is known about the singers, except for their names and ages and the fact that most of them probably lived in Bershad prior to the war, as, immediately after liberation, Bessarabians and Bukovinians were allowed to leave Ukraine, and most of them went to Romania, whereas Soviet citizens stayed in Bershad.[16] However, the songs that they sang probably circulated among all ghetto residents, not just Soviet-born ones.

Of the informants, seven were 18 or younger, all of them in school: 18-year-old Genya Soyfer; 17-year-old Sonya Reyber, Shmerl Guber, and Zunye Shtindler; 16-year-old Yosif Vartshak and Shmuel Korman; and 15-year-old Lyonya Shikhtman. Together, they contributed nineteen songs, most of which referred in one way or another to life under occupation. One of the most prolific singers was Genya Soyfer, who performed seven songs in Yiddish and one in Russian. Six of her songs directly depicted the wartime experience. The seventh, 'Falik the Partisan', probably dated to the Russian civil war but still resonated with the times, as it told of a brave Jewish man who became a partisan and was killed.[17] Beregovsky's team recorded three of Soyfer's songs. She can be heard performing them in a deep contralto voice. She sounds experienced: she carries the tune confidently and never stumbles over the words. She had learned the songs, some of which she dated to 1942 or 1943, in the ghetto, and continued performing them after liberation. It was not unusual for informants to remember the year when they first heard a song, sometimes linking it to an event in the ghetto.[18]

Music historians have established that during the Holocaust music served several functions. It provided relief, comfort, and entertainment; it helped people to grieve; and it created ways to remember appalling losses, including the death of loved ones.[19] Above all, the songs provide insights into what their audience found entertaining and worthy of remembering, and sometimes of sharing with others: insights that are hard to obtain from later oral testimonies or memoirs. In this chapter, I argue that in addition to such functions, the songs performed by Jewish children in Transnistria can serve as windows onto how young people made sense of the war as it was unfolding, and how they used music to document the atrocities they witnessed. Where possible, I compare the songs with the later testimonies of child survivors from the same places. I base most of my discussion on the lyrics, although I occasionally also bring the melodies into consideration.

Avrom-Itsye and His Wagon: Singing the Daily Deaths

In the Bershad ghetto, people lived under the constant threat of death from hunger, disease, and the brutality of the Romanian guards. Because of the lack of suitable housing and heating, the cold brought sickness, and sickness brought death. Zinaida Lubman remembered that every morning started with a horse and buggy collecting bodies and taking them to a place where men would grab legs, arms, and hair and dump them into open pits.[20] Between 1941 and 1944 more than 13,000 ghetto residents died of starvation or typhus.[21] By August 1942 only 10,000 people remained, with 150 to 200 people dying daily during that winter, mostly from typhus. Everyone was scared of Romanian Jews because 'they brought typhus and tuberculosis to the ghetto', Frida Muchnik recalled.[22] Miriam Valdman, from Bessarabia, concurred. Relations between local and foreign Jews were strained, because the locals blamed foreign Jews for bringing sickness and lice with them.[23]

Zinaida Lubman recalled the arrival of Jews from Bukovina, Romania, and Bessarabia:

They were called 'refugees', they were half-alive, half of them were shot on the way there. They were naked, shoeless, and it was winter, during the worst frost, snow. They were not fed on the way, they were dying. Bershad was a small town, it was impossible to accommodate so many people comfortably. The typhus epidemic began too. Refugees were settled in collective farms' barns, no windows, doors, ceilings. People were dying under the open sky and in empty houses.[24]

One song by Genya Soyfer, written by Bershad ghetto inmate Boris Zitserman, described conditions in the ghetto as they appeared to people who just arrived there. The song, titled by Beregovsky 'In Obodivker Camp', was set to the satirical, cheerful tune of a pre-war folk song 'Dzhankoy', one of the most famous Yiddish folk songs ever written. It described the happy life on a Soviet Jewish *kolkhoz* (collective farm) at Dzhankoy in Crimea, where Jews defied the stereotype of being incapable of hard physical work. 'In Obodivker Camp' tells what happened to these Jewish *kolkhozy* after the German invasion.

In Obodivker Camp

If you travel to Balanivke,
It's not far from Obodivke,
There's a dear camp there.

Jews serve time there, day and night,
Without drinking or eating.
Hitler, the thief, says:
That's how it has to be.

And the corpses lie and rot
And you begin to shudder,
And why does a Jew suffer like this?

Avrom-Itsye sits in the wagon.
It breaks his heart to say it aloud;
He's already making his sixth trip today.

The administration ordered him
To deal with all the corpses,
And his hair's standing on end with 'joy'.

In the *kolkhoz* there in a corner,
A girl dies, oy, of hunger
And here they play a round of poker.

> And the Bershad cemetery
> Accepts into the world to come
> As many people as there are.
>
> Oh, woe, misery, misery,
> Jews are good for nothing;
> They're waiting for the lucky day.[25]

In his short memoir about the Bershad ghetto, survivor Naum Kerpilevich noted that he could recite 'In Obodivker Camp' in Russian. He explained that Avrom-Itsye was the owner of a thin horse and a wagon. Every morning, he started his day by riding around the ghetto collecting bodies, and then dumping them outside the ghetto's iron gates that the guards would open for him.[26] Another Bershad survivor, Matvei Geyzer, in an interview with *Russkii Bazar*, mentioned that people called the horse a 'shvartser mes' (black corpse). He remembered that Avrom-Itsye was a deportee from Edintsy in Romania and had once worked as a professional cab driver. 'According to rumour the entire road from Edintsy to Bershad was the burial place of his children, parents, and relatives, all of whom died on the way.' Geyzer confirmed that Boris Zitserman wrote the song, saying 'I still get chills from his words.'[27] It is hard to say whether Geyzer, who was 4 years old at the time of the liberation, would have remembered Avrom-Itsye and his horse if not for Zitserman's composition.

Like many songs from Bershad and other parts of Transnistria, 'In Obodivker Camp' documents atrocities in specific detail. 'Jews serve time ... without eating or drinking'; 'corpses lie and rot'; 'a girl dies ... of hunger' in a corner where men play poker, an image that also hints at sexual violence: maybe the girl is discarded in the corner, or maybe men gambled for her, or maybe she suffered some other abuse. To Avrom-Itsye's horror, the cemetery is the liveliest place in Bershad. The song paints a picture of devastation and hopelessness, and the loss of self-worth that so many people experienced.

In contrast, the words are set to the humorous, fast-paced tune of 'Dzhankoy', making 'In Obodivker Camp' almost impossible to sing with sadness, underscoring the satire. The emphasis falls on 'lagerl' (dear camp), 'Gitler-ganev' (Hitler, the thief), 'zekstn tur' (sixth trip), and the slightly vulgar expression 'toygn yidn af kapores' (Jews are good for nothing). It is not clear whether people laughed as well as cried when they listened to the song. Maybe laughter came from recognizing the tune and hearing different content, thus heightening the parody. Maybe laughter came from a sense of relief that one could still sing about something unbearable. Or maybe people did not laugh at all but found the tragedy expressed in the piece bearable only because of the cheerful tune.

The Jewish Ghetto Leadership and Relations between Local Inmates and Refugees

The Jewish council in Bershad, popularly known as the *obshchina*, was established in September 1941. Shoykhet Eli Marchak, a resident of Łódź who moved to Bershad shortly before the war, became the head of the *obshchina*.²⁸ Soon after he assumed the post, the Jewish inmates organized a small bakery in the building of the synagogue.

From October 1941, when refugees from Bessarabia and Bukovina began to arrive, Marchak appealed to the Romanian authorities to accept money from the Romanian Jews to allow them to stay in Bershad.²⁹ The *obshchina* expanded to include Romanian Jews, who had had positions of power before the war and knew how to communicate with the Romanian authorities. They included M. Farfel, I. Perlmuter, lawyer Mikhael Shrentsl, Dr Fleyshman, and locals Gedaliya Shulman, V. Dolgonos, and I. Sobelman. Marchak remained the leader. The first actions of the *obshchina* were to establish a ghetto police and a Jewish labour committee, headed by Benjamin Korse.³⁰

The Romanian authorities used Jews for forced labour: to collect firewood, build roads, and manufacture clothing, with the *obshchina* in charge of recruiting and delivering workers. Children as young as 8 were forced to work, if they were deemed strong enough. Jews felled trees and cleaned streets, were employed in workshops and factories (producing furniture, sugar, and electrical goods, and canning), or had duties inside the ghetto (at the pharmacy, town hall, hospital, school, and orphanage). Others were unemployed due to a shortage of work and the necessary tools. In return for their labour most received little or no compensation, and were therefore forced to barter for food or to work for Ukrainian peasants, exposing themselves to the risk of being shot if caught outside the ghetto.³¹

Inside the ghetto, a balance had to be found between working in order to eat and avoiding strenuous work in order to survive. One of the most popular songs of the Bershad ghetto that addressed these challenges was called 'In the Cold Days'. It commented on working conditions, attitudes towards the ghetto's leadership, and other aspects of life in the ghetto. Also written by Zitserman, it tells the chilling story of a Bershad resident who was deported to Balta and Savran, and both times managed to escape back to Bershad. Beregovsky recorded it from two different teenagers, including Genya Soyfer, who did not seem to know the author of the song but remembered almost all of its verses:

> *In the Cold Days*
>
> In the cold days,
> I was taken to Balta.
> I made my escape from there,
> And found my way back home.
>
> As soon as I got here,
> The *plutonier* caught me.
> I spun around this way and that,
> And a gendarme caught me.
>
> My tools were taken away,
> And I was sent to Savran.
> I escaped from there anyway,
> And was found back home.

> I hear knocking at my door:
> There are four police.
> I sneak out of my bed in secret,
> Filled with fright.
>
> Secretary Perlmuter
> Screams: 'People, bribe me!'
> Vilnits is proud of himself.
> He shares profits with the *pretor*
>
> Snub-nosed Perlmuter
> Carries a bucket of water in Balta.
> He took bribes,
> So he has been sent to Balta.[32]

According to his son, Efim Alexandrov-Zitserman, Boris Zitserman grew up in Bershad. The song was based on his personal experience of deportation, escape, and return to Bershad, which had by then become a ghetto.[33]

The song also probably refers to an episode at the end of 1942, when 500 Bershad Jews were moved to Savran to ease overcrowding. By then, most Savran Jews had either been deported to the nearby Obodivker camp or killed. Savran was a village in the Transnistria region near Odessa, where a camp for Jews from Bessarabia and Bukovina operated between 1942 and 1944. Alternatively, the song might refer to the events of September 1943, when Romanian authorities from Savran arrived in Bershad to recruit skilled workers for their workshops.[34] The song mentions tools, which provides a clue, but it is not clear why the person had to run away again. Given that Savran was located in Golta district, known for having the worst conditions in Transnistria, with the shortest life expectancy for prisoners and harshest work conditions, it is no wonder that people tried to run away.[35] Most people sent to Savran in 1943, if they survived, remained there until the Red Army liberated the camp on 24 April 1944. Another possibility is that the song refers to an episode in which sixty to seventy children were moved to an orphanage in Balta in late November 1942.[36] Genya Soyfer mentioned that she first heard the song in 1942, but it is possible that some verses were changed or added later. Without a doubt, however, any Bershad ghetto audience would have understood the references to Balta and Savran.

Similarly, such an audience would have recognized and probably laughed at the descriptions of the guards, the Romanian authorities, the ghetto's leadership, and even the character's loss of his tools (having tools could mean a less strenuous work assignment). Members of the Romanian police and other authorities are referred to by their titles—gendarme, *pretor* (a judicial and administrative police functionary), and *plutonier* (chief gendarme)—whereas members of the Jewish leadership are presented by their last names. The song emphasizes the difficult relationship between the ghetto leadership and other Jews, accusing Perlmuter, for example, of bribery and shady dealings with the Romanian authorities and wishing him ill. In fact, emotionally the strongest, funniest, and most sarcastic parts of the song, including the wish for revenge, are not directed at the Romanian guards but at Jews in positions of power. In her study of post-war trials of Jewish leaders of Transnistrian ghettos, historian Diana Dumitru showed that numerous Soviet trial testimonies declared that bribes were paid to avoid dangerous work assignments or deportations to the east.[37] It is the betrayal of 'their own' rather than the invaders that seemed to offend the most, and the song emphasizes that emotion.

The Bershad ghetto audience could relate to the ordeals of the protagonist. People could laugh bitterly at the bribing incidents and laugh wholeheartedly at 'snub-nosed Perlmuter'. As they listened to the song, they could take pleasure in being able to look at their own troubles from a distance. It is a local and contextualized story, something that mattered and might be funny there and then, without the full knowledge of what was happening to Jews in other ghettos. Today the song provides scholars with insight into a sentiment that is almost entirely absent from later testimonies. Interviews recorded decades afterwards discuss bribery and collaboration but rarely mention the names of the guilty. In contrast, in many of these songs the names are central.

This song seemed to have been popular in Bershad. The day after recording Genya Soyfer's version, Beregovsky met Shmuel Korman, who sang a longer version with a few extra verses at the beginning and the end. It began with the following lines:

> From the Dniester to the Bug,
> They drive Jews and they beat them.
> *Refrain*
> Ay, ay, ay, ay, ay, ay, ay.
>
> The *obshchina* sits and thinks
> About whom to take tonight.
> *Refrain*
>
> As soon as I heard they were coming for me,
> I left through the back door.
> *Refrain*[38]

These verses take accusations against Jewish community leaders to a new level. They are the ones responsible for deportations, rather than the nameless 'they', the Nazis, of the first verse. The *obshchina* is seen as something artificial and ultimately negative, and thus subjected to condemning ridicule. The extra verses at the end of the song also heap ridicule on community leaders:

> Snub-nosed Perlmuter
> Is carrying pails of water in Balta.
> Grishe Baytlman, for fear,
> Is carrying pails of filth in Balta.
> And the Balta colonel
> Is flaying Zinkuzan.
> Meyer Kovel with the fat belly
> Doesn't want thick broth anymore.[39]

Grigori Baytlman from Bukovina was a member of the *obshchina* leadership. Beregovsky's notes refer to Zinkuzan as the commandant of the Bershad ghetto and Meyer Kovel as a community member who traded currency. These men were mercilessly ridiculed, probably to the complete delight of listeners who suffered from their abuses. I think, however, that these last two verses made the song too specific for anyone not from Bershad. Genya Soyfer's version would have been the more popular, with its more generic escapes, difficult living conditions, black market economy, and desire for revenge.

According to historian Faina Vinokurova, the Jewish community leadership in the ghetto helped organize certain institutions of mutual support, including orphanages, hospitals, and several small industries.[40] Some testimonies mention these organizations favourably. For example, in her interview for the University of Southern California Shoah Foundation, survivor Mina Schachter said that Bershad was considered better than other ghettos, such as Yampol, because there was a hospital there.[41] Diana Dumitru pointed out that when nominating ghetto leaders, the Romanians selected individuals who could keep the imprisoned community peaceful and obedient to the real rulers, the Romanians. Vadim Altskan emphasized that Romanian Jews most frequently represented ghetto populations because of their linguistic abilities, community leadership experience, adaptability, and entrepreneurial skills.[42]

Dumitru observed that, immediately after the war, Soviet-born survivors often spoke of the discrimination that they had suffered as a group at the hands of the ghetto leadership.[43] In their memoirs and interviews, some survivors, usually those born in Bershad, recalled the corruption of the *obshchina*. Frida Muchnik said her mother bribed Jewish officials to keep the police away from their house. Abram Mitsel remembered many acts of extortion by Jewish community leaders, who demanded jewellery in exchange for keeping people out of the labour camps.[44] Importantly, survivors from Bukovina often emphasized that the leaders of the ghetto helped them get out of hard work or obtain little perks, such as access to food packages or medicine.[45]

Testimonies also sometimes provide examples of mutual help between Romanian and Ukrainian Jews. For example, in her interview Lea Ishak (Katz), from Bukovina, mentioned that Ukrainian Jewish landlords, the Ledermans, treated her family as their own. They had a son and a daughter who treated them very kindly: the boy gave them some food. Lea explained that the Lederman family were originally from Bershad, and therefore had more food and property.[46]

In the songs, such co-operation and support are entirely absent. Even more lighthearted pieces focus on ridicule rather than support of others. For example, on 8 August 1945, Shmuel Korman performed a song he called 'At the Jewish Market', which also ridiculed Bessarabian Jews, even in the context of the starvation that was occurring in Bershad:

> *At the Jewish Market*
> Pinkhes runs with the chickens,
> Reb Yokl Kop with the potato cakes.

Tsipe runs like mad,
With the sour cream in a pot,

Refrain
And the *shompol*'s ready to jump,
So that bones resound,
So that people remember this forever and ever.

Yukl with the sliced meat,
Fayvish with the fat.
Yosl runs with the candies,
Moyshe with the salt.

Refrain

Two women from Savran run,
And they beat and grab each other:
One of them has
Stolen a customer from the other.

Refrain

The Bessarabian thieves, oy,
Seize the moment—
Here comes trouble!—they shove
Their hands into their pockets.

Refrain[47]

The song is similar to others that circulated in the ghettos of Vilna, Łódź, Warsaw, and elsewhere where food was precious.[48] What locates the song is the mentioning of Savran, where most prisoners died from starvation and disease. The *shompol* mentioned in the refrain was a long metal rod for cleaning guns that the Romanian gendarmes would use to beat Jews. So the ridicule of starving Bessarabian Jews fighting for a piece of food at the market turns into a condemnation of the guards.

When it comes to describing the relationship between the *obshchina* and the ghetto residents or Romanian and Ukrainian Jews, both songs and testimonies speak of tensions, disagreement, and bitterness. However, testimonies and memoirs were usually created decades later with the goal of leaving a legacy for the future, so some of the tensions are downplayed or omitted entirely. In contrast, the songs were created at the time of the events they depict, and were intended to entertain people who were suffering from corrupt officials and intra-group tensions. Possibly they were also written for revenge—a person might have been unhappy about a work assignment or an insult—thus a song. The difference in purpose leads to different content: testimonies need to tell a more general story, whereas a song loses its edge if it does not describe a specific offender. Songs circulating among teenagers contain rage, anger, and other emotions that they experienced as they lived through imprisonment. Surprisingly, they contain almost nothing about the loss of the past but everything about fixing the present.

Sexual Violence

Sexual violence and the threat of it were constant. In Bershad, Frida Muchnik recalled that girls were 'abused in a beastly manner'.[49] She survived because her mother hid her in the basement of the house where they lived. As far as the ghetto officials were concerned, Frida never existed. Sofya Degtyareva wrote in her short memoir that, after her mother died from starvation in Bershad, she and a few other girls were forced to publicly undress and dance naked in the streets: 'Once Germans made us go into the river, and stole our clothes.'[50] Another survivor, Mikhail Portnoy, wrote that he could still see the faces of the Jewish girls he saw publicly raped and then killed.[51] Raia Kuperstein remembered soldiers taking women and girls for 'labour', usually a code for rape. In such cases, the women were not killed, and they told other women of the abuse.[52] For reasons that still need to be explored, these themes are barely present in the songs by young people recorded in Bershad. However, a song from Genya Soyfer's repertoire, 'The Sun Sets in Transnistria', which was probably addressed to a non-Jewish audience, deals with an aspect of sexual violence. The only Russian-language song in her repertoire, set to the tune of the popular Soviet song 'Spyat kurgany temnye', it calls for women to 'be patient' and not 'go out' with the enemy:

The Sun Sets in Transnistria

The sun sets in Transnistria.
The field is warm.
The sun above Transnistria
Will also set.

Dear girls,
Do not lose patience.
The Reds will still come.
Peace will come.

Do not walk with Germans.
Germans are not good.
They are all cursed.
They are drinking your blood.

But on Russian lands,
Under the hammer and sickle,
Our brothers, our sisters
Are spilling their blood.[53]

The song, not unusually, blames the women for promiscuity rather than condemning the German soldiers for sexual violence. Choosing German rather than the less familiar Romanian soldiers to condemn probably meant hope for a larger, more general audience, not only those familiar with the realities of Bershad. But what is unusual is that this piece elaborates on the war and on the fact that soldiers of the Red Army were 'our' brothers and sisters. It is Soyfer's only piece articulating solidarity between Jews and non-Jews, and it acknowledges that the Jews of Transnistria were in fact Soviet citizens, a theme that once again is almost absent from the songs collected from children in Bershad. I think it comes up in the context of condemning collaboration only to emphasize the resilience and bravery of Jews, something that seemed to matter to all the young singers in Bershad.

Fighting with Guns and with Words: Anger and Resistance

Two main resistance groups operated in the Bershad ghetto: one led by Lev Voskoboynikov (eighty-four members), the other by Iosif Binder (forty-five members). Binder's group contacted a partisan detachment commanded by Iakov Talis that was based in the Bershad area. Talis was a Red Army officer who managed to escape from a POW camp and settled in the Bershad ghetto in 1941. The groups kept in close touch with the Soviet partisans working in the area, supplying them with money, medicine, and clothes. Sometimes, partisans also found shelter in the ghetto. Binder and Talis were supported by Mikhael Shrentsl, who helped to transfer some of the food and medication that arrived in Bershad from the Bucharest Jewish community to the partisans.[54] In retaliation for helping the partisans, Romanian gendarmes shot 173 Jews on 11 February 1944, and 154 more on 11 March. Among the victims were Eli Marchak and Iosif Binder.[55] Shrentsl was publicly tortured and eventually killed.[56]

Songs addressed resistance with extreme specificity but did not mention any of these episodes. Instead, Genya Soyfer performed for Beregovsky a piece called 'Moyshe, the Polish Jew', written by Boris Zitserman and Peysi Liberman. The piece was also performed by Ida Liberman, which is suggestive of its popularity. Its message, however, is the opposite of 'In the Cold Days' and 'At the Jewish Market'. Instead of condemning the ghetto leadership of Bershad or the Bessarabian marketgoers, the song praises ghetto resistance, including co-operation with partisans.

The song probably refers to an episode that took place in the summer of 1943, when Jewish partisans, in co-operation with a resistance group in the ghetto led by Efim Lebedev, helped 900 Jews escape from a labour camp in the village of Slivino near Nikolaev, where they had been building a bridge.[57] In the aftermath of this action, seventeen members of Efim Lebedev's group were arrested and shot.[58]

Moyshe, the Polish Jew
Once at two in the morning,
When Slivino camp was locked up,
All around a dead silence,
The night full of gloom.
Liber and Moyshe, the Polish Jew,
Went up to the Don Cossack.
They told the watchman quietly,
they'd give him whatever he wanted,
as long as the two of them
could get across the barbed wire

>   And escape from the terror and suffering
>   And no longer be held captive.
>   'Come on over here, Jews,
>   'When you hear a shot from my gun.
>   'Come over as fast as you can.'
>   Once at two in the morning,
>   When Slivino camp was locked up,
>   Over to the Jews' barracks, oy,
>   Came the Don Cossack.
>   'Oy, come on over here, Jews,
>   'When you hear the shot from my gun.
>   'Oy, come on over here, Jews,
>   Because your time to live is over.'
>   The night was dark,
>   The Jews' barracks stood there,
>   And outside on the black earth
>   Lay bodies killed by gunfire.
>   Once at two in the morning,
>   When Slivino camp was locked up,
>   The night full of gloom,
>   Liber and Moyshe the Polish Jew
>   Were no longer in the Jews' barracks.[59]

Among the Jewish prisoners of Transnistria, Nikolaev was feared, and for good reason. Unlike Bershad, it was under German occupation. The rumours circulated that after a week or two German guards simply shot workers to make room for new ones. The song combines the structure of a folk ballad with the content of a historical chronicle. Unlike 'In the Cold Days', the song does not name villains or mention Romanians or Germans. Instead, it refers to the guards as 'Don Cossacks', meaning soldiers of the Vlasov Army enlisted to guard such camps. The presence of Cossacks in the song harks back to pre-war Yiddish pogrom songs, in which Cossacks are condemned for killing Jews. But the location in 'Slivino camp' and the slim possibility of escaping alive ultimately locate the song in 1943.

Although the song's characters are named, I was unable to establish which historical figures they were based on (although Liber was probably related to Ida Liberman). The song starts with an exact time of night, but no date is given, suggesting that it probably fills the gaps left by lack of knowledge of some facts with imagination. The song's ending, both tragic and romantic, celebrates heroism and laments that in the labour camp only death frees a person from slavery. One can see why the song appealed to teenagers: it has just the right mixture of romanticism, bravery, anger, and inspiration. Above all, it sings of resilience: something that young people truly needed in Bershad.

'Trees Blaze and It Wails and It Burns', another song that Genya Soyfer performed, picks up on notions of collective fate and hopelessness and also introduces the theme of anger against God (not just against Romanians, Germans, Cossacks, and the

Jewish leadership). Beregovsky recorded five versions of this composition during his field trip, three of them in Bershad (by Soyfer, Shmerl Guber, and Zunye Shtindler).

Trees Blaze and It Wails and It Burns

Trees blaze and it wails and it burns.
Jewish victims fall from murderous hands.
> *Refrain*
> *Re'ey adoynoy* [See, Lord!]

Why do they beat us so?
Where is your mercy, God?
> *Refrain*

Little tiny children [ripped] from their mother's breast.
They beat them mercilessly; they throw them onto the garbage.
> *Refrain*

Little old men with grey beards,
They lie with their faces, oy, on the ground.
> *Refrain*

Little tiny children [ripped] from their mother's cradle.
They beat them mercilessly; they bear the name 'Jew'.
> *Refrain*

God take a look, a glance at your Jews.
Put an end to the slaughter and let it be enough.
> *Refrain*

God take a look, a glance at Ukraine.
Put an end to the slaughter and let it be enough.
> *Refrain*[60]

Other versions of the song have an additional two verses and a different refrain

On the roads from the *kolkhozy* and everywhere,
Jews lie around: no one knows where they perish.
> *Refrain*
> Oh woe, oh how can it be?
> Dear God, why don't you respond to the people?
> Have mercy already, *re'ey adoynoy*
> Take a look from on high, a glance at your Jews,
> Put an end to the slaughter and let it be enough.

In the Jewish cemetery blows a harsh wind.
Jews lie around like dogs.
> *Refrain*[61]

This song depicts violence against Jews not specifically in Bershad but throughout Ukraine. Rather than focusing on a specific cemetery or village, it speaks of nameless *kolkhozy*, nameless Jewish bodies, and nameless murdered children. The song is addressed to God, with a lot of anger, accusing God of abandoning the Jews, withdrawing his compassion, and allowing senseless violence. The combination of a bitter conversation with God and the casual description of *kolkhozy*, the comparison of Jews to dogs, perhaps borrowed from Nazi imagery, and talk of victimized defenceless 'men with grey beards' and 'tiny babies' creates a chilling sense of all-encompassing rage and hopelessness. It combines a light-hearted pre-war tune and cantorial elements from Hebrew prayers in the refrain, parodying both as inadequate to address reality.

Given that this was one of the most popular songs recorded in 1945, although dated by informants to 1942, it is worth thinking about what made it both appealing and memorable. Maybe it was the context of continued victimization as their homeland, the USSR, turned against them after the war through the discriminatory policies of the mid-1940s towards Jews, or a sense of God punishing innocent people and a loss of hope for the future. Written in 1942, the most difficult year of the Bershad ghetto, when so many people died and the hope of liberation by the Red Army was slim, addressing God seemed like the only, desperate, option. The song was, I think, one of the first pieces designed as a commemorative prayer for those Bershad ghetto inmates who never lived to see liberation. But as far as I know, this song has never been performed in public.

One striking absence from the repertoire of Bershad teenagers is any mention of war between Germany and the Soviet Union. In most songs, the war seems to be exclusively against Jews rather than against Soviet citizens more generally, probably because they had so little information about what was going on in other places. Only one song includes a reference to the Red Army. It was recorded under the name 'The Jewish Song'.

> *The Jewish Song*
> Once we Jews used to live during the best times.
> We did not know any exploitation.
> Germans came with their long guns,
> And our lives became cursed.
>
> > *Refrain*
> > Oy, oy, oy, dear Jews,
> > Sing a little song
> > Of our lives.
>
> Once Jews did not know about camps,
> Never saw any ghettos.
> But the Germans came with their long guns,
> And the crying began.
>
> > *Refrain*
>
> Take Nikolaev, take Varvarovke,
> Women in Tulchin.

> We are jealous of the dead.
> We hope for the Reds.
> They should come and help.
>
> *Refrain*[62]

The song's geographical scope is wider than usual: it includes Nikolaev, with its ghetto and labour camp, on the Southern Bug. The song also mentions Varvarovka, a village in the Nikolaev region and home to a labour camp where Jews lived in cowsheds and worked on roads, ports, and bridges. Few people survived the labour and living conditions of Varvarovka, especially those who worked on the port in Nikolaev.[63] In the Tulchin ghetto, created on 1 September 1941, north-west of Bershad, only women were allowed to leave its limits, but if they did and went to the market, they were also disproportionately punished or killed. On 7 December 1941 all the Jews of Tulchin were forced to move into one building, a former Jewish school, and the next day eighty of them committed suicide. Five days later, on 12 December, more than 3,000 Jews were deported to Pechora, where most of them perished.[64] The song hints at the story by emphasizing the voices of women and including the common trope of being 'jealous of the dead'.

At first glance, the abrupt ending of the song does not quite fit the grim storyline, but in fact it evokes 'the best times' before the exploitation expressed in the opening two lines. The last two lines are also the only ones that are filled with hope, and this hope is associated with the arrival of the Red Army. It is noteworthy too that although the expectation of liberation is high, the 'Reds' are not referred to as 'ours', as they are in Russian songs of the time, where the two words are used interchangeably. This usage never occurs in the Bershad repertoire of 1945. This is probably because the writers of the songs did not fully associate themselves with the Soviet Union, either because they had not been Soviet citizens before the war or because Soviet citizens were hostile to or ambivalent about them during the occupation.[65] Of course, this attitude would soon change when many of the former prisoners were drafted into the Red Army, days after liberation. This happened, for example, with Boris Zitserman, author of many of the songs discussed here. But at the time when liberation could only be anticipated, the Red Army did not seem to be theirs. Songs of the time are rare historical sources where this attitude can still be found.

Orphans

A children's home gave the orphans of Bershad a greater chance of survival than in many other parts of Transnistria. In autumn 1941 money sent by the Central Bureau of Romanian Jews was used to rent a four-room house, in which 122 children between the ages of 5 and 16 were placed. In spring 1942 the *obshchina* rented a room and housed an additional ten orphans who had been released from hospital after recovering from typhus. In addition, 135 children were placed with families. Another sixty to seventy children were moved to an orphanage in Balta in late November 1942. Teachers educated the orphaned children, and, as of the second half of 1943, a Jewish

Romanian school for all the ghetto children was in operation. In January 1943 the number of registered Jewish orphans in Bershad was 257, probably the highest of any ghetto in Transnistria.[66] In early March 1944 orphans younger than 15 were allowed to go to Romania, with the majority of them taking the opportunity.

Among the children sent to Balta and then to Romania was Batiyah Veysman, who lost her parents soon after the family arrived in Bershad. Kind people took her to a hospital. The doctor, named Doctor Weiner, a relative on her mother's side, did not recognize her at first. He gave her crutches because she was unable to stand on her own. At the hospital she was fed only once a day; when she was transferred to the orphanage, she got food three times a day. She remembers that they also tried to teach the children there.[67]

Not all ghetto orphans ended up in orphanages. Some supported themselves by begging.[68] No humiliation can compare to that of stretching out one's hand and asking for charity, one survivor explained.[69] Others wrote about the experience only briefly, if at all. Itzhak Shekhtman wrote one line about this aspect of his life in Bershad ghetto: 'Mother died, my three sisters and I stayed. Then I got sick with typhus. When the summer came, my sister and I were able to sneak out of the ghetto and beg there.'[70]

It seems that because the Bershad ghetto had an orphanage, fewer orphans had to rely on begging, and fewer beggars' songs were recorded there compared with other places, such as Pechora, where begging was often the only way to get by. Still, themes of orphanhood appear in some of the songs performed by young singers. For example, on 14 August 1945 Yosif Vartshak performed a lengthy song for Beregovsky called 'An Orphan'. Although it lacked any specific connection to Bershad, it addressed a subject that resonated with many people and probably led to donations for the performer. Here is a fragment:

> *An Orphan*
>
> The street is black with many people.
> A hearse is standing there.
> The old women shed many tears.
> The men stand sorrowfully silent.
> They've brought her out now,
> And they drive her away quickly,
> And after the hearse runs
> A child, crying...
>
> *Refrain*
> 'Oy, oy, oy, Mom come back
> 'For just one moment.
> 'Don't you hear my cry?
> 'I'm lonely as a stone.
> 'Oy, oy, oy Mom come back,
> 'Come, I want to see you,
> 'And if you can't come to me,
> 'Then take me to you.'[71]

The song goes on to tell of the father's second marriage, the wicked stepmother, and the ordeals of the orphan. Ironically, because the song does not talk about bodies in the street, starvation, and humiliation, it almost sounds benign, telling of the suffering of an orphaned child in pre-ghetto times.

Liberation

The Red Army liberated the Bershad ghetto on 14 March 1944. Survivors remember exactly what they were doing on that day. Frida Blyam recalls that she rejoiced the moment she heard Russian being spoken.[72] Suffering and hardship, however, did not end with liberation. Almost immediately, many survivors had to face news of dead family members. Matvei Geyzer wrote this poignant account:

When Bershad was liberated, people went to dig out the ditch where the Germans dumped the shot bodies. There was a horrible scream: people argued over the dead. Not everyone could recognize 'theirs'. It was wet, damp, and windy. I still remember that wind and that Jewish moan. People who are alive are fighting, because they are deciding whose dead relative it is. But we recognized our uncle David immediately. He was shot the night when all the partisans were shot.[73]

Naum Kerpilevich remembers that German POWs were ordered to dig out the bodies. His father was also found among those in the ditches.[74]

Some survivors remember that immediately after liberation they started to walk home. Klara Lubarskaya recalled that on 15 March 1944 she and her family members walked all the way to their native village of Soroki in Bessarabia.[75] Similarly, Fanya Portnaya and her mother set out for their home in Zguritsa. But because Zguritsa was 128 kilometres west of Bershad, the family relied on help from Red Army soldiers, who, for the modest fee of home-made vodka, gave them rides part of the way.[76]

Only one song performed for Beregovsky's team by the young people of Bershad ghetto spoke of liberation, that of Zunye Shtindler.

I'm Going Back Home

> *Refrain*
> I'm going back home,
> Because I'm not used to this.
> Home, home, back home.
> I'm leaving you behind the joys of Bershad.
> I'm a guy from Bessarabia.
> I'm going home to my own land.
>
> At home, I wore shoes and galoshes;
> I came here, and I'm dying for a penny.
>
> *Refrain*

> At home I rode on a white horse;
> I came here, and we're lying six feet under.
>
>> *Refrain*
>
> At home I had a bakery;
> I came here, and we're lying in a pigsty.
>
>> *Refrain*
>
> At home at my mother's, I was the handsomest;
> we came here, and we're lying in a cowshed without windows.
>
>> *Refrain*
>
> At home, we rode in a horse-drawn carriage;
> I came here, and they've ruined me.
>
>> *Refrain*
>
> At home, I lay in a nickel bed;
> we came here, and my wife divorced me.
>
>> *Refrain*[77]

The joy and relief are understated, the anger explicit. The nostalgia for pre-war life in Bessarabia in this song is almost palpable: references to bakeries, white horses and carriages, and metal beds plated with nickel to prevent corrosion: all these things seemed like luxuries in the Soviet Union and were simply unobtainable in the ghetto. Unlike later testimonies, the song does not mention the Red Army or the Soviet Union and does not name a specific home town or village in Bessarabia. Home seems to be anywhere but Bershad.

Conclusion

The songs Beregovsky and his team recorded in Bershad in 1945 reveal almost nothing about the performers' life experiences, where they lived or worked. They might have been deportees from Bessarabia or Bukovina, or natives of Bershad. They might have been orphans, half-orphans, or living with both parents. They might have known Perlmuter and Avrom-Itsye personally or never met either of them. Similarly, there is little knowledge to be gleaned about the life of Boris Zitserman, the 15-year-old poet who wrote many of the songs.

The Bershad musical archive, however, brings to life the actual voices and language of the young Jewish survivors in 1945. The songs provide an authentic, concise narrative of the tragedy of Jewish life during the war as perceived by the ghetto's youngest prisoners. They tell of cold weather, rampant disease, and crowded living conditions. They speak of the deportation of Jews from Bessarabia, Bukovina, and all over Transnistria, the corruption of the ghetto leadership, the dreams of resistance, the anger against God, the praise for Jewish heroes, the condemnation of collaborators, and the calls for commemoration of the dead.

The songs provide an almost unparalleled insight into what teenagers found relevant, comforting, or amusing in the conditions of the Bershad ghetto. The songs had a direct relevance to their lives: they provided emotional outlets, they inspired, and they comforted. Unlike some other Holocaust songs that circulated in the ghettos of Łódź, Warsaw, and Vilna, these were not theatrical, they were not performed by professional actors but instead relied on amateur performers to circulate. In other words, these are the songs that teenagers sang to each other.

It is also possible that, in addition to entertaining, music provided information about the course of the war, about impending round-ups, and events happening in other places. In the absence of functioning professional media, such as newspapers, radio, or even information bulletins, songs summarized and spread rumours, presenting the news in a catchy and easy-to-memorize way.

One striking feature of the lyrics is how little they borrow from professional Yiddish poets. There is no discernible influence of Leyb Kvitko, Itsik Fefer, Peretz Markish, or other Soviet authors. Instead, the rhymes and imagery seem to come from simple folk songs. The tunes, on the other hand, often came from Soviet films or radio programmes, and very often they were not Jewish. This pattern seems to hold not just for Bershad, but also for other Transnistrian ghettos. It is hard to say what this means, except for the fact that pre-war songs set to lyrics by Soviet Yiddish poets did not seem to make much of an impression on the young Jewish audience of Bershad.

Compared to the songs by adults that Beregovsky's team recorded, teenage music is much more specific and historical.[78] Adults enjoyed pre-war 'non-political' ballads, tragic or comic songs, comforting oldies, and favourites from their youth, whereas teenagers were busy creating their own youth culture, one that developed in the midst of hunger, cold, public executions, and everyday violence. The tone of most pieces is the mood of teenagers, with their acute emotions, raw anger, and heightened sense of fairness and justice.

When teenagers who lived through similar circumstances in other ghettos were interviewed, they sometimes challenged their interviewers' assumptions. This happened, for example, when psychologist David Boder interviewed an 18-year-old survivor of Buchenwald, Abe Mohnblum, in 1946, Mohnblum confronted him with the assertion that 'psychologists do not know the most important things', and insisted that his life experience could prove it.[79] The teenagers of the Bershad ghetto were not formally interviewed by psychologists or, indeed, historians, but they shared similar attitudes. They were angry, disoriented, mostly orphaned or separated from parents and other family members, and deeply disappointed with adults: the Nazis who invaded their homes, the Jewish leadership of the *obshchina* who failed to protect them, and the Ukrainian bystanders who did nothing to help them. All that is left of these sentiments are the songs that Beregovsky recorded in 1945.

As with any collective memory, this one proves selective: the Beregovsky archive never mentions a mother abandoning her child to ensure her own survival, and examples of Soviet atrocities are rare. There is no way of knowing, either, what the informants chose not to sing for Beregovsky and his colleagues or what the ethnographers chose not to record. Even with these limitations, however, the songs provide a unique glimpse into the daily life of Jewish children during the darkest chapter of Jewish history in Europe. They reveal what mattered most to people at the time, how children and adults made sense of their experiences, how young people documented history using poetic forms, and how Yiddish-speakers began to form a collective narrative of what happened to them as victims of war.

The teenagers of the Bershad ghetto went through horrific suffering, and the fact that they wrote songs and performed them to make sense of their experience deserves attention. I have read dozens of testimonies from Bershad and interviewed a number of survivors, but if I were asked to summarize their stories in the fewest possible words, I would rely on one or two songs from Genya Soyfer's repertoire. They include all the essentials of the historical record, the atrocities, the hardships, and the anger, and they name the villains. And they do so in a loud and confident voice that demands not to be ignored. I think we should oblige.

Notes

Thank you to Natalia Aleksiun, François Guesnet, Diana Dumitru, Doris Bergen, and Naomi Seidman for helpful comments and suggestions. I should like to thank John Goddard and Daniel Rosenberg for help in editing this article; Cara Bruni for helping to catalogue the songs; Eli Jany for poetic translations of Yiddish songs into English; and Miriam Schwartz for translating and summarizing Hebrew-language interviews from the USC Shoah Foundation. All errors are my own.

1 Natsional'na biblioteka Ukrayiny imeni V. I. Vernads'koho, Kyiv (hereafter NBU), Manuscript Department, f. 190, spr. 132, l. 37; 'Mames gruv / My Mother's Grave', on *Yiddish Glory: The Lost Songs of World War II*, CD (Six Degrees, 2018); trans. Tova Benjamin.

2 D. Deletant, 'Transnistria', in G. D. Hundert (ed.), *YIVO Encyclopedia of Jews in Eastern Europe* (New Haven, Conn., 2008). On the Holocaust in Transnistria, see J. Ancel, *The History of the Holocaust in Romania* (Lincoln, Neb., 2012); D. Deletant, 'Ion Antonescu and the Holocaust in Romania', *East Central Europe*, 39 (2012), 61–100; D. Ofer, 'The Holocaust in Transnistria: A Special Case of Genocide', in L. Dobroszycki and J. S. Gurock (eds.), *The Holocaust in the Soviet Union: Studies and Sources on the Destruction of the Jews in the Nazi-Occupied Territories of the USSR, 1941–1945* (Armonk, NY, 1993), 133–54: 143; D. Dumitru and J. Carter, 'Constructing Interethnic Conflict and Cooperation: Why Some People Harmed Jews and Others Helped Them during the Holocaust in Romania', *World Politics*, 63 (2011), 1–42; S. Suveica, 'The Local Administration in Transnistria and the Holocaust: Two Case Studies', *Holocaust: Studii şi cercetări*, 7/8 (2015), 97–109; F. A. Vinokurova, 'The Holocaust in Vinnitsa Oblast', in M. Wiener (ed.), *Jewish Roots in Ukraine and Moldova* (New York, 1999), 332–5; D. Dumitru, *The State, Antisemitism, and Collaboration in the Holocaust: The Borderlands of Romania and the Soviet Union* (Cambridge, 2016); V. Solonari, *A Satellite Empire: Romanian Rule in Southwestern Ukraine, 1941–1944* (Ithaca, NY, 2019).

3 Based on manual counting of original pieces in NBU, f. 190, spr. 147 (96 songs), 157 (52 songs), 132 (42 songs), 148 (73 songs).

4 B. Werb, 'Fourteen Shoah Songbooks', *Musica Judaica*, 20 (2013–4), 39–116: 96.

5 I. Sergeeva, 'Fonoarkhiv evreiskoi narodnoi muzyki; istorya, soderzhanie fondov i perspektivy razvitiya', *Rukopysna ta knyzhkova spadshchyna Ukrayiny*, 12 (2007), 80–92: 88.
6 L. Sholokhova, *Fonarkhiv evreiskogo muzykalnogo naslediya. Kollektsiya fonograficheskikh zapisei evreiskogo fol'klora iz fondov Instituta rukopisii Natsional'noi biblioteki Ukrainy im. V. I. Vernadskogo: Annotirovannyi katalog fonotsilindrov, notnykh i tekstovykh rasshifrovok* (Kyiv, 2001).
7 E. V. Khazdan, 'Velikaya Otechestvennaya voina v evreiskom fol'klore (po materialam iz sobraniya M. Ya. Beregovskogo)', *Vremennik Zubovskogo instituta*, 6 (2011), 96–105: 101.
8 See S. Kassow, *Who Will Write Our History? Emanuel Ringelblum, the Warsaw Ghetto, and the Oyneg Shabes Archive* (Bloomington, Ind., 2007).
9 The only documents produced by the victims of the Holocaust in the Soviet Union during and immediately after the war were the testimonies collected in the Black Book (I. Ehrenburg and V. Grossman, *The Complete Black Book of Russian Jewry*, trans. and ed. D. Patterson (London, 2017)) and documents amassed by the Extraordinary State Commission for Ascertaining and Investigating Crimes Perpetrated by the German-Fascist Invaders (Gosudarstvennyi arkhiv Rossiiskoi Federatsii, Moscow, f. 7021, 'Materialy Chrezvychainoi gosudarstvennoi komissii po rassledovaniyu zlodeyanii nemetsko-fashistskikh zakhvatchikov').
10 On the ghettos in Transnistria, see A. Bărbulescu, 'The Underlife of Transnistria's Ghettos: Recategorizing and Reframing Social Interaction', *Journal of Holocaust Research*, 35 (2021), 196–213; D. Ofer, 'The Ghettos in Transnistria and Ghettos under German Occupation in Eastern Europe', in C. Dieckmann and B. Quinkert (eds.), *Im Ghetto 1939–1945: Neue Forschungen zu Alltag und Umfeld* (Göttingen, 2009), 30–53.
11 O. Creangă and A. Kruglov, 'Berşad', trans. K. Luf, in United States Holocaust Memorial Museum, *Encyclopedia of Camps and Ghettos, 1933–1945*, iii: *Camps and Ghettos under European Regimes Aligned with Nazi Germany*, ed. J. R. White and M. Hecker (Bloomington, Ind., 2018), 606–8: 606.
12 Ibid.
13 Ibid.
14 Ibid. 607.
15 Khazdan, 'Velikaya Otechestvennaya voina v evreiskom fol'klore', 100.
16 V. Altskan, 'The Closing Chapter: Northern Bukovinian Jews, 1944–1946', *Yad Vashem Studies*, 43/2 (2015), 51–81; see also 'Bershad' (1995): Elektronnaya evreiskaya entsiklopediya website, visited 7 July 2022.
17 NBU, f. 190, spr. 147, l. 163.
18 For example, NBU, f. 190, spr. 147, l. 37.
19 S. Gilbert, *Music in the Holocaust: Confronting Life in the Nazi Ghettos and Camps* (Oxford, 2005); see also A. Fisher and A. Gilboa, 'The Role of Music amongst Musician Holocaust Survivors before, during, and after the Holocaust', *Psychology of Music*, 44 (2016), 1221–39; A. L. Wlodarski, *Musical Witness and Holocaust Representation* (Cambridge, 2015).
20 Zinaida Lubman, in *Kolokola pamyati: Vospominaniya byvshikh uznikov getto i kontslagerei, prozhivayushchikh v gorode Ashdod (Izrail')*, ed. Y. Helmer (Ashdod, 2005), 41–4: 44.
21 F. Vynokurova, 'The Fate of Bukovinian Jews in the Ghettos and Camps of Transnistria, 1941–1944: A Review of the Source Documents at the Vinnytsa Oblast State Archive', trans. V. Bobrov, *Holocaust and Modernity*, 2/8 (2010), 18–26.
22 Frida Muchnik, interview with Zhanna Litinskaya (May 2004): 'Interviews in Ukraine', Centropa: Trans.History website, visited 13 May 2022.

23 University of Southern California Shoah Foundation, Los Angeles, Visual History Archive (hereafter VHA), interview 9372: Miryam Valdman (11 Feb. 1996; Heb.).
24 Zinaida Lubman, in *Kolokola pamyati*, 42.
25 NBU, f. 190, spr. 147, ll. 166–8.
26 Naum Kerpilevich, in *Kolokola pamyati*, 392–5: 392.
27 M. Nemirovskaya and V. Shintser, 'Mal'chik iz getto: Istoriya dalekaya i blizkaya' (5–12 Oct. 2006): *Russkii Bazar* website, visited 7 July 2022.
28 Creangă and Kruglov, 'Berşad', 607.
29 'Istoriya mestechka Bershad': Evreiskaya Bershad" (17 Aug. 2010): Moye Mestechko Bershad website, visited 7 July 2022.
30 In 1941 and 1942 the commander of the Romanian gendarmerie was Lieutenant George Petresku, who allowed Ukrainian peasants to trade in the ghetto and also helped to provide soap and other disinfection materials during the typhus pandemic of winter of 1941 (ibid.).
31 Creangă and Kruglov, 'Berşad', 607.
32 NBU, f. 190, spr. 132, ll. 206–7.
33 Efim Alexandrov-Zitserman, telephone call with author, 11 Nov. 2021.
34 Sheyndla Blyakher, in *Kolokola pamyati*, 331–3: 333.
35 D. Deletant, 'Ghetto Experience in Golta, Transnistria, 1942–1944', *Holocaust and Genocide Studies*, 18 (2004), 1–26. I would like to thank Diana Dumitru for drawing my attention to this reference.
36 Creangă and Kruglov, 'Berşad', 607.
37 D. Dumitru, 'The Gordian Knot of Justice: Prosecuting Jewish Holocaust Survivors in Stalinist Courts for "Collaboration" with the Enemy', *Kritika*, 22 (2021), 729–56: 740.
38 NBU, f. 190, spr. 147, ll. 145–7.
39 Ibid.
40 Vinokurova, 'The Holocaust in Vinnitsa Oblast', 6.
41 VHA, interview 50942: Mina Schachter (2 July 2000; Heb.).
42 V. Altskan, 'Soviet Archival Sources for Studying the Jewish Experience during the Holocaust', in Center for Advanced Holocaust Studies, United States Holocaust Memorial Museum, *Ghettos 1939–1945: New Research and Perspectives on Definition, Daily Life and Survival. Symposium Presentations* (Washington DC, 2005), 147–57.
43 Dumitru, 'The Gordian Knot of Justice', 738.
44 Frida Muchnik, interview with Zhanna Litinskaya; Abram Mitsel, in *Kolokola pamyati*, 48–9: 48.
45 Dumitru, 'The Gordian Knot of Justice', 738; see also Ofer, 'The Ghettos in Transnistria', 43, 48.
46 VHA, interview 51091: Lea Ishak (3 Aug. 2000; Heb.).
47 NBU, f. 190, spr. 147, ll 142–4.
48 S. L. Kremer, *Women's Holocaust Writing: Memory and Imagination* (Lincoln, Neb., 1999), 42, 45–6.
49 Frida Muchnik, interview with Zhanna Litinskaya.
50 Sofya Degtyareva, in *Kolokola pamyati*, 37.
51 Mikhail Portnoy, ibid. 50–3: 52.
52 VHA, interview 14630: Raia Kuperstein (8 May 1996; Heb.).
53 NBU, f. 190, spr. 147, l. 148.

54 R. Baron, 'Gore i stradaniya ne minuli nikogo', in B. Zabarko (ed.), *'My khoteli zhit'…'*: *Svidetel'stva i dokumenty* (Kyiv, 2013), 488–90: 490; I. A. Altman, *Kholokost na territorii SSSR: Entsiklopediya* (Moscow, 2009), 86.
55 Creangă and Kruglov, 'Berşad', 607.
56 Altman, *Kholokost na territorii SSSR*, 87.
57 Deletant, 'Ghetto Experience in Golta', 16–17; see also Altman, *Kholokost na territorii SSSR*, 87.
58 Baron, 'Gore i stradaniya ne minuli nikogo', 490. For more on Slivino camp, see M. D. Goldenberg (ed.), *Sud'by evreev Nikolaevshchiny v period Velikoi Otechestvennoi voiny 1941–1945 gg.* (Nikolaev, 2012), 294; Altman, *Kholokost na territorii SSSR*, 909.
59 NBU, f. 190, spr. 132, ll. 198–205.
60 NBU, f. 190, spr. 147, ll. 137–9.
61 NBU, f. 190, spr. 147, l. 140.
62 NBU, f. 190, spr. 132, ll. 208–9; trans. Anna Shternshis.
63 Altman, *Kholokost na territorii SSSR*, 131.
64 Ibid. 990.
65 I thank François Guesnet for this insight.
66 Creangă and Kruglov, 'Berşad', 607.
67 VHA, interview 45001: Batiyah Veysman (3 June 1998; Heb.).
68 Dumitru, *The State, Antisemitism, and Collaboration in the Holocaust*, 196–200.
69 Mikhail Portnoy, in *Kolokola pamyati*, 50.
70 Itzhak Shekhtman, ibid. 65.
71 NBU, f. 190, spr. 132, ll. 189–90.
72 F. Blyam, 'Malo nas ostalos' v zhivykh…', in *'My khoteli zhit'…'*, 89–90: 89.
73 M. Geizer, 'Koe-chto o moei zhizni', in *'My khoteli zhit'…'*, 179–83: 181.
74 Naum Kerpilevich, in *Kolokola pamyati*, 392.
75 K. Lubarskaya, ibid. 41–2: 42.
76 F. Portnaya, ibid. 54–9: 59.
77 NBU, f. 190, spr. 147, ll 134–6.
78 NBU, f. 190, spr. 147.
79 A. Mohnblum, 'What Is Man?', in D. P. Boder, *I Did Not Interview the Dead* (Urbana, Ill., 1949), 95–126: 126.

Jewish Child Survivors in the Aftermath of the Holocaust

JOANNA MICHLIC

> The last two decades have been marked by a steadily increasing interest in the history of children during and in the aftermath of the Second World War; this might be described as the children's turn in Holocaust studies. Today, we have a wide range of case studies of Jewish children under Nazi occupation in both western and eastern Europe, studies of children in concentration camps, and child survivors' early post-war lives. Other important areas which have been the subject of research are the resettlement of Europe's unaccompanied and displaced children in the aftermath of the Second World War, the (transnational) reconstruction of Jewish families, mental and medical problems among young survivors in the aftermath the Holocaust, and the memories and self-representation of child survivors. Over the past two decades, scholars and wider audiences have also paid more attention to the wartime diaries of older Jewish children and teenagers. One currently growing area is the history of hidden children during the Holocaust, whose wartime and post-war experiences and memories were barely known to historians in the early 1990s.

It is over. Our liberation has come, but she wears a prosaic face. No one has died of joy. No one has gone mad with excitement. When we used to dream of freedom, we bathed her with our tears. We crowned her with the garlands of our smiles and dreams. Now that she is here, she looks like a beggar and we have nothing to give her. With what desperation did we call for her in those dark days. With what power did her far-off shimmer flesh out our thin bodies? Now she is here and she beckons to us from every corner. She is right before our eyes, yet we cannot see her. She begs us: 'Touch me . . . enjoy me . . .' But we are tired. Our past, like a hawk, circles overhead, fluttering its black wings, devouring our days with horrible memories. It poisons our nights with terror. Poor, sad Freedom! Will she ever have the strength to free us from those dark shadowy wings?

Chava Rosenfarb, 'Bergen-Belsen Diary, 1945'

For years my own feelings lay dormant like a fossil inside an amber bead. Now, fifty years after the war ended, I want to uncover my past and learn who I was . . . For years I did not speak about the war. People were killed. Parents watched their children slain. I survived. What was there to tell? Only the dead can tell. But when my older son, Daniel, went to school, his teacher asked me to meet with the students to tell them about my life.

Miriam Winter, Trains, 1997

THE FIRST PASSAGE is from the diary of Chava Rosenfarb (1923–2011), today an acclaimed Yiddish writer, dated 8 May 1945 when she was 22 years old.[1] The second is an excerpt from the memoir of Miriam Winter (1933–2014), a professor of theatre studies in the United States and a hidden child survivor, who was, like

Rosenfarb, born in the great multicultural city of Łódź.[2] Their writings encapsulate some central aspects of the Holocaust experience for young Jews: anxiety, fear, trauma, and silence.

The war forced young Jews to suppress pivotal aspects of their own identity in order to survive. When that pressure abated, many pursued a sudden compelling search for their pre-war and wartime selves while experiencing an overwhelming sense of the irreparable loss of their families and of their childhoods. Post-war memoirs and testimonies of young survivors are imbued with the realization that wartime experiences have a profound, long-term effect on people's lives, even those who achieved what is regarded as a successful family and professional life.[3] The memoirs constitute a body of evidence regarding the young survivors' apprehensions about their identities, their continuous mourning for their murdered families, and their explorations and interrogations of their own memories and their own past selves during and after the Holocaust. They reveal the ongoing long shadow of the Holocaust on their adult lives.

The mortality rate for Jewish children during the Holocaust, as for elderly Jews, was especially high. According to reliable estimates, only 6 to 11 per cent of Europe's pre-war Jewish children, who had numbered between 1.1 and 1.5 million, survived, compared with 33 per cent of the adults.[4]

The Under-Researched History of Young Jewish Survivors

Lawrence Langer convincingly argued that by dividing the history of the Holocaust into two, that of the perpetrators and that of the victims, conventional historians have failed the victims and privileged the perpetrators, merely because the Nazi regime produced official documents.[5] These conventional historians created narratives concerned mainly with the perpetrators, while ignoring or marginalizing the victims. They failed the youngest victims and survivors most by denying them not only agency but also a legitimate place as a subject of historical enquiry.

However, in the last two decades there has been a steady increase in interest in the history of children during and after the Second World War which can be described as a 'children's turn' in Holocaust studies. The first two pioneering studies in English of Jewish children in Nazi-occupied Europe were Debórah Dwork's *Children with a Star*, published in 1991,[6] which gives an overview of the different fates of Jewish children, and Nicholas Stargardt's *Witnesses of War*, published in 2005.[7] *Witnesses of War* demonstrates the merits of a history of children written from a child's point of view and places children's experiences within broader social and cultural contexts of the Second World War. Today, there is a wide range of case studies of Jewish children under Nazi occupation in both western and eastern Europe, studies of children in concentration camps and of child survivors' early post-war lives. Other important research areas are the resettlement of Europe's unaccompanied and displaced children following the Second World War, the (transnational) reconstruction of Jewish families, mental and medical problems among young survivors, and the memories and self-representation of child survivors.[8]

Over the past two decades more attention has been paid to the wartime diaries of older Jewish children and teenagers, the many 'Anne Franks' of eastern Europe, who, before they were murdered, left poignant, adult-like reflections about life, love, and the everyday struggles of young lives confined in ghettos.[9] These diaries, written during the Holocaust, provide a glimpse into the world of the young generation, the majority of whom perished voiceless, never having had a chance to leave their own testimony.

The Hidden Children

One current growing area in the study of Jewish children during the Holocaust is the history of hidden children, whose wartime and post-war experiences and memories were barely known to historians in the early 1990s. Today, hidden children have well-established and active social networks, foundations, and associations not only in the United States, Canada, Australia, and western Europe, but also in post-communist eastern Europe.

Hidden children are part of the remarkable global social movement of memory among survivors, committed to the reconstruction of their pre-war and wartime childhood and their post-war youth, which are characterized by a twisted sense of split identities and complicated family histories. Like other child survivors, many hidden children are the driving force behind specific commemoration ceremonies in their new homelands and those of their ancestors. Some take on the role of survivor-educators, 'professional survivors',[10] by teaching about their experiences and the Holocaust in schools, colleges, and universities and by public engagement, promoting tolerance and multicultural understanding.

Many child survivors have deposited their interviews and memoirs in archives such as Yad Vashem in Jerusalem, the United States Holocaust Memorial Museum in Washington DC, the Imperial War Museum in London, and smaller local archives and museums. Between 1981 and 1995 the Fortunoff Video Archive for Holocaust Testimonies at Yale University collected 34,000 testimonies, while between 1994 and 2002 Steven Spielberg's Shoah Foundation at the University of Southern California collected 52,000.[11] At the same time, there are child survivors who avoid giving public interviews or testimonies, and may never be ready to do so. There are many reasons for their silence, including family concerns, psychological reservations, personal life trajectories, or drastically violent memories of wartime and early post-war experiences, such as emotional and sexual assault by those who were supposed to be their guardians.

Studies of child survivors' testimonies unsettle a number of assumptions and popular conceptions about the Holocaust. First, they shatter the commonly accepted notion that the Holocaust ended in 1945. This sense that the Holocaust is an ongoing trauma is poignantly expressed by Thomas Buergenthal, an internationally acclaimed American human rights lawyer and judge, and a child survivor whose father was a Polish Jew from Galicia and whose mother was a German Jew. He said: 'That story, after all, continues to have a lasting impact on the person I have become.'[12]

Secondly, an examination of child survivors' accounts questions the heroic and martyrological traditions that tend to sentimentalize Jewish children and Jewish families and fail to recognize the complexity of the dilemmas they faced during and after the Holocaust. For example, in the early post-war period, some hidden children struggled to function in the newly reconstructed family units, in which their surviving parents had become forgotten and emotionally distant figures because of the long years of separation or because widowed parents remarried after the war.[13] As a result, these children sometimes yearned for a reunion with their wartime rescuers. Of course, this pattern was common among hidden children from all over Nazi-occupied Europe, as revealed in a powerful documentary film *Secret Lives* by Aviva Slesin,[14] herself a hidden child from Lithuania.

Third, child survivors' testimonies reveal how extremely vulnerable young fugitives were in the world of adults under the conditions of war and genocide in Poland and other eastern European countries. Although some rescuers treated their young charges with love, compassion, and dedication, as if they were their own children, there were also what I call 'rescuer-abusers' who tormented them mentally and physically and treated them as a source of free labour. A history of mistreatment of Jewish child fugitives by those who were supposed to rescue and care for them has not yet been written,[15] although there are studies of certain categories of rescuers, such as those who did it for profit.[16] My own research, examining cases of everyday intimate relations between rescuers and their young Jewish charges, reveals a disturbing picture.[17] What should have been a safe shelter was often a space of daily suffering, isolation, loneliness, and even sexual abuse. The reasons behind such abuse seem to have been anti-Jewish prejudice, consciousness of the Nazi persecution of Jews and the calculating understanding that Jews were simply disposable in their eyes and that no one was likely to help the fugitives, and the pure cruelty of some individuals. Children articulated their confusion, fear, and helplessness in the face of dependency on abusive individuals and how they coped. Their recollections of threats of denunciation and of crying and begging for their lives to be spared for one more day provide a brutal and disturbing picture of rescue as a grey zone in which human greed, lack of compassion or respect for a young life, and exploitation were central to the relationships between Jewish children and their rescuers.[18] From the point of view of the hidden children, hard work, making yourself as useful and as indispensable as possible, wit and intelligence in dealing with the rescuer-abusers, and sheer luck were the only means that guaranteed their survival.

Some children who had been hidden in Polish villages and exposed to mental and physical abuse and long hours working in the fields recalled shortly after the war that they did not care about living any longer. A good illustration of the loss of the will to live are brief early post-war recollections of their responses to local battles between the encroaching Russian army and the retreating Germans in the second half of 1944. Unlike their rescuers, the children did not flee to safe shelters but stayed in the fields, risking being killed by bombs or bullets.[19]

Their testimonies reveal their mental and emotional fragility, lack of confidence, and confusion about their identity after the loss of their parents and the long, cruel years in hiding with rescuer-abusers, which led to them developing pathological dependencies on them.

After the Soviets came, the people started to tell me: 'The Germans cannot kill you any longer, you are free.' But I did not believe my luck. In the spring of 1946 I converted to Christianity as a way of thanking [the Wajdzik family] for sheltering me. I wanted to simply give them my soul. After, I went to visit my parents' grave: that is, the ditch where they were buried. I put violet flowers there and cried a lot. Today I do not cry any longer, my heart has hardened out of fear, because of my experiences ... Later one of my cousins found me and wanted to take me away from them, but they demanded 'a half a million for the child'. He did not have the money, because he served in the army, and left. I did not even want to say 'Goodbye' to him, I was so stupid. I wanted to remain with them forever and to be a Pole, I was so used to that life. But my cousin told the Jews about my existence, and they took me from the Wajdziks. At the first attempt to take me away, I ran off and walked 7 kilometres back to the farmer. At the end, the police had to come to take me away. They held me by my hands and legs because I did not want to go with them. The Jews placed me in the orphanage, and now I feel good.[20]

Some orphaned children who had survived the war, mostly through using their wits and determination, did not wish to be dependent on adults after the war. Their wartime experiences made them prone to distrust all adults, Jewish and non-Jewish alike. The daily experiences during the war also taught them to be tough, bold, and impudent in dealing with adults. As during the Holocaust, in the early post-war period they continued to be proactive and determined to make their own decisions about their future.[21]

Child survivors constituted the most affected and vulnerable social group in the turbulent early post-war period. For many, who were well looked after and loved by their Christian Polish rescuers, the appearance of a forgotten or an unknown relative meant a messy and frightening disruption of what they regarded as a solid family life and a happy childhood. Therefore, it took them a while to adjust to leaving the familiar and stable environment in which they had lived for two, three, or even in some cases five or six years. The youngest children, those born on the eve of or during the war, were the most shocked by the visits of strangers who came to claim them, since in their eyes they had never had any other family or ethnic, social, and cultural background than that of their rescuers. Unlike some of the older children, they did not have any memories of their biological parents or of the main facets of Jewish identity. Thus, they had to adjust not only to their new Jewish guardians but also to a new social identity. Jewish identity was a totally new, frightening, and foreign terrain, a terra incognita.

The end of the war did not bring an end to the confusion and vulnerability of the young survivors in the world of adults. The key features of their early post-war experience were shattered dreams and a deeply felt sense of orphanhood buried beneath the surface of their joy at having survived. Other features included different and often contradictory expectations of behaviour and educational and career choices between the young survivors and their newly appointed guardians, and a lack of understanding and sympathy on the part of some adoptive parents and institutionalized authorities in the West. Despite obvious differences between then and now, perhaps these unsettling findings about young Jews during and after the Holocaust constitute important lessons on how young victims of current and future genocides and wars should be treated.

Many Czech, Slovak, Polish, and Hungarian Jewish children found themselves in the displaced persons camps in the American, British, and French zones of Germany and made their new post-war homes in the West: in the US, Canada, and Australia, and to a lesser extent in the United Kingdom and France. Many child survivors, the full orphans, were shattered by the painful knowledge that no one would 'come for them', because their immediate and extended families had been totally destroyed. As a result, they were attracted not only in an ideological but also primarily in a practical and existential sense to Zionism as the only way to build a future life.[22] The children's homes and kibbutzim that mushroomed in the early post-war period were the formative centres for young survivors in which the yearning for the 'dreamed' safe Jewish homeland crystallized. These children emigrated, mostly illegally, to Palestine/Israel between 1945 and 1950, but the sense of orphanhood did not disappear easily in their new homeland, as is expressed in a simple poem by an unnamed child survivor written in Kibbutz Mishmar Ha'emek, in 1946:

> I have so much of everything
> But I have no parents
> At the same time
> I hear the wind whisper
> Child, don't listen to that voice
> There are many children like you
> Who have no mothers
> So don't cry
> You must sing, study, and dance
> And build our land.[23]

Other orphaned children were adopted by unknown Jewish relatives or complete strangers in the United States through a variety of Jewish charities such as the European Jewish Children's Aid, which became part of the United Services for New Americans. The 'lucky ones', who were reunited with at least one surviving biological parent or other close relative, emigrated to the West after their newly reconstituted families met all the bureaucratic criteria and achieved the difficult task of proving that they were 'blood relatives', often without possessing crucial documents such as birth and death certificates.

The post-Holocaust history of young east European Jews encompasses many transnational aspects, such as the reconstitution of their families, adoption, and a variety of life trajectories, including first loves, marriages, life-long friendships, and family-like relationships among those who met in children's homes and kibbutzim.

It is a history that must be approached through a transnational lens. To understand the short- and long-term impact of the Holocaust on young survivors and the post-1945 multi-generational Jewish family, it is also illuminating to study that history in both the wartime and post-war historical contexts rather than treating these two periods separately.

The growing awareness of the inevitable passing of the survivor generation, gravely accelerated by the COVID pandemic, makes interpretation of the Holocaust memories of adult and child survivors by the 'second' and 'third' generations a compelling and timely research subject. The subject engages not only historians, psychologists, sociologists, and literary scholars, but also neuroscientists, who have recently claimed that it is possible to identify the mode of transmission of Holocaust survivors' stress to their offspring through their genes: 'the epigenetic inheritance'.[24]

Since 1977 there has been a growing global outpouring of fictional and life writing and visual artistic works by the second generation, known as 'the heirs of the Holocaust',[25] a term coined by Helen Epstein, the pioneering voice of the second generation who made 'an unidentifiable group identifiable'.[26] There have also been a number of fictional works by the third generation, such as Jonathan Safran Foer's *Everything is Illuminated* (2002), Andrew Wiener's *The Marriage Artist* (2010), and Nathan Englander's *What We Talk About When We Talk About Anne Frank* (2012), and the emergence of new Holocaust memorialization projects. The latter include getting tattoos of a survivor's concentration-camp number by the grandchildren of Holocaust survivors as a way of remembering and raising awareness of the Holocaust.[27] According to Michael Berenbaum, transmitting memories of the Holocaust with one's own body is a manifestation of a broader transition from 'life' to 'historical memories': 'We're at that transition, and this is sort of a brazen, in-your-face way of bridging it.'[28]

However, despite the current impressive research into the history of Jewish childhood under the Nazis, and of child Holocaust survivors, there are still many questions about the wartime experiences of Jewish families and certain groups of Jewish children in German-occupied Europe and about how the Holocaust affected child survivors and the second and third generations. These questions require various historical, ethnographic, sociological, and anthropological approaches, different analytical tools, and research into previously unavailable or ignored archival collections. With the endorsement of the child-centred historical methods and interdisciplinary approaches, there is no doubt that the field will continue to thrive and bear new fruit.

Notes

1   C. Rosenfarb, 'Bergen-Belsen Diary, 1945' [excerpts], trans. G. Morgentaler (27 Jan. 2014), 8 May 1945: Tablet website, visited 14 May 2022. The diary was written in the displaced persons camp at Bergen-Belsen after the liberation of the concentration camp on 15 April 1945. Excerpts from it were first published as *Fragmentn fun a togbukh* as an addendum to Rosenfarb's first collection of poems, *Di balade fun nekhtikn vald* (Montreal, 1948). They

were translated into English by Goldie Morgentaler, Rosenfarb's daughter and a professor of English at the University of Lethbridge.

2   M. Winter, *Trains: A Memoir of a Hidden Childhood during and after World War II* (Jackson, Mich., 1997).

3   There is a lack of studies on the cultural, social, and economic achievements of young east European Jewish survivors in the West. For an interesting analysis of socio-economic achievements of young Jewish refugees from German-speaking Europe in the United States, see G. Sonnert and G. Holton, *What Happened to the Children Who Fled Nazi Persecution* (New York, 2006).

4   For a short overview of the history of Jewish children during the Holocaust, see K. Nili, 'Children', in *The Holocaust Encyclopedia*, ed. W. Laqueur (New Haven, Conn., 2001), 115–19; for a rich collection of published primary sources on children during the Holocaust, see P. Heberer, *Children during the Holocaust* (Lanham, Md., 2011).

5   See L. L. Langer, *Holocaust Testimonies: The Ruins of Memory* (New Haven, Conn., 1991).

6   D. Dwork, *Children with a Star: Jewish Youth in Nazi Europe* (New Haven, Conn., 1991).

7   N. Stargardt, *Witnesses of War: Children's Lives under the Nazis* (London, 2005).

8   On the historiography of the subject, see J. B. Michlic, 'Mapping the History of Child Holocaust Survivors', in A. Helma (ed.), *No Small Matter: Features of Jewish Childhood* (Oxford, 2021), 79–102.

9   See e.g. R. Spiegel, *Renia's Diary: A Young Girl's Life in the Shadow of the Holocaust*, trans. A. Blasiak and M. Dziurosz (London, 2019); *The Diary of Dawid Sierakowiak: Five Notebooks from the Łódź Ghetto*, ed. A. Adelson, trans. K. Turowski (New York, 1996); J. Feliks Urman, *I'm Not Even a Grown-Up*, ed. and trans. A. Rudolf (London, 1991).

10 A. Sheftel and S. Zembrzycki, 'Professionalizing Survival: The Politics of Public Memory among Holocaust Survivor-Educators in Montreal', *Journal of Modern Jewish Studies*, 12 (2013), 210–31.

11 On the revival of interest in the testimony of Holocaust survivors, see G. Hartman, *The Longest Shadow: In the Aftermath of the Holocaust* (Bloomington, Ind., 1996); see also A. Wieviorka *The Era of the Witness*, trans. J. Stark (Ithaca, NY, 2006), 107–18.

12 T. Buergenthal, *A Lucky Child: A Memoir of Surviving Auschwitz as a Young Boy* (New York, 2009), p. xiii.

13 On the difficulties of reconstituting Jewish families in post-war Holland, see D. L. Wolf, *Beyond Anne Frank* (Berkeley, Calif., 2007), esp. ch. 6.

14 A. Slesin (dir.), *Secret Lives: Hidden Children and Their Rescuers during WWII*, documentary (Ann Rubenstein Tisch, Aviva Slesin, and Toby Appleton Perl, 2002); see D. Kher, 'Film in Review. "Secret Lives": Hidden Children and Their Rescuers during WWII' (16 May 2003): *New York Times* website, visited 14 May 2022.

15 See O. Orzeł (ed.), *Dzieci żydowskie w czasach Zagłady: Wczesne świadectwa 1944–1948: Relacje dziecięce ze zbiorów Centralnej Żydowskiej Komisji Historycznej* (Warsaw, 2014). Many of the fifty-five early post-war Jewish children's testimonies in this collection speak directly about mistreatment and abuse.

16 On rescuers for profit, see J. Grabowski, *Rescue for Money: Paid Helpers in Poland, 1939–1945* (Jerusalem, 2008); A. Wierzcholska, 'Helping, Denouncing, and Profiteering: A Process-Oriented Approach to Jewish–Gentile Relations in Occupied Poland from a Micro-Historical Perspective', in H. Kubátová and J. Láníček (eds.), *Jews and Gentiles in Eastern Europe During the Holocaust in History and Memory* 23 (2017), 34–58. Joanna Tokarska-

Bakir questions the use of the terms 'righteous' and 'unrighteous' (see J. Tokarska-Bakir, 'The Unrighteous Righteous and the Righteous Unrighteous', *Dapim*, 24 (2010), 11–63).

17 J. B. Michlic, *Piętno Zagłady: Wojenna i powojenna historia oraz pamięć żydowskich dzieci ocalałych w Polsce* (Warsaw, 2020), 248–52; ead., 'What Does a Child Remember? Recollections of the War and the Early Postwar Period among Child Survivors from Poland', in ead. (ed.), *Jewish Families in Europe, 1939–Present: History, Representation, and Memory* (Waltham, Mass., 2017), 153–72.

18 See Michlic, 'What Does a Child Remember?' 162–3.

19 See Michlic, *Piętno Zagłady*, 126–7.

20 Archiwum Żydowskiego Instytutu Historycznego, Warsaw, 301/2731: Gizela Szulberg, testimony for Centralny Komitet Żydów w Polsce, recorded by Ida Gliksztejn, 3 Sept. 1947 (Pol.), p. 3; see also Michlic, *Piętno Zagłady*, 250–1.

21 See Michlic, *Piętno Zagłady*, 252–3.

22 See A. J. Patt, *Finding Home and Homeland: Jewish Youth and Zionism in the Aftermath of the Holocaust* (Detroit, 2009).

23 Kibbutz Mishmar Ha'emek Archive, Kevutsat shaḥar: 'Mipenei shehaḥayim sheli lefanai' (1949); cited in M. Balf, 'Holocaust Survivors on Kibbutzim: Resettling Unsettled Memories', in D. Ofer, F. S. Ouzan, and J. Baumel Schwartz (eds.), *Holocaust Survivors: Resettlement, Memories, Identities* (New York, 2011), 165–83; see also J. B. Michlic, 'Rebuilding Shattered Lives: Some Vignettes of Jewish Children's Lives in Early Postwar Poland', in Ofer, Ouzan, and Baumel Schwartz (eds.), *Holocaust Survivors*, 46–87.

24 On the subject of epigenetic inheritance, see e.g. D. Samuels, 'Do Jews Carry Trauma in Our Genes? A Conversation with Rachel Yehuda' (11 Dec. 2014): Tablet website, visited 14 May 2022; H. Thomson, 'Study of Holocaust Survivors Finds Trauma Passed on to Children's Genes?' (21 Aug. 2015): *The Guardian* website, visited 14 May 2022; M. Shapiro, 'Intergenerational Transmission of Trauma: How the Holocaust Transmits and Affects Child Development', Working Papers Series, Hadassah-Brandeis Institute Project on Families, Children and the Holocaust, Brandeis University.

25 H. Epstein, 'Heirs of the Holocaust' (19 June 1977): *New York Times* website, visited 14 May 2022.

26 D. Lipstadt, 'Children of Jewish Survivors of the Holocaust: The Evolution of a New-Found Consciousness', *Encyclopedia Judaica Year Book*, 1988/9, pp. 139–50.

27 For a critical assessment of Holocaust tattoos, see Y. Miller, 'Holocaust Tattoos: Isn't There a Better Way to Educate?' (22 Oct. 2012): *Haaretz* website, visited 14 May 2022.

28 Cited in J. Rudoren, 'Proudly Bearing Elders' Scars, Their Skin Says "Never Forget"' (1 Oct. 2012): *New York Times* website, visited 14 May 2022; see also 'A Tattoo to Remember', audio recording (30 Sept. 2012): *New York Times* website, visited 14 May 2022.

The Rehabilitation of Jewish Child Holocaust Survivors, Poland, 1944–1947

BOAZ COHEN

> The rehabilitation of Jewish child survivors of the Holocaust, scarred by their wartime experiences, was a priority for the re-established Jewish community in Poland in the early post-war years. Educators and pedagogues worked to help the children overcome their mistrust, self-hate, and anger and to integrate them into society. This work of rehabilitation needs to be understood in the framework of the perception of these children by the adults entrusted with their care, and of the challenges they presented to their educators and to the Jewish community in general. The educational practices that were developed and the concerns underlying these practices are best seen in the children's homes they established. The children who found shelter there posed an educational and behavioural challenge to their carers, and significant attempts had to be made to re-establish trust and identity, including innovative forms of self-government and children's courts.

IN LATE 1944 a bitter argument took place in the offices of the Jewish Committee in liberated Kraków. It was provoked by a gang of teenage Jewish survivors who were engaging in all sorts of unruly behaviour and criminal activity. A 9-year-old boy survivor, who was not accepted into the gang, attempted suicide by jumping from a third-floor window. He was only saved by his coat catching on the window and the timely intervention of one of the older boys. The head of the Jewish Committee, a camp survivor whose own 16-year-old son had been beaten to death before his eyes, argued for the expulsion of the gang:

For these thieves, swindlers, and robbers, we have to fight with the authorities so that we can cater to their needs? For them, we have to beg, to risk antisemitic attacks! No, I will not let them stay here in the institution! [He himself took them all in.] They might murder other children . . . they demoralize them . . . they disgrace all Jews . . . We never had thieves and robbers . . . No, we cannot be responsible for them. They should leave the house now! Return all they got from us.[1]

Arguing with the head of the committee was a young female survivor, Lena Küchler (Kichler), who had taken a break from her doctorate in educational psychology at the Jagiellonian University in Kraków to take care of the surviving Jewish children housed in appalling conditions on the top floor of the committee headquarters.

'Did you ever contemplate the fact that these children survived the war because of the behaviours for which you are blaming them?' she asked. 'These children survived the war by stealing and lying. They had to learn to lie to save their lives.' These behaviours could not easily be abandoned since they had been their best weapons during the war. They could not be expected now to lay down 'the weapons to which they owe their survival'. Moreover, she argued, 'is it their fault that they were forced to be like this in order to survive?' 'So what', he replied. 'Should we give them a reward for this? Are they not responsible for their actions? Do you not want them punished? Should they be allowed to continue to rob, swindle, and attack the weaker ones?' Küchler was adamant that punishment was not the answer:

> What will punishment help? It will only amplify their anger at the injustice done to them and drive them to further resistance! Do not forget that these are war children, and in war there is a different moral code; in war the strongest, the cruellest, and the most cunning survive... You will not root out this behaviour by punishment. This can be taught only by a long and slow educational process: love, understanding, until their own 'moral self' will awaken to judge their deeds.[2]

Lena Küchler-Silberman (1910–87) spent the war under an assumed Polish identity which allowed her to rescue Jewish orphans from the Warsaw ghetto and place them in convents. She had been a teacher before the war and was married with a baby girl who died young. Her husband, believing he had a better chance of survival alone, deserted her. Following liberation, she began her doctoral thesis. A chance encounter with neglected child survivors at the Kraków Jewish Committee headquarters changed the course of her life. Through the committee, she established an orphanage in Zakopane, a resort in the Tatra mountains. She subsequently smuggled the children from Poland to France with the aid of the American Orthodox Jewish relief organization Va'ad Hahatsalah, and into a children's home under the auspices of the Œuvre de Protection des Enfants Juifs, a socialist-Zionist organization, where she remained with them until their emigration to Israel in 1949. She was a dedicated and gifted educator whose 'children' kept in touch with her for decades afterwards.

Küchler was not alone in undertaking educational work with Jewish child survivors in post-war Poland, and the problems she had to deal with were also not unique. Jewish educators, mainly survivors themselves, took on the gargantuan task of rehabilitating the children and addressing their problems. Of course, not all the children adopted a pattern of criminal behaviour like that described above. Yet they all carried the scars of persecution and war. They had experienced multiple traumas: loss of family, separation, abuse, deprivation, and sickness, and their medical condition was poor. They had a strong mistrust of adults and a dislike of authority. Those who had survived by hiding with Christian families or in convents were unsure of their Jewish identity and saw it as a liability in a world that had just allowed the murder of millions of Jews and where hostility towards them was still rampant.[3]

This chapter will explore the rehabilitative work with Jewish child and teenage survivors in the aftermath of the Holocaust in Poland. It will look at the perception of these children by the adults with whom they were in contact and the educational challenges they presented to their educators and to the Jewish community in general.

The educational practices developed and the concerns underlying them will be investigated, with a focus on the setting up of orphanages. Throughout the world, millions of children—scarred, dispossessed, deported, and orphaned—had to be taken care of and rehabilitated in the aftermath of the Second World War. They were the victims of a modern, total, and global war, and their rehabilitation posed challenges to the emerging post-war world.[4] This chapter, however, focuses on the rehabilitation of Jewish children, who were specifically targeted for annihilation by the genocidal policies of the Nazis and their collaborators in Poland, where the Germans murdered a large proportion of the 6 million Jewish victims of the Holocaust and where, after the war, great efforts were made to rehabilitate the very few Jewish children that survived.[5]

Heroes or Ruffians?

Similar arguments to the one described above took place all across post-war Europe. The surviving children captivated the Jewish public and were seen as heroes and the hope of a national future, but at the same time they posed educational and behavioural challenges to post-war Jewish society.[6]

On 19 and 20 September 1945 the Jewish Historical Commission in Poland held its second meeting for activists from across the country. One of the issues debated was 'the psychology of young Jews during the Nazi occupation, based on the information collected by the commission'.[7] Noe Gruss, himself a Holocaust survivor, opened the discussion with a presentation on the subject. Based on his observations in the orphanages, he claimed that 'the children are spiritually more mature, more capable of resistance, and more balanced than before the war'. In his view, during the war, the children had developed a '"practical intellect" . . . that in many cases helped save their lives'. Moreover, he claimed, the children's testimonies and the diaries of their experiences showed 'that the behaviour of the Jewish children contained ethical and moral elements . . . more than once they displayed heroism and a strong will, which was not concerned only for their own good'.[8] These testimonies and diaries bear witness to their 'premature maturity'. The children 'occupy their minds with questions of social justice, religious faith and the lack of religious faith, the meaning of courage, life, and death . . . They want to avenge themselves on their enemies, but are also extremely grateful to the people who helped them in their time of need.'[9]

But Gruss's idealized depiction of the surviving Jewish children was not easily accepted by his colleagues on the commission. It was regarded as 'too one-sided'; he had a 'too optimistic depiction of the matter', argued survivor historian Philip Friedman. 'We must not say that, after all they have lived through, the children have no psychological problems.' These problems were bound to have behavioural implications: 'One can state that the children are wild. They lack ethical restraints and education.'[10] Another participant, Bolesław Drobner, noted that Gruss omitted to mention the 'internal conflicts' of those children 'who had been brought up in a different religion'.[11] Many of the children were indeed displaying very challenging behaviour, as the children of the Kraków orphanage testified many years later. Nathan, 15 years old at the time, stated:

What a child I was, I was all in pieces and had to put myself together like a jigsaw puzzle... We roamed the streets. What did we do there? If there was a chance to steal something, we stole it—generally food. I had a few true friends but to the others it was 'Move aside I'm walking here.' I also had scores to settle with the teachers... but I settled them quickly... I put them through living hell... If someone did not grant me respect it was very bad for him... They had to grant me respect... We were people without mercy. Completely without mercy... Cross us? Pay the price.[12]

Historian Nahum Bogner, a child survivor who spent the war hiding in the forest and joined the group later, concluded: 'In 1945 everyone came from very bad places, they looked for their families and found no one... That rage had to be expressed.'[13]

Recounting another violent outburst by Nathan (whom she referred to as Shaul), this time directed at the medical team who tried to check his many wounds, Küchler wrote:

How dare I be angry at him? What did I do for him? He has all the justification to blame people/humanity. They killed his mother, father, and brother... took his childhood, made him an invalid, took one of his eyes... and the wounds to his soul are even worse... Why am I surprised that he has lost his trust in people?... His aggressiveness is just a form of self-preservation.[14]

Kraków was not unique. Anna Nathanblut, who headed the orphanage in Lublin, wrote of 'orphaned, homeless children, dressed in rags, faces pale from hunger, roaming the streets'.[15] One of these children from Lublin testified:

One day I came upon several food stalls... one sold candies, chocolate, sausages, and rolls, these were things I had not tasted for five years... I managed to steal some candies and chocolate and moved aside to devour the chocolate. I then went to another stall that had sausages and tried to repeat my performance, but the Polish woman noticed and started shouting... I was frightened and ran away.[16]

The unruly behaviour did not cease with the end of the war. In Küchler's orphanage, a staff member on duty during noon recess heard suspicious noises coming from the room of the teenage boys. From the door she heard sobs and sounds of a scuffle. On forcing open the door, blocked by an iron bed, she saw that one of the boys was about to be hanged from the light fitting. The other boys were just about to kick over the stool he was standing on. In the nick of time the hanging was stopped. The boy had been tied up and a rag stuffed down his throat to prevent him from shouting; he was blue, and mouth-to-mouth resuscitation was needed. Unlike those of the other children, the boy's father had survived and was now the physician at the orphanage, and the boy used this to avoid doing his share of the chores. The fact that his father wanted to marry Küchler and thus possibly take her away from the children did not help. 'In the forest, people like that were hanged by their legs', said one of the boys. 'Those who did not obey the commander's orders were "put down".' Another added: 'In the camp they would also hang people, and we had to watch.' And a third boy said: 'At our camp, the veteran prisoners threw people like him on the barbed wire.'[17]

This incident brought Küchler close to breaking point. She recalls asking herself: 'Who is to be blamed here? The boys? Me? The boy's father? Or all of society? Would the children have done it if they had not seen behaviour like that in the camps, the forests and the towns? If they had not learned from the Germans to despise the weak, and follow a ritual of cruelty and brute force?'[18] She told the boys, 'we all carry the Nazi poison in our veins and this poison will destroy us if we do not cleanse ourselves of it'. This extreme event underscores the educational challenges posed by children and teenagers who were carrying the emotional and behavioural scars of their recent experiences. It was not only in Poland that their behaviour elicited negative reactions. Judith Hemmendinger, who worked with child and teenage survivors from Buchenwald in homes run by the Œuvre de Secours aux Enfants in France, spoke of the exasperation of the director of one of them over the boys' aggressiveness towards him: 'He believed they were true psychopaths, cold and indifferent by nature', she recounts, for otherwise, 'how could they survive camp life?'[19] Both sides to the argument agreed that care for the child survivors was a priority and a major Jewish responsibility, but that the children were not always making it easy for caregivers and policy-makers to administer this care.

The pertinent issues and practices debated by Jewish educators in post-war Poland and some of the educational strategies they adopted in their quest to rehabilitate the children are discussed in this chapter. Specifically, it will address the issues of trust and identity and the practices of self-government and schooling. A way had to be found to help the children grow up and assume their role in Jewish society. For that, issues of trust and identity had to be worked through and moral agency and education developed. The discussion is thematic and spans the early post-war years up to 1947. This was a time of fluidity and social and political change, yet the themes appear throughout the period.[20]

Regaining Trust

In January 1945 the American *Journal of Educational Sociology* devoted a whole issue to 'the Jew in the postwar world'.[21] In a paper on cultural reconstruction, Aryeh Tartakower, a Polish-born sociologist who had been the director of the Department of Relief and Rehabilitation of the World Jewish Congress during the Second World War, addressed the problems of Jewish child survivors in Europe. One of them was the issue of trust:

How can the child who witnessed and survived the inferno of Jewish life under Nazi domination be converted into a member of human society with a more or less normal attitude, not only toward the Germans, but toward other nations as well? A child who has seen the passive indifference of the surrounding population, and in many cases the active participation in deeds of terror, must inevitably come to a realization that all humanity is corrupt and foul. No real cultural reconstruction will be possible, unless this educational problem is solved first.[22]

The caretakers working with child survivors in Poland concurred with this analysis. Lena Küchler described the children she met in the Jewish Committee headquarters in Kraków: 'They trusted no one. They declined to tell the truth since they were sure it could harm them—while lying and deceit would save them. For them, the war was not yet over.'[23] Years later, she addressed this issue again: 'These children lost their faith in humanity, because from an early age, they saw only evil', and therefore 'all people were perceived as evil unless proven otherwise'.[24]

Chasia Bielicka, a 24-year-old survivor of the Białystok ghetto and a member of Hashomer Hatsa'ir, a left-wing Zionist youth movement, was the leader of the first Koordynacja orphanage, established in Łódź in March 1946.[25] She also spoke of the educational challenges of children who 'had no faith, not in anyone and not in anything'; they 'had given up on life'; and it was very hard 'to bring them back some sort of belief, to love, to believe'.[26]

The need to be patient with the children and to believe in them emerges frequently in the testimonies of educators and caregivers. Lena Küchler was convinced that, first and foremost, 'we have to give them time . . . to educate them . . . to help them regain their trust in people . . . and then there is a chance that the good inherent in them will emerge'.[27] In the face of challenging behaviour, patience was paramount, 'we need a lot of patience for these children . . . much compassion . . . and love. We can't be offended by their behaviour, we should understand them . . . [they are] miserable, not evil.'[28]

The children had to be accepted unconditionally and loved. 'They had to be given a ceaselessly warm home', wrote Bielicka. 'Only thus could I earn their trust and give them a sense of well-being. I hugged them, caressed them, held them in my arms, and woke up at any hour of the night when they needed me . . . I made each child feel that I was his or hers alone but also reinforced the sense of family togetherness.'[29] Nesia Orlovits, a Holocaust survivor who directed a Hashomer Hatsa'ir orphanage, also saw love as necessary to regain trust:

First and foremost, we have to gain the children's trust. In the face of all the hate, all the evil they encountered, we have to infuse them with huge doses of love, unrestricted love, motherly love, in all its manifestations and with all its exaggerations. In the face of the hostile environment, we have to establish for them a home radiating warmth and security, each child has to feel that 'here you are a king'.[30]

Yeshayayu Drucker explained the importance of the loving and warm approach to the children as practised in the Zabrze orphanage: 'The children have suffered enough and now they need warmth and even more than that, so that they will feel as in their parents' home.'[31]

By 1947 some educators were having second thoughts about the centrality of love in the rehabilitative process. A three-day conference of heads of Jewish orphanages was held in Kraków between 12 and 14 December of that year under the patronage of the Central Committee of Jews in Poland. One of the speakers stated:

In the first stages of organizing our children's homes, we consciously applied the principle of tenderness and affection—perhaps in excessive amounts—towards children. It was a sad consequence of our post-war reality, as Jewish children, who had been abused, beaten and tortured, were, first of all, starving for warmth. Therefore, we tried to surround them with warmth, cordiality, and love, in order to give them back their childhood years, the joy of life, and fill that terrible void in their souls.[32]

Yet, he claimed, this might have resulted in overcompensation for the lost childhood and warmth that led to the children being constantly reminded that they were victims of war and 'the conviction that as a result, they have special rights, privileges and favours'. 'It is absolutely necessary to put an end to this', he concluded.[33]

The use of the terms 'warmth', 'love', and 'family' underscores the fact that many caretakers and educators based their educational work on identifying and addressing the emotional needs of the children. Their own Holocaust experiences and loss influenced how they perceived the loss experienced by the children. They believed they could help the children regain trust through accepting them as they were and providing them with love and affection. 'Being there' for the children, and showing a commitment to them, was their strategy to help them regain their trust in the world.

Reclaiming Jewish Identity

One child survivor, Paula Weinstein, wrote years later:

After the war I did not want to return to Judaism. I was Christian. I prayed. I believed. I couldn't believe in the God [of the Jews]. For me, it was a fact that God didn't help me, but Jesus did . . . The Jews were murdered and the Christians weren't. So, what sort of God is this? Jesus is OK, he helps, and he saves. The God of the Jews does not care about his Jews.[34]

'Of the word "Jew"', recounted Küchler about her first encounters with child survivors, 'the children were afraid as if of fire . . . Throughout the war years it was synonymous with the greatest calamity, something related to guilt, almost a crime—and a fear from all it entails . . . therefore, they would not reveal their Jewish names.'[35] The children remembered their harrowing experiences during the Holocaust—the loss and trauma and suffering—as the consequence of being Jewish. This was a liability in their eyes. Children denied being Jewish. Anna Nathanblut spoke in her memoirs of one child, P., who refused to stay in the orphanage and shouted incessantly, 'Why did you bring me here? I'm not Jewish.'[36]

The identity crisis of Jewish child survivors in Poland has been researched by, among others, Joanna Michlic, Nahum Bogner, and Emuna Nahmani Gafni.[37] This chapter examines how educators addressed the problem. The issue was not only reclaiming personal Jewish identity, it was also how these Christianized Jewish children related to Jews in general, whom they regarded as an alien and menacing 'Other'. Many of them, especially girls who had been hidden in convents, adopted a Christian identity that included a certain antisemitism. 'I'm not going to stay with Jews', a new arrival, Irka, told Bielicka, when she got to her orphanage just before the Passover meal, and she refused to eat 'matzah made from the blood of a Christian child'.[38] Bielicka recalled hearing sobbing from the girls' room at Easter: some of the girls were kneeling and crying. '"Jesus won't forgive us," they wailed. "It's Easter today and we're with the Jews. We're not praying, we're not going to church, and there's not even one cross on the wall!"'[39] In Bielicka's eyes, the terror of the girls was directly connected to their strict convent education.

But the girls were terribly afraid: living with Jews, without prayer-books, without beads and without a crucifix . . . The transition from a strict rigid life that left no room for free will, wishes or requests was hard for them. They still feared the punishment that surely awaited them for living among Jews, failing to observe the religious precepts and refraining from prayer.[40]

'Some of the children were saturated with antisemitism', recounted Yeshayahu Drucker about the Zabrze orphanage.[41] This led to conflicts. Küchler described one incident in which the convent girls complained that the boys were grabbing their crosses. The boys had experienced life in concentration or labour camps or hiding out in forests, unlike many of the girls, who had survived in Polish homes or convents. One of the boys explained that 'such girls should not be here . . . They spit when they hear the word Jew. Let them go back to their convents and their priests.' He explained that he tore a crucifix off a girl because: 'I can't take this anymore! Did we suffer in the woods, fight and almost die so that these girls would come here to insult us?'[42]

To children who complained about children identifying with Christianity in the orphanage, Küchler answered: 'You are trying to force them to discard their faith that is everything to them now, their treasure . . . The faith that they believe saved them. When you tear off their crosses you are using force, violence.' One boy countered: 'So we have to stand aside and see them pray all day and look down on the Jews?' Küchler responded: 'Unfortunately, yes . . . The more you pressure them the more they will resist. You should give them space . . . let them be . . . These things will sort themselves out with time.' Those children who saw themselves as Christian needed to have 'full freedom to practise their faith', even when this was anathema to the surviving members of their families, the other children, and the staff.[43]

This conversation encapsulates the approach of many educators to the problem. It was obvious that acceptance and patience were needed. Thus, Bielicka believed that 'by denying them what they believed in, I could only break them, not build them'. She decided to approach the issue indirectly: 'Not to destroy their belief system but to build on it an alternate one.' Unlike those children who had lost their faith in religion or humanity, 'with children who believed in something, I could find a way'.[44] Carefully, Bielicka developed an approach which evolved from her work with the children and her wish to bring them back into a normal life: not criticizing the children's Christian identity but respecting their commitment to it, while infusing them with a positive Jewish identity.

I sat with them, and started to draw a line between the war years and the present, to differentiate between the need to deny Judaism in order to escape death and the privilege of returning to Judaism as free people. I tried to draw a line between the appalling loneliness of living with a false identity and the privilege of being a part of a large family of children who, although parentless, have brothers and sisters, a home, and a nation.[45]

Her goal was to bring them back into the Jewish community and the Jewish people, to transfer 'belief in Jesus to belief in the Jewish people and the Land of Israel'. This was not a clash between two religious creeds: the orphanages were usually secular institutions and stressed a national Jewish identity. Bielicka's motto was 'love of the Jewish people, of the Land of Israel . . . love of humanity'. It was bound to be a long process. 'I didn't take away their crosses', said Bielicka. 'They first wore them openly, then under their shirts and finally took them off, and packed them away as a memento.'[46]

An interesting example of the tension involved in bringing children back to Judaism can be found in the Zabrze orphanage, which had been established by the Committee of Jewish Religious Communities headed by Rabbi Dr David Kahane, chief Jewish chaplain of the Polish army. It was financed by Va'ad Hahatsalah, Rabbi Dr Solomon Schonfeld of Agudat Israel from London, and the American Jewish Joint Distribution Committee. Yeshayahu Drucker, also an army chaplain, was entrusted with recovering hidden Jewish children and overseeing the orphanage. It was officially a religious institution, and thus it could be expected that the demand that children adopt Jewish religious practices would result in a head-on collision, but this was not the case. While the orphanage was nominally an Orthodox institution, the attitude to religious observance in it was very lenient. The director, Nehama Geler, also a survivor, was very dedicated to the children but not religious. There was a Jewish studies teacher 'who made great efforts to rekindle the Jewish religious flame in the children's souls, but unfortunately not always successfully'. While the sabbath was observed in the orphanage, the children did not go to synagogue regularly, and even then only the boys.[47] The synagogue was across the street, 'but they only went when I was there', Drucker said.[48] It was obvious to Drucker and Geler that patience was needed to facilitate the readoption of a Jewish identity. The Jewish community of Zabrze complained to the Committee of Jewish Religious Communities. Here too, there were those who did not accept Drucker and Geler's approach on religious grounds, but, in general, the committee backed them and their educational policy. 'It was not possible, sometimes, for the children, to make the transition from a Polish Christian education to a Jewish way of life—a measured educational approach was needed', wrote Rabbi Kahane. 'The fatherly, lenient approach of Drucker set the tone at the home.'[49] Not only was there a lenient attitude to Jewish ritual but also an understanding of the children's Christian spiritual needs. This was manifested by

Drucker taking some children to church when they wanted to go.[50] Drucker himself recounted the story of a teenager who was reunited with her grandfather who took away her cross by force. 'He couldn't understand why she had to be Christian', he said, 'and did not know how to convince her to return to Judaism by her own choice. Her younger relatives at least, should have known to give her more kindness: she was lonely.'[51]

The readoption of a Jewish identity was a long process that was not always resolved in the immediate post-war years. Some children chose to stay at the convent where they had been hidden, or with their non-Jewish rescuers. Some of these eventually found their way back to the Jewish people and identity; others never did. The Christian identity formed at a young age left traces even on child survivors who made their way to Israel and raised Israeli Jewish families.

The Involved Child: Honing Social Skills and Values

Jewish educators and caretakers believed that the young survivors should be involved in the management of their orphanages and in their education. During the war many of them had had to make decisions for themselves, to make hard choices, and to bear the consequences. Educators and caretakers wanted to take into account this ability and to use it in the rehabilitative process. Immediately after the war this was done on an ad hoc basis. While many caregivers had strong personalities and charisma, they also believed in self-government in the orphanages, even on a limited scale. It was seen as central to their efforts to help the children re-establish social skills, moral judgement, self-confidence, and trust. Lena Küchler formed a children's court in her orphanage to deal with disputes and disciplinary problems, and Nesia Orlovits established a child-directed 'secretariat' in hers. Chasia Bielicka explained: 'Precisely because I don't have the personality to be a guard or an enforcer of orders, perhaps, I felt I had to provide the little ones with mechanisms of organization and order for sound independent life.'[52] She did this by establishing children's commissions for every aspect of life at the orphanage, each headed by one of the teenagers. 'All members carried equal weight in making decisions. I provided guidance and counsel but wholeheartedly accepted decisions that clashed with my views.'[53] She saw the older children in the orphanage as her partners in the educational work and decision-making:

They displayed an uncommon responsibility and total devotion to action. They were more than helpful elders; they were also my closest friends. With them I could share agonies and fears and speak about pain and anguish. Together we engaged the Polish kids in a stone-throwing battle in a public park. Together we set out at night to find children who had run away because they wanted to be elsewhere.[54]

The concept of children's self-government in orphanages had its roots in pre-war educational ideologies, especially that of Janusz Korczak. A physician and educator, Korczak directed an orphanage for Jewish children in Warsaw before the war and was also involved with one for non-Jewish children. His pedagogy stressed children's rights to respect, autonomy, and honour. Their concerns and requests were addressed as seriously as those of adults. Korczak stressed that children should not be talked down to, but rather listened to in a spirit of dialogue. Self-government was an important pillar of the educational work in the orphanage, and manifested itself through the children's court.[55] Korczak believed that the court would advance children's rights, and a constitution would ensure a serious and fair examination of their concerns. 'The child is entitled to be taken seriously, that his affairs be considered fairly. Thus far, everything has depended on the teacher's goodwill or his good or bad mood. The child has been given no right to protest. We must end despotism.'[56] The caretakers and educators discussed in this chapter had no direct links to Korczak, who was murdered with the children and the rest of his staff in Treblinka in 1942, and none of them mentioned him in this context. Yet it can be surmised that his ideas, about which he wrote and published widely, were certainly an inspiration to many of the educators.[57]

Self-government and the children's courts were two of the issues debated at length at the conference of heads of Jewish orphanages in Kraków in December 1947. H. Mark gave a lecture titled 'Children's Self-Government at a Children's Home'. He claimed that children's self-government was critical to their rehabilitation. 'What are our educational goals?', he asked:

We strive for the physical and moral rebirth of children, the young, after the most terrible of wars, which brought so much material and moral ruin upon the world. We must restore our children's disturbed spiritual balance, raise their sense of dignity, as well as self and national worth, develop their socialization and independence, an active attitude towards life and instil a conscious discipline.[58]

He claimed that these goals could not be met by the 'pep-talks, beliefs, or detached attitudes' that disregarded the 'organization of our children's lives and the life relations they enter into'. They could be achieved 'only by placing the children in such conditions that would make it necessary for them to adopt an active attitude to life, to adopt a socially beneficial attitude'. Self-government, he claimed, embodied these conditions. He stressed the importance of children's courts for both practical and moral reasons:

A penalty imposed by a peer court is often less painful and yet more effective than if we had applied it. Since we entrust children with work in so many important sections, then we should also grant them the freedom to reward and punish their colleagues for their attitude towards the work of the children's collective.[59]

Anton Makarenko, the famous Soviet educator who introduced self-government for juvenile delinquents in his children's colony in Gorky and similar institutions in the 1920s, was also an inspiration for implementing self-government. His writings were very influential in the communist and socialist circles from which, by 1947, most of the directors of orphanages came.[60] One of the directors asked whether 'children's self-government has good educational results only when applied to children who are difficult to manage'. His answer was that 'The experience of many educators, including the outstanding expert on the soul of a child, Janusz Korczak', demonstrated the 'great educational achievements' of self-government. This was an important issue for the educators, who were aware that, unlike orphanages before the war, whose populations came from the lower strata of society, post-war orphanages had a large proportion of children from families that had belonged to the middle class and to the social and professional elite. This had to be taken into account in educational work.[61]

There was also opposition to children's self-government among the staff of the orphanages: 'educators become demoralized, feel declassed and deprived of authority. This often leads to misunderstandings [and] disputes.' Mark argued that, accorded self-government, 'children become arrogant; they are disrespectful towards their educators'. Thus, the caretakers' authority would be undermined, children would 'not listen to their elders and become know-it-alls'. For the staff, the 'immensity of the task of working with the self-government organization' and its discontents would bring a 'reluctant response' to the idea, making for a 'primitive form [of self-government], and is limited to children fulfilling certain order-related functions, regulated by educators'. This would result in 'external forms of self-government', not bounded or grounded 'by the very idea of self-government, which would fill the forms with proper life. Thus empty, superficial forms are created, which are bound to die.' What was needed, maintained Mark, was a gradual and systematic introduction of self-government 'according to a pre-arranged and carefully considered plan of action' that he described at length.[62]

Children's courts also drew criticism. Łabędź, the director of the Zatrzebie orphanage, claimed that the courts 'were unnecessary'. Mark himself, who supported them, quoted a dissertation by Przanowski: 'The institution of peer courts is at the very least redundant, and perhaps even harmful. When there are judges, there will be cases to be tried.' He concluded with a question to the participants: 'Should peer courts be introduced as separate institutions?'[63]

Giving child survivors a role in the running of their orphanage and the ability to pass judgement on their peers was based on pre-war educational ideologies. It was also a response to the needs of the hour, as trust had to be regained and the children had to grow up and find their place as active and valuable members of society and the state. Self-government and children's courts were regarded as one of the tools for this task.

Back to School

To Jewish leaders and educators in the post-war world, it was obvious that the young generation was uneducated and illiterate. Aryeh Tartakower termed this 'enforced illiteracy': the problem of 'tens and perhaps thousands of Jewish children who, during five years of the war, were deprived of every possibility of acquiring even the minimum of education'.[64] For the educators, it was obvious that a return to schooling was of paramount importance once the primary physical rehabilitation was taken care of. It was time 'to wage war on the children's illiteracy. It was bound to be more difficult and harder to win', wrote Lena Küchler.[65]

Bielicka explained: 'This was one issue about which I refused to compromise; I made compromises, but not about studying. This was a matter of principle: a child has to go to school, and this is your school, this is what we have and this is where you study.' Bielicka chose not to send the children to Polish state schools. First, she had the option, in Łódź, of a Jewish school with a Zionist orientation. Secondly, in her view, sending child survivors to Polish state schools would undo efforts to help them reclaim their Jewish identity. The children were still unsure of their regained Jewish identity, and 'placing them again among Poles and reconnecting them to their recent past would have made a Jewish children's home untenable'.[66] In big cities, it was possible to send children to Jewish schools, but, where these were not available, there were other problems. Küchler's orphanage was situated in Zakopane in Podhale at the foot of the Tatra mountains, and the children had no option but to attend the local schools. The schools initially refused to admit them. One headmaster explained that his teachers were opposed to testing Jewish children to determine which class they should attend. The other headmaster was more straightforward. He explained that during the war the Germans had co-opted the local population, accepted them as ethnic Germans and collaborators, and fuelled their antisemitism. The school population, he explained, was deeply antisemitic and would not accept Jewish children.[67]

Küchler had to obtain the support of the school superintendent in person, and teachers were forced to co-operate. However the problems were not over. The schools were a hostile environment for Jewish children. Often, they were ignored by the teachers and attacked by their fellow students. 'They want to beat us up', the boys told Küchler. 'And do you hit back?', she asked, and received the answer: 'Sometimes, sometimes we curse them and sometimes we hit back. It is worst after school on our way back [to the orphanage], then they set upon us and beat us up.'[68] Although the staff of the orphanage tried to take precautions, the situation deteriorated. One day, after bullying at school and with no support from the teachers, the children were physically attacked by the Polish pupils from the school on their way back to the orphanage. Only the opportune arrival of one of the caretakers from the orphanage stopped the assault. Küchler described the return of the children: some were bloody, some had lost teeth, and some were wounded in the head or in the limbs. 'All were scratched and dishevelled, they were all black and blue and their clothes dirty with snow and mud . . . nothing was left of their school bags and school caps.'[69] This led Küchler to the decision to take all the boys out of the state school.

It is obvious that such antisemitic attacks hindered the rehabilitation process. In the evening after the attack, Küchler went to check on the boys. 'I found Mrs Roza the caretaker holding 9-year-old Salush in her arms, cradling him like a baby. He was crying uncontrollably, repeating one question again and again "So why were my mummy and daddy killed?"'[70] The region was home to antisemitic groups that murdered Jewish survivors, and anti-Jewish sentiment was open and widespread. The attacks on the orphans exacerbated the feeling of insecurity and trauma for children and staff and were a prime reason for Küchler smuggling the whole orphanage out of Poland.[71] Anna Nathanblut also recorded antisemitic violence against her children. She recalled that, unexpectedly for the Polish attackers, the older boys from the orphanage fought back, returning home bruised and dishevelled. The girls and the younger boys did not fight back, but they did lodge complaints. 'Attempts at intervention by the orphanage at the school brought no results.'[72]

Returning to schooling was a central experience in some orphanages, especially those that did not have a Zionist orientation. Good schooling ensured the integration of the children into Polish society and a return to a 'normal' childhood. Mina Kaplan, an educator at the orphanage in Lublin, wrote about the preparation for schooling and the excitement this evoked. As she recorded in her diary on 1 September 1945:

> The 7-year-olds are already enrolled in the school. 'I will also go to school', shouts Dorotska, 'we will have notebooks, books and pencils, we're grownups already' . . . The girls got white collar aprons—a sign of being a student, each embroidered with their name. They take good care of them and take them off when they come back from school. All day they sing a song I taught them 'We are going to school.'[73]

Anna Nathanblut wrote about the older children: 'They really wanted to study, but this did not come easily to them. They worked hard, but the results were mediocre. The lack of schooling for years has caused this. Sonia, one of the girls, wanted to be a teacher. She also had difficulties. With much effort she began to advance.' Others were quick to grasp their studies: 'Rachelka . . . was interested in all sorts of problems, she wanted to study and understand everything: her dream was to be a physician.' One of the halls was set aside for homework with benches and tables, and the children organized decorations and a wall newspaper.[74]

The antisemitic and violent school experiences of Lena Küchler's and Mina Kaplan's wards exemplify the immediate post-war years in Poland. As the situation stabilized, discussions regarding schooling for child Holocaust survivors became more common. One of the issues discussed at the conference of heads of Jewish orphanages in Kraków in December 1947 was the relationship with the schools the children went to and homework. Apparently, doing homework clashed with the children's chores at the orphanages, which were also held to be educational. However, as the pedagogical director of the orphanage in Legnica, 'Citizen Kleper', maintained, 'the children are so preoccupied with studying and doing their homework that placing [extra] responsibilities on them . . . leads to a work overload'.[75]

Schooling and learning were of paramount concern after the war. Jewish children were sent to school at an early stage after liberation—even to schools that did not welcome them. It seems that, to Jewish adults, 'enforced illiteracy' was a curse that must be erased. Moreover, returning to school meant that children could regain a 'normal' childhood. It was a step that showed continuity with their pre-Holocaust life, on the one hand, and a hope for a better future in which they would participate as educated citizens on the other.

Conclusion

The experience of the Holocaust marked the lives of the few Jewish children who survived in Poland. Jewish leaders and educators had no textbooks or manuals to show them how to rehabilitate the children, and had to develop strategies and practices as they worked with the children themselves. The pedagogical philosophies and practices of the pre-war years had to be adapted for children who had been persecuted, interned, hunted, and tortured on a massive scale. As orphanages were established, the educators and caretakers had to develop and constantly adjust their practices and educational approaches. This was done through trial and error and an awareness of the children's reactions and needs.

This chapter has described some of the challenges faced by adults, many of them Holocaust survivors themselves, working with children and young people, and how they addressed and tried to overcome them. Their focus was on issues of identity, trust, self-government, and schooling. At the time, these were deemed crucial in the rehabilitation process, and they certainly were.

Yet there is still much research to be done into the post-war rehabilitation of child survivors of the Holocaust. What was the role of religious education, faith, and adherence to Judaism? I have examined the challenge posed by the involvement of many of the children in Christianity during the war and the understanding of the caretakers that patience was of paramount importance, but the positive aspect of Jewish religiosity for the rehabilitation process has yet to be researched. Another issue is that of sexuality and sexual abuse, which was certainly an issue for adolescent survivors. Many children, both girls and boys, had been victims of sexual abuse or witnesses to it.[76] How did caretakers address this issue? The poor medical condition of the children is mentioned in many reports, but there has been no in-depth analysis of medical rehabilitation, particularly in relation to Jewish children. Likewise, little research has been undertaken into children's disabilities, both those they were born with and those caused by their wartime experiences, and how they were dealt with after the war.[77]

For the researcher living in the twenty-first century, one aspect of post-war rehabilitation of children in Poland stands out. Psychologists and other mental health professionals are not mentioned, and there is no trace of their input. This is unlike research on the rehabilitation of children in the DP camps and in Britain that is now focused on the work of American-trained social workers in the camps and of Anna Freud and her colleagues in the UK.[78] It is not clear whether this was the result of the interests of researchers or whether it reflects the reality of the time.

This chapter should be seen as part of a larger endeavour to explore the rehabilitation work done in Poland and all over Europe with child survivors of the Holocaust. What is needed now is an attempt to compare the Polish case with similar work in Europe and elsewhere. The rehabilitation of Jewish child survivors is thus part of the work on 'war orphans' and the millions of other children who lived through the world war and were affected by it. Yet it is a distinct chapter, as Jewish children were specifically condemned to death by the Nazis for being Jewish and, as such, were survivors of genocide. It is my hope that this research will not only enhance our historical knowledge but also help rehabilitative work with child survivors of genocides and war-affected children today.[79]

Notes

This research was made possible thanks to a grant from the Israeli Ministry of Science and Technology (Medicine, Illness and Childhood in the Holocaust and Beyond: Multi-Disciplinary Research on the Holocaust and its Relevance to the Twenty-First Century). Many thanks to my colleague, Dr Verena Buser, for her valuable insights and comments.

1 L. Küchler-Silberman, *Me'ah yeladim sheli* (Jerusalem, 1959), 188; Eng. edn.: *One Hundred Children*, adapted by D. C. Gross (Garden City, NY, 1961); see also ead., *Mayne kinder* (Paris, 1948); Heb. edn.: *Anu ma'ashimim* (Merchavia, 1961). *Me'ah yeladim sheli* was joined by *Hame'ah ligevulam* (Tel Aviv, 1969) and *Beit imi* (Tel Aviv, 1985) to form a trilogy. Lena Küchler expressed dissatisfaction with the translations of her works (see Ghetto Fighters' House Archives, 29625/12), so I have used the original Hebrew editions.
2 Küchler-Silberman, *Me'ah yeladim sheli*, 188.
3 See, inter alia, J. B. Michlic, *Jewish Children in Nazi-Occupied Poland: Survival and Polish–Jewish Relations during the Holocaust as Reflected in Early Postwar Recollections* (Jerusalem, 2008); ead., 'The Raw Memory of War: The Reading of Early Postwar Testimonies of Children in Dom Dziecka in Otwock', *Yad Vashem Studies*, 37/1 (2009), 11–52; ead., '"Who am I?" The Identity of Jewish Children in Poland, 1945–1949', *Polin*, 20 (2007), 97–121; ead., '"The war began for me after the war": Jewish Children in Poland, 1945–49', in *The Routledge History of the Holocaust*, ed. J. C. Friedman (New York, 2011), 482–97; ead., 'Rebuilding Shattered Lives: Some Vignettes of Jewish Children's Lives in Early Postwar Poland', in D. Ofer, F. S. Ouzan, and J. Tydor Baumel-Schwartz (eds.), *Holocaust Survivors: Resettlement, Memories, Identities* (New York, 2011), 46–87; E. Nachmany Gafny, *Dividing Hearts: The Removal of Jewish Children from Gentile Families in Poland in the Immediate Post-Holocaust Years* (Jerusalem, 2009); N. Bogner, *At the Mercy of Strangers: The Rescue of Jewish Children with Assumed Identities in Poland* (Jerusalem, 2009); N. Freeman, '"Our children are our future": Child Care, Education, and Rebuilding Jewish Life in Poland after the Holocaust, 1944–1950', Ph.D. thesis (Ohio State University, 2022).
4 T. Zahra, *The Lost Children: Reconstructing Europe's Families after World War II* (Cambridge, Mass., 2011).
5 It is estimated that one and a half million Jewish children were murdered in the Holocaust. Only 11 per cent survived the war in Nazi-occupied Europe, the lowest survival rate of any demographic group (D. Dwork, *Children with a Star: Jewish Youth in Nazi Europe* (New Haven, Conn., 1991), p. xxxiii n. 27). Nahum Bogner estimates that only 5,000 Jewish children survived in Poland, just 3 per cent (Bogner, *At the Mercy of Strangers*, 15). The number of Polish Jewish children in Poland rose to 28,000 with the return of Polish Jews who had spent the war in the unoccupied Soviet Union. Immediate post-war estimates suggest that there were 150,000 Jewish child survivors in Europe (180,000 with those returning from the Soviet Union) (Dwork, *Children with a Star*, p. xxxiii n. 27).

6 See D. Doron, *Jewish Youth and Identity in Postwar France: Rebuilding Family and Nation* (Bloomington, Ind., 2015).
7 YIVO Archives, New York, RG 1258: 'Barikht fun der tsvayter visnshaftlekher baratung fun der tsentraler historisher komisye in poyln dem 19-tn un 20-tn September 1945'.
8 Ibid.
9 Ibid.
10 Ibid.
11 Ibid.
12 A. Margolin and O. Schwartz (dirs.), *My Hundred Children*, documentary (JCS Productions, 2003).
13 Ibid.
14 Küchler-Silberman, *Me'ah yeladim sheli*, 239.
15 Yad Yaari Archive, Givat Haviva, 9-1-2/000021/000205: Anna Nathanblut, memoirs (1962).
16 D. Tocker, 'Beit hayeladim milublin', Ph.D. thesis (Tel Aviv University, 2008), 11.
17 Küchler-Silberman, *Me'ah yeladim sheli*, 273–8.
18 Ibid. 277.
19 J. Hemmendinger, *Survivors: Children of the Holocaust* (Bethesda, Md., 1986), 23; see also J. Hemmendinger and R. Krell, *The Children of Buchenwald: Child Survivors and Their Post-War Lives* (Jerusalem, 2000).
20 On post-war Poland and its Jews, see J. T. Gross, *Fear. Anti-Semitism in Poland after Auschwitz: An Essay in Historical Interpretation* (Princeton, NJ, 2006); A. Kichelewski, *Les Survivants: Les Juifs de Pologne depuis la Shoah* (Paris, 2018).
21 *Journal of Educational Sociology*, 18/5 (1945): *The Jew in the Postwar World*.
22 A. Tartakower, 'Problems of Jewish Cultural Reconstruction in Europe', *Journal of Educational Sociology*, 18 (1945), 271–7.
23 Küchler-Silberman, *Me'ah yeladim sheli*, 177.
24 Margolin and Schwartz (dirs.), *My Hundred Children*.
25 Koordynacja was a Zionist organization which located children rescued by Christian families and convents in order to reclaim them for the Jewish people.
26 Hebrew University of Jerusalem, Oral History Division (hereafter OHD), interview 68/26: Hasia Bornstein (Bilitzka) [Chasia Bielicka] (28 Oct. 1970; Heb.).
27 Küchler-Silberman, *Me'ah yeladim sheli*, 188.
28 Ibid. 239.
29 C. Bornstein-Bielicka and N. Izhar, *One of the Few: A Resistance Fighter and Educator, 1939–1947*, trans. N. Greenwood (Jerusalem, 2009), 322; Heb. orig.: *Aḥat mime'atim: darkah shel loḥemet umeḥanekhet 1939–1947* (Tel Aviv, 2003), 279.
30 N. Orlovits-Reznik, *Ima, hamutar kevar livkot?* (Ramat Gan, 1964), 43.
31 OHD, interview 68/28: Yeshayayu Drucker (27 Dec. 1970; Heb.).
32 Archiwum Żydowskiego Instytutu Historycznego, Kraków, 303/IX, 'Centralny Komitet Żydów w Polsce: Wydział Oświaty, 1945–1950', 67: 'Zjazd kierowników domów dziecka przy CKŻP dn. 12-14.12.1947 r.', 22–3 (3–4).
33 Ibid. I believe that this is an uncommon view not shared by most educators. I have not found any other statements like this.
34 Pola Weinstein (b. 1933), in *Dapei edut*, 4 vols. (Lohamei Haghetaot, 1984), iii. 1002; quoted in Nachmany Gafny, *Dividing Hearts*, 286.
35 Küchler-Silberman, *Me'ah yeladim sheli*, 177.

36 Anna Nathanblut, memoirs.
37 See Michlic, *Jewish Children in Nazi-Occupied Poland*; ead., 'The Raw Memory of War'; ead., '"Who am I?"'; ead., '"The war began for me after the war"'; ead., 'Rebuilding Shattered Lives'; Bogner, *At the Mercy of Strangers*; Nachmany Gafny, *Dividing Hearts*.
38 Bornstein-Bielicka and Izhar, *One of the Few*, 323; see eaed., *Aḥat mime'atim*, 280.
39 Bornstein-Bielicka and Izhar, *One of the Few*, 326; see eaed., *Aḥat mime'atim*, 283.
40 Bornstein-Bielicka and Izhar, *One of the Few*, 326; see eaed., *Aḥat mime'atim*, 283.
41 Yeshayayu Drucker, OHD interview.
42 Küchler-Silberman, *Me'ah yeladim sheli*, 204.
43 Ibid.
44 Hasia Bornstein, OHD interview.
45 Ibid.
46 Ibid.
47 Yeshayayu Drucker, OHD interview.
48 Ibid.
49 D. Kahane, *Aḥarei hamabul: ḥayei hakehilot bepolin le'aḥer hasho'ah* (Jerusalem, 1981), 54.
50 See Nachmany Gafny, *Dividing Hearts*, 113.
51 Yeshayayu Drucker, OHD interview.
52 Bornstein-Bielicka and Izhar, *One of the Few*, 344; see eaed., *Aḥat mime'atim*, 300.
53 Bornstein-Bielicka and Izhar, *One of the Few*, 344–5; see eaed., *Aḥat mime'atim*, 300.
54 Bornstein-Bielicka and Izhar, *One of the Few*, 329; see eaed., *Aḥat mime'atim*, 285.
55 See *Selected Works of Janusz Korczak*, selected by M. Wolins, trans. J. Bachrach (n.d.): Janusz Korczak Association of Canada website, 'Publications', visited 17 May 2022.
56 J. Korczak, 'The Court of Peers', in *Selected Works of Janusz Korczak*, 312–24: 313.
57 This can also be seen in the movie *Unzere kinder* which is set in an orphanage for surviving Jewish children and features the renowned Jewish comedians Shimon Dzigan and Israel Shumacher, Niusia Gold, and a cast of Jewish children, many of them survivors. The directors chose to place the discussion about the appropriate way to rehabilitate the children under a large portrait of Korczak (see N. Gross and S. Goskind (dir.), *Unzere kinder* (Kinor, 1948)).
58 'Zjazd kierowników domów dziecka przy CKŻP dn. 12-14.12.1947 r.', 22–3 (3–4).
59 Ibid.
60 For English translations of Makarenko's educational writings, see 'Anton Semyonovich Makarenko, 1888–1939' (n.d.): Marxist Internet Archive website, visited 17 May 2022.
61 'Zjazd kierowników domów dziecka przy CKŻP dn. 12-14.12.1947 r.', 22–3 (3–4).
62 Ibid.
63 Ibid. Opposition to children's courts by members of staff had existed before the war. In a critical review of the running of the children's home in Helenówek published in 1932 by one of the staff, he relates an incident in which the children's court asked for permission to try a teacher who had wronged a student but was refused, since it had no jurisdiction. The title given to this episode was 'The Teacher Can Do Anything . . .'. See S. Martin, *For the Good of the Nation: Institutions for Jewish Children in Interwar Poland. A Documentary History* (Brighton, Mass., 2017), 113–15. In Korczak's orphanage, on the other hand, teachers and he himself were tried by the court.
64 Tartakower, 'Problems of Jewish Cultural Reconstruction in Europe', 271.
65 Küchler-Silberman, *Me'ah yeladim sheli*, 242.

66 Hasia Bornstein, OHD interview.
67 Küchler-Silberman, *Me'ah yeladim sheli*, 289; for a general picture, see D. Engel, 'Patterns of Anti-Jewish Violence in Poland, 1944–1946', *Yad Vashem Studies*, 26 (1998), 43–85.
68 Küchler-Silberman, *Me'ah yeladim sheli*, 306.
69 Ibid. 308.
70 Ibid. 309.
71 On the murder of Jewish survivors in the area and attacks on the orphanage, see K. Panz, '"The children are in a state of true panic": Postwar Anti-Jewish Violence in Podhale and Its Youngest Victims', *Yad Vashem Studies*, 46/1 (2018), 103–40.
72 Anna Nathanblut, memoirs.
73 Yad Vashem Archives, Jerusalem, O33/8797: Mina Kaplan-Halberstadt, diary, 26 June–24 Dec. 1945 (1 Sept. 1945).
74 Anna Nathanblut, memoirs.
75 'Zjazd kierowników domów dziecka przy CKŻP dn. 12-14.12.1947 r.', 6.
76 B. Chalmers, *Betrayed: Child Sex Abuse in the Holocaust* (Tolworth, Surr., 2020).
77 R. Balint, 'Children Left Behind: Family, Refugees and Immigration in Postwar Europe', *History Workshop Journal*, 82 (2016), 151–72.
78 R. Clifford, *Survivors: Children's Lives after the Holocaust* (New Haven, Conn., 2020).
79 For such work, see the Western Galilee College 'Children of War, Holocaust and Genocide' project, headed by the author and Dr Verena Buser.

5. CHILDHOOD IN POST-1945 POLAND

Beyond Post-Holocaust Trauma
Polish Jewish Childhood in Dzierżoniów, Lower Silesia, 1945–1950

KAMIL KIJEK

> Dzierżoniów was one of the largest Jewish settlements in Lower Silesia. Its Jewish population included many children, and their paths into adulthood provide a unique perspective on the post-war period in Poland. For young Jews the experience of growing up in Lower Silesia, among relatively strong and pluralistic Jewish communities, was very different from that in the in post-Holocaust landscape of central Poland. It was not defined mainly by antisemitism, assimilation, or concealing one's Jewish identity, but by a unique mixture of older pre-1945 Jewish traditions and the new post-Holocaust reality, including educational opportunities unavailable to their parents' generation. The long-term processes that affected this generation of Polish Jews in communist Poland, metropolitanization and professionalization while maintaining a strong Jewish identity, made its members not unlike their counterparts in non-communist centres of the post-Holocaust Jewish world.

Introduction

This chapter is a case study of the experience of childhood and adolescence among members of the Polish Jewish community in the first years after the Holocaust. That experience will be described with reference to Dzierżoniów, a small town in the south-west of present-day Poland, in Lower Silesia, a part of pre-war Germany which, after the Second World War, fell within the borders of the new Polish state.[1] The town was known as Reichenbach when it was in Germany, and briefly as Rychbach between spring 1945 and spring 1946.

The community was unusual in post-Holocaust Poland, in that Dzierżoniów, for several years after the end of the Second World War, had a large and visible Jewish population. Jewish life there was representative of the broader situation in post-war Lower Silesia as a whole, which was home to around half of all Polish Jews, the vast majority of whom lived in Jewish communities organized around a dense network of institutions and who made no attempt to hide their identity. In this sense, many of the places in Lower Silesia (as well as Łódź and Szczecin in other parts of the country) differed markedly from hundreds of towns and villages in central Poland.[2] The experiences of Jewish children and adolescents were therefore quite different from those described in the existing literature on the subject, where they are associated with such post-Holocaust processes as assimilation, fear, and the concealment of Jewish identity.[3]

The central issue addressed in this chapter is the dialectic between, on the one hand, the destruction, rupture, and revolution introduced into the life of Polish Jews by the Holocaust and communism, and, on the other, the continuity and the survival to a greater or lesser extent of pre-war and sometimes centuries-old forms of Jewish culture, and the influence of this dialectic on the experience of Jewish childhood. A second issue concerns the sources of post-war Jewish identity. This was influenced not only by family life and Jewish organizations and institutions but also by the institutions of the communist state and the public sphere which it dominated. The overlapping impact of all these cultural institutions determined the basic framework in which Jewish childhood was experienced and served to shape the generation of Polish Jews growing up after the Holocaust in a specific way.

This chapter also aims to illuminate the consequences of the Holocaust. The Holocaust was inevitably the principal context for Jewish adolescence and childhood, not only because of the personal trauma suffered by children and their parents, which was then reflected in the children's upbringing, but also, in a broader sense, as a historical event which all but destroyed the civilization of Polish Jews. This did not mean that everything which defined Jewish childhood in Poland was new. Parents, teachers, and the social environment in which children lived and grew up were all marked not only by the trauma of the Holocaust but also by their pre-1939 experience. As I will endeavour to show, the patterns of childhood and adolescence and the subsequent life trajectories of the Jewish children of Dzierżoniów were not all that different from those of their Jewish contemporaries in the United States, western Europe, and Israel.

This does not of course mean that Jewish childhood in Dzierżoniów after the Holocaust did not have its own distinctive characteristics. The trauma of the Holocaust and the unique experience of exile in the Soviet Union, as well as post-war antisemitism and the authoritarian political culture, all had a significant influence. The premise of this chapter is simply that, despite these influences, Jewish childhood in Dzierżoniów between 1945 and 1950 was also defined by the more general processes taking place in the Jewish world on both sides of the Iron Curtain: processes such as the gradual decline of the modernist, ideological political culture; professionalization and the growing importance of formal education; metropolitanization; and the development of the transnational aspect of Jewish identity.

The main source materials used in this chapter are interviews recorded by me and other individuals and institutions with a number of Jewish inhabitants of Dzierżoniów, some of whom remained in Poland and some of whom left. This is augmented by material created by Polish Jews and their institutions and by people from abroad and foreign institutions engaged in the rebuilding of the Polish Jewish community. This chapter focuses on the experiences of childhood and adolescence in Dzierżoniów between 1945 and 1950, in other words of those who spent at least a few years there and were under 18 in 1950. It should be noted that the boundaries between 'childhood', 'youth', and 'adulthood' in this period were exceptionally fluid. During and after the war many minors—some orphaned, some not—were obliged to take responsibility for their own lives or were held in the care of various institutions, and their education was delayed. Their experiences in wartime and afterwards certainly did not constitute a classic 'childhood'. The sources refer to 'children' as being persons under the age of 10 and to 'young people' as being teenagers under 18. The first part of the chapter concentrates on various policies in relation to children and sets out the general conditions of life in Dzierżoniów. The second part focuses on the perspectives and memories of those who grew up in the post-war Jewish community.

The principal heuristic premise of this chapter is the conviction expressed by Carlo Ginzburg and others that the aim of 'microhistory' is not to convey new historical details but to depict broader historical processes in a new light.[4] It is, in my view, just such a light that selected elements of Jewish childhood in Dzierżoniów can shed on the first years after the Holocaust. From the perspective of the present day or from the perspective of Poland after March 1968, they take on an irresistible logic, a teleology of the inexorable disappearance of the Jewish world in Poland, of fear, and of communist assimilation. This inevitability is less obvious and more ambivalent from the perspective of a Jewish child in Dzierżoniów in 1945.

Jews in Lower Silesia, 1945–1968: The Wider Context

After the Second World War, Lower Silesia was part of the so-called 'Recovered Territories', the eastern territories of Germany which were incorporated into the new Polish state. In May 1945 the only sizeable groups of Polish citizens in the region were forced labourers and concentration camp inmates. Of the approximately 18,000 prisoners at the huge concentration camp at Gross-Rosen, as many as 10,000 were Polish Jews, most of them held in one of the subcamps near Rychbach. Whereas the Poles and Jews from other countries quickly left for their pre-war homes, many Polish Jews had nowhere to go. On 13 May 1945 they established a committee to look after and provide subsistence for the survivors.[5] On 17 June 1945, after the committee had established contact with the Central Committee of Jews in Poland (Centralny Komitet Żydów w Polsce; CKŻP) in Warsaw and gained the support of the authorities, it became the Provincial Committee of Polish Jews (Wojewódzki Komitet Żydów Polskich; WKŻ), with its headquarters in Rychbach.[6] The decision was taken to make Lower Silesia one of the centres of the post-war Jewish community. Holocaust survivors soon began to pour in from central Poland, German concentration camps, and the former eastern parts of Poland which were now part of the USSR. At the end of June 1945 there were 2,000 Polish Jews in Rychbach; by the end of 1945 that number had doubled.[7]

An unusual set of circumstances influenced the selection of Lower Silesia as the site of Jewish settlement. For the new Polish authorities, the presence of Polish Jewish Holocaust survivors and the restoration of a Jewish community on previously German soil was an excellent means of proving their legitimacy to the international community. Furthermore, the authorities were subject to international criticism because of the high level of antisemitism in Poland and the attacks on Jews returning to their homes and attempting to reclaim their property, and preferred to move as many Jews as possible to new territories.[8] By summer 1945 some of the German inhabitants had already fled, and it was obvious that the rest would soon be deported. For Jews, it was significantly easier to find accommodation and employment there. For much the same reasons, Jewish settlement in Lower Silesia was of interest to those Jewish leaders who believed in the possibility of rebuilding Jewish life in Poland. Lower Silesia offered an opportunity for significantly larger and more closely knit Jewish communities, whose members would not have to conceal their identity. It also offered the possibility of establishing a dense network of institutions and through them the chance of developing a broadly secular Jewish national culture.[9]

Apart from the uncertain political environment and the reluctance of most Polish Jews to remain in a country which had become a cemetery for their families and friends and in which an aggressive antisemitism was rampant, the fundamental fact which put the future of the Lower Silesian Polish Jewish community in doubt was its demographic situation. Among the former prisoners of the concentration camps and the Jews who arrived from central and eastern Poland, there were almost no children (or indeed elderly people).[10] In January 1946, only 155 of the 3,873 people registered with the Rychbach District Jewish Committee (Powiatowy Komitet Żydowski; PKŻ) were under the age of 14.[11] That situation was to change with the arrival in Lower Silesia of Polish Jews who had spent the war in the Soviet Union. There, entire families had managed to survive. The decision to resettle the majority of these 200,000 or so Polish Jews in Lower Silesia was taken in the late summer of 1945. News had begun to spread about the successful establishment of a local Jewish community, the development of institutions, and the ease with which newcomers could find accommodation and employment there, and it was viewed as the most suitable place for Jewish settlement both by the authorities and by the leaders of the CKŻP.[12] This body estimated that as many as 25,000 of all repatriates would be children.[13] It was they who were to decide the future of the Jewish nation in Poland.

The first trains carrying Jewish repatriates from the USSR began to arrive in Lower Silesia in February 1946. By May 1946 Dzierżoniów, two smaller neighbouring towns, and a handful of local villages were home to over 15,000 Jews.[14] In Dzierżoniów itself, the number of Jewish inhabitants tripled in the first half of 1946, and by August it had reached 12,000 or over half of the total population. In reality, because those who left were not deregistered, this figure was undoubtedly lower, probably around 9,000.[15] At the same time, the second half of 1946 saw the greatest exodus of Jews from Poland in the post-war period, precipitated, amongst other things, by the bloody pogrom in Kielce.[16] It is generally accepted that around 63,000 Jews left Poland at this time.[17] Many also left Lower Silesia, but the percentage leaving was lower than in many other places. In December 1947, a year after the end of the wave of emigration, there were still 6,712 Jews in Dzierżoniów, making up 30 per cent of its population and around 10 per cent of all Jews in Lower Silesia.[18] The demographic structure of the community had also returned to normal, so that by autumn 1946 children under the age of 14 constituted 25 per cent of Dzierżoniów's Jewish population.[19]

The percentage of Jews in the overall population of Dzierżoniów and its neighbouring towns between 1945 and 1950 was exceptional, in comparison both with that in Poland as a whole and that in post-Holocaust Europe more generally. A distinguishing feature of Jewish life there was its unusually extensive political, social, and cultural pluralism. Communists were active, but so were the political parties and youth organizations of all the main Zionist movements (illegally in the case of the right-wing Revisionists) and those of the socialist Bund. Semi-officially, the Orthodox Agudat Israel and the Zionist-religious Mizrachi party also operated there, making use of the organizational structures of the Congregations of the Mosaic Faith (as the religious Jewish communities were now termed). Aid flowed into the town from the American Jewish Joint Distribution Committee and other international philanthropic Jewish organizations. The PKŻ, the local religious congregation, party units, and youth organization cells all helped to arrange work, accommodation, health care, various forms of social assistance for the Jewish population, and cultural institutions, farms and kibbutzim, schools, orphanages, and after-school daycare centres for the children of working parents.[20]

Zionist and Orthodox groups, which as a matter of principle did not envisage a Jewish future in Poland, worked towards the departure from Poland of as many Jews as possible. Communists and Bundists, on the other hand, worked towards the rebuilding of the community *in situ*. For all the parties and organizations, children were a crucial issue. Another key player with a direct impact on Jewish children was the state. Its educational activities and general ideological influence were at times compatible and at times incompatible with the activities of Jewish institutions. These issues also had both a direct and an indirect bearing on Jewish parents, on non-Jewish contemporaries, and on the wider social environment in which the Jewish children of Dzierżoniów grew up.

The years 1949 and 1950 were a turning point in the life of the Jewish community in Poland. The installation of a full communist dictatorship; the associated closure of all non-communist Jewish institutions, including the committees which had until then been responsible for organizing Jewish community life; the nationalization of Jewish schools; the elimination of the private sector; the ban on all contact with western Jewish organizations uncontrolled by the state; and the drastic deterioration of relations with Israel triggered a further exodus of Jews.[21] Between autumn 1949 and summer 1951 around 28,000 people emigrated:[22] fewer than 3,000 Jews remained in Dzierżoniów.[23] Although Stalinism did not spell the end of Jewish life in Poland, and some aspects of it continued to function, that life was fundamentally altered, and with it the nature of childhood and adolescence. The analysis which follows focuses on the period before that turning point.

Childhood and Youth in the Shadow of Ideology and Politics

Of the political movements which believed not only in the future of individual Jews but also in the survival of the entire nation and its culture in post-Holocaust Poland, the two most important were communism, represented by the Jewish Fraction of the Polish Workers' Party, and socialism, represented by the Bund. In Rychbach, by early summer 1945, issues pertaining to children and young people were a key aspect of these parties' activity in the PKŻ, and seeing to their welfare, securing their future in Poland, and winning over Jewish parents were critical elements of their political programmes. In July 1945, when there were still very few Jewish children in the region, the PKŻ was already engaged in establishing a school in Rychbach. In an effort to encourage the small number of young Jews to take part in the harvest festival, the committee announced a competition for a 'Hymn to New Life in Rychbach', to promote the notion of staying and building a new and better Jewish future there.[24] On 30 August 1945, at a meeting of activists from the various Jewish youth organizations in Lower Silesia, the communist representative declared: 'Young Jews in Poland will make every effort to ensure that Lower Silesia, where Jewish life is centred, sees a flourishing of Jewish culture, prosperity, and a national community of Polish Jews' —thus confirming the key role of children and young people in the planned rebirth of the Jewish community in Poland.[25]

Earlier, in July 1945, a decision had been made to transfer one of the largest Jewish children's homes then operating in Poland from Lublin to Pieszyce, near Rychbach.[26] The main reason for this move, apart from the desire to bolster the Lower Silesian Jewish community, was security: the wave of anti-Jewish violence sweeping through central and eastern Poland was far less pronounced there. The first Jewish orphans (150 children) arrived in Rychbach and Pieszyce from Lublin in August 1945, and classes for the youngest children, including lessons in Yiddish, started at the home the following month.[27]

From the very beginning, the Zionists were also interested in Lower Silesia, and issues concerning children and young people. Their aim was to encourage as many Jews as possible to leave Poland, to secure their settlement in Palestine, and to build a Jewish state there.[28] Children and young people were just as important for the future of their movement as they were for those of their ideological opponents. At the end of July 1945 the Palestine-based Liaison Office of the global Hashomer Hatsa'ir movement prepared its members in Poland for the anticipated repatriation of hundreds of thousands of Polish Jews from the USSR. Its instructions on establishing kibbutzim and *hakhsharot* to prepare repatriates for emigration and life in Palestine stressed the importance of undertaking different work with adults and with young people. The latter were to be organized, as far as possible, into separate kibbutzim in order to maximize the movement's ideological influence over them.[29] As early as July 1945 Hashomer Hatsa'ir sent out activists across Lower Silesia with the primary aim of involving as many young Jews as possible in its activities.[30] Kibbutzim were organized in Rychbach and its surrounding area. A kibbutz run by the umbrella organization Hehaluts was operating in Pieszyce by September 1945, and Gordonia and Hashomer Hatsa'ir were preparing to set up their own kibbutz nearby.[31]

Also evident from the very start was the characteristic ideological maximalism of all the Jewish parties. Each was convinced that only the realization of its particular vision could open the door to a better future and that the methods of its rivals would inevitably lead to catastrophe. A political culture of this sort, one of the legacies of the pre-war period, was the cause of intense rivalry between the various Jewish groups (often despite their purported formal co-operation), and it was children who were at the heart of this rivalry. In September 1945 Jewish communists in Rychbach accused Natan Blit, the director of the Pieszyce children's home, of having too much freedom of action. The autonomy of the establishment and its non-adherence to communist goals and ideals were said to be 'unhealthy'.[32] Opinions such as this gave rise to fierce battles between communists and Zionists over their influence on children and young people. These battles were waged from the very beginning of the WKŻ's operation in Rychbach. In July 1945 Jakub Egit, the communist chairman of the PKŻ, evicted the kibbutz of Hehaluts and the League for Labour Palestine from the committee's premises where it was based, on the grounds, later shown to be unproven, that it was engaged in anti-Soviet agitation.[33] One of the principal allegations against Zionists in Lower Silesia was their encouragement of children to leave Poland and the damaging effect of their ideology on the young.[34] This was the primary justification for the unsuccessful protest by the WKŻ and PKŻ against the opening of the Hebrew Tarbut school in Dzierżoniów in September 1946.[35]

The bitter rivalry between the Jewish political camps even affected a difficult and painful issue close to the heart of all Jews: the removal of Jewish children from the Christian homes and institutions where they had survived the Holocaust.[36] Thus a Zionist report emphasized the success achieved in this field by Orthodox Jews, who operated in Poland without official consent and were financially supported by Va'ad Hahatsalah and the worldwide Agudat Israel. Hehaluts set about establishing its own children's homes.[37] In autumn 1945 a heated dispute broke out between communists and Zionists in Rychbach concerning the transfer by the latter of the last remaining children from the children's home in Pieszyce to their special kibbutz for orphans in Sosnowiec, whence they intended to remove them from Poland. The fact that workers from the home participated in this action triggered an angry reaction from the communists and Bundists on the WKŻ.[38] Less than a year later they responded with furious indignation when Zionists from the Ihud party removed Jewish children from a convent near Dzierżoniów and transferred them to their own kibbutz, not the committee's children's home.[39] This 'battle for children' was not of course peculiar to Dzierżoniów or indeed to Jewish life in Poland. Although there were distinctive local features which derived from the uniqueness of the Jewish experience during the Holocaust, it was part of the broader European phenomenon of renationalizing children after the Second World War. Post-war states and communities, devastated and fragmented by the war, were now engaged in restoring law and order. An important element of that process was the reconstruction of cohesive national identities for the new post-war generations.[40]

The rivalry between communists and Zionists should not, however, disguise the important fact that both parties employed the same modernist model of political culture. This model, developed over the preceding decades and especially in the interwar period, posited the primacy of a deeply internalized ideology, an all-embracing dedication, and subordination to the cause, discipline, and a conviction that the political movement in question was building a new and glorious future.

It was undoubtedly this model of political culture which characterized Zionist activism in Dzierżoniów. In April 1946, according to a report from the local leader of Hashomer Hatsa'ir in Bielawa (a town bordering on Dzierżoniów with a similarly high percentage of Jewish residents), one of the most important recent events organized at his kibbutz was a trip to the nearby Sowie mountains, during which the young Hashomer members 'marched in orderly formation through the whole of Bielawa ... singing Hebrew and Soviet songs'. At the Passover seder organized that month at the Hashomer kibbutz in Dzierżoniów, behind the speakers delivering their solemn addresses hung portraits of Theodor Herzl and Joseph Stalin.[41]

In June 1946 all the young Jews of Dzierżoniów, regardless of political sympathy, were mobilized to take part in the People's Referendum, the aim of which was to legitimize Poland's ruling bloc and the reforms it intended to introduce (see Figure 1). Both the state and virtually every Jewish institution recruited young people to organize and participate in rallies and to go and visit Jewish homes in person.[42] The same took place on an even greater scale during the parliamentary elections in January 1947.[43] A report on the first year's activity of the WKŻ repeatedly underlined that 'new life' was the watchword of the Jewish community. For communists and Bundists, one of the key elements of this 'new life' was to be Jewish labour in state factories, to which Jews had had only very limited access before the war. Particular attention was paid to the employment in those factories of young Jews.[44] The Zionists carried out their programme of productivization mainly through *hakhsharot*, so-called 'productivization centres', and agricultural labour on their kibbutzim. Through youth education of this sort, they too drew on memories of the interwar period and their ideological traditions and symbols. Towards the end of July 1946, the Hashomer Hatsa'ir kibbutz in Bielawa organized a large harvest festival, to which the entire local Jewish community was invited. The festival's main stage was decorated with the emblems of Keren Kayemet Leyisra'el and Keren Hayesod, the two most important organizations involved in raising funds from around the world for the development of the Jewish community in the Land of Israel, and popular Hebrew kibbutz songs were sung. Accounts of the festival recorded that 'the atmosphere and overall impact was such that it seemed as if this was not all taking place on land which only a short time earlier had belonged to the Nazis but in the Land of Israel'.[45]

The celebrations to mark the second anniversary of the establishment of the local community also harked back to the interwar traditions of Lower Silesian political culture. The principal celebrations took place in Dzierżoniów on 22 June 1947 and

Figure 1 The Bund party headquarters and a Bundist 'tavern for workers' (named Arbeter Vinkl after a famous workers' centre in pre-1939 Warsaw) in the old town square of Dzierżoniów, with posters urging local Jews to vote 'Yes' three times in the forthcoming referendum on 30 June 1946
Archiwum Katedry Judaistyki im. Tadeusza Taubego, University of Wrocław

were attended by representatives of the state and the CKŻP in Warsaw. In keeping with the modernist model of political culture, and also in response to the trauma of the Holocaust, these celebrations expressed a collective faith in the building of a new and glorious future, and young people played a key role in the day's events. The 10,000 Jews from Lower Silesia who were present watched with admiration as a procession of young Jews marched past under the red banners of the communists, the Bund, and Po'alei Tsiyon Left and the white and blue banners of numerous other Zionist organizations.[46]

Communists and Bundists were united in their desire to have the maximum possible influence over young people's social and political awareness. However, Zionists too shared the same aspirations, something which was not incompatible with their plans to secure the departure from Poland of as many Jews as possible, and especially children and young people. Aware that not all Polish Jews would be able or would immediately want to emigrate, they set out to ensure that they were engaged in every facet of Jewish life in Poland. For them too the principal objective was ideological mobilization.[47] This was why, in April 1946, when allocating newly arrived repatriates to its kibbutzim in Dzierżoniów and Bielawa, Hashomer Hatsa'ir separated children aged 12 to 16 from their parents and housed them in special accommodation. The parental presence was thought to undermine the all-important ideological influence of the organization.[48] In this period, the priority was emigration to the Land of Israel. When organizing the departure of its young members to displaced persons camps in Germany, Austria, and Italy, Hashomer Hatsa'ir also organized the departure of their parents and siblings. Nonetheless, whenever possible, it sought to divide them into separate groups, so that the young people would remain together even after their departure.[49] In its instructions dated 18 August 1946, the Central Committee of Hashomer Hatsa'ir in Poland, located in Łódź, stipulated that the movement's local activists who were organizing emigration from Lower Silesia were 'required to ensure that the groups which are leaving do so as part of the kibbutzim. It is essential to make sure that children do not travel together with their parents.' The intention was to uphold the 'organizational cohesion of the movement' not only within Poland but also in the displaced persons camps in the American zone of occupied Germany.[50] Equally, when in late 1946 and 1947 Jewish emigration from Poland virtually ceased and the Zionist movement began to prepare for long-term activity among those Jews who remained, it continued to maximize its ideological work with young people, premised on the pre-war concept of 'the sons' revolt' and the building of a strong Zionist identity among the young, so as to encourage widespread opposition to the destructive 'spirit of the diaspora'. This spirit was supposedly passed on to children by their parents, who were fearful of leaving Poland, but above all by the communist-controlled Jewish committees and their schools.[51]

It should be stressed that the ideological maximalism of the main Jewish political movements was seldom foreign to Jewish parents themselves, the vast majority of whom had grown up during the interwar period and had encountered the burgeoning Jewish parties and youth organizations. The language, slogans, symbols, and methods which they now employed on their children would have been entirely familiar to them. The powerful secularizing tendencies of the interwar period and their experience of the Holocaust and of life in the USSR meant that most young post-war parents, who had grown up in traditional Jewish families, now abandoned Orthodox Judaism. This rebellious generation was also characterized by its fierce criticism of the pre-war Jewish economic structure; its distaste for the petty trading practised by most of its parents' generation; its coming of age during the economic and political crisis of the 1930s; and its experience of the antisemitism and widespread discrimination against Jews of that period. This generation was therefore united not only by its experience of the Holocaust and exile in the USSR but also by its formative experiences during the 1930s, its terrible fear of fascism, and its quest for political programmes which promised a new and better future, whether in Poland or in Palestine.[52] After the war, many of these people embraced the programme put forward by Jewish communists with great hope and confidence, welcoming their vision of building a new Poland which would confront religious prejudice and antisemitism and ensure work and support for all its citizens. Zionists also endorsed this programme in the early post-war years.[53]

Michał Teitelbaum was born in 1947, a few months after his parents' return from the USSR, and grew up in Dzierżoniów hearing about his father's devout family of petty traders from Kielce, of his 'father's disappearances from the synagogue to join the illegal cells of a communist organization', and of how he had to start work in a factory at the age of 11. His father believed that the new Poland in which his son was now to grow up was a repudiation of that past.[54] Izaak Gingold, born in the same year in Bielawa, was also brought up on the recollections of his father, a textile worker in a Bielawa factory who had learned his trade before the war in his home town of Tomaszów Mazowiecki, where he worked only seasonally and often suffered from hunger and unemployment. Gingold's father too, through his trade union activism, had joined the communist movement before the war and as a result had spent two and a half years in prison. He survived the war in the Soviet part of Ukraine until the end of June 1941, and thereafter in central Asia.[55] For this group of Jewish parents, the notion of a 'new life', so powerfully present in state and official Jewish discourse in Poland in the immediate post-Holocaust period, was not simply a propaganda slogan. It spoke directly to their pre-1939 experiences, to their painful memories of the poverty and discrimination of those years, and to their dreams of a better world. This was why the notion was so potent and therefore so central to the lives of many Jewish children in this period. They were to be raised in a world which was completely different from that in which their parents had grown up, a world of equal opportunities, good prospects, and a bright future.

The idea of a new life and a Poland that was radically different from that of the pre-war years, an idea inevitably bound up with negative memories of growing up at that time and, in particular, memories of economic deprivation and ethnic discrimination, also had an impact on Jewish families which had no pre- or post-war communist leanings and which were sceptical about both communism and their own future in Poland. These were not mutually exclusive. The immediate post-war years were a time of ambivalence, a time when life in Poland simultaneously involved both opportunity and risk. Chaim Pertman and Frida Szarfstein had been brought up before the war in a small shtetl, Wohyń Podlaski. Both had grown up in very poor and religious artisan families. As was typical for members of their generation, their working lives began as soon as they left elementary school, and after acquiring the necessary tailoring skills they left for Warsaw to look for work. They married at the beginning of October 1939 when Chaim Pertman returned home from the Polish army. In

November the Pertmans decided to escape to the Soviet Union. Until 1941 they lived and worked in Brest; after June 1941, together with the thousands of other Jews fleeing the invading German forces, they ended up far to the east, in Astrakhan and then Kazakhstan. The Pertmans fled to the USSR, not as the result of any belief that the USSR would offer equal status to Jews but simply through fear of further German atrocities of the sort they had witnessed at the beginning of the occupation in Warsaw and Wohyń. In contrast to many of their contemporaries, they did not rebel against their family environment or their parents' beliefs. Frieda Pertman, the granddaughter of a ritual slaughterer and a religious teacher, ate her first consciously non-kosher meal during her period of exile and hunger in the Soviet Union. She described her wartime experiences as having taken place in a foreign country which was dangerous and at times hostile. She viewed post-war Poland and its communists with a similar mistrust, including the Jewish communists whom she knew from the streets of Dzierżoniów. Yet she also recalled the significance of the post-war changes, the opportunities for work and study, the chance of a different life for herself and her husband and above all for their children, who would have had none of those advantages if they had grown up in a poor artisan family before the war.[56]

At the same time, however, the ambivalence of the wartime and post-war experience could have the opposite effect. A majority of the Jewish inhabitants of Dzierżoniów had survived the war in the Soviet Union. It was there that, for the first time, they had the opportunity of living in a state which on a daily basis promised freedom and equality to all its citizens, regardless of their nationality or faith. It was there that they were able for the first time to contrast slogans about building a glorious new world and a future that was quite different from the past with the reality of a state which was both steeped in modernist culture and authoritarian in its political structure. The contrast, even for Polish communists, was not favourable and often led to wariness about the post-war reality in Poland too. Szlomo (Sam) Ponczak was born in Warsaw towards the end of 1937. In the winter of 1940/1, as a small child, he crossed the German–Soviet border with his mother in order to join her communist husband, who had fled there at the very beginning of the war. He spent his early childhood in Siberia and central Asia. In his recollections, the feelings of a 4- or 5-year-old child are inextricably bound up with the feelings of his parents, as conveyed to him during family discussions after the war. The predominant impression was of overwork and exploitation, with the experience of exile seen as a battle for survival in a Soviet state which was at times brutal and indifferent to the suffering of its citizens and inhabitants.[57] In contrast to the Holocaust, the struggle for survival in the Soviet Union was not something which could be discussed in public in communist Poland in the early post-war period, so those experiences were forced into the private, domestic sphere, and sometimes lived on only in the memories of those who had been affected by them.[58]

The post-war ambivalence which resulted from the specific dialectic between the interwar and wartime experiences of Jewish parents had a marked influence on their children. On the one hand, they were brought up in a political culture and amid symbols which their parents knew well; on the other hand, they learned to keep a certain critical distance from them. Jewish parents, whether they aligned themselves with communists or Zionists, were very familiar with the top-down, centralized nature of those movements and were fully aware of their authoritarian reach and their desire to have the maximum possible impact on their children. At the same time, their wartime experiences, their time in the Soviet Union, and the obvious divergences between the lofty slogans of communists or Zionists and post-war reality meant that they approached the communist state and the various Jewish organizations with some caution and tried to minimize their influence over their children. Thus Jewish childhood in Dzierżoniów after the war was also marked by the process, seen throughout the Western world, of a gradual retreat from radical, collectivist ideologies towards more individualist lifestyles and values, and a liberal political culture.[59] Another factor which may have had a bearing on this process was the pluralism and richness of Jewish life in post-war Dzierżoniów.

Social Density, Political Pluralism, and the Open Jewish Identity

A key influence on the complexion of childhood and adolescence in Dzierżoniów between 1945 and 1950 was the size and density of its Jewish community. Dzierżoniów was a small town in which Jews formed a large part of the population. They lived close together and made regular use of the main streets, on most of which stood Jewish institutions of various sorts: the headquarters of political parties, various schools, a co-operative, an after-school daycare centre, a nursery, a canteen, and the health centre run by the Society for Safeguarding the Health of the Jewish Population. The town was regularly the scene of large Jewish public gatherings, such as celebrations of the anniversaries of the Warsaw ghetto uprising or the beginning of post-war Jewish settlement of Lower Silesia. Jewish political parties and movements, including Zionist ones, took part in state festivals, such as the May Day parade (see Figure 2). Dzierżoniów was unique in this sense, and visiting members of western Jewish communities (many of whom were of Polish descent) were struck by how different it was from the hundreds of other towns in Poland in which only the ruins of Jewish houses remained. Józef Tenenbaum, president of the American and World Federation of Polish Jews, described his impressions of Dzierżoniów in spring 1946:

The largest Jewish community was in Rychbach (Reichenbach), a former German spa which had become a Polish-Jewish settlement, with a Jewish majority, a Jewish militia, and a Jewish life charged with vigour and activity ... I was struck by the sound of Yiddish everywhere, Yiddish posters, large streamers in Yiddish calling for May Day celebrations, Yiddish theater bills ... I have even heard some of the non-Jewish Poles massacre this tongue with an atrocious Polish accent as if in the recognition that Yiddish was the official language of the 'Jewish town'.[60]

The Dzierżoniów phenomenon was even noted in the reports sent to Palestine by Zionist emissaries, who were fundamentally hostile to any prolongation of the

Figure 2 The Zionist Freiheit–Hehaluts Hatsa'ir and Dror youth movements during the 1946 May Day parade in Dzierżoniów
Archiwum Katedry Judaistyki im. Tadeusza Taubego

presence of a large Jewish community in Lower Silesia. One of these reports, from October 1946, stated:

Lower Silesia is effectively a separate state-within-a-state . . . The majority of Polish Jews are based here, as are most of our kibbutzim and the heart of our movement . . . Rychbach has 5,000 Jews . . . Poles refer to this town as 'Żydbach' since, especially during the repatriation, it was full of Jews. All the kibbutzim here are still operating. The Tarbut school and the Jewish school are still operating . . . Our [Hashomer Hatsa'ir] kibbutz is functioning and owns a workshop and a bakery. Our regional headquarters is based in Dzierżoniów.[61]

The density, visibility, and openness of Jewish life all served to increase the sense of security of the community members. That in turn had a material influence on the upbringing of children, on how they moved around the town, and on how their Jewish identity was passed down to them. Although, even there, the situation was far from ideal, the everyday experience of being a Jew in public was not predominantly associated, as it was in many other places in Poland, with shame or fear.[62] Tauba Gingold, who was from Bessarabia and met her husband Jeszaja in the Soviet Union before moving with him to Bielawa, recalled that during this period she would speak to her children in Yiddish not just at home but also in the street.[63] Szlomo Ponczak recounted how, at the peak of the repatriation, he would go twice a week with his father to the railway station. On the way there they would pass the premises of the PKŻ, which would always be surrounded by hundreds of Jews speaking Yiddish. At the station nearby, his father would ask in the trains conveying the repatriates for news of their pre-war family and friends. This was how the Ponczaks found the Pertman family. The Pertman family had originally intended to go to Legnica, but when they came across their pre-war friends, the Ponczaks, they decided to stay in Dzierżoniów. The father of the family, Chaim Pertman, joined the '9 May' Jewish tailors' co-operative, at the core of which were Jewish shoemakers and tailors who knew each other from their pre-war shtetls (Międzyrzecz Podlaski and Wohyń).[64] The strength of these pre-war ties in Dzierżoniów was underlined in an interview recorded for the USC Shoah Foundation by Mojżesz Jakubowicz, chairman of the local branch of the Jewish Social and Cultural Association from the second half of the 1950s until his death in 2003 and leader of the town's Jewish community. Thus, on the board of the Jewish hosiery co-operative sat people who were friends from pre-war Warsaw; Jews from Kosów Huculski were on the board of the kilim co-operative; and Jews from Ozorków, Łódź, and Białystok led the textile-makers. Jews from Międzyrzec predominated in the '9 May' co-operative so that, as he put it, 'some Jakubowicz from Nowy Sącz had no chance there'.[65] He, as a young communist, was critical of social networks of this sort, but they were crucial for many other Jews, including children, who built their lives among them, in a Jewish space and with a sense, so vital after the Holocaust, of relative security.

The history of the Turbiner family is particularly revealing of pre-war and wartime networks of family and friends and their continuation after the Holocaust. The whole family, Beniamin and Estera Turbiner, their two children, and Beniamin's parents, hid during the Holocaust in a dugout in a village near Parczew in the district of Lublin, assisted by their Ukrainian neighbours, Konstanty and Maria Supruniuk. After the war, the Turbiner family 'adopted' their rescuers as it were, and brought them to Dzierżoniów (see Figure 3). The Turbiners were a religious family who observed *kashrut*, celebrated Jewish holidays, and hosted the Supruniuks at their family table.[66]

Social and occupational contacts of this sort created substitutes for the wider Jewish family: they stood in for murdered brothers, sisters, grandparents, and cousins. In many such patchwork families not only was Yiddish habitually spoken but children also had unrestricted access to pre-war memories and culture. Thus the Jewishness of children growing up in the Dzierżoniów environment was not a Jewishness which was dissociated from or stripped of the past, but nor was it an identity forged solely of grief and fear. It was nonetheless plainly a different identity, one shaped in different circumstances to those which had obtained before the war. A phenomenon which was undoubtedly new was that some Jewish families, or at least families considered by their neighbours to be Jewish, had non-Jewish members. This came about mainly because many of the Polish Jews who moved from the USSR to Poland arrived with their non-Jewish spouses. Thus although Michał Teitelbaum was raised in a Jewish environment and in Jewish institutions, his mother was a non-Jew from Moldavia, whom her father had met when he was a soldier in the Red Army.[67] The wife of Mojżesz Jakubowicz was also Russian.[68] The children of these marriages were generally considered to be Jews by both their Jewish and their non-Jewish neighbours, if their parents functioned mainly in the Jewish environment.

Figure 3 Konstanty and Maria Supruniuk in Dzierżoniów after the war

Shlomo Turbiner's private family photograph

This was the case regardless of their actual halakhic status. The Jewish identity of these children was also undoubtedly reinforced by their upbringing.

The fact that the identity of these children and adolescents was so overt served to boost the activity of the various institutions which had been set up to cater for them. From spring 1946 there was a fully functioning Jewish school in Dzierżoniów, teaching Yiddish, Jewish history and culture, and even (although to a much more limited extent) Hebrew and classes in Judaism, Jewish holidays, and the Jewish community in Palestine.[69] A Hebrew school opened in September 1946. By 1947 there were five Jewish schools in Dzierżoniów and its neighbouring towns and seven other children's institutions: children's homes, nurseries, boarding schools, and after-school daycare centres for children and adolescents.[70] In Dzierżoniów itself there was a Jewish sports club which attracted many young people.[71] Frieda Pertman recounted her delight at the level of care and the quality of education offered in the Jewish nursery, where her son was looked after by a pre-war pupil and colleague of Janusz Korczak.[72] The brothers Pinkus and Szlomo Turbiner continued their education, after the war, at the Association of Children's Friends (Towarzystwo Przyjaciół Dzieci; TPD) school in Dzierżoniów and through courses in radio construction run by the Association for the Promotion of Skilled Trades.

For all the ideological purism of youth organizations and their uncompromising rivalry for absolute influence over children and adolescents, participation in those organizations had a paradoxical effect, namely the development of an ideologically pluralist awareness and identity among young people. Young Jews had access to many organizations, and participation in multiple organizations meant that none of them could be sure of an ideological monopoly over its members. Szlomo Ponczak, who grew up in a communist family, was taken to meetings at the Hashomer Hatsa'ir youth centre by a Jewish classmate from his TPD school and went on a Hashomer summer camp in 1947. At that camp, despite the fact that his own parents' views were (at least at that time) quite incompatible, he wore the Hashomer Hatsa'ir uniform, sang Hebrew songs, listened to stories about the illegal emigration of Jews from Poland, and was himself encouraged to emigrate.[73]

Religious Jews were probably dealt the most devastating blow by the Holocaust. Very few survived and even fewer kept their faith after the war. Sociological research on the Jewish community in 1948 revealed most community members to be unequivocally non-practising non-believers.[74] Furthermore both the state and Jewish institutions were controlled by people who were hostile to all religions, including Judaism. Lower Silesia, in particular, was dominated by secular parties and Jewish circles engaged in the construction of a new life. In their understanding, 'new' meant 'secular'. However despite these unfavourable circumstances, without state backing, and in the face of open hostility from the PKŻ, religious Jews, bolstered by the international Orthodox community, also managed to establish a stronghold in Dzierżoniów. Its strength was evident in the first half of 1946 during the greatest wave of repatriation from the USSR. According to a report by Rabbi Dr Solomon Schonfeld, one of the leaders of the British branch of Agudat Israel who visited Poland in February and March 1946, the faith congregations competed to good effect with the committees in arranging assistance for the repatriates and preparing them to emigrate from Poland. In Dzierżoniów, some repatriates were accommodated in the synagogue building, where they had access to kosher food.[75]

For obvious reasons, the work of the local Orthodox institutions also focused on children and adolescents. In March 1946 the Congregation of the Mosaic Faith in Dzierżoniów received one of the highest subsidies allocated by Va'ad Hahatsalah to Jewish communities in Poland, 250,000 zlotys.[76] A yeshiva operated in the town until August 1946, when its twenty-three students joined 1,000 others whom Va'ad Hahatsalah, in collaboration with the Zionist Bricha, assisted in moving out of Poland.[77] Despite this, in autumn 1946 the semi-official Orthodox party Agudat Israel still ran four kibbutzim for religious youth in Dzierżoniów and its surrounding towns and villages.[78] The town had a permanent rabbi, a ritual bath, and a kosher shop.[79] Moreover in April 1948 the London *Jewish Chronicle* reported that 'Jewish communists have lost their battle against circumcision': the number of circumcisions had steadily increased, especially in western Poland where Dzierżoniów was situated.[80]

Did this mean that, at least until 1950, the Orthodox community grew in size? Not necessarily. The film *Yidishe yishev in nidershlezye*, commissioned by the CKŻP in the spring of 1947 and intended to assist fundraising efforts among western Jewish communities, singled out Dzierżoniów as a unique place, where the synagogue was always full on important holidays and traditional-looking Jews were a normal, everyday sight.[81] Similar images appear in the photographs of Jewish life in the town commissioned by the CKŻP and taken at around the same time. The presence of religious Jews, especially older males whose appearance caused them to stand out, on the streets of Dzierżoniów was undoubtedly a consequence of the size of the Jewish population and the strength of its institutions (see Figure 4). At the same time, however, the Orthodox community was focused on emigration and was vigorously supported in this by its international institutions.[82] Moreover the photographs from Dzierżoniów reveal a clear generational divide. Traditional prayer shawls, wigs, hats, and overcoats are only worn by members of the older generation. In contrast to the

Figure 4 Religious Jews on the streets of Dzierżoniów, 1946
Archiwum Katedry Judaistyki im. Tadeusza Taubego

photographs from hundreds of towns and villages in the interwar period, there are no Jewish boys with sidelocks, hasidic coats, or the characteristic head coverings of Orthodox Jews (see Figure 5). Secularization was also a very powerful force in the town, all the more so as it was not a new trend resulting from the Holocaust but the intensification of an existing pre-war trend. Szymon Tenenbaum, recalling after several decades the Dzierżoniów and Bielawa of the late 1940s, associated truly religious convictions, daily prayers, the observance of *kashrut*, and other halakhic practices predominantly with older people. He observed:

People who had lived their whole life like this were to a greater or lesser extent devout. They missed going to the *mikveh* [ritual bath] on Friday, they were used to eating kosher food. A person like that would have got used to this over the course of his life and so would look for like-minded people. They would quickly find common ground and formed these groups of religious Jews. But the young people [were no longer interested].[83]

At the same time, however, the Orthodox presence and the diversity of Jewish religious life in Dzierżoniów meant that secularization was not all-embracing. Elements of Jewish religious tradition were present in many, and probably most, Jewish homes, including communist ones. Thus while Judaism was not the dominant feature of Jewish childhood in Dzierżoniów in the immediate post-Holocaust years, it was nonetheless an important one.

Figure 5 Three Jewish generations on the streets of Dzierżoniów, 1946, clearly showing the generational aspect of post-war secularization
Archiwum Katedry Judaistyki im. Tadeusza Taubego

Szlomo Ponczak's is a good example of a Jewish childhood in a town where attachment to Jewish tradition was an optional but nonetheless significant part of growing up. On the one hand, his parents sent him to a non-Jewish TPD school; on the other, despite—or maybe because of—their unequivocally communist views, they did not want their son to be wholly cut off from the world of his forebears and so sent him for a time to classes at the (unauthorized) ḥeder.[84] Beniamin Turbiner was religious throughout his long life until his death in Dzierżoniów in 1997, and regularly attended synagogue in the 1940s. His teenage sons attended with their parents only during important Jewish holidays. However, they also learned elements of Jewish tradition, halakhic principles, Hebrew and the Bible outside the home, in the ḥeder and at the Ihud kibbutz in Dzierżoniów, which they regularly attended after school.[85] Pinkus Turbiner even completed *hakhsharah* training at the kibbutz in preparation for emigration to Palestine, although in 1950, when his turn came to leave, his father refused to allow him go.[86]

In this context, the distinctively transnational nature of the Polish Jewish community in the first years after the Holocaust is highly relevant. Many members of the community thought about emigrating; many, including those who planned to remain in Poland for a short or perhaps a longer period, had families abroad; and the Jewish media in Poland was full of news from the Jewish world. Most of the activities of Jewish committees, religious congregations, kibbutzim, and other Zionist organizations were funded from abroad, from institutions such as the Joint Distribution

Committee, the Jewish Labour Committee, and Va'ad Hahatsalah. Until 1950 relations with all these organizations were not blocked by the communist authorities. They played a vital role in Dzierżoniów too, not least through their socializing effect on its Jewish children. As an example, in August 1946, in Dzierżoniów alone, the PKŻ received 2,967 letters addressed to local Jews from family members, friends, and acquaintances abroad. Most of those letters came from the United States.[87] Jewish children had an acute awareness of the Jewish world outside Poland: of having aunts, uncles, and other relatives abroad, and other members of families that had been ravaged by the Holocaust. They were also aware of the influence of foreign Jewish communities on the material aspects of their lives since, through the Jewish committees, they received clothes, toys, and food from them.[88]

The Jewish transnationalism in post-war Dzierżoniów was also apparent in the community's active, daily interest in the question of Palestine and the desire of the worldwide Jewish community to establish a Jewish state there. The majority of those leaving Poland between 1945 and 1948 were bound for Palestine, and many Dzierżoniów Jews had family members, friends, or acquaintances there. The developing interest and attachment to Palestine as a new and important centre of the Jewish world, a sense of pride in Jewish achievements there, and the thought of it as a haven if things in the diaspora took a turn for the worse were the continuation of tendencies which were already strong in the 1930s,[89] and which were further boosted by the Holocaust. It is very clearly on display in a photograph taken at the headquarters of the Polish Socialist Party in Dzierżoniów on 29 November 1947, where the whole Jewish community, including the children, can be seen listening to a radio broadcast of the vote taking place at the United Nations headquarters in New York on the partition of Palestine and the creation of a Jewish state (Figure 6).

This type of transnationalism was a further significant element of Jewish childhood in Dzierżoniów. Alongside the town's political, organizational, and cultural pluralism, it too served to dilute the influence of the dominant communist ideology, of state propaganda and control over the Jewish community. The children growing up there had an awareness that they were part of a wider Jewish world which extended beyond the borders of Poland and whose centre lay elsewhere, in the United States or in Palestine/Israel.

Memories of the Holocaust, Antisemitism, and Insecurity: 1945–50 and Beyond

Even taking all the above into account, it is important to bear in mind that childhood and adolescence in Dzierżoniów in the late 1940s were certainly not wholly carefree, unaffected by fear, or open to the unrestricted manifestation of every aspect of Jewish identity. Everything was overshadowed not only by the trauma of the Holocaust, whether experienced directly or through stories of murdered family members, but also by its central presence in Jewish discourse in early post-war Poland. Until 1946 and the mass repatriation of Jews from the USSR, Dzierżoniów's Jewish community

Figure 6 Mass assembly of Dzieżoniów Jews listening to a radio broadcast of the UN decision on the partition of Palestine, 29 November 1947
Beit Lohamei Hagetaot Archive, 16817

consisted mainly of Holocaust survivors. Yaacov Pat, who visited Dzierżoniów and its surrounding area in 1946, devoted an entire chapter of his moving and shocking account of post-Holocaust Poland to his conversations with children at the Janusz Korczak Children's Home in Pieszyce. All the luxury of the former German palace in which this establishment was based could not efface the deep trauma which the Holocaust had inflicted on the children. They had lost not only their parents and siblings but often also their names, which some of them could not remember. All had serious psychological damage; some, like Fela from Kraśnik near Lublin, who had been shot in the hand, were also physically disabled.[90] One resident of the Pieszyce children's home, 11-year-old Lena Atlas, did not give her account until 1948, and three years after the end of the war and her own survival of the Holocaust she still had problems with her Jewish identity: it was always associated in her mind with fear.[91] This sort of trauma remained with Jewish child survivors of the Holocaust for the rest of their lives.[92]

The trauma of the Holocaust not only affected those children who experienced it personally, whether in ghettos, forests, dugouts, or hidden in convents or with Christian families. Children who returned to Poland after the war from the Soviet Union also experienced it indirectly. As Szlomo Ponczak recalled:

The situation after the war was that not many Jews had survived. I remember that those who had survived and knew one another from town or from Warsaw, where they had met, would gather at our house in Dzierżoniów and would sometimes sit up all night talking and crying and drinking, who knew who had been killed, who had been in Auschwitz, who had survived. And I sat there too, I was a small boy, and I understood what they were talking about and these are the things I remember from listening to their conversations.[93]

Perhaps just as significant and traumatic, especially for Jewish children, was the experience of post-war antisemitism which aroused fear and amplified the trauma caused by the Holocaust. Antisemitism was evident in Dzierżoniów too, and it also affected the lives of the youngest members of the Jewish community there. Jews were physically attacked in the town, and on occasion killed. For this reason, by 1946 an armed Jewish Patrol Service, set up with the support of the authorities and run by the committees, had four stations in Dzierżoniów and its surrounding area and access to eight rifles.[94] The local kibbutzim also had access to firearms. This, however, was not enough to prevent the killing of Saul Zilberberg, a young guard at the Ihud kibbutz in Dzierżoniów, who was shot at his post by unknown persons in September 1946.[95] One of Szlomo Turbiner's most vivid memories from his first years in Dzierżoniów was of hearing about the death of his uncle, who was killed by members of the Polish anti-communist underground in Parczew.[96] It is clear that pogroms were also feared: a report written by the Polish correspondent of a Jewish newspaper in Great Britain noted that in December 1947 rumours of Jews attacking a Christian boy in order to obtain his blood had almost led to mass violence: 'The attacks were planned, and word sent to surrounding villages calling on supporters to be ready for the "day of reckoning" with the Jews'. The author of this report stressed the fear which was felt at the time by the local Jewish community.[97]

The Jewish experience in Dzierżoniów was also marked by everyday antisemitism. Before he was sent to the TPD school, Szlomo Ponczak spent a few days at the state school. During breaks, several Jewish pupils were attacked by their Christian classmates. Ponczak recalled that: 'As a young boy, I was absolutely terrified. I still thought that Hitler was going to kill me . . . I remember how, after a while, I just didn't want to be a Jew any more. And I spoke to a Polish boy and asked him how to become a Christian.'[98]

Experiences of this sort were a common phenomenon for Jewish children throughout Poland, as was their fear of identifying with a community which, even after the war, was so strongly stigmatized and attacked.[99] What undoubtedly distinguished Ponczak's fate from that of many other Jewish children growing up elsewhere in Poland was that in Dzierżoniów he was surrounded by hundreds of Jewish contemporaries and numerous Jewish institutions. Nonetheless, such experiences inevitably gave rise to feelings of being different and meant having to confront the fact that Jews were still not accepted by many people in Poland, including immediate neighbours.[100]

In his research on the psycho-social consequences of the Second World War, post-war deprivation, and the growth in everyday violence and crime, Marcin Zaremba has established that a common phenomenon in this period was 'pathological familialism'. The essence of this was a drastic decline in collective confidence and an increased mistrust of strangers. This in turn caused people to confine themselves to their immediate social, and especially family, circles and to view any people or institutions which were outside those circles with suspicion.[101] Among Jews all this was intensified by the trauma of the Holocaust and antisemitic violence. The phenomenon undoubtedly also had an impact on Jewish children, who grew up in an atmosphere of uncertainty and with a mistrust of both the non-Jewish environment and state institutions. This uncertainty and mistrust were factors in the fundamental dilemma of the years 1945 to 1950, namely whether to stay or to leave.

Interviews conducted with those who did not emigrate immediately after the war show the scale of this dilemma: very few of them were unequivocally in favour of either one course of action or the other. It was often chance which determined whether or not families left, and when. The Pertmans had thought about emigrating from the very first day they returned from the USSR. They made efforts to move to Argentina but could not get a visa. They were also refused a certificate for legal entry into Palestine. In the second half of 1946 they were packed and ready to cross the Czechoslovak border illegally with one of the kibbutzim, but did not in the end do so because Frieda Pertman suddenly fell seriously ill. Eventually, in 1948, they moved to Wrocław. They emigrated to Israel only in 1957, later moving to the United States.[102] Szlomo Turbiner left for Israel with his wife shortly after their marriage in the same year. His brother, Pinkus, even though he had almost emigrated with the Ihud kibbutz in 1949, only left for the United States after the antisemitic campaign of 1968.[103] Michał Teitelbaum left Dzierżoniów with his family a year later.[104] Szymon and Dora Tenenbaum seriously considered emigrating to Israel in 1949 to join Dora's father, a pre-war Mizrachi party activist who had moved there three years earlier. Szymon even went so far as to visit Israel, but having seen for himself how harsh conditions were in the newly established state he decided that, as a dentist with a stable job, he would be much better able to provide for his family back in Bielawa. The Tenenbaums never left Poland. One of their sons decided to leave after 1968, but the rest of their children and grandchildren remained in Poland and moved to bigger towns. The Gingold family also stayed, despite the discrimination they encountered both in 1956 and in 1968.

There can be no doubt that for Jewish children and adolescents, an open and multidimensional Jewish identity and a rootedness in Polish and state culture went hand in hand with an ambivalence and an uncertainty derived from personal experience of the place of Jews in Poland. To a lesser extent and in a different context, the features of Jewish life in Dzierżoniów described above were also present between 1950 and 1968, despite the two great waves of antisemitism of that period. Those experiences still await more extensive research, free from past paradigms.

Conclusion

In the years 1945 to 1950 Jewish childhood in Dzierżoniów was different from Jewish childhood in other parts of Poland, where there was no significant Jewish presence. The communist state's ideological offensive and the associated pressure to assimilate were a part of life in Dzierżoniów; however, that pressure was defused by the pluralism, richness, and density of Jewish social and cultural life. Attempts at extreme political indoctrination were offset by the wartime experiences of parents, part of a general post-war process of gradual loss of faith in extreme ideological politics. Jewish children in Lower Silesia grew up in a Jewish cultural continuum, one that in the post-Holocaust period was relative but nonetheless meaningful. It was made up of both a rootedness in modernist interwar political culture and the continued functioning of elements of Jewish cultural tradition, including religion. Jewish children growing up in Dzierżoniów were taught at home and in schools and other institutions about the culture and history of the Jewish nation, including the history of the Holocaust (see Figure 7). They were also brought up with an awareness of their permanent, deep, and unbreakable links with the Jewish world on the other side of the Iron Curtain.

Despite the antisemitism and other problems associated with being a Jew in Poland, there is no doubt that Jewish children in Dzierżoniów benefited from educational opportunities which had not been available to their parents' generation. The tailor's son Szlomo Ponczak passed his matriculation exams in Wrocław and, by way of Israel and Argentina, ended up in the United States, where he completed an MBA and worked as a manager in the semiconductor industry in Baltimore. His childhood friend from Dzierżoniów and Wrocław, Lusiek (Allan) Pertman, the son of the Wohyń tailors Frieda and Chaim, emigrated to Israel with his parents midway

Figure 7 Holocaust commemoration service in the Dzierżoniów synagogue, 1946
Archiwum Katedry Judaistyki im. Tadeusza Taubego

through high school and after a few months moved to the United States, where he studied electronics and spent his working life as an engineer in the US Navy. Lusiek's sister Rita graduated in business studies in the United States and runs her own stockbroking firm. Szymon Tenenbaum, the son of an unqualified worker from Warsaw, finished secondary school after the war, attended university, and worked as a dentist for several decades. All his children completed their studies in Poland. The life trajectories of these people, and of hundreds of other Jewish children from Dzierżoniów in the second half of the 1940s, demonstrate that the processes which determined the centres of Jewish life after the Holocaust, processes such as metropolitanization and professionalization, also encompassed the Polish Jewish community. An analysis of these processes, and the others referred to above, de-exoticizes the post-Holocaust history of the Jews in Poland and reintegrates it into the global history of Jews in the second half of the twentieth century.

Translated from the Polish by Anna Podolska

Notes

Research for this article was funded by Narodowe Centrum Nauki (grant no. UMO-2018/31/B/HS3/00228: The Last Polish Shtetl? The Dzierżoniów Jewish Community, Jewish World, the Cold War and Communism, 1945–1950) and the Czech Science Foundation (grant no: 16-01775Y: Inclusion of Jewish Citizens in Postwar Czechoslovak and Polish Societies).

1 S. Siebel-Achenbach, *Niederschlesien 1942 bis 1949: Alliierte Diplomatie und Nachkriegswirklichkeit* (Würzburg, 2006); R. M. Douglas, *Orderly and Humane: The Expulsions of the Germans after the Second World War* (New Haven, Conn., 2012); D. T. Curp, *A Clean Sweep? The Politics of Ethnic Cleansing in Western Poland, 1945–1960* (Rochester, NY, 2006).

2 On the post-Holocaust Jewish community of Radom, a medium-sized town in central Poland, see Ł. Krzyżanowski, *Ghost Citizens: Jewish Return to a Postwar City* (Cambridge, Mass., 2020).

3 See E. Koźmińska-Frejlak, 'Po Zagładzie: Praktyki asymilacyjne Ocalałych jako strategie zadomawiania się w powojennej Polsce 1944–1950', Ph.D. thesis (University of Warsaw, 2019); K. Auerbach, *The House at Ujazdowskie 16: Jewish Families in Warsaw after the Holocaust* (Bloomington, Ind., 2013). On the differences between the socialization of Jewish children in large cities such as Warsaw and in Lower Silesia, see M. Starnawski, *Socjalizacja i tożsamość żydowska w Polsce powojennej: Narracje emigrantów z pokolenia Marca '68* (Wrocław 2016), 175–81.

4 C. Ginzburg, 'Microhistory: Two or Three Things that I Know about It', *Critical Inquiry*, 1 (1993), 26–34; id., 'Microhistory' (25 June 2015): YouTube website, visited 17 May 2022.

5 Archiwum Państwowe we Wrocławiu (hereafter APWr), 82/415/0/1/5, 'Sprawozdania opisowe z działalności WKŻ' (1945–9), fos. 37–8: report on WKŻ activities, May 1945–April 1946; J. Turkow, *Nokh der bafrayung (zikhroynes)* (Buenos Aires, 1959), 230–1.

6 APWr, 82/415/0/1/1, 'Protokoły z posiedzeń WKŻ' (1945), fo. 1: minutes of first WKŻ meeting, Rychbach, 18 June 1945; Y. Egit, *Tsu a naye lebn* (Wrocław, 1947), 19–31; id., *Grand Illusion* (Toronto, 1991), 44–54.

7 APWr, 82/415/0/1/1, fo. 6: minutes of WKŻ meeting, Rychbach, 5 July 1945;

82/415/0/1/5, fo. 20: report on WKŻ activities, June–Dec. 1945 (early 1946); fo. 39: report on WKŻ activities, June 1945 – Apr. 1946.
8 D. Engel, 'Patterns of Anti-Jewish Violence in Poland, 1944–1946', *Yad Vashem Studies*, 26 (1998), 43–85; J. T. Gross, *Fear. Anti-Semitism in Poland after Auschwitz: An Essay in Historical Interpretation* (Princeton, NJ, 2006).
9 B. Szaynok, *Ludność żydowska na Dolnym Śląsku, 1945–1950* (Wrocław, 2000), 19–25; K. Kijek, 'Aliens in the Land of the Piasts: The Polonization of Lower Silesia and Its Jewish Community in the Years 1945–1950', in T. Grill (ed.), *Jews and Germans in Eastern Europe: Shared and Comparative Histories* (Oldenburg, 2018), 236–9.
10 This was a universal phenomenon among Holocaust survivors throughout Europe (see A. J. Patt, *Finding Home and Homeland: Jewish Youth and Zionism in the Aftermath of the Holocaust* (Detroit, 2009), 21–2).
11 Report on WKŻ activities, June–Dec. 1945.
12 APWr, 82/415/0/1/1, fo. 24: minutes of WKŻ meeting, Rychbach, 14 Sept. 1945; J. Adelson, 'W Polsce zwanej Ludową', in J. Tomaszewski (ed.), *Najnowsze dzieje Żydów w Polsce w zarysie (do 1950 roku)* (Warsaw, 1993), 387–477: 390, 397; Szaynok, *Ludność żydowska na Dolnym Śląsku*; H. Shlomi, 'Reshit hahitargenut shel yehudei polin beshilhei milḥemet ha'olam hasheniyah', in ead. (ed.), *Asupat meḥkarim letoledot she'erit hapeletah hayehudit bepolin 1944–1950* (Tel Aviv, 2001), 78–81.
13 Wiener Holocaust Library, London (hereafter WHA), 27/15/78, 'Poland: Correspondence 10 Aug 1945 – 11 Oct 1956', 28/22: CKŻP, letter to Central British Fund, 22 Mar. 1946. Helena Datner estimated that 28,000 Jewish children returned to Poland from the Soviet Union in 1946 (H. Datner, 'Dziecko żydowskie (1944–1968)', in F. Tych, M. Adamczyk-Garbowska (eds.), *Następstwa zagłady Żydów: Polska 1944–2010* (Lublin, 2012), 245–81: 248–9).
14 Goldstein-Goren Diaspora Research Center Archive, Tel Aviv, Abraham A. Berman Bequest, P-70, folder 141: WKŻ, letter to CKŻP, 4 May 1946.
15 B. Szaynok, 'Żydzi w Dzierżoniowie (1945–1950)', in S. Ligarski and T. Przerwa (eds.), *Dzierżoniów – wiek miniony* (Wrocław, 2007), 25–33: 29; APWr, 82/415/0/1/9, 'Protokoły i sprawozdania KŻ w Dzierżoniowie i Pieszycach' (1945–8), fo. 6: report on PKŻ activities, Aug. 1946.
16 See esp. J. Tokarska-Bakir, *Pod klątwą: Społeczny obraz pogromu kieleckiego*, 2 vols. (Warsaw, 2018); Gross, *Fear*, 81–166.
17 A. Stankowski, 'Nowe spojrzenie na statystyki dotyczące emigracji Żydów z Polski po 1944 roku', in G. Berendt, A. Grabski, and A. Stankowski (eds.), *Studia z historii Żydów w Polsce* (Warsaw, 2000), 103–51: 109.
18 APWr, 82/415/0/2/56, 'Sprawozdania statystyczne komitetów ludnościowych za miesiąc grudzień' (1947), fo. 11: PKŻ, report on the number of Jewish inhabitants, Dzierżoniów, Dec. 1947 (7 Jan. 1947).
19 APWr, 82/415/0/1/9, fo. 21: report on PKŻ activities, Sept. 1946; fo. 86: report on PKŻ activities, Dec. 1946.
20 On the history of the Jewish community in post-war Dzierżoniów, see B. Lavi, 'The Community which "Sat on the Suitcases" (Dzierżoniów)', *Kwartalnik Historii Żydów*, 262 (2017), 245–71; Szaynok, 'Żydzi w Dzierżoniowie', 25–34; A. Grużlewska, *Polish Jerusalem: The Phenomenon of the Jewish Settlement in the County of Dzierżoniów 1945–1950* (Dzierżoniów, 2019).
21 A. Grabski, *Centralny Komitet Żydów w Polsce (1944–1950)* (Warsaw, 2015), 192–248.

22 D. Stola, *Kraj bez wyjścia? Migracje z Polski, 1949–1989* (Warsaw, 2010), 61; A. Stankowski, 'Nowe spojrzenie na statystyki dotyczące emigracji Żydów z Polski po 1944 roku', 116.
23 G. Berendt, *Życie żydowskie w Polsce w latach 1950–1956* (Gdańsk, 2008), 95.
24 APWr, 82/415/0/1/1, fo. 2: minutes of WKŻ meeting, Rychbach, 3 July 1945; fo. 7: minutes of WKŻ meeting, Rychbach, 5 July 1945.
25 Hashomer Hatsa'ir Archives, Givat Haviva (hereafter HHA), 1–2, 49(1): Hashomer Hatsa'ir representative, report concerning a meeting of activists from Jewish youth organizations WKŻ HQ, Rychbach, 1 Sept. 1945.
26 APWr, 82/415/0/1/1, fo. 11: minutes of WKŻ meeting, Rychbach, 29 July 1945.
27 APWr, 82/415/0/1/1, fo. 18: minutes of WKŻ meeting, Rychbach, 8 Aug. 1945; fo. 25: minutes of WKŻ meeting, Rychbach, 14 Sept. 1945. On the history of this children's home between 1944 and 1945 when it was still based in Lublin, see P. Nazaruk, 'Żydowski sierociniec w Lublinie (1944–1945)' (n.d.): Ośrodek 'Brama Grodzka: Teatr NN' website, visited 18 May 2022.
28 For overviews of Zionism in the first years of post-Holocaust Poland, see D. Engel, *Bein shiḥrur liveriḥah: nitsolei hasho'ah bepolin vehama'avak al hanhagatam, 1944–1946* (Tel Aviv, 1996); N. Aleksiun, *Dokąd dalej? Ruch syjonistyczny w Polsce (1944–1950)* (Warsaw, 2002).
29 Hashomer Hatsa'ir Liaison Office, letter to activists in Poland, 27 July 1945.
30 HHA, 1-2, 50(2): letter (Wrocław) to Hashomer Hatsa'ir Central Committee, Poland, 26 July 1945.
31 HHA, 1-2, 48(1): report of a meeting of the Hashomer Hatsa'ir cell in Rychbach, 10 Aug. 1945; letter (Waldenburg [Wałbrzych]) to Hashomer Hatsa'ir Central Committee, Poland, 11 Oct. 1945; 'Szraga' (Peterswaldau [Pieszyce]), letter to Hashomer Hatsa'ir Central Committee, Poland, 2 Sept. 1945.
32 APWr, 82/415/0/1/1, fo. 25: minutes of WKŻ meeting, Rychbach, 14 Sept. 1945.
33 HHA, 1–2, 48(1), letter (Rychbach), 6 Aug. 1945; 49(2): report on CKŻP delegation investigating the expulsion of the Rychbach kibbutz, 10 Aug. 1945; Engel, *Bein shiḥrur liveriḥah*, 115–16.
34 APWr, 82/415/0/1/9, fo. 12: minutes of PKŻ meeting, Dzierżoniow, 5 Aug. 1945; fo. 33: minutes of PKŻ meeting, Dzierżoniow, 16 Sept. 1945; HHA, 1–2, 49(10): report on Hashomer Hatsa'ir activity in Lower Silesia, 9 July 1946.
35 Lavon Institute Archives, Tel Aviv, Po'alei Tsiyon Smol-IV 407-1, folder 26{Hebrew 22}: WKŻ, letter to Po'alei Tsiyon Left, Dzierżoniów Branch, 3 Sept. 1946. The Hebrew school in Dzierżoniów opened despite the protests and continued to function for the following two years.
36 See H. Datner, *Po Zagładzie: Społeczna historia żydowskich domów dziecka, szkół, kół studentów w dokumentach Centralnego Komitetu Żydów w Polsce* (Warsaw, 2016), 26–34; E. Nachmany Gafny, *Dividing Hearts: The Removal of Jewish Children from Gentile Families in Poland in the Immediate Post Holocaust Years* (Jerusalem, 2009).
37 HHA, 1–2, 48(3): Palestinian emissary, report on the Jewish community in Poland and the Zionist movement in the first weeks of the repatriation from the USSR (n.d.).
38 HHA, 1–2, 48(1): Szraga, letter to Hashomer Hatsa'ir Central Committee, Poland (n.d.); 48(5): management of the children's home, letter to the Jewish Committee in Peterswaldau [Pieszyce], 28 Aug. 1945; 49(1): Hashomer Hatsa'ir representative, report on a meeting of Jewish youth organization activists, WKŻ headquarters, Rychbach, 1 Sept. 1945.
39 APWr, 82/415/0/1/1, fo. 10: minutes of WKŻ meeting, Rychbach, 29 July 1945.
40 T. Zahra, *The Lost Children: Reconstructing Europe's Families after World War II* (Cambridge Mass., 2015), 119–20, 122–45.

41 HHA, 1–2, 50(2): report on Hashomer Hatsa'ir activity, Lower Silesia, 17 Apr. 1946.
42 APWr, 82/415/0/1/5, fo. 85: report on PKŻ activities, July 1946.
43 APWr, 82/415/0/1/9, fos. 86–7: report on PKŻ activities, Dec. 1946.
44 APWr, 82/415/0/1/5, fo. 105: report on PKŻ Youth Department activities, 1–20 July 1946.
45 HHA, 1-2, 50(1): Hashomer Hatsa'ir Central Committee, Poland, letter to all cells in Poland, 28 July 1946.
46 'Tsvay yoriker yubilei fun yid. yishev in nidershlezye', *Dos naye lebn*, 22 June 1947, p. 1; Y. Egit, 'Tsu naye dergreihungen', *Dos naye lebn*, 22 June 1947, p. 2; G.B. 'Jubileusz żydowskiego osiedla na Dolnym Śląsku', *Mosty*, 27 June 1947, p. 4; APWr, 82/415/0/1/9, fos. 107–8: report on WKŻ Special Commission activities, July 1946 (16 Aug. 1946).
47 Palestinian emissary, report on the Jewish community in Poland and the Zionist movement in the first weeks of the repatriation from the USSR.
48 HHA, 1–2, 50(2): report on Hashomer Hatsa'ir activity, Lower Silesia, 17 Apr. 1946.
49 HHA, 1–2, 50(2): report on the organization of the departure of members of youth kibbutzim and their parents from Lower Silesia, 28 July 1946.
50 HHA, 1–2, 50(2): Hashomer Hatsa'ir Central Committee, Poland, letter to 'Sonia', 18 Aug. 1946.
51 HHA, 1–2, 50(4): Hashomer Hatsa'ir Bulletin, 4 Sept 1946; Hashomer Hatsa'ir Bulletin, 22 Oct. 1946; 49(4): minutes of special meeting of Hashomer Hatsa'ir Central Committee, Poland, 18 Oct. 1946; minutes of meeting of Hashomer Hatsa'ir Central Committee, Poland (late July or Aug. 1946).
52 K. Kijek, *Dzieci modernizmu: Świadomość, kultura i socjalizacja polityczna młodzieży żydowskiej w II Rzeczypospolitej* (Wrocław, 2017); K. B. Moss, *An Unchosen People: Jewish Political Reckoning in Interwar Poland* (Cambridge, Mass., 2021).
53 N. Aleksiun, 'Zionists and Anti-Zionists in the Central Committee of the Jews in Poland: Cooperation and Political Struggle, 1944–1950', *Jews in Eastern Europe*, 2 (1997), 32–50.
54 Michał Teitelbaum, interview with author, Petah Tikvah, 11 Aug. 2008.
55 Tauba and Izaak Gingold, interview with author, Bielawa, 20, 24 Nov. 2008.
56 Frieda Pertman, interview with author, Baltimore, 20–1 Feb. 2009.
57 Shlomo Ponczak, interview with author, Baltimore, 16 Feb. 2009.
58 See E. R. Adler, *Survival on the Margins: Polish Jewish Refugees in the Wartime Soviet Union* (Cambridge, Mass., 2020); M. Nesselrodt, *Dem Holocaust entkommen: Polnische Juden in der Sowjetunion, 1939–1946* (Berlin, 2019); K. Friedla, '"From Nazi Inferno to the Soviet Hell": Polish-Jewish Children and Youth and Their Trajectories of Survival during and after the Second World War', *Journal of Modern European History*, 19 (2021), 274–91.
59 T. Judt, *Postwar: A History of Europe since 1945* (New York, 2005); T. Judt and T. Snyder, *Thinking the Twentieth Century* (New York, 2012), 210–48.
60 J. Tenenbaum, *In Search of the Lost People* (New York, 1948), 253. For similar accounts by foreign activists and Jewish journalists from Dzierżoniów, see e.g. Y. Pat, *Ash un fayer: iber di khurves fun poyln* (New York, 1946), 212–19; Eng. trans.: *Ashes and Fire*, trans. L. Steinberg (New York, 1947); S. L. Schneiderman, *Between Fear and Hope* (New York, 1947), 229–36; P. Novick, *Eyrope - tsvishn milkhome un sholem* (New York, 1948), 106–25.
61 HHA, 1–2, 51(1): Hashomer Hatsa'ir Regional Committee, Lower Silesia, letter to Hashomer Hatsa'ir Supreme Council, Palestine, 5 Oct. 1946.
62 On the prevalence of such experiences in many other parts of Poland, see Krzyżanowski, *Ghost Citizens*; M. Tsanin, *Iber shteyn un shtok: a rayze iber hundert khorev-gevorene kehiles in poyln* (Tel Aviv, 1952); Pol. trans.: M. Canin, *Przez ruiny i zgliszcza: Podróż po stu zgładzonych gminach żydowskich w Polsce*, trans. M. Adamczyk-Garbowska (Warsaw, 2018).

63 Tauba and Izaak Gingold, interview with author.
64 Shlomo Ponczak, interview with author; Frieda Pertman, interview with author. On the importance of interwar networks for the post-Holocaust Lower Silesian community, see M. Shulshtayn, *Tsvishn ruinen un rushtovanyes (fun rayze in poyln)* (Paris, 1949), 83–4.
65 University of Southern California Shoah Foundation, Los Angeles, Visual History Archive, interview 29827: Mojżesz Jakubowicz (27 Feb. 1997; Pol.).
66 Shlomo Turbiner, interview with author, Rehovot, 25 Aug. 2008.
67 Michał Teitelbaum, interview with author.
68 Mojżesz Jakubowicz, Visual History Archive interview; J. Wiszniewicz, *Życie przecięte: Opowieści pokolenia Marca* (Wołowiec, 2018), 217.
69 APWr, 82/415/0/1/5, fo. 50: report on WKŻ activities, Jan.–June 1946; fo. 57: report on WKŻ Schools Department activities, June 1946; fo. 60: report on WKŻ Schools Department activities, Apr. 1946; fos. 61–2: report on WKŻ Schools Department activities, May 1946; APWr, 82/415/0/1/4, 'Zjazdy i konferencje' (1949), fo. 8: minutes of conference of presidents and secretaries of Jewish committees in Lower Silesia, 7–8 Sept. 1946; Datner, *Po Zagładzie*, 73–80.
70 'Jewish Life in Poland', *Jewish Chronicle*, 1 Sept. 1947, pp. 3–4.
71 APWr, 82/415/0/1/5, fos. 83–4: report on WKŻ activities, July 1946.
72 Frieda Pertman, interview with author.
73 Shlomo Ponczak, interview with author.
74 I. Hurwic-Nowakowska, *Żydzi polscy (1947–1950): Analiza więzi społecznej ludności żydowskiej* (Warsaw, 1996), 184.
75 WHA, 27/15/78, 28/18–19: report on Dr Schonfeld's second visit to Poland, Feb.–Mar. 1946.
76 Yeshiva University Archives, New York, 1969.099, 'Vaad Hatzala Collection', Box 32, folder 102: list of financial allocations for the communities in Poland, Feb.–Mar. 1946.
77 Yeshiva University Archives, 1969.099, Box 18, folder 104: list of people extricated from Poland by Va'ad Hahatsalah, Aug. 1946.
78 WHA, 27/15/78, 28/114: Rabbi Shonfeld, Council of Polish Agudists, letter to secretary of Central British Fund, 13 Nov. 1946.
79 Frieda Pertman, interview with author; Shimon and Dora Tenenbaum, interview with author, Bielawa, 12 Aug. 2009.
80 WLA, Microfilm Collection, Reel 190, II.22.H: newspaper clipping, 'Jewish Communists on Circumcision', *Jewish Chronicle*, 4 Sept. 1948.
81 'The Jewish Settlement in Lower Silesia, 1947: Yiddish Film' (2 Dec. 2012): YouTube website, visited 17 May 2022.
82 On Jewish religious life and its decline in the first years of post-Holocaust Poland, see A. Cichopek-Gajraj, *Beyond Violence: Jewish Survivors in Poland and Slovakia, 1944–1948* (Cambridge, 2014), 210–12.
83 Shimon and Dora Tenenbaum, interview with author.
84 Shlomo Ponczak, interview with author.
85 Shlomo Turbiner, interview with author.
86 Ibid.
87 APWr, 82/415/0/1/9, fo. 6: report on PKŻ activities, Aug. 1946.
88 Frieda Pertman, interview with author.
89 Moss, *An Unchosen People*.

90 Pat, *Ash un fayer*, 310–13; id., *Ashes and Fire*, 224–6.
91 Archiwum Żydowskiego Instytutu Historycznego, Warsaw, 301/3364: Lena Atlas, testimony for Centralny Komitet Żydów w Polsce, 13 Mar. 1948 (Pol.).
92 See J. Michlic, 'What Does a Child Remember? Recollections of the War and the Early Postwar Period among Child Survivors from Poland', in ead. (ed.), *Jewish Families in Europe, 1939–Present* (Waltham, Mass., 2017), 153–72; ead., 'A Young Person's War: The Disrupted Lives of Children and Youth', in S. Giglotti and H. Earl (eds.), *A Companion to the Holocaust* (Hoboken, NJ, 2020), 295–310; S. Moskovitz, *Love Despite Hate: Child Survivors of the Holocaust* (New York, 1988).
93 Shlomo Ponczak, interview with author.
94 APWr, 82/415/0/1/5, fo. 69: report on WKŻ Jewish Self-Defence Command activities, Apr.–July 1946 (1 Aug. 1946).
95 HHA, 1–2, 51(1): Hashomer Hatsa'ir Central Committee, Poland, letter to Hashomer Hatsa'ir Supreme Council, Palestine, 5 Oct. 1946.
96 Shlomo Turbiner, interview with author. On 5 February 1946, a unit of the anti-communist underground which occupied the town for a few hours shot three previously disarmed and captured Jews, including Mendel Turbiner, and also robbed members of the local Jewish population (A. Grabski, 'Antysemicki pogrom jako kolejne polskie powstanie? Na marginesie pracy o pogromie w Parczewie w 1946 r.', *Kwartalnik Historii Żydów*, 258 (2016), 550–7; Adelson, 'W Polsce zwanej Ludową', 401).
97 WHA, Reel 189, II.22.A: newspaper clipping, 19 Dec. 1947.
98 Shlomo Ponczak, interview with author.
99 J. B. Michlic, '"Who am I?" Jewish Children's Search for Identity in Post-War Poland, 1945–1949', *Polin*, 20 (2007), 108–17.
100 On the very similar experiences of Jewish students in Polish state schools in the interwar period, see K. Kijek, 'Between Love of Poland, Symbolic Violence and Anti-Semitism: On the Idiosyncratic Effect of the State Education System among the Jewish Youth in Interwar Poland', *Polin*, 30 (2018), 237–64.
101 M. Zaremba, *Wielka Trwoga: Polska, 1944–1947* (Kraków, 2012), 124–9, 409–18.
102 Frieda Pertman, interview with author.
103 Shlomo Turbiner, interview with author.
104 Michał Teitelbaum, interview with author.

Blurred Spots of Revolution
Polish Communists of Jewish Origin and Their Early Political Socialization

ŁUKASZ BERTRAM

> Politics was central to the lives of the young Polish Jews who grew up in the Second Polish Republic. Public and private accounts and interviews with family members provide an insight into the childhood and adolescence of Polish Jewish communists who came of age and became radicalized at this time. Produced after the war under communism, this documentation shows how this cohort understood itself and its path to Marxism-Leninism and political activism. Idealizing their choice of the communist option and their leftist childhood, they largely downplay the importance of Jewishness and the role of antisemitism in family socialization and the move to modern politics. Although communists came to the movement with very different backgrounds, motivations, and hopes, within it they encountered—and often contributed to—pressure towards a specific uniformity. In the case of communists of Jewish origin, this pressure largely took the form of strategies aimed at erasing the Jewish component of their biographies.

THE LITERATURE on Jews and communism is so extensive that merely a survey of its many aspects could form the basis of several articles.[1] The goal of this chapter is therefore to look at the childhood, adolescence, and early adulthood of participants in the pre-war Polish communist movement with Jewish roots from a particular angle. My aim is first to ascertain how the members of this group (re)constructed their own Jewishness and Polishness with reference to these stages of their lives, and its significance—together with their experiences of antisemitism—for the process of political socialization and their commitment to communism. Secondly, I analyse individual strategies for constructing past experiences,[2] the conscious and dynamic reinterpretations made by active subjects.[3] I am interested in the dependence of such narratives on the time and place of their creation. Accordingly, I analyse, on the one hand, their authors' views, emotions, and attitudes at the time and, on the other, the political context. To do so, I trace continuities and tensions in memoirs and autobiographies published in the Polish People's Republic, in exile outside Poland and after the fall of communism in 1989; in the questionnaires and CVs produced for the Communist Party; and in oral history interviews.[4] I consider the language, including the ideological language, used by communists not only to set out their political views but also, as has been argued by Wiktor Marzec, to create a particular sense of self in which political participation made possible the construction of a narrative of their own lives.[5] I also examine how origins and national self-identification relate to such aspects of biography as social background and the position occupied in public life before and after the war, while reflecting on the similarities and differences in the experience of intellectuals and workers.

A key issue is the dynamics behind the presence or absence of material on Jewishness and antisemitism in communist ego-documents. Therefore I highlight the 'blurred spots' in personal narratives which, for a variety of reasons, became the object of deliberate or unconscious attempts to erase aspects of one's history.

Finally, I raise the question of the extent to which the forms and consequences of youthful political engagement and the strategies adopted by communists of Jewish origin in constructing their narratives about these experiences were specific to them, compared to those of different backgrounds within the movement.

Introductory Remarks: Concepts, Language, Sources

I use the term 'political socialization' to refer to the processes by which an individual's political attitudes, views, and other dispositions are shaped. These are processes which continue throughout their whole life; however, the phases analysed in this chapter have particular intensity and importance. My view is that, contrary to some discussions of political socialization,[6] these processes are not one-sided but involve active and subjective engagement on the part of the socialized individual and are concerned not only with the maintenance of social stability but also with the possibility of dissent and change.

Tackling a theme of this kind requires an analytical language and terms which will, on the one hand, distinguish the individuals examined as a group, and on the other avoid essentialism and arbitrary categorization, while also taking into account the patterns of self-identification. A straightforward differentiation of 'Poles' and 'Jews' will not fulfil these conditions. Even if the aim is to provide statistical analysis, this has to be done with appropriate reservations and nuance, treating these terms as points of departure rather than as fixed categories. A whole spectrum of identities is to be found between them, such as 'Polish Jews', 'Poles of Jewish origin', 'Jewish Poles',[7] and even, to use Isaac Deutscher's phrase, 'non-Jewish Jews'.[8] A differentiation is sometimes made between 'communist Jews' and 'Jewish communists': according to this, the first group felt practically no link with Jewishness, seeing communism as a route through which they could dissolve national particularism, whereas the second group saw it as a chance to gain equality and foster the development of Jewish culture.[9] The sociologist Jaff Schatz, author of a now classic study of the subject, uses both 'Jewish communists of Poland' and 'Polish-Jewish communists'.[10] As a general rule, I regard the phrase 'communists/individuals of Jewish origin' as giving rise to the fewest problems. It captures the objective aspect of coming into the world in a family belonging—to varying degrees—to a minority culture within Polish society, but does not arbitrarily determine the self-identification of particular individuals, which could be as 'Polish', 'Jewish', 'internationalist', or anywhere in a triangle whose points are demarcated by these three attributes.

In this chapter, it is impossible not to refer to the issue of transformation and the dynamics of the public identity of communists of Jewish origin (indeed not only of communists and not only of those of Jewish origin) as manifested in the Polonization of names and surnames after 1944. This subject deserves a separate, in-depth study and is beyond the scope of this chapter, which focuses on earlier experiences. At this point, I will emphasize only that, in presenting personal information, I include both those surnames which were an aspect of the identity and experiences of childhood and youth and those which were used after the war. I posit that both were equally 'true' or 'real' at various stages of the owner's life and that changing a surname is an important aspect of the dynamics and complexity of human experience, both personal and public.

In this chapter, I use the terms 'Polish communist movement' or 'Polish communism', despite the fact that, on the one hand, a major proportion of its members were Jews, Ukrainians, or Belarussians and, on the other, that it was also part of a transnational movement, which inclines some scholars to perceive it—wrongly—as a phenomenon grafted onto the banks of the Vistula in an artificial way, as a facade or cover. In fact, as in other countries, it grew out of both the October revolution and local radical-left traditions.[11]

Some further remarks concerning my sources are in order. This chapter is based, mostly, on Polish-language personal files, memoirs, and interviews (with both activists and their family members), whose authors were born, as a rule, in the first fifteen years of the twentieth century, were characterized by a high degree of Polonization, did not abandon communism before 1939, survived the war and occupation, and held high political posts in the 1940s and 1950s. As a result, this is a group of limited representativeness both within the communist movement as a whole and among those of Jewish origin who were part of it. Although it included both members of the pre-war intelligentsia and workers, practically speaking it contains no individuals with a deep-rooted experience of the poorly assimilated 'Jewish street'. Despite this limitation, it is possible to identify an entire set of problems significant for the history of the communist movement and Polish Jews in these documents.

The majority of the sources concerning the subjective, personal experiences of Jewishness and engagement in communism during the Second Polish Republic were created some time later. Ego-documents, such as diaries or private letters, from before 1939 are very scarce, as they were lost during the war or were never written, since the activists of illegal, underground, and repressed organizations were not inclined to produce them. The same conditions made it impossible for the communist movement to gather personal information concerning its adherents, so that the statistically 'objective' data on their social composition are also based largely on estimates. Regardless of whether the authors of documents created after 1945 lived in Poland or elsewhere or were at a given moment in favour of or opposed to the prevailing order in Poland, these are narratives which were reconstructed and filtered through later experiences and interpretations. This is not to belittle their value but to draw attention to the complexity and ambiguity which also characterize, albeit in a different way, sources created 'on the spot', as I shall show below.

Absent and Returning Jewishness

A tendency which should be noted from the very outset was for Polish communists of Jewish origin to blur their Jewishness or to erase it completely from their biographies. A characteristic feature of many memoirs published by members of the Communist Party of Poland (Komunistyczna Partia Polski; KPP) in the Polish People's Republic from 1956 to 1989 was the marginalization of or outright failure to reveal or reflect on their Jewish roots or youthful Jewish identity.[12] The topic does appear in some publications but in an extremely perfunctory manner (as in the discussion of nationality barriers in the educational system) and with almost no contextualization.[13] This same principle can be observed in the CVs produced for the party, which should also be treated as conscious self-presentations.

Clearly, both subjective and objective factors stood behind these omissions, the first of which was linked with people's desire to cut themselves off from the past of those for whom Polishness was a basic positive point of reference, who considered themselves Polish and wanted to be perceived as such, or who, as committed internationalists, did not attach much importance to national issues. The reluctance to delve into the realm of the personal could also stem not only from the aim of extinguishing Jewishness but also from individual subjectivity in general, which, from the perspective of the pursuit of the great goal of the revolutionary cause, was insignificant.[14] The objective factors, in turn, could be related to the politics of memory of the Polish United Workers' Party (Polska Zjednoczona Partia Robotnicza; PZPR), which constantly sought national legitimation of its authority and was hostile—in the face of antisemitism expressed in the stereotype of *żydokomuna* (antisemitic stereotype of Judaeo-communism)—to the proclamation of 'Jewishness' by a significant proportion of the pre-war membership of the KPP. There did exist such items as the Yiddish-language edition of KPP documents published in 1959 and some Yiddish memoirs, but their public impact was inevitably very limited because of the language barrier.[15]

Interviews with the children of communists conducted in the course of my doctoral research revealed that the pre-war past was often a powerful taboo or, at best, only reluctantly addressed.[16] Equally, publications appearing after 1989 show that Jewishness was something not spoken of aloud but present below the surface, in hints and understatements which generated tension and unease.[17] The trauma of the Holocaust and the fear of antisemitism undoubtedly cast a shadow. In the case of some communists, those most disillusioned, there was a general reluctance to return to or recount the past which stemmed, above all, from a reluctance to remember a deep youthful engagement with the movement and to confront cognitive and emotional dissonances between the present and the past.

It should be noted that a similar silence can be found in, for example, the memoirs of Jan Trusz (1913–2004), a communist of Ukrainian origin, published at the beginning of the 1980s. He wrote at length about life in a village near Chełm, but his

Ukrainian background was mentioned only tangentially, in the form of a passing reference to a political organization that his brother had joined.[18]

Significantly more references to Jewish experiences can be found in memoirs written or published in Poland after 1989, those published earlier in the underground press or in exile, and those which were never published but remained in archives or in the desk drawers of their authors.[19] Here too, both objective and subjective factors were in play. Gone were the institutionalized norms imposed by the censor's office or by the party itself to determine party memory, and in their place was a significant growth of Jewish history and memory in the public sphere and in scholarly research.[20] Some of those authors were by then disillusioned or embittered and had rejected party discipline or broken the personal ties which had imposed political and social self-censorship. Testimonies of a Jewish childhood could also survive within family memory despite the marginalization and erasing of the Jewish aspects of personal histories.

Landscapes of Childhood

What were the patterns, then, of communists' accounts of childhood or early youth and the place of 'Jewishness' or 'Polishness' in the lives of their families? I will start with the landscape of childhood—that is, the early socialization—of three inhabitants of Lwów (Lviv) born into intellectual or bourgeois households: Józef Kowalczyk (Izajasz Sznajder; 1903–89), the son of a musician, and Roman Werfel (1906–2003) and Adam Schaff (1913–2006), both sons of lawyers.[21] They lived in milieus in which adherence to Polishness (or at least the aspiration to acculturate) was unquestioned,[22] where the portrait of an ancestor who had taken part in the January insurrection hung on the wall,[23] and the head of the family was both a Zionist and a Polish patriot.[24] School was another element of childhood, where scuffles took place with more pious Jewish schoolmates outraged by the ham sandwiches brought from home[25] or which took the form of a secular Jewish institution, where Hebrew was taught but where Polish language and culture were also part of the curriculum.[26] If an account of religious practices appears, it is in the form of reminiscences of a 'loosely Jewish' family, infrequently attending services in Polish in the progressive synagogue.[27] Similar themes of the interweaving of traditions and the maintenance of forms of Jewish identity alongside participation in Polish culture and modern political ideologies (such as Zionism and socialism) can be found in the early stages of the lives of many other, more or less well-known, figures in the Polish communist movement.[28]

Maria Kamińska (née Eiger; 1897–1983), hailing from a family of wealthy Warsaw and Łódź industrialists, described her family environment as 'assimilated through and through', devoid of any religious traditions, and largely indifferent to the Yiddish language or newspapers. At the same time, its members considered themselves to be Jewish Poles or Poles of Jewish origin.[29] The Jewish component of this designation reflected what 'had been' part of the daily experience of the family to a significantly greater degree than what 'was now', and might also reflect how the Eigers were perceived within their social milieu. By way of digression, it can be said that—unlike many of her comrades—Kamińska included the above references to her parents' roots in her fascinating memoirs, published in 1960, which had something to do, perhaps, with her strong and uncompromising personality. In this regard, a notably broader picture appears in the memoirs published in the 1990s by Celina Budzyńska (née Wleklińska; 1907–93), one of the most important Polish-language memoirs of the fully assimilated Polish intelligentsia of Jewish origin, which also shows a few interconnected families seeking a response to the challenges of the zeitgeist at the beginning of the twentieth century in various variants of leftism.[30]

These processes extended across a spectrum, ranging from assimilation—that is, rejecting a former identity in favour of a different majority group within a given society—to acculturation—that is, adopting the culture of a dominant group while retaining a sense of belonging to one's own.[31] There were tendencies to Jewish acculturation or assimilation not only to Polishness (which was characteristic for Lwów, as mentioned above) but also to Germanness (in Greater Poland, and Austrian Silesia) and to Russianness (in eastern parts of the former Polish–Lithuanian Commonwealth).[32]

For such people, communist activity did not constitute 'red assimilation' in the strong sense of the term, where the choice of communism enabled a rapid transformation of identity and entry into the sphere of the majority culture. As is clear from these accounts, access to the KPP manifested itself more as an intensification and strengthening of a process already begun within the family. All these narratives, however, were produced by people coming from the better situated and educated strata of society and who, after the Second World War, often also had close links with the cultural and intellectual world and held high-profile positions as Marxist philosophers, party ideologues, press editors, and so on. But there was also Helena Kamińska (née Frenkel; 1905–98), who hailed from a poor Warsaw family of artisans and had completed only primary education: she did not learn Yiddish until she wound up in prison.[33] Eugenia Pelowska (1911–78), the daughter of a leather-goods seller in Warsaw, combined communist activism with working in a wellington-boot factory or tea-packing plant and, lacking knowledge of Yiddish, could not work in party cells in Warsaw's Muranów district, which was largely inhabited by Jews.[34]

The circumstances of socialization and the associated questions of identity were obviously not static but themselves constituted the nexus of dynamic processes. An important pattern which often emerges from the analysis of the youth of communists of Jewish origin (although not only them) are the tensions, or at least the differences, between generations within the family, the processes of transformation captured 'in the act of becoming'. Ostap Dłuski (né Adolf Langner; 1892–1964) remembered his Galician grandfather, who wore a traditional beard, as a positively exotic figure. As a grown man, Dłuski had a problem similar to that of Pelowska: addressing Jewish cells of the KPP, he needed a translator.[35] Situated halfway between these experiences was his father, who taught Judaism in the gymnasium of his native Buczacz.

The teenage years, which are of particular interest here, were a time of breakthroughs and ruptures. The 15-year-old Roman Zambrowski (1909–77) from Warsaw, grandson of a rabbi (but also the son of a mother indifferent to religion), refused to say Kaddish for his father, who had died in exile.[36] The daughter of Salomon Natanson (1904–86), who was known after the war as Józef Kowalski and was one of the party's most prominent historians, recalled that her father had broken with religion at the age of 13 and therefore just at the moment when, as a Jewish child, he should have celebrated his barmitzvah and his traditional entry into adulthood.[37]

In 2005 Julian Gren (né Szmul Gringras; 1911–2007), an engineer, activist with the Communist Union of the Youth of Poland (Komunistyczny Związek Młodzieży Polski; KZMP) and the communist student organization Życie in the 1930s, and deputy minister of several industrial departments after the war, composed an extensive account of his own youth. He was born into the family of a prosperous photographer from Kielce. He remembered his petit bourgeois home as bilingual, moderately observant of religious traditions, but also marked by generational division, in that his parents still maintained a kosher household but the children did not observe *kashrut* (here too, ham sandwiches make an appearance). Of the stage through which the family was passing, Gren said: 'It wasn't assimilation, but there was a tendency that way, probably.' He himself, according to this account and the stories recalled by his son, completely abandoned religion as a teenager and, as a pupil at a Jewish Polish-language gymnasium in Kielce (he later switched to a state school), would throw stones at *ḥeder* students and very much desired to cut himself off from Jewishness in favour of Polishness, embodied also by the Polish girls whose attention he wished to attract.[38]

The processes of inter-generational change and modernization took place in very different social environments. In another affluent petit bourgeois household, that of the Goldwags, religious feast days were treated very seriously and the parents, effectively, did not know Polish, using Russian instead. The children, meanwhile, spoke Polish amongst themselves—and it was Polish, perhaps, that became the code for the inner-generational transfer of subversive ideas, since three of the four young Goldwags joined the KPP.[39] The father of Necha Zalcman (Stanisława Sowińska; 1912–2004), the impoverished cantor of a Łódź synagogue, spoke hardly any Polish, wore traditional dress, and agonized over his daughter's hobnobbing with non-Jews —but her points of departure and those of her siblings were Zionism, communism, the radio, and the novels of Zola.[40] Juliusz Hibner (1912–94) remembered some tensions in the family home in Tarnopol which he confided to family memory. His father, an impoverished merchant, and his mother wanted their children to be educated in a secular school which they also attended on Saturdays—although they were not permitted to take writing materials on that day, in order to observe the sabbath.[41]

These experiences do not give the whole picture, however. The difficulties created by Pelowska's and Dłuski's inability to speak Yiddish point to the existence of wide circles of communists and their sympathizers on the Jewish street who were not 'professional revolutionaries' (that is de facto underground white-collar workers) or intellectuals but unqualified workers and unemployed people, separated by solid barriers from the culture of the majority. Admittedly, in the younger generation of Jews whose socialization took place in the Second Polish Republic, there were very few who had no contact at all with Polish culture and language or the modern educational system: for this generation, the processes of political radicalization or cultural modernization—secularization, Polonization, and so on—were intensified. However, the autobiographies written by young Jews for the competitions organized by YIVO in the 1930s reveal a world of young people for whom Yiddish continued to be their first language; the world of their childhood was one of tradition and material scarcity or outright poverty, and their communist world was made up of a loose group of peers similar to them not only in terms of class but also of 'ethnicity'.[42] For one 14-year-old girl, getting in touch with communists coincided with learning to read and write.[43] This experience was therefore characterized by a deep ambivalence: to choose communism constituted an aspiration to attain some form of personal modernity and involved the rejection of the world of one's Jewish childhood; yet socialization at this level of the communist movement continued to take place within a Jewish and Yiddish milieu.[44]

This is part of a wider issue. The experience of many communists, regardless of their ethnic background, from the lower social strata, the proletariat, the peasantry, or the poorer petite bourgeoisie, who were never to become leaders, professional revolutionaries, or 'public intellectuals', remains largely unexplored. What is involved here is not the movement's head or backbone but its muscles, people who worked in workshops and factories and sometimes left the party, forced by material circumstances or loss of contact with the clandestine organization. Jews from this stratum, poorly educated and sometimes more weakly assimilated or acculturated, with little social capital in Polish society, had less chance of surviving the Holocaust.[45] Many of those who did survive did not possess sufficient cultural, political, or social capital to find themselves prominent positions in the political field (especially in the realm of culture).[46] Still others, even if they did achieve high office in post-war Poland, never wrote or published memoirs, nor did they meet anyone who would be willing to listen to their story. The grass-roots history of Polish communism—for example, of radicalized farm labourers or Jewish tailors' apprentices—is thus a neglected topic. The analysis produced a few years ago by Piotr Laskowski of the memoirs (in Polish and Yiddish) of a female Jewish communist active among Jewish domestic servants is an excellent beginning which, it is hoped, will stimulate more extensive research in this direction in Poland,[47] especially in the context of recent research into the experiences of the unprivileged throughout Polish history.[48]

Jewishness, Antisemitism, Politics

At some point, the individuals whose experiences and narrative-building strategies I analyse in this chapter made the momentous political choice of linking themselves to a socially stigmatized and fiercely repressed movement with radical and maximalist aims. Needless to say, a comprehensive look at the complicated combination of motivations and factors leading an individual to a communist organization is not possible here. The aim of this section is to elicit the relationship between radical left-wing engagement and 'ethnic' origin. Communists of Jewish origin came to the movement by the same routes as their Polish or Ukrainian comrades. Sometimes they followed in the footsteps of their parents or older siblings but also, on occasion, rebelled against them. They were fascinated by Żeromski's novels. Marxism seemed to them the key to understanding the world. They agonized over their own poverty or exclusion and matured to a sense of moral dissent to the injustices they observed. They encountered communist mentors and guides in high schools and universities or in factories and workshops. Is it then possible to draw out the specifics of their experience of becoming communist—or the ways in which they reconstructed the process subsequently?

In the group of 214 communists which I studied previously, the median age of joining the communist organization was 19, and a fifth had joined by the age of 16: they were therefore at an age at which elements of political socialization have been identified as being particularly strong.[49] In this regard, a certain difference can be observed between activists of Jewish origin and the rest. Among the Jews (74 individuals), 33 per cent had joined a communist organization before the age of 17; the median age of joining was 18. In the non-Jewish group (140 individuals), 12 per cent had joined before they were 17, and the median age of joining was 19.[50]

The memoirs of Romana Granas (1906–87), published towards the end of the 1950s, offer an incisive insight into such adolescent political experience. In the first years of the Second Polish Republic, as a 15-year-old student at the Łódź gymnasium, she joined a leftist study circle which then became a communist group. The girls read Lenin as much out of ideological fascination as out of concern not to compromise themselves in front of the boys, and their first tasks for the party were greeted as a confirmation of their maturity.[51] Thus the political and social circles of teenage revolutionaries created a space both for transition between different phases of life and for the coexistence of their elements, such as 'youthful' adventure and 'mature' political consciousness.

Entry into communist organizations was quite often preceded by involvement in political youth circles of a different ideological character, such as the Bundist youth movement Tsukunft, or the Zionist Hashomer Hatsa'ir.[52] On the one hand, joining any group constituted a choice which could determine one's entire future; on the other, the boundaries between particular ideological milieus were sometimes vague, and there are many examples of young people moving between different groups as they sought better answers to the questions that troubled them. This raises the question of the extent to which involvement with a Zionist youth group was primarily an expression of internalized identification with its ideas and the resulting Jewish self-identification, or whether it was more a question of conforming to family expectations, a social rather than ideological affinity. As the biography of a certain

Lwów communist demonstrates, one might join Hashomer Hatsa'ir under the influence of one's peers and leave it as the result of a conscious recognition that one was opposed to Zionism; the next stage of the journey towards communism progressed thanks to friends from the KZMP along with the reading of political works.[53] Very similar questions can be posed with regard to communists from rural backgrounds who passed through the peasant youth movement as teenagers.

A frequent element of communist memoirs is the emphasis on the leftist political socialization that those who entered the movement had previously experienced in their family home. The childhood landscape of Celina Budzyńska was peopled, as far back as she could remember, by the activists of the Social Democracy of the Kingdom of Poland and Lithuania (Socjaldemokracja Królestwa Polskiego i Litwy; SDKPiL), the Polish Socialist Party: Left (Polska Partia Socjalistyczna–Lewica; PPS–L), and the Polish Socialist Party: Revolutionary Faction (Polska Partia Socjalistyczna–Frakcja Rewolucyjna; PPS–FR) who passed through her parents' house: a refuge for 'illegals', scene of party meetings, and a place for storing subversive literature. Ten-year-old Celina delivered parcels and messages for her favourite uncles, who, after 1918, became leaders of the KPP.[54] It was therefore no surprise that on entering the communist youth movement in 1922, she had the feeling that her whole 15-year-old life had been preparing her for this.[55] The CVs produced for the party also mention an atmosphere where, for example, 'the Bund tradition dominated' and where 'the epoch of the great tremors of 1917–18–19' resonated loudly;[56] in another case, the father sympathized with the Russian Socialist Revolutionaries, whereas the mother displayed 'a social attitude typical of the Jewish intellectual milieu, fluctuating between the influences of the workers' movement and the nationalist position of the petite bourgeoisie'.[57] Communists of Jewish origin did not differ particularly from their Polish comrades, who also willingly remembered their fathers —for example, radical, anti-clerical peasants. But here, too, the norm of blurred Jewishness comes to the fore. Esfira Mirer (Edwarda Orłowska; 1906–77), an underground activist of the Communist Party of Western Belarus and after the war head of the Women's Department of the PZPR Central Committee among other things, evoked in her autobiography, written in 1946, how strongly her father's tales of tsarist exploitation spoke to her childish imagination: 'With the whole of my childish heart, I detested the tsar who oppressed and tormented poor workers and peasants . . . I was religious, and in my prayers I begged God to punish the tsar and relieve the fate of the wronged and oppressed.'[58] However, it is not related to which God, in what language, and according to which rituals that had been imparted to her in the process of socialization Esfira prayed.

What clearly distinguished communists of Jewish origin when it came to constructing their world-views, emotions, resentments, and political commitments was the experience of various forms of antisemitism: beginning with the school system which assigned to Jews the roles of outsider and inferior, to the blocking of certain social positions (for instance, in state institutions), through to hateful language and physical violence.[59] In an autobiography written for one of the YIVO competitions, a young Jew who had passed through both communist and Zionist organizations stated explicitly: 'I love Poland ... but I do not love the Poland which hates me for no reason!'[60] Another author, from a working-class background, asked, after the KPP had been dissolved: 'Who will defend our rights? Who will defend the national minorities? There will be no one to demand equal rights for the Jewish masses.'[61] According to Kamil Kijek, communism was particularly appealing to the better-assimilated or acculturated inhabitants of larger cities, since greater contact with a Polish environment meant that they were also more exposed to confrontations with antisemitism, which gave rise to a disposition to protest and oppose in the most radical way possible.[62]

However, the avoidance of any mention of antisemitism as a meaningful aspect of daily life or as a factor leading to the choice of communism in the post-war CVs produced for the party or the memoirs of activists is very striking. Even a perfunctory comment by an industrial activist after the war about 'racist harassment', because of which, towards the end of the 1930s, he lost his job on the construction of the main railway station in Warsaw, seems quite exceptional.[63] It was certainly not in the interests of the party authorities to preserve the memory of the widespread nature of anti-semitism in pre-war Poland. It would appear that particular communists themselves also did not wish to devote much attention to this aspect of their own lives. One reason could be the tendency, which I have already alluded to, to blur their Jewish past. Another was probably the belief that ethnicity was of little importance. For some, it was also possibly psychologically uncomfortable to reconstruct their story with themselves in the role of victim, someone weaker or inferior, a role which would not fit easily into the framework of a narrative about rebellion, awareness, and the empowerment of an equally weak and inferior proletariat. At the same time, the communist-leaning authors of the autobiographies written for the YIVO competitions, under entirely different conditions, do seem to accentuate more strongly the topics of social injustice and the poverty in which they grew up.[64] Did they write about Jewish poverty and injustice—or poverty and injustice in general? It is difficult to decide. On the one hand, the straightforward ideological message of communism steered them in the direction of universalism; on the other, the poverty of the Jewish street was what they knew best.

In this context, documents created after 1989, in exile or circulated within the family, provide a rather different picture to the documents prepared for the party or memoirs published in the 1960s and 1970s. The memory of antisemitic violence constitutes an important feature of the unpublished memoirs of Stanisława Sowińska, which I have already discussed, in which Jewishness itself also appears as something familiar and remembered with nostalgia.[65] Similarly, some of the last remaining witnesses described, for example, how nationalists threw them out of lecture halls.[66] The daughter of Jakub Berman, who was, in the 1930s, secretary of the KPP subdivision for the intelligentsia, recollected how her parents sent her to a Jewish primary school in Warsaw because they were concerned about antisemitism.[67] Julian Gren observed: 'Even before the war I'd dreamed of a Poland where life would be good and fair. Where Jews wouldn't be discriminated against, where there would be no antisemitism. That was a dream of mine, probably straight out of books by Żeromski who was my idol at the time.'[68] It is worth drawing attention to the connection this personal account makes with the content of youthful reading, as Yuri Slezkine puts it: 'putting books to the test of life and putting life to the test of books'.[69] This is a theme which often features in communist socialization, most frequently, however, in terms of finding in Marxism a comprehensive explanation of the causes of the injustices and deprivation experienced.

In an interview recorded in France, Juliusz Hibner, explaining his communist commitment, observed: 'It is not easy to come to terms with manifestations of discrimination and humiliation in a country in which you feel yourself to be a normal citizen.'[70] This son of a 'proletarianized' trader managed to graduate from the gymnasium and begin study at university, as had been his dream, but was unable to complete his course, as he was forced to flee Lwów pursued by the police. Nevertheless, he defined himself as one who had advanced socially and gained capital that should have secured him a better position on the social ladder but who came up against barriers which derived exclusively from his ethnic origin. Michał Dichter (1912–82), who also managed to break free of 'Galician poverty' in Borysław and to finish his studies at the Lwów Polytechnic in the 1930s, would recount within his family circle the difficulties that even educated Jews encountered in gaining employment in the oil industry.[71] Coming from a completely different background, Adam Schaff also identified his youthful political commitment with the sense that, as a Jew in Poland, despite being raised in material comfort and gaining cultural capital in the form of an education, certain routes of advancement were closed to him. He also referred to a still earlier experience: during the Lwów pogrom in November 1918, when he was 5 years old, Polish soldiers had entered his home, and he was later to discover photos in his father's drawer of the dead victims of those events.[72]

The year 1920 was also a significant moment of political socialization. Hersz (Grzegorz) Smolar (1905–93) related to his sons the moment at which he felt safe for the first time on the streets of his native Zambrów. It was in the summer of that year, after the Red Army had occupied the town, when as a 15-year-old he acted as a representative of the new authorities.[73] A time that has gone down in official Polish historical memory as marked by the threat of Soviet subjugation was, for this Jewish boy from a petit bourgeois family, a time not only of entry into political maturity but also of emancipation from fear. It is worth stressing, however, that the Polish–Bolshevik war could also be a formative moment for future non-Jewish communists, such as two gymnasium pupils from Nowy Sącz who tried to cross the front line and join the Red Army.[74] A similar sense of agency and empowerment to that experienced by Smolar could also have been felt by contemporary farm labourers, hoping for an end to exploitation with the arrival of the Red Army. Similarly, reports of clashes between workers and the army in Kraków in November 1923 contributed to the leftist radicalization of the young, regardless of their ethnic or social background.[75]

In the context of family socialization, it seems important to ask how involvement with communism on the part of young boys and girls was received by their closest relatives. How did families react, for example, to the fact that their sons and daughters chose radically different values and points of reference? The tension between the world of Jewish tradition and the world of modern politics sometimes had a humorous character, for example in the case of a young female communist from a traditional family, who had to supply male members of the organization—who were both comrades-in-arms and friends with whom she spent her free time—with women's hats, since her father, as pious as he was short-sighted, would not countenance her receiving young male visitors.[76] In other cases, however, there was a much more dramatic rupture: the abandonment of the family home or rejection by the family. This breach was particularly sharp if an individual transformed him- or herself into a professional revolutionary, a functionary of the underground party living in a closed conspiratorial community, existing between prison and whatever district they might be sent to next by the party leadership, counting only on being able to establish themselves there for a few months before once again finding themselves in prison or compelled to flee.

The image of somewhat alienated young communists who had broken away completely from the environment of their earlier socialization is confirmed by many sources. They were shaped by factors inherent to the communist movement (a tendency to construct a dichotomous vision of the world divided into 'the good', on the side of the revolution, and 'the bad'—everything else) and also by the environment in the broadest sense (such as state persecution and anti-communist public discourse). But this is not the complete picture. The majority of communists, whether Polish, Jewish, or Ukrainian, were not professional revolutionaries. They studied at gymnasia and universities, and, above all, they worked (or struggled to find work), most often in factories, workshops, or on farms, and maintained and entered various non-communist networks, including those of their families. There were undoubtedly those who, having chosen revolution, found themselves in a social vacuum which could only be filled by the illegal community of comrades who became their new and most important reference group. However, even in the accounts of those illegals most dedicated to the cause, there is interwoven the motif of fathers and mothers making their way to prison with parcels, running between lawyers, and putting parental love and loyalty above their failure to understand and even their revulsion at the ideas professed by their children.

It has rightly been noted that people of Jewish origin aspiring to leave their environment often found themselves in a state of awkward suspension, no longer belonging to the world of their family but not accepted by society either, as Jews or as communists: Kamil Kijek termed this position one of 'double alienation'.[77] Of course, Polish, as well as Jewish or Polish Jewish, fathers and mothers were to be found among the parents visiting their precious children in prison. It is easy, too, to imagine a devout Catholic father being concerned about visits to his growing daughter from strange boys who might lead her astray, or a 'native Polish' family expelling a wayward communist son from their midst—or the son himself, feeling absolute alienation in 1930s Poland. However, objective conditions meant that this sense of estrangement and suspension was likely to be stronger among men and women of Jewish origin. This leads to the question of how important were the ties with their communist peers, linked both by ideas and by friendship and love, in overcoming this sense of isolation.[78]

Similarities and differences in communist experience can also be found in many other areas. There is still no comprehensive study of the political repression of communists by the Polish state apparatus, in spite of the progress of historical study in other areas since 1989. It therefore remains to be empirically verified, for example, whether revolutionaries with Jewish surnames and physiognomies were, generally speaking, treated differently by the police, courts, or prison warders from their 'ethnically Polish' comrades, and how this translated into the specific accounts of Sanacja prisons, which are one of the most important elements of the legacy of the Party History Department of the Central Committee of the PZPR. Another important theme in the context of the relationship between youth and politics is what consequences there were for the views and emotions of communists on finding themselves, at the age of 15 or 16, under arrest or even in prison.[79] On the one hand, there was the fearful reaction, 'What will my parents say?'; on the other, there ensued a radicalization of attitudes towards state institutions and the state itself.[80]

The Dynamics of Self-Identification

Finally, there remains the question of how these young people, as communists, formulated their views of their origins: what was the nature of their national self-identification, their personal sense of ties with the tradition of their ancestors, and their more broadly understood attitude to Jewishness? To what extent did they feel themselves to be 'Jewish' or 'Polish', or did they strive to rise above these distinctions in favour of an internationalist identity, parallel to the Bolshevization, and then Stalinization, of the communist world movement, creating a strongly pro-Soviet or Comintern identity?[81]

Were they 'Jewish communists' or 'communist Jews'? In a memoir written in exile in the 1980s, Artur Kowalski (1911–90), a bitterly disillusioned former communist, declared that at the beginning of the 1930s, as a 20-year-old member of the Łódź KZMP, he identified with the party rather than any country or nation, and saw himself not so much as a citizen of the world as of the Comintern. When he was active in Belgium or France, it was all the same to him whether he wrote in French, Yiddish, or Polish—though Polish was closest to him.[82] The slogan of internationalism undoubtedly reflected a promise, appealing to many individuals, of overcoming social divisions, economic crises, and the growing strength of nationalists. Were individuals of Jewish descent more 'receptive' to constructing an internationalist identity for themselves? A conducive factor might be the uneasy state of suspension between two reference groups: the Jewish, from which the individual wished to cut themselves free, and the Polish, to which they aspired but which was closed to them by barriers of antisemitism.[83]

The very concept of an 'international communist' has at least two interlinked dimensions: of identity and of function. An international communist could just as easily be a cosmopolitan of Jewish origin who felt equally at home in Warsaw and in Paris, a local activist, or a miner in the nationally and linguistically mixed region of Upper Silesia. An example of an international communist who could also be at home in different environments was Bolesław Bierut (1892–1956), an 'ethnic Pole', who, as an emissary of the Comintern, worked for several years at a high level in the communist parties of Bulgaria, Austria, and Czechoslovakia.

It would be a serious exaggeration to argue, nevertheless, that all communists fully internalized internationalist slogans or national nihilism. The people who have been mentioned in this chapter so far aspired to or identified with Polishness in various ways—and they did not reject this identification on becoming communists. However—and here lurks one of the many complexities of the communist habitus—their Polishness was often closely intertwined with internationalism and even pro-Soviet sentiments.

The memoirs of Sygmunt Stein (1899–1968), who left the movement following disagreements and disappointments over the civil war in Spain, provide both similarities and differences to the narratives analysed above. He wanted to remain Jewish while becoming communist, but in his case too the old identities mixed with the new ones. He wrote his memoirs in exile in France at the beginning of the 1960s and published them in Yiddish. As his daughter recounted, as a teenager, by linking himself with the Bund and then with the communists, he cut himself off from his devout family near Lwów, from the *ḥeder* which he attended and from the *peyes* which he wore as a boy and which he cut off himself (unfortunately, it is not known under what circumstances this took place).[84] He did not, however, abandon his passionate love of Jewish culture (again, there is no further information on how he understood this), 'which melted into an integral whole with an unbreakable faith in the historic role of the Soviet Union'.[85] Meanwhile, Dawid Sfard (1903–81), a poet writing in Yiddish, attended his father's funeral in the 1930s and, in contrast to Zambrowski, said Kaddish, despite being a member of the KPP.[86] After the war, Sfard would go on to be active in the Social and Cultural Society of Jews in Poland and would leave for Israel during the antisemitic campaign of 1967–8, whereas in France, Stein would go on to function in circles publishing in Yiddish. The lives and choices of these two follow the pattern of 'Jewish communists' rather than 'communist Jews'.

The documents produced in the Soviet Union by Polish communists who went there to study in political schools, worked in Comintern departments, took part in KPP congresses (of which all but the first took place in the USSR), or travelled there for medical treatment are very useful in understanding their attitudes to their origins. In 1936 Roman Zambrowski, then 27, explained to the Comintern authorities: 'Though I am a Jew by descent, I regard myself as a Pole. I do not know the Yiddish language, I am offended by certain Jewish national characteristics, I was brought up on Polish history and literature.'[87] But nothing is simple in the biography of an individual or, indeed, in the files of the Comintern. Four years earlier, in a participants' questionnaire for the Sixth Congress of the KPP, Zambrowski listed his nationality as 'Jewish'.[88] Is this an example of the dynamics of self-identification, the record of a process of change which took place in an individual over the space of several years, filled not only with activism and political socialization but also with reflection on the past, the future, and one's place in the world? Was Zambrowski making a radical break between 'objective' origin and its 'subjective' appraisal? Or maybe one of these statements—or perhaps both of them—constituted an expression of his adaptation to the expectations and norms prevailing in political structures?

Participants' questionnaires from KPP congresses contain examples of people with Jewish roots entering their nationality as Polish and Jewish or declaring themselves to be Poles of Jewish origin. There are even more intriguing entries: at the Fifth Congress of the KPP in 1930, Solo Stramer (Roman Kornecki; 1905–84) clearly first gave his nationality as 'Polish', only to cross it out and correct it to 'Jewish'.[89] This is not an entry where it is easy to make a slip from carelessness or a lapse of memory. Was he concerned that someone would question this first declaration and refuse to legitimize it? Or perhaps he judged that it was necessary to 'open up' completely to the party, allow it to X-ray his whole life, to the point of admitting to a 'truth' with which he felt no personal connection? It should be remembered that the beginning of the 1930s was a point of transition for the communist movement from its Bolshevik to its Stalinist phase, which was linked with growing xenophobia in the USSR, the marriage of revolution with Great Russian nationalism, the constant mobilization of 'vigilance', and the accelerating ritual of self-criticism and purges.[90] The last two congresses of the KPP took place in a very specific atmosphere: on the one side, there was the imposition of Stalinist uniformity on the entire communist movement; on the other was the triumph of the radical 'minority' faction of the KPP which had just taken control of the party, marking it even more strongly with an atmosphere of suspicion and caution.[91]

It is very difficult therefore, looking at Zambrowski, Kornecki, and dozens of their comrades, to mark the boundary between the complexity of national self-identification, a deep internalization of political norms, conformism within the movement, and the tactical game being played in this field, where not only recognition was at stake but also survival (at this time primarily politically but, within a few years, also literally physically). When Zambrowski was formulating his declaration in 1936, the first wave of Stalinist purges against 'internal enemies' was already under way—the atmosphere grew more tense, and he himself became the object of suspicion and denunciation. By then, communists understood the need to choose their words carefully in order to minimize the risk of being accused—for example, of 'Jewish nationalism'.

Intriguing clues are also provided by sources of a completely different kind: university records preserved from the time of the Second Polish Republic. The questionnaires the students were asked to fill out were not detailed, but they did include questions about nationality, on the basis of which non-obvious dynamics can also be traced. Gren and another member of the KZMP and Życie, Rubin Filderbaum (Roman Fidelski; 1912–88; minister of machine industry, 1955–6), when starting out at the Warsaw University of Technology at the end of the 1920s, declared their nationality to be 'Polish'. In somewhat later documents, however, they changed this to 'Jewish'.[92] What role was played here by the growing radicalization and antisemitic violence for which Polish educational institutes became an arena in this decade? Was the modification an expression of solidarity with the persecuted, even when a particular individual wished—like Gren—to dissociate himself from Jewishness? In the case of the communists, who were radically opposed to the social order, a less likely explanation perhaps would be conformism with regard to external factors demanding the 'exposure' of Jews 'pretending' to be Poles. The situation is further complicated by the fact that Filderbaum, who initially identified himself with Polishness, during his first years as a student was active in Pochodnia. This was a twin organization to Życie, except that it focused on Jewish students. Unfortunately, Fidelski did not leave any testimony explaining these choices and their circumstances.

A necessary comment to conclude this section: questions analogous to those concerning the tension between 'Jewishness', 'Polishness', Sovietness', and 'internationalism' in the socialization of communists of Jewish origin may also be posed with regard to 'ethnically Polish' revolutionaries. For example, there was Roman Śliwa (1904–44), who maintained during a police interrogation that he was a Pole 'because I speak Polish and live in Poland. Otherwise, as a worker, there is nothing further binding me to Poland.'[93] It is impossible to tell to what extent this was a fully internalized radicalism and to what extent the adoption of a radical position in the face of a political enemy in the course of a highly emotional interaction. Nevertheless, questions concerning this dimension of the relationship between 'Polishness' and 'communism' and also the sense of 'Polishness' among representatives of the peasant class at this time certainly remain open.[94]

Conclusion

All the blurring and refocusing outlined above, the ambivalences and tensions, mean that the answer to whether there was a specifically Jewish experience of childhood and youth as a road to communism is bound to be complicated. Although there was no crystallized Jewish 'interest group' within the Polish communist movement,[95] there certainly existed a Jewish experience of communism and communist socialization—just as there existed a women's, peasant, or intellectual experience of it. There was a communism of the Jewish street, just as there was a communism of the Ukrainian village, of the farmsteads of Mazovia, and of remote hamlets in Polesie. The Jewish street or the milieu of young, radicalized Jews choosing between the KZMP, the Bund, and left Zionism sometimes functioned as a 'separate Jewish subculture'[96] or a distinct group or even sub-group within the cultural formation of communism.[97]

The lower the rung of the KPP/KZMP organizational structure, the less the degree of assimilation or acculturation, and 'Jewish' cells could function without any contact with 'Polish' ones.[98] However, the Jewish street is one thing; the experiences of the majority of people whom I have discussed in this chapter—Jews who were communists, professional revolutionaries, or assimilated members of the intelligentsia—are quite another.

Communists functioned in a space in which diversity and uniformity clashed. It can be clearly seen through the prism of their biographies that the history of this movement is marked by complicated relations between 'communism' and 'communisms', between the top-down Comintern model and local specifics, and the psychological and social dispositions of individuals. Communists came to the movement bringing very different baggage, class and national backgrounds, motivations, and hopes, but within it they encountered—and often contributed to—pressure towards a specific uniformity. Regardless of the fact that this uniformity was never complete, it was strongly in evidence in the narrative strategies presented in this chapter. In the case of communists of Jewish origin, the pressure for uniformity largely led to the erasure of the Jewish component of their lives. Sometimes this was supplemented by attempts to cut themselves off from the world of their childhood and youth, but sometimes this uniformity was marked by a state of tension with tenacious memories, sentiments, and traumas.

Translated from the Polish by Anna Zaranko

Notes

1 See, inter alia, K. Auerbach, *The House at Ujazdowskie 16: Jewish Families in Warsaw after the Holocaust* (Bloomington, Ind., 2013); J. Brun-Zejmis, 'National Self-Denial and Marxist Ideology: The Origin of the Communist Movement in Poland and the Jewish Question, 1918–1923', *Nationalities Papers*, 22/S1 (1994), 29–54; M. Checinski, *Poland: Communism, Nationalism, Anti-Semitism* (New York, 1982); P. Hanenbrink, *A Specter Haunting Europe: The Myth of Judeo-Bolshevism* (Cambridge, Mass., 2018); R. Levy, *Ana Pauker: The Rise and Fall of a Jewish Communist* (Berkeley, Calif., 2001); M. Mishkinsky, 'The Communist Party of Poland and the Jews', in Y. Gutman, E. Mendelsohn, J. Reinharz, and C. Shmeruk (eds.), *The Jews of Poland between Two World Wars* (Hanover, NH, 1989), 56–74; J. Nalewajko-Kulikov, *Obywatel Jidyszlandu: Rzecz o żydowskich komunistach w Polsce* (Warsaw, 2009); J. Schatz, *The Generation: The Rise and Fall of the Jewish Communists of Poland* (Berkeley, Calif., 1991); P. Wróbel, 'Failed Integration: Jews and the Beginning of the Communist Movement in Poland', *Polin*, 24 (2012), 187–222.

2 W. Marzec, *Rebelia i reakcja: Rewolucja 1905 roku i plebejskie doświadczenie polityczne* (Łódź, 2016), 198.

3 A. Giza-Poleszczuk, 'Autobiografia: Między symbolem a rzeczywistością', *Kultura i Społeczeństwo*, 34/1 (1990), 95–109: 96–7.

4 After the war activists were regularly asked to fill in questionnaires for the personnel departments of the party, including basic facts concerning social origin, families, political affiliations, education, and so on. A short narrative CV was often attached to these questionnaires.

5 Marzec, *Rebelia i reakcja*, 200.
6 See e.g. D. Easton and R. D. Hess, 'The Child's Political World', *Midwest Journal of Political Science*, 6 (1962), 229–46; R. D. Hess and J. V. Torney, *The Development of Political Attitudes in Children* (Chicago, 1967); R. M. Merelman, 'The Role of Conflict in Children's Political Learning', in O. Ichilov (ed.), *Political Socialization, Citizenship, Education and Democracy* (New York, 1990), 47–65; K. M. Słomczyński and G. Shabad, 'Can Support for Democracy and the Market be Learned in School? A Natural Experiment in Post-Communist Poland', *Political Psychology*, 19 (1998), 749–79.
7 See A. Landau-Czajka, *Syn będzie Lech…: Asymilacja Żydów w Polsce międzywojennej* (Warsaw, 2006); A. Molisak and Z. Kołodziejska (eds.), *Żydowski Polak, polski Żyd: Problem tożsamości w literaturze polsko-żydowskiej* (Warsaw, 2011).
8 I. Deutscher, 'Message of the Non-Jewish Jew', *American Socialist*, 5 (1958), 6–10.
9 Nalewajko-Kulikov, *Obywatel Jidyszlandu*, 198.
10 Schatz, *The Generation*.
11 E. J. Hobsbawm, *Revolutionaries: Contemporary Essays* (London, 1973), 3.
12 See R. Granas, *Gruba Ceśka* (Warsaw, 1958); L. Krzemień, *Kropla w potoku* (Warsaw, 1982); J. S. Ludwińska, *Życie nielegalne* (Warsaw, 1988); E. Orłowska, *Pamiętam jak dziś* (Warsaw, 1973).
13 F. Kalicka, *Dwa czterdziestolecia mojego życia: Wspomnienia 1904–1984* (Warsaw, 1989), 38; A. Zatorska, *Spoza smugi cienia* (Kraków, 1982), 8, 18–19. In these cases the original surnames of the authors appear, but they are the only hint of their Jewish roots.
14 For a similar pattern in the autobiographies of activists in the workers' movement, see Marzec, *Rebelia i reakcja*, 213.
15 *Unter der fon fun k.p.p.: artikln, zikhroynes, dokumentn*, ed. H. Goldfinger, M. Mirski, and S. Zachariasz (Warsaw, 1959).
16 See Ł. Bertram, *Bunt podziemie, władza: Polscy komuniści i ich socjalizacja polityczna do roku 1956* (Warsaw, 2022).
17 See R. Gren, *Krajobraz z dzieckiem* (Warsaw, 1996).
18 J. Trusz, *Z doświadczeń pokolenia* (Warsaw, 1981), 15.
19 See C. Budzyńska, *Strzępy rodzinnej sagi* (Warsaw, 1997); B. Puchalska, 'Było to tak…: Rozmowy z Juliuszem Hibnerem', *Zeszyty Historyczne*, 124 (1998), 33–178; A. Schaff, *Pora na spowiedź* (Warsaw, 1993); id., *Próba podsumowania* (Warsaw, 1999); Biblioteka Narodowa, Warsaw, Magazyn Rękopisów, 14256: S. Sowińska, 'Okrutne lata' (before 1994); S. Stein, *Moja wojna w Hiszpanii. Brygady Międzynarodowe: Koniec mitu*, trans. B. Szwarcman-Czarnota (Kraków, 2015); T. Torańska, *Oni* (Warsaw, 2004); Eng. trans.: *'Them': Stalin's Polish Puppets*, trans. A. Kolakowska (New York, 1987).
20 See N. Aleksiun, 'Polish Historiography of the Holocaust: Between Silence and Public Debate', *German History*, 22 (2004), 406–32.
21 At the same time, their accounts represent three different types of source material: memoirs written before 1989 but unpublished (Józef Kowalczyk, 'Z dawnych przeżyć', photocopy of unpublished memoir (n.d.), in author's possession); memoirs published after 1989 (Schaff, *Pora na spowiedź*); accounts recorded in the 1980s and originally published in the underground press (Roman Werfel, interview, in Torańska, *Oni*, 105–41; ead. *Them*, 85–122).
22 Kowalczyk, 'Z dawnych przeżyć', 1.
23 Roman Werfel, interview (Torańska, *Oni*, 109; ead., *Them*, 88).
24 B. Chwedeńczuk, *Dialogi z Adamem Schaffem* (Warsaw, 2005), 17, 23.

25 Roman Werfel, interview (Torańska, *Oni*, 110; ead., *Them*, 89).
26 Schaff, *Pora na spowiedź*, 15.
27 Roman Werfel, interview (Torańska, *Oni*, 110; ead., *Them*, 89).
28 E. Krasucki, *Międzynarodowy komunista: Jerzy Borejsza. Biografia polityczna* (Warsaw, 2009), 29–38; A. Sobór-Świderska, *Jakub Berman: Biografia komunisty* (Warsaw, 2009).
29 M. Kamińska, *Ścieżkami wspomnień* (Warsaw, 1960), 16, 184–5, 188.
30 Budzyńska, *Strzępy rodzinnej sagi*, 12–70.
31 On the distinction between assimilation and acculturation, see Landau-Czajka, *Syn będzie Lech…*; see also Schatz, *The Generation*, 35–6.
32 See J. Better, *Dziecko Gułagu: Okruchy wspomnień z nieludzkiej ziemi* (Warsaw, 2017), 11–24; W. Mędrzecki, *Kresowy kalejdoskop: Wędrówki przez ziemie wschodnie Drugiej Rzeczypospolitej 1918–1939*, e-book (Kraków, 2018), locs. 533–51.
33 Archiwum Akt Nowych, Warsaw (hereafter AAN), 2/1581/0 'Zbiór relacji dotyczących ruchu robotniczego', 1956–89, R-182, fo. 57: Helena Kamińska, account for PZPR, 31 May 1966.
34 AAN, 2/1582/0 'Zbiór akt osobowych działaczy ruchu robotniczego', 1918–1990, 13316, fo. 14: E. Pelowska-Waluk, CV, 18 Oct. 1949.
35 Wiktor Dłuski, oral history interview with author, 18 Feb. 2015.
36 See M. Szumiło, *Roman Zambrowski, 1909–1977: Studium z dziejów elity komunistycznej w Polsce* (Warsaw, 2014), 22–7.
37 Tatiana Kowalska, oral history interview with author, 30 Nov. 2015.
38 Julian Gringras (Gren), interview with Anka Grupińska (July 2005): Centropa website, visited 19 May 2022; Roman Gren, e-mail to author, 10 June 2017.
39 Maria Krych, interview with Agata Gajewska (Oct.–Dec. 2004): Centropa website, visited 19 May 2022.
40 Sowińska, 'Okrutne lata'.
41 Urszula Hibner, oral history interview with author, 30 Sep. 2015.
42 YIVO Archives, New York, RG 4 (Autobiographies of Jewish Youth in Poland); *Awakening Lives: Autobiographies of Jewish Youth in Poland before the Holocaust*, ed. J. Shandler (New Haven, Conn., 2002); *Ostatnie pokolenie: Autobiografie polskiej młodzieży żydowskiej okresu międzywojennego*, ed. A. Cała (Warsaw, 2003); *Alilot ne'urim: otobiyografiyot shel benei no'ar yehudim mipolin bein shetei milḥamot ha'olam*, ed. I. Bassok (Tel Aviv, 2011).
43 Urszula Hibner, oral history interview with the author.
44 See K. Kijek, *Dzieci modernizmu: Świadomość, kultura i socjalizacja polityczna młodzieży żydowskiej w II Rzeczypospolitej* (Wrocław, 2017).
45 B. Engelking, *Zagłada i pamięć: Doświadczenie Holocaustu i jego konsekwencje opisane na podstawie relacji autobiograficznych* (Warsaw, 1994), 46.
46 On the situation of former KPP members living in poverty, working as janitors, and so on after the war, see AAN, 2/1354/0 'Polska Zjednoczona Partia Robotnicza: Komitet Centralny w Warszawie' ([1905–1947] 1948–1990), 191–217: documents concerning former members of the KPP.
47 P. Laskowski, '"Zaczęłam filozofować, rozmyślać, szukać odpowiedzi na dręczące mnie kwestie": Wspomnienia Edwardy (Etli) Bomsztyk: biografia, emancypacja, polityka', *Praktyka Teoretyczna*, 23/1 (2017), 84–129.
48 See A. Leszczyński, *Ludowa historia Polski: Historia wyzysku i oporu. Mitologia panowania* (Warsaw, 2020); K. Pobłocki, *Chamstwo* (Wołowiec, 2021); M. Rauszer, *Siła podporządkowanych* (Warsaw, 2021).

49 These figures are not exact. Some people were actively collaborating and identifying themselves with the organizations long before becoming members; others never joined them, remaining merely fellow travellers.
50 Bertram, *Bunt, podziemie, władza*, 416.
51 Granas, *Gruba Ceśka*, 14–18.
52 M. Kozłowska, *Świetlana przyszłość? Żydowski Związek Młodzieżowy Cukunft wobec wyzwań międzywojennej Polski* (Kraków, 2016); E. Margalit, 'Social and Intellectual Origins of the Hashomer Hatzair Youth Movement, 1913–1920', *Journal of Contemporary History*, 4 (1969), 25–46.
53 AAN, 2/1354/0, CKXX/14972, fo. 11: Zygfryd Sznek, CV, 30 Oct. 1944.
54 Budzyńska, *Strzępy rodzinnej sagi*, 71–80, 84–94.
55 Ibid. 155.
56 AAN, 2/1354/0, 237/XXIII-620, fo. 18: Jerzy Tepicht, CV, 6 Dec. 1948.
57 AAN, 2/1354/0, CKXX/19118, fo. 5: Aleksander Dyszko-Wolski, CV, 18 Sep. 1945.
58 AAN, 2/1354/0, 237/XXIII-886, fo. 20: Edwarda Orłowska, CV, 20 Nov. 1946.
59 See, inter alia, N. Aleksiun, 'The Cadaver Affair in the Second Polish Republic: A Case Study of Practical Antisemitism?', in R. Fritz, G. Rossolinski-Liebe, and J. Starek (eds.), *Alma Mater Antisemitica: Academic Milieu, Jews and Antisemitism at European Universities between 1918 and 1939* (Vienna, 2016), 203–20; A. Cała, *Żyd – wróg odwieczny? Antysemityzm w Polsce i jego źródła* (Warsaw, 2012); K. Kijek, 'Between a Love of Poland, Symbolic Violence, and Antisemitism: The Idiosyncratic Effects of the State Education System on Young Jews in Interwar Poland', *Polin*, 30 (2018), 237–64; id., *Dzieci modernizmu*, 250–89; G. Krzywiec, *Polska bez Żydów: Studia z dziejów idei, wyobrażeń i praktyk antysemickich na ziemiach polskich początku XX wieku (1905–1914)* (Warsaw, 2017); J. B. Michlic, *Poland's Threatening Other: The Image of the Jew from 1880 to the Present* (Lincoln, Neb., 2006); E. Melzer, *No Way Out: The Politics of Polish Jewry, 1935–1939* (Cincinnati, 1997); Nalewajko-Kulikov, *Obywatel Jidyszlandu*, 68–75; S. Rudnicki, 'From "Numerus Clausus" to "Numerus Nullus"', *Polin*, 2 (1987), 246–68.
60 YIVO Archives, RG 4, Autobiography 3598: 'Abraham Rotfarb' (Pol., 1939); quoted in Kijek, *Dzieci modernizmu*, 285; A. Rotfarb, 'Pamiętnik żydowskiego młodzieńca', in *Ostatnie pokolenie*, 87–126: 119.
61 YIVO Archives, RG 4, Autobiography 3629: 'Kola' (Yid., 1939), 98–9; quoted in Kijek, *Dzieci modernizmu*, 311.
62 Kijek, *Dzieci modernizmu*, 317.
63 AAN, 2/1354/0, CKXX/19118, fo. 19: Aleksander Wolski, CV [19 Feb. 1949?].
64 YIVO Archives, RG 4, Autobiography 3587: 'Heniek G.' (Pol., 1934); Heniek G., 'Mój pamiętnik', in *Ostatnie pokolenie*, 71–86: 80; YIVO Archives, RG 4, Autobiography 3598: 'Abraham Rotfarb'; Rotfarb, 'Pamiętnik żydowskiego młodzieńca', 114.
65 They were written in a prison cell, where the author ended up between 1949 and 1954 as a victim of the Stalinist purges, and re-edited twenty years later. The antisemitic current in the PZPR was the main reason for Sowińska's disillusionment. See S. Sowińska, *Gorzkie lata: Z wyżyn władzy do stalinowskiego więzienia*, ed. Ł. Bertram (Warsaw, 2017).
66 Maria Jakubowicz, oral history interview with the author, 10, 17 Feb., 10 Mar. 2015.
67 L. Tychowa and A. Romanowski, *Tak, jestem córką Jakuba Bermana* (Kraków, 2016), 25.
68 Julian Gringras, interview with Anka Grupińska.
69 Y. Slezkine, *The House of Government: A Saga of the Russian Revolution* (Princeton, NJ, 2017), 64.

70 Puchalska, 'Było to tak…', 37.
71 Wilhelm Dichter, e-mail to author, 22 July 2019. In a CV from 1945, Dichter highlighted rather his working-class background and experiences with poverty (AAN, 2/1354/0, CKXX/8950, fo. 11: Michał Dichter, CV, 19 Apr. 1945).
72 Schaff, *Pora na spowiedź*, 13–22; see also K. Kijek, '"Naród słabych i skrzywdzonych": Wojny i rewolucja lat 1914–1921 w pamięci młodzieży żydowskiej okresu międzywojennego', *Studia Judaica* (Kraków), 18 (2015), 85–104.
73 Eugeniusz Smolar, oral history interview with the author, 20 Apr. 2017.
74 AAN, 2/1581/0, R-83, fo. 10: Tadeusz Kropczyński, account for PZPR, 8 June 1961.
75 Granas, *Gruba Ceśka*, 43–4; W. Gomułka, *Pamiętniki*, 2 vols. (Warsaw, 1994), i. 92–4; W. Sokorski, *Wspomnienia* (Warsaw, 1990), 12–13.
76 Ryszard Kole, oral history interview with the author, 24 July 2014; Krzemień, *Kropla*, 128.
77 Kijek, *Dzieci modernizmu*, 291; see also Landau-Czajka, *Syn będzie Lech…*, esp. 24–5, 53–74, 87–8, 93–107, 131–6.
78 For the most comprehensive picture of the strength of political and personal ties in the clandestine peer community of communists, see Budzyńska, *Strzępy rodzinnej sagi*.
79 See H. Wajn, 'Młodzi komuniści w więzieniach (1918–1939)', *Pokolenia*, 2 (1967), 19–35.
80 Granas, *Gruba Ceśka*, 29–32.
81 J. Holzer, 'Jedyna ojczyzna proletariatu – ZSRR: w dobrym i złym to jest mój kraj', in T. Szarota (ed.), *Komunizm: Ideologia, system, ludzie* (Warsaw, 2001), 9–16; K. McDermott and J. Agnew, *The Comintern: A History of International Communism from Lenin to Stalin* (London, 1996).
82 As a journalist in the Federal Republic of German, Kowalski decided not to return to Poland during the 1967–8 antisemitic campaign (A. Kowalski, *Kochałem ją nad życie: Wspomnienia byłego komunisty* (San Jose, Calif., 1986), 119; see also D. Kowalski, 'Ein "typischer Kosmopolit?" Über die Vorgeschichte der antisemitischen Kampagne von 1967/68 in Polen', 'Mimeo: Blog der Doktorandinnen und Doktoranden am Dubnow-Institut' (17 June 2019): Dubnow-Institut website, visited 19 May 2022).
83 A. Kainer [S. Krajewski], 'Żydzi a komunizm', *Krytyka: Kwartalnik polityczny*, 15 (1983), 189–91; Landau-Czajka, *Syn będzie Lech…*, 396; Schatz, *The Generation*, 66–7.
84 O. Stein, 'Nota biograficzna Sygmunta Steina napisana przez jego córkę', trans. J. M. Kłoczowski, in Stein, *Moja wojna w Hiszpanii*, 317–21: 317.
85 Stein, *Moja wojna w Hiszpanii*, 12.
86 Nalewajko-Kulikov, *Obywatel Jidyszlandu*, 107.
87 Rossiiskii gosudarstvennyi arkhiv sotsial'no-politicheskoi, Moscow, f. 459, op. 252, d. 121: Roman Zambrowski files 1, fo. 67: Comrade Wiktorowicz's explanations, 14 Aug. 1936; quoted in Szumiło, *Roman Zambrowski*, 29–30.
88 AAN, 2/1287/0 Komunistyczna Partia Polski, 158/I-6, t. 16, fo. 58: Roman Zambrowski, questionnaire for the Sixth Congress of the KPP, Oct. 1932.
89 AAN, 2/1287/0, 158/I-5, t. 5, fo. 45: Roman Kornecki, questionnaire for the Fifth Congress of the KPP, Aug. 1930.
90 See W. J. Chase, *Enemies Within the Gates? The Comintern and the Stalinist Repression, 1934–1939* (New Haven, Conn., 2002).
91 See G. Simoncini, *The Communist Party of Poland 1918–1929: A Study in Political Ideology* (New York, 1993), 189–226.

92 Archiwum Politechniki Warszawskiej, 11773: Rubin Fliderbaum, questionnaire, 29 Aug. 1929; questionnaire, 4 Oct. 1934; 12576, Szmul Gringras, application to the rector, 17 Dec. 1932.

93 AAN, 2/1582/0, 5875, fo. 27: trial of Roman Śliwa (transcript), 8 Jan. 1934; quoted in P. Gontarczyk, *Polska Partia Robotnicza: Droga do władzy, 1941–1944* (Warsaw, 2006), 85.

94 See M. Łuczewski, *Odwieczny naród: Polak i katolik w Żmiącej* (Toruń, 2012); M. Przeniosło, 'Stosunek chłopów Królestwa Polskiego do wojsk i władz rosyjskich, niemieckich i austriackich w latach 1914–1918', *Dzieje Najnowsze*, 30/4 (1998), 43–61.

95 Mishkinsky, 'The Communist Party of Poland and the Jews', 63.

96 Kijek, *Dzieci modernizmu*, 312.

97 I use the phrase 'cultural formation of communism' following Eryk Krasucki (E. Krasucki, *'A jednak coraz silniej wierzę': Życie i los Witolda Kolskiego (1902–1943)* (Szczecin, 2019), 17).

98 Szumiło, *Roman Zambrowski*, 47–50; Kijek, *Dzieci modernizmu*, 316–17; Schatz, *The Generation*, 55; Wróbel, 'Failed Integration', 213, 220.

Index

A

Abel, Tema 345, 348
Abersteld, Doris 352
Abraham 'the Angel', R. 31
Abrahamowicz, Janina 337
Abrahamowicz, Teresa 337
Abramovitsh, Sholem Yankev (Mendele Moykher Sforim), on childhood 44, 50–6, 60
Abramowicz, Olek 252
abuse, sexual 413
acculturation 453
  in state schools 200
Agudat Israel 310, 407, 422, 424, 434
Ahad Ha'am 56, 298
ailments, childhood 100–11
Akiva, R. 24
Aleksiun, Natalia 356
Alexandrov-Zitserman, Efim 372
Alryyes, Ala 47–8
Altskan, Vadim 374
American Jewish Joint Distribution Committee, *see* JDC
amulets 108, 110, 112
An-sky, S. 142
antisemitism 457–9
  of clergy 330
  of converted Jews 406–7
  experienced by children 254–5
  in late 1930s 213
  in Nowy Dwór 185
  post-war 439
  in public schools 97
  in state schools 411–12
Antończyk, Anna 336
Appenszlak, Jakub 355
Ariès, Philippe 19, 105
art, Jewish 299–303
Asch, Shalom 298
Ashkenazi, R. Judah ben Simeon 150
Asnyk, Adam 272
assimilation 452–3
Association of Children's Friends (Towarzystwo Przyjaciół Dzieci; TPD) 433
Association of Handicraft Workshops for Jewish Girls in Lwów 293
Astman, Genya (Genia) 278, 280–1, 283
Atlas, Lena 438

autobiographies 44–9, 182
  competitions 2
  fictional 53
  sponsored by YIVO 248, 251, 254, 455, 457–8
  of young people 200
autograph books of Polish Jewish schoolgirls 267–90
Avinum, Sara, *see* Jabłonska, Sara
Avrom-Itsye 370
Awin, Józef 294, 300

B

Baal Shem Tov 22–4
  Shivḥei habesht 21–4
baby farming 148
Ba'er heitev 150
Bais Yaakov schools for Orthodox girls 251–2
Bałaban, Majer 256, 297
Balsam, Jenny 344–5, 347
Balsam, Max 345
Balta 371–3, 381–3
Bander, J. 276–7
baptism:
  and conversion 336
  of Jewish children 336
Baran, Janina, *see* Leiman, Halina
Baron, Devorah 49
barrenness 124
Bar-Yishay, Nina 90
Bar-Yosef, Hamutal 59
Baudouin de Courtenay, Jan 91, 95
Bauman, Janina 252–3
Bauman, Zygmunt 242
Baytlman, Grigori 373–4
beauty contests for children 242–3
Beck, Jadwiga 302
Beck, Józef 302
Beck, Walenty 270
Beit Hillel 124
Beit Shammai 124
Bellak, Elizabeth (Ariana) 67, 70–4, 76, 79
Bełza, Władysław 208–9, 267
Berdichevsky, Mikhah Yosef 58
Beregovsky, Moisey 365–89
Berenbaum, Michael 396
Berkowitz, Esther 345–6, 350, 353
Berland, Felicja and Sara 245
Berler, Ruzena 351–3

Berlin, Moisei 147
Berman, Jakub 458
Bernfeld, Siegfried (Selig) 317–19
Bershad:
  ghetto 367–89
  Jewish Council in 370, 374–5, 381
  orphans in 381–2
  resistance groups in ghetto 377–81
  violence, sexual, in ghetto 376–7
Besht, *see* Baal Shem Tov
Besser, Gusta 349, 352–3
Bezalel School of Arts and Crafts 300
Bialik, Hayim Nahman 50, 298, 303
Białystok ghetto 404
Bielicka, Chasia 404, 406–8, 411
Bierut, Bolesław 462
Bikel, Genia 349–50
Binder, Iosif 377
Blit, Natan 424
Bloch, Gerta 275
Blum, Paula 354
Blyam, Frida 383
Boder, David 385
Bodwińska, Danuta 267
Bogner, Nahum 402, 405
Bojdak, Czesław 335
Borysław, pogrom in 273
Botticini, Maristella 134
boyhood:
  boys and the supernatural 113
  in 19th-c. Hebrew literature 42–64
  Jewish 46–9
breastfeeding 124–5
  in the Bible 123
  colostrum 128, 131–2
  in exile 351–2
  halakhah on 141, 147
  in medieval Ashkenazi society 126
  Mishnah on 141
  post-partum 125
  remarriage while 129
  Shulḥan arukh on 128–9
  see also wet nurses; wet-nursing
Brod, Max 313
Brodziński, Kazimierz 272
Budzyńska, Celina 453, 457
Buergenthal, Thomas 392
Bund 164, 423
Bunem, R. Simha, of Przysucha, childhood 23

C
caregivers for Jews in the Soviet Union 344
caregiving in exile 352–3
Catholic institutions and Jews in Kraków 327–41

Celnik, William 209
CENTOS 89–103, 163, 167, 295
  journals on children 89
Central Committee to Care for Jewish War
    Orphans in Galicia (Centralny Komitet
    Opieki nad Żydowskimi Sierotami
    Wojennymi w Galicji) 293
Central Committee of Jews in Poland (Centralny
    Komitet Żydów w Polsce; CKŻP) 405, 420
Central Organization for the Care of Jewish
    Children in Poland (Centralna Organizacja
    Opieki nad Dziećmi w Polsce) 94–5
Centralna Organizcja Opieki nad Dziećmi w Polsce,
    see Central Organization for the Care of
    Jewish Children in Poland
Centralny Komitet Opieki nad Żydowskimi
    Sierotami Wojennymi w Galicji, *see* Central
    Committee to Care for Jewish War Orphans
    in Galicia
Centralny Komitet Żydów w Polsce, *see* Central
    Committee of Jews in Poland
child labour:
  and loss of education 220–40
  in Palestine 225
childbirth:
  in exile 346–8
  on sabbath 124, 126
childhood:
  ailments 100–11; *munkalb* 110; *wasermun* 110
  in Hebrew literature 42–64
  rationalist and sentimentalist views of 20–1
  role of father in 47–8
  role of mother in 57–8
  Romantic perception of 54
  symbolic reversion to 115
  see also boyhood
children:
  baby farming 148
  'battle for children' 424
  beauty contests for 242–3
  as caregivers 105
  in Catholic institutions 327–41
  childcare 89–103; by children 226–7
  'children's talk' 48–9
  as curers 113–14
  and demons 112
  in hasidic courts before 1939 19–41
  holidays of, in interwar Poland 241–66
  Holocaust survivors 390–8; memoirs 392–8;
    rehabilitation of 390–417
  Home for Displaced Children, Kraków 338
  letters of in Hebrew 181–98
  mortality, infant and child 109–10, 122–39, 148
  as narrators 45

orphanages, self-government in 408–10; *see also* orphanages; orphans
in Polish Jewish families in the Soviet Union 342–64
refugee 309–26
separated from parents 427
and traditional medicine 104–21
as tutors 231–3
working, letters to *Mały Przegląd* 220–40
Chovav, Yemima 128
Cierniak, Józef 212–14
circumcision 109, 124, 126, 130, 348
concealment of 335
in exile 347
increase in 434
remedies 115
CKŻP, *see* Central Committee of Jews in Poland
Clara de Hirsch Home for Working Girls 296
colostrum 131–2
feeding with 128
Comintern 462
communism:
becoming communist 456
and the Jewish community 422–47
Communist Party of Poland (Komunistyczna Partia Polski; KPP) 451, 453, 457–8, 462–3
Communist Union of the Youth of Poland (Komunistyczny Związek Młodzieży Polski; KZMP) 454, 457, 461, 464
communists:
Jewish 428
Polish Jewish, childhood of 448–70
concentration camps, *see* Gross-Rosen; Pechora
convents, transfer of Jewish children from 424
conversion:
to Catholicism 336, 394
to Christianity 405–6
fears of 313
Council to Aid Jews (Żegota) 333
courts, hasidic, children in 19–41
craft workshops for girls 293–4
Cweigel, Mireczka 244
Czaczkes, Lieba 280, 284
Czerwiński, Sławomir 303

D

Danziger, Shraga, Feivel 22
degeneration, perceived Jewish 165–6
Degtyareva, Sofya 376
Deutscher, Isaac 449
Di kinder-velt 249
Dichter, Michał 459
Dłuski, Ostap (Adolf Langner) 453
Dmowski, Roman 185

Dolgonos, V. 371
Don, Rivka 189–90
Dos elendste kind 91, 95–6
Dos kind 89–91, 93–5, 97–8
Dos shutsloze kind 92–4
Drobner, Bolesław 401
Drucker, Yeshayahu 404, 406–8
Dubrinski, Moyshe 99
Dulz, Yehoshua 191
Dumitru, Diana 373–4
Dwork, Debórah 391
Dziecko 94
Dzierżoniów:
education in 433–4
Polish Jewish childhood in, 1945–50 418–47
Tarbut school in 424

E

Ecker, Janina, *see* Leiman, Halina
Eckstein, Zvi 134
education:
on country estates 72–3
in Dzierżoniów 433–4
in exile 354–5
girls' 27–8
Jewish, in Lower Silesia 423
language of instruction 201
national-patriotic 208–9
in Polish schools 97
state, reports by teachers 202–19
for women 291–308
Zionist 317–19
see also schools
educators, Jewish, of Holocaust survivors 400–17
Egert, Marceli (Martek) 274
Egit, Jakub 424
ego-documents 181–4, 450
Eiger, R. Avraham, of Lublin 25
Eisenstain, Wuna 276
emigration:
to Israel 427
to Palestine 186, 188, 194, 235, 395, 436–7
from Poland 1949–51 422
employment for Jews 425
Endecja 185
Ender, Markus 213
Engel, Alfred 313, 316–17
Engelberg, Romek 277–8
Englander, Nathan 396
Enlightenment, ideas of childhood in 43
Epstein, Helen 396
Epstein, R. Kalonymos Kalman of Kraków 21
estates, country:
languages on 80–1
raising children on 65–88

etrog, traditions associated with 107, 109
European Jewish Children's Aid 395
Even, Yitzhak 28–9
evil eye 114
Evreiskii Komitet Pomoshchi Zhertvam Voiny, *see* Jewish Committee for Aid to Refugees
exile:
 caregiving in 352–3
 childbirth in 346–8
 circumcision in 47
 education in 354–5
 living spaces in 353–5

F
Falimirz, Stefan 128
Farbówna, U. 272
Farfel, M. 371
favus (scalp infection) 167
Fedorow, Ewa 270
Feierberg, Mordekhai Ze'ev 44–5, 56–60
Fenster, Helen 342–3, 345
Filderbaum, Urbin (Roman Fidelski) 464
Finkler, Golda 25–8, 39, 46
Fisz, Pepka 270, 279
Fleck-Kesslerowa, Antonia 301
Fleischer, Nina 283
Fleyshman, Dr 371
Foer, Jonathan Safran 396
folk music, Jewish instrumental 366
Fortunoff Video Archive for Holocaust Testimonies 392
Fraenklowa, Eliza 297
Frankel, Giza 303
Frenkel, Riva 347, 350
Freud, Anna 413
Freud, Sigmund 256
Freymann, Helena 282
Fried, Gavriel 188–9
Friedländer, Michał 92
Friedman, R. Avraham Yaakov, of Sadegura 28
Friedman, R. Israel, of Ruzhin 31
Friedman, Philip 401
Frishman, David 58
Froków, Ernuśka 244
Fudem, Gizela 202

G
Galen 106
Galicia, Jewish landowners in 65–88
Garmada, Ludwik 210–11
Gastwirth, Jacob 213
Gazit, Shlomo, *see* Grzywacz, Shlomo
Geler, Nehama 407
Gergel, N. 91

Gertner, Ginka 244
Geyzer, Matvei 370, 383
ghettos, *see* Bershad; Białystok; Kraków; Łódź; Pechora; Tulchin; Vilna; Warsaw; Yampol
Gingold, Izaak 428
Gingold, Tauba 431
Gingold family 440
Gintsburg, Mordekhai Aharon, autobiography 44–9
Ginzburg, Carlo 420
girls:
 as caregivers 113
 in childhood narratives 49
 craft workshops for 293–4
 refugee 313–14
Glauberman, R. Yisrael Binyahim 33
Gleichenhaus, Mareczek 244
Gloger, Zlota 354
godparents 114
Goethe, Johann Wolfgang 271
Goldberg, Helen 346
Goldwag family 454
Goldwasser, Monika 337
Gordon, Yehuda Leib 46
Gordonia 257, 424
Gotfreidówna, Marylka 244
Gottlober, Avraham Ber 46
Granas, Romana 456
Great Children's Beauty Contest 242
Greenshpan, Zvi 193
Greenwald, Dr 175
Gren, Julian (Szmul Gringas) 454, 458–9, 464
Gringas, Szmul, *see* Gren, Julian
Gross, Lena 333
Gross-Rosen concentration camp 420
Gruen, Freda 349
Gruss, Noe 401
Grzywacz, Shlomo (Marek Kaczyński, later Shlomo Gazit) 336
Guber, Shmerl 368
Gurecki, Moshe 189
Gurfinkiel, Beniek 244

H
hakhsharah 231, 436
Halberstam, R. Hayim, of Sandz 30
 childhood 23
Hamelits 140
Handlowa, J. 271
Hanoar Haivri Akiba 257
Hanoar Hatsioni 257
Hapstein, R. Yerahmiel Moshe, of Kozienice 25
Harari, Rea 353
Hashomer Hatsa'ir 235, 251, 404, 423–7, 433, 456–7

hasidim 252-3
  childhood among 19-41
  see also *tsadikim*
Hatsofeh 146
Haynt 168
health:
  childhood illnesses 110-11
  health policy 164-5
  Jews and health 165-6
  name-changing after illness 115
  Shema and healing 114
  urine as diagnostic tool 107
Hebrew, teaching of 317, 319
  ḥeder 47-8, 52, 57-8
  rejection of 315-16, 318
Hehaluts 424
Heller, Celia 200, 209
Heller, Hersz Luzer 169
Hemmendinger, Judith 403
Hershkowitz, Joe 213
Hertzberg, Frances 347, 350-1
Herzl, Theodor 298
Hibner, Juliusz 454, 459
Hillel 298
Hine, Lewis 3
Hippocrates 106
Hirsz, Ludwik 276
Hlond, August, Primate of Poland 330
Holocaust:
  children's memories of 437-40
  Fortunoff Video Archive for Holocaust Testimonies 392
  Jewish child survivors 390-8
  saving Jewish children during 327-41
Home for Displaced Children, Kraków 338
Horodezky, R. Baruch 26
Horodezky, Shmuel Abba 26-8, 35
Horowitz, Rose 352-3
humours, theory of 111
  and conception 106
Hundert, Gershon D. 14, 241

I
identification, self- 461-4
identity, Jewish open 430-7
Ihud, and 'battle for children' 424
Imrot shelomoh 106-8
Indelman, C. 94
Infeld, Olga 275
intermarriage 432-3
International Health Division 165
internationalism 461-2
Ishak (Katz), Lea 374
Israel of Ruzhin, R. 19

J
Jabłonska, Sara (Sara Warszawiak, later Sara Avinum) 334-5
Jakubowicz, Mojżesz 432
JDC, *see* Joint Distribution Committee
Jędrzejewicz, Janusz 201, 207
Jewish Committee for Aid to Refugees (Evreiskii Komitet Pomoshchi Zhertvam Voiny) 167
Jewish Committee in Kraków 390-1
Jewish Council in Bershad 370-5
Jewish Ethnographic Program 142
Jewish Fraction of the Polish Workers' Party 423
Jewish Historical Commission in Poland 401
Jewish Labour Committee 437
Jewish National Fund 182-3, 190, 252
Jewish Patrol Service 439
'Jewish Polishness' 355
Jewish Relief Committee 293
Jewish Rescue Committee 293
Jewish Society for the Protection of Girls and Women 296
Jewish Women's Sports Association in Poland (Zrzeszenie Żydowskich Kobiecych Stowarzyszeń Sportowych w Polsce) 164
Jewishness:
  erased or blurred 451, 457-8
  rejection of 454
JNF, *see* Jewish National Fund
Joint Distribution Committee (JDC) 90, 93-7, 162-3, 166, 185, 255-6, 293-4, 407, 422, 436
  and childcare 167
  and summer camps 167-8
Jung, Carl 24
Jurand, Lena 250

K
Kacyzne, Alter 3
Kahane, R. David 407
Kalb, Sister Emanuela 337
Kalish, Ita 26-9
Kalish, R. Itzhak 26
Kalish, R. Menachem Mendel, of Otwock 26
Kamińska, Helena (née Frenkel) 453
Kamińska, Maria (née Eiger) 452-3
Kamiński, Maksymilian 337
Kanevski, Shmuel 151
Kaplan, Marion 292
Kaplan, Mina 412
Karim, Anna (Anna Badowska) 336
Karmoil, Fela 353
Karp, Ethel 348-50, 353
Karp, Gecel 348-9
kashrut, observance of 454

Katcherginsky, Shmerke 366
Katz, Samuś 244
Keff, Bożena 269, 284
Kelly, Catriona 20
Kempler, Anita 338
Kempler, Bernhard 338
Keren Hayesod 425
Keren Kayemet Leyisra'el 425
Kerpilevich, Naum 370, 383
Kessler, Ewa 277-8
kibbutzim:
　in Lower Silesia 423-4
　for orphans 424
　in Rychbach and Pieszyce 424
Kielce, pogrom in 421
Kijek, Kamil 200, 209, 458, 460
Kimelman, Jadwiga 82
Kimelman, Moses and Isak 82
Kimelman, Oswald 82
Kindergarten of the Zionist Central Committee 314-17
Kirszenbaum, Broneczka 244
Kitsur shulḥan arukh 109
Klaften, Aleksander 293
Klaftenowa, Cecylia 291-308
Kofler, Oskar 66
Kofman, Moshe 188, 191
Kohn, Józef 89, 93
Komunistyczna Partia Polski, *see* Communist Party of Poland
Komunistyczny Związek Młodzieży Polski, *see* Communist Union of the Youth of Poland
Königsberg, Dawid 74
Königsberg, Edward (Edzio) 74
Königsberg, Hersz 75
Königsberg, Hilary Hilel 74-5, 77
Königsberg, Kos (Kohos) 75, 77
Königsberg, Marcel 77-9
Königsberg, Maria (née Spiegel) 74-5, 77
Königsberg, Roza Steckel 75
Koplowicz, Rachel 347, 350-1
Korczak, Janusz (Henryk Goldszmit) 91-2, 98, 220-1, 223, 243, 251, 408-10
Koretz, Irena 267-90
Koretz, Józef 269-70
Koretz, Olga 270-1
Koretz, Rozalia 270
Korman, Shmuel 368, 373-4
Kornecki, Roman 463
Korse, Benjamin 371
Kosińska, Izabella 272
Kovel, Meyer 373-4
Kowalczyk, Józef (Izajasz Sznajder) 452
Kowalska, Tatiana 454

Kowalski, Artur 461
Kowalski, Józef 454
KPP, *see* Communist Party of Poland
Krajoznawstwo 163
Kraków:
　ghetto 329, 338-9
　Jews in Catholic institutions in 327-41
　orphanage 402
Kraszewski, Józef Ignacy 272
Kreitenberg, Marlene 350
Kriegel, J. 274
Küchler(-Silberman) (Kichler), Lena 390-1, 399, 402-5, 408, 411-12
Kupershmidt, Sholem 366
Kuperstein, Raia 376
Kurek-Lesik, Ewa 328
KZMP, *see* Communist Union of the Youth of Poland

L
Łabędź, director of Zatrzebie orphanage 410
Landau, Giza 278, 281, 283
Landau, Jan 94
landowners, Jewish, in Galicia 65-88
Langer, Lawrence 391
Langner, Adolf 453
Lanzman, Mordechai 191
Lapterowa, Franciszka 297
Laskowski, Piotr 455
Latawiec, Józefa and Tadeusz 327, 332
Lauf, Anita 274
Łazowertówna, Nacia 244
League for Labour Palestine 424
Lebedev, Efim 377
Lederman family 374
Lednicki, Aleksander 91
Leiman, Halina (Janina Baran, later Janina Ecker) 327, 331-3
Lender, Regina 342, 345, 353
Lender-Młynek-Platkowski clan 342
Lenin, Vladimir 456
Lerich, Yisrael 187-8, 190-3
Lerman (Livne), Ze'ev 194
Lermontov, Mikhail 152
Lerner, Ruvim 366
letters by children 181-98
Letzer, Klara 278, 281, 283
Lev, Erez 184
Levi Yitzhak of Berdichev, R. 22
Levine, Yehudah Leib 28, 32-3
Levinson, Abraham 183
Levinson, Avrum 91, 93, 96
Lewin, Gerchon 170
Libera, Zbigniew 111

Liberman, Ida 377–8
Liberman, Peysi 377
Liebentritt, Luiza Lotta (née Kimelman) 82
Lieber, Blanka 283
Lilienblum, Moshe Leib 46
Lilientalowa, Regina 2
Łódź ghetto 366
Löwenkron, Rachela 274
Lower Silesia:
    education, Jewish, in 423
    Jewish settlement after Holocaust 420–2
    Jews in, 1945–68 420–68
    kibbutzim in 423–4
    secularism in 434–5
    Zionists in 423
Lubarskaya, Klara 383
Lubenfeld, Nina 352
Łubieńska, Róża 332, 338
Lubman, Zinaida 368–9
lullabies sung by non-Jewish wet nurses 152
Luzzatto, Samuel David, autobiography 63 n.10
Lwów pogrom 459

M

Machay, Fr. Ferdynand 337
Magid of Mezerich 31
Maimon, Solomon, autobiography 45, 47
Main Welfare Council (Rada Główna Opiekuńcza; RGO) 331, 334
Makarenko, Anton 409–10
Mały Przegląd (children's supplement to *Nasz Przegląd*) 98, 243, 249, 251, 253–5
    letters to, from working children and young people 220–40
Manekin, Rachel 313
Manskleid, Tolek 283
Maramorosch, Karl 66
Marchak, Shoykhet Eli 370–1, 377
Marenfeld, Rachel 347
Marenfeld, Sara 353
Maresky, Sonia 278
Mark, H. 409–10
Mark, Zvi 24
marriage:
    during the war 345–6
    hasidic 30
    remarriage and breastfeeding 147, 153
Marxism 456
Matthews Grieco, Sara 132, 144
Matuszewska, Stefania 275
Maza, Sarah 1
Mazurkiewicz, Wojciech 213–14
medicine:
    classical 105

diagnosis of illness 111
folk 105
German and Slavonic 111–13
traditional Jewish 104–21
urine as diagnostic tool 107
see also health
Megilat setarim 24
Meir, Golda 145
melamed 47–9, 52
Melcerowa, Róża 296
memoirs 453, 456
Mendelbaum, R. Baruch, of Turów 32
Mendele Moykher Sforim, *see* Abramovitsh
messianism 24–5
Metzendorf, Barbara 333
Meynekes rivko 128–9, 131
Michalska, Iwona 92
Michlic, Joanna 405
Mickiewicz, Adam 272–4, 303
midwives 130
Mifalot elokim 107
Milewski, Włodek 282
Minority Treaty, and school language 201
Mintz, Alan 46
Mintz, Rachel 194
Mintz, Steven 1
Mirer, Esfira (Edwarda Orłowska) 457
Mishnah:
    on breastfeeding 141
    on infant development 124
Misky, Ludwik 297–8, 300
Mitsel, Abram 374
Mittelmann, Berta 275
Mizrachi party 422
Mocny, Jureczek 244
Mohnblum, Abe 385
Mościcki, Ignacy 303
Moshe of Kobrin, R. 28
Muchnik, Frida 369, 374, 376
Muszka, Eidelheit 280, 284

N

Nachmani Gafni, Emuna 405
Nahash, Yosef ('Snake') 190, 192
Nahman of Bratslav, R. 25, 29
    childhood 23–4
Nahum of Chernobyl 31
Nasz Przegląd 222, 242
Natanson, Salomon (Józef Kowalski) 454
Nathanblut, Anna 402, 405, 412
nationality, decision on 463–4
neonatal care 122–39
    bathing newborns 127–8
    biblical and talmudic concepts 123–5

neonatal care (*cont.*):
   in early modern Poland 127–31
   isolation of newborns 132
   in medieval Ashkenazi communities 125–6
   Mishnah: on breastfeeding 141; on infant development 124
   and modern medicine 131–3
   naming 126
   wrapping and salting newborns 123–4, 126–7, 131
Neustadt, Leib 93–4
Newerly, Igor 221
Neymanowicz, Jerzyk 244
Nikolaev 378, 380–1
Nordau, Max 300
Nowy Dwór Mazowiecki 181–98
Noyshtot, L. 91
Nussbaum-Hilarowicz, Józef 293

O

Oberklaid, Frania 345, 348, 355–6
Oberklaid, Pinkas 345
Obóz Zjednoczenia Narodowego 213
Obshchestvo Zdravookhraneniya Evreev, *see* Society for the Protection of the Health of the Jews
obshchina, *see* Bershad, Jewish Council in 370
Œuvre de Protection des Enfants Juifs 400
Œuvre de Secours aux Enfants 403
Opieka nad dzieckiem 94
Orlovits, Nesia 404, 408
Orłowska, Edwarda 457
Ornstein, Hela 280–1
orphanages 354
   Jewish survivors in 401
   Kraków 402, 409; Albertine 334–5
   Legnica 412
   Łódź 404
   Lublin 402, 412
   self-government by children in 408–10
   Vienna 312
   Zabrze 404, 406–7
   Zakopane 400, 411
   Zatrzebie 410
   ZPP 354
orphans, Jewish 2–3, 89–103, 394–5
   adoption of by hasidim 31
   Central Committee to Care for Jewish War Orphans in Galicia 293
   kibbutz for 424
   refugee 312
   rescue from Warsaw ghetto 400
   in Rychbach and Pieszyce 423
Orthodox institutions in Dzierżoniów 434–5
Orthodox Judaism, abandonment of 427

OZE, *see* Society for the Protection of the Health of the Jews

P

Palestine:
   emigration to 186, 188, 194, 235, 395, 436–7
   pen pals in 181–98
   views of young Jews on 98–9
   working in 235–6
Pappenheim, Bertha 296
Pat, Yaakov 438
Patak, Erna 314–15
Patron, Stefanek 244
Pechora:
   concentration camp in 365
   ghetto 381–2
Peker, Michał (Meir) 89, 92–6
Pelowska, Eugenia 453
pen pals, in Palestine 181–98
People's Referendum 425
Perec, Abram 94
Peretz, Isaac Leib (Yitskhok Leibush) 58, 298
Perlmuter, I. 372–3
Perlmutter, Rita 352
Perlov, Yaakov Yitzhak 36
Perlov, Yisrael 32
Perlov, R. Yitzhak 32
Pertman, Chaim 428–9, 432, 440–1
Pertman, Frida Szarfstein 428–9, 432
Pertman, Frieda 433, 440–1
Pertman, Lusiek (Allan) 441–2
Pertman, Rita 442
Pieszyce:
   children's home in 423, 438
   Jewish orphans in 423
Pilch, Jan 335
Pilch, Julia 335
Piłsudski, Józef 185, 207, 252, 298
Pines, Yehiel Mikhel 151
Pinkus, Adela 244
Pinsker, Leon 298
Pirkei avot 298
Pius XII, Pope 330
PKŻ, *see* Rychbach District Jewish Committee
Platkowski, Fela and Yeshayahu 345
Plesser, Zvi, letters to 184–93
Plotz, Judith 51
pogroms, fear of 439
   see also Borysław; Kielce; Lwów
Pol, Wincenty 283
Polish Socialist Party: Left (Polska Partia Socjalistyczna–Lewicka; PPS-L) 457
Polish Socialist Party: Revolutionary Faction (Polska Partia Socjalistyczna–Frakcja Rewolucyjna) 457

Polish United Workers' Party (Polska Zjednoczona Partia Robotnicza) 451, 457, 461
Polonization of names 450
Polska Partia Socjalistyczna–Frakcja Rewolucyjna, see Polish Socialist Party: Revolutionary Faction
Polska Partia Socjalistyczna–Lewicka, see Polish Socialist Party: Left
Polska Zjednoczona Partia Robotnicza, see Polish United Workers' Party
Polski Punki 348
Pomeranc-Melcer, Róża 92–3
Ponczak, Szlomo (Sam) 429, 431–3, 436, 438–9, 441
Portnaya, Fanya 383
Portnoy, Mikhail 376
Post, Rózia 272
Powiatowy Komitet Żydowski, see Rychbach District Jewish Committee
PPS–FR, see Polish Socialist Party: Revolutionary Faction
PPS–L, see Polish Socialist Party: Left
pregnancy 107–9
　attempts to end 348–50
　foetus, discovering sex of 106–7
prison, Jews in 460–1
Prokop-Janiec, Eugenia 199
prose, Hebrew, development of 43
proverbs, Yiddish and Polish 4
Provincial Committee of Polish Jews (Wojewódzki Komitet Żydów Polskich) 420, 424–5
Przegląd Społeczny 89–96
punishment, corporal 190
Pushkin 273
PZPR, see Polish United Workers' Party

R
Rabinowicz, R. Yehoshua Heschel, childhood of 23
Rada Główna Opiekuńcza, see Main Welfare Council
Randmesser, Karol 274
Rath, Moses 317
Ravitzky, Eliezer 186–8
Rechter, David 310
Refa'el hamalakh 107–8, 112, 114
refugee children, Galician, in Austria 309–26
Reichenbach, see Rychbach
Reichenstein, Ada 298
Reiss, Bobuś 244
repatriation of Polish Jews from the Soviet Union 342–64
rescuers of child refugees 393–5
resistance groups in Bershad ghetto 377–81

Reyber, Sonya 368
RGO, see Main Welfare Council
Richard, Helena H. 297
Riis, Jacob 3
Ringelblum, Emanuel 366
Ringelblum Archive 90
Rivlin, A. 195
Rochel Feyga 30
Rokeah, Yssachar Dov, R. 30
Rosenblatt, Albina 291, 302
Rosenblit, Marsha 310
Rosenfarb, Chava 390–1
Rosner, Alexander 338
Rotenstreichowa, Fryderyka 302
Rotfarb, Abraham 1
Rousseau, Jean-Jacques 43–5
Rubin, Y. 91
Rudaev, Moshe Yosef 145–6
Rutowski, Tadeusz 293
Rychbach 418, 420
　Jewish orphans in 423
　Jews in 431
Rychbach District Jewish Committee 421, 423, 437

S
sabbath, childbirth on 124, 126
Salka, Sara 270
Sanacja movement, and education 207
Sapieha, Archbishop Adam Stefan 330–2
Savran 371–2, 375
Schachter, Mina 374
Schachter, Toba 343, 345, 353, 355
Schaff, Adam 452, 459
Schaff, Maks 96
Schaikewitz, Nachum Meir (Shomer) 143
Schattner, Bertha 352
Schatz, Borys 300
Schatz, Jaff 449
Schenirer, Sarah 251–2
Schneerson, R. Menachem Mendel 40 n.76
Schonfeld, R. Solomon 407, 434
schools:
　elementary 202
　Hebrew 181–98
　private Jewish 201
　see also Bais Yaakov; education; *ḥeder*; state schools; Tarbut schools
Schriebman, Jean 353–4
Schwalbe, Dr 175
Schwarz-Hiller, Rudolf 311
Schwarzman, Fanny 143
SDKPiL, see Social Democracy of the Kingdom of Poland and Lithuania
secularism in Lower Silesia 434–5

Segal, Erna 309
Seidman, Naomi 252
Sfard, Dawid 462
Shabad, Tsemakh 93, 173
Shalit, Moyshe 91
Shalom Shekhna, son of R. Abraham 'the Angel' 31
Shapira, R. Pinhas Yosef 33
Shapiro, R. Avraham Elimelekh, of Grodzisk 25
Shapiro, Malka 25–6
Shargorodskaya, Hine 366
Shaykes, Ida 366
Shekhinah, lamenting for 22
Shekhtman, Itzhak 382
Shema and healing 114
Shikhtman, Lyonya 368
Shimkovitch, Joseph 184
Shivḥei habesht 21–4
Shlomo Efraim 25
Shlomo of Karlin 31
Shneyorson, M. 91, 93
Shoah Foundation 213, 392
Sholem Aleichem 298
Sholokhova, Lyudmila 366
Shrentsl, Mikhael 371, 377
Shtindler, Zunye 368, 379, 383
Shulḥan arukh 127–8, 150
  on breastfeeding 141, 151
Shulman, Gedaliya 371
Siennik, Marcin 128
Silkes, Genia 1
Sinkoff, Nancy 296
Slesin, Aviva 393
Slezkine, Yuri 459
Śliwa, Roan 464
Śmigly-Rydz, Edward 207
Smolar, Hersz (Grzegorz) 459
Smolenskin, Peretz 298
Sobelman, I. 371
Sochaczewska, Eścia 272, 284
Social and Cultural Society of Jews in Poland 462
Social Democracy of the Kingdom of Poland and Lithuania (Socjaldemokracja Królestwa Polskiego i Litwy) 457
social work 295
socialism 423
socialization, political 449
Society for the Promotion of Vocational Education among Jews in Lesser Poland (Związek dla Szerzenia Wykształcenia Zawodowego wśród Żydów w Małopolsce) 292, 298–303
Society for the Protection of the Health of the Jewish People (Towarzystwo Ochrony Zdrowia Ludności Żydowskiej), *see* TOZ

Society for the Protection of the Health of the Jews (Obshchestvo Zdravookhraneniya Evreev) 163
Society for the Rescue of Abandoned Jewish Children in Galicia and Bukovina 293
Socjaldemokracja Królestwa Polskiego i Litwy, *see* Social Democracy of the Kingdom of Poland and Lithuania
Sofrin, R. Itzhak Yehudah Yehiel, childhood of 23
Sokolow, Nahum 242
songs, Yiddish, from the ghetto 365–89
  'At the Jewish Market' 374–5
  'Dzhankoy' 369–70
  'I'm Going Back Home' 383–4
  'In the Cold Days' 371–4
  'In Obodivker Camp' 369–70
  'The Jewish Song' 380–1
  'Moyshe, the Polish Jew' 377–8
  'An Orphan' 382–3
  'The Sun Sets in Transnistria' 376–7
  'Trees Blaze and It Wails and It Burns' 378–80
  see also lullabies
Soranus of Ephesus 125
Sosnowiec 424
Sotsyalistishe Kinder Farband 164
Soviet Union, Polish Jewish families with children in, 1939–46 342–64
Sowińska, Stanisława 454, 458
Soyfer, Genya 368–9, 371–4, 376–9
Spiegel, Bernard 67, 71, 73–5, 83
Spiegel, Henryk 74, 83
Spiegel, Hinda 74
Spiegel, Józek 74
Spiegel, Markus 74
Spiegel, Renia (Aurelia), diary 65–88
Spiegel, Róża (née Finkel) 71, 73–4
Spiegel, Salomea (née Solowiec) 74
Spiegel, Witek 74
Spielberg, Steven 392
Stargardt, Nicholas 391
state schools:
  acculturation in 200
  antisemitism in 411–12
  ghetto benches in 214–15
  in Tarnów, Jews in 199–219
Steckel, Paja 74
Steckel (Stöckel), Jakob 75
Steedman, Carolyn 51
Stein, Sygmunt 462
Stein, Zygmunt 272
Stöckel, Józek (Józef Salomon) 78
Stöckel, Ludwik 78–9
Stöckel, Osias 75, 78
Stöckel, Pesia (née Krasucka) 78

Storch, Miriam 350, 352–3
Stout, Pola 298
Stramer, Solo (Roman Kornecki) 463
Stricker, Robert 310, 315
summer camps 162–80, 189, 247–8, 250–1, 433
　activities in 172–5
　Hebrew 186
　Jewish 255–8
　in North America 163–4
　Orthodox 257
summer holidays, religious objection to 250–1
superstitions about children 110
Supruniuk, Konstanty and Maria 432–3
Sussman, Beatrice 354
Szczecińska, Ziuta and Genia 244
Szereszowski, Rafał 90
Szkoła Zawodowa Żeńska Towarzystwa
　Warsztatów Rękodzielniczych dla Dziewcząt
　Żydowskich, *see* Women's Vocational School
　of the Association of Handicraft Workshops
　for Jewish Girls
Sznajder, Izajasz 452
Szpiegiel, Czesław 74
Szpiegiel, Mojżesz 74–5
Szwarc, Chunka 244
Szwarc, Majer Berisz (Meir) 270
Szwarc, Mania 270
Szwarc (Schwarz), Klara 269–90
Szyfman, Nusia and Ina 245
Szyk, Artur 303

T

Taffet, Gershon 279
Talis, Iakov 377
Tarbut schools:
　in Baranowicze (Baranavichy) 194
　in Nowy Dwór, children's letters 181–98
Tarnów, Jews in state schools in 199–219
Tartakower, Aryeh 403–4, 410
Taubenfeld, Alicja 333
Taylorism 297
Tchernichowsky, Shaul 298
Teicher, Janka and Niuta 277–8
Teitelbaum, Michał 428, 432
Tenenbaum, Dora 440
Tenenbaum, Józef 294, 430
Tenenbaum, Szymon 435, 440, 442
Thon, Yehoshua (Ozjasz) 91
Thorsh, Dr 175
Thumim, R. Boruch Frenkl 30
Titelbaum, Michał 440
Toledot adam 108
Topór, Kubuś 244

Towarzystwo Ochrony Zdrowia Ludności
　Żydowskiej, *see* TOZ
Towarzystwo Przyjaciól Dzieci, *see* Association of
　Children's Friends
TOZ 162, 166–7
　day camps 169–70
　summer camps 162–80; attendance at 170–2;
　　financing of 168–70
TPD, *see* Association of Children's Friends
Transnistria during Romanian occupation 365–89
Trunk, Yehiel Yeshaya, and Ita Yelin 142
Trunk, R. Yisrael Yeshoshua, of Kutno 145, 150
Trusz, Jan 451–2
tsadikim 113
　child leaders 31–6
　children of 19–41
　daughters of 27
Tshernovitsh, S. 91
Tsukunft 164, 456
　camps 257–8
Tulchin 380
　ghetto 381
Turbiner, Beniamin 432, 436
Turbiner, Estera 432
Turbiner, Pinkus 433, 436, 440
Turbiner, Szlomo 433, 439–40
Twersky, R. Aharon, of Chernobyl 30
Twersky, Avraham 34
Twersky, Baruch Asher, of Chernobyl 34
Twersky, R. Gedaliah, of Malin 26
Twersky, Haya 27
Twersky, R. Menahem Nahum, of Warsaw 27, 32
Twersky, R. Mordechai, of Shpikov 27, 30
Twersky, R. Shlomo Bentsion 32, 34–5
Twersky, Yitzhak Nahum 27
Twersky, Yohanan 27, 49 n.46
TWR, *see* Women's Vocational School of the
　Association of Handicraft Workshops for
　Jewish Girls

U

underground, Polish 331
Union of Jewish Women 298
Union of Polish Patriots (Związek Patriotów
　Polskich) 343, 348, 352, 355
　orphanages 354
Union of Warsaw Jews 343
United Services for New Americans 395
United States Holocaust Memorial Museum 392
Unzer kind 89–91, 93–4
Uri of Strelisk 22
Ussishkin, Mr 190

V

Va'ad Hahatsalah 400, 407, 424, 434, 437
Valdman, Miriam 369
Vartshak, Yosif 368, 382
Varvarovka 380, 381
Veysman, Batiyah 382
Vilna:
  ghetto 366
  Tarbut Teachers' Seminary 182–3
Vindman, Yosef 98–9
Vinokurova, Faina 374
violence:
  anti-Jewish 411–12, 423, 439
  sexual, in Bershad ghetto 376–7
Vishniac, Roman 3
Vlasov Army 378
vocational training 99
Voskoboynikov, Iosif 377

W

Wachs (Waks), Ewa 74–5
Wachs (Waks), Lila 74–6
Wachtel, Jakób 203–4, 207, 209–10
Wajdzik family 394
Wajnberg, Zosia 244
Wajnrybówna, Zosia 244
Walzman, Freda 350–1, 355
Wandervogel 163
Warsaw ghetto 366, 400
  uprising 355
Warszawiak, Sara, *see* Jabłonska, Sara
Web, Marek 90
Wechsler, Cecylia 293
Weichardt, Teodor Tomasz 133
Weiler, Dozia 280–1
Weinreb, Zygmunt 335
Weinstein, Paula 405
Weinstock, Leon 93
Weissblumówna, H. 248
Weitzman, Marta 283
Werfel, Roman 452
Wesołowska, Janina 278–9
wet nurses 123, 125, 128–30
  Christian 130
  live-in 142–3
  live-out 143–8
  non-Jewish 124, 126, 141, 149–51
  on the sabbath 129
  and substitution of babies 140, 144–5
  wages of 148–9
wet-nursing:
  of abandoned babies 148
  attitudes and perceptions 141–2
  and immunity 132–3
  in the late Russian empire 140–61
  and substitution of babies 140, 144–5
Wiener, Andrew 396
Wienerówna, Runa 275
Winter, Daniel 390
Winter, Miriam 390–1
WKŻ, *see* Provincial Committee of Polish Jews
Wojewódzki Komitet Żydów Polskich, *see* Provincial Committee of Polish Jews
Wojtas, Dorota 207
Wolf, Bronia 275
Wolkun, Hannah 354
women:
  and war relief 292–3
  work of 294–7
Women's International Zionist Organization 296, 298
Women's Vocational School of the Association of Handicraft Workshops for Jewish Girls (Szkoła Zawodowa Żeńska Towarzystwa Warsztatów Rękodzielniczych dla Dziewcząt Żydowskich; TWR) 291
Wulman, Lejb 162, 169
wunderkind in Jewish cultural contexts 22
WUZET, *see* Society for the Promotion of Vocational Education among Jews in Lesser Poland

Y

Yad Vashem 392
Yampol ghetto 374
yenuka 31–6
  mothers of 35
  in the Zohar 22
Yiddish 79
  during the war 365–89
  in Dzierżoniów 430–2
  importance of 298–9
  lack of 453
  not a minority language 201
  proposal to publish in Latin letters 222–3
  songs from the ghetto 365–89
Yidishe Arbeter Froy Organizatsye 164
Yisrael Hayim, son of R. Abraham 'the Angel' 31
YIVO autobiographical essays project 1–2, 76–9, 182, 237, 243, 248, 251, 254, 457–8
Yurin, Dr 175

Z

Zak, Yakov 151
Zalcman, Necha (Stanisława Sowińska) 454
Zambrowski, Roman 454, 462–3
Zapolska, Gabriela 27–87

Zaremba, Marcin 439
Zarzycki, Adolf 205, 207, 212–14
Zechariah Mendel ben Arieh Leib, R. 150
Żegota 333
Zeidah laderekh 126
Zeitlin, Aharon 91
Zenner, Herman Steinkohl 83
Żeromski, Stefan 302
Zevi of Zhidachov, R. 23
Zhitlowsky, Chaim 91
Ziemiańska, Franciszka 338
Zilberberg, Saul 439
Zilberfarb, Moyshe 91
Ziller, A. 273
Zinkuzan 373–4
Zionism 100, 234–5, 257, 395
  'mild' 297–8
Zionist Women's Association 314
Zionists 98, 427–8
  and 'battle for children' 424
  child 193–4, 193
  Habonim summer camps 164
  Hitachdut 169

in Lower Silesia 423
and refugee children 309–26
and relief for refugees 310–26
Zisfain, Bronia 346, 353
Zisfain, Jacob 346
Zitserman, Boris 369–72, 377, 381, 384
Zloch, Stephanie 201
ZPP, *see* Union of Polish Patriots
Zrzeszenie Żydowskich Kobiecych Stowarzyszeń
  Sportowych w Polsce, *see* Jewish Women's
  Sports Association in Poland
Zucker, Esther 190
Zunser, Miriam Shomer 143
Związek dla Szerzenia Wykształcenia Zawodowego
  wśród Żydów w Małopolsce, *see* Society for
  the Promotion of Vocational Education
  among Jews in Lesser Poland
Związek Patriotów Polskich, *see* Union of Polish
  Patriots
Życie 454, 464
żydokomuna (antisemitic stereotype of Judaeo-
  communism) 451
żydzi, capitalization of 210